Microcomputer Architecture and Programming

The 68000 Family

JOHN F. WAKERLY
Stanford University

WILEY

JOHN WILEY & SONS, INC.
New York • Chichester • Brisbane • Toronto • Singapore

Cover Art: Jana Brenning

Library of Congress Cataloging in Publication Data:

Wakerly, John F.
    Microcomputer Architecture and Programming

    Bibliography: p.
      1. Motorola 68000 series microprocessors — Programming.
2. Computer architecture   I. Title

QA76.8.M6895W35   1989   005.265   88–27849
ISBN 0–471–85319–4

Printed in the United States of America

10 9 8 7 6 5 4 3 2 1

To Michael

I never met a Mike
I didn't like

Preface

The "microcomputer revolution" is best understood by realizing that a micro-computer is just an inexpensive computer. The basic principles of computer organization and programming have changed very little as a result of this revolution. The major impact of the proliferation of microcomputers has been to heighten the need for programmers who understand basic computer principles and who know how to apply them.

The purpose of this book is to explain basic computer architecture and programming using microcomputers as examples. We emphasize basic principles rather than details of a particular microcomputer's instruction set. Still, we must use *some* specific computer organization for examples. Therefore, we explain basic principles using Motorola 68000-family processors. Building on these basic principles, we also describe and compare other important microprocessors.

Mac Notes

Our discussions of the Motorola 68000 are not inseparably tied to a particular programming environment, but our assembly language examples follow Motorola standards. In addition, *Mac Notes* are provided to help students who happen to be working in the Macintosh environment.

The book is organized into three parts. Part 1 contains four chapters of introductory material that each reader may or may not have studied before. The heart of the book is Part 2, nine chapters that describe basic principles of computer organization and assembly language programming, using the 68000 as the main example. Part 3 presents additional details of advanced processors and peripherals in the 68000 family, and concludes with case studies of other popular microprocessors—the DEC PDP-11 and LSI-11, the Motorola 6809, and the Intel 80x86 family—and a hypothetical stack machine. Throughout the book, *marginal notes* alert the reader to important concepts and definitions.

marginal notes

USES OF THIS BOOK

This book is suitable for an introductory course on (micro)computer organization and assembly language programming, typically the third programming course in a computer science or computer engineering curriculum. (The first two courses usually cover programming principles in a high-level language such as Pascal, C, or FORTRAN.) Such an introductory course would make use of the basic principles in Parts 1 and 2 of this book and may also refer to one or more of the processor descriptions in Part 3. This book treats all of the topics recommended for course CS 3 and stresses techniques of good programming style as recommended in the ACM's Curriculum '78 (*Comm. ACM*, Vol. 22, No. 3, March 1979, pp. 147–166).

The development of concepts in Parts 1 and 2, and the consistent use of these concepts to describe different processors in Part 3, make this book also suitable for a course on "comparative computer architectures" or "microcomputer architectures." Such a course examines and compares the structure and features of several different computers.

A third use of this book is as a reference, both by students who have used it in a course and by practicing computer professionals. The book is organized into well-structured topic areas to facilitate reference use, and there is a comprehensive index as well.

CHAPTER DESCRIPTIONS

Chapters 1 through 4 comprise Part 1, introductory and remedial material that is used in the remainder of the book.

- Chapter 1 defines terms and discusses fundamental concepts, so that a serious student without a previous or recent programming course can understand the rest of the book.

- Chapter 2 describes the Pascal programming language. The remainder of the book uses Pascal both for documenting algorithms and for precisely defining the internal operations of a computer, and so a reading knowledge of simple Pascal programs is useful. This chapter can serve either as a review of Pascal or as a quick introduction.

- Chapter 3 introduces data structures including arrays, records, stacks, and queues; these data structures are used later in descriptions of several aspects of computer organization and programming.

- Chapter 4 presents basic concepts of the number systems and arithmetic operations used in typical computers.

Part 2 describes basic principles that are applicable to all computers, using the Motorola 68000 as a specific example.

- Chapter 5 describes a useful subset of the instructions, organization, and assembly language of the Motorola 68000 processor.

- Chapter 6 describes assembly language programming in more detail, including topics of assembler operation, relocation and linking, position-independent code, macros, and structured assembly languages.

- Chapter 7 is an encyclopedia of commonly used addressing modes, including all of the 68000's modes. Basic concepts of memory mapping and memory management are also covered.

- Chapter 8 explains the formats and effects of computer operation types, including the encodings, options, and effects of all of the 68000's instructions.

- Chapter 9 begins with a discussion of procedures and functions in Pascal and then relates these high-level concepts to subroutine calling and parameter-passing conventions in assembly language programs. It also covers concepts of recursion and coroutines.

- Chapter 10 discusses input/output architecture and software concepts.

- Chapter 11 covers interrupts, traps, and direct memory access, and includes complete coverage of the 68000's interrupt system.

- Chapter 12 introduces the advanced concepts of processes, shared data structures, and reentrancy.

- Chapter 13 contains often-neglected introductory material on software engineering and the program development process, including documentation standards and debugging practices.

Part 3 consists of Chapters 14 through 19. The first two of these chapters cover advanced topics in the 68000 family:

- Chapter 14 covers the extended programming models, addressing modes, and instructions of the MC68010, MC68020, and MC68030 processors.

- Chapter 15 covers the MC68851 PMMU and MC68881 FPU, the MC68020 and MC68030 on-chip caches, the MC68030 on-chip MMU, the MC6850 serial interface, and the MC68230 parallel interface and timer.

Using the basic principles that were presented in Part 2, each of the remaining chapters describes the architecture of a specific microcomputer:

- Chapter 16 describes a simple accumulator machine, the Motorola 6809.

- Chapter 17 presents an older but historically very significant general register architecture, the PDP-11 and LSI-11.

- Chapter 18 descr bes a somewhat twisted but commercially very important architecture, the Intel 80x86 family, including the extended features of the 80286 and 80386 processors.

- Chapter 19 contains a very quick description of a hypothetical stack machine based on the PDP-11, and a discussion of the pros and cons of pure stack architectures.

The processor descriptions in Part 3 are fairly detailed, so that readers can make intelligent judgments about the processors. For example, all of the addressing modes and instructions of each processor are explained. However, in the interest of brevity, not all of the details of assembly language, instruction side-effects, and development system operation are included. A reader who wishes to write and run programs for one of the Part 3 processors may wish to supplement the material in this book with documentation from the processor's manufacturer.

Two appendices appear at the end of the book. Appendix A describes the ASCII character code and special characters used in CRT terminals. Appendix B describes the asynchronous serial communication protocol commonly used with CRT terminals.

HOW THIS BOOK WAS PREPARED

The text of this book was formatted using Don Knuth's TEX manuscript preparation language, along with Leslie Lamport's LATEX macro package and my own book-format customizations. The text files were created using the very capable and speedy Epsilon text editor, an EMACS-like editor from Lugaru Software that runs on my IBM PC-AT compatible computer.

The figures were created using Cricket Draw, an object-drawing program that runs on my Apple Macintosh II. The Macintosh and the AT are linked by a TOPS network from Sun Microsystems, so that the figures and text can be merged when TEX runs on the AT. The `psfigtex` macro package, written by Trevor Darrell, merges the PostScript figure files created by Cricket Draw with the PostScript page files created from TEX's `.DVI` output files by the ArborText `DVIPS` output driver. The page files for early drafts of the book were printed on my Apple LaserWriter, and the negatives of the final pages were run on my Linotronic 100, a 1270 dpi phototypesetter.

It might be interesting to consider the fact my most recent keystrokes went through two 8-bit microcontrollers (in the keyboard and PC-AT), an 80286 (in the PC-AT), an MC68020 (in the Mac), and two MC68000s (in the phototypesetter) before being rendered onto film. Older keystrokes, lifted from my 1981 *Microcomputer Architecture and Programming*, went through a Southwest Technical Products 6800 system and an Onyx Z8000-based Unix system before arriving at the PC-AT. Amazing! Even more amazing is the fact that all this equipment is still sitting in my basement.

ERRORS

It has been said that there is no such thing as a completely debugged program, only a program with undiscovered bugs. The same thing is true of books. I am anxious to learn of errors in this book so that they may be fixed in future printings, editions, and spin-offs. (Text files stick around forever—I actually encountered a few typos in files derived from my 1981 book while working on this one.) Therefore I will pay $4 to the first finder of each undiscovered error, be it technical, typographical, or otherwise. Please send your comments to me at Computer Systems Laboratory, Stanford University, Stanford CA 94305.

Any reader can request an up-to-date list of discovered errors by writing to me at the above address and enclosing a stamped self-addressed envelope. Only one ounce of first class postage will be needed, I hope.

ACKNOWLEDGEMENTS

Many people deserve thanks for making this book possible. My sponsoring editor at Wiley, Gene Davenport, gets the credit (or blame) for tricking me into writing this sort of book and its predecessor in the first place. He tricked me by sending me other microcomputer book proposals to review, to which I would always respond, "No, they've got it all wrong; if they were smart, they'd do it *this* way." Eventually I had to back up my reviews by actually writing a book *this* way. Now I suppose that some other authors will review *my* book and be motivated to write their own improved versions.

Actually, my notions of how to write an assembly language book were originally inspired by Harold Stone and his minicomputer-era book, *Introduction to Computer Organization and Data Structures* (McGraw-Hill, 1972). The opportunities that he gave me to see "inside" the book preparation process on that and several other projects made the whole process less scary. However, I'm still trying to catch up with him on number and quality of books published.

Instructors Timothy Chou and John Gill and over 600 students who took Stanford's introductory computer organization and assembly language programming course during the last three years used draft manuscripts during this book's preparation. Timothy formally reviewed the near-final manuscript and suggested many improvements based on his classroom experinece.

Comments from students and several anonymous reviewers were also very helpful. In addition to suggesting or otherwise motivating many improvements, the students spotted dozens of typographical and technical errors whose fixes are incorporated in the typeset book. James Loan was the clear winner, having spotted over 20 errors.

Recently I have been giving students an incentive of $4 for each new error they find. I offered them the option of putting their names in the preface instead of giving them money, but I had no takers. Oh well.

My friend Roger King was a great help when I was setting up the hardware and software tools that made the writing and production of this book possible. The folks at Apple Computer and, in particular, Developer Services, were very helpful in providing me with Macintosh resources. The Macintosh documentation was a joy to read.

On the production side, thanks go to Madelyn Lesure for patiently coaching me on the book design and layout, and to Jana Brenning for a beautiful cover design. Jim Kalopp at CopiGraphics did a nice job of printing and binding the draft manuscripts used by students and reviewers over the last few years. Most recently, Dick Sommers of Dick's Typesetter Service and Charles Collier of Collier Instruments helped me figure out how to use my Linotronic 100 typesetter.

My programmer, technician, and daughter's chauffeur, Matthew Kaufman, has made the most visible and useful contributions to this book. He drew all of the figures (though he may not admit to Figure 14–30, which he considers *very* silly), wrote several Macintosh and Unix utilities for handling the figures and text, and prepared the index. If you are a professor at UC Santa Cruz using this book, and a smart-alec student wearing bright colors tells you that *he* wrote the book, that's Matthew. On the other hand, if you are a co-ed, he's really quite nice and he *may* be available.

When I started writing this book in earnest, in January 1987, I took a leave of absence from my job at DAVID Systems, Inc. I was going to write this and a companion volume on the 80x86 family, all in less than a year! To my friends at DAVID, I can only say, thanks for the leave, and sorry I never made it back!

Of course, I must thank my wife Kate for putting up with the late hours and frequent pressures that come with a writing project such as this. My four-year-old daughter Susanne is starting to wonder why I'm always at home, working in the basement, so it must be time to finish up and get this book rolling off the presses.

John F. Wakerly
Mountain View, California
July 23, 1988

Preface to Instructors

The information in this preface is intended to help instructors weave their way through all the material in this book. Readers who are using the book as a reference should simply consult the appropriate section or the index to find what they're looking for.

From the Contents you can see that this book has been organized into logical topic areas, with thorough coverage of each topic. As a result, the book is a comprehensive reference containing far more information than would ever be used in an introductory course on computer organization and assembly language programming. Typical courses might cover only half to two-thirds of the material in Parts 1 and 2, and at most one additional processor from Part 3.

When I started writing this book, a number of reviewers suggested that the book be organized as a narrative that introduces small pieces of each topic as needed, so that the Contents would read like a typical instructor's lecture outline. The problem with this approach is that it requires *me* to decide what material should be covered and in what order. But why trust me to decide? Even in my own teaching, I don't follow exactly the same outline from quarter to quarter!

Therefore, I chose an organization that allows you as an instructor to assemble topics easily into an optimal course outline for your own student population and time schedule. This requires you to do a little more work up front than simply "following the book," but there are two benefits. First, you can find almost all of the material that *you* want to cover in this book, without requiring a lot of supplementary reading material. Second, when the course is over, your students have a comprehensive reference in which they can find even the material that you didn't want to cover.

A POSSIBLE COURSE OUTLINE

On the chance that it may make your job a little easier, I'll tell you about the course format that we use at Stanford. The goal is to teach assembly language programming and basic computer organization from a programmer's point of view to students who have previously had one or two programming courses in a high-level language. The academic quarter is ten weeks long with thirty 50-minute lectures.

TABLE 1   Computer Organization and Assembly Language Programming course outline.

Essential topics	Reading	Lectures
Introduction and course overview		0.5
Review of Pascal	2.1–2.9	1.0
Computer data types	1.6, 4.12	0.5
Positional number systems	4.1–4.4	1.0
Complement number systems	4.5–4.6	1.0
Basic computer organization	1.3, 5.1–5.7	1.5
Basic assembly language	5.8–5.10	0.5
Simple addressing modes	5.12, 7.1–7.2.4	0.8
Simple operations	8.1–8.6	0.8
Programming assignment #1	Notes	0.4
Assemblers and loaders	6.1–6.3	1.0
Condition codes, branches	8.7	0.5
Subroutines	5.13, 8.8	0.5
How to write programs and use the lab	Notes, 13.3, 13.5	1.0
Advanced addressing modes	7.2.5–7.3.6,	1.0
Addressing-mode applications	3.1–3.4	2.0
Miscellaneous operations	8.9–8.12	0.5
Programming assignment #2	Notes	0.5
Subroutines and parameters	9.1–9.3.6	2.0
Input/Output	10.1–10.3	1.5
Terminals and interfaces	A, 15.6	0.5
Queues	3.5, 9.3.7	1.0
Interrupts	11.1–11.4	1.5
Programming assignment #3	Notes	0.5
Interrupt processes	12.1–12.5	2.0

Optional topics	Reading	Lectures
Program development techniques	13.1–13.6	1.0
Recursion	9.4	1.0
Coroutines	9.5	1.0
Relocation and linking	6.4	0.5
Macros	6.5	0.5
Dynamic storage and lists	3.6–3.9	1.0
Multiplication and division	4.8–4.9, 8.10	1.0
Decimal arithmetic	4.10, 8.11	0.5
Floating-point arithmetic	4.11,15.3	1.0
Stack machines	19.1–19.4	1.0
DMA, block I/O devices	11.4, Notes	1.0
Serial I/O protocols and devices	B.1–B.2, 15.6	1.0
MC68010 and MC68020 architecture	14.1–14.9.6	2.0
68020 operating system support, PMMU	14.9.7, 15.4	3.0
Architecture of another processor	16, 17, or 18	2.0–3.0

Table 1 gives an outline of the topics that we cover, the corresponding reading material, and the approximate number of lectures we spend on each topic. Topics in the first part of the table are always covered, and we pick up topics from the second part of the table toward the end of the quarter according to time and interest.

USE OF PASCAL

In the first lecture or so, we handle administrative chores and describe the philosophy and a few salient features of Pascal, and then ask students unfamiliar with Pascal to skim Chapter 2. Although we use Pascal for explaining computer operations and as a documentation language for some assembly language programming examples, students need not be Pascal programmers to use this book. A reading knowledge of elementary Pascal programs is all that is required to understand the Pascal examples in this book.

PROGRAMMING ENVIRONMENT AND ASSIGNMENTS

Our course uses a real 68000-based computer for all example programs, and we require students to write several programs and run and debug them on the real hardware. The course outline requires careful planning to introduce topics and still leave enough time for corresponding programming assignments, especially in a 10-week quarter.

We currently use the Macintosh as the development and execution environment. This has the obvious advantage of allowing students to use their own systems as well as the countless Macs scattered around campus. However, we still use electronic mail on a central campus machine to communicate with the students outside the classroom.

We specifically use the Macintosh 68000 Development System (MDS) environment from Consulair Corp. It comes with an editor, assembler, linker, and interactive debugger, and is simple enough for a Mac novice to master in a few weeks. In the first week of class, we encourage anyone who has not used a Macintosh to at least learn the editor.

The first nontrivial programming assignment requires only knowledge of basic operations (load, store, add, branch) and addressing modes (register, immediate, absolute). In the Macintosh environment, we've also had to introduce based addressing very early in the lecture material. We give the students a Pascal algorithm for a problem such as binary-to-ASCII conversion (Exercise 5.23) or prime factors (Exercise 8.29). Input/output, if any, is performed using utility programs in the computer's ROM monitor. The students learn how to use the assembler and other software tools, they learn the basic features of the 68000 processor, and they get their first taste of debugging.

The second programming assignment uses advanced addressing modes and nontrivial data structures. At this point, we also make sure that the student understands subroutines and parameter passing, and we introduce notions of hierarchical program design. Handouts for the assignment usually include an initial program design that breaks down the problem into several modules with well-defined interfaces; the student's job is to design and code the internals of each module. Typical assignments have included included queue modules, linked list managers, and a recursive quicksort.

The third programming assignment introduces students to a multiple process environment. Although designing an I/O interrupt handler is an excellent vehicle for this material, this is difficult to do in the Macintosh environment.

Instead, we have the students implement a small multitasking kernel in which processes freely return control to the kernel when they are done and the kernel reschedules the next process. Once again, we give the students module specifications and let them design and code the internals.

When assignments are due, we ask the students to submit both a disk and a source listing. Naturally, we highly recommend that students maintain backups while they are in development.

ADDITIONAL MATERIALS

This book attempts to cover all software aspects of 68000-family processors, and so students should not need a 68000 processor reference manual.However, such a manual could be a useful adjunct for students who might benefit from a more encyclopedic description of the processor's instruction set.

This book does not describe all of the idiosyncrasies of different assembly languages and development systems for the 68000. Therefore, instructors and readers must refer to appropriate technical literature for their own needs. One or more system-specific documents may be needed:

- *Assembly language reference manual* (published by the processor manufacturer or cross-assembler vendor). This manual describes the syntax of the assembly language.

- *Development system software reference manual* (published by the development system manufacturer). This manual describes the development tools—editor, assembler, debugger—and how to use them.

- *Development system hardware reference manual* (published by the development system manufacturer). This manual describes the physical operation of the development system (e.g., how to turn it on), and any built-in program facilities (e.g., I/O and utility programs, debugging commands).

- *Lab procedures and configuration guide* (usually prepared by the instructor). If the students use the school's equipment, these few pages give them administrative information such as sign-up policy and lab hours, and describe the lab equipment and its configuration.

At Stanford, Consulair's MDS documentation provides the equivalent of the first two items, and general Macintosh documentation provides the third.

Instructors interested in more information on our particular way of teaching the computer organization and assembly language course using the Motorola 68000 can find it in the Instructor's Manual for this book, available from the publisher or from me at Computer Systems Laboratory, Stanford University, Stanford CA 94305. You will receive a fact sheet and course outline; sample programming assignments, exams, and solutions; solutions for many of the exercises; oversize copies of all the book's figures, suitable for transparencies; and a list of jokes to use at appropriate places in your lectures.

Contents

PART 3 / ADDITIONAL TOPICS   465

C H A P T E R   1

Introduction to Computers and Programming

1.1   WHAT IS A COMPUTER?

A computer is a large room full of equipment, clicking and clanking, whirring and flashing, satisfying the data-processing needs of a large organization. It monitors inventory, bills customers, pays creditors, edits and types reports, sends out personalized advertising notices, communicates with other computers, and, most importantly, prints payroll checks every second Wednesday. On some days it seems like the computer does everything but cook lunch.

A computer is a rack of equipment and a teleprinter in one corner of a scientist's laboratory. It controls an experiment by means of electrical impulses and mechanical actuators, and monitors its progress with temperature, pressure, and motion sensors. When the experiment is completed, the computer analyzes and graphs the results. Each morning when the scientist turns the computer on, it prints out, "Good morning, Susanne!"

A computer is a small box that sits in the hobby room where the ham radio used to be. It has a keyboard, a video display, a speaker, a tiny printer, and a slot that gobbles floppy disks with information stored on them. The computer stores correspondence, recipes, and financial records, gives educational quizzes to the children, calculates the tax refund every April 14 (including of course its own deduction as a business expense), engages opponents in tournament-level chess, and plays the *Star Trek* theme in four-part harmony and stereo. The computer owner's old-fashioned friends warn, "Watch out—the computer can take over your mind!"

A computer is a miniature electronic circuit deep inside a home appliance. It *does* cook lunch, but that's about all.

All of the above answers are valid, roughly spanning (but not defining) four categories of computers: maxicomputers, minicomputers, microcomputers, and microcontrollers. Even though the computers described above have widely varying sizes, capabilities, and costs, they share a great many characteristics and operating principles. The goal of this text is to describe general principles of computer architecture and programming that apply to computers of any category. However, we draw most of our examples from computers that we now classify as "microcomputers"—hence the title of the text.

Taken as a whole, a computer is an incredibly complex system, with many more levels of detail than, say, the noncomputer part of an automobile. Fortunately, a computer system *is* structured into many levels, so that it is easy to understand if taken one level at a time.

hardware
architecture

The lowest level in a computer is its *hardware*—the electronic circuits from which it is built. The next level is its *architecture*—the interconnection of hardware elements and the structure and features perceived by someone using the machine (some people may refer to this area as hardware also). The highest (and

software
program

most noble?) level is *software*—the sequences of instructions, or *programs*, that make the computer do useful work. Each of the above levels could be further decomposed into additional levels. In the next few sections we give a "bottom-up" description of the hardware, architecture, and software of modern computer systems.

1.2   DIGITAL COMPUTER HARDWARE

analog computer

Most computers in use today are digital, as opposed to analog. An *analog computer* represents numbers by a continuously varying phenomenon such as pressure, position, or voltage. Slide rules and specialized calculating wheels

electronic analog
computer

are examples of analog computers. An *electronic analog computer* performs a computation by means of an electrical circuit whose operating characteristics emulate the desired computation. For example, addition of two numbers can be emulated by a circuit whose output voltage is the sum of two input voltages; the value of e^{-t} can be obtained by timed observations of the voltage across a capacitor as it discharges through a resistor. Electronic analog computers have been used most often for simulation of physical systems modeled by complicated differential equations.

digital computer
digit

The distinguishing characteristic of a *digital computer* is that it stores and manipulates entities representing *digits*. Most of the physical phenomena that have been exploited in modern computer technology have one of two stable states, thereby representing one of two digits. Hence, digital computers process

binary digit
bit

binary digits, or *bits*; a bit has the value 0 or 1.

Examples of the physical phenomena used to represent bits in some modern computer technologies are presented in Table 1–1. With most phenomena, there is an undefined region between the 0 and 1 states (e.g., voltage = 1.5, dim light, and capacitor slightly charged). This undefined region is necessary so that the

TABLE 1–1 Physical states representing bits in different computer logic and memory technologies.

| Technology | State Representing Bit | |
	0	1
Transistor-transistor logic	0–0.8 volts	2.0–5.0 volts
Fiber optics	Light off	Light on
Dynamic memory	Capacitor discharged	Capacitor charged
Nonvolatile, erasable memory	Electrons trapped	Electrons released
Bipolar read-only memory	Fuse blown	Fuse intact
Charge-coupled device memory	No charge	Charge present
Bubble memory	No magnetic bubble	Bubble present
Magnetic tape or disk	No flux reversal	Flux reversal
Polymer memory	Molecule in state A	Molecule in state B

Notes: A *positive logic* convention is assumed. In *negative logic*, the state correspondences are simply reversed.

0 and 1 states can be unambiguously defined and reliably detected. Noise can more easily corrupt results if the boundaries separating the 0 and 1 states are too close.

digital logic
gate

Digital logic is used to manipulate bits inside a computer. The basic logic elements are *gates*, which take one or more bits as inputs and produce one bit of output. Figure 1–1 shows three basic gates, AND, OR, and NOT (or INVERTER), and their function tables. Any desired logic function can be developed from these basic gates. For example, a circuit that adds two 16-bit numbers

combinational

could be designed using about 250 of these gates. Gates are *combinational* logic elements—they accept their inputs, combine them, and produce an output immediately, in less than 10 nanoseconds (10×10^{-9} seconds) in typical technologies.

memory element
S-R flip-flop

Memory elements are used to retain logic values in a digital circuit. The basic memory element is the *S-R flip-flop* shown in Figure 1–2. Normally both inputs to the flip-flop are 0. If a logic 1 is momentarily applied to the S input, the Q output will go to the value 1. Because of the feedback of Q into the bottom OR gate, Q will remain at 1 even after the S input returns to 0. The Q

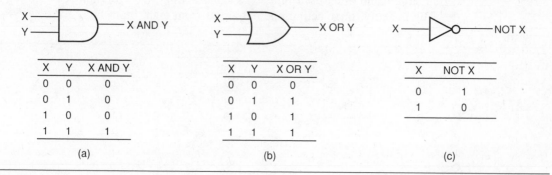

X	Y	X AND Y
0	0	0
0	1	0
1	0	0
1	1	1

(a)

X	Y	X OR Y
0	0	0
0	1	1
1	0	1
1	1	1

(b)

X	NOT X
0	1
1	0

(c)

FIGURE 1–1 Logic gates: (a) AND; (b) OR; (c) NOT.

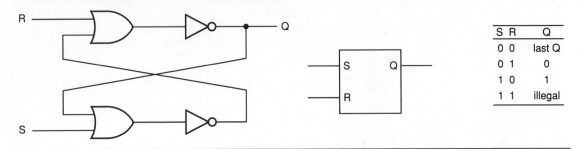

S R	Q
0 0	last Q
0 1	0
1 0	1
1 1	illegal

FIGURE 1–2 A simple S-R flip-flop: (a) circuit; (b) symbol; (c) function table.

output can be reset to 0 by momentarily applying a 1 to the R input. Hence the flip-flop can be used to store one bit of information.

The function table for a more complicated flip-flop is shown in Figure 1–3. This *positive edge-triggered D flip-flop* has two inputs, CLK (clock) and D (data). Each time the CLK input changes from 0 to 1, the value on the D input is sampled and transferred to the Q output. At all other times, the value of Q is held at its current value and the D input is ignored. D flip-flops are grouped together into *registers* to store multi-bit quantities in a computer. For example, 16 D flip-flops form a register that stores a 16-bit number. Although flip-flops are the most common storage element in a computer processor, other memory elements shown in Table 1–1 are typically used to store large quantities of information in the main memory or mass storage devices in a computer.

Computer logic elements are manufactured as *integrated circuits (IC)*, tiny electronic circuits etched in rectangular chips of silicon no larger than a centimeter on a side. The smallest ICs contain only a small number of individual logic gates or flip-flops and are called *small-scale integration (SSI)* circuits. SSI circuits in computer systems today are used mainly for miscellaneous, irregular control functions. Larger, more regular control and data manipulation functions are performed in *medium-scale integration (MSI)* circuits. A typical MSI circuit contains 10 to 100 individual gates and flip-flops arranged to perform a well-structured and often-used function such as adding two 4-bit numbers, storing an 8-bit quantity, or selecting one output bit from eight input bits.

positive edge-triggered D flip-flop

register

integrated circuit (IC)

small-scale integration (SSI)

medium-scale integration (MSI)

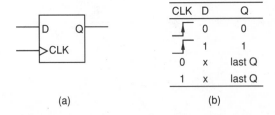

CLK	D	Q
↑	0	0
↑	1	1
0	x	last Q
1	x	last Q

(a) (b)

FIGURE 1–3 Positive edge-triggered D flip-flop: (a) symbol; (b) function table.

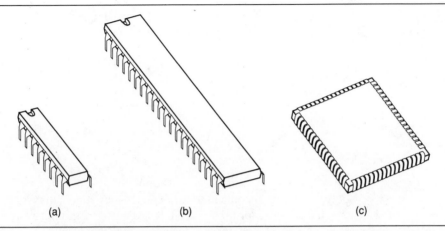

(a)   (b)   (c)

FIGURE 1–4   Examples of integrated circuit packages (actual size): (a) 16-pin (typical SSI and MSI); (b) 40-pin (LSI microprocessor); (c) 68-pin (VLSI microprocessor).

large-scale integration (LSI)

very large scale integration (VLSI)

programmable logic device (PLD)

High-level system functions requiring more than 100 gates are performed by *large-scale integration (LSI)* and *very large scale integration (VLSI)* circuits. The dividing line between LSI and VLSI is fuzzy; it is sometimes given as 100,000 devices (transistors or diodes).

The smallest function that might be classified as LSI is a 4×4-bit register file; larger functions falling into the LSI category include memories storing up to 64 Kbits[1], 8-bit and 16-bit microprocessors, memory management units, serial communication circuits, and peripheral device controllers. *Programmable logic devices (PLDs)* are an important class of LSI parts that have eliminated 90% of the SSI and MSI parts in many systems. A PLD contains gates, flip-flops, input pins, and output pins whose interconnection may be "programmed" by a pattern that is loaded into the device when the device is first used.

VLSI parts include 256-Kbit and larger memories, sophisticated 16-bit microprocessors and microcomputers, and 32-bit processors (which perhaps should no longer be called "micro"!).

Figure 1–4 gives an indication of the physical size and packaging of digital ICs. Larger circuits generally require larger packages, both to contain the larger silicon chip and to provide more input/output pins. However, some very large regular circuits such as memories can still be squeezed into a small package.

A complete computer system may contain anywhere from 1 to 100,000 integrated circuit packages, and so system packaging techniques obviously can

K
M

[1]In normal business jargon, the letters "K" and "M" refer to the quantities 1,000 and 1,000,000, respectively. However, in computer memory jargon, these letters are used to refer to the quantities 2^{10} (1,024) and 2^{20} (1,048,576), as recommended by the American National Standards Institute (ANSI). Warning: If you apply for a programming job and ask for a salary of $40K, don't expect $40,960!

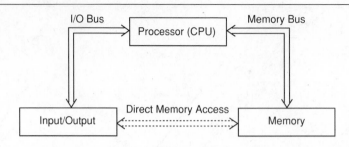

FIGURE 1–5   Block diagram of a typical computer.

vary widely. The microcontroller that cooks your lunch may occupy only a few square inches on a printed circuit board inside the microwave oven; the major packaging challenge for its designers may have been to shield it from microwave interference. On the other hand, the large mainframe computer that prints payroll checks while you eat may fill a room; the major challenge for its designers may have been in cooling and air conditioning.

1.3 BASIC COMPUTER ORGANIZATION

processor

central processing unit (CPU)

A computer system consists of three major subsystems: processor, memory, and input/output (I/O), as shown in Figure 1–5. The *processor* (or *central processing unit*, *CPU*) is the heart of the computer. As shown in Figure 1–6, a simple processor contains control circuits for fetching and executing instructions, an arithmetic logic unit for manipulating data, and registers for storing the processor status and a small amount of data. It also has interface circuits for controlling and communicating with the memory and I/O subsystems.

register-transfer level description

The block diagram in Figure 1–6 is a rather incomplete description of a processor. A *register-transfer level description* of a processor indicates the names and functions of registers and computation units, and describes the operations and interactions of these units for every instruction that the processor can execute. In Chapter 5, we'll use the programming language Pascal as a register-transfer language to describe the operation of the Motorola 68000 processor.

memory

main memory

bus

location

address

The *memory* (or *main memory*) of a computer contains storage for instructions and data, and is tied to the processor via the Memory Bus in Figure 1–5. A *bus* is simply a bundle of wires or any other physical medium for transferring information. A computer memory has some number of *locations*, each of which stores a b-bit quantity. Associated with each location in the memory is a unique binary number called the *address*. If there are n locations, then the addresses range from 0 to $n - 1$.

random access

The key feature that distinguishes main memory from other forms of storage in a computer is *random access*—the processor has equally fast access to every location in memory. Random access memory is analogous to a wall of

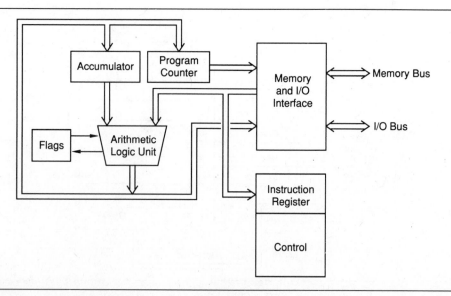

FIGURE 1–6   Block diagram of a simple processor.

post office boxes; a postal clerk can deposit mail in any box with equal ease. Compare this with the *serial access* method of a letter carrier who visits locations sequentially, in the order of the route. Magnetic tapes provide serial-access memory in computer systems.

Figure 1–7 shows how the processor accesses main memory in a typical small computer system. The memory is an array of n locations of b bits each. To read the data stored at location X, the processor places the number X on the Address Bus, and activates a Read control signal; the memory responds by placing the contents of location X on the Data Bus. To write a value V at location X, the processor places X on the Address Bus and V on the Data Bus and activates Write; the memory immediately writes the value V in the specified location. Subsequent reading of address X will now return the value V.

input/output (I/O)
peripheral device

The *input/output (I/O)* subsystem contains *peripheral devices* for communicating with, observing, and controlling the world outside the computer. Peripheral devices include terminals, printers, communication devices, and mechanical sensors and actuators. Also included in the I/O subsystem are *mass storage devices* such as magnetic tapes and disks. These devices are used to store information not needed in the main memory at all times, such as applications programs and text files. Not all computers have mass storage devices, but all useful computers have at least one peripheral device, since by definition a peripheral is the computer's only means of communicating with the outside world.

mass storage
device

The processor writes and reads information to and from peripherals by means of I/O instructions that place commands and data on the I/O Bus. In many computers, both main memory and peripherals share the same physical

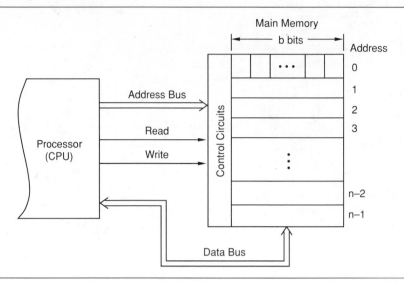

FIGURE 1–7   Main memory in a typical computer.

bus. Going one step further, some processors communicate with their peripherals using registers that masquerade as memory locations—the I/O registers are accessed with the same buses, control signals, and instructions as main memory. The Motorola 68000 is such a processor, as we'll see in Chapter 10.

In simple computer systems, there is no direct path from peripherals to main memory; the only way to transfer data between a peripheral and memory is for the processor to read it from the peripheral and store it in memory, or vice versa. However, systems requiring a higher data transfer rate incorporate *direct memory access (DMA)*, a link between a special peripheral controller and memory that allows a peripheral to read and write memory without processor intervention; DMA is explained in Chapter 11.

direct memory access (DMA)

1.4 COMPUTER SYSTEM SOFTWARE

software

program
data base
file
input
data
machine language

Computer *software* consists of the instructions and data that the computer hardware manipulates to perform useful work. A sequence of instructions for a computer is called a *program*. The data manipulated by a program may be called a *data base*, a *file*, *input*, or simply *data*, depending on its nature and extent (and, to some degree, the whims of the speaker!).

The most primitive instructions that can be given to a computer are those interpreted directly by hardware, in the *machine language* of the computer. Machine language instructions are encoded as strings of bits in the computer's main memory, and are fetched and executed one by one by the processor. Machine instructions perform primitive operations such as "add 3 to register D1," "store the contents of register D1 into memory location 16," "add the contents of memory location 132 to register D2," or "jump to the instruction sequence starting at location 208 if register C is zero."

assembly language assembler

Since it is difficult for humans to read and recognize strings of bits, machine language programs are written in *assembly language* and translated into bit strings by an *assembler*. Assembly language represents machine instructions by mnemonic names and allows memory addresses and other constants to be represented by symbols rather than bit strings.

mnemonic

For example, the machine instruction that adds 3 to register D1 might be encoded as the bit string 0101 011 000000 001. Here 0101nnn000000ddd is the general format for the instruction "Add small integer N to Data Register," the nnn field contains the binary representation of "3", and the ddd field selects a particular data register D1. In assembly language, the same instruction could be written as ADD #ADJ,D1, where ADD is the instruction *mnemonic* and ADJ is a symbolic constant whose value is defined elsewhere in the program to be 3. The assembler translates the symbolic instruction ADD #ADJ,D1 into the bit string 0101 011 000000 001.

Assembly language is used for much computer software, most often in small computers or microcontrollers and in frequently invoked program modules in large computers. However, often it takes several assembly language instructions to perform operations that can be stated in one line in English, such as "Set *W* equal to *W* plus *X* minus *Y* divided by *Z*," or "Repeat the next sequence of instructions until *X* is less than 0 or *Y* equals *Z*."

high-level language statement

Studies have shown that both the time to write and debug a program and the difficulty of understanding and maintaining it are proportional to the number of instructions, with little dependency on the complexity of each instruction. Therefore, most programs are written in *high-level languages* that allow common operations such as expression evaluation, repetition, assignment, and conditional action to be invoked in a single high-level *statement*. Furthermore, *structured high-level languages* such as Pascal impose a programming discipline that makes programs easier to design, understand, and maintain.

compiler

Few computers can execute a high-level language directly. Therefore, most programmers use a *compiler* to translate a high-level language program into a sequence of machine instructions that performs the desired task. Since five to ten machine instructions are generated for each high-level statement, the savings in programming time and cost over an equivalent assembly language program should be obvious.

Still, there are some arguments to support programming in assembly language. Since assembly language allows the programmer to write *any* sequence of machine instructions, it is always theoretically possible to write an assembly language program that is at least as compact and efficient as the machine language program emitted by a compiler. Depending on the compiler, the computer, and the application, a compiled program might be anywhere from 0% to 300% longer and slower than the *optimal* machine language program, but it may be substantially better than a machine language program written by a person with average skills (and patience!).

The reduced development cost and enhanced maintainability of high-level language programs almost always outweigh their inefficiencies. In most development projects, the cost of more memory to store longer programs is less than the cost of hiring more programmers, especially since in a large project it may take four times as many programmers to write a program twice as long. This is not a criticism of programmers; rather it indicates the nonlinear increase in the time spent communicating as the size of the project increases.

The speed of high-level language programs is usually not a problem. If a program is found to be too slow, it can often be improved without rewriting much of it. In a typical program, 10% of the written program accounts for 90% of its execution time. Critical subprograms, once identified, can be rewritten and optimized in either the original high-level language or assembly language.

coding
code
programming

Since machine instructions in a computer are en*coded*, the act of writing instructions in any language has come to be known as *coding*, and the written instructions are called *code*. Coding is just a small part of *programming*, which is the overall process of designing, specifying, documenting, coding, and debugging programs.

software tool

Assemblers and compilers are not the only *software tools* that a programmer may encounter. Other useful tools related to program development are interpreters, simulators, and on-line debuggers. Like a compiler, an *interpreter* processes a high-level language program. Unlike a compiler, an interpreter actually executes the high-level language program one statement at a time, rather than translating each statement into a sequence of machine instructions to be run later. A *simulator* is a program that simulates individual machine instructions, usually on a machine other than the one being simulated. A typical use of a simulator is to test programs to be run on a processor before the processor hardware is available. An *on-line debugger* executes a program on a machine one or a few instructions at a time, allowing the programmer to see the effects of small pieces of the program and thereby isolate programming errors (*bugs*).

interpreter

simulator

on-line debugger

bug
text editor
text formatter

Text editors are used to enter and edit text in a general-purpose computer, whether the text is a letter, a report, or a computer program. *Text formatters* read text with imbedded formatting commands and produce pretty, formatted documents such as this book. Text editors and formatters belong to the area of computing known as *word processing*.

word processing

operating system

In a medium to large computer system, cooperating programs run under the control of an *operating system*. An operating system schedules programs for execution, controls the use of I/O devices, and provides utility functions for all of the programs that run on the computer. Programs and text stored on disks and other mass storage devices are managed by a *file system*, a collection of programs for reading, writing, and structuring such information in *files*. The operating systems in most computers include file systems. Even a very small computer with no mass storage or file system has a simple operating system, at least to monitor inputs and accept commands from the outside world.

file system
file

1.5 ALGORITHMS

algorithm

primitive

"Computers are stupid; they won't do anything unless they're told, and once told, they'll perform *exactly* as specified, even if it's stupid." This is an often-heard and accurate description of the computational capability of computers. A computer requires a precise sequence of instructions to perform any task; such a sequence is called an *algorithm.*

To be an algorithm, a sequence of instructions must satisfy two important properties. First of all, each instruction must be taken from the set of basic operations, called *primitives*, available in the machine that runs the algorithm. Thus, the algorithm for multiplying 119 by 102 may be just one instruction in a machine with multiplication as a primitive; it may consist of a few additions and shifts in a machine with these operations as primitives; and it consists of 102 additions of 119 in a machine with only addition and counting as primitives.

Second, an algorithm must produce a result in a finite number of steps. Not only does this mean that the algorithm itself contains a limited number of instructions, but also that any instructions specifying enumeration, repetition, or trial and error will eventually terminate. For example, a sequence of instructions that tries to compute all of the prime numbers can't be an algorithm, since there are an infinite number of primes.

Even when a problem has a finite solution, a particular sequence of instructions to find the solution may never terminate. Consider the following sequence of instructions to divide a positive number X by 5:

(1) Set Q equal to 0.

(2) Set X equal to $X - 5$ and set Q equal to $Q + 1$.

(3) If X is between 0 and 4, then terminate; the quotient is Q and the remainder is X. Otherwise, return to step 2.

This sequence works fine if X is initially 5 or larger. However, it never terminates if X is initially between 0 and 4. The first time that the test in step 3 is encountered, X will be negative, and it will just keep getting more negative with successive repetitions of steps 2 and 3. This example is typical of a common error in computer "algorithms"—an instruction sequence that works most of the time, but fails because of unexpected test results in one or more special cases.

The example could be modified in step 3 above to test only for X less than or equal to 4. Then it will terminate, but still produce incorrect results for X between 0 and 4. The following algorithm terminates and produces correct results for all positive values of X:

(1) Set Q equal to 0.

(2) If X is between 0 and 4, then terminate; the quotient is Q and the remainder is X. Otherwise, set X equal to $X - 5$ and set Q equal to $Q + 1$.

(3) Return to step 2.

Even "correct" algorithms can be improved upon. The algorithm above relies on the user to supply a positive value of X; if X is initially negative, the sequence above never terminates. Robust algorithms always check that their inputs are within an allowed range. Formulating correct and robust algorithms is one of the most important aspects of programming.

1.6   COMPUTER DATA TYPES

data type

Although we may sometimes think that computers manipulate only numbers, in reality they process many different types of data (*data types*). In fact, it is fair to say that most of the input and output of computers today is nonnumeric.

Recall that the basic unit of information storage in a digital computer is the *bit*, which has a value of either 0 or 1. Obviously a single-bit data type is not very useful for numeric computation, since it only allows us to count from 0 to 1! Nevertheless, the bit is a very useful data type if we interpret its values

TRUE
FALSE
logical type
boolean type
boolean algebra

1 and 0 to represent two logic values, TRUE and FALSE. The resulting data type is called *logical* or *boolean*, after George Boole, who invented a mathematical system forming the basis for the two-valued *boolean algebra* used in digital logic design. The boolean type has many uses in a program, for example, to save the results of comparisons, to mark special cases, and in general to distinguish between two possible outcomes or conditions.

bit string

By assembling two or more bits into a *bit string*, we can represent more than two values or conditions. The bits in a string of n bits can take on 2^n different combinations of values. For example, a 4-bit string has 16 different values, and Table 1–2 shows several different ways of assigning meanings to the 16 combinations. In Chapter 4, we shall look at many different systems for assigning numeric values to bit strings. However, we can also assign nonnumeric meanings as shown by the last three columns in the table. It is usual to associate a numeric name with each unique bit string even if the bit string represents a nonnumeric value. For example, referring to the fifth column of Table 1–2, we might say, "The number 5 represents the color green."

byte

Strings of eight bits are usually referred to as *bytes*. The name "byte" was invented at IBM in the early days of electronic computers. The name for a string

nibble

of four bits is fancifully derived from the byte—the *nibble*.

word
word length

A bit string manipulated by a computer in one operation is usually called a *word*. Some computers have a *word length* as short as 4 bits, others as long as 64 bits or more. Many minicomputers and microcomputers have standardized in using "word" to describe 16-bit strings, and using "longword" or "double word" to describe 32-bit strings. Some large computers, such as the IBM 370, use

nibble
byte
word
longword
quadword

"word" to describe a 32-bit string, and use "double word" and "half word" to describe 64-bit and 16-bit strings, respectively. We will adopt standard micro-computer usage in this text: *nibble* = 4 bits; *byte* = 8 bits; *word* = 16 bits; *longword* = 32 bits; *quadword* = 64 bits.

TABLE 1–2   Values and meanings of 4-bit strings.

String	Unsigned Integer	Signed Integer	Unsigned Fraction	Color	City	Food
0000	0	+0	0	Black	St. Louis	Hot dog
0001	1	+1	$1/16$	Brown	Miami	Pizza
0010	2	+2	$1/8$	Red	Chicago	Hamburger
0011	3	+3	$3/16$	Orange	San Francisco	Steak
0100	4	+4	$1/4$	Yellow	Detroit	Chocolate cake
0101	5	+5	$5/16$	Green	New York	Pudding
0110	6	+6	$3/8$	Blue	Boston	Banana cream pie
0111	7	+7	$7/16$	Violet	Houston	Pretzel
1000	8	−8	$1/2$	Gray	Denver	Oatmeal
1001	9	−7	$9/16$	White	Memphis	Broccoli
1010	10	−6	$5/8$	Silver	Portland	Cream cheese
1011	11	−5	$11/16$	Gold	Milwaukee	Beer
1100	12	−4	$3/4$	Tan	Seattle	Ice cream
1101	13	−3	$13/16$	Indigo	Juneau	Asparagus
1110	14	−2	$7/8$	Pink	Honolulu	Mystery meat
1111	15	−1	$15/16$	Puce	Albuquerque	Escargot

Bits, nibbles, bytes, and words are easy data types to classify because they require differing amounts of storage in the computer memory. There are other data types that are classified not by how much storage they take, but how they are interpreted and used by the computer hardware and software. For example, a microcomputer might define the following four data types, all using a 16-bit word:

- *Unsigned integer.* The word represents an unsigned integer between 0 and 65,535.

- *Signed integer.* The word represents a signed integer between −32,768 and +32,767.

- *Address.* The word represents an address in a memory with a maximum size of 65,536 bytes.

- *Logical array.* The word contains 16 independent boolean flags.

Even though all four data types could be stored exactly the same way in the computer's memory, they may be manipulated by the hardware and software differently. For example, an arithmetic operation on an unsigned integer "overflows" when the correct result is less than 0 or greater than 65,535, while an operation on a signed integer overflows when the result is less than −32,768 or greater than 32,767.

The same computer might define three different data types employing a 32-bit longword:

- *Long signed integer.* The longword represents an integer in the range $-2,147,483,648$ to $+2,147,483,647$.

- *Floating point.* The longword represents a number in the range $-1.7 \cdot 10^{38}$ to $+1.7 \cdot 10^{38}$.

- *Long address.* The low-order 24 bits of the longword are used as an address in memory and the high-order 8 bits are not used.

supported data type

A data type is said to be *supported* by a computer if the computer's instruction set contains operations that manipulate data and produce results according to the data type's interpretation of bit strings.

1.7 CLASSIFICATION OF COMPUTERS

Computers can be examined from several different viewpoints and classified according to many different criteria. We shall describe one classification here in order to clarify our own use of computer jargon.

Computers are classified as supercomputers, maxicomputers, midicomputers, minicomputers, and microcomputers according to system size. We'll give a rough definition of each category and then explain:

supercomputer

- *Supercomputer:* a very high performance computer for large scientific or "number-crunching" applications, costing millions of dollars. Examples: CRAY–II, ILLIAC IV.

maxicomputer

- *Maxicomputer:* a large, high-performance, general-purpose computer system costing over a million dollars. Examples: CYBER 76, IBM 3090.

midicomputer

- *Midicomputer:* a general-purpose computer lying between minis and maxis in performance and price. Examples: VAX–8600, HP 3000.

minicomputer

- *Minicomputer:* a general-purpose computer, often tailored for a specific, dedicated application, costing between $20,000 and $200,000. Examples: VAX–8200, PDP–11/84.

microcomputer

- *Microcomputer:* a computer whose CPU is a microprocessor, often configured for a specific, dedicated application and costing well under $20,000. Examples: MicroVAX–2000, Macintosh, IBM PC, Sun-386i.

Before we continue, we should clarify the meanings of four other terms that use the prefix "micro":

microprocessor

- *Microprocessor:* a complete processor (CPU) contained in one or a few LSI circuits, used to build a microcomputer in the context above. Examples: MC68000, 80386, MC6809.

microcomputer
single-chip
* microcomputer*

- *Microcomputer:* in another context, a processor, memory, and I/O system contained in one LSI circuit, often referred to as a *single-chip microcomputer* for clarity. Examples: MCS–51, MC68HC11.

microcontroller

- *Microcontroller:* a processor, memory, and I/O system contained in one or a few LSI circuits, tailored to an application that hides the general-purpose data-processing capabilities of the computer from the users. Examples: processors used in microwave ovens, automobiles, electronic games.

microprogrammed
* processor*
microinstruction
microprogramming

- *Microprogrammed processor:* a particular type of processor in which the control hardware executes each machine instruction as a sequence of primitive *microinstructions. Microprogramming* refers to writing sequences of microinstructions, *not* the programming of microprocessors. Examples of microprogrammed processors: MC68000, 80386.

The definitions of computer classes are vague for a number of reasons. Advances in technology tend to blur classifications based on hardware design or performance. For example, many contemporary microcomputers outperform the maxicomputers of 15 years ago.

A classification based on application is also imprecise, because computers of different sizes and costs are often used in the same application, simply depending on the size and requirements of the application. For example, an individual author may use a dedicated microcomputer in the basement for word processing, while in a large company many users may share word-processing facilities on a maxicomputer.

Cost is the best single characteristic for distinguishing the above computer classes. As time goes on, advances in technology make higher performance available for the same price, matching the demands of users of a particular computer class for better capabilities for the same price. Furthermore, as time goes on, new computer classes are created by new applications and classes of users. "Personal computers" and "workstations" are examples of such classes.

Because the definition of computer classes is fuzzy, different people sometimes place the same machine in different categories. However, most machines at any given time will clearly fall into one class or another. Rather than trying to be more precise, we close this section by noting that computer classification is really important only to authors who feel obliged to write about it. The general concepts of computer architecture and programming discussed in Part 2 are applicable to computers of all classes.

R E F E R E N C E S

Digital computer hardware, including gate-level design, MSI and LSI building blocks, memory systems, I/O devices and interfaces, and system design, is discussed in detail in several texts. Worthwhile texts include *Logic Design*

Principles by Edward J. McCluskey (Prentice-Hall, 1986), *Computer Design* by Glen G. Langdon (Computeach Press, 1982), *Microcomputer Interfacing* by Harold S. Stone (Addison-Wesley, 1982), and *Microprocessor-Based Design* by Michael Slater (Mayfield, 1987).

There are many more dimensions to computer architecture than we can possibly cover or even mention in an introductory text. However, *Structured Computer Organization* by Andrew S. Tanenbaum (Prentice-Hall, 1984, 2nd ed.) has good coverage of several important levels—digital logic, microprogramming, machine language, assembly language, and operating system. *Computer Hardware/Software Architecture* by Wing Toy and Benjamin Zee (Prentice-Hall, 1986) also describes several levels, from operating systems and high-level languages down to instruction set design, and it even contains a chapter on fault-tolerant computing.

You can sample some advanced concepts in hardware organization in *Principles of Computer Structures* by D. P. Siewiorek, C. G. Bell, and A. Newell (McGraw-Hill, 1982) and *High-Performance Computer Architecture*, by H. S. Stone (Addison-Wesley, 1987). A collection of papers on all the machines produced by Digital Equipment Corporation, *Computer Engineering* by C. G. Bell, J. C. Mudge, and J. E. McNamara (Digital Press, 1978), is especially recommended for hardware engineers; it contains a wealth of practical insight not found in ordinary textbooks. It also has a chapter on seven different ways to classify computers, for those of you who found the last section of this chapter unsatisfactory.

Computer software has dominated hardware in cost for some time now, and the importance of the field is probably best evidenced by your own interest in it. There are many software areas that merit your additional study; we'll mention them as they occur in later chapters.

One somewhat nebulous area not covered in this book is *how to program*. We introduce some rules and tools and give examples, but we do not describe the actual creative process of writing a program. We hope that most readers will have already experienced this creativity by writing programs in a high-level language. If not, there are some books that can help. *An Introduction to Programming and Problem Solving with Pascal* by G. M. Schneider, S. W. Weingart, and D. M. Perlman (Wiley, 1982, 2nd ed.) has an extended discussion of how to develop algorithms. Both this book and *Software Tools in Pascal* by Brian W. Kernighan and P. J. Plauger (Addison-Wesley, 1981) show the step-by-step construction of many Pascal programs. Even if you think you already know how to write programs, read *The Elements of Programming Style* by Kernighan and Plauger (McGraw-Hill, 1978) to see whether you know how to write *good* programs.

C H A P T E R 2

The Programming Language Pascal

Pascal is a "structured" high-level language that allows programs and data to be defined in a natural, hierarchical fashion. In addition to having widespread use on large computers in the academic, scientific, and business communities, Pascal is one of the most popular high-level languages for microcomputers. Pascal compilers exist for all major microcomputers; several microcomputer chip manufacturers provide Pascal-based software; and there was even a microcomputer (the Pascal Microengine by Western Digital Corp.) that had primitive Pascal "P-code" as its machine language.

The language's designer, Niklaus Wirth, named Pascal after the French philosopher, but not because of Pascal's teachings. Wirth said in a letter to *Electronics*[1]

> Actually, I am neither capable of fully understanding his philosophy nor of appreciating his religious exaltations. Pascal, however, was (perhaps one of) the first to invent and construct a device that we now classify as a digital computer. He did so at the age of 16, when he was called upon by his father, who was a tax collector, to assist in the numerous and tedious calculations.

This chapter provides a brief description of the programming language Pascal. It serves as an introduction for a reader with no previous exposure to Pascal, and as a review for a reader who has used it before.

The description of Pascal in this chapter is not complete. Some features of Pascal are described elsewhere in this book: arrays in Sections 3.1 and 3.2, records and pointers in Sections 3.3 and 3.6, and procedures, functions, and their parameters in Sections 9.1 and 9.2. Some Pascal features have been omitted completely: set types, file handling, formatted input/output, and implementation

---

[1] Vol. 51, No. 26, 21 December 1978, p. 6.

*Pascal
    implementation*

dependencies. (A *Pascal implementation* consists of the compiler and run-time environment for a particular computer system.)

Nevertheless, the subset of Pascal presented here is quite adequate for giving algorithmic descriptions of data structures, assembly language programs, and computer instruction sets in later chapters. In fact, it covers enough of the language to write rather powerful "real" Pascal programs. The reader who plans to write and run "real" Pascal programs should still consult the reference manual for the compiler being used, and possibly one of the Pascal books listed at the end of this chapter.

2.1   OVERVIEW

declaration

Three key elements contribute to making Pascal a "structured" language: declarations, block structure, and procedural code. *Declarations* require the programmer to supply certain information to the compiler about the structure of the program—the name and types of all variables that will be used, and the names of all labels referenced by discontinuities in program flow (GOTO statements). They also allow a good programmer to give optional information to the compiler and to improve program readability in a number of ways: by defining identifiers that convey the meaning of program constants, by restricting the range of variables to allow automatic error checking, and by explicitly defining data structures in a way that the compiler supports and a reader understands.

*block structure
statement
simple statement
assignment
    statement
structured
    statement
compound
    statement*

Figure 2–1 illustrates the *block structure* of Pascal programs. *Statements* specify the actions in a program; Pascal defines both simple and structured statements. A *simple statement* performs a single action; for example, the *assignment statement* x := (3+y)/7 computes the value of the expression (3+y)/7 and assigns it to the variable x. A *structured statement* contains one or more other statements and controls them by well-defined rules. The most important structured statement is the *compound statement*, a list of other statements bracketed by the words BEGIN and END. Another example is the FOR statement, which repeats a statement a predetermined number of times.

Now here's where block structure comes in: a structured statement can control *any* statement, including another structured statement. If we draw each statement as a block, the program shown in Figure 2–1 looks like a "nested" set of blocks. Block structure lets Pascal programs reflect a natural method of problem solving: repetitively and conditionally executing simple instruction sequences.

procedural code

Procedural code is the name used to describe a program that is decomposed into modules with well-defined interfaces and interactions. Procedural code

top-down design

results from a *top-down* approach to program design, wherein a program is defined in terms of a few high-level modules (procedures and functions), each of which is defined in terms of lower-level modules.

*procedure
function*

A *procedure* is a defined sequence of declarations and statements that can be invoked by a single statement. A *function* is defined similarly, but is

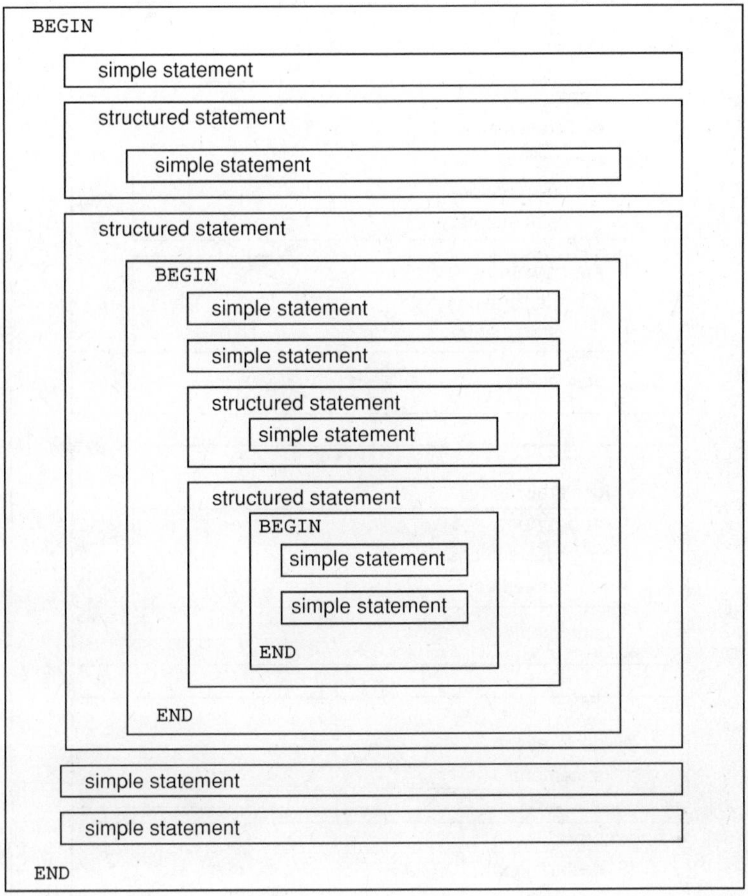

```
BEGIN

    simple statement

    structured statement
        simple statement

    structured statement

        BEGIN

            simple statement

            simple statement

            structured statement
                simple statement

            structured statement
                BEGIN
                    simple statement

                    simple statement

                END

        END

    simple statement

    simple statement

END
```

FIGURE 2–1   Block structure in Pascal.

invoked by writing the function name in an expression, as one would normally use a variable name. Besides including a number of predefined procedures and functions, Pascal allows each program to define its own procedures and functions. As shown in Figure 2–2, Pascal supports top-down design by using the same general structure for procedures and functions as it does for programs, and by allowing each procedure or function to define its own subservient procedures and functions.

scope

The *scope* of an item defined within a program or procedure is the part of the program in which that definition is recognized. In Figure 2–2, the scope of an item defined in a given block is limited to that block and all the smaller blocks

global
local

contained in it. Items defined in the outermost block are called *global*; items defined in an inner block are *local* to that block. Thus, the programmer may

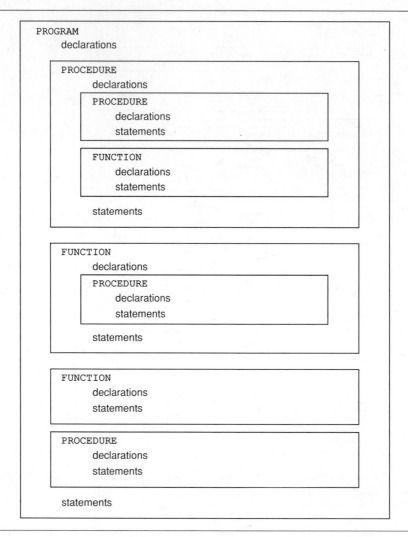

FIGURE 2–2   Program, procedure, and function structure in Pascal.

define local variables, data structures, and procedures within one block without concern about possible conflicts in other blocks at the same or higher levels.

To give you a preview of what an actual Pascal program looks like, a complete program is shown in Table 2–1. Like all good programs, the example is self-contained so that someone conversant in the language can readily understand it without any other documentation. Details of Pascal are discussed in the rest of this chapter.

TABLE 2-1   Pascal program to simulate a simple adding machine.

```
PROGRAM AddingMachine (input,output);
{ This program simulates a simple adding machine with 13 keys:
      0-9  Digits -- entered one digit at a time, left to right.
      C    Clear -- sets the accumulated sum to zero.
      +    Plus -- adds the current number to the accumulated sum.
      S    Stop -- stops the machine (and program).
   The keys are simulated by reading characters one at a time from the
   input.  The current number and sum are printed after each C, +, or S
   operation.  Illegal characters clear the sum and current number.      }
VAR
   sum, number : integer;  charIn : char;
PROCEDURE PrintNums;        {Print current number and sum so far.}
   BEGIN writeln (number,sum) END;
PROCEDURE InitNums;         {Clear current number and sum and print them.}
   BEGIN sum := 0;  number := 0;  PrintNums;  END;
FUNCTION DigitVal (c : char) : integer;  {Evaluate a digit from 0 to 9.}
   BEGIN
      {The value of a digit is the value of its numeric character
        code minus the value of zero's numeric character code.}
      DigitVal := ord(c) - ord('0');
   END;
BEGIN  {Main Program}
   InitNums;  read(charIn);  {Initialize variables; get first char.}
   WHILE charIn <> 'S' DO  {Read a character at a time.}
      BEGIN
         IF (charIn >= '0') AND (charIn <= '9') THEN  {If charIn is a digit...
               multiply current number by 10 and add charIn's digit value.}
            number := number*10 + DigitVal(charIn)
         ELSE IF charIn = 'C' THEN InitNums  {Clear sum on 'C'.}
         ELSE IF charIn = '+' THEN    {Add on '+'.}
            BEGIN sum := sum + number;  PrintNums;  number := 0  END
         ELSE InitNums;  {Clear sum and number on bad input characters.}
         read(charIn);  {Always get next character.}
      END;
   PrintNums;
   writeln('All done -- bye');  {Got an 'S' -- stop.}
END.
```

2.2 VOCABULARY

special symbol

At the very lowest level, a Pascal program is just a series of letters, digits, and special symbols recognized by the compiler. A *special symbol* may be a single character or a pair of characters, as shown in Table 2–2. There are two symbols

TABLE 2-2   Special symbols in Pascal.

;	:	.	,	'	<	>	{	}	(	)	[	]
&	=	+	−	*	/	:=	<=	>=	<>	..		

TABLE 2–3   Pascal reserved words.

AND	DIV	FILE	IN	OF	RECORD	TYPE
ARRAY	DO	FOR	LABEL	OR	REPEAT	UNTIL
BEGIN	DOWNTO	FUNCTION	MOD	PACKED	SET	VAR
CASE	ELSE	GOTO	NIL	PROCEDURE	THEN	WHILE
CONST	END	IF	NOT	PROGRAM	TO	WITH

reserved word

in this list that you don't see—space and "newline" (or carriage return). In addition, the language defines *reserved words* shown in Table 2–3. All other symbols in a program are groups of characters that form numbers, identifiers, or strings. Throughout this text, we use `Courier` for all characters in Pascal and assembly language programs, and Pascal reserved words are printed in UPPER CASE.

number

fixed-point notation

scientific notation

identifier

standard identifier

  Numbers are written in decimal either in *fixed-point notation* (`17`, `-999`, `123.456`, `0.0000000005168`) or in *scientific notation*, (`17E0`, `-0.999E3`, `123456E-3`, `5.168E-10`), where `E` means "times 10 to the power of." An *identifier* is a series of letters and digits beginning with a letter. A program may contain arbitrarily defined identifiers with length limited only by the input line, but the first eight characters of each distinct identifier must be unique. Also, some identifiers called *standard identifiers* are predefined in any Pascal implementation; they may be redefined by the programmer, but it's usually best not to. The standard identifiers included in every Pascal implementation are shown in Table 2–4; a particular implementation may define additional ones.

  Good programmers choose identifier names that are descriptive of the identifiers' meaning or function. Different programmers use different conventions for separating the words in multi-word identifiers. For example, some Pascal compilers treat the underline character as a letter, which allows a programmer to use identifiers such as `item_count`, `stack_size`, and `get_next_char`. Pascal implementations accepting both upper- and lower-case characters support the convention used by many Pascal programmers and in this book:

- Reserved words are written in lower case for simplicity when typing real programs, in upper case for emphasis in printed text.

- The "body" of an identifier is written in lower case.

TABLE 2–4   Standard identifiers in Pascal.

Files	Constants	Types	Procedures		Functions		
input	false	boolean	get	readln	abs	odd	arctan
output	true	integer	new	reset	chr	ord	succ
	maxint	real	pack	rewrite	cos	pred	trunc
		char	page	unpack	eof	sin	eoln
		text	put	write	exp	sqr	round
			read	writeln	ln	sqrt	

- User-defined program, procedure, and function names begin with an upper-case letter; all other identifiers begin with a lower-case letter.

- The first letter of the second and successive words in a multi-word identifier is capitalized.

Thus, `head`, `itemCount`, and `stackSize` may be variable names, while `Sort`, `GetNextChar`, and `TicTacToe` are user-defined program, procedure, or function names. In standard Pascal, matching upper- and lower-case letters appearing in identifiers and reserved words are equivalent. Forgetting to capitalize a letter doesn't bother the compiler, only a copy editor!

string   A *string* is a sequence of characters enclosed in single quotes, for example, `'string'`. Capitalization in strings *is* significant. A quote is included in a string by writing it twice, `'Don''t think twice, it''s alright!'`.

comment   A sequence of characters other than braces, `{}`, enclosed by braces, is
separator called a *comment* and is ignored by the compiler. Comments, spaces, and newlines are used as *separators*. One or more separators *must* occur between consecutive Pascal reserved words and identifiers. No separators are *required* between a special symbol and any other character sequence, but one or more separators *may* occur. A program can be written with a minimum number of separators, but a look at the programming examples in this and other chapters should show the desirability of freely using separators to improve readability.

2.3   PROGRAM STRUCTURE

Viewed from the highest level, a Pascal program consists of declarations and
declaration statements. *Declarations* appear at the beginning of the program and specify such things as the program's name, the names and types of constants and variables that it uses, and the definitions of functions and procedures that it uses.
statement *Statements* specify the actions performed by the program.
program   Formally, a *program* is defined to be a program heading and a block
syntax diagram followed by a period. This format can be described by a *syntax diagram* as shown in Figure 2–3(a). In a syntax diagram, rectangular boxes surround the names of the program elements that are defined elsewhere, such as "*program heading*" and "*block*." Circles or rounded boxes surround special symbols and reserved
syntax words. A syntax diagram defines only the *syntax* of a program element—its
semantics format. Its meaning or *semantics* must be described separately.
        The description of a program is refined in Figure 2–3(b) and (c). A
program heading *program heading* consists of the reserved word `PROGRAM`, followed by an iden-
`PROGRAM` tifier, followed by a list of one or more identifiers enclosed in parentheses,
block followed by a semicolon. A *block* consists of six parts in a prescribed order; all parts except the statement part are optional.
        The program heading is always the first line of a Pascal program and gives its name and the files that it accesses:

```
PROGRAM Example (input,output);
```

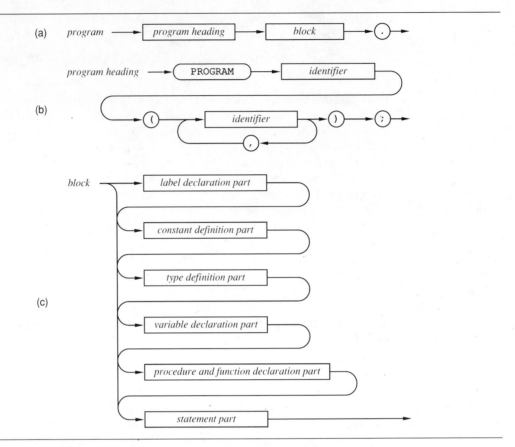

FIGURE 2–3   Syntax diagrams: (a) program; (b) program heading; (c) block.

The program named **Example** reads from the standard file **input**, and sends its results to the standard file **output**. The identities of the files **input** and **output** are implementation dependent. For example, in a timesharing system, both **input** and **output** might be named files in the user's directory; and in a personal computer, **input** might be a keyboard and **output** a display screen. A program may access additional files by specifying them in the program heading, but general file handling in Pascal is beyond the scope of our discussion.

Figure 2–3 defined a block as five optional declaration parts and a statement part. Each of the declaration parts is described in later sections; the statement part *statement part* is defined in Figure 2–4. A *statement part* is simply a *compound statement*— *compound* a sequence of *statements* bracketed by the reserved words **BEGIN** and **END**. *statement* A *statement* may be one of many different kinds of statements, as shown in **BEGIN** Figure 2–5. These statements are defined in Sections 2.7 through 2.9. **END** An example of a simple program is given in Table 2–5. In this example, *statement* the label, constant, type, and function and procedure declarations are "empty."

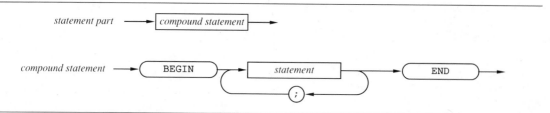

FIGURE 2–4   Syntax diagrams for statement part and compound statement.

2.4 DECLARATIONS

Declarations appear at the beginning of a block, as defined in the previous section. Every Pascal program contains at least one block; a procedure or function definition also contains a block, and hence declarations. Syntax diagrams for declarations are given in Figure 2–6.

label declaration part
LABEL

The *label declaration part* of a block gives a list of labels used in the block, for example:

    LABEL 17, 6851, 357;

label

A *label* in Pascal is an unsigned integer of up to four digits. Labels are used to mark statements referenced by GOTO statements, as described later; every label

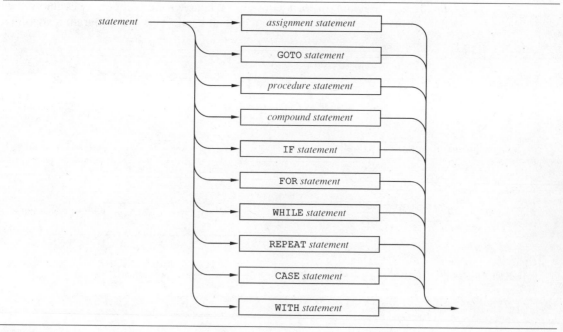

FIGURE 2–5   Syntax diagram showing many different kinds of statements.

TABLE 2–5   A simple Pascal program.

```
PROGRAM Example (input,output);
VAR x, square, recipr : real;
BEGIN
  read(x);
  square := x*x;
  recipr := 1/x;
  write('Square of', x, 'is', square, 'reciprocal is', recipr)
END.
```

constant definition part
CONST

must be declared before it is used. If there are no labels in the program, the label declaration part is "empty"—it contains no characters.

The *constant definition part* uses the reserved word CONST to introduce a list of identifier/constant equations terminated by semicolons:

```
CONST pi = 3.14159265;
  first = 1;   last = 50;
  heading = 'Areas of circles';
```

The type of each identifier is implied by the type of the constant with which it is equated; types are discussed in the next section. If no constants are to be defined, this declaration is omitted.

The constant definition part provides a nice facility present in assembly language but missing from most high-level languages—the ability to define an identifier as a synonym for a constant. Whenever the compiler encounters such an identifier, it replaces it with the constant itself. This aids program readability,

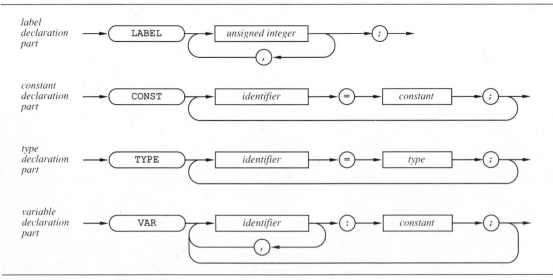

FIGURE 2–6   Syntax diagrams for declarations.

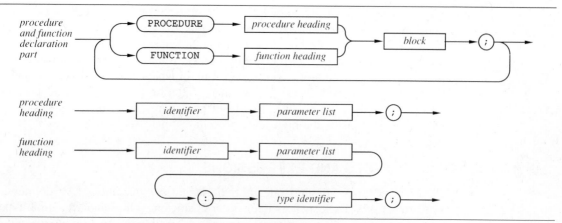

FIGURE 2–7   Procedure and function declaration part syntax diagram.

since a well-chosen name has more meaning than a number. More significantly, it enhances program portability and maintainability, since the programmer can change important parameters such as input range or internal data structure size in a single declaration line without searching the entire program for occurrences of the changed parameters.

The *type definition part* contains a list of identifier/type equations. Section 2.6 will show two ways to create user-defined types in a Pascal program. If a program defines no new types, the type definition part is omitted.

Every variable used in a Pascal program must be declared in the *variable declaration part*, which begins with the reserved word VAR and contains a list of identifier/type associations. Each such association contains one or more identifiers and a type, and declares each identifier to be a variable of that type:

```
VAR
    count, id, nScores : integer;
    average, sigma : real;
    inputChar : char;
    greater, finished : boolean;
    stripe1, stripe2, stripe3 : colorCode;
```

The type may be a standard type or a type previously defined in the type definition part. Every nontrivial program has at least one variable, and so the variable declaration part always appears in a program block. However, it is possible to define a procedure or function with no local variables, in which case this part is omitted.

The syntax for the *procedure and function declaration part* is shown in Figure 2–7. Each procedure or function declaration is similar in structure to the program itself; "block" has the same definition given in the previous section. The *procedure heading* or *function heading* gives the name of a procedure or function and lists its parameters as described in detail in Chapter 9. If there are no parameters, then the parameter list is empty. Simple examples of procedure and function declarations were given in Table 2–1.

At this point, you should observe the "recursive" nature of a procedure or function declaration—since it contains a block, it may define its own procedures and functions. This allows top-down design, in which a procedure can define its own subservient procedures. Rather than cluttering up the high-level program description with a lot of little low-level procedures, the low-level procedures can be defined inside the high-level procedures that use them.

2.5   STANDARD DATA TYPES AND EXPRESSIONS

simple type

structured type

Pascal data types fall into one of two categories. A *simple type* defines an ordered set of values, such as integers or characters. The standard simple types `integer`, `real`, `char`, and `boolean` are described in this section. A *structured type* is characterized by the type(s) of its components and a structuring method, as described in Chapter 3.

expression
relational expression
relational operator

Data may be compared and combined in *expressions*. A *relational expression* compares two arguments of like type using one of the *relational operators*:

=	equal
<	less than
>	greater than
<=	less than or equal
>=	greater than or equal
<>	not equal

arithmetic expression

boolean expression

An *arithmetic expression* combines arguments of type `real`, `integer`, or subrange of `integer`, and produces results in one of these types according to rules given in the next two subsections. A *boolean expression* combines `boolean` arguments and produces a `boolean` result as discussed in the final subsection.

2.5.1   Integer

`integer`
`maxint`

The value of an `integer` variable or constant is a whole number in the range `-maxint` to `+maxint`, where `maxint` is an implementation-dependent constant. As discussed in Section 4.5.4, most modern computers use two's-complement representation for integers, so that $maxint = 2^{w-1} - 1$, where w is the word length of the machine or a multiple thereof. For example, in a typical 16-bit microprocessor Pascal, `maxint` = 32,767. An `integer` constant is a sequence of decimal digits, possibly preceded by a plus or minus sign.

The arithmetic operators add (+), subtract (−), and multiply (*) in Pascal yield `integer` results when applied to `integer` operands. There are two "division" operators that yield `integer` results: `DIV` produces a truncated quotient, for example, $9 \text{ DIV } 4 = 2$; and `MOD` produces the remainder, for example, $9 \text{ MOD } 4 = 1$. The "normal" division operator (/) when applied to `integer` operands yields a result of type `real`, for example, $9/4 = 2.25$.

`DIV`
`MOD`
`/`

2.5.2   Real

real
*floating-point
 number*

A `real` value is an element of an implementation-dependent subset of the real numbers, called the *floating-point numbers* of the machine. Floating-point representations allow both positive and negative numbers, and typically allow absolute values as small as 10^{-38} and as large as 10^{38} (refer to Section 4.11). A `real` constant is a signed sequence of decimal digits possibly including a decimal point, or a number in scientific notation. The magnitude of a `real` constant must begin with a digit, so we write `0.005` or `5E-3`, not `.005` or `.5E-2`.

+

–

*

/

There are four operations that can be applied to `real` operands: addition (+), subtraction (−), multiplication (*), and division (/). Division always produces a `real` result; the other operations produce a `real` result whenever at least one of the operands is type `real`.

trunc
round

An expression that produces an `integer` result can be assigned to a `real` variable; the result will be automatically converted to `real`. However, a `real` result cannot be assigned to an `integer` variable. The standard functions `trunc` and `round` may be used to convert a `real` result to `integer` by truncation and rounding, respectively.

precedence

As in most other high-level languages, multiplication and division operations in Pascal have *precedence* over addition and subtraction in expressions, and parentheses may be used freely. Thus, the right-hand and left-hand sides of the equations below are equivalent:

```
a*b+c*d = (a*b)+(c*d)
a+b/c+d = a+(b/c)+d
a*b/c = (a*b)/c
```

Although the precedence is well defined, parentheses should be used whenever it isn't obvious. Parentheses may affect `integer` operations more than `real`:

```
5.0*3.0/2.0  =  (5.0*3.0)/2.0  =  5.0*(3.0/2.0)  =  7.5
5*3 DIV 2  =  (5*3) DIV 2  =  7  <>  5*(3 DIV 2)  =  5
```

2.5.3   Char

char

A value of the type `char` is an element of a set of characters used to communicate with the computer. Both the set of characters recognized (and printed) by a machine, and the internal bit strings used to represent those characters, are implementation dependent. However, there exists a standard character set and bit-string encoding used by almost all computers except IBM mainframes. This is the ASCII code, described in Appendix A.

A character enclosed in single quotes (apostrophes) denotes a constant of type `char`. The set of characters is assumed to be ordered. In most implementations, the ordering will be the same as the numerical ordering of the corresponding bit strings. Thus, in ASCII, `'A'<'B'`, `'Q'<'q'`, and `'+'<'P'`.

TABLE 2–6   Boolean operators in Pascal.

x	y	NOT x	x OR y	x AND y
false	false	true	false	false
false	true	true	true	false
true	false	false	true	false
true	true	false	true	true

2.5.4 Boolean

boolean
NOT
unary operation
binary operation
AND
OR

A boolean value is always either true or false. Pascal defines the logical negation operator, NOT, which returns the complement of a boolean operand x, as shown in Table 2–6. Negation is called a *unary operation* because it has only one operand; a *binary operation* has two operands. Pascal defines two binary operations on boolean operands, AND and OR, also shown in the table. Boolean operands can be combined by these logical operations to make complex program decisions.

When operands of other types are compared by relational operators, the result of the comparison is a value of type boolean. For example, if j is an integer, the expression j>1 yields true only if the value of j is greater than 1, false otherwise; 1=1 always yields true; and 5<2 always yields false. More examples of boolean expressions are given below, assuming cnt and limit are type integer, inChar is char, and testOK is boolean.

```
cnt <= 50
(cnt < limit) AND (inChar <> '.')
((cnt > (limit-10)) AND (inChar = '?')) OR NOT testOK
```

As with arithmetic expressions, Pascal has a well-defined operator precedence, but it's best for clarity and safety to use parentheses around all subexpressions where the precedence isn't obvious.

2.6 USER-DEFINED TYPES

Pascal provides several classes of user-defined types. This section describes the simplest of these—enumerated and subrange types. User-defined types help make better programs in a number of ways. Enumerated types allow a nonnumeric problem to be stated more clearly than the alternative of writing a long series of constant declarations equating identifiers with numbers (e.g., black=0; brown=1; red=2; ...). Subrange types restrict the range of variables, thereby allowing a compiler to perform more thorough error checking and possibly create more efficient programs.

Set types, not described in this book, provide a natural means of expression for many combinatorial problems. And structured types, which are discussed in Chapter 3, allow explicit definition of complex data structures in a manner understandable by both the compiler and a human reader.

2.6.1 Enumerated Types

enumerated type

type definition part

TYPE

In Section 1.6 we indicated that a bit string need not represent a number, that it could represent an element of any set of related objects. Recognizing that computers process much nonnumeric data, Pascal provides a formal mechanism for defining nonnumeric *enumerated types* and allowing the program to refer to such data values by nonnumeric names. A program may introduce a new enumerated type in the *type definition part*; three such types are defined below:

```
TYPE
    color = (black,brown,red,orange,yellow,green,blue,violet,
        grey,white,silver,gold,tan,indigo,pink,puce);
    city = (stLouis,miami,chicago,sanFrancisco,detroit,
        newYork,boston,houston,denver,memphis,portland,
        milwaukee,seattle,juneau,honolulu,albuquerque);
    direction = (north,south,east,west);
```

Once a new type has been defined, variables of this type may be declared, for example:

```
VAR
    birthplace, origin, destination : city;
    route, alternate : direction;
    favorite : color;
```

Variables of enumerated types may also be declared without naming the type, for example:

```
VAR route, alternate : (north,south,east,west);
```

The identifiers listed in a type definition become the constants of the defined type. A variable may be assigned the value of any variable or constant of the same type, but expressions and mixed assignments are not allowed. For example, the first four assignment statements below are valid; the last three are not.

```
{valid}
    origin := chicago;
    favorite := puce;
    alternate := route;
    route := north;
{invalid}
    destination := west;
    favorite := birthplace;
    birthplace := origin OR destination;
```

ordinal number

ord

When they are listed in the type definition, the constants of an enumerated type acquire an ordering: they are assigned *ordinal numbers*, consecutive integers beginning with 0. The compiler uses the ordinal number to represent the constant in the computer's memory. The predefined function ord returns the ordinal number for a variable or constant of any enumerated type, for example,

```
ord(white) = 9
ord(sanFrancisco) = 3
ord(north) = 0
```

pred
succ

The predefined functions `pred` and `succ` use this ordering to return the predecessor and successor of an argument:

```
pred(green) = yellow
succ(east) = west
pred(milwaukee) = portland
succ(west) = ?  {undefined}
pred(black) = ?  {undefined}
```

Besides assignment, the only operation allowed on enumerated types is comparison by the relational operators. When two arguments are compared, the result is obtained by comparing their ordinal numbers. For example,

```
(chicago > sanFrancisco) = (2 > 3) = false
```

The preceding discussion also applies to the predefined standard types `integer`, `char`, and `boolean`. Thus, we can make several useful statements.

```
pred(29) = 28
succ(-5) = -4
ord(false) = 0
ord(true) = 1
false < true
succ('i') = 'j'
pred('8') = '7'
ord('9') <> 9
ord('9') - ord('0') = 9
```

The statements about characters are guaranteed true only if characters have the ordinal values implied by the ASCII encoding (Appendix A). For example, `succ('i')='j'` is false in the EBCDIC encoding used in IBM mainframe computers. Therefore, statements that assume a contiguous ordering of the characters should be avoided. Still, standard Pascal makes the following guarantees:

(1) The ordinal values of `'0'-'9'` are ordered and contiguous.

(2) The ordinal values of `'A'-'Z'` are ordered but not necessarily contiguous.

(3) The ordinal values of `'a'-'z'` are ordered but not necessarily contiguous.

2.6.2 Subrange Types

subrange type
host type

The values in a *subrange type* are a contiguous subset of a *host type*, which may be any enumerated type or simple type other than `real`. A subrange type is defined in the type definition part by giving constants (in the host type) for first and last values in the subrange, separated by "`..`". For example,

..

```
TYPE
   digit = 0..9;
   digitChar = '0'..'9';
   colorCode = black..white;
```

defines the three subranges `digit` of `integer`, `digitChar` of `char`, and `colorCode` of the enumerated type `color`. Subrange variables may be defined much like variables of an enumerated type, for example:

```
VAR
   units, tens, hundreds : digit;
   outChar : digitChar;
   band1, band2, band3 : colorCode;
   index : 1..100;
```

Subrange variables may be used in expressions and on the left-hand side of assignment statements anywhere that the associated scalar type would be allowed. However, an attempt to assign a subrange variable a value beyond its range causes an error when the program is run.

An `integer` variable, especially when used for counting, indexing, or enumeration, seldom takes on unpredictable values in a program. Subrange types let the programmer inform the compiler of the allowable range of such variables in normal operation, so that abnormal operation due to bad inputs or programming errors can be detected by simple range checks automatically inserted into the program by the compiler. Subrange types are also essential to the syntax of Pascal, for they are used in `CASE` statements and `ARRAY` declarations, as described in Sections 2.8.6 and 3.1, respectively.

2.7 SIMPLE STATEMENTS

statement

Statements are the sequences of reserved words, identifiers, and symbols that specify the actions in a Pascal program. The statements in each block of a Pascal program are executed sequentially, in the order in which they were written. Pascal statements are classified into two types: simple and structured. A *simple statement* is a statement that contains no other statement. The three types of nontrivial simple statements will be described in this section. The *empty statement*, which consists of no characters and performs no action, is also a simple statement. The discussion of structured statements in the next section will show that there *are* good uses for the empty statement.

simple statement

empty statement

2.7.1 Assignment Statements

assignment statement

:=

An *assignment statement* assigns the value of an expression on the right-hand side of the symbol `:=` to a variable on the left-hand side. The variable and the expression must have the same type, with two exceptions: (a) if the expression is `integer` or a subrange thereof, the variable may be `real`; (b) the expression type may be a subrange of the variable type, or vice versa. Several examples of assignment statements have already been given; Table 2–7 gives some more.

TABLE 2–7 Examples of assignment statements.

```
VAR
  i, j, k : integer;
  a, b, c : real;
  outChar, inChar : char;
  done, valid : boolean;
BEGIN
  ...
  i := j + k - 1;
  a := j + k - 1;
  k := j*i + 5;
  b := a*b/c;
  c := b*a/1E10;
  inChar := 'q';
  outChar := inChar;
  valid := (i < j) AND ((inChar <> outChar) OR (c > 3.14));
  done := NOT valid;
  ...
END.
```

2.7.2 The GOTO Statement

GOTO statement

Any Pascal statement may be preceded by the construct "*label* :", where *label* is a unique 1- to 4-digit unsigned integer that has been listed in the label declaration part. The GOTO *statement* has the form "GOTO *label*", and has the effect of transferring control to the labeled statement; that is, the next statement executed after the GOTO will be the labeled statement, and execution of the program will continue from this new point.

The use of the GOTO statement is generally discouraged, because the resulting "jumping around" of control is difficult to follow (and therefore, difficult to debug and verify its correctness). The "structured statements" in the next section offer a much more regular and readable means of program control. Examples will demonstrate this by showing all of the extra statements that are needed in the absence of structured statements.

The most frequent legitimate use of GOTO is to jump out of a structured statement on some abnormal termination condition. Jumping *into* a structured statement from outside yields unpredictable results.

2.7.3 Procedure Statements

procedure
procedure
  statement

A *procedure* is a defined sequence of declarations and statements (i.e., a block) that can be invoked by a single statement, called a *procedure statement*. Procedures are discussed in detail in Chapter 9, but we'll introduce them here.

Pascal has four built-in procedures that allow a program to read and write data. They may be invoked by the following procedure statements:

read
input

- **read**(*var1*,*var2*,...,*varn*)—reads from a standard file named `input` and assigns values to the listed variables. The types of the input values must match the corresponding variables.

readln

- **readln**(*var1*,*var2*,...,*varn*)—same as **read**, except a new input line is started after the last variable has been read.

write
output

- **write**(*expr1*,*expr2*,...,*exprn*)—writes the values of the listed expressions to a standard file named `output`.

writeln

- **writeln**(*expr1*,*expr2*,...,*exprn*)—same as **write**, except a new output line is started after the last expression has been written.

These procedures can also read and write files other than the standard input and output, and take simple data-formatting specifications. Pascal has several other built-in procedures dealing with input and output; their effects are somewhat implementation dependent and in any case beyond the scope of our discussion.

Like any other high-level language, Pascal allows and encourages user-defined procedures. Consider the task of printing the reciprocal, square, and integer part of a `real` variable a, as in the program fragment below:

```
VAR a, recipr, square : real; int : integer;
  ...
  recipr := 1/a;
  square := a*a;
  int := trunc(a);
  writeln(a,recipr,square,int);
```

If we wanted to do the same with variables b, c, and d, we could write three similar sequences, changing a to b, c, and d in each one, but still using `recipr`, `square`, and `int` for temporary storage. Table 2–8 shows how a procedure can instead be declared and invoked to compute the desired functions on arbitrary `real` values. If the input values to this program are 4.5 1.7 0.5 6.8, then the output will be as follows:

```
4.5000    0.2222   20.2500    4
1.7000    0.5882    2.8900    1
0.5000    2.0000    0.2500    0
6.8000    0.1471   46.2400    6
```

formal parameter

actual parameter

The variable x in the procedure declaration in Table 2–8 is called a *formal parameter*; the variables a, b, c, and d in the `PrintVal` procedure statements are called *actual parameters*. When a procedure statement is encountered, the actual parameters are substituted for the formal parameters in the body of the procedure before it is executed. In Pascal, there are a number of possible ways that this substitution can take place, as discussed in Section 9.2.

By requiring only one copy of a commonly used sequence of instructions, a procedure can save time during program development and space during program execution. Procedures (and functions) are essential to the "structure" of Pascal

TABLE 2–8   Program using a procedure.

```
PROGRAM Print4Values (input,output);
{Declare variables used by the program}
VAR a, b, c, d : real;
{Declare the printing procedure}
PROCEDURE PrintVal (x : real);
  {declare local variables}
  VAR recipr, square : real; int : integer;
  BEGIN  {This is the statement part of the procedure}
    recipr := 1/x;
    square := x*x;
    int := trunc(x);
    writeln(x,recipr,square,int);
  END;
{Now comes the statement part of the main program}
BEGIN
  read(a,b,c,d);
  PrintVal(a);
  PrintVal(b);
  PrintVal(c);
  PrintVal(d);
END.
```

or any other computer language, high-level or assembly. The use of procedures contributes to program modularity, readability, and testability by breaking down a problem into a structured group of smaller problems with well-defined interfaces.

2.8 STRUCTURED STATEMENTS

structured statement

A *structured statement* contains one or more additional statements as components. Pascal defines a set of structured statements that allow decision and repetition in a program, and together handle the most common program control situations. In the remainder of this chapter, we describe all of Pascal's structured statements except WITH, which is used in conjunction with RECORD variables as described in Section 3.3.

The decision and repetition statements in Pascal can be contrasted with the primitive capabilities of typical computer machine languages. A typical machine primitive tests a condition and, based on the outcome, either jumps to a different sequence of instructions or continues the current instruction sequence. This is roughly equivalent to the following Pascal statement:

IF *condition* THEN GOTO *label*

When we discuss the Pascal decision and repetition statements, we shall compare them with sequences using only the above primitive.

2.8.1 Compound Statements

*compound
 statement*
BEGIN
END

A *compound statement* is a sequence of statements separated by semicolons and bracketed by the reserved words BEGIN and END:

```
BEGIN
    statement-1;
    statement-2;
    ...
    statement-n-1;
    statement-n
END
```

A syntax diagram was shown in Figure 2–4. We have already seen many examples of compound statements, since the statement part of a program, procedure, or function must be a compound statement.

Each statement within a compound statement can be any simple or structured statement; the structured statements may include more compound statements. This "recursive" definition is essential to the structure of Pascal. It is responsible for the power of the rest of the structured statements—an IF, FOR, WHILE, REPEAT, or CASE statement can control a complex structured statement just as easily as it controls a simple assignment statement.

semicolon usage

One thing to notice about the definition of a compound statement is that the semicolon is a statement *separator* rather than a statement *terminator*. Some block-structured languages, most notably C, PL/1, and PL/M, use the semicolon as a terminator—*every* statement must be followed by one. In Pascal, the last statement in a compound statement is *not* followed by a semicolon. Nevertheless, the following compound statement is still legal:

```
BEGIN
    temp := x;
    x := y;
    y := temp;
END
```

It contains *four* statements, the last being the empty statement. Even though the extra semicolon is shunned by purists, it is still a good idea to include it, to avoid the error of forgetting it when appending additional statements. However, semicolons cannot be used indiscriminately after every statement in Pascal—the next subsection will show why.

2.8.2 The IF Statement

IF *statement*
THEN

The decision primitive in a Pascal program is the IF *statement*; its basic format is

IF *condition* THEN *statement*

where *condition* may be any boolean expression and *statement* may be any statement, simple or structured. The *statement* is executed only if *condition* has the value true.

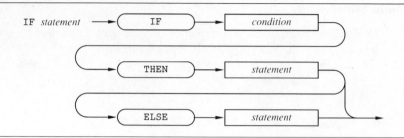

FIGURE 2–8   Syntax diagram for IF statement.

Quite often it is necessary to choose between two alternative actions, depending on a condition. This is accomplished in Pascal by appending an ELSE *clause* to an IF statement:

> IF *condition* THEN *statement1* ELSE *statement2*

If *condition* is true, then *statement1* is executed; otherwise *statement2* is executed. In assembly language or in any language with only a primitive test and jump facility, an IF–THEN–ELSE statement would have to be implemented as follows:

```
IF condition THEN GOTO labelA;
statement2;
GOTO labelB;
labelA : statement1;
labelB : ... ;
```

A syntax diagram for IF is shown in Figure 2–8 and an example program using IF statements is presented in Table 2–9. It should be noted from the IF syntax and from the examples that a semicolon is *not* used to separate the ELSE clause from the IF clause. The examples also show how IF statements may be combined. When an IF statement contains a compound statement, any of the components of the compound statement may of course be IF statements. The last part of the example shows a *compound* IF *statement*, where the ELSE clause of each succeeding IF statement is another IF statement. This is a useful and common structure. On the other hand, consider an IF statement wherein the THEN clause contains another IF clause:

```
IF condition1 THEN
   IF condition2 THEN statement1
ELSE statement2;
```

From the statement indentation, it appears that the ELSE clause belongs to the first IF. However, the language syntax attaches the ELSE clause to the nearest IF that doesn't have one, the opposite of the way we've formatted it. Even though the language is unambiguous, the THEN IF construct should be avoided because of the confusion it can introduce. The ambiguity can be resolved by

TABLE 2–9   Program using IF statements.

```
PROGRAM Iffy (input,output);

VAR radius, area, diameter : real;
    hour, minute, number : integer;
    inchar : char;

BEGIN

{Find the radius and diameter of a circle of a given area.}
  read(area);
  IF area >= 0 THEN
    BEGIN
      radius := sqrt(area/3.1416);
      diameter := 2*radius;
      writeln('For a circle with area', area, 'the radius is',
          radius, 'and the diameter is', diameter);
    END
  ELSE writeln('Negative area (', area, ') not allowed');

{Convert 24-hour time to 12-hour time.}
  read(hour,minute);
  IF (hour < 0) OR (hour > 23)
       OR (minute < 0) OR (minute > 59) THEN
    BEGIN {If input out of range, set to default.}
      hour := 0;  minute := 0;
    END;
  IF hour <= 11 THEN
    BEGIN
      IF hour = 0 THEN hour := 12;
      writeln('Time is', hour, ':', minute, 'AM');
    END
  ELSE
    BEGIN
      hour := hour - 12;
      if hour = 0 THEN hour := 12;
      writeln('Time is', hour, ':', minute, 'PM');
    END;

{Read a hexadecimal-digit character and convert to an integer.}
{Assumes ASCII ordering of characters.}
  number := -1;
  read(inchar);
  IF (inchar >= '0') AND (inchar <= '9') THEN
    number := ord(inchar) - ord('0')
  ELSE IF (inchar >= 'a') AND (inchar <= 'f') THEN
    number := ord(inchar) - ord('a') + 10
  ELSE IF (inchar >= 'A') AND (inchar <= 'F') THEN
    number := ord(inchar) - ord('A') + 10
  ELSE writeln(inchar, ' -- not a hexadecimal digit');
  writeln('The decimal value of ', inchar, ' is', number);
END.
```

negating *condition1* and reversing the order of the clauses if *statement2* isn't also an IF, or by simply using BEGIN–END to bracket the subordinate IF statement:

```
IF condition1 THEN
   BEGIN IF condition2 THEN statement1 END
ELSE statement2;
```

2.8.3 The FOR Statement

FOR *statement*
DO
TO

The FOR *statement* provides a means of repeating a statement a predetermined number of times; its general format is

```
FOR control := first TO last DO statement
```

Here *control* is a declared variable, and *first* and *last* are expressions, all of the same simple type (excluding real). The *first* and *last* expressions are evaluated at the beginning of the FOR statement execution, and the value of *first* is assigned to *control*. Then the value of *control* is compared to *last*; if (*control* > *last*) is false, then *statement* is executed once, *control* is bumped to its successor value, and the whole process is repeated. Otherwise the FOR statement terminates. An equivalent sequence can be written using only primitive tests and jumps as follows:

```
control := first;
temp := last;
labelA : IF (control > temp) THEN GOTO labelB;
statement;
control := succ(control);
GOTO labelA;
labelB : ... ;
```

Here temp is a variable, with type compatible with *first* and *last*, that is not otherwise defined in the program. There is one slight exception to the equivalency—in standard Pascal the value of *control* is undefined after exiting the FOR statement, even when GOTO is used to exit.

DOWNTO

The reserved word TO in a FOR statement may be replaced with the reserved word DOWNTO, resulting in a FOR statement that counts down instead of up. In this case, pred(*control*) produces the next value of *control* after each iteration, and (*control* < temp) is the termination criterion. Figure 2–9 is a syntax diagram for both types of FOR statements.

iteration

Each execution of *statement* above is called an *iteration* of the FOR loop. Since *first* and *last* are expressions, the number of iterations may be different each time the FOR statement is executed, even though the number is fixed once a particular execution is begun. Also, because *control* is checked at the *beginning* of each iteration, it is possible for *statement* to be executed zero times. Table 2–10 gives examples of FOR statements.

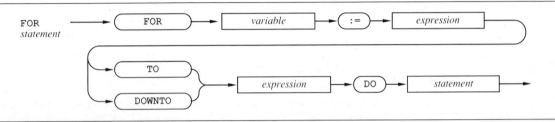

FIGURE 2–9   Syntax diagram for FOR statement.

2.8.4 The WHILE Statement

WHILE *statement*

In contrast with the FOR statement, which produces a predetermined number of iterations each time it is executed, a WHILE *statement* repeats a number of times determined by computation within the WHILE statement itself. The format of a WHILE statement is shown in Figure 2–10 and below:

WHILE *condition* DO *statement*

Here *condition* is any boolean expression and *statement* is of course any state-

TABLE 2–10   Program using FOR statements.

```
PROGRAM FourFORloops (input,output);
VAR
  i, power, n, m, nsum : integer;
  char1, char2, pchar : char;
  innum, sum : real;
BEGIN
{Print a table of integers and squares.}
  FOR i := 1 TO 10 DO writeln(i,i*i);
{Print a table of powers of 2.}
  power := 1;
  FOR i := 0 TO 10 DO
    BEGIN writeln(i,power); power := power*2 END;
{Read two characters and print all the ones between.}
  readln(char1,char2);
  IF char1 < char2 THEN
    FOR pchar := char1 TO char2 DO writeln(pchar)
  ELSE FOR pchar := char1 DOWNTO char2 DO writeln(pchar);
{Compute sums of n groups of input numbers.}
  read(n);   {Number of groups to be summed.}
  FOR nsum := 1 TO n DO
    BEGIN
      sum := 0;  read(m);   {Number of components in this group.}
      FOR i := 1 TO m DO
        BEGIN read(innum); write(innum); sum := sum+innum END;
      writeln(sum);
    END;
END.
```

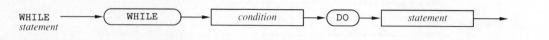

FIGURE 2–10 Syntax diagram for WHILE statement.

ment. The WHILE statement evaluates *condition* and then executes *statement* if *condition* is true; this process repeats as long as *condition* continues to be true. Obviously, the variables affecting *condition* must be modified within *statement* if the WHILE statement is ever to terminate. Some examples of WHILE statements are given in Table 2–11.

A primitive sequence equivalent to WHILE is shown below:

```
labelA : IF NOT condition THEN GOTO labelB;
statement;
GOTO labelA;
labelB : ... ;
```

TABLE 2–11 Program using WHILE statements.

```
PROGRAM Whilst (input,output);
VAR
  n, power, nnums, hour : integer;
  innum, sum : real;
BEGIN
{Print a table of powers of 2.}
  n := 0; power := 1;
  WHILE power < (maxint DIV 2) DO
    BEGIN writeln(n,power); n := n + 1; power := power*2 END;
  writeln(n,power);   {Print last table entry.}
{Average a sequence of nonnegative numbers.}
  sum := 0; nnums := 0;
  write('Input sequence:'); read(innum);
  WHILE innum >= 0 DO {Any negative number terminates sequence.}
    BEGIN
      sum := sum + innum; nnums := nnums + 1;
      write(innum); read(innum);
    END;
  writeln; writeln(nnums, 'numbers, average is', sum/nnums);
{While away the hours.}
  read(hour); {Out-of-range hour terminates loop.}
  WHILE (hour >= 0) AND (hour <= 23) DO
    BEGIN
      IF hour = 0 THEN writeln('Hour 0 is midnight')
      ELSE IF hour < 12 THEN
          writeln('Hour', hour, 'is', hour, 'AM')
      ELSE IF hour = 12 THEN writeln('Hour 12 is noon')
      ELSE writeln('Hour', hour, 'is', hour-12, 'PM');
      read(hour);
    END;
END.
```

It is clear from this sequence that the WHILE statement can have zero iterations if *condition* is already false when the WHILE statement is encountered. Also, you may notice a similarity to the FOR statement. A FOR statement can actually be simulated using the WHILE:

```
control := first;
temp := last;
WHILE control <= temp DO
   BEGIN
      statement;
      control := succ(control);
   END;
```

However, the FOR statement should still be used when appropriate because it is easier to read, and because as a restricted case it allows the compiler more opportunity for optimization.

2.8.5 The REPEAT Statement

REPEAT *statement*
UNTIL

The REPEAT *statement* is similar in effect to the WHILE, except that it tests a condition *after* each iteration; its syntax is shown in Figure 2–11 and below:

REPEAT *statement-1; statement-2; ...; statement-n* UNTIL *condition*

There are three differences from a WHILE statement: the REPEAT statement always has at least one iteration; a false rather than true condition continues the iterations; and a series of statements, not just one, may be controlled. The last difference occurs because the compiler treats the reserved word REPEAT as if it were really REPEAT BEGIN, and UNTIL as if it were END UNTIL.

Because the condition test is at the end of the loop, the primitive equivalent of a REPEAT statement is a little simpler than that of a WHILE:

```
labelA : statement;
IF NOT condition THEN GOTO labelA;
```

WHILE statements are used more commonly than REPEAT, because in most situations it is important to be able to execute a loop zero times. However, Table 2–12 shows two situations where the REPEAT statement is preferred. In the first sequence, a loop is executed for cases up to *and including* a termination case, saving complexity over the corresponding WHILE statement in Table 2–11. In the second sequence, REPEAT is necessary because the termination condition is indeterminate until the loop is executed the first time.

REPEAT
statement

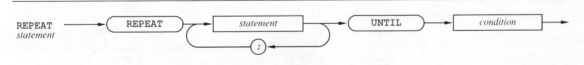

FIGURE 2–11   Syntax diagram for REPEAT statement.

TABLE 2–12   Program using REPEAT statements.

```
PROGRAM Repetitious (input,output);
VAR
  n, power  : integer;
  inchar : char;
BEGIN
{Print a table of powers of 2.}
  n := 0; power := 1;
  REPEAT
    n := n + 1; power := power*2; writeln(n,power);
  UNTIL power > (maxint DIV 2);
{Read and print a sentence.}
  REPEAT
    read(inchar); write(inchar);
  UNTIL inchar = '.';
END.
```

With any of the repetitive statements (REPEAT, WHILE, and FOR), it is sometimes necessary to terminate the loop because of some unusual condition. Often it is impractical to include all of the unusual termination conditions in the basic termination clause, especially if the conditions do not arise until the middle of the loop. The simplest solution in this situation is to jump out of the repetitive statement with a GOTO for each unusual condition. Because GOTOs are "unstructured," some Pascal implementations provide an EXIT statement that terminates a repetitive statement from within.

2.8.6   The CASE Statement

CASE statement

The CASE *statement* is just a multivalued generalization of IF. While IF executes one of two statements according to a boolean value, a CASE statement selects among a number of statements according to a value from an enumerated or *OF* subrange type. The syntax of a CASE statement is shown in Figure 2–12. Here *selector* *selector* is an expression whose value belongs to one of the types integer, *case list* boolean, or char, or to an enumerated or subrange type. The *case list* has one or more elements, each of which has a list of constants of the same type as *selector*, and a *statement* to execute if the *selector* has one of the listed values.

An example of a CASE statement with four selector values and three possible outcomes follows.

```
TYPE myCases = 1..4;
VAR which : myCases;
    ...
  CASE which OF
    1 : write('This is case 1');
    2 : write('But this is case 2');
    3,4 : write('This could be either case 3 or case 4');
  END;
```

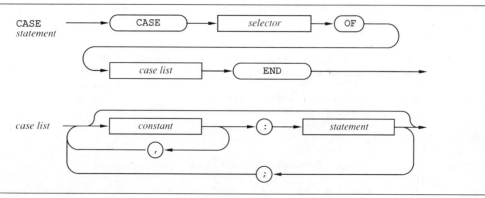

FIGURE 2-12   Syntax diagram for `CASE` statement.

The semicolon after the last case list element is optional. Each distinct value of *selector* may appear in only one case list element. It is advisable that every possible value of the scalar or subrange type of *selector* be specified in some case list element, since the behavior of the case statement may be undefined if *selector* takes on an unrepresented value (however, this event should cause a run-time error according to the Pascal standard).

To write the equivalent of a `CASE` statement using only primitive test and jump instructions, a separate test and jump is needed for each case. However, the `CASE` statement can be implemented efficiently in most computers by means of a jump table. Many problems naturally break down into a few cases, where the `CASE` statement is ideal. The `CASE` statement may also be used to decode commands and to classify objects. Table 2-13 shows an example of this.

R E F E R E N C E S

The computing exploits of Blaise Pascal and many others are described in *The Computer from Pascal to von Neumann*, by Herman H. Goldstine (Princeton University Press, 1972). This book has a wealth of historical information and good references to original source material.

The original definition of the standard Pascal language was published in the *Pascal User Manual and Report* by Kathleen Jensen and Niklaus Wirth (Springer-Verlag, 1974). As the language grew in popularity, several variants and extensions appeared, but at the same time an international effort was made to standardize the language. The result was *Specification for the Computer Programming Language Pascal*, standard 7185, published by the International Standards Organization (ISO) in 1982. The ISO standard defines two versions of the language, "Level 0" (regular Pascal) and "Level 1" (regular Pascal plus conformant arrays). The Level 0 standard has also been adopted by the American National Standards Institute and the Institute of Electrical and Electronics

TABLE 2–13   Program using a CASE statement.

```
PROGRAM ClassifyOrClassyIf (input,output);
{
  This program reads a lower case letter and classifies it
  according to certain characteristics.  The program assumes that
  inputs are in the ASCII character set so that the subrange
  'a'..'z' contains only the lower case letters.  The program
  may not work with other character sets.
}
TYPE letter = 'a'..'z';
VAR inchar : letter;
  vowel, hexdigit, dull, descender, multistroke : boolean;
BEGIN
  vowel := false; hexdigit := false; dull := false;
  descender := false; multistroke := false;
  read(inchar);
  CASE inchar OF
    'a','e' : BEGIN vowel := true; hexdigit := true END;
    'i' : BEGIN vowel := true; multistroke := true END;
    'o','u' : vowel := true;
    'y' : BEGIN vowel := true; descender := true END;
    'b','c','d','f' : hexdigit := true;
    'g','p','q' : descender := true;
    'j' : BEGIN descender := true; multistroke := true END;
    't','x' : multistroke := true;
    'h','k','l','m','n','r','s','v','w','z' : dull := true;
  END;
  writeln(inchar, ' has the following properties:');
  IF vowel THEN writeln('It is a vowel.')
  ELSE writeln('It is a consonant.');
  IF hexdigit THEN writeln('It is a hexadecimal digit.');
  IF descender THEN writeln('It has a descender.');
  IF multistroke THEN
      writeln('You must lift your pen to write it in script.');
  IF dull THEN writeln('It is a very boring character.');
END.
```

Engineers (ANSI/IEEE770X3.97-1983). Jensen and Wirth's *Pascal User Manual and Report* has been updated by A. B. Mickel and J. F. Miner to incorporate the new standard (Springer-Verlag, 1985, 3rd ed.).

Many tutorial texts on Pascal are available. Two good books at the introductory level are *An Introduction to Programming and Problem Solving with Pascal* by G. M. Schneider, S. W. Weingart, and D. M. Perlman (Wiley, 1987, 2nd ed.) and *Oh! Pascal!* by Doug Cooper and Mike Clancy (W. W. Norton, 1985, 2nd ed.); both are lucid and complete and have good bibliographies of their own. Several texts are based on personal-computer Pascal implementations; for example, *Turbo Pascal® A Problem Solving Approach* by Elliot B. Koffman describes a popular implementation by Borland International for IBM-compatible personal computers.

If you're interested in the inner workings of Pascal compilers, from syntax analysis through the run-time environment of compiled programs, Per Brinch Hansen's *On Pascal Compilers* (Prentice-Hall, 1985) is a good starting point.

EXERCISES

2.1   What are the advantages of using a CONST declaration to declare constants, as opposed to defining variables with the same names and assigning constant values to them at the beginning of the program?

2.2   What is the initial value of a Pascal integer variable, before any assignments have been made to it?

2.3   Why do you suppose that Pascal labels the targets of GOTO statements with numbers instead of descriptive alphanumeric identifiers?

2.4   Assuming that the variable declarations in Table 2–7 have been made, explain whether or not each of the following assignment statements can be compiled without type-matching or other errors.

```
k := j*i + 5;
j := (i + k)/2;
b := a*c/1.1E10;
i := (j + m) MOD k;
k := ord(inChar);
done := (a = 2);
valid := valid OR (j = k) OR NOT done;
a := b*c - k + succ('a');
outChar := pred(inChar);
```

2.5   Replace the following compound IF statement with a less confusing IF that has the same effect.

```
IF x >= 0 THEN
   BEGIN
     IF x <= 10 THEN
       BEGIN
         IF x = 0 THEN result := 0 ELSE result := x;
       END
     ELSE result := sqrt(x)
   END
ELSE IF x < -20 THEN result := sqrt(-x + 10)
ELSE result := -x;
```

2.6   The program in Table 2–9 sets hour and minute to 0 if either is out of range. Modify the program so that it instead prints an error message for out-of-range inputs, and prints the time only if both inputs are in range.

2.7   Modify the program in Table 2–9 so that it writes number only if a valid hexadecimal digit was received.

2.8   Find a simpler statement equivalent to the following IF statement.

```
IF x > y THEN greater := true ELSE greater := false;
```

2.9   The adding-machine program in Table 2–1 fails if the input ever causes `sum` or `number` to be greater than `maxint`. Modify the program so that it detects "overflow" and prints a message whenever it occurs.

2.10   Eliminate the GOTOs in the following program fragment.

```
IF x = 1 THEN GOTO 1;
IF x = 2 THEN GOTO 2;
IF x = 3 THEN GOTO 3;
IF x = 4 THEN GOTO 4;
5:   statement-a;
4:   statement-b;
3:   statement-c;
2:   statement-d;
1:   statement-e;
```

2.11   Write the output values produced by the first two FOR loops in Table 2–10.

2.12   Are the following two statements equivalent? Why or why not?

```
FOR i := 1 TO n DO
  IF prod < (maxint DIV i) THEN prod := prod*i
  ELSE n := i;

BEGIN
  i := 1;
  WHILE i <= n DO
    BEGIN
      IF prod < (maxint DIV i) THEN prod := prod*i
      ELSE n := i;
      i := i + 1;
    END;
END;
```

2.13   Assuming that `maxint` $= 2^{15} - 1$, write the table of powers of two produced in Table 2–11. Repeat for Table 2–12.

2.14   Are the following two statements equivalent? Why or why not?

```
WHILE condition1 DO
  WHILE condition2 DO
    statement;

WHILE condition1 AND condition2 DO
  statement;
```

2.15   Give a general format for replacing a **REPEAT** statement with an equivalent sequence using **WHILE**.

2.16   Give the general format of a **CASE** statement that replaces an **IF** statement.

2.17   Eliminate the `read` operation in Table 2–13 and instead provide a FOR statement to classify all of the lower-case letters.

2.18   (Electrical engineers only) Write a sequence of Pascal statements that computes the resistance of a resistor, assuming that its color code is contained in three variables, `stripe1`, `stripe2`, `stripe3`, of the subrange type `colorCode`.

CHAPTER 3

Data Structures in Pascal Programs

data structure

Niklaus Wirth, the designer of Pascal, once wrote a programming book called *Algorithms + Data Structures = Programs*. From the previous chapters, you already have a good idea of what programs and algorithms are. To find out what data structures are, just subtract, and you don't have to read this chapter....

Seriously, Wirth's equation indicates the fundamental importance of data structures in programming. A *data structure* can be defined as a collection of related data and a set of rules for organizing and accessing it. A list of the members of a family is an example of a simple data structure; a family tree is a more complex example.

The choice of a data structure obviously affects what we can do with the data. With either a family list or a family tree, we can sort the names alphabetically, determine whether or not a given name is in the family, find the persons with the longest and shortest names, and so on. But only with the family tree can we determine the relationships of people as siblings, cousins, parents, spouses, and children, and determine how many generations are represented.

Even when two data structures contain exactly the same information, the choice between the two may affect the efficiency of accessing the information, depending on the application. For example, the telephone company gives its customers a phone book sorted by last name. But it also sells the same data sorted by street address to the perpetrators of nuisance calls.

Another factor is the amount of storage needed to contain the data structure. Suppose that we want to store all of the prime numbers between 1 and 1000. There are 168 such numbers, and so we could allocate 168 words of memory and store one number in each. In a computer with 16-bit memory words, this would require a total of 2688 bits of memory. Alternatively, we could allocate only 1000 bits of memory, one for each number in the range 1 to 1000. Each bit in this "bit map" would be set to 1 if the corresponding number were prime, 0 if not.

In this chapter, we'll learn how data structures can be defined and manipulated in Pascal programs. When we discuss the Motorola 68000 family in Part 2, we'll see how strongly the instruction set influences the way data structures are set up and manipulated in assembly language programs.

3.1   ONE-DIMENSIONAL ARRAYS

array
one-dimensional
array

The simplest and most familiar type of data structure is the array. An *array* is an ordered list of data components of the same type. A *one-dimensional array* specifies each component by the array name and its position in the array. A simple example of a one-dimensional array of 10 integers is shown in Table 3–1. As shown in the table, array components are customarily stored in sequential locations in memory; we visualize the array as shown in Figure 3–1. A one-

vector

dimensional array is sometimes called a *vector*.

TABLE 3–1   An array `ints` of 10 integers.

Array Element	Hex Address in Memory	Value
ints[1]	2300	119
ints[2]	2302	−17
ints[3]	2304	−88
ints[4]	2306	24
ints[5]	2308	0
ints[6]	230A	27
ints[7]	230C	−99
ints[8]	230E	32
ints[9]	2310	6
ints[10]	2312	−51

Notes: Address sequence assumes each integer occupies two bytes in a byte-addressable computer.

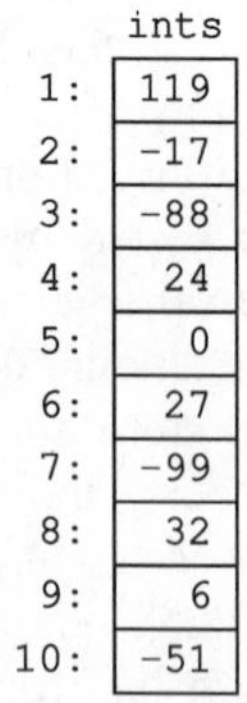

```
            ints
    1:   119
    2:   -17
    3:   -88
    4:    24
    5:     0
    6:    27
    7:   -99
    8:    32
    9:     6
   10:   -51
```

FIGURE 3–1   Visualization of a one-dimensional array.

TABLE 3–2   Characteristics of arrays in different high-level languages.

Language	Index of First Element	Index of Last Element	Multidimensional Arrays?	Conformant Arrays?
Algol	Declared	Declared	Yes	Yes
Basic	0 or 1	Declared or default	Yes	No
C	0	Declared	Yes	Yes
Fortran	1	Declared	Yes	No
Pascal	Declared	Declared	Yes	Maybe[1]
PL/1	1	Declared	Yes	Yes
PL/M	0	Declared	No	No

Notes: (1) "Level 0" standard Pascal does not support conformant arrays, while "Level 1" Pascal
does, as discussed in the references at the end of Chapter 2.

array name
index value

The primary characteristics of an array are its name, the type of its components, and the indices of its first and last components. A high-level language program does not specify the actual addresses in memory used by an array; each component of the array is referenced by the *array name* (e.g., `ints`) and an *index value* (e.g., `[3]`) giving the component's position in the array. Different high-level languages impose different restrictions on arrays, as shown in Table 3–2. Some languages fix the index number of the first array component, while others allow an arbitrary first index. Some allow *conformant arrays*, in which the starting and ending indices can be inputs to the program or even values computed by the program, rather than fixed when the program is written. Most languages allow *multidimensional arrays*, with elements whose positions are specified by two or more indices.

conformant array

multidimensional array

To see the usefulness of being able to specify the first index of an array, consider a 100-component array containing the gross national product (GNP) for each year in the 19th century. Pascal allows the starting and ending indices to be specified as follows:

ARRAY
OF

```
VAR gnp : ARRAY [1801..1900] OF real;
```

In a language that forces the first index to be 1, we would have two less desirable alternatives. We could declare an array `biggnp` of 1900 components and waste the first 1800; or we could declare an array `shfgnp` of 100 components and compute `index := year-1800` and access `shfgnp[index]` to get the GNP for `year`.

An array is the simplest of structured types in Pascal. The syntax diagram for defining an *array type* is shown in Figure 3–2. Thus, the general format of an array variable declaration is

array type

```
VAR
    identifier :   ARRAY [index type] OF component type;
```

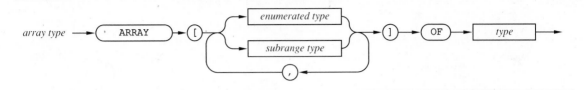

FIGURE 3–2   Syntax diagram for array type.

index type
component type

where *index type* is any enumerated or subrange type (not `integer` or `real`), and *component type* is any type. The following variable declarations make use of example types that were defined in Section 2.6.

```
VAR
   population : ARRAY [city] OF integer;
   opposite : ARRAY [direction] OF direction;
   digitCount : ARRAY [digit] OF integer;
   paintSupply : ARRAY [color] OF real;
```

Going one step further, Pascal also allows user-defined types that are arrays. Array types may be defined in the type definition part of a program; array variables may then be declared by referring to the defined type, as shown in the following examples.

```
TYPE
   vector = ARRAY [1..50] OF real;
   cityNums = ARRAY [city] OF integer;
   mapLinks = ARRAY [direction] OF direction;
VAR
   a, b, c : vector;
   population, elevation : cityNums;
   opposite, clkwise, cclkwise : mapLinks;
```

A simple application of an array is shown in Table 3–3, a Pascal program that averages and normalizes students' scores on an exam. The scores must be stored in an array so that each score can be normalized after the highest score is determined. Since Pascal does not allow conformant arrays, the program declares an array with size equal to the maximum number of students ever expected. Each time the program is run, it reads the number of scores to be handled on that particular run, followed by the scores themselves.

At this point, a few words should be said about validity checking of inputs to a program. It is standard programming practice to check the "reasonableness" of inputs to a program if inputs outside a specified range will cause abnormal program behavior or nonsensical results. The program in Table 3–3 fails if the number of scores (`nscores`) is greater than 100 or less than or equal to 0. For example, if `nscores` is greater than 100, the program will attempt to access array components beyond the declared range of the array. If `id` and `nscores` were of type `integer`, a good Pascal compiler would generate code that checks these values against the array boundaries each time the array is

TABLE 3–3   Pascal program using an array of numbers.

```
PROGRAM Normalize (input,output);
{
  This program reads exam scores and places them in an array.
  It computes and prints the average score, normalizes all scores
  according to the highest, and prints the normalized scores.
}
CONST maxscores = 100;  {maximum number of scores}
TYPE idnum = 1..maxscores;
VAR id, nscores : idnum;
  score : ARRAY [idnum] OF real;
  sum, hiscore, avg : real;
BEGIN
  read(nscores);  {Read number of scores for this run.}
  writeln('Number of scores for this run: ',nscores);
  sum := 0; hiscore := 0;
  FOR id := 1 TO nscores DO
    BEGIN
      read(score[id]);  {Read score}
      sum := sum + score[id];  {Get sum for average.}
      IF score[id] > hiscore THEN
        hiscore := score[id];  {Get highest score for normalization.}
    END;
  writeln('Highest score is: ',hiscore);
  avg := sum/nscores;   {Compute average and print results.}
  writeln('Average score is: ',avg);
  writeln('Normalized average is: ',avg/hiscore);
  writeln('Input and normalized scores are: ');
  FOR id := 1 TO nscores DO  {Print normalized scores.}
    writeln(id,score[id],score[id]/hiscore);
END.
```

accessed. However, restricting these variables to be in the subrange 1..100 allows more efficient checks—a check is required only when a new value is assigned to id or nscores. In an assembly language program, it is always up to the programmer to provide such checks.

Strings of characters are stored as arrays in Pascal. For example, a line of text to be displayed on a terminal could be declared as follows:

```
VAR
    line : ARRAY [1..80] OF char;
```

PACKED   Pascal array declarations may use the reserved word PACKED to tell the compiler that array elements are to be packed as efficiently as possible into the computer's memory words, for example:

```
VAR
    line : PACKED ARRAY [1..80] OF char;
```

Theoretically, the use of PACKED should have no effect on the results of the program's execution, but it sometimes can in strange boundary cases. In any case, it definitely affects both the size and execution time of the program. Packing obviously reduces data storage requirements, but it usually increases program size and execution time because of extra instructions for packing and unpacking.

Character strings are very common data structures in typical program applications, yet standard Pascal handles them rather awkwardly. In standard Pascal, a string is an array, and the length of an array is fixed. Real programs must deal with strings of differing lengths, some of which are not known until the program is run (for example, user inputs).

In standard Pascal, there are two equally unsatisfactory methods of dealing with variable-length strings: (1) using different array sizes for different string lengths, and (2) using a single maximum array length for all strings. The first method, though it uses memory efficiently, makes string handling a nightmare, because a different string-handling routine must be provided for each string length (standard Pascal does not support conformant arrays); variable-length user input strings cannot be handled at all. The second method, though it allows a uniform set of string utility routines to be used, requires length information to be somehow imbedded in each string, and uses memory inefficiently, especially if the longest string is much longer than the average.

Because of these difficulties, many extended Pascals, including UCSD Pascal, Microsoft Pascal and MacPascal, provide a special "string" array type and built-in utilities for dealing with variable-length strings. In this book, however, we don't have to deal with strings and so we can stick with standard Pascal.

3.2   MULTIDIMENSIONAL ARRAYS

Although a computer's memory is one-dimensional, a program can define multidimensional arrays and map them into the one-dimensional memory. For example, consider a 3×2 matrix A,

$$A = \begin{bmatrix} 1 & 2 \\ 3 & 4 \\ 5 & 6 \end{bmatrix}$$

There are two obvious ways of storing the components of A in memory. They could be stored one row at a time, forming the sequence 1, 2, 3, 4, 5, 6; this storage sequence is called *row-major order*. Or the components could be stored one column at a time, 1, 3, 5, 2, 4, 6, in *column-major order*.

row-major order
column-major order

Pascal allows a multidimensional array to be declared as a one-dimensional array whose components are arrays. This means that the 3×2 array above could be declared as a one-dimensional array of three components of type "row," each of which was itself an array of two components:

```
TYPE
   row = ARRAY [1..2] OF integer;
   a3by2array = ARRAY [1..3] OF row;
VAR a : a3by2array;
```

Storing each row sequentially in memory by normal array storage rules results in row-major storage order. A component of A in row i, column j, would be referenced as `a[i][j]`.

The above declaration can be abbreviated so that the definition of `row` is incorporated in the definition of `a3by2array`:

```
TYPE a3by2array = ARRAY [1..3] OF ARRAY [1..2] OF integer;
```

Pascal syntax allows this form to be further abbreviated by simply indicating the name of the array and the range of each of its dimensions:

```
TYPE a3by2array = ARRAY [1..3, 1..2] OF integer;
```

The array type need not be named if it is only used once, so we may write:

```
VAR a : ARRAY [1..3, 1..2] OF integer;
```

The array references are also abbreviated; `a[i][j]` becomes `a[i,j]`. Declarations of arrays with three or more dimensions extend this syntax in the obvious manner; a $5 \times 19 \times 6$ array is declared below.

```
VAR b : ARRAY [0..4, 2..20, 10..15] OF real;
```

A useful application of a multidimensional array is shown in Table 3–4. This Pascal program reads four exam scores for each student in a class of up to 100 students and stores them in a two-dimensional array. It then computes the class average for each exam, each student's average for the four exams, and the overall class average for four exams.

3.3 RECORDS

record
field name

As we've shown in the previous sections, an array is a data structure whose elements all have the *same* type and are accessed by *position*. A *record* is a data structure whose elements may have *different* types and are accessed by *field name*.

record type

In Pascal, we usually define the format of a record—the names and types of its fields—in an explicit *record type* definition using the syntax in Figure 3–3

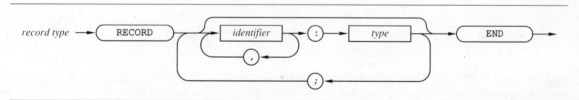

record type → RECORD → *identifier* → : → *type* → END →

FIGURE 3–3   Syntax diagram for record type.

TABLE 3–4   Pascal program using a multidimensional array.

```
PROGRAM Average (input,output);
{
  This program reads four exam scores for each student and places
  them in an array.  It computes and prints the average score of
  each student for four exams, the average for each exam over all
  students, and the average of all students over all exams.
}
CONST
  maxStudents = 100;   {Maximum number of students handled}
  nExams = 4;   {Number of exams}
TYPE
  idNum = 1..maxStudents;
  examNum = 1..nExams;
VAR
  id, nStudents : idNum;
  exam : examNum;
  score : ARRAY [idNum,examNum] OF real;
  sum, average : real;
BEGIN
  read(nStudents);   {Read number of students for this run.}
  FOR id := 1 TO nStudents DO
    FOR exam := 1 TO nExams DO
      read(score[id,exam]);   {Read scores.}

  writeln('Average for each student: ');
  FOR id := 1 TO nStudents DO   {Get average for each student.}
    BEGIN
      sum := 0;
      FOR exam := 1 TO nExams DO
        sum := sum + score[id,exam];
      average := sum/nExams;
      writeln(id,average);
    END;

  writeln('Average for each exam: ');
  FOR exam := 1 TO nExams DO   {Get average for each exam.}
    BEGIN
      sum := 0;
      FOR id := 1 TO nStudents DO
        sum := sum + score[id,exam];
      average := sum/nStudents;
      writeln(exam,average);
    END;

  sum := 0;
  FOR exam := 1 TO nExams DO   {Get average for all exams.}
    FOR id := 1 TO nStudents DO
      sum := sum + score[id,exam];
  average := sum/(nExams*nStudents);
  writeln('Average for all exams: ',average);
END.
```

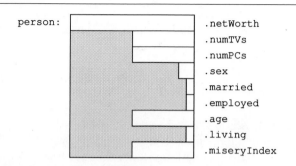

person:

- .netWorth
- .numTVs
- .numPCs
- .sex
- .married
- .employed
- .age
- .living
- .miseryIndex

FIGURE 3–4   Visualization of a person record.

(see also Exercise 3.9). An example of a Pascal record type definition is shown below:

```
TYPE
  person = RECORD
             netWorth: real;
             numTVs, numPCs: integer;
             sex: (male, female, unknown, uncommitted);
             married, employed: boolean;
             age: integer;
             living: boolean;
             miseryIndex: integer;
           END;
```

Here, the programmer has defined all of the essential characteristics of a person as elements of a single data structure. Once the person type has been defined, the program may declare any number of variables of this type. In a program that keeps track of a family of four, we might declare four such variables:

```
VAR
  mother, father, sister, brother: person;
```

We visualize each variable of type person as shown in Figure 3–4. Notice that we have drawn different fields with different widths to emphasize the fact that fields in a record may have differing types and may therefore require differing amounts of storage. However, each variable of type person requires exactly the same amount of storage and has the same layout in memory as shown in the figure.

Two pieces of information are needed to reference information in a record variable: the name of the variable and the name of the desired field within it. In Pascal, we give this information as the variable name, followed by a period, followed by the field name, as in the following program fragment:

```
inheritance = mother.netWorth + father.netWorth;
IF sister.sex = male THEN error; {probably}
father.age := father.age + 1;
mother.age := mother.age - 1;
```

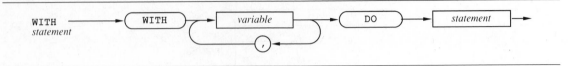

FIGURE 3–5   Syntax diagram for WITH statement.

WITH *statement*   The Pascal WITH *statement* allows us to shorten portions of programs that make multiple references to the same record variable. Unlike other Pascal structured statements that perform decision or repetition, WITH is merely a notational shorthand with the general syntax shown in Figure 3–5, where each *variable* is a single record. The Pascal compiler in effect searches the *statement* part of a WITH statement for identifiers which are field names of one of the *variables* and treats each one as as if it were preceded by its variable name and a period.[1] Thus, the following WITH statement computes the miseryIndex for father:

```
WITH father DO
  BEGIN
    miseryIndex = numPCs - numTVs + (abs(age-21) div 10);
    IF NOT employed THEN
      miseryIndex := miseryIndex + 5;
    IF mother.age < age THEN
      miseryIndex := miseryIndex - 5;
    IF NOT living THEN miseryIndex := 0;
  END;
```

Quite often, we may imbed many, many variables of a given record type in a larger data structure. For example, if we wrote a program to keep track of the successes and failures of the 100 students in the Class of '89, we might declare the following array:

```
VAR
  classOf89A: ARRAY [1..100] OF person;
```

Here, each element of classOf89A is not a simple type, such as integer, but a structured type, a record with the format shown previously in Figure 3–4. We could visualize the array as having 100 copies of the figure strung out in memory. With the array definition, we could determine the net worth of the entire class using a program fragment such as the following:

```
totalNetWorth := 0.0;
FOR i := 1 TO 100 DO
  totalNetWorth := totalNetWorth + classOf89A[i].netWorth;
```

Arrays of records are very useful data structures for storing the characteristics of a number of similar entities. However, we close this section by revisiting

---

[1]If two or more *variable*s are listed in the WITH statement, they must be of different record types. Otherwise the compiler has no way of deciding which variable name is to be matched with each field name.

the idea that there are many alternative data structures for storing a given set of information. In particular, instead of an array of records, the information about the Class of '89 could be structured as a record of arrays:

```
VAR
   classOf89R = RECORD
                   netWorth: ARRAY [1..100] OF real;
                   numTVs, numPCs: ARRAY [1..100] OF integer;
                   sex: ARRAY [1..100] OF
                      (male, female, unknown, uncommitted);
                   married, employed: ARRAY [1..100] OF boolean;
                   age: ARRAY [1..100] OF integer;
                   living: ARRAY [1..100] OF boolean;
                   miseryIndex: ARRAY [1..100] integer;
                END;
```

With this definition, we visualize the nine 100-element arrays of differing types strung out in memory to form one giant record. Going one step further, we could drop the record structure altogether, leaving us with nine independent arrays.

Which data structure is best? For the Class of '89, the array of records seems most "natural," since it groups together all of the information about one student into a single logical element. However, the correct answer to our question depends on how the data structure will be used—issues of program efficiency, robustness, and readability all come into play. Rather than dwell on these issues, which are beyond the scope of this text, we'll simply show how the choice of data structures dictates the use of different memory-addressing modes when we discuss based, indexed, and other addressing modes in Sections 7.3 and 7.5.

3.4 STACKS

pushdown stack

top of stack
last-in, first-out
LIFO
stack pointer (sp)

A *pushdown stack* (or simply a *stack*) is a one-dimensional data structure in which values are entered and removed one item at a time at one end, called the *top of stack*. A stack operates on a *last-in, first-out* basis, and is therefore sometimes called a *LIFO*.

As illustrated in Figure 3–6, a stack consists of a block of memory and a variable called the *stack pointer (sp)*. In this example, the stack pointer always points to the item stored at the top of stack, which is customary in microcomputer systems because of the hardware's addressing modes that support stacks (see Section 7.2.5). It is also possible to define the stack so that the stack pointer points to the location just above the top item in the stack.

push

In the stack of Figure 3–6, an item is entered by a *push* operation that stores the item at the top of stack and points the stack pointer at the next available memory location. An item is removed by a *pop* (or *pull*) operation that backs up the stack pointer by one memory location and removes the item stored there.

pop
pull

A pushdown stack operates like the "IN" basket of a harried engineer. Each time a new task arrives, the current task is pushed down in the stack of

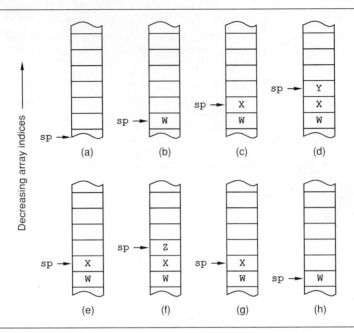

FIGURE 3–6   A pushdown stack: (a) at initialization; after (b) pushing W; (c) pushing X; (d) pushing Y; (e) popping Y; (f) pushing Z; (g) popping Z; (h) popping X.

work, and the new task is started. Once a task is completed, the engineer returns to the previous one.

stack overflow

If the harried engineer is given too many tasks, some of them will be lost or forgotten. The pushdown stack will likewise *overflow* if too many items are pushed onto it, as limited by the size of the memory block allocated for it. What happens at overflow depends on details of the stack's programming. A good program should either guarantee that stack overflow can never occur or provide a means of detecting it, since undetected overflow almost always causes program failure.

stack underflow

There is one situation that the pushdown stack encounters that a harried engineer never sees—trying to remove an item from an empty stack. This is called *underflow* and, left undetected, can be just as disastrous to a program as overflow.

One way to program a stack in Pascal is to declare an array `stack` and an integer variable `sp` to point into it. In our examples, the stack grows in the direction of *decreasing* array indices and therefore *lower-numbered* memory addresses (which are at the *top* of Figure 3–6). This is customary in microcomputer systems because of the hardware's addressing modes that support stacks (refer to Section 7.2.5 again). However, it is possible and even natural in other environments to define stacks that grow in the direction of increasing array indices and memory addresses.

The elements of `stack` can be of any type; we use type `char` in our example:

```
CONST stackSize = 100;
VAR
  stack : ARRAY [1..stackSize] OF char;
  sp : integer;
  ...
```

At the beginning of any program that uses a stack, the stack should be initialized to be empty:

```
BEGIN
  sp := stackSize + 1;   {Point just past stack area}
  ...
```

An item `x` can be pushed onto the stack by the following sequence:

```
{Push x}
  sp := sp - 1;
  stack[sp] := x;
```

and popped by the following sequence:

```
{Pop x}
  x := stack[sp];
  sp := sp + 1;
```

However, the first sequence fails if we try to put too many items in the stack. An explicit test for overflow should be included as shown below.

```
{Check and push x}
  IF sp > 1 THEN
    BEGIN sp := sp - 1; stack[sp] := x END
  ELSE
    {Overflow, report error};
```

Likewise, the program should check that the stack is not empty before attempting to pop an item:

```
{Check and pop x}
  IF sp <= stackSize THEN
    BEGIN x := stack[sp]; sp := sp + 1 END
  ELSE
    {Underflow, report error};
```

A simple program that makes use of a stack to reverse the order of a character string is shown in Table 3–5.

Another application of stacks is shown in Table 3–6, a program that reads and sorts a sequence of numbers using two stacks. Figure 3–7 illustrates the operation of the sorting program. One stack, `stackL`, stores numbers in ascending order, with the largest number at the top of stack. The other, `stackH`, stores numbers in descending order, with the smallest at the top of stack. Furthermore, the number at the top of `stackL` is always less than or equal to the number at the top of `stackH`. To enter a new number, we transfer items from

TABLE 3–5 Program to reverse character strings.

```
PROGRAM Reverse (input,output);
{
  This program reads and prints a line of text terminated by a
  period and saves it in a stack.  It then empties the stack,
  printing each character as it is removed.
}
CONST maxLen = 80;  {maximum length of a string}
  endChar = '.';  {string termination character}
VAR sp : integer;
  stack : ARRAY [1..maxLen] OF char;  inChar : char;
BEGIN
  sp := maxLen + 1; read(inChar); write('Input string is: ');
  WHILE inChar <> endChar DO
    IF sp > 1 THEN
      BEGIN  {Stack not full.}
        sp := sp - 1; stack[sp] := inChar;  {Push the char.}
        write(inChar); read(inChar); {Print this char and read next.}
      END
    ELSE
      BEGIN  {Stack full.}
        write('!! String too long !!');  {Error message.}
        inChar := endChar;  {Force a terminator.}
      END;
  writeln; write('Reversed string is: ');
  WHILE sp <= maxLen DO  {Pop a char and print it.}
    BEGIN  write(stack[sp]); sp := sp + 1  END;
END.
```

stackL to stackH or from stackH to stackL so that the value of the new number lies between the values of the top of stackL and the top of stackH. Then we can push the new number onto either stack (stackL in the program) and maintain the sorted property of the stacks. When all input numbers have been processed in this manner, we move all of stackL into stackH, and then emptying stackH produces the sorted input numbers in ascending order.

Stacks are important data structures in several areas of systems programming. Algorithms for expression evaluation in compilers and interpreters depend on stacks to store intermediate results. Block-structured high-level languages such as Pascal keep local data and other information on a stack. Parameters of a procedure in a block-structured high-level language program are usually passed on a stack, and assembly language programs sometimes use this convention as well. And, as we shall see later, all contemporary microprocessors, including the 68000, provide hardware stacks to store return address and status information during subroutine calls and interrupt servicing. In assembly language programs, the hardware stack pointer SP contains an absolute memory address, rather than an index into an array.

TABLE 3–6   Sorting program using stacks.

```
PROGRAM StackSort (input,output);
{
  This program reads a sequence of integers between -99 and +99,
  terminated by any number outside this range. As it reads the
  numbers, it sorts them using two stacks, stackL and stackH.
  After processing the last number, it prints the sorted series.
}
CONST
  maxLen = 200;  {Maximum length of a series.}
  stackSize = 201;  {Size needed in worst case.}
  minNum = -99;  maxNum = +99; {Allowable input range.}
VAR
  spL, spH, inNum, nNums : integer;
  stackL, stackH : ARRAY [1..stackSize] OF integer;

PROCEDURE PushH(v : integer); {Push v onto stackH.}
  BEGIN spH := spH - 1; stackH[spH] := v END;
FUNCTION PopH : integer; {Pop an integer from stackH.}
  BEGIN PopH := stackH[spH]; spH := spH + 1 END;
PROCEDURE PushL(v : integer); {Push v onto stackL.}
  BEGIN spL := spL - 1; stackL [spL] := v END;
FUNCTION PopL : integer; {Pop an integer from stackL.}
  BEGIN PopL := stackL[spL]; spL := spL + 1 END;

BEGIN
  spL := stackSize; stackL[spL] := minNum - 1;  {Initialize stacks.}
  spH := stackSize; stackH[spH] := maxNum + 1;
  read(inNum); nNums := 1;
  writeln('Input sequence: ');
  WHILE (inNum >= minNum) AND (inNum <= maxNum)DO  {Process inputs.}
    BEGIN
      {Make top of stackL <= inNum}
      WHILE stackL[spL] > inNum DO PushH(PopL);
      {Make top of stackH >= inNum}
      WHILE stackH[spH] < inNum DO PushL(PopH);
      PushL(inNum); {Now we have the right spot for inNum.}
      nNums := nNums + 1; {Keep track of how many inputs.}
      write(inNum);  {Print inNum.}
      IF nNums <= maxLen THEN  {If no overflow possible...}
        read(inNum)  {...get next inNum.}
      ELSE
        BEGIN  {Otherwise, print error message...}
          writeln('*** Too many inputs');
          inNum := minNum - 1;  {...and force termination.}
        END;
    END;
  {Finished all inputs, now move everything into stackH.}
  WHILE spL < stackSize DO PushH(PopL);
  writeln; write('Sorted sequence: '); {Print contents of stackH.}
  WHILE spH < stackSize DO write(PopH);
END .
```

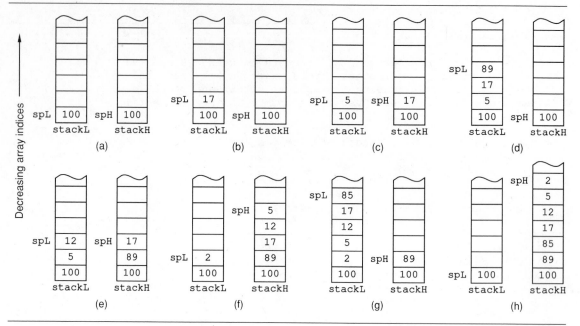

FIGURE 3–7   Contents of stacks used in sorting program: (a) at initialization; (b)–(h) after inputs 17, 5, 89, 12, 2, 85, –100.

3.5   QUEUES

queue
tail
head
first-in, first-out
FIFO
enqueue

dequeue

A *queue* is a one-dimensional data structure in which data is entered at one end, called the *tail*, and removed at the other, called the *head*. As illustrated in Figure 3–8, a simple queue consists of a block of memory and two variables to store pointers to the head and tail locations. Since a queue operates on *first-in, first-out* basis, it is often called a *FIFO*.

In the queue of Figure 3–8, a datum is entered by an *enqueue* operation that stores the datum at the location specified by `tail` and then advances `tail` to the next available memory location. Data is removed by a *dequeue* operation that reads the datum specified by `head` and then advances `head` to point to the next item in the queue. The queue is empty whenever `head` equals `tail`.

A queue could be declared and initialized in Pascal as follows:

```
CONST queueSize = 100;
VAR queue : ARRAY [1..queueSize] OF char;
    head, tail : integer;
BEGIN
    head := 1; tail := 1;
```

As in a stack, the elements in a queue can be of any type.

The queue as described so far has limited usefulness, since we exhaust the storage space in an array of `queueSize` items as soon as `queueSize` items have been enqueued, even if most of them have been subsequently removed.

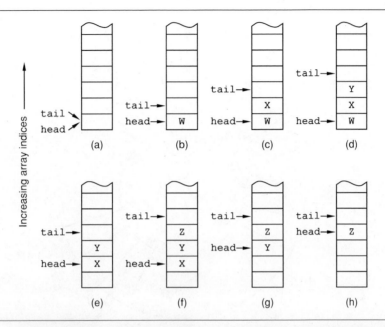

FIGURE 3–8   A simple queue: (a) at initialization; after (b) enqueueing W; (c) enqueueing X; (d) enqueueing Y; (e) dequeueing W; (f) enqueueing Z; (g) dequeueing X; (h) dequeueing Y.

What we need is a way to recover the space that is freed as items are dequeued, so that the queue overflows only if there are too many items actually stored in the queue. This can be done quite simply by viewing the storage array as a *circular buffer* as shown in Figure 3–9, wrapping around to the beginning when the end is encountered. Then an item **x** can be enqueued and dequeued as follows:

circular buffer

```
{enqueue x}
    queue[tail] := x; tail := tail + 1;
    IF tail > queueSize THEN tail := 1;
```

```
{dequeue x}
    x := queue[head]; head := head + 1;
    IF head > queueSize THEN head := 1;
```

queue overflow

Like a stack, a queue can overflow if we try to put too many items in it. This condition can be detected by `tail` "catching up" with `head` and attempting to pass it. From Figure 3–8 it might appear that `tail` is always greater than or equal to `head`, so that overflow could be detected by the condition `tail<head`. However, due to the queue's circular nature, `tail<head` can occur in normal operation, and so a strict equality check is needed before an item is enqueued:

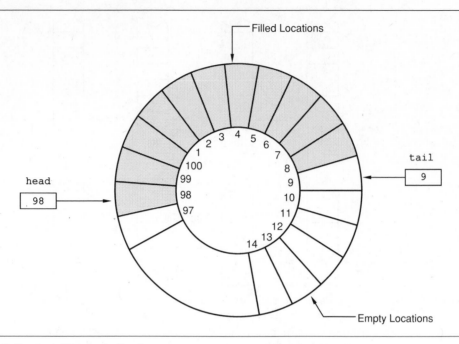

FIGURE 3–9   Circular buffer for queue.

```
{check and enqueue x}
   temp := tail + 1;
   IF temp > queueSize THEN temp := 1;
   IF temp = head THEN {overflow, report error}
   ELSE BEGIN queue[tail] := x; tail := temp END;
```

When `tail` is just one less than `head`, no more items can be stored in the queue, even though there is still one free memory location. Otherwise, we would have `head=tail` for a full queue, which is indistinguishable from the criterion for an empty queue. Therefore the queue can hold only `queueSize-1` items. This makes sense if one considers that there are `queueSize` possible values of the (circular) distance from `head` to `tail`, corresponding to a range of 0 to `queueSize-1` items stored in the queue.

queue underflow   A robust program also checks for underflow before it dequeues an item:

```
{check and dequeue x}
   IF head = tail THEN {underflow, report error}
   ELSE BEGIN
        x := queue[head]; head := head + 1;
        IF head > queueSize THEN head := 1;
      END;
```

There is another, somewhat different way of designing a queue, wherein the head is fixed at the bottom of the memory buffer. Rather than move the head pointer when an item is removed, we can move all of the items in the

TABLE 3–7   Word queue and output program.

```
PROGRAM WordQueue (input,output);
{
  This program enqueues a sequence of words, where each word is
  terminated by a space and the sequence is terminated by a
  period. Each time a '!' is received, it dequeues and prints
  one word. The '!' is not enqueued.
}
CONST qLen = 200;   {queue length}
  endChar = '.';   {input terminator}
  space = ' ';   {word separator}
  dumpChar = '!';   {command to print one word}
VAR inChar : char;
  queue : ARRAY [1..qLen] OF char;
  head, tail, temp, : integer;
  wordFlag : boolean;
BEGIN
  head := 1; tail := 1; read(inChar); {Init queue and get first char.}
  WHILE inChar <> endChar DO {Process a character at a time.}
    BEGIN
      IF inChar <> dumpChar THEN
        BEGIN  {Enqueue the character.}
          temp := tail + 1;
          IF temp > qLen THEN temp := 1;
          IF temp <> head THEN
            BEGIN queue[tail] := inChar; tail := temp END;
        END {Lose characters on overflow.}
      ELSE
        BEGIN  {Dump one word to output.}
          wordFlag := true;
          WHILE (head<>tail) AND wordFlag DO
            BEGIN
              wordFlag := queue[head] <> space;
              write(queue[head]); head := head + 1; {Dequeue, print char.}
              IF head > qLen THEN head := 1;
            END;
          writeln;  {Start a new line after each printed word.}
        END;
      read(inChar);   {Get next char.}
    END;
END.
```

queue down in memory. This is seldom done in programs, because of the large overhead of moving each item, one by one. However, hardware FIFO chips quite commonly use this technique, because compact shift register circuits can be designed to do all the moving in parallel.

A contrived example of a text input/output program that makes use of a queue is given in Table 3–7. The program reads a sequence of characters and places them in a queue. Whenever the character "!" is received, the first word in the queue is dequeued and printed, where a word is defined to be a sequence of nonspace characters terminated by a space. Thus, the order of the input characters is preserved, and the words are printed in the order in which they were received.

Queues are quite common in operating systems of large computers, where they are used to store requests for service in the order they are received, and then grant service on a first-come, first-served basis as the necessary resources become available. Queues are also a very natural data structure to use in the input/output software of any computer. When different devices and programs have varying speeds, a queue can be used to temporarily store data from a fast device or program and later transfer it to another device or program upon demand, without mixing up its order. A program that uses queues for input/output processing is presented in Section 12.5.

In our Pascal examples, we have used arrays to store queue data, and so `head` and `tail` have been indices into the arrays. In an assembly language program, the array index computation can be avoided by storing absolute memory addresses in `head` and `tail`. A set of assembly language queue manipulation subroutines are presented in Section 9.3.

3.6   DYNAMIC VARIABLES AND POINTERS

Most variables and data structures in a Pascal program are explicitly named and declared at the beginning of the program, and they are given fixed locations in memory when the program is compiled. However, there are two exceptions to this rule.

local variable

Local variables of a procedure or function are declared at compile time, but they are assigned locations each time that the procedure or function is called. The locations are in an anonymous pushdown stack that is created by the compiled code. By "anonymous," we mean that this stack is not explicitly declared in the source code; the compiler simply creates it as part of the "run-time environment" of the compiled code. We'll take a closer look at this stack in Chapter 9.

dynamic variable

Dynamic variables aren't even declared at compile time. They spring into existence as requested while the program is executing, each time the program

`new`
heap

explicitly calls a built-in procedure called `new`. Memory for these variables is allocated from another pool of memory, often called the *heap*, which is part of the run-time environment of the compiled code. Dynamic variables are discussed in the remainder of this subsection.

pointer variable

A *pointer variable* points to a dynamic variable. A given pointer variable may point to different dynamic variables at different times during a program's execution. However, it may only point to dynamic variables of one certain type, as determined by pointer variable's declaration:

```
TYPE
  agePointer = ^integer;
VAR
  myAge, yourAge, oldest : agePointer;
```

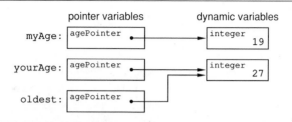

FIGURE 3–10   Pointer variables and dynamic variables.

Here `agePointer` is defined to be a *pointer type* that points to dynamic variables of type `integer`, and `myAge`, `yourAge`, and `topAge` are declared to be pointer variables. A possible configuration of these variables is shown in Figure 3–10; the label in the upper left-hand corner of each box indicates the variable's type. Notice that the dynamic variables are anonymous—unlike `myAge`, `yourAge`, and `oldest`, they have no identifiers.

What is the value of a pointer variable? In our figures, it is drawn as an arrow. In most Pascal implementations, the value of a pointer variable is the address of a memory location, which in turn is an integer. However, unlike other integers, the value of a Pascal pointer variable cannot be incremented, decremented, added to other integers, or even printed. Therefore, to stay out of trouble, and to relieve stress on the word "pointer," we'll think of a pointer

arrow

variable as simply containing an *arrow* for the balance of this chapter.

Like all Pascal variables, a pointer variable's initial value when a program begins execution is undefined. There are three ways to assign a value to a pointer variable *pointvar*:

(1) Execute the assignment statement "*pointvar* := nil". The reserved word

nil

nil denotes a value that may be assigned to any pointer variable and means "this arrow points to nothing."[2]

(2) Execute the assignment statement "*pointvar* := *pv*", where *pv* is a pointer variable that has the same type as *pointvar* and that has a defined value. A copy of *pv*'s value is made, so that now both *pointvar* and *pv* contain arrows to the same dynamic variable (or `nil` if *pv* was `nil`).

new

(3) Call the procedure `new(pointvar)`. A new dynamic variable is created and an arrow to it is stored in *pointvar*. Note that at this time, the value of *pointvar* is defined but the value of the new dynamic variable not.

Since dynamic variables are anonymous, the only way to reference their values is through pointer variables. The Pascal syntax *pointvar*^ means "the

---

[2]We break with our convention of capitalizing reserved words in this one case. It doesn't seem right to highlight a word that means nothing!

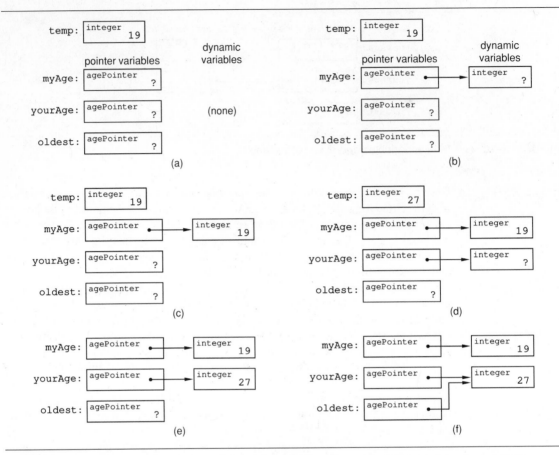

FIGURE 3–11   Values of pointer and dynamic variables after executing each line of a program.

dynamic variable that *pointvar* points to," or simply "what *pointvar* points to." Consider the following program fragment, where **temp** is an integer variable:

```
read(temp);                                    {a}
new(myAge);                                     {b}
myAge^ := temp;                                 {c}
read(temp);   new(yourAge);                     {d}
yourAge^ := temp;                               {e}
IF myAge^ > yourAge^ THEN oldest := myAge
ELSE oldest := yourAge;                         {f}
```

Figure 3–11 shows the creation of dynamic variables and the values of variables during the program's execution. Study the program fragment and the figure carefully, since they illustrate the subtle distinction between accessing a pointer variable (e.g., **yourAge**, an arrow) and referencing what it points to (e.g., **yourAge^**, an integer).

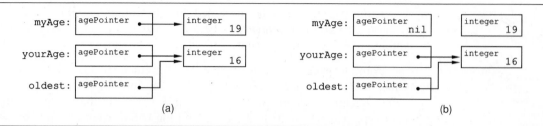

FIGURE 3–12   More fiddling with pointers and dynamic variables.

Notice that at the end of the program fragment, two pointer variables contain arrows to the same dynamic variable. If we subsequently execute the statement,

```
yourAge^ := 16;                                     {a}
```

then as shown in Figure 3–12(a), we change the value of only one dynamic variable, and we don't change any pointer values, yet we change the values of two pointer references—`yourAge^` and `oldest^`—even though `oldest^` was never explicitly mentioned. In another example that might bother you, suppose we execute the statement,

```
myAge := nil;                                       {b}
```

Now `myAge` points to nothing, and nothing points to the first dynamic variable, as shown in Figure 3–12(b). That poor dynamic variable is now not only anonymous, but also unattached, unreferenceable, and perhaps even unloved!

dispose

Pascal provides a built-in procedure, `dispose`, for humanely terminating the existence of unwanted dynamic variables. In many Pascal implementations, executing the procedure `dispose`(*pointvar*) returns the storage that was used by *pointvar*^ to the heap, where it can be allocated by `new` to other dynamic variables. In any case, it is an error to attempt to access a dynamic variable after it has been `dispose`d of.

The key ideas for pointer and dynamic variables are summarized below:

- A *pointer type* is defined in the type definition part as ^*anytype*.

- A *pointer variable* is a variable of a pointer type ^*anytype*. Its value is `nil` or an arrow to a dynamic variable of type *anytype*.

- A *dynamic variable* of type *anytype* is created by calling `new`(*pointvar*), where *pointvar* is a variable of type ^*anytype*.

- A dynamic variable is referenced by the syntax *pointvar*^, where *pointvar* is a pointer variable containing an arrow to the dynamic variable.

- A dynamic variable may be discarded and its storage possibly reclaimed by calling dispose(*pointvar*), where *pointvar* is a pointer variable containing an arrow to the dynamic variable to be discarded.

The example program fragment that we presented in this section is not terribly useful, but in general pointers and dynamic references are very useful for creating dynamic data structures such as linked lists. In these applications, the pointer type usually points to a record, and the record itself contains one or more fields of a pointer type, as we'll see in the next two sections.

3.7   ONE-WAY LINKED LISTS

linked list

link

one-way linked list

successor
predecessor

Stacks and queues allow data to be entered or removed at one end of the data structure, but not in the middle. A *linked list* is a one-dimensional data structure that allows data to be entered and removed at arbitrary locations. To get this flexibility, each item in the list has an associated *link* that points to the next item.

Figure 3–13 provides a conceptual view of a *one-way linked list*. (Two-way linked lists are discussed in the next section.) There is a pointer variable called head that points to first item in the list. Items in a list are typically records with the same format; each has one field (link) that points to the next item, and one or more fields that contain data. Note that in our illustrations of lists, we sometimes use X as the name of x^, the item currently referenced by a pointer variable x, even though x^ has no name from the Pascal point of view.

The "next item" after an item X in the list is called the *successor* of X; the item before X is called the *predecessor* of X. If an item X has no successor, then its link is set to nil.

To insert a new item Q in the list after an item P, we simply make Q's link point to the old successor of P, and make P's link point to Q. To delete the item Y after an item X, we make X's link point to Y's successor.

Pascal's pointer and record data types are ideal for defining linked lists and other dynamic data structures. It is also possible to define linked lists using only the array type, using array indices as pointers (see Exercise 3.23).

As an example, we will define a "class list" containing student names and exam scores. Each element of the list is a record containing a name, an exam score, and a pointer to another record:

```
TYPE
  studentPointer = ^student;
  student = RECORD
              link : studentPointer;
              name : ARRAY [1..20] OF char;
              score : real;
            END;
```

This declaration defines the student record type but does not create any student records. Records are allocated from the Pascal heap as needed by

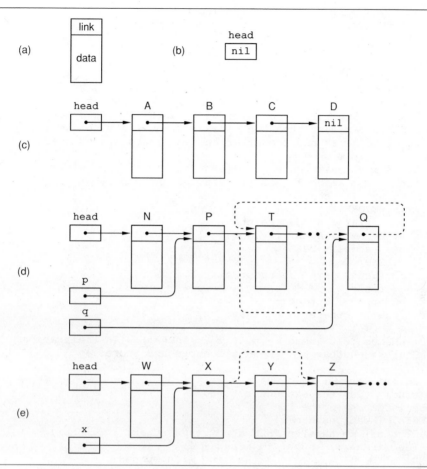

FIGURE 3–13   One-way linked lists: (a) general format of a list item; (b) an empty list; (c) a list with four items; (d) inserting an item Q after item P; (e) deleting the successor of X.

calls to the **new** function, as described in the previous section. We also define a few variables of type `studentPointer` to be used in the examples that follow:

```
VAR
    head, p, q, x: studentPointer;
```

Now suppose q points to an item Q we wish to insert after an item P, pointed to by p. Assuming that storage for Q has already been allocated and its data fields have been filled, the insertion can be accomplished as follows:

```
{insert item q^ after item p^}
    q^.link := p^.link; {The link field of what q points to (Q)
                              is set equal to
                         the link field of what p points to (P)}
    p^.link := q; {The link field of what p points to (P)
                         is set equal to q (a pointer to Q)}
```

TABLE 3–8   Name and exam score sorting program.

```
PROGRAM ClassList (input,output);
{
  This program reads a sequence of names and exam scores separated
  by spaces, one name/score pair per line, with the entire sequence
  terminated by a line starting with a period. As the program reads
  each name/score pair, it enters it into a linked list that is kept
  sorted by name. After all name/score pairs have been read, all
  entries with scores less than the class average are ruthlessly
  deleted, and the names and scores of the survivors are printed.
}
CONST listLen = 100;  nameLen = 20;  {List and name lengths}
      endChar = '.'; space = ' '; {Terminator and separator}
TYPE studentPointer = ^student;
     student = RECORD
                  link : studentPointer;
                  name : ARRAY [1..nameLen] OF char;
                  score : real;
               END;
VAR head, stud, prev, next : studentPointer;
    sum, avg : real;
    nNames, nChar, j : integer;
    inChar : char;  greater : boolean;
BEGIN
  sum := 0; nNames := 0; head := nil; read(inChar); {Initialization}
  WHILE inChar <> endChar DO  {Read all names and scores.}
    BEGIN
      nNames := nNames + 1;  nChar := 1;
      new(stud); {Get new student record.}
      WHILE inChar <> space DO
        BEGIN  {Read one name.}
          IF nChar <= nameLen THEN stud^.name[nChar] := inChar;
          read(inChar);  nChar := nChar + 1;
        END;                        {Pad end with spaces}
      FOR j := nChar TO nameLen DO stud^.name[j] := space;
      readln(stud^.score);  {Get score and start new line}
      sum := sum + stud^.score;  {Add to sum for average.}
      prev := nil; next := head;  {Point to class list head.}
      greater := false;
      WHILE (next <> nil) AND (NOT greater) DO
        BEGIN  {Chase down list until end or greater name found.}
          FOR j := nameLen DOWNTO 1 DO
            greater := next^.name[j] > stud^.name[j])
              OR ((next^.name[j] = stud^.name[j]) AND greater);
          IF NOT greater THEN {Get next item}
            BEGIN prev := next; next := next^.link END;
        END;  {Then insert new item.}
      IF prev = nil THEN {Insert afer head.}
        BEGIN stud^.link := head; head := stud END
      ELSE {Insert after prev.}
        BEGIN stud^.link := next;  prev^.link := stud END;
      IF nNames < listLen THEN read(inChar)
      ELSE inChar := endChar;  {Terminate if too many names.}
    END;
```

TABLE 3–8   (continued)

```
avg := sum/nNames;   {Compute average.}
writeln('Average score:', avg, 'Lower scores will be purged!');
prev := nil; next := head;
WHILE next <> nil DO   {Purge scores lower than class average.}
   BEGIN
     IF next^.score < avg THEN {Purge item next^}
       BEGIN
         IF prev = nil THEN head := next^.link
         ELSE prev^.link := next^.link
         dispose(next);
       END
     ELSE {Skip over item next^}
       BEGIN prev := next; next := next^.link END;
   END;
next := head; writeln; {Now print the remaining sorted list.}
WHILE next <> nil DO
   BEGIN
     FOR j := 1 TO nameLen DO write(next^.name[j]);
     writeln(next^,score); next := next^.link;
   END;
END.
```

Deleting an item is even simpler; the following statement deletes the successor of an item X, pointed to by x:

```
{delete item x^}
  IF x^.link <> nil THEN x^.link := (x^.link)^.link
       {The link field of what x points to (X)
            is set equal to
        a pointer to X's successor}
  ELSE {error, item x^ has no successor};
```

Table 3–8 is a program that reads names and exam scores one at a time, entering each one into the class list, always keeping the list sorted by name. The program starts with the list head (head) equal to nil, and no student records created. As each name/score pair is read, the program creates a student record by calling new and stores the new information in the new record. Then starting at the head, it scans down the list until a record with an alphabetically greater name or the end of the list is found. It enters the new record before the greater record, or at the end of the list if no name was greater. After all name/score pairs have been read, the program unsympathetically deletes the entries for all of the unfortunate students whose scores were less than the class average, and prints the remaining sorted list.

In our example, we used new to create records dynamically and we used Pascal pointers to access the records. It is also possible to create records as elements of a fixed array, and to access them using array indices. However, this introduces two forms of overhead. First, we may waste memory because we must declare an array of the maximum number of records that we ever expect to encounter; dynamic records consume memory only as needed. Second, we waste time because the program must convert an array index into an absolute memory address every time an index is used, whereas a pointer is already an absolute memory address in most Pascal implementations. We'll see this difference between indexed addressing and pointers more clearly when we study addressing modes in Chapter 7.

3.8   TWO-WAY LINKED LISTS

The list insertion and deletion operations described so far operate on the *successor* of a list item (insert Q after P, delete successor of X). Suppose we are handed pointer `x^` and `y^` to a list item X and a new item Y and told, "Insert Y in front of X." Or suppose we are simply told "Delete X." Both of these operations must change the link of X's *predecessor*. If all we have is a pointer to X, the only way to find X's predecessor is to start at the beginning of the list and search until X is found. Thus, to insert an item in front of X, we have the following code:

```
{insert item Y in front of item X}
  IF head = nil THEN {error, list is empty}
  ELSE IF head = x THEN {X is at head of list}
    BEGIN head := y; y^.link := x END
  ELSE BEGIN {X is somewhere down the list}
    prev := head;
    WHILE (prev^.link <> nil) AND (prev^.link <> x) DO
      prev := prev^.link; {search down the list}
    IF prev^.link = x THEN
      BEGIN prev^.link := y; y^.link := x END
    ELSE {error, item X not found};
  END;
```

Deleting item X is not much simpler:

```
{delete item X}
  IF head = nil THEN {error, list is empty}
  ELSE IF head = x THEN {X is at head of list}
    head := head^.link
  ELSE BEGIN {X is somewhere down the list}
    prev := head;
    WHILE (prev^.link <> nil) AND (prev^.link <> x) DO
      prev := prev^.link; {search down the list}
    IF prev^.link = x THEN prev^.link := (prev^.link)^.link
    ELSE {error, item X not found};
  END;
```

If X is the last item in the list, we search the entire list before finding X. If we frequently insert or delete at the end of the list, it may be worthwhile to avoid the overhead of searching by using a two-way linked list.

two-way linked list

In a *two-way linked list*, each list item has two links; `succlink` points to the successor of the item and `predlink` points to the predecessor. An additional pointer variable `tail` always points to the last item in the list. Now we can always find an item's predecessor or successor in one step, but we have more links to update each time that we insert or delete an item:

```
{insert item Y in front of item X}
  y^.succlink := x;
  y^.predlink := x^.predlink;
  IF x^.predlink = nil THEN head := y {start of list}
  ELSE (x^.predlink)^.succlink := y; {middle of list}
  x^.predlink := y;


{insert item Y after item X}
  y^.succlink := x^.succlink;
  y^.predlink := x;
  IF x^.succlink = nil THEN tail := y {end of list}
  ELSE (x^.succlink)^.predlink := y; {middle of list}
  x^.succlink := y;


{delete item X}
  IF x^.predlink = nil THEN head := x^.succlink {start of list}
  ELSE (x^.predlink)^.succlink := x^.succlink; {middle of list}
  IF x^.succlink = nil THEN tail := x^.predlink {end of list}
  ELSE (x^.succlink)^.predlink := x^.predlink; {middle of list}
```

These operations are illustrated in Figure 3–14.

Even more complicated linked data structures can be devised. The number and type of links in a data structure can be tailored to the application. For example, we could have a variable number of "child" links in a family tree, or links to several other different types of records in a "student information record." An important programming challenge, from the simplest list structure to the most complex, is maintaining list pointer consistency and avoiding "spaghetti" data structures.

3.9 LIST STORAGE MANAGEMENT

So far, we have assumed that there is always enough storage available on the Pascal heap to create new list items when we call new, and we have assumed that space is efficiently reclaimed when we use dispose to release deleted list items. However, we can't always get by so easily.

In some Pascal implementations, dispose(x) does not reclaim the memory used by x, so that the heap can be exhausted by a simple loop such as the following:

```
WHILE condition DO
  BEGIN new(x); compute; dispose(y) END;
```

Even though this loop uses a constant amount of memory (since it releases an item for each one that it consumes), it will eventually eat through all available free memory.

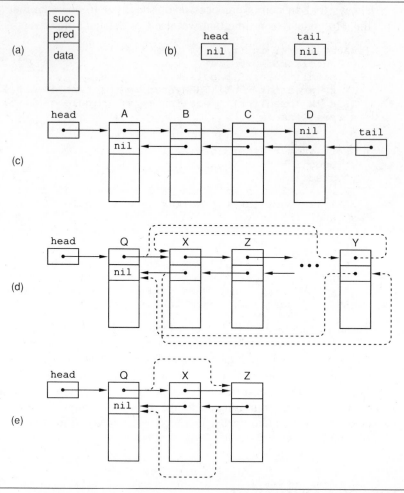

FIGURE 3–14   Two-way linked lists: (a) general format of a list item; (b) an empty list; (c) a list with four items; (d) inserting item Y in front of item X; (e) deleting item X.

In programs written in other high-level languages or in assembly language, we simply don't have the Pascal `new` and `dispose` functions available, and so we have to manage list storage ourselves. In this section, we'll show how to manage list storage using Pascal examples, without `new` and `dispose`, which can be adapted to other languages.

free list   The easiest way to keep track of available list storage is by use of a *free list*, a list of all the unused blocks. At system initialization, we chain all of the available blocks together into the free list. When we want to add a new item to an active list, we remove the first block from the free list and use it to store the

new item. When we delete an item from an active list, we return the block to
the free list.

Once again we'll use the class list example from Section 3.7, but we'll
explicitly create an array sm of records instead of allocating them with new:

```
CONST listSize = 100; null = 0;
TYPE studentPointer = [1..listSize];
     student = RECORD
                  link : studentPointer;
                  name : ARRAY [1..20] OF char;
                  score : real;
               END;
VAR head, free, stud, prev, next : studentPointer;
    sm: ARRAY [1..listSize] OF student;
```

We now use indices into the sm array rather than Pascal pointers to point to
list items. (Unfortunately, in standard Pascal, pointer variables can only point
to dynamic variables allocated by new.) A free list containing unused student
records could be initialized as follows:

```
head := null;  {init head of class list}
free := 1;      {init free list}
FOR next := 1 TO listSize - 1 DO {chain list items}
   sm[next].link := next + 1 END;
sm[listSize].link := null; {terminate free list}
```

Now when we need a new item, we take it from the free list rather than calling
new:

```
{obtain new item stud from free list}
  IF free <> null THEN
    BEGIN
       stud := free;  {get first item on free list}
       free := sm[free].link;  {delete from free list}
    END
  ELSE {error, out of free space};
```

Once we have stud, the index of the new item, we can manipulate stud and
insert the new item in the class list. When we delete an item from the class list,
we return it to our free list instead of calling dispose:

```
{delete item next, where prev points to its predecessor}
  IF prev = null THEN head := sm[next].link   {Delete}
  ELSE sm[prev].link := sm[next].link;
  sm[next].link := free;   {Return to free list}
  free := next;
```

*garbage
collection*

An alternative to systematically returning deleted items to a free list is a
technique known as *garbage collection*. Whenever the free list becomes empty,
an audit is made of all the active lists that share it. Any list item that does not
appear in some active list is assumed to be garbage and is returned to the free
list. This eliminates the overhead of updating the free list with each deletion in
favor of a periodic, possibly more efficient garbage collection operation.

Garbage collection is essential in complicated list-processing applications where several lists may contain the same item or sublist—when we delete an item from one list, we don't know whether there are other lists still pointing to the same item and therefore we *can't* return it to the free list. Free-list management and garbage collection are an integral part of the run-time packages of list-processing languages such as LISP and are invisible to the programmer.

One typical application uses lists to implement queues. Consider a computer that distributes messages to 100 different destinations in a network. Assuming that we can sometimes generate messages for a particular destination faster than we can transmit them, we must provide a message queue for each destination to store pending messages temporarily. Suppose that in the worst case, we might have to queue 20 messages for a particularly busy destination. Therefore, providing a separate maximum-length queue for each destination using the structure in Section 3.5 would require storage for $100 \cdot 20 = 2000$ messages. If each message block is 100 characters long, we need 200,000 characters of memory!

On the other hand, we may know that there will never be more than 100 outstanding messages in the system, even if some destinations have 20. Therefore, we can allocate a free list with 100 message blocks, and program each queue to be a linked list that uses this free list. During normal operation, most queues would be empty or near-empty, but there would be sufficient free space that a few queues could become very large if they needed to. By sharing one free list, we can do the job with only 10,000 characters of storage.

REFERENCES

Since 1968, the best reference on data structures has been Donald E. Knuth's *Fundamental Algorithms* (Addison-Wesley, 1973, 2nd ed.). Knuth's treatment of data structures is especially applicable for assembly language programmers, since examples are given in the assembly language of a fairly general, hypothetical machine called MIX. Advanced data structures and techniques applicable to sorting and searching are covered in Knuth's *Sorting and Searching* (Addison-Wesley, 1973).

Wirth's *Algorithms + Data Structures = Programs* (Prentice-Hall, 1976) begins with a description of basic data structures in the context of Pascal programs, and continues with a study of some useful algorithms and data structures. His latest revision of the book is based on Modula-2, his extension to Pascal, and is titled simply *Algorithms & Data Structures* (Prentice-Hall, 1986). Apparently too many wiseguys were abusing the original title.

Other books that combine data structures and Pascal include *A Second Course in Computer Science with Pascal* by Daniel D. McCracken (Wiley, 1987), *Advanced Programming and Problem Solving with Pascal* by G. M. Schneider and S. C. Bruell (Wiley, 1987, 2nd ed.), and *Data Structures Using Pascal* by A. M. Tenenbaum and M. J. Augenstein (Prentice-Hall, 1986, 2nd ed.).

Also based on Pascal, *Data Structures & Program Design* by R. L. Kruse (Prentice-Hall, 1987, 2nd ed.) is an especially readable introductory text—it's printed in two colors!

EXERCISES

3.1 Write a Pascal program that reads a series of input characters one at a time and places them in an array. Assume that there are three predefined constants of type `char`: `backspace`, `endofline`, and `endoffile`. Whenever a `backspace` is received, the previously stored character should be deleted from the array. When `endofline` is received, all valid characters in the array should be printed, and character collection should restart at the beginning of the array. When an `endoffile` is received, the array contents should likewise be printed, but the program should then terminate.

3.2 Write a Pascal program that reads a series of 100 integers into an array and then sorts them as follows. Compare the first two items in the array and swap them if the first is larger. Compare the second and third items and swap them if the second is larger. Continue in this manner until that last two items in the array have been compared and possibly swapped. At this point, the largest number is the last item in the array, but the other items are still unsorted. So, repeat this process on the first 99 items in the array, then the first 98, and so on, until the entire array has *bubble sort* been sorted. *Note:* This sorting algorithm, called a *bubble sort*, isn't very efficient.

3.3 Write a Pascal program that reads a series of 100 integers into an array and then *selection sort* sorts them using the following algorithm, called a *selection sort*. Find the smallest number and exchange it with the first number in the array; find the second smallest number and exchange it with the second number in the array; continue in this manner until all numbers have been processed. After sorting the numbers, the program should print the sorted series. (*Hint:* After each iteration, the next smallest number can be found by starting the search one location deeper in the array.)

3.4 Write a Pascal program that computes the prime numbers from 2 to 1000 using a `boolean` array `prime [2..1000]`. Initialize all the array elements to `true`. Starting with array element 2·2, mark all of the array elements corresponding to multiples of 2 as `false`. Continue with multiples of 3, 4, 5, and so on, until all nonprime numbers have been marked, and then print the primes.

3.5 Optimize the preceding program by only marking multiples of known primes; that is, do not mark multiples of 4, 6, 8, 9, and so on, since they are already marked when this step is reached.

3.6 The programs in Table 3–3 and Table 3–4 begin by reading the number of students to be handled on a particular run of the program. This requires the input file to contain this number, and is a source of error when the input file is modified. Show a way to modify the input format and the programs so that the student count is not needed.

3.7   Given an $m \times r$ matrix A and an $r \times n$ matrix B, the matrix product $A \cdot B$ is an $m \times n$ matrix C, where each element C_{ij} of C is given by the following equation:

$$C_{ij} = \sum_{1 \le k \le r} A_{ik} \cdot B_{kj}$$

Write a Pascal program that reads two matrices A and B and computes and prints their product. Assume that the maximum value of m, n, and r for any run of the program is 20, but read their actual values at the beginning of the program.

3.8   Rewrite the Pascal program in Table 3–4 so that the first and last FOR loops are eliminated.

3.9   The programming examples in Section 3.3 showed TYPE definitions followed by use of the defined types in variable declarations. Alternatively, a record type could be defined in the variable declaration itself, for example,

```
VAR
    familyIncome: RECORD
                    mother, father, sister, brother: real;
                  END
```

However, assuming this is the only place that this type is used, in this example it would make more sense to simply define four variables, motherIncome, fatherIncome, sisterIncome, and brotherIncome of type real. Under what circumstances would an imbedded type definition make more sense?

3.10 Write declaration, initialization, "check and push," and "check and pop" sequences in Pascal for a stack in which sp always points at the location just past the top stack item.

3.11 Write declaration, initialization, "check and push," and "check and pop" sequences in Pascal for a stack that grows by *incrementing* rather than decrementing the stack pointer.

3.12 Rewrite the Pascal program in Table 3–6 so that the constants minNum-1 and maxNum+1 do not have to be stored as the first elements in the stack to force termination of the second and third WHILE loops. How does this affect the speed of the WHILE loops?

3.13 Rewrite the Pascal program in Table 3–6 so that both stacks share a single array. One stack starts at the first location of the array and grows by incrementing the stack pointer; the other starts at the last location and grows by decrementing the stack pointer. With this arrangement, how big an array is needed to sort a sequence of 200 integers?

3.14 Assuming that the high-level language does *not* perform bounds checking on stack access, suggest a method of detecting stack overflow that allows "postmortem" detection of stack overflow without requiring a check before every push operation. Indicate any assumptions required for the method to be effective.

3.15 Write declaration, initialization, "check and enqueue," and "check and dequeue" sequences in Pascal for a queue that can actually store queueSize items in an array of size queueSize. (*Hint:* In order to do this, an extra variable will be needed to distinguish between full and empty when head = tail.)

3.16 Write declaration, initialization, "check and enqueue," and "check and dequeue" sequences in Pascal for a queue that fixes the head at the bottom of a memory buffer and shifts down the entire contents of the queue when an item is deleted. Using this technique, how many items can be stored in a buffer of size `queueSize`?

3.17 Show how to eliminate the variable `wordFlag` in Table 3–7 by using a `GOTO` statement in the innermost `WHILE` loop. Is this a reasonable use of `GOTO`? Suggest how an `EXIT` statement could be added to Pascal to provide a more structured way of terminating loops in situations like this.

3.18 Modify the program in Table 3–7 so that multiple spaces can be used to separate words. The output of the program should be the same whether a single space or multiple spaces are used.

3.19 Ask your favorite engineer if his or her "IN" basket is a stack or a queue. Ask the same question to a few experienced computer scientists and learn about all kinds of unusual and fascinating data structures.

double-ended 3.20 A *double-ended queue* (sometimes called a *dequeue*) may have items added or
queue   removed at either end. The variables required for such a structure are the same as
dequeue   for a normal queue—head, `tail`, and a storage block. However, there are four
                     ways to access the queue:

   (1) Enqueue item **x** at the head.

   (2) Enqueue item **x** at the tail.

   (3) Dequeue item **x** at the head.

   (4) Dequeue item **x** at the tail.

   Write instruction sequences, including error checking, for these functions. Note that (2) and (3) are the access methods for a normal queue, while (1) and (3) [or (2) and (4)] give behavior analogous to a stack.

3.21 Suppose the last two lines in the example program in Section 3.6 are replaced with the following:

```
IF mySalary^ > yourSalary^ THEN topSalary^ := mySalary^
ELSE topSalary^ := yourSalary^;
```

   What is the effect? How can you make it better?

3.22 Rewrite the string comparison code in Table 3–8 so that the FOR loop starts with item 1 and works up to item `nameLen`.

3.23 Rewrite the program in Table 3–8 to use `student` records stored in an array rather than dynamic records created by `new`. Declare an array containing `listLen` records at the beginning of the program and use array indices as pointers.

3.24 The program in Table 3–8 must treat the `head` as a special case in both list insertions and deletions. Rewrite the program using the `link` field of an extra `student` record to store the list head, eliminating the special-case code.

3.25 Why did we use the identifier `prev` instead of `pred` for predecessors in the linked-list examples in Section 3.6?

3.26 Write a Pascal program that reverses the order of a one-way linked list, using as little intermediate storage as possible.

3.27 Repeat the previous problem using a stack to store the links.

3.28 Show how to add a single `tail` pointer to a one-way linked list in order to allow efficient appending to the end of the list. Write instruction sequences that perform each of the following functions, correctly updating `tail` as well as the other pointers: (a) append item `q` at the end of the list; (b) insert item `q` after item `p`; (c) delete the successor of item `x`.

3.29 Convince yourself that the instruction sequences given for inserting and deleting items in a two-way linked list are correct for the following special cases by working them out by hand:

    (1) inserting after the head in an empty list;

    (2) inserting in front of the tail in an empty list;

    (3) deleting the item in a list with only one item.

3.30 Write a Pascal program that reverses the order of a two-way linked list.

3.31 In manipulations of two-way linked lists, the special-case operations involving `head` and `tail` may be eliminated as in Exercise 3.24. Rewrite the insertion and deletion code in Section 3.8 and resketch Figure 3–14 assuming that the head and tail of the list are stored in the `succlink` and `predlink` fields of an otherwise unused item. *Hint:* At initialization, `head` and `tail` should point to this item, rather than contain `nil`.

3.32 Suppose elements of a two-way linked list are always accessed by scanning the list in one direction or the other, so that we always know either the predecessor or the successor of the current list item. Then instead of storing both predecessor and successor links with each list item, we can store a function of the two links such that, given the value of one link, we can derive the other from the stored function value. Describe two functions that have this property and require no more storage for the function value than for one link.

3.33 Add free-list maintenance to the program in Table 3–8. Define the procedures `GetFree` and `PutFree` to get items from the free list and return surplus items to the free list. Provide appropriate error checks to determine whether the free list is empty.

CHAPTER 4

Number Systems and Arithmetic

The study of computer number systems and arithmetic is essential for understanding how computers process numeric data. And, like all mathematics, number systems can be put to good use in everyday affairs too, if you just look hard enough. Here are some examples from my own experience:

- Correctly decorating the cake for my wife's 31st birthday with only five candles.
- Making my checkbook look like it had a large positive balance when it was really in the red.
- Finding HFC in the phone book after my efforts to hide the negative balance failed.

In the first crisis above, a binary number system saved the day. In the second, a system called ten's complement came in handy. And in the last case, remembering how characters are represented by numbers in a computer helped me to understand why HFC isn't listed between Heywood and Hiatt in the white pages. After reading this chapter, you too will be able to apply different number systems to your personal affairs, and you'll understand computer arithmetic as well.

4.1 POSITIONAL NUMBER SYSTEMS

positional number system
weight

Positional number systems are used in all computers and almost all day-to-day business of people. In a *positional number system*, a number is represented by a string of digits where each digit position has an associated *weight*. For example, the value D of a 4-digit decimal number $d_3d_2d_1d_0$ is

$$D = d_3 \cdot 10^3 + d_2 \cdot 10^2 + d_1 \cdot 10^1 + d_0 \cdot 10^0$$

Each digit d_i has a weight of 10^i. Thus, the value of 6851 is computed as follows:

$$6851 = 6 \cdot 1000 + 8 \cdot 100 + 5 \cdot 10 + 1 \cdot 1$$

A decimal point is used to allow negative as well as positive powers of 10 in a decimal number representation. Thus, $d_1 d_0 . d_{-1} d_{-2}$ has the value

$$D = d_1 \cdot 10^1 + d_0 \cdot 10^0 + d_{-1} \cdot 10^{-1} + d_{-2} \cdot 10^{-2}$$

For example, the value of 34.85 is computed as:

$$34.85 = 3 \cdot 10 + 4 \cdot 1 + 8 \cdot 0.1 + 5 \cdot 0.01$$

base
radix

In a general positional number system, each digit position has an associated weight of b^i, where b is called the *base* or *radix* of the number system. The general form of a number in such a system is

$$d_{p-1} d_{p-2} \cdots d_1 d_0 . d_{-1} d_{-2} \cdots d_{-n}$$

radix point

where there are p digits to the left of the point and n digits to the right of the point, called the *radix point*. The value of the number is

$$D = \sum_{i=-n}^{p-1} d_i \cdot b^i$$

the summation of each digit times the corresponding power of the radix. If the radix point is missing, it is assumed to be to the right of the rightmost digit.

Except for possible leading and trailing zeroes, the representation of a number in a positional number system is unique. (Obviously, 34.85 equals 034.85000, and so on.) The leftmost digit in such a number is called the *high-order* or *most significant digit*; the rightmost is the *low-order* or *least significant digit*.

high-order digit
most significant digit
low-order digit
least significant digit
binary radix
bit

The *binary radix* is used in almost all computers. The allowable digits, 0 and 1, are called *bits*, and each bit d_i has weight 2^i. Using subscripts to indicate the radix of a number, we show examples of binary numbers and their decimal equivalents below.

$$10001_2 = 1 \cdot 16 + 0 \cdot 8 + 0 \cdot 4 + 0 \cdot 2 + 1 \cdot 1 = 17_{10}$$
$$101010_2 = 1 \cdot 32 + 0 \cdot 16 + 1 \cdot 8 + 0 \cdot 4 + 1 \cdot 2 + 0 \cdot 1 = 42_{10}$$
$$110.011_2 = 1 \cdot 4 + 1 \cdot 2 + 0 \cdot 1 + 0 \cdot 0.5 + 1 \cdot 0.25 + 1 \cdot 0.125 = 6.375_{10}$$

MSB
LSB

The leftmost bit of a binary number is called the *high-order* or *most significant bit (MSB)*; the rightmost is the *low-order* or *least significant bit (LSB)*.

TABLE 4–1   Binary, decimal, octal, and hexadecimal numbers.

Binary	Decimal	Octal	3-Bit String	Hexadecimal	4-Bit String
0	0	0	000	0	0000
1	1	1	001	1	0001
10	2	2	010	2	0010
11	3	3	011	3	0011
100	4	4	100	4	0100
101	5	5	101	5	0101
110	6	6	110	6	0110
111	7	7	111	7	0111
1000	8	10	—	8	1000
1001	9	11	—	9	1001
1010	10	12	—	A	1010
1011	11	13	—	B	1011
1100	12	14	—	C	1100
1101	13	15	—	D	1101
1110	14	16	—	E	1110
1111	15	17	—	F	1111

4.2   OCTAL AND HEXADECIMAL NUMBERS

octal number system
hexadecimal number system

Other radices besides 2 and 10 are important for computer users. In particular, the radices 8 and 16 provide convenient representations for numbers in a computer. The *octal number system* uses radix 8, while the *hexadecimal number system* uses radix 16. Table 4–1 shows the binary integers from 0 through 1111 and their octal, decimal, and hexadecimal equivalents. The octal system requires 8 digits, and so the digits 0–7 of the decimal system are used. The hexadecimal system requires 16 digits, so the letters A–F are used in addition to digits 0–9.

The octal and hexadecimal number systems are useful for representing binary numbers because their radices are powers of 2. Since a string of three bits can take on eight different combinations, it follows that each 3-bit string is uniquely represented by one octal digit, according to the third and fourth columns of Table 4–1. Likewise, a 4-bit string is represented by one hexadecimal digit according to the fifth and sixth columns of the table.

binary to octal or hexadecimal conversion

Thus, it is very easy to convert a binary number to octal (or hexadecimal). Starting at the binary point and working left, we simply separate the bits into groups of three (or four) and replace each group with the corresponding octal (or hexadecimal) digit. Two examples are shown below.

$$101011000110_2 \ = \ 101\ 011\ 000\ 110_2 \ = \ 5306_8$$
$$= \ 1010\ 1100\ 0110_2 \ = \ AC6_{16}$$

$$11011001110101001_2 \ = \ 011\ 011\ 001\ 110\ 101\ 001_2 \ = \ 331651_8$$
$$= \ 0001\ 1011\ 0011\ 1010\ 1001_2 \ = \ 1B3A9_{16}$$

Notice in the examples that zeroes can be freely added on the left to make the total number of bits a multiple of 3 or 4 as required.

If a binary number contains digits to the right of the binary point, we can convert them by starting at the binary point and working right. As before, zeroes can be freely added as required (this time on the right), as shown in the example below.

$$11.1010011011_2 \ = \ 011\,.\,101\,001\,101\,100_2 \ = \ 3.5154_8$$
$$= \ 0011\,.\,1010\,0110\,1100_2 \ = \ 3.A6C_{16}$$

octal or hexadecimal to binary conversion

Conversion from octal or hexadecimal to binary is easy too. We simply replace each octal or hexadecimal digit with the corresponding 3- or 4-bit string. The examples below also show that we can convert from octal to hexadecimal or vice versa by converting first to binary.

$$1573_8 \ = \ 001\,101\,111\,011_2 \ = \ 0011\,0111\,1011_2 \ = \ 37B_{16}$$

$$A748_{16} \ = \ 1010\,0111\,0100\,1000_2 \ = \ 001\,010\,011\,101\,001\,000_2 \ = \ 123510_8$$

$$3.145_8 \ = \ 011\,.\,001\,100\,101_2 \ = \ 0011\,.\,0011\,0010\,1000_2 \ = \ 3.328_{16}$$

Most computer software uses either octal or hexadecimal numbers to describe binary numbers in the machine; hexadecimal numbers are normally used with the Motorola 68000. A 16-bit word takes on 65,536 values, a range of 0–177777 in octal, or 0–FFFF in hexadecimal.

The choice between octal and hexadecimal representations is almost entirely a documentation convention. Perhaps the only hardware impact of the choice can be seen in ancient computers in museums and science-fiction movies, which had front panels with lights and switches arranged in groups of either three or four!

4.3 GENERAL POSITIONAL NUMBER SYSTEM CONVERSIONS

In general, conversion between two bases cannot be done by simple substitutions; arithmetic operations are required. In this section, we show how to convert a number in any base to base 10 and vice versa, using base-10 arithmetic.

base-b to decimal conversion

In Section 4.1, we indicated that the value of a number in any base is given by the formula

$$D \ = \ \sum_{i=-n}^{p-1} d_i \cdot b^i$$

where b is the base of the number and there are p digits to the left of the radix point and n to the right. Thus, the value of the number can be found by converting each digit of the number to its base-10 equivalent and expanding the formula using base-10 arithmetic. Some examples are given below:

$$1BE8_{16} \;=\; 1 \cdot 16^3 + 11 \cdot 16^2 + 14 \cdot 16^1 + 8 \cdot 16^0 \;=\; 7144_{10}$$

$$F1AC_{16} \;=\; 15 \cdot 16^3 + 1 \cdot 16^2 + 10 \cdot 16^1 + 12 \cdot 16^0 \;=\; 61868_{10}$$

$$437.5_8 \;=\; 4 \cdot 8^2 + 3 \cdot 8^1 + 7 \cdot 8^0 + 5 \cdot 8^{-1} \;=\; 287.625_{10}$$

$$122.1_3 \;=\; 1 \cdot 3^2 + 2 \cdot 3^1 + 2 \cdot 3^0 + 1 \cdot 3^{-1} \;=\; 17.\overline{3}_{10}$$

The overbar in the last example indicates a repeated decimal.

A shortcut for converting whole numbers to base 10 is obtained by rewriting the expansion formula as follows:

$$D \;=\; ((\cdots((d_{p-1}) \cdot b + d_{p-2}) \cdot b + \cdots) \cdot b + d_1) \cdot b + d_0$$

That is, we start with a sum of 0; beginning with the leftmost digit, we multiply the sum by b and add the next digit to the sum, repeating until all digits have been processed. For example, we can write

$$F1AC_{16} \;=\; (((15) \cdot 16 + 1) \cdot 16 + 10) \cdot 16 + 12$$

decimal to base-b conversion Although the formula above is not too exciting in itself, it forms the basis for a very convenient method of converting a decimal number D to a base b. Consider what happens if we divide the formula by b. Since the parenthesized part of the formula is evenly divisible by b, the quotient will be

$$Q \;=\; (\cdots((d_{p-1}) \cdot b + d_{p-2}) \cdot b + \cdots) \cdot b + d_1$$

and the remainder will be d_0. Thus, d_0 can be computed as the remainder of the long division of D by b. Furthermore, the quotient Q has the same form as the original formula. Therefore, successive divisions by b will yield successive digits of D from right to left, until all the digits of D have been derived. Examples are given below.

$$179 \div 2 = 89 \text{ remainder } 1 \quad (\text{LSB})$$
$$\div 2 = 44 \text{ remainder } 1$$
$$\div 2 = 22 \text{ remainder } 0$$
$$\div 2 = 11 \text{ remainder } 0$$
$$\div 2 = 5 \text{ remainder } 1$$
$$\div 2 = 2 \text{ remainder } 1$$
$$\div 2 = 1 \text{ remainder } 0$$
$$\div 2 = 0 \text{ remainder } 1 \quad (\text{MSB})$$

$$179_{10} = 10110011_2$$

$$467 \div 8 = 58 \text{ remainder } 3 \quad \text{(least significant digit)}$$
$$\div 8 = 7 \text{ remainder } 2$$
$$\div 8 = 0 \text{ remainder } 7 \quad \text{(most significant digit)}$$
$$467_{10} = 723_8$$

$$3417 \div 16 = 213 \text{ remainder } 9 \quad \text{(least significant digit)}$$
$$\div 16 = 13 \text{ remainder } 5$$
$$\div 16 = 0 \text{ remainder } 13 \quad \text{(most significant digit)}$$
$$3417_{10} = D59_{16}$$

4.4 ADDITION AND SUBTRACTION OF NONDECIMAL NUMBERS

Addition and subtraction of nondecimal numbers by hand uses the same technique that we learned in grammar school for decimal numbers; the only catch is that the addition and subtraction tables are different. Table 4–2 is the addition *binary addition* and subtraction table for binary digits. To add two binary numbers X and Y, we add together the least significant bits with an initial carry (c_{in}) of 0, producing sum ($x + y + c_{in}$) and carry (c_{out}) bits according to the table. We continue processing bits from right to left, including the carry out of each column in the next column's sum. Some examples of decimal additions and the corresponding binary additions are shown below, with the carries shown as a bit string C.

C		101111000		C		001011000
X	190	10111110		X	173	10101101
Y	+ 141	+ 10001101		Y	+ 44	+ 00101100
$X + Y$	331	101001011		$X + Y$	217	11011001
C		011111110		C		000000000
X	127	01111111		X	170	10101010
Y	+ 63	+ 00111111		Y	+ 85	+ 01010101
$X + Y$	190	10111110		$X + Y$	255	11111111

TABLE 4–2 Binary addition and subtraction table.

c_{in} or b_{in}	x	y	$x + y + c_{in}$	c_{out}	$x - y - b_{in}$	b_{out}
0	0	0	0	0	0	0
0	0	1	1	0	1	1
0	1	0	1	0	1	0
0	1	1	0	1	0	0
1	0	0	1	0	1	1
1	0	1	0	1	0	1
1	1	0	0	1	0	0
1	1	1	1	1	1	1

binary subtraction   Subtraction is performed similarly, using borrows (b_{in} and b_{out}) instead of carries:

B		001111100		B		011011010
X	229	11100101		X	210	11010010
Y	$-\ 46$	$-\ 00101110$		Y	$-\ 109$	$-\ 01101101$
$X-Y$	183	10110111		$X-Y$	101	01100101

B		010101010		B		000000000
X	170	10101010		X	221	11011101
Y	$-\ 85$	$-\ 01010101$		Y	$-\ 76$	$-\ 01001100$
$X-Y$	85	01010101		$X-Y$	145	10010001

comparing numbers   A very common use of subtraction in computers is to compare two numbers. For example, if the operation $X-Y$ produces a borrow out of the most significant bit position, then X is less than Y; otherwise X is greater than or equal to Y. The use of subtraction for comparing numbers will be explored in detail in Sections 8.4 and 8.6.

Addition and subtraction tables can be developed for octal and hexadecimal digits, or any other desired base. However, few computer scientists bother to memorize these tables, for a number of reasons. Subtraction tables are never needed, since subtraction can always be performed using complement number systems and addition as shown in the next section. Even addition is seldom done by hand, especially in high-level language programming. Hard-core assembly language programmers can purchase a hex calculator from Texas Instruments or Casio to facilitate calculations in binary, octal, or hexadecimal.

If the calculator's battery wears out, some mental shortcuts can be used to facilitate nondecimal arithmetic. In general, each column addition (or subtraction) can be done by converting the column digits to decimal, adding in decimal, and converting the result to corresponding sum and carry digits in the nondecimal base. (A carry is produced whenever the column sum equals or exceeds the base.) Since the addition is done in decimal, we rely on our knowledge of the decimal addition table; the only new thing that we need to learn is the conversion from decimal to nondecimal digits and vice versa. The sequence of *hexadecimal* steps for mentally adding two hexadecimal numbers is shown below.

addition

C	$1\ 1\ 0\ 0$	1	1	0	0
X	$1\ 9\ B\ 9_{16}$	1	9	11	9
Y	$+\ C\ 7\ E\ 6_{16}$	$+\ 12$	7	14	6
$X+Y$	$E\ 1\ 9\ F_{16}$	14	17	25	15
		14	$16+1$	$16+9$	15
		E	1	9	F

4.5 REPRESENTATION OF NEGATIVE NUMBERS

So far, we have dealt only with positive numbers, but there are many ways to represent negative numbers. In everyday business, we use the signed-magnitude system, but most computers use a complement number system. All of the important systems are covered in this section.

4.5.1 Signed-Magnitude Representation

signed-magnitude system

The representation of decimal numbers used in everyday business is called the *signed-magnitude system*. In this system, a number consists of a magnitude and a symbol indicating whether the magnitude is positive or negative. Thus we interpret decimal numbers $+98$, -57, $+123.5$, and -13 in the usual manner. In the decimal number system, we make the convention that the sign is interpreted as "+" if no sign symbol is present. There are two possible representations of zero, "+0" and "−0", but both have the same value.

sign bit

The signed-magnitude system can be applied to binary numbers quite easily by using an extra bit position to represent the sign (the *sign bit*). Traditionally, the most significant bit (MSB) is used as the sign bit (0 = plus, 1 = minus), and the lower-order bits contain the magnitude. Thus, we can write several 8-bit signed-magnitude integers and their decimal equivalents:

$$00101011_2 \ = \ +43_{10} \qquad\qquad 10101011_2 \ = \ -43_{10}$$
$$01111111_2 \ = \ +127_{10} \qquad\qquad 11111111_2 \ = \ -127_{10}$$
$$00000000_2 \ = \ +0_{10} \qquad\qquad 10000000_2 \ = \ -0_{10}$$

The signed-magnitude system contains an equal number of positive and negative integers. An n-bit signed-magnitude integer lies within the range $-(2^{n-1} - 1)$ through $+(2^{n-1} - 1)$, with two possible representations of zero.

signed-magnitude addition rules

To add two signed-magnitude numbers, we follow the rules that we learned in grammar school. If the signs are the same, we add the magnitudes and give the result the same sign. If the signs are different, we subtract the smaller magnitude from the larger and give the result the sign of the larger. To subtract signed-magnitude numbers, we change the sign of the subtrahend and proceed as in addition.

4.5.2 Complement Number Systems

complement number systems

Negative numbers in a computer are usually represented by *complement number systems*. While the signed-magnitude system negates a number by changing its sign, a complement number system negates a number by taking its complement as defined by the system. Taking the complement is more difficult than changing the sign, but two numbers in a complement number system can be added or subtracted directly without the sign and magnitude checks required by the signed-magnitude system. We shall describe two complement number systems, called the "radix complement" and the "diminished radix-complement."

In any complement number system, we always deal with a fixed number of digits, say n. We shall further assume that the base or radix is b, and that numbers have the form

$$D = d_{n-1}d_{n-2} \cdots d_1 d_0.$$

so that the radix point is on the right and the number is an integer. If any operation produces a result that requires more than n digits, we throw away the extra high-order digit(s). If a number D is complemented twice, the result is always D.

4.5.3   Radix-Complement Representation

radix-complement system

10's complement

In a *radix-complement system*, the complement of an n-digit number is obtained by subtracting it from b^n. In the decimal number system, the radix complement is called the *10's complement*. Some examples using 4-digit decimal numbers (and subtraction from 10,000) are shown below.

Number	10's complement
1849	8151
2067	7933
100	9900
7	9993
8151	1849

Observe that the 4-digit 10's complement of 100 is 9900, not 900, and the 10's complement of 7 is 9993, not 3. Since complement number systems only work with a fixed number of digits, four in this example, we treat numbers with fewer digits as if they had leading zeroes; we'll say more about this in the next subsection.

In general in the radix-complement system, the complement of an n-digit number D is obtained by subtracting it from b^n. If D is between 1 and $b^n - 1$, this subtraction will result in another number between 1 and $b^n - 1$. If D is 0, the result of the subtraction is b^n, which has the form $100 \cdots 00$, where there are a total of $n + 1$ digits. We throw away the extra high-order digit and get the result 0. Thus there is only one representation of zero in a radix-complement system.

computing the radix complement

From the preceding discussion, it would seem that a subtraction operation is needed to compute the radix complement of a number. However, this subtraction is avoided by rewriting b^n as $(b^n - 1) + 1$ and $b^n - D$ as $((b^n - 1) - D) + 1$. The number $b^n - 1$ has the form $mm \cdots mm$, where $m = b - 1$ and there are n m's. For example, 10,000 equals 9,999 + 1. If we define the complement of a digit d as $b - 1 - d$, then $(b^n - 1) - D$ is obtained by complementing the digits of D.

TABLE 4–3 Digit complements.

Digit	Binary	Octal	Decimal	Hexadecimal
			Complement	
0	1	7	9	F
1	0	6	8	E
2	–	5	7	D
3	–	4	6	C
4	–	3	5	B
5	–	2	4	A
6	–	1	3	9
7	–	0	2	8
8	–	–	1	7
9	–	–	0	6
A	–	–	–	5
B	–	–	–	4
C	–	–	–	3
D	–	–	–	2
E	–	–	–	1
F	–	–	–	0

Therefore, the radix complement of a number D is obtained by complementing the individual digits of D and adding 1. You should mentally confirm that this trick works for the 10's-complement examples above. The digit complements for binary, octal, decimal, and hexadecimal numbers are presented in Table 4–3.

4.5.4 Two's-Complement Representation

two's complement For binary numbers, the radix complement is called the *two's complement*. In this system, a number is positive if the most significant bit is 0 and negative if it is 1. The decimal equivalent of a two's-complement binary number is computed the same as for an unsigned number, except that the weight of the most significant bit is -2^{n-1} instead of $+2^{n-1}$. The range of representable numbers is $-(2^{n-1})$ through $+(2^{n-1} - 1)$. Some examples of 8-bit numbers and their two's complements are shown below.

$$17_{10} = 00010001_2$$
$$\Downarrow \quad \text{(complement bits)}$$
$$11101110$$
$$+1$$
$$\overline{11101111_2} = -17_{10}$$

$$-99_{10} = 10011101_2$$
$$\Downarrow \quad \text{(complement bits)}$$
$$01100010$$
$$+1$$
$$\overline{01100011_2} = 99_{10}$$

$$119_{10} = 01110111_2 \qquad\qquad -127_{10} = 10000001_2$$
$$\Downarrow \text{ (complement bits)} \qquad\qquad \Downarrow \text{ (complement bits)}$$
$$10001000 \qquad\qquad\qquad 01111110$$
$$\underline{+1} \qquad\qquad\qquad\qquad \underline{+1}$$
$$10001001_2 = -119_{10} \qquad\qquad 01111111_2 = 127_{10}$$

$$0_{10} = 00000000_2 \qquad\qquad -128_{10} = 10000000_2$$
$$\Downarrow \text{ (complement bits)} \qquad\qquad \Downarrow \text{ (complement bits)}$$
$$11111111 \qquad\qquad\qquad 01111111$$
$$\underline{+1} \qquad\qquad\qquad\qquad \underline{+1}$$
$$1\,00000000_2 = 0_{10} \qquad\qquad 10000000_2 = -128_{10}$$

extra negative number

In the two's-complement number system, zero is considered positive because its sign bit is 0. Since two's-complement has only one representation of zero, we end up with one extra negative number, -2^{n-1}, that doesn't have a positive counterpart. As shown in the preceding example, an attempt to negate this number gives us back the number itself. However, arithmetic operations can still give correct results when this number appears as an intermediate result, as long as we never attempt to negate it.

We can convert an n-bit two's-complement number X into an m-bit one, but some care is needed. If $m > n$, we must append $m - n$ copies of X's sign bit to the left of X (see Exercise 4.17). That is, we pad a positive number with 0's and a negative one with 1's. If $m < n$, we discard X's $n - m$ leftmost bits; however, the result is valid only if all of the discarded bits are the same as the sign bit of the result (see Exercise 4.18).

signed vs unsigned numbers

Even with these rules, we can have "interpretation" errors, as in the question, "What is the 8-bit two's-complement equivalent of 1010_2?" Simple, you say—extend the sign bit to obtain 11111010_2. However, this answer is wrong if the number was supposed to be interpreted an *unsigned* number, in which case the proper procedure would be to pad it with 0's, obtaining 00001010_2. This sort of error occurs in assembly language programs and even in some high-level languages quite often, so please beware and be aware of the difference between signed and unsigned numbers!

The two's-complement system is used in all minicomputers and microcomputers, and almost all large computers in operation today. However, for completeness, we'll also briefly discuss the diminished radix-complement and ones'-complement systems.

4.5.5 Diminished Radix-Complement Representation

diminished radix-complement system

In a *diminished radix-complement system*, the complement of an n-digit number D is obtained by subtracting it from $b^n - 1$. This can be accomplished by complementing the individual digits of D, *without* adding 1 as in the radix-complement

9s' complement   system. In decimal, this is called the *9s' complement*; some examples are given
below.[1]

Number	9s' complement
1849	8150
2067	7932
100	9899
7	9992
8150	1849

4.5.6   Ones'-Complement Representation

ones' complement   The diminished radix-complement for binary numbers is called the *ones' complement*. As in two's complement, the most significant bit is the sign, 0 if
positive and 1 if negative. Thus there are two representations of zero, positive
zero $(00\cdots00)$ and negative zero $(11\cdots11)$. Positive number representations
are the same for both ones' and two's complements. However, negative number
representations differ by 1. A weight of $-(2^{n-1}-1)$, rather than -2^{n-1}, is given
to the most significant bit when computing the decimal equivalent of a ones'-
complement number. The range of representable numbers is $-(2^{n-1}-1)$ through
$+(2^{n-1}-1)$. Some examples of 8-bit numbers and their ones' complements are
given below.

$$17_{10} = 00010001_2 \qquad\qquad\qquad -99_{10} = 10011101_2$$
$$\Downarrow \qquad\qquad\qquad\qquad\qquad \Downarrow$$
$$11101110_2 = -17_{10} \qquad\qquad\qquad 01100010_2 = 99_{10}$$

$$119_{10} = 01110111_2 \qquad\qquad\qquad -127_{10} = 10000000_2$$
$$\Downarrow \qquad\qquad\qquad\qquad\qquad \Downarrow$$
$$10001000_2 = -119_{10} \qquad\qquad\qquad 01111111_2 = 127_{10}$$

$$0_{10} = 00000000_2 \text{ (positive zero)}$$
$$\Downarrow$$
$$11111111_2 = 0_{10} \text{ (negative zero)}$$

The main advantages of the ones'-complement system are its symmetry and
the ease of complementation. However, addition of ones'-complement numbers
is somewhat more difficult than for two's-complement numbers. Also, number-
testing hardware in a ones'-complement machine must always check for both

punctuation   [1]The apparent inconsistency in punctuation of 10's and 9s' complements can be explained. If
the radix point is considered to be just to the right of the leftmost digit, then the largest number is
$9.99\cdots99$ and the 10's complement of D is obtained by subtracting it from 10 (singular possessive).
Regardless of the position of the radix point, the 9s' complement is obtained by subtracting D from
the largest number, which has all 9s (plural).

representations of zero, or always convert $11\cdots11$ to $00\cdots00$. The ones'-complement system is used in some Control Data Corporation computers, but is seldom considered for new computer designs. It is still a useful system for certain software checksum applications.

4.5.7 Excess Representations

excess-B
representation

bias

excess-2^{m-1}
system

Yes, the number of different systems for representing negative numbers *is* excessive, but there's just one more for us to cover. In *excess-B representation*, an *m*-bit string whose unsigned integer value is M ($0 \le M < 2^m$) represents the signed integer $M - B$, where B is called the *bias* of the number system.

For example, an *excess-2^{m-1} system* represents a number X in the range -2^{m-1} through $+2^{m-1}-1$ by the *m*-bit binary representation of $X + 2^{m-1}$ (which is always nonnegative and less than 2^m). The range of this representation is exactly the same as *m*-bit two's-complement numbers. In fact, the representations of any number in the two systems are identical except for the sign bits, which are always opposite. (Note that this is true only when the bias is 2^{m-1}.)

We'll see the most common use of excess representation when we discuss floating-point number systems in Section 4.11.

4.6 TWO'S-COMPLEMENT ADDITION AND SUBTRACTION

4.6.1 Addition Rules

A table of decimal numbers and their equivalents in different number systems, Table 4–4, reveals why the two's complement is preferred for arithmetic operations. If we start with 1000_2 (-8_{10}) and count up, we see that each successive two's-complement number all the way to 0111_2 ($+7_{10}$) can be obtained by adding 1 to the previous one, ignoring any carries beyond the fourth bit position. The same cannot be said of signed-magnitude and ones'-complement numbers. Because ordinary addition is just an extension of counting, two's-complement numbers can thus be added by ordinary binary addition, ignoring any carries beyond the MSB. The result will always be the correct sum as long as the range of the number system is not exceeded. Some examples of decimal addition and the corresponding 4-bit two's-complement additions confirm this.

two's-complement
addition

$$
\begin{array}{rl}
+3 & 0011 \\
+\ +4 & +\ 0100 \\
\hline
+7 & 0111
\end{array}
\qquad
\begin{array}{rl}
-2 & 1110 \\
+\ -6 & +\ 1010 \\
\hline
-8 & 1\ 1000
\end{array}
$$

$$
\begin{array}{rl}
+6 & 0110 \\
+\ -3 & +\ 1101 \\
\hline
+3 & 1\ 0011
\end{array}
\qquad
\begin{array}{rl}
+4 & 0100 \\
+\ -7 & +\ 1001 \\
\hline
-3 & 1101
\end{array}
$$

TABLE 4–4   Decimal and 4-bit numbers.

Decimal	Two's Complement	Ones' Complement	Signed Magnitude	Excess 2^{m-1}
−8	1000	—	—	0000
−7	1001	1000	1111	0001
−6	1010	1001	1110	0010
−5	1011	1010	1101	0011
−4	1100	1011	1100	0100
−3	1101	1100	1011	0101
−2	1110	1101	1010	0110
−1	1111	1110	1001	0111
0	0000	1111 or 0000	1000 or 0000	1000
1	0001	0001	0001	1001
2	0010	0010	0010	1010
3	0011	0011	0011	1011
4	0100	0100	0100	1100
5	0101	0101	0101	1101
6	0110	0110	0110	1110
7	0111	0111	0111	1111

4.6.2   A Graphical View

Another way to view the two's-complement system uses the 4-bit "counter" shown in Figure 4–1. Here we have shown the numbers in a circular or "modular" representation. Starting with the arrow pointing to any number, we can add $+n$ to that number by moving the arrow n positions clockwise, where n is between 0 and 7. It is also evident that we can subtract n from a number by moving the arrow n positions counterclockwise.

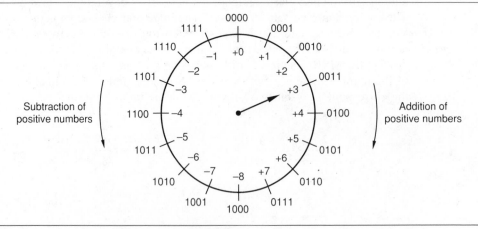

FIGURE 4–1   A modular counting representation of 4-bit two's-complement numbers.

What is most interesting is that we can also subtract n (or add $-n$) by moving the arrow $16 - n$ positions clockwise. Notice that the quantity $16 - n$ is what we defined to be the 4-bit two's complement of n, that is, the two's-complement representation of $-n$. This graphically supports our earlier claim that a negative number in two's-complement representation may be added to another number by simply adding the 4-bit representations using ordinary binary addition. Adding a number in Figure 4–1 is equivalent to moving the arrow a corresponding number of positions clockwise.

4.6.3 Overflow

overflow

If an addition operation produces a result that exceeds the range of the number system, *overflow* is said to occur. Addition of two numbers with different signs can never produce overflow, but addition of two numbers of like sign can, as shown by the following examples.

$$
\begin{array}{rl}
-3 & 1101 \\
+ \quad -6 & + \ 1010 \\
\hline
-9 & 1\,0111 = +7
\end{array}
\qquad\qquad
\begin{array}{rl}
+5 & 0101 \\
+ \quad +6 & + \ 0110 \\
\hline
+11 & 1011 = -5
\end{array}
$$

$$
\begin{array}{rl}
-8 & 1000 \\
+ \quad -8 & + \ 1000 \\
\hline
-16 & 1\,0000 = +0
\end{array}
\qquad\qquad
\begin{array}{rl}
+7 & 0111 \\
+ \quad +7 & + \ 0111 \\
\hline
+14 & 1110 = -2
\end{array}
$$

overflow rules

Fortunately, there is a simple rule for detecting overflow in addition: an addition overflows if the signs of the addends are the same and the sign of the sum is different from the addends' sign. The overflow rule is sometimes stated in terms of carries generated during the addition operation: an addition overflows if the carry bits into and out of the sign position are different. Close examination of Table 4–2 shows that the two rules are equivalent.

An overflow rule may also be stated in terms of Figure 4–1. Starting with the arrow pointing at any number, adding a positive number causes overflow if the arrow is advanced through the $+7$ to -8 transition. Adding a negative number to any number causes overflow if the arrow is advanced through the -1 to $+0$ transition.

Most computers have built-in hardware for detecting overflow.

4.6.4 Subtraction Rules

two's-complement subtraction

Two's-complement numbers may be subtracted as if they were ordinary unsigned binary numbers, and appropriate rules for detecting overflow may be formulated. However, two's-complement subtraction is seldom performed directly. Rather, the subtrahend is negated by taking its two's complement and then the minuend and subtrahend are added, following the normal rules for addition. Negating the subtrahend and adding the minuend can be accomplished with only one addition operation as follows: perform a bit-by-bit complement of the subtrahend and add the complemented subtrahend to the minuend with an initial carry of 1 instead of 0. Examples are given below.

$$
\begin{array}{r}
&&& 1 \text{ --- initial carry} \\
+4 & 0100 & 0100 \\
-\ +3 & -\ 0011 & +\ 1100 \\
\hline
+1 && 1\,0001
\end{array}
$$

$$
\begin{array}{r}
&&& 1 \text{ --- initial carry} \\
+3 & 0011 & 0011 \\
-\ +4 & -\ 0100 & +\ 1011 \\
\hline
-1 && 1111
\end{array}
$$

$$
\begin{array}{r}
&&& 1 \text{ --- initial carry} \\
+3 & 0011 & 0011 \\
-\ -4 & -\ 1100 & +\ 0011 \\
\hline
+7 && 0111
\end{array}
$$

Overflow in subtraction can be detected by examining the signs of the minuend and the *complemented* subtrahend, using the same rule as in addition. Or, using the technique in the examples above, the carries into and out of the sign position can be observed and overflow detected irrespective of the signs of inputs and output, again using the same rule as in addition.

An attempt to negate the "extra" negative number results in overflow according to the rules above, when we add 1 in the complementation process:

$$
\begin{array}{r}
-(-8) = -1000 = & 0111 \\
+ & 0001 \\
\hline
& 1000 = -8
\end{array}
$$

However, this number can still be used in additions and subtractions as long as the final result does not exceed the number range:

$$
\begin{array}{r}
&&&&& 1 \text{ --- initial carry} \\
+4 & 0100 &&& -3 & 1101 & 1101 \\
+\ -8 & +\ 1000 &&& -\ -8 & -\ 1000 & +\ 0111 \\
\hline
-4 & 1100 &&& +5 && 1\,0101
\end{array}
$$

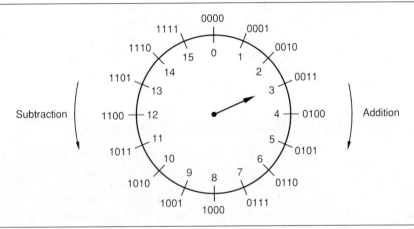

FIGURE 4–2   A modular counting representation of 4-bit unsigned numbers.

4.6.5 Two's-Complement and Unsigned Binary Numbers

Since two's-complement numbers are added and subtracted by the same basic binary addition and subtraction algorithms as unsigned numbers of the same length, a computer needs only one type of addition or subtraction instruction to handle numbers of both types. However, a program must interpret the results of such an addition or subtraction instruction differently depending on whether it thinks it is dealing with signed numbers (e.g., −8 through +7) or unsigned numbers (e.g., 0 through 15).

signed vs
unsigned
numbers

We have already shown a graphical representation of the 4-bit two's-complement system in Figure 4–1. We can relabel this figure as shown in Figure 4–2 to obtain a representation of the 4-bit unsigned numbers. The binary combinations occupy the same positions on the wheel, and a number is still added by moving the arrow a corresponding number of positions clockwise, and subtracted by moving the arrow counterclockwise.

An addition operation exceeds the range of the 4-bit unsigned number system in Figure 4–2 if the arrow moves clockwise through the 15 to 0 transition. In this case a "carry" is said to occur; in a paper-and-pencil addition this carry would be indicated by a carry out of the most significant bit position.

Likewise a subtraction operation exceeds the range of the number system if the arrow moves counterclockwise through the 0 to 15 transition. In this case a "borrow" is said to occur; in a paper-and-pencil subtraction this borrow would be indicated by a borrow in the most significant bit position.

From Figure 4–2 it is also evident that we may subtract an unsigned number n by counting *clockwise* $16 - n$ positions. This is equivalent to *adding* the 4-bit two's-complement of n. The subtraction produces a borrow if the corresponding addition of the two's complement *does not* produce a carry.

In summary, in unsigned addition the carry or borrow in the most significant bit position indicates an out-of-range result. In signed, two's-complement addition the overflow condition defined earlier indicates an out-of-range result. The carry from the most significant bit position is irrelevant in signed addition in the sense that overflow may or may not occur independently of whether or not a carry occurs.

4.7 ONES'-COMPLEMENT ADDITION AND SUBTRACTION

Another look at Table 4–4 helps to explain the rule for adding ones'-complement numbers. If we start at 1000_2 (-7_{10}) and count up, we obtain each successive ones'-complement number by adding 1 to the previous one, *except* at the transition from 1111_2 (negative 0) to 0001_2 $(+1_{10})$. To maintain the proper count, we must add 2 instead of 1 whenever we count past 1111_2. This suggests a technique for adding ones'-complement numbers: perform a standard binary addition, but add an extra 1 whenever we count past 1111_2.

ones'-complement addition

Counting past 1111_2 during an addition can be detected by observing the carry out of the sign position. Thus the rule for adding ones'-complement numbers can be stated quite simply. Perform a standard binary addition; if there is a carry out of the sign position, add 1 to the result. This rule is often called

end-around carry

end-around carry. Examples of ones'-complement addition are given below.

+3	0011		+4	0100		+5	0101
+ +4	+ 0100		+ −7	+ 1000		+ −5	+ 1010
+7	0111		−3	1100		−0	1111

−2	1101		+6	0110		−0	1111
+ −5	+ 1010		+ −3	+ 1100		+ −0	+ 1111
−7	1 0111		+3	1 0010		−0	1 1110
	+ 1			+ 1			+ 1
	1000			0011			1111

Following the two-step addition rule above, the addition of a number and its ones' complement produces negative 0. In fact, an addition operation using this rule can never produce positive 0 unless both addends are positive 0.

Some hardware adder circuits perform ones'-complement addition in one step by connecting carry output from the MSB directly to the LSB carry input. Unless the carry output is forced to 0 before the addition is begun, this can actually cause an ambiguity or even an oscillation when a number and its complement are added, and the result can be either positive or negative 0.[2] Except for this case, end-around carry causes no ambiguity.

[2]For example, see "One's Complement Adder Eliminates Unwanted Zero," by J. Wakerly, *Electronics*, Vol. 49, No. 9, 5 February 1976, pp. 103–105.

ones'-complement subtraction

As with two's-complement, the easiest way to do ones'-complement subtraction is to complement the subtrahend and add. Overflow rules for ones'-complement addition and subtraction are the same as for two's-complement. Ones'-complement operations can be performed on two's-complement machines by using `Add with carry` and `Subtract with carry` instructions.

4.8   BINARY MULTIPLICATION

In this section we describe algorithms for signed and unsigned binary multiplication. Many computers implement these or similar algorithms in machine instructions. However, small computers omit these instructions to save hardware, and so the algorithms must be implemented in software using addition and shifting as primitives.

The algorithms in this and the next section are described in Pascal. However, they can be easily translated into the assembly language of most computers.

4.8.1   Unsigned Multiplication

shift-and-add multiplication

In grammar school we learned to multiply by adding a list of shifted multiplicands computed according to the digits of the multiplier. The same method can be used to obtain the product of two unsigned binary numbers:

```
      11                   1011     multiplicand
   ×  13                ×  1101     multiplier
   ─────                ─────────
      33                   1011    ⎫
      11                   0000    ⎬ shifted multiplicands
   ─────                   1011    ⎭
     143                  1011
                        ─────────
                        10001111    product
```

Forming the shifted multiplicands is trivial in binary multiplication, since the only possible values of the multiplier digits are 0 and 1.

Instead of listing all the shifted multiplicands and then adding, in a computer it is more convenient to add each shifted multiplicand as it is created to a *partial product*. The previous example is repeated in Table 4–5 using this technique.

partial product

When we multiply an n-bit word and an m-bit word in a computer, the resulting product will take at most $n + m$ bits to express. Therefore, a typical multiplication algorithm multiplies two n-bit words and produces a $2n$-bit double-word product. Table 4–6 shows an algorithm that multiplies two positive integers `mpy` and `mcnd`, and produces a positive integer product stored in `hiProd` and `loProd`.

`bit`
`word`

Table 4–6 uses Pascal to describe operations on binary words by introducing types `bit` and `word`. The resulting Pascal operations are straightforward.

TABLE 4–5   Multiplication with partial products.

1011	multiplicand
× 1101	multiplier
00000000	partial product
1011	shifted multiplicand
00001011	partial product
0000	shifted multiplicand
00001011	partial product
1011	shifted multiplicand
00110111	partial product
1011	shifted multiplicand
10001111	product

Bshr

Bshl
Badd

Variables of type `bit` can have the values 0 and 1. A `word` is defined as an array of `bit`s, numbered right to left from 0 to `highbit`.

We define a Pascal function `Bshr(X,Cin,Cout)` which shifts a word X one position to the right as shown in Figure 4–3(a). The vacated MSB is filled with the `bit` value `Cin`; the value of the lost LSB is placed in the VAR parameter `Cout`.[3] Similarly, the `Bshl` function performs a left shift as shown in Figure 4–3(b). Finally, we have the addition function `Badd(X,Y,Cin,Cout)` in Figure 4–3(c), which adds two words X and Y with an initial carry of `Cin`, using unsigned binary addition as in Section 4.4; `Cout` is set to 1 if the operation produces a carry from the MSB, to 0 otherwise.

[3]Since `Cin` is a value parameter, and `Cout` is a VAR parameter, function calls such as `Bshr(hiProd,C,C)` behave properly: the old value of C, before the function call, is shifted in, and the new value of C, after the function call, is what was shifted out.

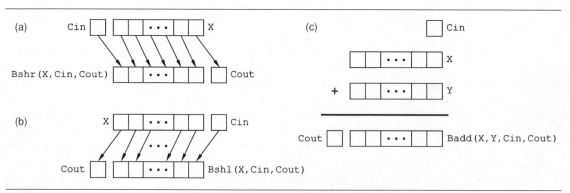

FIGURE 4–3   Pascal bit-manipulation functions: (a) `Bshr(X: word; Cin: bit; VAR Cout: bit)`; (b) `Bshl(X: word; Cin: bit; VAR Cout: bit)`; (c) `Badd(X,Y: word; Cin: bit; VAR Cout: bit)`.

TABLE 4–6   Program to multiply two 16-bit unsigned integers.

```
PROGRAM UnsignedMultiply (input,output);
CONST
  highbit = 15;
TYPE
  bit = 0..1;
  word = ARRAY [0..highbit] OF bit;
VAR
  cnt : integer;
  mpy, mcnd, hiProd, loProd : word;
  C : bit;

{ See figure for description of the next three functions; the
  bodies of all functions and procedures are left as an exercise. }
FUNCTION Bshr(X : word; Cin : bit; VAR Cout : bit) : word;
  BEGIN ... END; {Shift word right with carry in and out}
FUNCTION Bshl(X : word; Cin : bit; VAR Cout : bit) : word;
  BEGIN ... END; {Shift word left with carry in and out}
FUNCTION Badd(X, Y : word; Cin : bit; VAR Cout : bit) : word;
  BEGIN ... END; {Add two words with carry in and out}
PROCEDURE ClearWord(VAR X : word);
  BEGIN ... END; {Set all the bits of X to 0.}
PROCEDURE ReadWord(VAR X : word);
  BEGIN ... END; {Read in a word.}
PROCEDURE WriteWord(X : word);
  BEGIN ... END; {Write out a word.}


BEGIN   {UnsignedMultiply program body}
  ClearWord(loProd);  ClearWord(hiProd);   {Initialization}
  ReadWord(mpy);   ReadWord(mcnd);   {Get operands.}
  FOR cnt := 0 TO highbit DO
    BEGIN   {Process the multiplier one bit at a time.}
      {If multiplier LSB is 1, add multiplicand to high-order
          product, setting C according to carry from MSB.}
      IF mpy[0] = 1 THEN hiProd := Badd(hiProd,mcnd,0,C) ELSE C := 0;
      {Shift hiProd right, put C into MSB, and put lost LSB into C.}
      hiProd := Bshr(hiProd,C,C);
      {Shift loProd right, picking up the LSB that was lost from hiProd.}
      loProd := Bshr(loProd,C,C);
      {Now move the next bit of multiplier to the LSB position.}
      mpy := Bshr(mpy,0,C);
    END;
  WriteWord(hiProd);  WriteWord(loProd);
END.
```

Figure 4–4 illustrates the operation of the multiplication program. Like the example in Table 4–5, it processes the low-order bits of the multiplier first. However, instead of shifting the multiplicand left, it "positions" the multiplicand under the high-order word of the partial product, and shifts the partial product right.

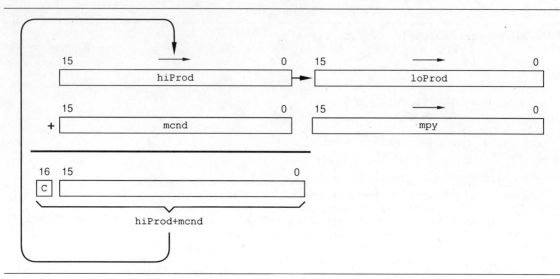

FIGURE 4–4   Variables used by multiplication algorithm.

The number of iterations of the loop in Table 4–6 equals the number of bits in the multiplier. In each iteration, if the LSB of mpy is 1, then mcnd is added to hiProd. This addition may result in a carry that sets C; if the addition is not performed, C is cleared. In this way, the resulting high-order partial product (hiProd and C) may be shifted right one position, and the LSB is shifted into loProd. After being shifted into loProd, a product bit never changes.

At the beginning of the multiplication, loProd has no information in it, while mpy is full of multiplier bits to be processed. At the end, loProd is filled with the low-order product bits, while mpy has been emptied. Close examination of the program leads us to conclude that both mpy and loProd may be combined into one variable. In fact, this trick is used in most hardware multipliers to save circuitry.

4.8.2   Signed Multiplication

Multiplication of signed numbers can be accomplished using unsigned multiplication and the usual grammar school rules: perform an unsigned multiplication of the magnitudes and make the product positive if the operands had the same sign, negative if they had different signs. This is very convenient in signed-magnitude systems.

two's-complement multiplication   In the two's-complement system, a complement operation is required to get the magnitude of a negative number, and the unsigned product must be complemented if a negative result is required. This overhead leads us to seek a more efficient way of performing two's-complement multiplication.

Conceptually, unsigned multiplication is accomplished by a sequence of unsigned additions of the shifted multiplicands; at each step, the shift of the multiplicand corresponds to the weight of the multiplier bit. The bits in a two's-complement multiplier have the same weights as an unsigned multiplier, except for the MSB, which has a negative weight. It follows that we can perform two's-complement multiplication by a sequence of two's-complement additions of shifted multiplicands, except for the last step, which is a subtraction. This leads us to the two's-complement multiplication algorithm shown in Table 4–7.

BaddV

Bcom

In order to do a signed operation, we must introduce another addition function, `BaddV(X,Y,Cin,OV)`, which is unconcerned with the carry out of the MSB of an addition, but which instead detects two's-complement overflow and sets `OV` accordingly. We also introduce the function `Bcom(X)`, which returns the bit-by-bit complement of a word `X`. Using these functions, the statement `BaddV(hiProd,Bcom(mcnd),1,V)` performs a two's-complement subtraction `hiProd-mcnd` in the last part of the program.

multiplication overflow

Note that although overflow may occur during the individual addition and subtraction steps that make up the multiplication algorithm, the multiplication itself never overflows, because the product of two n-bit two's-complement numbers is guaranteed to fit in $2n$ bits.

You are encouraged to explore the subtleties of the algorithm in Table 4–7 by working several examples with 4-bit two's-complement numbers. Like the unsigned algorithm, the signed algorithm can be modified to use the same variable for `mpy` and `loProd`.

4.9 BINARY DIVISION

4.9.1 Unsigned Division

The simplest binary division algorithm is also based on the technique that we learned in grammar school, as shown in Table 4–8. In both the decimal and binary cases, we mentally compare the reduced dividend with multiples of the divisor to determine which multiple of the shifted divisor to subtract. In the decimal case, we first pick 11 as the smallest multiple of 11 less than 21, and then pick 99 as the smallest multiple less than 107. In the binary case, the choice is somewhat simpler, since the only two choices are zero and the divisor itself. Still, a comparison operation *is* needed to pick the proper shifted divisor.

division overflow

Unsigned division in a computer processor is complementary to multiplication. A typical division algorithm accepts a double-word dividend and a single-word divisor, and produces single-word quotient and remainder. Such a division *overflows* if the divisor is zero or the quotient would take more than one word to express. The second situation occurs only if the divisor is less than or equal to the high-order word of the dividend.

Table 4–9 presents a division algorithm that can be easily converted into an assembly language program for most microprocessors. It divides a double-word unsigned integer `hiDvnd,loDvnd` by a single-word divisor `dvsr`, and

TABLE 4–7 Program to multiply two 16-bit two's-complement integers.

```
PROGRAM SignedMultiply (input,output);

CONST
  highbit = 15;
TYPE
  bit = 0..1;
  word = ARRAY [0..highbit] OF bit;
VAR
  cnt : integer;
  mpy, mcnd, hiProd, loProd : word;
  C, V, sign : bit;

{ Procedure and function declarations are same as in UnsignedMultiply,
  plus the following.}

FUNCTION BaddV(X,Y : word; Cin : bit; VAR OV : bit) : word;
  BEGIN ... END; {Like Badd, but no Cout.  Instead, sets OV on
          two's-complement overflow.}
FUNCTION Bcom(X : word) : word;
  BEGIN ... END; {Complements the bits of X.}

BEGIN  {UnsignedMultiply program body}
  ClearWord(loProd);  ClearWord(hiProd);  {Initialization}
  ReadWord(mpy);  ReadWord(mcnd);  {Get operands.}
  FOR cnt := 0 TO highbit - 1 DO
    BEGIN {Process all mpy bits except MSB.}
      {If multiplier LSB is 1, add multiplicand to high-order
          product, set V to 1 on two's-complement overflow.}
      IF mpy[0] = 1 THEN hiProd := BaddV(hiProd,mcnd,0,C,V) ELSE V := 0;
      {Figure out the correct sign of the sum.}
      sign := hiProd[highbit];
      IF V = 1 THEN sign := 1 - sign; {Complement sign if V = 1.}
      {Shift hiProd right, replicate the correct sign of
          the result, and put the lost LSB into C.}
      hiProd := Bshr(hiProd,sign,C));
      {Shift loProd right, picking up the LSB that was lost from hiProd.}
      loProd := Bshr(loProd,C,C);
      {Move the next bit of mpy to the LSB position.}
      mpy := Bshr(mpy,0,C);
    END;
  {Process the sign bit of mpy.}
  {If mpy's LSB is 1, subtract multiplicand from high-order
      product, setting V to 1 on two's-complement overflow.}
  IF mpy[0] = 1 THEN hiProd := BaddV(hiProd,Bcom(mcnd),1,V) ELSE V := 0;
  {Shift hiProd right, give it the correct sign, and put LSB into BC.}
  sign := hiProd[highbit];  IF V = 1 THEN sign := 1 - sign;
  hiProd := Bshr(hiProd,sign,C);
  {Shift loProd right, picking up the LSB that was lost from hiProd.}
  loProd := Bshr(loProd,C,C);
  WriteWord(hiProd);  WriteWord(loProd);
END.
```

TABLE 4–8   Example of long division.

19	10011	quotient
11)217	1011)11011001	dividend
11	1011	shifted divisor
107	0101	reduced dividend
99	0000	shifted divisor
8	1010	reduced dividend
	0000	shifted divisor
	10100	reduced dividend
	1011	shifted divisor
	10011	reduced dividend
	1011	shifted divisor
	1000	remainder

produces single-word quotient `quot` and remainder `rmdr`. The relationships of these variables are shown in Figure 4–5.

Beq
Bls

The algorithm begins by checking for the two overflow conditions, using two more new bit-manipulation functions `Beq` and `Bls`. `Beq(X,Y)` returns `true` if its two bit-array arguments are equal, `false` otherwise; `Bls(X,Y)` returns `true` if `X` is lower than or the same as `Y` when both are interpreted as unsigned numbers.

If there is no overflow, the quotient is initialized to zero and the division loop is executed once for each quotient bit (i.e., 16 times for a 16-bit quotient). Each time that the loop is entered, it is known that `hiDvnd` is strictly less than

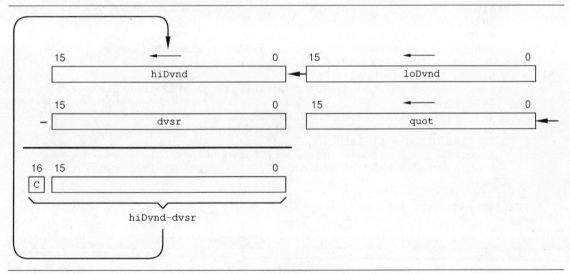

FIGURE 4–5   Variables used by unsigned division algorithm.

TABLE 4–9   Program to divide two unsigned integers.

```
PROGRAM UnsignedDivide (input,output);

CONST
  highbit = 15;
TYPE
  bit = 0..1;
  word = ARRAY [0..highbit] OF bit;
VAR
  cnt : integer;
  hiDvnd, loDvnd, dvsr, quot, rmdr : word;
  C, V, sign : bit;
  flag: boolean;

{ Procedure and function declarations are same as in the multiply programs,
  plus the following.}

FUNCTION BeqZ(X : word) : boolean;
  BEGIN ... END; {Returns true if and only if all the bits of X are 0.}

FUNCTION Bls(X,Y : word) : boolean;
  BEGIN ... END; {Returns true if and only X < Y (unsigned interpretation).}

BEGIN
  ReadWord(hiDvnd);  ReadWord(loDvnd);  ReadWord(dvsr);  {Get operands.}
  IF BeqZ(dvsr) THEN writeln('Error, division by 0 not allowed')
  ELSE IF Bls(dvsr,hiDvnd) THEN writeln('Error, quotient too big')
  ELSE
    BEGIN
      ClearWord(quot);
      FOR cnt := 0 TO highbit DO
        BEGIN
          {Make room for next quotient bit.}
          quot := Bshl(quot,0,C);
          {Shift double-word dividend left one bit, old MSB ends up in C.}
          loDvnd := Bshl(loDvnd,0,C);
          hiDvnd := Bshl(hiDvnd,C,C);
          {Set flag if shifted dividend definitely greater than divisor.}
          flag := C = 1;
          {Do trial subtraction, set C if the result is positive.}
          hiDvnd := Badd(hiDvnd,Bcom(dvsr),1,C);
          IF flag OR (C = 1) THEN
             quot[0] := 1  {Positive result, set quotient bit.}
          ELSE hiDvnd := Badd(hiDvnd,dvsr,0,C); {Negative, restore hiDvnd.}
        END;
      rmdr := hiDvnd;
      WriteWord(quot); WriteWord(rmdr);
    END;
END.
```

dvsr. Therefore, shifting the double-word dividend left one bit makes the 17-bit word consisting of C and hiDvnd still less than $2 \cdot$ dvsr. If this quantity is greater than or equal to dvsr, then a 1 is placed in the quotient and dvsr is subtracted, once again leaving hiDvnd less than dvsr. The shifting function Bshl was shown in Figure 4–3(b).

The comparison of C, hiDvnd and dvsr is somewhat involved. First, flag is set true if C=1; if flag is true, then C, hiDvnd is a full 17-bit number and therefore definitely greater than dvsr, a 16-bit number. Next, a "trial subtraction" is made by the statement Badd(hiDvnd, Bcom(dvsr), 1), which subtracts dvsr from hiDvnd. Since a borrow is the complement of a carry, this operation sets C to 1 if there was no borrow out of the MSB, to 0 otherwise. If flag is true or no borrow was produced, then C, hiDvnd was greater than dvsr and a 1 bit is placed in the quotient. Otherwise, the value of hiDvnd before the operation is restored by adding dvsr to it.

At each iteration, quot is shifted left one bit to make room for the next quotient bit. At the end of 16 iterations, the quantity left in hiDvnd is the remainder.

As in the multiplication algorithms, we have one variable being filled with result bits while another is being emptied. Thus, quot and loDvnd may share the same variable. Again, this trick is often implemented in hardware. Also, like the multiplication algorithms, the division algorithm is best understood by working several examples and special cases with 4-bit numbers.

restoring division
nonrestoring division

This division algorithm is usually called *restoring division*. There is also a *nonrestoring division* algorithm that avoids the restoring addition step in the divide loop; most hardware dividers use it for its speed. However, in assembly language programs, nonrestoring division gives at best only marginally faster performance than restoring division, and so we don't cover it here.

4.9.2   Signed Division

As in multiplication, there are special techniques for performing division directly on two's-complement numbers; these techniques are often implemented in hardware dividers. However, in assembly language programs, the easiest way to divide two's-complement numbers is to convert them to positive numbers, perform restoring division, and convert the results back to the appropriate sign.

two's-complement division

The restoring division algorithm is somewhat simplified in this case because negative numbers produced by trial subtractions are now representable within the word length of the operands. Adapting the previous program, the divisor, remainder, and quotient are now 15 bits plus sign, and the dividend is 31 bits plus sign. The new program is shown in Table 4–10. The signs of the divisor and dividend are tested at the outset, and both operands are made positive for the division algorithm. The results are converted to the proper signs at the end. The conversions are done so that the remainder has the same sign as the dividend, so that the remainder plus the divisor times quotient equals the original dividend.

TABLE 4–10   Program to divide two's-complement integers.

```
PROGRAM SignedDivide (input,output);

CONST
  highbit = 15;
TYPE
  bit = 0..1;
  word = ARRAY [0..highbit] OF bit;
VAR
  cnt : integer;
  hiDvnd, loDvnd, dvsr, quot, rmdr, zero : word;
  C, V, sign : bit;
  negDvsr, negDvnd: boolean;

{ Procedure and function declarations are same as in UnsignedDivide.}

BEGIN
  ClearWord(zero);   {Initialization}
  ReadWord(hiDvnd);  ReadWord(loDvnd);  ReadWord(dvsr);   {Get operands.}
  negDvsr := dvsr[highbit] = 1;  negDvnd := hiDvnd[highbit] = 1;
  IF negDvsr THEN dvsr := Badd(Bcom(dvsr),zero,1,C); {Make dvsr positive.}
  IF negDvnd THEN   {Make dvnd positive.}
    BEGIN   {A 'double precision' negate.}
      loDvnd := Badd(Bcom(loDvnd),zero,1,C);
      hiDvnd := Badd(Bcom(hiDvnd),zero,C,C);
    END;
  IF BeqZ(dvsr) THEN writeln('Error, divide by 0 not allowed')
  ELSE IF Bls(dvsr,hiDvnd) THEN writeln('Error, quotient too big')
  ELSE
    BEGIN {Compute quotient and remainder.}
      quot := zero;
      FOR cnt := 0 TO highbit - 1 DO
        BEGIN
          quot := Bshl(quot,0); {Make room for next quotient bit.}
          loDvnd := Bshl(loDvnd,0); {Shift double-word dvnd left one bit.}
          hiDvnd := Bshl(hiDvnd,BC);
          hiDvnd := Badd(hiDvnd,Bcom(dvsr),1); {Do trial subtraction.}
          IF hiDvnd[highbit]=0 THEN
            quot[0] := 1 {Positive result, set quotient bit.}
          ELSE
            hiDvnd := hiDvnd + dvsr; {Negative - restore hiDvnd.}
        END;
      IF negDvnd THEN rmdr := Badd(0,Bcom(hiDvnd),1)
      ELSE rmdr := hiDvnd;   {Remainder gets sign of dividend.}
      IF (negDvsr AND (NOT negDvnd)) OR
         ((NOT negDvsr) AND negDvnd) THEN
           quot := Badd(Bcom(quot),zero,1,C);
      WriteWord(quot);  WriteWord(rmdr);
    END;
END.
```

4.10   BINARY-CODED DECIMAL REPRESENTATION

binary-coded decimal (BCD)

The *binary-coded decimal (BCD)* number system encodes the digits 0 through 9 by their 4-bit unsigned binary representations, 0000 through 1001. The codes 1010 through 1111 are not used. Conversions between BCD and decimal representations are trivial, a direct substitution of four bits for each decimal digit.

packed-BCD representation

Two BCD digits are placed in one byte in *packed-BCD representation*; thus one byte may represent the values from 0 to 99 as opposed to 0 to 255 for a normal unsigned 8-bit binary number. BCD numbers with any desired number of digits may be obtained by using one byte for each two digits.

As with binary numbers, there are many possible representations of negative BCD numbers. Signed BCD numbers have one extra digit position for the sign. Both the signed-magnitude and 10's-complement representations are popular. In signed-magnitude BCD, the encoding of the sign bit string is arbitrary; in 10's-complement, 0000 indicates plus and 1001 indicates minus.

BCD addition

Addition of BCD digits is similar to adding 4-bit unsigned binary numbers, except that a correction must be made if a result exceeds 1001. The result is corrected by adding 6; examples are shown below:

```
     5       0101                        4       0100
  +  9    +  1001                     +  5    +  0101
    14       1110                        9       1001
          +  0110 — correction

  10+4     1 0100


     5       0101                        9       1001
  + 11    +  1011                     +  9    +  1001
    16       1 0000                      18      1 0010
          +  0110 — correction                +  0110 — correction

  10+6     1 0110                     10+8     1 1000
```

Notice that the addition of two BCD digits produces a carry into the next digit position if either the initial binary addition or the correction factor addition produces a carry.

Although the BCD encoding's utilization of memory is less efficient than binary, BCD is still a useful encoding in applications with much I/O of decimal data, such as electronic cash registers, since it avoids conversions to and from binary at each I/O operation. Many computers have a full set of instructions for processing BCD data, including addition, subtraction, and conversions to and from binary. Other computers at least have a `Decimal adjust` instruction that allows the binary operations to be adapted to decimal data. Examples of signed and unsigned BCD operations using typical microprocessor instructions will be given in Section 8.11.

4.11 FIXED-POINT AND FLOATING-POINT REPRESENTATIONS

4.11.1 Fixed-Point Representation

All of the number systems that we've discussed so far fix the binary point to the right of the rightmost bit. Thus, a 16-bit unsigned number lies in the range 0 through +65,535:

$$0000000000000000._2 \ = \ 0_{10}$$
$$1100000000000000._2 \ = \ 49152_{10}$$
$$0010000000000000._2 \ = \ 8192_{10}$$
$$1000000000000000._2 \ = \ 32768_{10}$$
$$1111111111111111._2 \ = \ 65535_{10}$$
$$0000000000000001._2 \ = \ 1_{10}$$

This type of number system is most appropriate for programs that count objects or otherwise deal with integer quantities.

On the other hand, many programs must deal with fractional quantities. For example, in a scientific program that computes a table of positive sines, it might be convenient to fix the binary point to the right of the *leftmost* bit of a 16-bit number, as shown below:

$$0.000000000000000_2 \ = \ 0_{10}$$
$$1.100000000000000_2 \ = \ 1.5_{10}$$
$$0.010000000000000_2 \ = \ 0.25_{10}$$
$$1.000000000000000_2 \ = \ 1.0_{10}$$
$$1.111111111111111_2 \ = \ 1.999\,969\,482\,421\,875_{10}$$
$$0.000000000000001_2 \ = \ 0.000\,030\,517\,578\,125_{10}$$

The weights of the bits to the right of the binary point are negative powers of 2, as previously explained in Section 4.1. This example provides as many bits as possible to the right of the binary point for accurate representation of sine values less than 1, while still allowing the largest sine value (1.0) to be represented.

The numbers in the two examples above are related—if X is a number in the first example and Y is the corresponding number in the second example, then $Y = X \cdot 2^{-15}$, where 2^{-15} is called an *implicit scale factor*. In principle, a number system could use an arbitrary scale factor—2^{+15}, 2^{-25}, 3.14159, 10^9, and $186000 \cdot 60 \cdot 60 \cdot 24 \cdot 365$ might each be reasonable for some application. However, powers of 2 are preferred because multiplication or division by the scale factor is then accomplished by simply shifting the binary point.

*implicit scale
factor*

Addition and subtraction of numbers with implicit scale factors can be performed directly with normal binary addition and subtraction rules:

$$
\begin{array}{r}
x \\
+ \quad y \\
\hline
x + y
\end{array}
\qquad
\begin{array}{r}
X \cdot 2^{-15} \\
+ \quad Y \cdot 2^{-15} \\
\hline
(X + Y) \cdot 2^{-15}
\end{array}
$$

However, some adjustment for scale factors is needed when numbers are multiplied or divided:

$$
\begin{array}{r}
x \\
\times \quad y \\
\hline
x \cdot y
\end{array}
\qquad
\begin{array}{r}
X \cdot 2^{-15} \\
\times \quad Y \cdot 2^{-15} \\
\hline
(X \cdot Y \cdot 2^{-15}) \cdot 2^{-15}
\end{array}
$$

fixed-point representation

Number systems that fix the position of the binary point and require the programmer to keep track of implicit scale factors are called *fixed-point representations*. Because of the extra bookkeeping associated with implicit scale factors other than 1 (2^0), virtually all computer hardware and software for fixed-point numbers use an implicit scale factor of 1, so that the binary point is on the right as we have been assuming all along.

Regardless of the value of the scale factor, the "dynamic range" of a fixed-point number system is fairly limited. For example, the ratio between the largest and smallest nonzero numbers in a 16-bit fixed-point number system is about 2^{16}, even if the largest number is 2^{100}.

4.11.2 Basic Floating-Point Representation

floating-point representation

To avoid error-prone bookkeeping and to represent a large dynamic range of numbers with relatively few bits, a *floating-point representation* can be used to explicitly encode a scale factor in each number. For example, we could break up a 16-bit word into two fields as shown in Figure 4–6. The value of a number X in this format is $M \cdot 2^E$, where both M and E are encoded as unsigned binary numbers. The value M is called the *mantissa* of the number, and the explicit scale factor is 2^E, where E is called the *exponent* of the number. This is simply the binary equivalent of decimal scientific notation, which specifies numbers such as $34 \cdot 10^{29}$ and $186 \cdot 10^3$.

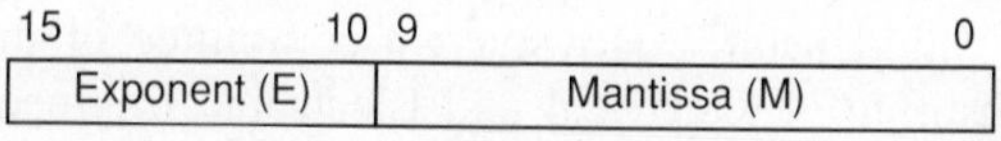

mantissa

exponent

15	10 9	0
Exponent (E)		Mantissa (M)

FIGURE 4–6   A 16-bit floating-point representation.

Some binary numbers and their decimal equivalents in the above floating-point system are shown below:

$$
\begin{array}{llllll}
E & M & & & & \\
000000 & 0000000000_2 & = & 0 \cdot 2^0 & = & 0_{10} \\
000000 & 1000000101_2 & = & 517 \cdot 2^0 & = & 517_{10} \\
001000 & 0100101101_2 & = & 301 \cdot 2^8 & = & 77\,056_{10} \\
111111 & 1111111111_2 & = & 1023 \cdot 2^{63} & = & 9\,435\,509\,593\,702\,435\,651\,584_{10}
\end{array}
$$

sex

precision

With only 16 bits, we can now represent very large numbers, the largest being over nine *sex*tillion. However, we haven't gotten something for nothing. By stealing six bits for the exponent field, we have reduced the resolution or *precision* of the number system to only 10 bits instead of 16. Given any real number between 0 and nine sextillion, we are very unlikely to be able to represent it exactly, and we'll typically encounter an error of 1 part in 2^{11} by picking the representable integer nearest to it. Compare this with the 16-bit integer fixed-point system—given any real number between 0 and $2^{16} - 1$, we can pick an integer within 0.5 of it, an error of 1 part in 2^{17} for the largest number.

Also note that the 16-bit floating-point system uses 16-bit strings inefficiently, since it can represent fewer than 2^{16} distinct numbers. For example, there are 64 different representations of zero (any exponent will do), and other numbers may have up to nine different representations (e.g., $1536_{10} = 3 \cdot 2^9 = 6 \cdot 2^8 = \ldots = 768 \cdot 2^1$).

Still, a floating-point system is very useful if we embellish it as described in the next subsection:

- To obtain adequate precision, we increase the number of mantissa bits.

- To represent both positive and negative numbers, we allocate one bit for the sign of the mantissa.

- To increase the dynamic range, we increase the number of exponent bits.

- To represent fractions, we allow both positive and negative exponents.

- To use bits more efficiently, we eliminate redundant representations of the same number.

4.11.3 IEEE Standard Floating-Point Representation

A variety of floating-point formats are used in different computers because of the many different choices for mantissa length, positioning of the radix point in the mantissa, exponent length and radix, encoding of negative numbers, and use of a "hidden bit." However, a committee of the Computer Society of the IEEE (Institute of Electrical and Electronic Engineers) worked for eight years, starting in 1977, to produce a standard floating-point format that was adopted by the IEEE in 1985 and that is now widely used in microprocessor systems.

FIGURE 4–7   IEEE standard 32-bit floating-point representation.

The IEEE standard defines single- and double-precision formats, as well as extended formats and exceptions to achieve the best possible floating-point results. We'll describe the basic elements of the 32-bit single-precision format in this subsection.

Figure 4–7 shows the layout of bits in the IEEE standard 32-bit format. Here the mantissa M is a 24-bit unsigned number with the binary point just to the right of bit position HB; there are 23 bits to the right of the binary point. (The "hidden bit" HB will be explained shortly.) Thus the smallest mantissa is $0.00\ldots00 = 0$, and the largest mantissa is $1.11\ldots11$, a number just 2^{-23} less than 2. The MS bit gives the sign of the mantissa, 0 for positive and 1 for negative.

The exponent E is an 8-bit excess-127 number (Section 4.5.7) in which the bit strings 00000000 and 11111111 are reserved for special cases. Thus the bit strings 00000001 (1) through 11111110 (254) represent the exponents -126_{10} through $+127_{10}$ respectively. The choice of excess-127 representation is appropriate for the ordering of numbers, as we'll see shortly.

There appear to be many different representations for some numbers in IEEE format, for example,

$$
\begin{array}{ccc}
MS & E & M \\
+1 = 0 & 01111111 & 10000000000000000000000 \\
 & (0) & (1.0) \\
= 0 & 10000000 & 01000000000000000000000 \\
 & (+1) & (0.5) \\
= 0 & 10000001 & 00100000000000000000000 \\
 & (+2) & (0.25)
\end{array}
$$

normalized representation

However, the IEEE format follows a convention that yields a unique, preferred, *normalized representation* for each number. A nonzero floating-point number is normalized if the leftmost bit of the mantissa is nonzero. Thus, the first representation of +1 above is the preferred one. The normalized representation of zero is all 0's.

By convention, all numbers in the IEEE format with a nonreserved exponent value (anything but 00000000 or 11111111) are normalized numbers. Therefore, the leading mantissa bit of a nonzero number is always 1. Instead of explicitly storing this bit (labeled HB in Figure 4–7), machines that follow the IEEE standard discard it when storing a floating-point number into a register or memory location. All operations on nonzero floating-point numbers assume that *hidden bit*

this *hidden bit* is 1. Thus, all 33 bits in the format of Figure 4–7 are packed into 32 bits of memory, and redundant 32-bit representations are eliminated.

zero

With normalized numbers, the smallest mantissa is 1.0 instead of 0, while the largest mantissa is still $2 - 2^{-23}$. In order to represent *zero*, the IEEE standard specifies that the hidden bit is 0 and the exponent is 2^{-126} if the exponent field is 00000000.

Some decimal numbers and normalized equivalents are shown below.

```
           MS    E      HB              M
 +3.000  =  0  10000000  1  10000000000000000000000
              (+1)             (1.5)

-17.375  =  1  10000011  1  00010110000000000000000
              (+4)             (1.0859375)

 +0.125  =  0  01111100  1  00000000000000000000000
              (-3)             (1.0)

 +0.000  =  0  00000000  0  00000000000000000000000
              (-126)           (0.0)
```

If two positive numbers X and Y are normalized, then we can guarantee that X is greater than Y if the exponent of X is numerically greater than the exponent of Y (see Exercise 4.35). Only if the exponents are equal does the relationship between X and Y depend on the values of the mantissas. Thus, the positioning of the MS, E, and M fields in Figure 4–7 makes it possible to compare 32-bit normalized floating-point numbers as if they were 32-bit signed-magnitude numbers; no unusual operations are needed.

Many other floating-point formats were developed before the IEEE standard came along. Among machines that predate it, the PDP-11 and VAX families use a format that is closest to the standard. In those machines, the binary point lies to the *left* of the hidden bit—mantissas are between 0.5 and 1—and the exponent uses excess-128 notation.

Many IBM computers use a 32-bit floating-point format with a major difference from the formats that we've seen so far: the exponent specifies a power of 16 instead of 2! The format contains a 7-bit exponent in excess-64 representation, a mantissa sign bit, and a 24-bit mantissa magnitude with radix point on the left (no hidden bit). The mantissa can be viewed as six 4-bit hexadecimal digits; the leading hexadecimal digit must be nonzero in a normalized number.

4.11.4 Floating-Point Operations

Now that we've studied some formats, it would be nice to be able to do some useful computation on floating-point numbers. A minimum set of floating-point operations includes addition, subtraction, multiplication, division, and comparison of floating-point numbers, and conversion to and from integer fixed-point format.

The exact rules for any of the above operations of course depend on the floating-point format, but there are some basic steps that are used universally. First, we note that a left shift of the binary point in the mantissa corresponds to a division by 2, and therefore can be compensated by increasing the exponent by 1. Likewise, a right shift of the binary point is compensated by decreasing the exponent by 1. Thus,

$$1101.001 \cdot 2^0 \ = \ .1101001 \cdot 2^4 \ = \ 1101001. \cdot 2^{-3}$$

fixed-to-floating conversion

A number can be converted from a fixed-point to a floating-point format as follows:

(1) Convert the number to the system used to represent the mantissa (e.g., signed magnitude).

(2) Starting with an exponent of 0, shift the mantissa's binary point to the left or right, adjusting the exponent accordingly, until the mantissa is normalized.

(3) Convert the resulting exponent into the appropriate representation (e.g., excess 127).

(4) Pack the mantissa sign, the normalized mantissa, and the exponent into the floating-point format.

floating-to-fixed conversion

To convert a number from floating-point to fixed-point format, we can simply expand the formula that defines the floating-point format, performing any necessary number system conversions along the way. Sometimes we will detect an overflow condition, a floating-point number too large for the fixed-point format. At other times we may encounter floating-point numbers that don't have an exact representation in the prescribed fixed-point format, in which case we must use approximate values obtained by truncating digits or rounding.

floating-point addition and subtraction

The algorithm for addition and subtraction of floating-point numbers has three steps:

(1) The radix points of the numbers are "aligned" so that both numbers have the same exponent. This is accomplished by "unnormalizing" the smaller operand so that the exponents of both operands are equal.

(2) The mantissas are added or subtracted.

(3) The result is normalized. Normalization is necessary because addition of mantissas may produce a result greater than 2 and subtraction may produce a result much less than 1 (assuming IEEE format).

floating-point multiplication and division

Multiplication and division of floating-point numbers do not require the radix points to be aligned, since multiplication or division of scale factors corresponds to addition or subtraction of exponents. Multiplication and division are accomplished as follows:

(1) The exponents are added (in multiplication) or subtracted (in division).

(2) The mantissas are multiplied or divided.

(3) The result is normalized.

Two approaches are possible for performing floating-point operations on a computer. Some computer systems have built-in hardware and instructions to process floating-point numbers in a prescribed format. For example, Motorola makes a "coprocessor" chip, called the MC68881, which may be installed in a 68000 system to perform floating-point operations.

Floating-point operations may also be performed by software. For example, in 68000 systems without a floating-point coprocessor, the 68000 processor automatically "traps" a program's attempts to execute floating-point instructions and gives control to a special software routine that performs these operations. However, software routines typically take 10 to 100 times longer than hardware to perform a given floating-point operation, and so the hardware approach is preferred for applications that make frequent use of floating-point operations.

4.12 CHARACTER CODES

text

ASCII

In Chapter 1, we pointed out that a bit string need not represent a number, and that in fact most input and output of contemporary computers is nonnumeric. The most common type of nonnumeric data is *text*, strings of characters from some character set. Each character is represented in the computer by a bit string according to an established convention.

The most commonly-used character code is *ASCII*, the American Standard Code for Information Interchange. ASCII represents each character by a 7-bit string, a total of 128 different characters as shown in Appendix A. Thus, the text string "Yeccch!" is represented by a rather innocent looking list of seven 7-bit numbers:

1011001   1100101   1100011   1100011   1100011   1101000   0100001

Some of the 7-bit strings in ASCII denote device control functions instead of "printing" characters. For example, CR (0001101) returns the print head or cursor on a printer or display to the first column, and LF (0001010) advances to the next line. Most of the other control characters are intended for use by data communication links, but different computer systems may use these characters for different functions.

Most computers manipulate an 8-bit quantity as a single unit, a byte, and store one character in each byte. The disposition of the extra bit when 7-bit ASCII is used depends on the system or program. Sometimes this bit is set to a particular value, sometimes it is ignored, and sometimes it is used to encode an additional 128 non-ASCII characters.

An important feature of ASCII is that the bit strings for letters and digits form a reasonable numerical sequence, so that text strings can be sorted by computer instructions that compare numerical values. The ASCII code chart may also explain why HFC, IBM, and TWA come before Haag, Iacocca, and Taaffe, respectively, in the phone book.

REFERENCES

Precise, thorough, and entertaining discussions of all of the topics in this chapter can be found in Donald Knuth's *Seminumerical Algorithms* (Addison-Wesley, 1969). Mathematically inclined readers will find Knuth's analysis of the properties of number systems and arithmetic to be excellent, and all readers should enjoy the insights and history sprinkled throughout the text.

Descriptions of arithmetic hardware as well as properties of various number systems appear in *Computer Arithmetic* by K. Hwang (Wiley, 1979). *Decimal Arithmetic* by H. Schmid (Wiley, 1974) contains a thorough description of techniques for BCD arithmetic.

A good discussion of floating-point number systems in general and the IEEE standard in particular can be found in *Introduction to Arithmetic for Digital Systems Designers* by Shlomo Waser and Michael J. Flynn (Holt, Rinehart and Winston, 1982). The standard itself was published in the August 1984 issue of *Computer* magazine (Vol. 17, No. 8) "Proposed Radix- and Word-Length Independent IEEE P854 Standard for Floating-Point Arithmetic," by W. J. Cody *et al.*, and is also available directly from the IEEE ("Binary Floating-Point Arithmetic," IEEE Standard 754-1985, publ. no. SH10116).

EXERCISES

4.1   How does one decorate a 31-year-old's birthday cake with only five candles?

4.2   Justify lighting only three candles on your birthday cake at the following ages: 3, 7, 13, 21, 31, 43, 57, 73.

4.3   Perform the following number system conversions:

(a) $1101011_2 = ?_{10}$ (b) $174003_8 = ?_{10}$

(c) $10110111_2 = ?_{10}$ (d) $67.24_8 = ?_{10}$

(e) $10100.1101_2 = ?_{10}$ (f) $F3A5_{16} = ?_{10}$

(g) $12010_3 = ?_{10}$ (h) $AB3D_{16} = ?_{10}$

(i) $7156_8 = ?_{10}$ (j) $15C.38_{16} = ?_{10}$

4.4   Perform the following number system conversions:

(a) $1101011_2 = ?_{16}$ (b) $174003_8 = ?_2$

(c) $10110111_2 = ?_{16}$ (d) $67.24_8 = ?_2$

(e) $10100.1101_2 = ?_{16}$ (f) $F3A5_{16} = ?_2$

(g) $11011001_2 = ?_8$ (h) $AB3D_{16} = ?_2$

(i) $101111.0111_2 = ?_8$ (j) $15C.38_{16} = ?_2$

4.5   Perform the following number system conversions:

(a) $125_{10} = ?_2$ (b) $3489_{10} = ?_8$

(c) $209_{10} = ?_2$ (d) $9714_{10} = ?_8$

(e) $132_{10} = ?_2$ (f) $23851_{10} = ?_{16}$

(g) $727_{10} = ?_5$ (h) $57190_{10} = ?_{16}$

(i) $1435_{10} = ?_8$ (j) $65113_{10} = ?_{16}$

4.6   Add the following pairs of binary numbers, showing all carries:

(a)   110101   (b)   101110   (c)   11011101   (d)   1110010
       + 11001   + 100101   + 1100011   + 1101101

4.7   Repeat the previous problem using subtraction instead of addition, and showing borrows instead of carries.

4.8   Add the following pairs of octal numbers:

(a)   1372   (b)   47135   (c)   175214   (d)   110321
      + 4631   + 5125   + 152405   + 56573

4.9   Add the following pairs of hexadecimal numbers:

(a)   1372   (b)   4F1A5   (c)   F35B   (d)   1B90F
      + 4631   + B8D5   + 27E6   + C44E

4.10   Give the 8-bit signed-magnitude, two's-complement, and ones'-complement representations for each of the following decimal numbers: +18, +115, +79, −49, −3, −100.

4.11   Suppose a $4n$-bit number B is represented by an n-digit hexadecimal number H. Prove that the two's complement of B is represented by the 16's complement of H. Make a similar statement that is true for the octal representation of a binary number.

4.12   Repeat the preceding problem using the ones' complement of B and the 15s' complement of H.

4.13   Indicate the most likely real balances in my checking account if the following balances appear: $9871.23, $9905.74, $123.46. For each of these balances, what should the new balance be if I deposit $102.99?

4.14 Given an integer x in the range $-2^{n-1} \le x \le 2^{n-1}-1$, we define $[x]$ to be the two's-complement representation of x, expressed as a positive number: $[x] = x$ if $x \ge 0$ and $[x] = 2^n - |x|$ if $x < 0$, where $|x|$ is the absolute value of x. Let y be another integer in the same range. Prove that the rules for two's-complement addition as defined in Section 4.6 are correct by verifying that the following equation is always true:

$$[x + y] \;=\; [x] + [y] \text{ modulo } 2^n$$

(*Hints:* Consider four cases based on the signs of x and y. Without loss of generality, you may assume $|x| \ge |y|$.)

4.15 Repeat the previous problem using the appropriate expressions and rules for ones'-complement addition.

4.16 Indicate whether or not overflow occurs when adding the following 8-bit two's-complement numbers:

(a)   11010100   (b)   10111001   (c)   01011101   (d)   00100110
     + 10101011   + 11010110   + 00100001   + 01011010

4.17 Show that a two's-complement number can be converted to a representation with more bits by "sign extension." That is, given an n-bit two's-complement number X, show that the m-bit two's-complement representation of X, where $m > n$, can be obtained by appending $m - n$ copies of X's sign bit to the left of the n-bit representation of X.

4.18 Show that a two's-complement number can be converted to a representation with fewer bits by removing higher-order bits. That is, given an n-bit two's-complement number X, show that the m-bit two's-complement number Y obtained by discarding the d leftmost bits of X represents the same number as X if and only if the discarded bits all equal the sign bit of Y.

4.19 Write the bodies of the Pascal functions and procedures `Bshr` through `Writeword` in Table 4–6.

4.20 Write the bodies of the Pascal functions `BaddV` and `Bcom` in Table 4–7.

4.21 Show how to implement the Pascal function `Bls` in Table 4–9 using `Badd` and `Bcom` as primitives.

4.22 Let X and Y be n-bit numbers, and let $\overline{Y}$ represent the bit-by-bit complement of Y. Prove that the operation $X - Y$ produces a borrow out of the MSB position if and only if the operation $X + \overline{Y} + 1$ *does not* produce a carry out of the MSB position.

4.23 In most cases, the product of two n-bit two's-complement numbers takes $2n - 1$ or fewer bits to represent. In fact, there is only one case in which $2n$ bits are needed—find it.

4.24 Prove that a two's-complement number can be multiplied by 2 by shifting it one bit position to the left, with a carry of 0 into the least significant bit position and disregarding any carry out of the most significant bit position, assuming no overflow. State the rule for detecting overflow.

4.25 State and prove correct a technique similar to the above, for multiplying a ones'-complement number by 2.

4.26 Describe a rule for dividing a two's-complement number by 2 by means of a right-shift operation. Give a Pascal statement that precisely defines the integer quotient obtained when the dividend is not a multiple of 2. Use only positive arguments with DIV and MOD, since standard Pascal allows their results with negative arguments to vary in different implementations.

4.27 Repeat the preceding exercise for ones'-complement numbers.

4.28 Rewrite the unsigned multiplication program in Table 4–6 so that mpy and loProd are the same variable.

4.29 Write a Pascal multiplication program that processes the multiplier bits from left to right, instead of right to left as in Table 4–6. State the advantages and disadvantages of this approach.

4.30 Rewrite the unsigned division program in Table 4–9 so that quot and loDvnd are the same variable.

4.31 Show how to subtract BCD numbers, by stating the rules for generating borrows and applying a correction factor. Show how your rules apply to each of the following subtractions: $9 - 3$, $5 - 7$, $4 - 9$, $1 - 8$.

4.32 How many different unnormalized (hidden bit = 0) representations does +1.0 have in IEEE floating-point format?

4.33 What is the smallest nonzero positive normalized number in IEEE floating-point format? What is the largest?

4.34 Show how the following numbers would be stored in a computer's memory in IEEE floating-point format: 17, 40, 9.25, 15/64, 7/1024.

4.35 Prove that if two numbers X and Y in IEEE floating-point format are normalized, then X must be greater than Y if the exponent of X is greater than the exponent of Y. (*Hint:* Consider the worst-case values of the exponents and mantissas.)

4.36 In IEEE floating-point format, the exponent field uses excess-127 representation, and so the "natural" value to use for the exponent when this field is 00000000 is 2^{-127}. Why do you suppose the standard specifies an an exponent of 2^{-126} in this case?

4.37 Why do HFC, IBM, and TWA come before Haag, Iacocca, and Taaffe, respectively, in the phone book?

C H A P T E R   5

Basic Computer Organization

A typical computer consists of a processor, memory, and input/output. All three of these subsystems have had major technological improvements since the first electronic digital computers were constructed in the 1940s. The improvements in processor and memory cost and performance due to integrated circuit technology in the last two decades have been breathtaking—for a few ounces of gold today, you can buy a business computer as powerful as a minicomputer that cost more than a three-bedroom house in 1980.

Despite the technological advances, the basic organization and operating principles of computers haven't changed too much. For example, in a 1946 description of the design of the first proposed electronic stored program computer, Burks, Goldstine, and von Neumann said[1],

> Conceptually we have ... two different forms of memory: storage of numbers and storage of orders. If, however, the orders to the machine are reduced to a numerical code and if the machine can in some fashion distinguish a number from an order, the memory organ can be used to store both numbers and orders.

To this day, almost all computers use the same "memory organ" for storing both data (numbers) and instructions (orders); such computers are often called "von Neumann machines." The early machines contain many other similarities to contemporary computers and precursors of their features.

In this chapter, we describe the basic organization and features of computer processors and memory. The discussion focuses on the Motorola 68000 family, a general-register processor whose details are described in later chapters.

---

[1] "Preliminary Discussion of the Logical Design of an Electronic Computing Instrument," in *Computer Structures: Readings and Examples*, by C. G. Bell and A. Newell (McGraw-Hill, 1971).

Of course, our discussion of the Motorola 68000 family does not touch upon every possible computer architecture or feature. While the 68000 family has a general-register architecture, other traditional architectures include accumulator-based processors and stack machines. Recently, so-called reduced-instruction-set computers (RISC architectures) have become popular.

Architectures quite different from the traditional and the popular have also been proposed, and many have even been built: machines whose data memory is a stack rather than an array; machines that process streams of data rather than streams of instructions; machines in which the processor sends instructions to memory instead of reading operands from it; and machines in which algorithms are defined by functional relations rather than by explicit steps to compute a result. Also, a very large number of computer systems have more than one processor. However, the general concepts discussed in this book and exemplified by the Motorola 68000 apply to the vast majority of computers in production and in use today.

5.1   MEMORY

memory
address
byte-addressable
  memory
word-addressable
  memory

A computer *memory* is simply an array of randomly accessible bit strings, each of which is identified by a unique *address*. If the smallest addressable bit string in the memory is a byte, then the memory is *byte-addressable*; if it is a word, then the memory is *word-addressable*. Most contemporary computers have byte-addressable memories.

5.1.1   Memory Organizations

Figure 5–1(a) provides a conceptual view of a memory with 2^{16} bytes; a 16-bit address uniquely specifies any byte in this memory. We shall always draw computer memories with the lowest-numbered address on top. By convention, the bits in a word or byte will be numbered from right to left starting with 0, so that the bit numbers correspond to the exponents of their unsigned numerical weights written as powers of 2 (e.g., bit 5 has a weight of $2^5 = 32$). Almost all minicomputers and microcomputers, including the 68000 family, follow this convention. Perversely, the IBM 370 family uses the opposite ordering. (That's OK—it was there first!).

Even if a computer has 16-bit or wider data paths and physical memory, the memory can still be byte-addressable. For example, Figure 5–1(b) shows the physical memory organization used in the Intel 8086 family. A 16-bit word in this figure consists of two consecutively numbered bytes. For example, "word 2" consists of bytes 2 and 3, and "word 4" consists of bytes 4 and 5. A word

aligned word
word boundary

that starts at an even address is said to be *aligned* on a *word boundary*. The organization of the 8086's physical memory system is such that both bytes of an aligned word can be accessed simultaneously.

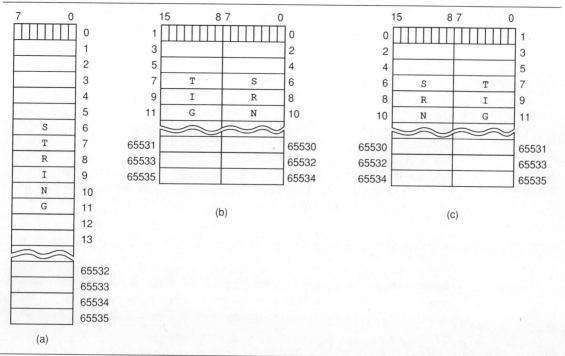

FIGURE 5–1   Memory organizations: (a) byte-addressable memory for an 8-bit processor;
(b) byte-addressable memory for a 16-bit processor (a so-called "Little Endian");
(c) alternative byte-addressable memory for a 16-bit processor (a "Big Endian" such
as the Motorola 68000).

nonaligned word   Many processors, including the 8086, allow *nonaligned words* to be accessed. For example, in Figure 5–1(b), "word 3" is a nonaligned word consisting
of bytes 3 and 4. Although a nonaligned word stores the same information as
an aligned word (2 bytes, 16 bits), the processor has to do more work to access
this information. To read "word 3" in Figure 5–1(b), the processor must first
read "word 2" and extract the low-order byte (3), and then read "word 4" and
extract the high-order byte (4). Thus, two memory accesses instead of one are
required when the desired word is nonaligned.

Manufacturers of processors that can access nonaligned words recommend
that programmers nevertheless arrange their programs so that words are aligned,
so that the programs will run faster. Some processors, including the Motorola
68000, avoid the problem altogether by forbidding access to nonaligned words;
thus, bytes 2 and 3 form a word but bytes 3 and 4 do not. In such a processor,
instructions that manipulate words must specify even addresses; instructions that
manipulate bytes may specify any address.

From the point of view of number theory, the arrangement of bytes in a
word as shown in Figure 5–1(b) is the natural one, since the least significant bits

are contained in the lower-numbered byte. Figure 5–1(c) shows an alternative method of addressing bytes in a 16-bit machine, with the lower-numbered byte on the left. This method is used in most 16-bit and 32-bit computers, including the Motorola 68000 family.

Although the equations relating bit and byte numbers are less elegant with the arrangement of Figure 5–1(c), some more practical problems of storing 8-bit characters in successive bytes are easier to deal with. In both Figure 5–1(b) and (c), the character string "STRING" is stored in sequential bytes beginning at byte address 6; Figure 5–1(c) is obviously easier to read. More importantly, the arrangement of Figure 5–1(c) has very tangible benefits when we use word instructions to do lexicographic sorting of strings (see Exercise 5.4).

We'll take another look at the memory organization for specific members of the Motorola 68000 family later, in Section 5.3.

5.1.2 Pascal Simulation of Processors and Memories

We can simulate the operation of a computer's processor and memory on another, larger computer by means of a Pascal program. Since the main memory of the simulated machine is just an array of bit strings, it can be defined by Pascal declarations as shown below for the memory of Figure 5–1(a).

```
TYPE
   byte = 0..255;
   address = 0..65535;
VAR
   MEM : ARRAY [address] OF byte;
```

The second line above defines a `byte` to be an element with 256 possible values, which can therefore be represented in 8 bits. The next line states that a valid `address` is an integer in the range of 0 through 65535. The last line defines the memory itself, an array of `byte`s, one `byte` per valid `address`. Since the total number of memory bytes is 2^{16}, an address may be specified by a 16-bit unsigned integer.

5.1.3 Memory Types

read/write memory (RWM)

volatile memory

read-only memory (ROM)

nonvolatile memory

programmable read-only memory (PROM)

Several types of memories are commonly used in computer main memory systems. With a *read/write memory (RWM)*, we can store data at any address and read back the stored information at any time. Most semiconductor RWMs are *volatile*, in that the stored information disappears when power is removed.

With a *read-only memory (ROM)*, we can read the contents of any address at any time, but data values can be stored only once, when the ROM is manufactured. The key advantage of a ROM is that it is a *nonvolatile*; that is, its contents are preserved even if no power is applied.

A *programmable read-only memory (PROM)* is similar to a ROM, except that the customer may store data values (i.e., "program the PROM") using a *PROM programmer*. A PROM chip is manufactured with all its bits at a par-

*PROM
  programmer*

*erasable
  programmable
  read-only
  memory
  (EPROM)*

*electrically
  erasable
  programmable
  read-only
  memory
  (EEPROM)*

*random-access
  memory (RAM)*

ticular value, typically 1. The PROM programmer can be used to set desired bits to the opposite value, typically by vaporizing tiny fuses inside the PROM corresponding to each bit.

An *erasable programmable read-only memory (EPROM)* is similar to a PROM, except that the EPROM can be "erased" to the all-1's state by exposing it to ultraviolet light. No, the light does not cause fuses to grow back! Rather, EPROMs use a different technology. The EPROM programmer forces electrons into tiny wells corresponding to each 0 bit, where they remain trapped unless excited by ultraviolet light. EPROMs are typically used during program development, where the program or other information in the EPROM must be repeatedly changed during debugging. Once a stable version of the program is finalized, a ROM or PROM may be used in production to save cost (ROMs and PROMs cost less than EPROMs of similar capacity).

An *electrically erasable programmable read-only memory (EEPROM)* is similar to an EPROM, except that it may be erased electrically. Special circuits inside an EEPROM drain the electrons from specified bits during programming operations. A "programming operation" for an EEPROM typically takes much longer than a read operation, and there may also be a limit on the number of times the EEPROM may be reprogrammed (say, 10,000 times). Therefore, EEPROMs are typically used for storing data that must be preserved when the equipment is not powered, but which must also be changed occasionally, such as the default configuration data for a smart terminal.

Every computer has RWM for storing variable data. Depending on the computer and the application, the programs may also be stored in RWM, or they may be stored in ROM, PROM, or EPROM.

All of the memories described above are *random-access memories*, because the processor has equally fast access to every memory location. However, computer jargon has developed so that the acronym "RAM" most commonly refers to read/write memory only. In this book, we'll follow the industry's practice of using "RAM" to refer to read/write random-access memories.

5.2 PROCESSOR ARCHITECTURES

Many different approaches have been taken in computer processor architectures. Before getting into the specifics of the Motorola 68000 architecture, we discuss the traditional approaches, of which the 68000 is just one example.

5.2.1 Accumulator Machines

*accumulator
  machine
accumulator*

The first computers, built in the 1940s and 1950s, were *accumulator machines*. The processor in such a computer has a single register, called an *accumulator*, in which arithmetic, logical, and comparison operations take place. All program variables are stored in main memory, and are transferred to the accumulator when they must be examined or combined with other variables. The high cost of registers and control circuitry compared with main memory motivated the use of accumulator-based architectures in early machines. Not surprisingly, the same kind of constraints led to the use of accumulator-based architectures in the first generation of minicomputers (e.g., DEC PDP-8 and HP 2116) and in the first generation of microprocessors (e.g., Motorola 6800 and Intel 8080). The Motorola 6809, described in Chapter 16, is a reasonable contemporary example of an accumulator-based architecture.

Let us use MEM(x) to denote the contents of the memory location in which program variable x is stored. For example, if the programmer decides to store variable x in memory location 1234, then MEM(x) means "the contents of memory location 1234." To execute the Pascal statement x:=y, an accumulator machine must execute two "machine instructions":

(1) Load accumulator with MEM(y).

(2) Store accumulator into MEM(x).

And to perform an arithmetic operation such as x:=y+z, it must execute three machine instructions:

(1) Load accumulator with MEM(y).

(2) Add to accumulator MEM(z).

(3) Store accumulator into MEM(x).

Thus, the machine instructions in an accumulator-based processor are concerned with moving data between the accumulator and main memory, and combining operands in main memory with the accumulator. A typical machine instruction uses two fields to specify what it does:

operation code (opcode)

- *Operation code (opcode).* Specifies the operation to be performed—load, store, add, and so on.

operand address

- *Operand address.* Specifies the memory address of one of the operands. The other operand is assumed to be the accumulator.

one-address machine

Because each instruction contains one memory address, accumulator-based processors are sometimes called *one-address machines.*

5.2.2 General-Register Machines

Accumulator-based processors have two significant performance disadvantages. First, main memory access time is slow compared with the access time for a processor register, yet every instruction must access main memory for one of its operands; so operand access is slow. Second, an instruction requires a relatively large number of bits to specify the address of a memory operand; there might be only 2^8 different operations (and 8 opcode bits), but 2^{32} memory addresses (and 32 address bits). Thus, instructions that specify memory operands are longer than ones that don't. Yet most instructions in an accumulator-based processor must specify a memory operand, and so programs are longer and slower than they might otherwise have to be.

general-register machine
general register

General-register machines overcome these problems by replacing the accumulator with a small set of *general registers* in which arithmetic, logical, and comparison operations take place. Frequently used program variables may be stored in registers and accessed more quickly than variables in main memory, overcoming the first problem above. A typical general-register machine has 8 or 16 general registers, so registers can be specified with only 3 or 4 instruction bits, overcoming the second problem. General-register architectures appeared in the second generations of mainframe computers (e.g., IBM 360/370), mini-computers (e.g., DEC PDP-11), and microprocessors (e.g., Zilog Z8000). The Motorola 68000 family is a good example of a general-register architecture.

Let us use REG(x) to denote the contents of a general register in which a program variable x is stored. For example, if the programmer decides to store variable x in general register 5, then REG(x) means "the contents of register 5." A general-register machine can execute the Pascal statement x:=y in only one machine instruction if both operands are stored in general registers:

- Load REG(x) with REG(y).

It can also execute arithmetic and logical operations in a single instruction if one of the source operands is the same as the result operand, as in x:=x+y:

- Add REG(y) to REG(x), store result in REG(x).

Both instructions above are potentially much shorter and faster than loads and adds in an accumulator machine.

Since most programs have dozens of variables, not all operands can be kept in general registers. Therefore, all general-register machines have instructions with one operand in memory and another in a register, such as the following:

- Load REG(x) with MEM(y).

- Store REG(x) into MEM(y).

- Add MEM(y) to REG(x), store result in REG(x).

- Add REG(y) to MEM(x), store result in MEM(x).

one-and-a-half address instruction

memory-to-register
register-to-memory

two-address instruction
three-address instruction

These are often called *one-and-a-half address instructions*, because they contain a full memory address and a short register number. The instructions that combine operands are also classified according to where they store the result; the third example above is a *memory-to-register instruction*, while the fourth is a *register-to-memory instruction*.

Some processors have *two-address instructions* that allow both operands to be in memory. The most general general-register machines have *three-address instructions* that allow all three operands of an operation like x:=y+z to be specified independently in memory or registers.

5.2.3 Stack Machines

stack machine
stack pointer (SP)

zero-address
machine

A *stack machine* has neither an accumulator nor general registers, only a *stack pointer (SP)* that points to the top of a pushdown stack in main memory. (Pushdown stacks were introduced in Section 3.4.) All operations except data movement are performed on operands at or near the top of the stack, and so typical instructions contain *no* memory addresses. Thus a stack machine is sometimes called a *zero-address machine*. Stack machines appeared in the second generation of mainframe computers (e.g., the Burroughs B5000) and minicomputers (e.g., the HP 300). Although many calculators, most notably Hewlett-Packard's, are stack machines, a popular microprocessor with a pure stack architecture has yet to appear. However, we'll describe a hypothetical stack machine based on the DEC PDP-11 and LSI-11 in Chapter 19.

Stack operations are very well suited for arithmetic expression evaluation, which accounts for their use in HP's hand-held calculators. Stack machines attempt to minimize instruction and program lengths by keeping "current" operands at the top of the stack and performing operations there, using zero-address instructions. For example, the addition instruction in a stack machine operates as follows:

- Pop the top two items off the stack, add them, and push the sum onto the stack.

However, complete programs also require initial values to be placed on the stack, and results to be stored away for later use, and so practical stack machines also have one-address instructions for loading and storing stack data:

- Push MEM(x) onto the stack.

- Pop stack and store into MEM(x).

A major disadvantage of pure stack machines compared with general-register machines is that the most frequently used operands are stored in relatively slow main memory rather than high-speed registers. Some commercial stack machines have minimized this problem by "shadowing" the top few stack locations in processor registers, but this complicates hardware design, especially in high-performance implementations. Thus, it seems that, for performance reasons, new architectures include hardware stacks only in conjunction with general registers and other features.

5.2.4 Other Processor Organizations and Classifications

Few real processors fall precisely into the categories of general-register, accumulator, and stack machines. For example, the 8086 has eight 16-bit registers that Intel calls "general registers" because they are treated the same in many operations. However, multiplication, division, and decimal operations can be performed on only one register (the "accumulator"), and each register is used differently in address calculations. Luckily, our purpose for classifying different machines is not to create a strict taxonomy; rather, it is to provide a framework for discussing and understanding diverse processor architectures.

Many "nontraditional" features have appeared in microprocessor architectures. One feature that we usually take for granted is that instructions and data are stored in the same memory. In most systems, this is necessary since instructions and data are interchanged by some program development tools. For example, a "loader" copies a saved program into memory and must treat it as data to do so. However, in dedicated applications such as electronic cash registers and automobile ignitions, there are no resident program development tools, and programs are never treated as data. Therefore, some microcontrollers such as the Intel MCS-51 store their instructions and data in different memories; their instructions do not allow program memory locations to be read and written as data. Such microcontrollers are *not* von Neumann machines in the purest sense.

working-register set

Another interesting concept is that of a *working-register set*. Instead of having just one set of general registers, some processors have many sets, using a "working-register pointer" to specify which set is currently in use. For example, the MCS-51 has four register sets, and the Texas Instruments 9900 can use a block of 16 words anywhere in its 32-Kword address space as its register set. Several recent VLSI processors have adapted this idea as *register windows*.

register windows

Here, working registers are allocated from a stack, and the top of the stack (a few hundred registers or so) is contained on-chip.

Processors may be classified by the size of the data that they process. Most contemporary processors can address and process data as small as a byte; some can even address individual bits in registers or memory. Except for character strings, the largest data type handled by a processor is usually four to ten bytes for floating-point operations.

n-bit machine

A particular processor is called an *n-bit machine* if the largest operand handled by the majority of its data operations is *n* bits. This is a characteristic of the processor registers and operations, not of the processor hardware design, the memory organization, or the memory bus. Thus, the 6809 is an 8-bit processor even though it has some 16-bit index registers and operations; the 8086 is a 16-bit processor even though its instructions are strings of 1 to 7 bytes; and the 68000 is a 32-bit processor even though the MC68000 chip has a 16-bit memory data bus and 16-bit internal data paths.

Processors may also be classified by their cost, as discussed in Section 1.7. They can also be classified by their addressing modes and by the size of the memory they can access, as discussed in Chapter 7.

5.3 68000-FAMILY PROCESSOR ORGANIZATION

The Motorola 68000 family contains several microprocessor chips that share a common base architecture. The family includes microprocessor chips with Motorola part numbers MC68000, MC68008, MC68010, MC68012, MC68020,

notation
68000
MC68020
and MC68030. In this book, we'll use the designation "68000" when discussing concepts or features that are common to the entire family, and we'll use a full part number such as "MC68020" when we need to limit the discussion to a specific family member.

Although they share a common base architecture, members of the 68000 family differ in several important ways:

- *Memory data bus width.* The width of the external data bus affects how quickly instructions and data may be moved between the processor and memory, but is otherwise transparent to program operation.

- *Memory address bus width.* All 68000-family processors use 32-bit addresses internally, but only a subset of these bits may be available on the external address bus, limiting the maximum size of physical memory attached to the processor.

- *Instruction set.* While all 68000-family processors share the same base instruction set, newer members have additional instructions and addressing modes. Still, the majority of instructions belong to the base instruction set, a tribute to the completeness of the original 68000 design.

- *Operating-system support.* Newer members of the 68000 family have additional features and instructions to support memory management and sophisticated operating systems.

- *Performance.* Some members of the 68000 family have additional hardware to speed up program execution.

68000-family differences
The differences among 68000-family members are summarized in Table 5–1; we mention these differences in later chapters as appropriate, and we discuss the advanced features of the MC68010 through MC68030 in detail in Chapter 14.

Memory size and organization is probably the single most important defining characteristic of a processor architecture. The MC68000 and MC68010 both access a 16-bit-wide memory with up to 2^{24} bytes (16 Mbytes), arranged as shown in Figure 5–2(a). The MC68020 and MC68030 access a 32-bit-wide memory with up to 2^{32} bytes (4 gigabytes), as shown in Figure 5–2(b).

notation
We'll use 32-bit numbers to represent 68000 addresses in this book. In fact, all 68000-family processors use 32-bit addresses internally, but most provide fewer bits on their external address bus, as we've indicated.

The 68000 has some instructions that can access only the lowest and highest 32 Kbytes of memory as shown in Figure 5–2(c). In these instructions, an address is contained in only 16 bits, and the corresponding 32-bit address is obtained by extending the most significant bit of the 16-bit address.

byte
word
longword
Most 68000 instructions can manipulate 8-, 16-, and 32-bit quantities, called *bytes*, *words*, and *longwords*. Most instructions occupy one to five words in memory; however, the additional addressing modes in the MC68020 and MC68030 can require instruction lengths of up to 11 words.

TABLE 5–1   Differences among 68000-family members.

Feature	MC68000/08[1]	MC68010/12[2]	MC68020/30[3]
Memory data bus width (bits)	16/8	16	8, 16, or 32
Memory address bus width (bits)	24/20	24/31	32
Internal data bus size (bits)	16	16	32
Word alignment of instructions	required	required	required
Word alignment of data	required	required	not required
Stack pointers	A7, A7'	A7, A7'	A7, A7', A7"
Additional control registers	none	SFC, DFC, VBR	SFC, DFC, VBR, CACR, CAAR
Additional bits in SR	none	none	T0, T1, M
Additional addressing modes	none	none	see Section 14.8
Additional instructions	none	see Section 14.2	see Section 14.9
Instruction continuation after bus error	no	yes	yes
On-chip memory management unit	no	no	no/yes
Instruction cache	none	3-word loops	64 longwords
Data cache	none	none	none/64 longwords

Notes: (1) The MC68000 and MC68008 instruction set architectures are identical. The MC68008
comes in a smaller package with fewer address bits and a narrower data bus, thereby
accessing a smaller physical memory at a slower rate, one byte at a time.

(2) The MC68010 and MC68012 instruction set architectures are identical. The MC68012
comes in a bigger package that provides more address bits, thereby accessing a larger
physical memory.

(3) The MC68020 and MC68030 instruction set architectures are identical. For improved
performance, the MC68030 has additional built-in hardware, including a data cache
and a memory management unit.

Figure 5–3 shows the internal organization of a typical 68000-family processor, whose registers and functional units are briefly described below:

program counter (PC)

- *Program counter (PC)*: a 32-bit register that holds the memory address of the next instruction to be executed.

instruction register (IR)

- *Instruction register (IR)*: a 16-bit register that holds the first word of the currently executing instruction.

effective address register (EAR)

- *Effective address register (EAR)*: a 32-bit register that, when required, holds a memory address at which the processor reads or writes data during the execution of an instruction.

general registers (D0–D7, A0–A7, A7')

data register

address register

user stack pointer (SP or USP)

supervisor stack pointer (SSP)

- *General registers (D0–D7, A0–A7, A7')*: a set of seventeen 32-bit registers containing data and addresses. Registers D0–D7 are called *data registers*, and A0–A7 and A7' are called *address registers*. Register A7 is the *user stack pointer (SP or USP)*, and A7' is the *supervisor stack pointer (SSP)*.

- *Temporary register (TEMP)*: a 32-bit register that holds operands or intermediate results during the execution of an instruction.

condition code register (CCR)

- *Condition Code Register (CCR)*: a set of 1-bit flags that the processor sets or clears during the execution of each data manipulation instruction.

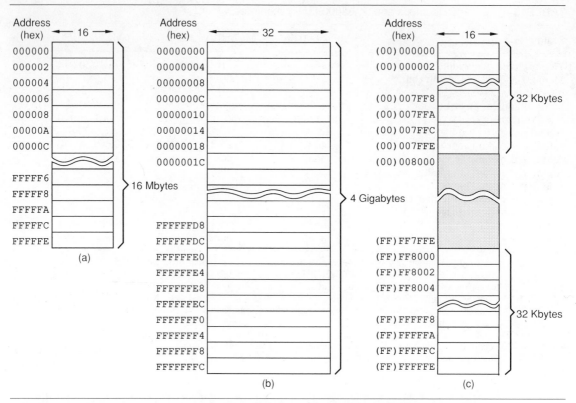

FIGURE 5–2 Memory addressing in the 68000 family: (a) MC68000 and MC68010; (b) MC68020 and MC68030; (c) region accessible by short, 16-bit addresses.

status register (SR)

- *Status register (SR)*: a 16-bit register whose high-order byte contains "processor control" bits and whose low-order byte is the CCR.

arithmetic and logic unit (ALU)

- *Arithmetic and logic unit (ALU)*: operates on one or two 8-, 16-, or 32-bit quantities, producing a like-sized result.

control unit

- *Control unit*: decodes instructions and controls the other blocks to fetch and execute instructions.

memory and I/O interface

- *Memory and I/O interface*: reads and writes memory and communicates with I/O (Input/Output) devices as commanded by the control unit.

Although all of the blocks above are essential to the internal operation of the 68000, only the registers PC, D0–D7, A0–A7, A7', and SR are explicitly manipulated by instructions and have values that are meaningful after each instruction's execution. Such registers comprise the *processor state*, and may be shown in a *programming model* for the processor, as in Figure 5–4. Only these registers are of concern to a programmer.

processor state

programming model

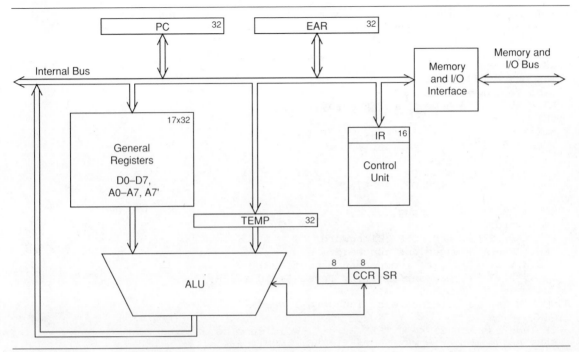

FIGURE 5–3   Organization of a 68000 processor.

5.4 INSTRUCTION PROCESSING CYCLE

The operation of the 68000 (or almost any other computer processor) consists of endless repetition of two steps: read the next instruction from memory (the *fetch cycle*) and perform the actions it requires (the *execution cycle*). This basic instruction cycle may be defined by an endless loop in Pascal:

fetch cycle
execution cycle

```
WHILE true DO  {Basic instruction processing cycle}
   BEGIN
      Fetch;
      Execute;
   END;
```

It is defined in more detail by the Pascal simulation in Table 5–2, and further developed in Section 5.11.[2]

---

[2]Note that the multiplications by 256 and 65536 shown in the `ReadMemWord` and `ReadMemLong` functions do not occur in real memory interface hardware. They simply get around the Pascal's limitations as a hardware simulation language—Pascal has no facilities for directly manipulating bit strings. The real hardware shifts or rearranges bytes, words, and longwords as they are received from memory to deliver properly sized operands as required.

Also, the real hardware uses special mode-dependent decoding for the general register array. That is, where the simulation "shadows" variables `SSP` and `USP` into `REG[A7]`, the real hardware decodes all instruction references to A7 and accesses either SSP or USP according to the current value of S.

TABLE 5-2   Basic instruction processing cycle of the 68000 processor.

```
PROGRAM S68000 (input,output);

CONST
  maxlong = 4398046511103;
  resetVector = 0;
  A7 = 15; {A7's number in REG array}
TYPE
  bit = 0..1;
  byte = 0..255;
  word = 0..65535;
  longword = 0..maxlong;
  regnum = 0..15; {D0-D7, A0-A7}
VAR
  MEM : ARRAY [0..maxlong] OF byte;
  IR : word;
  PC, EAR, TEMP, USP, SSP : longword;
  REG : ARRAY [regnum] of longword;
  T,S,X,N,Z,V,C : bit; {Component bits of SR}
  PPL : 0..7; {Processor Priority Level field in SR}

FUNCTION ReadMemWord(address: longword): word;
BEGIN
  IF (address MOD 2) <> 0 THEN Error  {Word must be at even address.}
  ELSE ReadMemWord := MEM[address]*256 + MEM[address+1];
END;

FUNCTION ReadMemLong(address: longword): longword;
BEGIN
  ReadMemLong := ReadMemWord(address)*65536 + ReadMemWord(address+2);
END;

PROCEDURE Fetch;
BEGIN
  IR := ReadMemWord(PC);  {Read instruction word.}
  PC := (PC + 2) MOD (maxlong+1);  {Bump PC to next instruction word.}
END;

PROCEDURE Execute;
BEGIN  {Will be defined later.}  END;

BEGIN  {Main program}
  SSP := ReadMemLong(resetVector);  {Initialize SSP and PC...}
  PC := ReadMemLong(resetVector+4); {  from vector in memory.}
  S := 1; PPL := 7; {Come up in supervisor mode, interrupts masked.}
  reg[A7] := SSP; {Accessing reg[A7] should be equivalent to accessing SSP.}
  WHILE true DO  {Basic instruction processing cycle}
    BEGIN
      Fetch;
      Execute;
    END;
END.
```

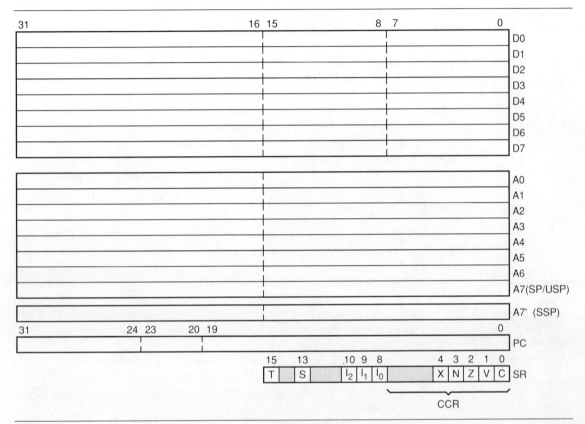

FIGURE 5–4   Programming model for the 68000.

The fetch cycle simply reads the first word of the instruction that PC points to, and adds two to PC to point to the next word in memory. The operations performed during the execution cycle depend on the instruction, and may include reading additional instruction words and updating PC accordingly. The use of a counter for PC is no accident. As observed by von Neumann[3],

> It is clear that one must be able to get numbers from any part of the memory at any time. The treatment in the case of orders can, however, be more methodical since one can at least partially arrange the control instructions in a linear sequence. Consequently the control will be so constructed that it will normally proceed from place n in the memory to place $(n + 1)$ for its next instruction.

[3]"Preliminary Discussion of the Logical Design of an Electronic Computing Instrument," in *Computer Structures: Readings and Examples*, by C. G. Bell and A. Newell (McGraw-Hill, 1971).

von Neumann
machine

In a von Neumann machine, the same memory contains both instructions and data, but it is impossible to distinguish between the two just by looking at the contents of memory. For example, in the 68000's memory, the word $4E75_{16}$ may represent either the opcode RTS or the integer $20,085_{10}$. Only the processor distinguishes between the two. During the fetch cycle, the processor interprets memory words as instructions. During the execution cycle, it interprets them as data. There are no other checks. If an error causes PC to point into a data area, the processor will blindly forge ahead, trying to interpret the data as a sequence of instructions. Likewise, if a program stores data words into the memory locations occupied by its own instructions, it will destroy itself.

5.5   INSTRUCTION SET

In this chapter, we introduce a subset of the 68000 instruction set; the full instruction set is covered in Chapter 8. Instructions in the subset are one to four words long.

opcode word
opcode
effective-address
(EA) field
operand

The first word of each instruction is called the *opcode word*. It contains an operation code (*opcode*) and zero, one, or two *effective-address (EA) fields*. The opcode uniquely specifies the operation to be performed, while each EA field specifies the register or memory location that contains an *operand* to be manipulated by the instruction.

If an operand is a variable stored in memory, then an additional instruction word may contain the address of the memory location. If the operand is an "immediate" constant, then one or two additional instruction words may contain the constant value.

As shown in Figure 5–5, the instructions in this chapter use six different formats for the opcode word, as required by different operations and operand types. There are many other formats used by the full 68000 instruction set.

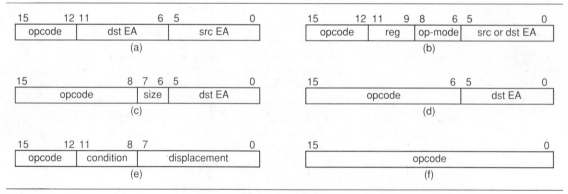

FIGURE 5–5   Format of the opcode word of typical 68000 instructions: (a) MOVE; (b) other double-operand; (c) single-operand; (d) JMP and JSR; (e) branch; (f) inherent addressing.

To understand why a particular set of formats is used in a given processor architecture, one must understand the goals, optimizations, and compromises of the architects, which is beyond the scope of this chapter. When you look at the formats in Figure 5–5, you'll often ask, "Why did they do *that*?" This question is easier to answer in view of the full 68000 instruction set, because there are many more instructions to be encoded, but even the full set of 68000 instructions is encoded somewhat irregularly (some would say cleverly).

Most of the 68000's data-manipulation instructions can operate on bytes, words, or longwords. The operand size is encoded as part of the opcode in MOVE instructions [Figure 5–5(a)], and in the size or op-mode field in other instructions [Figure 5–5(b,c)].

Instructions that reference memory contain a 6-bit EA field that specifies the location of the operand; MOVE contains two such fields. In all of these instructions, the EA field can specify one of several "addressing modes" as discussed shortly. Some addressing modes require an additional word or two of addressing information to be appended to the instruction, thus giving rise to two- to four-word instructions.

Table 5–3 lists a subset of the 68000's instruction set; the full instruction set is described in Chapter 8. There are several different formats for the opcode word, as was shown in Figure 5–5. Associated with each opcode word is an alphabetic *mnemonic* that we can use to name and recognize the instruction conveniently.

mnemonic

5.6 OPERANDS AND OPERATIONS

The first part of Table 5–3 contains double-operand instructions. Most instructions have three variations, indicated by ".B," ".W," and ".L" suffixes, for operating on byte, word, and longword data.

Each double-operand instruction has a "source" operand and a "destination" operand. The 68000 restricts the addressing modes that can be used to specify operands depending on both the type of the operand (source or destination) and the instruction (e.g., MOVE vs MOVEA). In Table 5–3, the most general source operand is denoted by src and may use any addressing mode. An "addressable" source operand (in Motorola parlance) is denoted by asrc and is forbidden to use certain addressing modes. Likewise, the most general destination operand dst is forbidden to use certain addressing modes, and a destination operand that may be only an address register or a data register is explicitly indicated (areg or dreg, respectively).

src
asrc

dst
areg
dreg
MOVE

Returning to the operations themselves, the MOVE instructions simply copy data from one place to another—the operand specified by the src field is copied to the place specified by the dst field, without disturbing the src data. Since src and dst may use different addressing modes to specify registers or memory locations, a MOVE instruction can copy from register to register, register to memory, memory to register, or memory to memory. The MOVEs are the only

TABLE 5–3   A subset of the instruction set of the 68000.

Mnemonic	Operands	Format	Opcode Word	XNZVC	Description
MOVE.B	asrc,adst	a	0001ddddddssssss	–**00	Copy asrc to adst (byte)
MOVE.W	asrc,adst	a	0011ddddddssssss	–**00	Copy asrc to adst (word)
MOVE.L	asrc,adst	a	0010ddddddssssss	–**00	Copy asrc to adst (long)
MOVEA.W	asrc,An	a	0011rrr001ssssss	–––––	Copy asrc to An (word)
MOVEA.L	asrc,An	a	0010rrr001ssssss	–––––	Copy asrc to An (long)
LEA.L	csrc,An	b	0100aaa111ssssss	–––––	Load An with address of csrc
ADD.B	asrc,Dn	b	1101rrr000ssssss	*****	Add asrc to Dn (byte)
ADD.W	asrc,Dn	b	1101rrr001ssssss	*****	Add asrc to Dn (word)
ADD.L	asrc,Dn	b	1101rrr010ssssss	*****	Add asrc to Dn (long)
ADDA.W	asrc,An	b	1101rrr011ssssss	–––––	Add asrc to An (word)
ADDA.L	asrc,An	b	1101rrr111ssssss	–––––	Add asrc to An (long)
AND.B	dsrc,Dn	b	1100rrr000ssssss	–**00	AND dsrc to Dn (byte)
AND.W	dsrc,Dn	b	1100rrr001ssssss	–**00	AND dsrc to Dn (word)
AND.L	dsrc,Dn	b	1100rrr010ssssss	–**00	AND dsrc to Dn (long)
CMP.B	asrc,Dn	b	1011rrr000ssssss	–****	Set CCR using Dn – asrc (byte)
CMP.W	asrc,Dn	b	1011rrr001ssssss	–****	Set CCR using Dn – asrc (word)
CMP.L	asrc,Dn	b	1011rrr010ssssss	–****	Set CCR using Dn – asrc (long)
CMPA.W	asrc,An	b	1011rrr011ssssss	–****	Set CCR using An – asrc (word)
CMPA.L	asrc,An	b	1011rrr111ssssss	–****	Set CCR using An – asrc (long)
CLR.B	ddst	c	0100001000dddddd	–0100	Set ddst to 0 (byte)
CLR.W	ddst	c	0100001001dddddd	–0100	Set ddst to 0 (word)
CLR.L	ddst	c	0100001010dddddd	–0100	Set ddst to 0 (long)
NOT.B	ddst	c	0100011000dddddd	–**00	Complement bits of ddst (byte)
NOT.W	ddst	c	0100011001dddddd	–**00	Complement bits of ddst (word)
NOT.L	ddst	c	0100011010dddddd	–**00	Complement the bits of ddst (long)
BNE	offset	e	01100110oooooooo	–––––	Branch if result nonzero (Z = 0)
BEQ	offset	e	01100111oooooooo	–––––	Branch if result zero (Z = 1)
JMP	cdst	d	0100111011dddddd	–––––	Jump to cdst address
JSR	cdst	d	0100111010dddddd	–––––	Jump to subroutine at cdst address
RTS		f	0100111001110101	–––––	Return from subroutine

Notes: asrc = any source operand, cannot be an address register in byte instructions.

    adst = any destination operand, cannot use immediate or relative addressing.

    csrc, cdst = control source or destination operand, cannot use register, auto-increment, auto-decrement, or immediate addressing modes.

    dsrc = data source operand, cannot be an address register.

    ddst = data destination operand, cannot use address register direct, immediate, or relative addressing.

    Dn = one of the data registers, D0–D7. An = one of the address registers, A0–A7.

    offset = 8-bit signed integer added to PC if branch is taken.

    s = bit in src field; d = bit in dst field; r = bit in reg (An or Dn) field; o = bit in offset field.

    Condition Code Bits:

        N—most significant bit of result was 1.

        Z—result was zero.

        V—operation caused two's-complement overflow.

        C—addition or subtraction caused a carry or borrow from most significant bit, or shift caused a 1 bit to "fall off" the end.

        X—when affected, same as C (but not always affected).

    Effects of instructions on condition code bits:

        –: not affected;

        1: always set to 1;

        0: always cleared to 0;

        *: set according to operation result as detailed above.

instructions in the 68000 that provide all these addressing options; other instructions do not provide memory-to-memory operation (except the specialized `CMPM`) or register-to-memory operation (except arithmetic on data registers).

The `MOVE` instructions affect four of the condition code bits as a side effect. The condition code bits, as discussed in detail in Chapter 8, store information about the results of most operations. For example, when affected the *zero bit (Z)* is set to 1 if the instruction produces a zero result (all bits 0), and to 0 if the instruction produces a nonzero result. An instruction that affects the Z bit can be followed by a *conditional branch instruction* to perform one of two possible actions depending on the value of Z, as we'll show at the end of this section.

`MOVEA` is a special version of the `MOVE` instruction used only when the `dst` operand is an address register. Its encoding is consistent with that of `MOVE`, and it differs only in that it does not affect the condition codes; this reflects the 68000 designers' philosophy that the "arithmetic" value of an address should have no significance, and that address registers should contain only addresses. In keeping with this philosophy, note also that instructions with single-byte operands cannot have an address register as a `src` or `dst` operand, since in the 68000 addresses are never as short as one byte.

The `LEA` instruction is sort of a half-hearted `MOVE`. Rather than actually read its operand, `LEA` merely computes the effective address of the operand and deposits it in an address register for later use. This instruction is a result of the 68000 designers' philosophy that, while 32-bit addresses are "expensive" (it would waste a lot of program memory to carry one or two addresses in every instruction), address *registers* are "cheap" (there are eight of them available). Therefore, if a memory operand is going to be referenced more than once, it makes sense to compute its address only once and keep the address lying around in an address register where it can be quickly and inexpensively used later as needed. We'll address this subject in more detail when we discuss indirect addressing in Section 5.12. But before leaving `LEA`, also notice that in keeping with the 68000 designers' philosophy about the nature of addresses, the `LEA` instruction does not affect the condition bits.

The `ADD` instructions perform a two's-complement addition of a source operand and a data register, and store the result in the data register. The condition codes are affected, so that an `ADD` may be followed by a conditional branch to test the value of the result. The `AND` instructions are similar to the `ADD`s, except that they perform a bit-by-bit logical AND of their operands.

The `ADDA` instructions add to an address register; there is no byte version of this instruction since addresses are never only 8 bits wide. An `ADDA` instruction is typically used to compute the address of a particular item in a complex data structure. Like other instructions with address-register destinations, `ADDA` does not affect the condition bits.

The `CMP` and `CMPA` instructions subtract a `src` operand from a register, and set the condition codes according to the result, without affecting either operand. Thus, `CMP` and `CMPA` may be used to compare two operands for equality or other relationships, without disturbing the current values of the operands.

zero bit (Z)

conditional branch instruction

MOVEA

LEA

ADD

AND

ADDA

CMP
CMPA

CLR
NOT

The second part of Table 5–3 contains instructions that have just one destination operand. The CLR instructions set their operand to 0, obviously useful for initializing variables. The NOT instructions complement each bit of their operand, useful in conjunction with AND instructions for isolating bits in a single byte or word where different bits or fields contain unrelated data. Note that these instructions do not work on address registers, once again because of the philosophy that addresses have no arithmetic or bitwise significance.

BNE
BEQ

The third part of Table 5–3 contains "program control" instructions that can affect the normally sequential fetching and execution of instructions. The BNE and BEQ instructions add an offset value to the PC if the Z bit is 0 or 1, respectively. Otherwise, execution continues with the next instruction. Thus, these instructions are comparable to a primitive Pascal "IF" statement:

```
          68000                                    Pascal

     MOVE.W XYZ,D0 (affects Z)              IF XYZ = 0
        BEQ    L1234   (tests Z)              THEN GOTO 1234;
        ...                                        ...
L1234   ...                                  1234: ...
```

The 68000 processor interprets the offset field of a branch instruction as a signed, two's-complement integer in the range -128 to $+127$. Since instructions must start on even addresses (word boundaries), the range is actually restricted to -128 to $+126$. At the time that the processor tests the branch condition, the PC is already pointing to the next instruction, and so the branch offset is limited to -128 to $+126$ bytes from the next instruction.

According to this convention, if the branch offset is 0, the next instruction should be executed whether the condition is true or false. However, since such an instruction performs no useful work and would therefore never be used, the 68000's designers used the offset=0 case to specify another instruction type, as explained in Section 8.6. Also, since instructions are aligned on word boundaries, odd offsets such as -127 are not used; the MC68020 uses this to encode yet another instruction type, as explained in Section 8.7. In the meantime, we won't use branch offsets of 0 or -127.

JMP

The JMP instruction in the 68000 is equivalent to the GOTO instruction in Pascal and most other high-level languages. It unconditionally transfers control to an instruction starting at the destination address. It does this by simply replacing the current value of the PC with the destination address.

JSR
RTS

The JSR and RTS instructions are used to call and return from subroutines, as we'll discuss in detail in Section 5.13.

5.7 ADDRESSING MODES

In the 68000, an operand is specified by a 6-bit source or destination EA field in the instruction, consisting of a 3-bit addressing mode designator and a 3-bit register number, as shown in Figure 5–6. In conjunction with the reg field, the eight mode combinations are used as follows:

```
11   9 8    6              5    3 2    0
   | reg | mode |              | mode | reg |
        (a)                        (b)
```

FIGURE 5–6   Operand effective-address (EA) fields in the 68000: (a) dst operand of MOVE instructions; (b) all other EA fields.

0 reg specifies a data register (D0–D7) that contains the operand.

1 reg specifies an address register (A0–A7) that contains the operand.

2–6 reg specifies an address register that is used, possibly in combination with other values, to determine the effective address of an operand in memory.

7 reg does not specify a register at all; instead, the three reg bits specify one of five addressing modes that do not use a general register; three combinations are left over for future expansion.

A full treatment of 68000 addressing modes is provided in Chapter 7, but for the moment we shall discuss the seven most important ones, which are summarized in Table 5–4.

register-direct addressing   In *register-direct addressing*, the operand is contained in one of the data registers D0–D7 or in one of the address registers A0–A7. As suggested by the dotted lines in Figure 5–4, word operations on the data registers use the low-

TABLE 5–4   Some addressing modes of the 68000.

Name	mode	reg	Notation	Operand	Extra Words
Data-register direct	0	0–7	Dn	Dn	0
Address-register direct	1	0–7	An	An	0
Immediate	7	4	#data	data	1 or 2
Absolute short	7	0	addr	MEM[addr]	1
Address-register indirect	2	0–7	(An)	MEM[An]	0
Based	5	0–7	disp16(An)	MEM[An+disp16]	1
Relative	7	2	raddr16(PC)	MEM[(raddr16-PLC)+PC]	1

Notes: Dn denotes a data register: D0–D7.
 An denotes an address register: A0–A7 or SP (same as A7).
 data is an 8- or 16-bit value as appropriate for the size of the operation.
 addr is the 16-bit absolute memory address of the operand.
 disp16 is a 16-bit value that is sign extended to 32 bits before being combined with the address register.
 raddr16 is a relative address within 32768 bytes of the instruction. The extension word contains a 16-bit displacement (raddr16-PLC, where PLC is the address of the extension word) that is sign extended to 32 bits and added to the PC to obtain the effective address of the operand when the instruction is executed.
 MEM[x] is the 8-, 16-, or 32-bit value beginning at memory address x, as appropriate for the size of the operation.

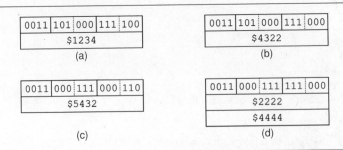

FIGURE 5–7 Encodings of various machine instructions: (a) MOVE.W #$1234,D5; (b) MOVE.W $4322,D5; (c) MOVE.W D6,$5432; (d) MOVE.W $2222,$4444.

order 16 bits, while byte operations use only the 8 low-order bits; the high-order bits in both cases are unaffected.

sign extension

Word operations on the address registers also use the low-order 16 bits, but a write operation into an address register extends the most significant bit of the low-order word into the high-order word. This is consistent with the short-addressing model of the 68000 memory in Figure 5–1(c), in which a 16-bit number can specify a memory address in the highest or lowest 32-Kbyte portion of a 4-gigabyte address space.

Byte operations are not allowed on address registers, since an "address" should normally be at least a 16-bit quantity. The full 68000 instruction set provides long-word operations on address registers, in order to handle addresses up to 32 bits long.

Register-direct addressing is not allowed with the 68000's JMP and JSR instructions, since it doesn't make sense to jump to a register.

immediate addressing

In *immediate addressing*, a 1- or 2-byte operand is contained in the second word of the instruction; with 1-byte operands, the high-order byte of the second word is unused. Thus, to place the value 1234_{16} in register D5, we could use the instruction, MOVE.W #$1234,D5. By convention, the notation "#" denotes an immediate operand, while the dollar sign ($) denotes a hexadecimal value. The machine language instruction occupies two words as shown in Figure 5–7(a).

notation
#
$

With immediate addressing, the operand is *constant* value. Immediate mode cannot be used for a "destination" operand, since it would require the instruction to modify itself. Thus, MOVE.W D5,#$1234 is not allowed.

absolute short addressing

In *absolute short addressing*, the instruction contains a 16-bit absolute memory address for the operand. The most significant bit of this 16-bit address is extended to produce a 32-bit address in the top or bottom 32 Kbytes of the address space, consistent with Figure 5–1(c). Thus, the instruction MOVE.W $4322,D5 [Figure 5–7(b)] reads the 16-bit value currently stored at memory location $4322 and copies (*loads*) it into register D5; the contents of memory are not disturbed. By convention, the absence of the modifier "#"

notation

denotes an absolute operand.

In the other direction, MOVE.W D6,$5432 [Figure 5-7(c)] *stores* the value of D6 into memory location $5432, without disturbing D6. Thus, an operand with absolute addressing is typically a *variable*, since the program may store different values into the specified memory location at different times.

Since MOVE instructions have two EA fields, they can perform memory-to-memory moves. For example, MOVE.W $2222,$4444 [Figure 5-7(d)] is a three-word long instruction that copies the contents of memory word $2222 to memory word $4444. Immediate-to-memory moves are also possible; for example, MOVE.W #$1234,$4444 loads memory word $4444 with the value $1234.

address-register indirect addressing

In *address-register indirect addressing*, the specified address register (An) contains the address of the operand. In this mode, not only is the operand a variable, but so is its address. Each time that the instruction is executed, the address register may "point to" a different memory location. This mode is useful for dealing with arrays, lists, and other data structures; we'll give an example in Section 5.12.

based addressing base address

In *based addressing*, the specified address register (An) contains a *base address* that is "near" the desired operand. The instruction contains a 16-bit, signed displacement value, disp16, which is added to the base address to obtain the effective address of the operand. Note that this sum is *not* written back into the address register, which remains unchanged.

Quite often, the base address is the starting address of a block of memory that has been reserved to store data. The displacement value disp16 specifies the relative position of a particular datum in that block.

While absolute addressing requires a particular datum to be stored at the same absolute address every time the program is executed, based addressing allows addresses to be changed. For example, before giving control to a user's program, an operating system could reserve a block of memory for the user program to store variables, and pass its base address to the user program in an address register, say A5. The user program would refer to all variables using based addressing with fixed displacements (disp16 values) from the base address contained in A5. This technique is used extensively in programs written for the Macintosh computer, as you'll soon see in "Mac Notes."

relative addressing

relative displacement

Relative addressing is used to access constant data that is stored in the same block of memory as the program instructions themselves. Instead of giving the absolute address of the operand, relative addressing specifies a *relative displacement*—the difference between the instruction address and the operand address. When the program runs, the instruction address (contained in the PC) and the relative displacement (contained in the extension word) are added to form the effective address of the operand. Instructions and operands that use relative addressing are *position independent*—the difference between instruction and the operand addresses remains constant even if the program and its constant data are picked up and moved to a different block of memory. Like based addressing, relative addressing is used extensively in position-independent programs written for the Macintosh and other computers, as we'll discuss in Section 7.4.

position independent

TABLE 5–5   Memory contents for a sequence of instructions and data.

Machine Language		Assembly Language			
Address (hex)	Contents (hex)	Label (sym)	Opcode (mnem)	Operand (sym)	Comments
00000000		*			Program to multiply MCND by MPY.
00000000			ORG	$1000	
00001000		*			
00001000	4240	MULT	CLR.W	D0	D0 will accumulate product.
00001002	3238		MOVE.W	MPY,D1	D1 holds loop count (multiplier).
00001004	101A				
00001006	670A		BEQ	DONE	Done if count is down to zero.
00001008	D078	LOOP	ADD.W	MCND,D0	Else add MCND to product
0000100A	101C				
0000100C	D27C		ADD.W	#-1,D1	and do loop MPY (D1) times.
0000100E	FFFF				
00001010	66F6		BNE	LOOP	
00001012	31C0	DONE	MOVE.W	D0,PROD	Save product.
00001014	1018				
00001016	4EF8		JMP	$8008	Return to monitor at $8008.
00001018	8008				
00001018	????	PROD	DS.W	1	Storage for PROD.
0000108A	007B	MPY	DC.W	123	Multiplier value.
0000108C	01C8	MCND	DC.W	456	Multiplicand value.
0000108E			END	MULT	

Symbol Table

DONE	00001012	LOOP	00001008	MCND	0000108C	MPY	0000108A
MULT	00001000	PROD	00001018				

Notes: hex = hexadecimal; sym = symbolic; mnem = mnemonic.

5.8 A MACHINE LANGUAGE PROGRAM

machine language program

Table 5–5 shows the values stored in memory for a sequence of instructions and data that form a program for multiplying 123 by 456. A list of machine instructions stored in memory, as defined by the two left-hand columns of the table, is called a *machine language program*. These two columns completely specify the operations to be performed by the computer. We shall explain the operation of the program shortly.

5.9 ASSEMBLY LANGUAGE

Obviously, the two left-hand columns of Table 5–5 don't mean much to a human reader. Fortunately for us, the Label, Opcode, and Operand columns describe the machine language program in symbolic form, using mnemonics for opcodes and alphanumeric labels for addresses and data values. The Comments column

*assembly
language
program
assembler*

pseudo-operations

ORG

DS.W

DC.W

END

*

$

*assembly time
run time*

gives an English explanation of what the program does. Together these four columns form an *assembly language program* that can be translated into machine language by a program called an *assembler*. The assembler produces, among other things, a listing of the equivalent machine language program as in the two left-hand columns of the table.

In addition to mnemonics for machine instructions, the assembler also recognizes *pseudo-operations* that control how the assembly language program is assembled. The four pseudo-operations used in Table 5–5 are described below:

- ORG (origin). The operand is the address at which the next instruction or datum is to be deposited when the program is loaded into memory. Subsequent instructions and data are deposited in successive memory addresses.

- DS.W (define storage—word). The operand is a number of memory words to be skipped without storing any instructions or data, thereby reserving space to be used by variables in a program.

- DC.W (define constant—word). The specified word value is stored into memory when the program is first loaded into memory, thereby establishing a constant value that may be accessed when the program is run.

- END (end assembly). This pseudo-operation denotes the end of the text to be assembled. Its operand, if present, is the address of the first executable instruction of the program.

The assembler also allows an entire line to be used as a comment:

- * (comment lines). Any line beginning with an asterisk is completely ignored by the assembler.

As discussed in Chapter 6, different assemblers for a particular processor may have different pseudo-operations and may also use different formats to specify various addressing modes and instructions. The examples that we give in the main text of this book are based on Motorola's assemblers for the 68000.

In all of the assembly language statements, numeric arguments are assumed to be given in decimal notation unless they are preceded by a dollar sign ($) for hexadecimal. When an identifier appears in the Label field, it is assigned the value of the Address field. For example, the values of LOOP and MCND are $1008 and $2004, respectively. When an identifier appears in the Operand field, the assembler substitutes the value that has been assigned to it. Therefore, the instruction ADD.W MCND,D0 is equivalent to ADD.W $2004,D0.

All of the above operations occur at *assembly time*; an identifier such as MCND refers to the memory address of a variable. At *run time*, when the program is executed, values stored in memory will be manipulated. Strictly speaking, we should refer to such a value as MEM[MCND]. However, when we discuss run-time operations, it is customary to use the identifier to refer to the value in memory itself. As a result, the comment Else add MCND to product really means Else D0 := D0 + MEM[MCND].

Mac Note

The programming environment and assembler pseudo-operations for the Macintosh are different in some respects from what we describe in the main text. *Mac Notes* will alert you to the most important differences.

Memory allocation in a typical Macintosh computer is shown in the figure to the right. In the Macintosh environment, a program has two parts, a code module and a data module, stored in separate areas of memory:

code module

- The *code module* contains the program's instructions and data constants. The Macintosh operating system loads the code module into an area of memory called the *application heap*.

application heap

data module

- The *data module* contains the program's variables. Just before the Macintosh operating system gives control to a program, it allocates space for its data module in an area of memory called the *application global space*.

application global space

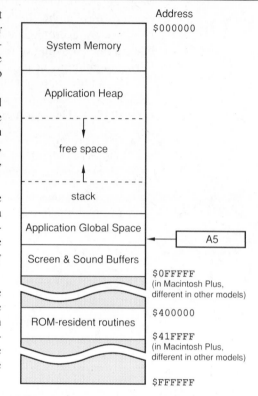

The application heap starts at a different absolute memory address in different Macintosh models, and may start at different locations even in the same Macintosh, depending on version of the operating system and what other resources (fonts, desk accessories, etc.) are installed. As a result, a Macintosh programmer cannot determine starting address of a program's code or data at the time the program is written, and so

ORG
relocation

the ORG pseudo-operation is not used. Instead, a program's code module is assembled as if it started at memory address zero, and the Macintosh operating system *relocates* it to the proper address when it is loaded.

Similarly, the address of a program's data module in the application global space is unknown when a Macintosh program is written. Before transferring control to a program,

A5

the operating system puts a pointer to this area in register A5. Thus, instead of using absolute addressing, a Macintosh program accesses its variables using based addressing with displacements relative to the contents of A5.

DS.W

As a result, the DS.W pseudo-operation for allocating variables is special in Macintosh assemblers. In standard 68000 assemblers, DS.W allocates variables "in-line" with instructions; for example, the PROD variable in Table 5–5 occupies the memory word immediately following the JMP instruction that preceded it. Macintosh assemblers keep track of variables separately from code; DS.W normally allocates variable words in the data module, and such variables are accessed in the application global space using based addressing with register A5.

The next Mac Note shows the results of these differences in the Macintosh version of our example program.

Mac Note

A few changes are needed to run our simple multiplication program in the Macintosh environment, as shown below. This listing is similar to what might be produced by the assembler in the Macintosh 68000 Development System (MDS) or the Macintosh Programmer's Workshop (MPW).

```
ADDR    CONTENTS    LABEL OPCODE  OPERAND      COMMENTS

0000                      INCLUDE MACLIB.ASM   ;Include useful definitions.
0000                                           ;Multiply MCND by MPY.
0000    4240        MULT  CLR.W   D0           ;D0 will accumulate product.
0002    323A 0014         MOVE.W  MPY,D1       ;D1 holds multiplier.
0006    670A              BEQ     DONE         ;Done if count reaches zero.
0008    D07A 0010   LOOP  ADD.W   MCND,D0      ;Else add MCND to product
000C    D27C FFFF         ADD.W   #-1,D1       ;  and loop MPY (D1) times.
0010    66F6              BNE     LOOP
0012    3B40 FEFE   DONE  MOVE.W  D0,PROD(A5)  ;Save product.
0016    A9F4              _ExitToShell         ;Return to operating system.
FEFE(D)            PROD  DS.W    1            ;Storage for PROD.
0018    007B        MPY   DC.W    123          ;Multiplier value.
001A    01C8        MCND  DC.W    456          ;Multiplicand value.
001C                      END
```

The reasons for these changes are discussed in the next two Mac Notes.

---

assembly time vs run time

The difference between assembly-time and run-time operations is probably the greatest single source of confusion to novice assembly language programmers, and so we'll explain it again. The assembler is a system program, a software tool, that translates lines of text into a sequence of instruction and data bytes that can be stored in the computer's memory; the assembler "goes away" before the machine language program that it produced is executed. As far as the assembler is concerned, an identifier such as PROD stands for the address that was assigned to it ($1018); the assembler is unconcerned with what may happen to the contents of the memory address $1018 when the program is run. Using an identifier frees the programmer from keeping track of the exact address at which an instruction or datum is located. Even though the identifier refers to an address, the programmer is usually more interested in the *contents* of the memory address at run time. Therefore the programmer informally uses the *name* of the address (PROD) to refer to its contents (MEM[$1018]), just to save typing.

Many instructions in the 68000 are more than one word long. It is therefore convenient to compress the program listing, showing all words associated with the same instruction on one line as in Table 5–6.

5.10 OPERATION OF A SIMPLE PROGRAM

We are now ready to explain the program in Table 5–6. It multiplies MCND by MPY by initializing the product to 0 and then adding MCND to it MPY times.

Notice that the values of the multiplier and multiplicand are "passed" to the program in fixed memory locations, $101A and $101C, that are initialized

TABLE 5–6 Compressed program listing.

Machine Language		Assembly Language			
Address (hex)	Contents (hex)	Label (sym)	Opcode (mnem)	Operand (sym)	Comments
00000000		*			Program to multiply MCND by MPY.
00000000			ORG	$1000	
00001000		*			
00001000	4240	MULT	CLR.W	D0	D0 will accumulate product.
00001002	3238 101C		MOVE.W	MPY,D1	D1 holds loop count (multiplier).
00001006	670A		BEQ	DONE	Done if count is down to zero.
00001008	D078 101C	LOOP	ADD.W	MCND,D0	Else add MCND to product
0000100C	D27C FFFF		ADD.W	#-1,D1	and do loop MPY (D1) times.
00001010	66F6		BNE	LOOP	
00001012	31C0 1018	DONE	MOVE.W	D0,PROD	Save product.
00001016	4EF8 8008		JMP	$8008	Return to monitor at $8008.
00001018	????	PROD	DS.W	1	Storage for PROD.
0000101A	007B	MPY	DC.W	123	Multiplier value.
0000101C	01C8	MCND	DC.W	456	Multiplicand value.
0000101E			END	MULT	

to 123 and 456 when the program is loaded. If, after loading the program, we start the program at location $1000, it will indeed compute the product of 123 and 456. Alternatively, if after loading the program we place different numbers in locations $101A and $101C, then the program will compute the product of the new numbers. In any case, the program "returns" its result by placing the result in memory location $1018, which may be examined by whoever ran the program in the first place.

Mac Note

There is one major difference in statement syntax between Macintosh assemblers and Motorola assemblers:

- Macintosh assemblers use semicolons for comments. The Comments field of a line begins with a semicolon, whether or not that line contains Label, Opcode, and Operand fields. A full-line comment also begins with a semicolon.

Another difference is a convenient feature found in many assemblers and high-level-language compilers:

- The INCLUDE pseudo-operation causes the assembler to read a designated text file and incorporate its lines as if they were included at this point in the current text file. In our example program, the MACLIB.ASM file does not generate any code, but merely contains definitions that allow a user program to access the operating system's global variables, data structures, and utility routines.

Other differences are more than syntactic; they occur because of the Macintosh's particular run-time environment, as discussed in our next Mac Note.

Mac Note

Macintosh and Motorola assemblers differ in the use of `DS.W`:

- In a Macintosh assembler, `DS.W` allocates variable storage in the data module, which is stored in a different area of memory than the code module.

In our example Macintosh program, the line `PROD DS.W 1` defines the variable `PROD` to be stored at an address $-\$102$ bytes from the base address of the application global space. (Why $-\$102$? We'll find out in the next Mac Note.) In the program listing, `$FEFE` is the two's-complement representation of $-\$102$, and the suffix (D) in the Address column reminds us that this value is an offset to data in the application global space, not an address in the instruction sequence (code module).

Related to the use of `DS.W`, the next important difference is in the way that instructions access variables:

- Variables are accessed using based addressing with a displacement from A5.

In our example program, the `MOVE.W D0,PROD(A5)` instruction that saves D0 into `PROD` explicitly specifies based addressing. At run time the processor adds the displacement `$FEFE` to the operating-system-supplied value in A5 to form `PROD`'s effective address.

Yet another difference is in the way that constants are accessed:

- Constants defined by the `DC.W` pseudo-operation are stored in the code module and are accessed by relative addressing.

The `DC.W` pseudo-operation in a Macintosh assembler defines constants that are stored in-line with the program's instructions, just as in Motorola's assemblers. The instructions that access these constants appear to be the same in both cases (e.g., `MOVE.W MPY,D1`). However, if you compare the Contents fields in the two listings you'll see that the assembled instructions are different. The Motorola assembler generates an instruction that uses absolute addressing, and the second word of the instruction contains an absolute address. Macintosh assemblers generate an instruction that uses relative addressing, and the second word of the instruction contains a relative displacement. Absolute addressing is almost never used in the Macintosh.

Suppose that the Macintosh program's code module is loaded into memory starting at address `$4800`. Then the instruction `MOVE.W MPY,D1` is stored at addresses `$4802` and `$4804` and `MPY` is stored at address `$4818`. When the instruction is executed, the processor adds the current value of the PC (`$4804`) to the displacement (`$0014`) to form the effective address of `MPY` (`$4818`). The code could be located anywhere in memory, and the correct address of `MPY` would still be calculated when the program runs.

- Macintosh programs are normally written to be position independent.

Our example Macintosh program is assembled as if its code begins at memory address 0. However, because it uses based addressing for variables and relative addressing for branches and constants, it is position independent—the program can be loaded anywhere in memory, without change, and it will still run correctly. This is not true for the original example, which *must* be loaded at address `$1000` to run properly. We'll have a lot more to say about position-independent code in Section 7.4.

Finally, notice that the Macintosh program returns control to the operating system using the statement `_ExitToShell`. This is not a machine instruction, but rather a "macro instruction" which is defined in `MACLIB.ASM`. The macro expands to a "trap" instruction with opcode word `$A9F4`, which returns control to the Macintosh operating system as explained in Section 11.3.

TABLE 5–7   Register and memory contents after executing instructions in multiplication program.

Step	Instruction	PC	D0	D1	Z	MEM[1018] (PROD)
0	. . .	1000	????	????	?	????
1	CLR.W D0	1002	0000	????	1	????
2	MOVE.W MPY,D1	1006	0000	007B	0	????
3	BEQ DONE	1008	0000	007B	0	????
4	ADD.W MCND,D0	100C	01C8	007B	0	????
5	ADD.W #-1,D1	1010	01C8	007A	0	????
6	BNE LOOP	1008	01C8	007A	0	????
7	ADD.W MCND,D0	100C	0390	007A	0	????
8	ADD.W #-1,D1	1010	0390	0079	0	????
9	BNE LOOP	1008	0390	0079	0	????
10	ADD.W MCND,D0	100C	0558	0079	0	????
11	ADD.W #-1,D1	1010	0558	0078	0	????
12	BNE LOOP	1008	0558	0078	0	????
	. . .					
367	ADD.W MCND,D0	100C	D950	0002	0	????
368	ADD.W #-1,D1	1010	D950	0001	0	????
369	BNE LOOP	1008	D950	0001	0	????
370	ADD.W MCND,D0	100C	DB18	0001	0	????
371	ADD.W #-1,D1	1010	DB18	0000	1	????
372	BNE LOOP	1008	DB18	0000	1	????
373	MOVE.W D0,PROD	1016	DB18	0000	0	DB18
374	JMP $8008	8008	DB18	0000	0	DB18

The program uses registers to accumulate the product (in D0) and to keep track of the multiplier count (in D1), because registers can be accessed faster than main memory in most computers, and hence the program will run faster. In fact, we could optimize the program to run even faster by placing MCND into a register (say D2) before entering the multiplication loop.

The program's execution is traced by Table 5–7, which shows the values of relevant registers and memory *after* each instruction is executed. Only the low-order words of PC, D0, and D1 are shown; the high-order words are not affected by this program. During its execution, the program executes 374 instructions, including three instructions in a loop that is executed 123 times.

So, the program begins by setting D0 to zero and copying MPY into D1. The MOVE instructions set the condition bits in CCR according to the value stored. In particular, the Z bit is set to 1 if a zero value (0000_{16}) was stored, or else Z is cleared to 0. Therefore, if MPY is zero, the Z bit is 1 when the BEQ DONE instruction is first reached, and the branch will be taken, leaving zero in D0. The purpose of this instruction is to exit the program with a product of 0 if the multiplier happens to be zero. Notice that the branch instruction gives a *relative offset* of $0A, so that either the next instruction (at address $1008) or the instruction at the branch offset (address $1008+$0A = $1012) is executed.

If the BEQ branch is not taken, then the two ADD instructions add MCND to the product in D0 and subtract 1 from the loop count in D1. Like a MOVE instruction, an ADD instruction sets Z to 1 if its result is zero. Thus, if D1 has *not* been reduced to zero, the BNE instruction will branch back to address $1008. (The 8-bit signed offset $F6, interpreted in two's-complement, equals -$0A; hence the branch is to address $1012-$0A = $1008.)

Eventually, after executing the loop 123 times, the program reaches the MOVE instruction at address $1012, which saves the accumulated product in memory. Finally, the program unconditionally jumps to address $8008, where we assume there exists a program that prints out or gives the user some way to examine the computation's result stored at location $1018.

5.11 PASCAL SIMULATION OF INSTRUCTION EXECUTION

S68000

Before giving more examples in the 68000 instruction set, we present a Pascal simulation that precisely defines the operation of each instruction covered in this chapter (the *S68000* subset of the 68000 instruction set). Table 5–8 contains the Execute procedure that goes with the simulation given in Table 5–2 on page 138.

The statement part of the procedure is a CASE statement, one case for each valid opcode. The Decode(IR) function is left as an exercise for the reader. This function, like the 68000 processor itself, examines all 16 bits of an opcode word to determine its validity and which case (instruction) to execute. Within each case, procedures such as SourceEA and DestEA are used to decode an addressing mode and compute an operand's effective address, which is deposited in EAR.

Table 5–8 also contains many auxiliary procedures and functions that are needed to make Execute work in the Pascal environment. Many of these routines contain arithmetic expressions, recursive function calls, and other constructs that do not occur as real operations in the hardware implementation of the 68000. Rather, they are simply a way of precisely defining and performing the necessary operations within the admittedly limited capabilities of the standard Pascal language. However, for pedagogical purposes, we have taken the liberty of using hexadecimal constants such as $FFFF that are not allowed in standard Pascal; you can easily translate them into decimal if you're so inclined.

Notice that the fetch cycle in Table 5–2 leaves the PC pointing to the word after the opcode word, regardless of whether this next word is the next instruction or part of the current instruction. The execution cycle in Table 5–8 reads one to three additional words and bumps PC past them only for instructions that require them so that, at the end of the execution cycle, PC always points to the first word of the next instruction.

If you are fluent in Pascal, you should study Table 5–8 to verify that each of the instructions that we've used so far does what you think it does, and also to get a preview of the instructions yet to come. If you're not fluent in Pascal, don't worry; it's not necessary to understand Table 5–8 to understand the 68000.

TABLE 5–8   S68000 instruction execution procedure and auxiliary procedures and functions.

```
PROCEDURE Execute;
TYPE
  bitnum = 0..31;
  EAfield = 0..7;
  EAtype = (src,dst);
VAR
  regEA : boolean; {regEA = true ==> EAR contains a register number.
       regEA = false ==> EAR contains a memory address. }

FUNCTION Power2(i: bitnum): long;
{Recursively compute 2 to the power i}
BEGIN  IF i = 0 THEN Power2 := 1 ELSE Power2 := 2*Power2(i-1)  END;

FUNCTION Bits(from, to: bitnum; lw: long): long;
{Get value of bit field in long word lw.  "from" is leftmost bit,
 "to" is rightmost bit.  Result is right-justified.                }
BEGIN  Bits := (lw DIV Power2(to)) MOD Power2(from-to)  END;

FUNCTION SignExtend(w: word): long; {Sign extend w to 32 bits.}
BEGIN   IF Bits(15,15,w)=0 THEN SignExt := w ELSE SignExt := $FFFF0000 + w  END;

FUNCTION ReadLong: long;  {Read longword whose address is in EAR.}
BEGIN
  IF regEA THEN ReadLong := REG[EAR];
  ELSE ReadLong := ReadMemLong(EAR);  {see Table 5-2}
END;

FUNCTION ReadWord: word;  {Read word whose address is in EAR.}
BEGIN
  IF regEA THEN ReadWord := Bits(15,0,REG[EAR]);
  ELSE ReadWord := ReadMemWord(EAR);  {see Table 5-2}
END;

FUNCTION ReadByte: byte;  {Read byte whose address is in EAR.}
BEGIN
  IF regEA THEN ReadByte := Bits(7,0,REG[EAR])
  ELSE ReadByte := MEM[EAR];
END;

PROCEDURE StoreMemWord(w: word);  {Store w at memory address given by EAR.}
BEGIN
  IF (EAR MOD 2) <> 0 THEN Error  {Word must be at even address.}
  ELSE BEGIN
        MEM[EAR] := Bits(15,8,w); MEM[EAR+1] := Bits(7,0,w);
      END;
END;

PROCEDURE StoreMemLong(lw: long);  {Store lw at memory address given by EAR.}
BEGIN
    StoreMemWord(Bits(31,16,lw),EAR); StoreMemWord(Bits(15,0,lw),EAR+2);
END;
```

TABLE 5–8   (continued)

```
PROCEDURE StoreLong(lw: long);   {Store lw in register or memory given by EAR.}
BEGIN
  IF regEA THEN REG[EAR] := lw ELSE StoreMemLong(lw,EAR);
END;

PROCEDURE StoreWord(w: word);   {Store w in register or memory given by EAR.}
BEGIN
  IF regEA THEN BEGIN
    IF EAR <= 7 THEN {Data register, don't touch high-order word.}
      REG[EAR] := Bits(31,16,REG[EAR])*$10000 + w
    ELSE {Address register, extend sign bit}
      REG[EAR] := SignExtend(w);
  END
  ELSE StoreMemWord(w,EAR);
END;

PROCEDURE StoreByte(b: byte);   {Store byte at addr given by EAR.}
BEGIN
  IF regEA THEN REG[EAR] := Bits(31,8,REG[EAR])*256 + b {Data registers only.}
  ELSE MEM[EAR] := b;
END;

PROCEDURE PushWord(w : word);   {Push a word onto the A7 stack}
  BEGIN REG[A7] := REG[A7] - 2; EAR := REG[A7]; StoreMemWord(w) END;

FUNCTION PopWord : word; {Pop a word from the A7 stack}
  BEGIN EAR := REG[A7]; REG[A7] := REG[A7] + 2; PopWord := ReadWord END;

PROCEDURE GetEA(srcdst: EAtype; mode, ereg: EAfield);
  BEGIN
    CASE mode OF
    0: BEGIN regEA := true; EAR := ereg END;              {Data-reg direct}
    1: BEGIN regEA := true; EAR := ereg + 8 END;          {Addr-reg direct}
    2: BEGIN regEA := false; EAR := REG[ereg+8] END;      {Addr-reg indirect}
    5: BEGIN regEA := false; EAR := PC; PC := PC + 2;     {Based}
            EAR := SignExt(ReadWord) + REG[ereg+8] END;
    3,4,6: Error;                                         {Unimplemented}
    7: CASE ereg OF
       0: BEGIN {Read next word and sign extend}         {Absolute short}
            regEA := false; EAR := PC; PC := PC + 2;
            EAR := SignExt(ReadWord);
          END;
       4: IF srcdst <> src THEN Error                     {Immediate}
          ELSE BEGIN regEA := false; EAR := PC; PC := PC + 2 END;
       5: IF srcdst <> src THEN Error                     {Relative}
          ELSE BEGIN regEA := false; EAR := PC;
                EAR := SignExt(ReadWord) + PC; PC := PC + 2 END;
       1,2,3,6,7: Error;                                  {Unimplemented}
       END; {CASE on ereg}
    END; {CASE on mode}
  END; {GetEA}
```

TABLE 5–8   (continued)

```
PROCEDURE SourceEA;
BEGIN   GetEA(src,Bits(5,3,IR),Bits(2,0,IR));   END;

PROCEDURE DestEA;
BEGIN   GetEA(dst,Bits(5,3,IR),Bits(2,0,IR));   END;

PROCEDURE MDestEA;
BEGIN   GetEA(dst,Bits(8,6,IR),Bits(11,9,IR));   END;

PROCEDURE DregEA;
BEGIN   EAR := Bits(11,9,IR); regEA := true; END;

PROCEDURE AregEA;
BEGIN   EAR := Bits(11,9,IR) + 8; regEA := true; END;

PROCEDURE Branch;   {Add 2's-complement number in IR low byte to PC}
BEGIN
  IF Bits(7,0,IR) = 0 THEN Error
  ELSE IF Bits(7,7,IR) = 0 THEN PC := (PC + Bits(7,0,IR)) MOD maxlong
  ELSE PC := (PC + Bits(7,0,IR) - 256) MOD maxlong;
END;

PROCEDURE SetNZVC(lw: long; len: integer);
{Set NZVC according to len-bit result lw}
BEGIN   N := ord(lw >= Power2(len-1)); Z := ord(lw = 0); V := 0; C := 0   END;

FUNCTION Add(a,b: long; cy: bit; len: integer): long;
{Perform len-bit addition of a, b, and cy}
VAR sum, maxn: long;
{Local functions}
  FUNCTION Pos(x: long): boolean;
    BEGIN   Pos := (x <  maxn)   END;
  FUNCTION Neg(x: long): boolean;
    BEGIN   Neg := (x >= maxn)   END;

BEGIN {Statement part of Add}
  maxn := Power2(len-1);
  sum := (a + b + cy) MOD (2*maxn);
  SetNZVC(sum,len);
  V := ord( (Pos(a) AND Pos(b) AND Neg(sum))
        OR (Neg(a) AND Neg(b) AND Pos(sum)) );
  C := ord((a+b+cy) >= 2*maxn);   X := C;
  Add := sum;
END;

FUNCTION Sub(a,b: long; borrow: bit; len: integer): long;
{Perform len-bit subtraction of a, b, and borrow}
BEGIN
  Sub := Add(a, (2*Power2(n-1)-1-b), (1-borrow),len);
  C := 1 - C;   X := C;
END;
```

TABLE 5–8   (continued)

```
FUNCTION Andr(a,b: long): long;
BEGIN
  IF (a = 0) OR (b = 0) THEN Andr := 0
  ELSE Andr := 2*Andr(a DIV 2, b DIV 2) + (a MOD 2)*(b MOD 2);
END;

FUNCTION Andd(a,b: long; len: integer): long;
VAR rslt: long;        {Perform len-bit logical AND of a and b}
BEGIN rslt := Andr(a,b); Andd := rslt;
      SetNZVC(rslt,Power2(len-1))        END;

BEGIN {Statement part of Execute}
  CASE Decode(IR) OF
  MOVE_B: BEGIN SourceEA; TEMP := ReadByte; MDestEA;
                StoreByte(TEMP); SetNZVC(TEMP,8); END;
  MOVE_W: BEGIN SourceEA; TEMP := ReadWord; MDestEA;
                StoreWord(TEMP); SetNZVC(TEMP,16); END;
  MOVE_L: BEGIN SourceEA; TEMP := ReadLong; MDestEA;
                StoreLong(TEMP); SetNZVC(TEMP,32); END;
  MOVEA_W:BEGIN SourceEA; TEMP := ReadWord; AregEA;
                StoreWord(TEMP); END;
  MOVEA_L:BEGIN SourceEA; TEMP := ReadLong; AregEA;
                StoreLong(TEMP); END;
  LEA_L:  BEGIN SourceEA; TEMP := EAR; AregEA;
                StoreLong(TEMP); END;
  ADD_B:  BEGIN SourceEA; TEMP := ReadByte; DregEA;
                StoreByte(Add(ReadByte,TEMP,0,8)); END;
  ADD_W:  BEGIN SourceEA; TEMP := ReadWord; DregEA;
                StoreWord(Add(ReadWord,TEMP,0,16)); END;
  ADD_L:  BEGIN SourceEA; TEMP := ReadLong; DregEA;
                StoreLong(Add(ReadLong,TEMP,0,32)); END;
  ADDA_W: BEGIN SourceEA; TEMP := ReadWord; AregEA;
                StoreWord((ReadWord + TEMP) MOD $10000); END;
  ADDA_L: BEGIN SourceEA; TEMP := ReadLong; AregEA;
                StoreLong((ReadLong + TEMP) MOD $100000000) ); END;
  AND_B:  BEGIN SourceEA; TEMP := ReadByte; DregEA;
                StoreByte(Andd(ReadByte,TEMP,8); END;
  AND_W:  BEGIN SourceEA; TEMP := ReadWord; DregEA;
                StoreWord(Andd(ReadWord,TEMP,16); END;
  AND_L:  BEGIN SourceEA; TEMP := ReadLong; DregEA;
                StoreLong(Andd(ReadLong,TEMP,32); END;
  CMP_B:  BEGIN SourceEA; TEMP := ReadByte; DregEA;
                TEMP := Sub(ReadByte,TEMP,0,8); END;
  CMP_W:  BEGIN SourceEA; TEMP := ReadWord; DregEA;
                TEMP := Sub(ReadWord,TEMP,0,16); END;
  CMP_L:  BEGIN SourceEA; TEMP := ReadLong; DregEA;
                TEMP := Sub(ReadLong,TEMP,0,32); END;
  CMPA_W: BEGIN SourceEA; TEMP := ReadWord; AregEA;
                TEMP := Sub(ReadWord,TEMP,0,16); END;
  CMPA_L: BEGIN SourceEA; TEMP := ReadLong; AregEA;
                TEMP := Sub(ReadLong,TEMP,0,32); END;
```

TABLE 5–8 (continued)

```
CLR_B:   BEGIN DestEA; StoreByte(0); SetNZVC(0,8); END;
CLR_W:   BEGIN DestEA; StoreWord(0); SetNZVC(0,16); END;
CLR_L:   BEGIN DestEA; StoreLong(0); SetNZVC(0,32); END;
NOT_B:   BEGIN DestEA; TEMP := ReadByte;
                StoreByte(Sub($FF,TEMP,0,8)); END;
NOT_W:   BEGIN DestEA; TEMP := ReadWord;
                StoreWord(Sub($FFFF,TEMP,0,16)); END;
NOT_L:   BEGIN DestEA; TEMP := ReadLong;
                StoreLong(Sub($FFFFFFFF,TEMP,0,32)); END;
BNE:     BEGIN IF Z = 0 THEN Branch; END;
BEQ:     BEGIN IF Z = 1 THEN Branch; END;
JMP:     BEGIN DestEA; IF regEA THEN Error; PC := EAR; END;
JSR:     BEGIN DestEA; IF regEA THEN Error; TEMP := EAR;
                PushWord(Bits(15,0,PC)); PushWord(Bits(31,16,PC));
                PC := TEMP; END;
RTS:     BEGIN PC := $10000*PopWord + PopWord END;
END; {CASE}
END; {Statement part of Execute}
```

5.12 INDIRECT ADDRESSING

indirect addressing

The program in Table 5–6 manipulated only simple variables and constants. More complicated data structures such as arrays, stacks, queues, records, and lists are used in almost all programs. Consider the problem of initializing the components of an array of five bytes to zero. An assembly language solution is shown in Table 5–9. Note that the operand expressions Q+1, Q+2, and so on are evaluated at assembly time. The choice of a five-component array above was very judicious—the corresponding program for a 100-component array would have 101 instructions! *Indirect addressing* avoids this problem by taking the

TABLE 5–9 Initializing an array the hard way.

Machine Language		Assembly Language			
Address (hex)	Contents (hex)	Label (sym)	Opcode (mnem)	Operand (sym)	Comments
00000000			ORG	$3000	Set components of Q to zero.
00003000	4238 3100	INIT	CLR.B	Q	First component.
00003004	4238 3101		CLR.B	Q+1	Second component.
00003008	4238 3102		CLR.B	Q+2	Third component.
0000300C	4238 3103		CLR.B	Q+3	Fourth component.
00003010	4238 3104		CLR.B	Q+4	Fifth component.
00003014	4EF8 8008		JMP	$8008	Return to monitor.
00003018			ORG	$3100	
00003100	???? ????	Q	DS.B	5	Reserve 5 bytes for array.
00003105			END	INIT	

TABLE 5–10   Initializing an array using indirect addressing.

Machine Language		Assembly Language			
Address (hex)	Contents (hex)	Label (sym)	Opcode (mnem)	Operand (sym)	Comments
00000000			ORG	$3000	Set components of Q to zero.
00003000	41F8 3100	INIT	LEA	Q,A0	A0 points to first component.
00003004	43F8 3105		LEA	QEND,A1	A1 points just past array end.
00003008	4210	ILUP	CLR.B	(A0)	Clear byte that A0 points to.
0000300A	D0FC 0001		ADDA.W	#1,A0	Point to next byte.
0000300E	B1C9		CMPA.L	A1,A0	Past the end?
00003010	66F6		BNE	ILUP	Nope, keep clearing.
00003012	4EF8 8008		JMP	$8008	Yep, return to monitor.
00003016			ORG	$3100	
00003100	???? ????	Q	DS.B	5	Reserve 5 bytes for array.
00003105		QEND	EQU	Q+5	Address of byte just past Q.
00003105			END	INIT	

address from an address register at run time. Thus we can write a loop to initialize an array, in which an address register points to a different array element on each iteration of the loop.

The program in Table 5–10 solves the array initialization problem using indirect addressing. As shown in Figure 5–8, it initializes A0 to point to the first component of Q, and A1 to point just past the last component of Q. Then it executes a loop that clears successive components of Q, incrementing A0 once per iteration of the loop. The CMPA instruction compares the contents of A0 with A1, which was initialized to contain the address just past the last array component. CMPA sets Z to 1 if A0 and A1 are equal, which causes the BNE instruction to terminate the loop.

Notice the use of the LEA instruction in Table 5–10, in particular the second one, which initializes A1. Performing this initialization outside the main loop reduces the length and execution time of the instructions inside the loop. An obviously less desirable alternative would have been to put the LEA instruction inside the loop, right before CMPA. An arguably less desirable alternative would be to eliminate the second LEA, and then to replace the CMPA instruction with CMPA #QEND,A0. While this would shorten the overall program length by one word, it increases the execution time of the loop. Also, this approach cannot be used in position-independent programs, as in the Macintosh, where the ending address of the array is not known at assembly time and must be computed at run time by an LEA instruction, as shown in the accompanying Mac Note.

Not only does the program in Table 5–10 occupy fewer bytes than the one in Table 5–9, but it also stays the same length for an array of any size. The program is easily modified to work on a different length array by changing the occurrences of the length "5" to the desired length.

Mac Note

As you know, variable storage in the Macintosh environment is allocated from the application global space, and variables are accessed using based addressing with A5. A Macintosh equivalent for the program in Table 5–9 is shown below.

```
ADDR    CONTENTS   LABEL OPCODE   OPERAND      COMMENTS

0000                      INCLUDE MACLIB.ASM  ;Include useful definitions.
0000                                          ;Set components of Q to zero.
0000    422D FEFB  INIT  CLR.B    Q(A5)       ;First component.
0004    422D FEFC        CLR.B    Q+1(A5)     ;Second component.
0008    422D FEFD        CLR.B    Q+2(A5)     ;Third component.
000C    422D FEFE        CLR.B    Q+3(A5)     ;Fourth component.
0010    422D FEFF        CLR.B    Q+4(A5)     ;Fifth component.
0014    A9F4             _ExitToShell         ;Return to operating system.
FEFB(D)            Q     DS.B     5           ;Reserve 5 bytes for array.
                         END
```

During the execution of a Macintosh program, A5 actually points into the middle of the application global area. As shown in the figure to the right, $20 bytes starting at the address contained in A5 are reserved for "application parameters" used by the operating system, and additional space is reserved for a "jump table" used by large applications. Application parameters and the jump table are accessed using based addressing with positive displacements from A5.

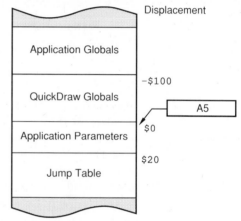

Additional space, usually $100 bytes, is reserved just below the address in A5 for "QuickDraw globals." QuickDraw is a set of graphics routines that form the basis for the Macintosh's user interface.

An application's global variables are allocated in the memory locations preceding the QuickDraw globals. Thus, in our example program, the displacement of Q with respect to A5 turns out to be $FEFB, or –$105 bytes ($100 bytes for QuickDraw globals plus 5 bytes for the length of Q).

Returning to our example program, array initialization using indirect addressing is accomplished in the Macintosh with very little change from Table 5–10. The first two instructions in original program loaded A0 and A1 with the effective addresses of Q and QEND, using **LEA** instructions with absolute addressing. The Macintosh version also uses **LEA** instructions, but with based addressing:

```
ADDR   CONTENTS   LABEL OPCODE   OPERAND      COMMENTS

0000   41ED FEFB  INIT  LEA      Q(A5),A0     ;A0 points to first component.
0004   43ED FF00        LEA      QEND(A5),A1  ;A1 points just past array.
```

The only other required changes are to include the **INCLUDE** statement, to replace **JMP** $8008 with **_ExitToShell**, and to remove the ORG statements.

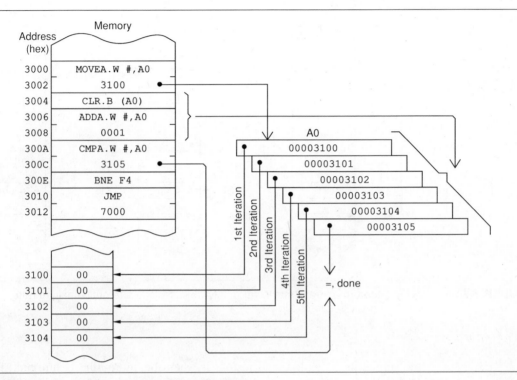

FIGURE 5–8   Effects of indirect addressing.

based addressing   *Based addressing* is a variation of indirect addressing in which the effective address is the sum of an address register and a fixed, signed displacement contained in the instruction. This addressing mode may be used to access data whose relative position in a block of memory is known at assembly time (and assembled into the instruction), but where the base address of the memory block is not determined until run time (and kept in the address register). This mode is used extensively in Macintosh programs, as shown in Mac Notes throughout this part of the book. It is also very useful for accessing records and subroutine parameters in any computer, as we'll show in Sections 7.3.2 and 9.3.6.

Many other variations on indirect addressing are found in the full 68000 and most other computers. These addressing modes are explored in Chapter 7.

5.13 SUBROUTINES

subroutine   A *subroutine* is the machine language equivalent of a procedure or function in Pascal: a sequence of instructions, defined and stored only once, that may be
call   invoked (or *called*) from many places. In order to use subroutines, we need
return address   instructions to save the current value of the PC (the *return address*) each time

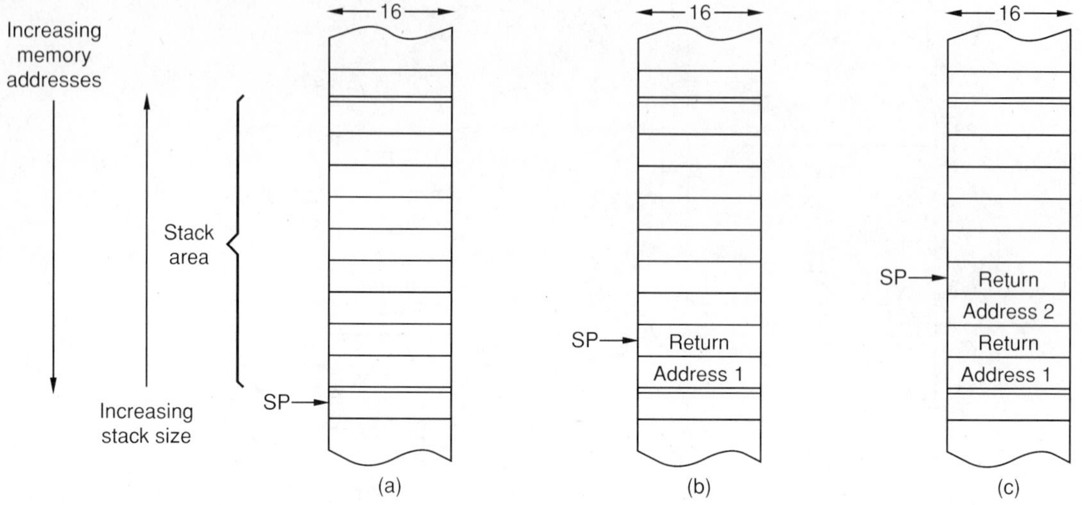

FIGURE 5–9   A 68000 return-address stack: (a) empty; (b) after one subroutine call; (c) after second (nested) subroutine call.

the subroutine is called, and restore it when the subroutine is finished. In the 68000, these instructions save and restore PC using a stack.

pushdown stack   A *pushdown stack* (or simply a *stack*) is a one-dimensional data structure in which values are entered and removed one item at a time at one end, called *top of stack*   the *top of stack*. A register called the *stack pointer (SP)* points to the top of *stack pointer (SP)*   stack. An item is entered by a *push* operation that advances the stack pointer to *push*   the next available memory location and then stores the item at the top of stack. *pop*   An item is removed by a *pop* (or *pull*) operation that removes the item at the top *pull*   of stack and then backs up the stack pointer. (See Section 3.4 for a discussion of stacks in Pascal programs.)

In the 68000, the JSR and RTS instructions perform subroutine calls and returns using address register A7 as a stack pointer. In 68000 assembly language *notation*   and documentation, the symbols "A7" and "SP" refer to the same register and may be used interchangeably.

Any 68000 program that uses subroutines is required to reserve a small area of memory for a pushdown stack for return addresses. At the beginning of such a program, the stack pointer SP must be initialized to point at this area using a MOVE.W #addr,SP instruction. As shown in Figure 5–9, SP points to the top item in the stack, or just past the stack area if the stack is empty. SP is decremented by 2 before storing each word on the stack, and incremented by 2 after popping each word. These operations correspond directly to auto-decrement and auto-increment addressing as described in Section 7.2.5. Since a return address may be up to 32 bits wide, two words on the stack are used for

TABLE 5–11   Program with two nested subroutines.

Machine Language		Assembly Language			
Address (hex)	Contents (hex)	Label (sym)	Opcode (mnem)	Operand (sym)	Comments
			ORG	$3000	PROGRAM Subrs(input,output);
00003000	...	SUBR2	...		PROCEDURE P2;
...	...		...		BEGIN
...	...		...		...
00003056	4E75		RTS		END;
00003058	...	SUBR1	...		PROCEDURE P1;
...	...		...		BEGIN
...	...		...		...
000030A2	4EB8 3000		JSR	SUBR2	P2; {Call P2}
000030A6	...	RET2	...		...
...	...		...		...
000030C4	4E75		RTS		END;
000030C5	3E7C 3FF0	MAIN	MOVE.W	#STK+$10,SP	BEGIN {Main program}
...	...		...		...
00003130	4EB8 3058		JSR	SUBR1	P1; {Call P1}
00003134	...	RET1	...		...
...	...		...		...
000031A8	4EF8 8008		JMP	$8008	END.
...			ORG	$3FF0	
00003FF0	???? ????	STK	DS.W	8	Allocate stack storage.
00004000		STKE	DS.W	0	Define stack end address.
00004000			END	MAIN	

each return address. As usual, the high-order word of 32-bit return address is stored in the lower-numbered address.

Table 5–11 outlines a Pascal program with two nested subroutines and the corresponding assembly language statements. The JSR addr instruction saves the address of the next instruction by pushing it onto the stack and then jumps to the instruction at location addr, the first instruction of the subroutine. At the end of the subroutine, RTS pops an address from the stack into PC, effecting a return to the original program sequence.

nested subroutine

A stack is the most appropriate data structure for saving return addresses, because it can store more than one return address when subroutines are *nested*, that is, when one subroutine calls another. The number of levels of nesting is limited only by the size of the memory area reserved by the programmer for the stack.

A detailed example program using subroutines is presented in Table 5–12. Before describing it, we should point out a few additional assembly language pseudo-operations and features that it uses:

JSR

RTS

TABLE 5–12 Program that uses subroutines to count the number of "1" bits in a word.

Machine Language		Assembly Language			
Address (hex)	Contents (hex)	Label (sym)	Opcode (mnem)	Operand (sym)	Comments
00000000			ORG	$2000	
00002000		SYSRET	EQU	$8008	Operating system address.
00002000	4FF8 2022	MAIN	LEA	STKE,SP	Initialize SP (A7).
00002004	3038 2010		MOVE.W	TWORD,D0	Get test word.
00002008	4EB8 2022		JSR	WCNT1S	Count number of 1s in it.
0000200C	4EF8 8008		JMP	SYSRET	Return to operating system.
00002010	5B29	TWORD	DC.W	$5B29	Test-word to count 1s.
00002012	???? ????	STK	DS.W	8	Space for 4 return addr's.
00002022		STKE	EQU	*	Initialization addr for SP.
00002022		*	Count the number of '1' bits in a word.		
00002022		*	Enter with word in D0, exit with count in D1.		
00002022	31C0 203C	WCNT1S	MOVE.W	D0,CWORD	Save input word.
00002026	1038 203C		MOVE.B	CWORDH,D0	Get high-order byte.
0000202A	4EB8 203E		JSR	BCNT1S	Count 1s.
0000202E	3E01		MOVE.W	D1,D7	Save '1' count.
00002030	1038 203D		MOVE.B	CWORDL,D0	Get low-order byte.
00002034	4EB8 203E		JSR	BCNT1S	Count 1s.
00002038	D247		ADD.W	D7,D1	Add high-order count.
0000203A	4E75		RTS		Done, return.
0000203C	????	CWORD	DS.W	1	Temporary word.
0000203E		CWORDL	EQU	CWORD+1	Low-order byte address.
0000203E		CWORDH	EQU	CWORD	High-order byte address.
0000203E		*	Count number of '1' bits in a byte.		
0000203E		*	Enter with byte in D0, exit with count in D1.		
0000203E	4241	BCNT1S	CLR.W	D1	Initialize '1' count.
00002040	41F8 205C		LEA	MASKS,A0	Point to 1-bit masks
00002044	43F8 2064		LEA	MASKE,A1	and end of masks.
00002048	1410	BLOOP	MOVE.B	(A0),D2	Get next bit mask.
0000204A	C400		AND.B	D0,D2	Is there a '1' there?
0000204C	6704		BEQ	BNO1	Skip if not.
0000204E	0641 0001		ADD.W	#1,D1	Else increment '1' count.
00002052	D0FC 0001	BNO1	ADDA.W	#1,A0	Point to next mask.
00002056	B1C9		CMPA.L	A1,A0	Past last mask?
00002058	66EE		BNE	BLOOP	Continue if not.
0000205A	4E75		RTS		Return.
0000205C		*	Define 1-bit masks to test bits of byte.		
0000205C	0102 0408	MASKS	DC.B	$1,$2,$4,$8,$10,$20,$40,$80	
00002060	1020 4080				
00002064		MASKE	EQU	*	Address just after table.
00002064			END	MAIN	

Symbol Table

BCNT1S	0000203E	BLOOP	00002048	BNO1	00002052	CWORD	0000203C
CWORDH	0000203C	CWORDL	0000203D	MAIN	00002000	MASKE	00002064
MASKS	0000205C	STK	00002012	STKE	00002022	SYSRET	00008008
TWORD	00002010	WCNT1S	00002022				

DS.B

- DS.B (define storage—byte). The operand specifies a number of memory bytes to be skipped without storing any instructions or data, thereby reserving space to be used by variables in a program.

DC.B

- DC.B (define constant—byte). The specified byte values are stored into memory when the program is first loaded into memory, thereby establishing a constant value that may be accessed when the program is run.

EQU

- EQU (equate). The identifier in the label field is assigned the value in the operand field, instead of the value in the address field. This makes the identifier a synonym for a constant value for the duration of the assembly process.

⋆

- ⋆ (program location counter). When used in an expression, the symbol "⋆" denotes the current address at which assembly is taking place.

The program in Table 5–12 contains a main program and two subroutines. The main program initializes SP to point to an 8-word stack. A stack of four words would have been sufficient for the two nested subroutines in this program, but it is a good practice to provide "headroom" in case programming errors, modifications, or interrupts (Chapter 11) increase the space required.[4]

The main program loads a 16-bit word into the low-order word of D0 and calls a subroutine WCNT1S that counts the number of 1 bits. WCNT1S splits the low-order word of D0 into two bytes and calls a subroutine BCNT1S to count 1's in each byte. The usefulness of subroutines is evidenced by the fact that BCNT1S can be called more than once and with a different byte to be converted each time.

Figure 5–10 shows the state of the stack after each instruction that affects it. When WCNT1S returns to the main program, the stack is again empty and D1 contains the 1s count. The main program terminates by jumping to the operating system.

The individual subroutines in Table 5–12 are worth discussing. On entry, WCNT1S expects the input word to be in D0, which it writes into a memory word that is read back as two individual bytes passed to BCNT1S. The memory write and reads are used because there are no instructions to directly break out the high-order byte of a register.

When BCNT1S is entered, it expects the input byte to be in D0. The subroutine checks each bit position for a 1 and maintains a count in D1 accordingly. It uses a table of eight "mask bytes," each having a 1 in a different bit position. At each iteration of the loop, A0 contains the address of a mask byte and a

---

[4]In fact, in a typical "real" program environment, a *much* larger stack would be provided, and the stack and all other read/write variables would be kept in an area of memory separate from the program itself. We have placed programs and data in the same area of memory in this and other examples in this chapter simply as a matter of convenience; you'll learn the reason for separating them in Section 7.4.

Mac Note

As usual, Macintosh assemblers operate somewhat differently from Motorola assemblers. The DC.B pseudo-operation in a Macintosh assembler generates a data constant in-line with instructions in the program's code module, and the constant is normally accessed using relative addressing. DS.B, on the other hand, allocates a variable in the application global space, and the variable is normally accessed using based addressing with A5. The program location counter (*) is generally the address in the code module at which *instructions* are being assembled. In the Macintosh environment, the operating system leaves SP pointing to a legitimate stack area when it transfers control to a user's program. With these ideas in mind, we can recode and reassemble the 1's-counting program of Table 5–12 as follows:

```
ADDR   CONTENTS  LABEL   OPCODE   OPERAND       COMMENTS

0000   303A 0008 START   MOVE.W   TWORD,D0      ;Get test word.
0004   4EBA 0006         JSR      WCNT1S        ;Count number of 1s in it.
0008   A9F4              _ExitToShell           ;Return to operating system.
000A   5B29      TWORD   DC.W     $5B29         ;Test-word to count 1s.
000C             ;        Count the number of '1' bits in a word.
000C             ;        Enter with word in D0, exit with count in D1.
000C   3B40 FEFE WCNT1S  MOVE.W   D0,CWORD(A5)  ;Save input word.
0010   102D FEFE         MOVE.B   CWORDH(A5),D0 ;Get high-order byte.
0014   4EBA 0010         JSR      BCNT1S        ;Count 1s.
0018   3E01              MOVE.W   D1,D7         ;Save '1' count.
001A   102D FEFF         MOVE.B   CWORDL(A5),D0 ;Get low-order byte.
001E   4EBA 0006         JSR      BCNT1S        ;Count 1s.
0022   D247              ADD.W    D7,D1         ;Add high-order count.
0024   4E75              RTS                    ;Done, return.
FEFE(D)          CWORD   DS.W     1             ;Temporary word.
0026             CWORDL  EQU      CWORD+1       ;Low-order byte address.
0026             CWORDH  EQU      CWORD         ;High-order byte address.
0026             ;        Count number of '1' bits in a byte.
0026             ;        Enter with byte in D0, exit with count in D1.
0026   4241      BCNT1S  CLR.W    D1            ;Initialize '1' count.
0028   41FA 001A         LEA      MASKS,A0      ;Point to 1-bit masks
002C   43FA 001E         LEA      MASKE,A1      ;  and end of masks.
0030   1410      BLOOP   MOVE.B   (A0),D2       ;Get next mask.
0032   C400              AND.B    D0,D2         ;Is there a '1' there?
0034   6704              BEQ      BNO1          ;Skip if not.
0036   D27C 0001         ADD.W    #1,D1         ;Else increment '1' count.
003A   D0FC 0001 BNO1    ADDA.W   #1,A0         ;Point to next mask.
003E   B1C9              CMPA.L   A1,A0         ;Past last mask?
0040   66EE              BNE      BLOOP         ;Continue if not.
0042   4E75              RTS                    ;Return.
0044             ;        Define 1-bit masks to test bits of byte.
0044   01020408 MASKS   DC.B     $1,$2,$4,$8,$10,$20,$40,$80
0048   10204080
004C             MASKE   EQU      *             ;Address just after table.
004C                     END
```

Notice that in the Macintosh version of the program, based addressing with respect to A5 is used to access CWORD, which is stored in the application global space. On the other hand, relative addressing is used by the JSR instructions and by the LEA instructions that compute the starting and ending addresses of the constant MASKS table, since jump targets and the MASKS table are part of the code module.

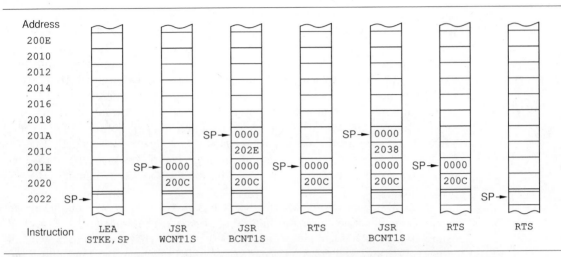

FIGURE 5–10   Stack contents after the execution of instructions in Table 5–12.

corresponding bit of D0 is tested using the AND.B D0,D2 instruction. AND.B produces a nonzero result if and only if the tested bit of D0 is 1.

Like procedures and functions in Pascal, subroutines are the key to the structure of assembly language programs. A typical program is divided into many "modules," each of which is a subroutine with inputs, outputs, and local data. Subroutines will be discussed in detail in Chapter 9.

REFERENCES

Little Endians
Big Endians

Students and practicing computer engineers alike have been curious and confused about bit and byte numbering in computers and networks. Danny Cohen gives an amusing and enlightening description of the "Little Endians" and the "Big Endians" in "On Holy Wars and a Plea for Peace" (*Computer*, Vol. 14, No. 10, October 1981, pp. 48–54). Hubert Kirrmann describes the ongoing battle in "Data Format and Bus Compatibility in Multiprocessors" in the August 1983 issue of *IEEE Micro* (Vol. 3, No. 4, pp. 32–47), which depicts the combatants on its front cover.

The best way to study computer organization is to examine the architectures of real machines, such as the 68000 family. The 68000 architecture was originally described by Skip Stritter and Tom Gunter in "A Microprocessor Architecture for a Changing World" (*Computer*, Vol. 12, No. 2, February, 1979). A description of the 68000 family and its evolution through the MC68020 can be found in "A Comparison of MC68000 Family Processors" by Thomas L. Johnson (*Byte*, Vol. 11, No. 9, September 1986). A very good architectural description of the latest member of the 68000 family, the MC68030, appears in Johnson's "The RISC/CISC Melting Pot" (*Byte*, Vol. 12, No. 4, April 1987).

Much of the architecture of the 68000 and many other microprocessors is based on the PDP-11, a very successful and important minicomputer architecture that was introduced by Digital Equipment Corporation (DEC) in 1970. The PDP-11 is described in Chapter 17 of this book. DEC extended the PDP-11 architecture in its current market-dominating family of 32-bit micro-, mini-, and maxicomputers, the VAX-11. The rationale and history of both the PDP-11 and VAX-11 designs are discussed in *Computer Engineering* by C. G. Bell, J. C. Mudge, and J. E. McNamara (Digital Press, 1978). Because of the VAX-11's popularity, there are many up-to-date textbooks, handbooks, and guides on VAX programming.

The Motorola 6809, described in Chapter 16, is a good example of an accumulator machine. And the Intel 8086, discussed in Chapter 18, is a good example of a machine architecture that doesn't know what it wants to be when it grows up—it evolved from an accumulator-based machine, the Intel 8008, and has been extended (so far) to the general-register Intel 80386.

Although we don't cover any real stack machines, a hypothetical stack machine based on the PDP-11 is described in Chapter 19. The HP3000 family is a popular midi/minicomputer family with a pure stack architecture.

Two of the first 16-bit microprocessor architectures—the the Texas Instruments 9900 and the Zilog Z8000—flourished for only a little while and then died. For the historically inclined, they are described in *Microcomputer Architecture and Programming* by John F. Wakerly (Wiley, 1981). This book also describes a very simple accumulator machine that happens to have separate memories for instructions and data—the Intel MCS-48.

Several textbooks discuss general computer organization from a hardware viewpoint, including *Digital Systems: Hardware Organization and Design* by F. J. Hill and G. R. Peterson (Wiley, 1980, 3rd ed.), *Computer Organization* by V. C. Hamacher, Z. G. Vranesic, and S. G. Zaky (McGraw-Hill, 1984, 2nd ed.), and *Computer Architecture and Organization* by John Hayes (McGraw-Hill, 1978). Probably the best overall efforts on classification and taxonomy of computer organizations appear in *Computer Structures: Readings and Examples* by C. G. Bell and A. Newell (McGraw-Hill, 1971) and *Principles of Computer Structures* by D. P. Siewiorek, C. G. Bell, and A. Newell (McGraw-Hill, 1982).

E X E R C I S E S

5.1 What is the relationship, if any, between the length of an instruction and the length of the data that it processes?

5.2 How many address bits are needed in a byte-addressable machine with 131,072 words of memory? What if it is a word-addressable machine? (Remember, one word contains two bytes.)

5.3   If manufacturers of processors that can access nonaligned words recommend that programmers nevertheless arrange their programs so that data words are aligned, why do they bother to allow nonaligned word access in the first place? Why don't they follow the 68000 approach and forbid nonaligned words? When are nonaligned words useful?

5.4   Two values may be arithmetically compared by subtracting them and determining whether the result is less than, greater than, or equal to zero. A typical processor has instructions for comparing bytes and for comparing words. Lexicographic sorting of a pair of ASCII character strings can be accomplished by comparing them a byte at a time, starting with the leftmost bytes, until an unequal byte is found. Discuss whether word-comparing instructions can be used to speed up the sorting, depending on whether the memory is organized as shown in Figure 5–1(b) or 5–1(c).

decimal instruction   5.5   A *decimal instruction* processes strings of decimal digits. Describe how the data for such an instruction could be stored in a binary memory, assuming that the desired memory organization could be described in Pascal as follows:

```
TYPE
  digit = 0..9;
  word = PACKED ARRAY [0..8] OF digit;
  address = 0..9999;
VAR
  MEM : ARRAY [address] OF word;
```

5.6   Draw a figure in the style of Figure 5–2 showing the physical organization of the MC68008's memory. How would you expect this organization to affect processor performance, compared with that of the MC68000/10 and the MC68020/30?

5.7   Classify the 68000's double-operand instructions in this chapter as 0-, 1-, $1^1/_2$-, or 2-address instructions.

5.8   In Table 5–5, why does the assembly language pseudo-operation DC.W 123 store the value 007B into memory instead of 0123?

5.9   Rewrite the 68000 program in Table 5–6 so that it multiplies longwords instead of words.

5.10   Write the Decode(IR) function for the 68000 simulation in Table 5–8.

5.11   The speed of a typical processor is limited by the speed of the memory. Therefore the execution time of each instruction depends mainly on the number of times that memory must be accessed to fetch and execute the instruction. As a first approximation for the MC68000, the total time to execute an instruction equals the number of memory words the instruction accesses (reads or writes) times the length of time for one access.

       Assuming that each access takes 0.5 microsecond, construct a table that shows the execution times for all of the instructions in Table 5–3. Note that, for most instructions, the total execution time depends on the addressing modes that are used, so your first task is to determine the execution times for the various addressing modes.

5.12   Repeat Exercise 5.11 for the MC68020/30, taking into account the 32-bit wide data bus. In your analysis, "average" the effects of instruction lengths that contain an odd number of words and the effects of even-length instructions that are not aligned on longword boundaries. That is, assume that a one-word instruction such as `MOVE.L DO,D1` takes only half a memory access, and that a four-word instruction such as `MOVE.L #$12345678,$ABCD` takes only two memory accesses, even if it is split across three memory longwords.

By making the above assumption, you are taking into account the fact that the MC68020/30 hardware uses any leftover half of a previously fetched longword before it fetches the next longword in a sequential instruction stream. The leftovers are wasted only if a branch instruction disrupts the sequential access pattern. Note that this averaging *cannot* be applied to data accesses; for example, a data byte read takes a full memory cycle, not 0.25. Why?

5.13   Using the table developed in Exercise 5.11 (or using real MC68000 times), calculate the execution time of one iteration of the inner loop of the program in Table 5–6.

5.14   Using the table developed in Exercise 5.11 (or using real MC68000 times), compare the execution times of the programs in Tables 5–9 and 5–10. Develop formulas that give the execution times of both programs as a function of the size of the array being initialized.

5.15   The recursive definition of the `Power2` function in Table 5–8 is concise but not particularly efficient to execute. Rewrite the function in three other ways: (a) iteratively, (b) using a `CASE` statement, and (c) using an array. Comment on the efficiency of each technique. How can the simulation's efficiency be further improved with the last technique?

5.16   The 68000 does not have `AND`, `CLR`, and `NOT` instructions that operate on address registers. What other instructions don't work on address registers? Why do you suppose the 68000 was designed in this way?

5.17   Suppose that the 68000's address-register indirect addressing mode is eliminated. Show how to rewrite the array initialization program in Table 5–10 using an instruction that modifies the `dst` part of another instruction. The new program should still be capable of initializing an array of any size with no increase in program length. Why is it a bad idea to write such "self-modifying code" in practice?

5.18   Suppose that the last instruction a 68000 subroutine executes before returning to its caller is to call another, nested subroutine. Show that the two-instruction sequence `JSR addr; RTS` can always be replaced by the single instruction `JMP addr`. Why is it a bad practice actually to do this?

5.19   If a 68000 "operating system" calls the main program in Table 5–12 using a `JSR MAIN` instruction, can the main program return to the operating system using an `RTS` instead of `JMP SYSRET`? Explain.

5.20   Suppose the `CMPA.L` instructions in Tables 5–10 and 5–12 are changed to `CMPA.W`. What difference, if any, does this make to the programs' operation?

5.21 Assemble the following 68000 subroutine by hand, producing a listing in the format of Table 5–6. While you're at it, add comments that explain what the subroutine does. (It's too bad that real assembler programs can't do this!)

```
              ORG      $3000
     START    LEA.L    VOLE,A0
              LEA.L    VOLE+LEN,A1
              CLR.B    STOAT
     LOOP     MOVE.B   (A0),D7
              ADD.B    STOAT,D7
              MOVE.B   D7,STOAT
              ADDA.W   #1,A0
              CMPA.L   A1,A0
              BNE      LOOP
              MOVE.B   STOAT,D7
              RTS
     STOAT    DS.B     1
     LEN      EQU      10
     VOLE     DS.B     LEN
              END      START
```

5.22 Rewrite the loop in the preceding program to execute more efficiently by eliminating variable STOAT in memory.

5.23 Write a 68000 subroutine that converts an 8-bit number DECNUM into a sequence of three ASCII characters, the digits of the corresponding unsigned decimal number. When the subroutine is entered, the input number is assumed to be contained in the low byte of D0 and, on exit, the result should be contained in three memory bytes, ASC2 (most significant), ASC1, and ASC0. Use the following algorithm:

```
ASC2 := 30H; ASC1 := 30H; ASC0 := 30H; {ASCII '0'}
WHILE DECNUM <> 0 DO
  BEGIN
    ASC0 := ASC0 + 1;
    IF ASC0 = 30H + 10 THEN
      BEGIN
        ASC0 := 30H;  ASC1 := ASC1 + 1;
        IF ASC1 = 30H + 10 THEN
          BEGIN ASC1 := 30H;  ASC2 := ASC2 + 1 END;
      END;
    DECNUM := DECNUM - 1;
  END;
```

5.24 Rewrite the 68000 simulator of Tables 5–2 and 5–8 efficiently in the C programming language, taking advantage of C's bit manipulation and shifting operations.

5.25 Suppose the 68000 architecture is to be redesigned so that instructions and data are in separate memories, each with its own 2^{32}-byte address space. Assume that the operands of all the instruction in the first two parts of Table 5–3 are in data memory, while the program control instructions have operands in instruction memory. Describe what additional instructions and/or addressing modes must be added to this table to make the new 68000 architecture practical. In particular, consider problems such as loading programs and reading look-up tables stored in instruction memory.

CHAPTER 6

Assembly Language Programming

machine language

Machine language and assembly language are not the same thing. The *machine language* of a computer is the set of bit strings recognized as instructions; the actions performed by each machine instruction are defined by the computer's hardware. *Assembly language* is a software tool, a symbolic language that can be directly translated into machine language by a system program called an *assembler*. The output of an assembler is an *object module* containing the bit strings that make up the machine language program, and information that tells a *loader* program where to place these bit strings in the computer's memory.

assembly language

assembler

object module

loader

The process of developing programs in assembly language is illustrated in Figure 6–1. A typical programmer uses a *text editor* to create a text file containing an assembly language program. The names *source file* and *source program* are often used for assembly language and high-level language text files. The assembler accepts a source program as input, checks for format errors, and produces an object module containing the machine language program. A loader then loads the object module into the memory of the target machine. There the machine language program is run, possibly with the aid of a *debugger*.

text editor

source file

source program

debugger

The loader, debugger, and machine language program described above *must* run on the target machine; the text editor and assembler may run there or on a different machine. An assembler that runs on one machine and produces object modules for another is called a *cross assembler*. For example, it is possible to create an assembly language program using a text editor on a laptop computer, transfer the source file using a serial data link to a large mainframe computer that runs a cross assembler, and transfer (or *download*) the object module to a loader in a local microcomputer using another serial data link.

cross assembler

download

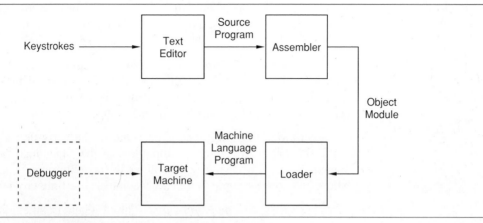

FIGURE 6–1   Assembly language program development.

6.1 ASSEMBLY LANGUAGE

Although every computer manufacturer defines a standard assembly language for a new machine when it is introduced, other vendors may define different assembly languages for the same machine. While the effect of each machine language instruction is fixed in hardware, the person who defines an assembly language is free to specify:

- a mnemonic for each machine language instruction;

- a standard format for the lines of an assembly language program;

- formats for specifying addressing modes and other instruction variations;

- formats for specifying character and integer constants in different bases;

- mechanisms for associating symbolic names with addresses and other numeric values;

- mechanisms for defining constant data to be stored in memory along with the instructions when the program is loaded;

- directives that specify how the program is to be assembled.

Normally, all assembly languages for a given machine agree on instruction mnemonics and addressing mode notations, but may differ on details like line formats, maximum identifier lengths, constant formats, and assembler directives. Although there can be many different assembly languages for a given machine, there are usually only a few important ones—the manufacturer's standard(s) and perhaps one or two different versions from independent software suppliers. There are several important assembly languages for the Motorola 68000:

cross macro assembly language

- *Cross macro assembly language.* This was Motorola's first assembly language for the 68000, used by a cross assembler that runs on mainframe computers. It generates "absolute code," as defined later.

resident assembly language

- *Resident assembly language* (the standard in this text). Motorola defined a slightly different assembly language that is recognized by the "resident assembler" that runs on Motorola's own 68000 development systems. It generates "relocatable code," as defined later.

Macintosh MDS assembly language

- *Macintosh MDS assembly language.* One of the early development environments for the Macintosh computer was the Macintosh 68000 Development System (MDS). The assembler in this environment is specifically tailored to create programs for the Macintosh run-time environment.

Macintosh MPW assembly language

- *Macintosh MPW assembly language.* The MDS environment is being gradually supplanted with the Macintosh Programmer's Workshop (MPW). Although somewhat more powerful than the MDS Assembler, the MPW assembler is also specifically tailored to the Macintosh environment.

Most of what we discuss in this chapter applies to all of these assembly languages, sometimes with a slight change in notation. However, where differences exist, we warn you and use Motorola's resident assembly language. Important characteristics of the MDS and MPW assemblers are highlighted in Mac Notes.

A 68000 assembler simplifies the programmer's job to some extent by recognizing alternate mnemonics for some instructions. For example, Table 5–2 showed `MOVEA.W`, `ADDA.W`, and `CMPA.W` instructions whose destination operand must be an address register. However, most 68000 assemblers accept the mnemonics `MOVE.W`, `ADD.W`, and `CMP.W` instead, automatically assembling the proper instruction when the destination operand is an address register.[1]

6.1.1 Assembly Language Formats

Examples of simple assembly language statements and programs were given in Chapter 5. Unlike Pascal programs, assembly language programs are usually line oriented, so that each assembly language statement is contained in a single line with a prescribed format. Each line has four fields arranged as shown below:

```
LABEL   OPCODE   OPERANDS   COMMENTS
```

label
symbol

The `LABEL` field is optional. A *label* is simply an identifier (or *symbol* in assembler parlance), that is, a sequence of letters and digits beginning with a letter. The maximum symbol length varies with different assemblers; most allow symbols at least six characters long. Like some Pascal compilers, many

---

[1] In many cases, the opcode bits of the assembled instruction are the same anyway, regardless of destination operand type. `MOVE.W` and `MOVEA.W` are considered to be different machine instructions only because they have different effects on the conditon codes.

assemblers allow symbols of arbitrary length, but only recognize the first six or eight characters.

symbol table

Every symbol in an assembly language program is assigned a value at the time that it is defined; the assembler program keeps track of labels and their values by an internal *symbol table*. For example, in the statement below,

```
START  MOVE.W   XX,D0      D0 := contents of memory location XX.
```

the value of the symbol START equals the memory address at which the MOVE.W instruction is stored. In general, the value of a symbol is the memory address at which the corresponding instruction or data value is stored. (An exception occurs for the EQU pseudo-operation discussed later.) Each symbol may be defined only once, but may be referenced as often as needed.

The OPCODE field contains the mnemonic of either a machine instruction or a pseudo-operation or assembler directive. In 68000 assembly language, many opcode mnemonics have a *size suffix* of .B, .W, or .L to indicate the size of the operands and operation. The size suffix is optional for operations that have only one size (such as LEA). In other cases, the assembler may use a default size (usually .W) if the programmer does not provide a size suffix, but this is a dangerous practice that often causes program bugs.

size suffix

Depending on the contents of the OPCODE field, the OPERAND field specifies zero or more operands separated by commas. An operand is an expression consisting of symbols, constants, and operators such as + and –. The simplest expression consists of a single symbol or constant.

decimal constant
$
hexadecimal constant
character constant

In 68000 assembly language, we use a sequence of digits to denote a *decimal constant*, and a sequence of hexadecimal digits preceded by $ to denote a *hexadecimal constant*. *Character constants* are surrounded by single quotes (e.g., 'A') and have the corresponding ASCII value.

Hexadecimal is the most convenient notation for data and address values in 8-, 16-, and 32-bit machines. Byte values are conveniently expressed in two characters, and 16- and 32-bit quantities are easily split into bytes. Compare with the difficulties encountered with decimal or even octal notation; for example, what word value is obtained by concatenating the bytes $235_8 . 312_8$?

The COMMENTS field is ignored by the assembler, but it is essential to good programming. This field should describe the algorithms and data structures used in the program. Assembly language programs in this book are commented either by English sentences or by Pascal-like pseudo-code.

fixed format

Many assembly languages, including 68000 assemblers covered in this book, accept *fixed-format* lines with the following restrictions:

- Fields are separated by one or more spaces or tabs.

- A label, if present, begins the line; it has no spaces or tabs preceding it. A line with no label begins with at least one space or tab.

- Multiple operands are separated by commas (or other punctuation marks in some cases); no spaces or tabs appear in the operand field.

- The comment field may start after a space or tab after the last operand (or opcode field if the instruction has no operand).

- A line beginning with an asterisk (*) is a full-line comment.

free format   *Free-format* assembly languages such as MDS and MPW, while still being line oriented, allow additional flexibility in the line format:

- A label may be immediately followed by a colon (:), in which case it may have spaces or tabs preceding it.

- Comments may start with a semicolon (;).

- Spaces may appear between operands if comments start with semicolons.

An example of a free-format assembly language is shown below:

```
START: MOVE.W (A0),Y ;These two lines are really tight.
 SUB.W QQ,ZEB
;        The rest of these lines are more typical.
NEXT:  ADD.W   ZEB,   D1   ;It's nice to make fields line up...
       MOVE.W  (A1),  ZEB  ;Where to put the semicolon is a
 LOOP: BEQ     FIRST;       matter of taste, but be consistent!
```

6.1.2   Pseudo-operations and the PLC

pseudo-operation   The assembly language program in Table 6–1 contains both machine instruc-
assembler   tions and pseudo-operations. *Pseudo-operations* (or *assembler directives*) tell
directive   the assembler how to assemble the program, and may or may not generate in-
                     structions or data. Table 6–2 lists standard 68000 assembler pseudo-operations;
                     we'll explain them shortly.

TABLE 6–1   Assembly language program for the 68000.

```
*                          Add the first 17 integers.
        ORG     $2000      Start at address 2000 hex.
START   CLR.W   SUM        Clear SUM.
        MOVE.W  ICNT,D0    Get initial value for CNT.
ALOOP   MOVE.W  D0,CNT     Save value of CNT.
        ADD.W   SUM,D0     Add to SUM.
        MOVE.W  D0,SUM
        MOVE.W  CNT,D0     Update CNT.
        ADD.W   #-1,D0
        BNE     ALOOP      Continue if CNT not zero yet.
        JMP     SYSA       Go to operating sys. when done.
SYSA    EQU     $8008      Operating sys. return address.
CNT     DS.W    1          Reserve storage for CNT.
SUM     DS.W    1          Reserve storage for SUM.
IVAL    EQU     17         Initial value is 17.
ICNT    DC.W    IVAL       Store initial value.
        END     START
```

TABLE 6–2   Assembly language pseudo-operations.

Name	Format	Description
Origin	ORG expr	PLC := expr;
Equate	label EQU expr	EnterSymbol(label,expr);
Define Constant (Byte)	label DC.B expr	EnterSymbol(label,PLC); MEM[PLC] := Bits(7,0,expr); PLC := PLC + 1;
Define Constant (Word)	label DC.W expr	AlignPLC; EnterSymbol(label,PLC); MEM[PLC] := Bits(15,8,expr); MEM[PLC+1] := Bits(7,0,expr); PLC := PLC + 2;
Define Constant (Long)	label DC.L expr	AlignPLC; EnterSymbol(label,PLC); MEM[PLC] := Bits(31,24,expr); MEM[PLC+1] := Bits(23,16,expr); MEM[PLC+2] := Bits(15,8,expr); MEM[PLC+3] := Bits(7,0,expr); PLC := PLC + 4;
Define Storage (Byte)	label DS.B expr	EnterSymbol(label,PLC); PLC := PLC + expr;
Define Storage (Word)	label DS.W expr	AlignPLC; EnterSymbol(label,PLC); PLC := PLC + 2*expr;
Define Storage (Long)	label DS.L expr	AlignPLC; EnterSymbol(label,PLC); PLC := PLC + 4*expr;
End Assembly	END expr	IF doingPass1 THEN GOTO Pass2 ELSE EndAssembly;

Notes: expr is any allowed expression.
      MEM[x] is loaded at load time.
      AlignPLC adds 1 to PLC if PLC is odd.
      label is optional except with EQU.
      EnterSymbol(label,expr) enters label into the symbol table with value expr.
      Bits(from,to,expr) returns the specified field of expr, as in Table 5–8 on page 156.

An assembler that processes the text in Table 6–1 produces a listing such as the one shown in Table 6–3. The assembler automatically numbers the lines of the text file to facilitate references and corrections to them. To keep track of where assembled instructions and data are to be loaded in memory, the assembler uses an internal variable called the *program location counter* (PLC). The second column in Table 6–3 shows the value contained in the PLC just before each line of code is assembled.

program location counter (PLC)

The PLC is initialized by means of the ORG pseudo-operation. It is updated after each line of assembly code is processed, normally by adding the length of the instruction or data just assembled. The current value of the PLC may be referenced in expressions by a special symbol such as *.

ORG

*

During the assembly of instructions, the PLC corresponds to the value

TABLE 6-3   Assembler listing for a program.

LN#	PLC	CONTENTS	LABEL	OPCODE	OPERAND	COMMENTS
1	00000000		*			Add the first 17 integers.
2	00000000			ORG	$2000	Start at address 2000 hex.
3	00002000	4278 2024	START	CLR.W	SUM	Clear SUM.
4	00002004	3038 2026		MOVE.W	ICNT,D0	Get initial value for CNT.
5	00002008	31C0 2022	ALOOP	MOVE.W	D0,CNT	Save value of CNT.
6	0000200C	D078 2024		ADD.W	SUM,D0	Add to SUM.
7	00002010	31C0 2024		MOVE.W	D0,SUM	
8	00002014	3038 2022		MOVE.W	CNT,D0	Update CNT.
9	00002018	0640 FFFF		ADD.W	#-1,D0	
10	0000201C	66EA		BNE	ALOOP	Continue if CNT not zero yet.
11	0000201E	4EF8 8008		JMP	SYSA	Go to operating sys. when done.
12	00002022		SYSA	EQU	$8008	Operating sys. return address.
13	00002022	????	CNT	DS.W	1	Reserve storage for CNT.
14	00002024	????	SUM	DS.W	1	Reserve storage for SUM.
15	00002026		IVAL	EQU	17	Initial value is 17.
16	00002026	0011	ICNT	DC.W	IVAL	Store initial value.
17	00002028			END		

SYMBOL TABLE:

SYMBOL	VALUE	SYMBOL	VALUE	SYMBOL	VALUE	SYMBOL	VALUE
ALOOP	00002008	CNT	00002022	ICNT	00002026	IVAL	00000011
START	00002000	SUM	00002024	SYSA	00008008		

that the hardware program counter (PC) has when the program runs. However, the PLC is not always the same as the run-time PC. For example, during the assembly of data constants, the PLC takes on values that the PC never has unless the program tries to execute its data as instructions!

symbol table

The assembler keeps track of user-defined symbols by means of a *symbol table*. Normally, when an identifier appears in the LABEL field, it is entered into the symbol table with the current value of the PLC. Notice that many of the symbols are used before they are defined; these are called *forward references*. The assembler resolves forward references by making two passes over the program, building the symbol table in the first pass and assembling the instructions in the second pass, as described in detail in the next section. (If this isn't clear, you may need a two-pass reading!)

forward reference

EQU

The EQU pseudo-operation is the only operation that does not assign the current PLC value to its label; the value of the EQU's operand is used instead. Thus, EQU can be used to assign a constant value to a symbol, much like a CONST definition in Pascal. It is possible to write a program without using EQU at all, but EQUs make programs more readable and easier to update. The program in Table 6-3 shows two different uses of EQU. In line 12, EQU is used to define an address while, in line 15, it is used to define a constant data value.

It is important to note that `EQU` directly affects only the symbol table generated during the assembly process; it does not cause any values to be stored in memory when the program is loaded. Therefore, the `PLC` is not changed by the `EQU` statements in Table 6–3.

`DC.B`
`DC.W`
`DC.L`

Constant values are stored in memory by the `DC.B`, `DC.W`, and `DC.L` pseudo-operations, which evaluate their operands at assembly time and store the resulting byte, word, or longword values in memory when the program is loaded. These pseudo-operations may have multiple operands separated by commas; the values are stored into successive memory locations.

The distinction between `EQU` and `DC` pseudo-operations has been known to escape some students, yet it is an extremely important distinction to understand. An `EQU` statement defines an *assembly-time constant*, making an association between a symbol and a number that is valid only during the assembly process. Any time that the assembler encounters the `EQU`'ed symbol, it substitutes the corresponding numeric value as if the number itself has been typed. Thus, the statement

assembly-time constant

```
SIZE     EQU      1000
```

allows a programmer to write the statement

```
        MOVE.W   #SIZE,D0
```

instead of

```
        MOVE.W   #1000,D0
```

If the programmer wants to change the "size" (`SIZE`), only the `EQU` statement defining `SIZE` must be changed; the programmer need not search the entire program for all `MOVE.W #1000,D0` instructions. Indeed, the latter procedure requires extraordinary care if the number 1000 is also used in other contexts unrelated to its use as `SIZE`.

run-time constant

A `DC` statement defines one or more *run-time constants*, numbers that are actually stored into the computer's memory when the program is loaded, numbers that are available for the processor to read while executing the program. Thus, the statement

```
ICNT     DC.W     17
```

sets aside a memory word in which the number 17 is stored when the program is loaded. In the assembler's symbol table, the value of the symbol `ICNT` is not 17 but *the address at which the number 17 is stored* ($00002026 in Table 6–3). Hence a program could load the number 17 into D0 with the instruction

```
        MOVE.W   ICNT,D0
```

which is a symbolic way of writing the instruction

```
        MOVE.W   $00002026,D0
```

Mac Note

The example program from Table 6–3 is rewritten and reassembled for the Macintosh as shown below.

```
ADDR    CONTENTS   LABEL    OPCODE    OPERAND        COMMENTS

0000    426D FEFC  START    CLR.W     SUM(A5)        ;Clear SUM.
0004    303A 001A           MOVE.W    ICNT,D0        ;Get initial value for CNT.
0008    3B40 FEFE  ALOOP    MOVE.W    D0,CNT(A5)     ;Save value of CNT.
000C    D06D FEFC           ADD.W     SUM(A5),D0     ;Add to SUM.
0010    3B40 FEFC           MOVE.W    D0,SUM(A5)
0014    302D FEFE           MOVE.W    CNT(A5),D0     ;Update CNT.
0018    D07C FFFF           ADD.W     #-1,D0
001C    66EA                BNE       ALOOP          ;Continue if CNT not 0 yet.
001E    A9F4                _ExitToShell             ;Go to oper. sys. when done.
FEFE(D)            CNT      DS.W      1              ;Reserve storage for CNT.
FEFC(D)            SUM      DS.W      1              ;Reserve storage for SUM.
0020              IVAL      EQU       17             ;Initial value is 17.
0020    0011      ICNT      DC.W      IVAL           ;Store initial value.
0022                        END
```

SYMBOL TABLE:

SYMBOL	VALUE	TYPE	SYMBOL	VALUE	TYPE	SYMBOL	VALUE	TYPE
ALOOP	00000008	code	CNT	FFFFFEFE	data	ICNT	00000020	code
IVAL	00000011	const	START	00000000	code	SUM	FFFFFEFC	data

A few changes have been made in the source text of this version because of the particular run-time environment for Macintosh programs:

- There is no ORG statement.

- Variables are accessed using based addressing with A5.

- The _ExitToShell macro returns control to the operating system.

The assembler handles some things differently too. Each symbol has an associated *type*:

code
- A code symbol represents the address of an instruction or data constant. Its value is a relative displacement from the beginning of the program's code module.

data
- A data symbol represents the address of a data variable. Its value is a displacement from the base address of the application global space, the address contained in A5 at run time.

const
- A const symbol represents a constant numeric value, usually assigned by EQU.

A Macintosh assembler handles operands differently depending on their type; for example, a code operand of an instruction is assembled using relative addressing. The assembler also checks for some errors based on symbol types; for example, a code symbol may not appear as a destination operand, since in the 68000 destination operands may not use relative addressing. Some Macintosh assemblers automatically use based addressing with A5 as the default for data operands; for example, if all of the "(A5)" suffixes were dropped in the program above, the MPW assembler would still produce the same object code.

This instruction reads the contents of memory location $00002026, and deposits this word (which happens to be 17) into D0.

Notice that the first action of DC.W and DC.L in Table 6–2 is AlignPLC. Since words and longwords must be aligned on word boundaries, DC.W and DC.L ensure that the PLC is even by adding 1 to it if it isn't already even, before setting aside any words in memory. An odd PLC value can result from previous byte pseudo-operations.

Character strings may be used with the DC.B directive to store ASCII characters in memory. For example,

```
HIMSG   DC.B    'Hello, world!'
```

stores a sequence of 13 ASCII characters into successive memory bytes beginning at the current PLC. The leftmost character in the string is stored at the lowest memory address. Numeric constants may be mixed with character constants in these directives; this capability is most often used to terminate a string with a zero byte, so that programs can detect the end of variable-length strings:

```
HIMSG   DC.B    'Hello, world!',0
```

DC.W and DC.L may also be used to store character strings; they pad the last word or longword with zero bytes if the string length is not a multiple of 2 or 4, respectively.

DS.B

We continue with a few more pseudo-operations. DS.B advances the PLC to reserve one or more memory bytes for storing variables, without causing the bytes to be initialized when the program is loaded. This is analogous to a variable declaration in Pascal, where the values of variables in a program or

DS.W
DS.L

procedure block are undefined when the block is entered. DS.W and DS.L are similar to DS.B; they reserve a specified number of words or longwords.

Like their DC counterparts, DS.W and DS.L align the PLC to a word boundary before reserving any memory words. Consider the following program fragment:

```
        ORG     $2000
STRING1 DC.B    'Slot Machine',0
STRING2 DC.B    'How much money do you have to start with?',0
        . . .
STRING9 DC.B    'Sorry, no credit!',0
        DS.W    0
SLOTSIM LEA     STKE,SP
        . . .
```

Here the pseudo-operation DS.W 0 is used to force the PLC to an even value before a sequence of instructions. This is particularly useful after a sequence of byte definitions where it's not obvious whether the PLC is left odd or even.

Unlike Pascal CONST and VAR declarations, the EQU, DC, and DS pseudo-operations may appear in the middle or at the end of an assembly language program. However, pseudo-operations that store constants or reserve memory

Mac Note

Most Macintosh assemblers, including MDS, automatically keep track of code and data modules separately. The assembler uses an internal variable, the program location counter (PLC), to keep track of the address at which instructions and run-time constants (defined by DC) are to be assembled. Rather than an absolute address, the PLC contains the relative displacement of the current instruction or data constant from the beginning of the program's code module.

In order to keep track of variable addresses, Macintosh assemblers such as MDS use a second internal variable, the *data location counter* (DLC). The DLC contains the displacement between the address of the last variable allocated and the base address of the application global space (contained in A5 at run time). The DLC is normally initialized to –$100 when assembly begins (to account for the space used by the QuickDraw globals), and manipulated only by DS pseudo-operations. A DS.size expr pseudo-operation causes the following assembler actions:

DLC

DS

(1) If size is W or L and DLC is odd, subtract 1 from DLC to force word alignment.

(2) Allocate space by subtracting the size of the data from DLC (e.g., if size is W, then DLC := DLC – 2*expr). Note that space is allocated in the direction of *decreasing* memory addresses.

(3) If a label is present, enter it into the symbol table with type data and value equal to the current DLC.

code module
data module

The MPW assembler can also keep track of code and data separately, but not automatically. In MPW, the programmer can declare an arbitrary number of independent code and data modules, each of which may be loaded into a separate area of memory. The assembler has a separate PLC or DLC for each one. This feature makes the MPW assembler much more powerful than MDS for developing large programs, but a bit inconvenient for small programs. Special pseudo-operations must be used to declare the names and the beginning and ending points of each code and data module, and special CODE and DATA directives are used to switch back and forth between modules.

Thus, to assemble any of our example Macintosh programs with MPW, we must add the following lines before the first executable instruction:

```
MAIN                    ;Start "MAIN" program module.
DATA    DECR            ;Start an associated data module
                        ;  in which DS's DECRement the DLC.
ORG     -$100           ;Subtract $100 from DLC to account for
                        ;  the space used by QuickDraw globals.
CODE                    ;Executable instructions follow.
```

Subsequently, each DS statement or contiguous list of DS statements must be preceded with a DATA directive, and followed with a CODE directive if any instructions or data constants follow it. If the DATA directive is omitted, then MPW's DS pseudo-operation allocates space in-line with instructions, as in the Motorola assemblers.

must not be used in the middle of a sequence of executable instructions. For example, consider the following program fragment:

```
        MOVE.W  SUM,D0
SUM     DS.W    1
        ADD.W   NEXT,D0
```

After executing the `MOVE.W` instruction, the computer will interpret whatever value happens to be stored in location `SUM` as an instruction, creating havoc by performing an unpredictable operation.

The assembler allows instructions and data to be mixed up as shown above, so it is up to the programmer to exercise care in allocating data areas in programs. In many program development environments, instruction areas and variable data areas must be strictly separated, either because the instructions are stored in ROM, or because instructions and data may be put in different areas in memory each time the program is loaded and runs, as in the Macintosh environment. In such environments, only `DC` (run-time constant) definitions can be used in the instruction area, and variables must be allocated by some other, environment-specific method. For example, the `DS` pseudo-operation does this in a special way in Macintosh assemblers, as described in the Mac Notes in this section. In any case, it is a good idea to get into the habit of grouping all variable and constant definitions together at one place in a program (or in a separate "include file") rather than scattering them all over the program text as they are needed.

`END`

The `END` pseudo-operation indicates the end of the assembly language program. In some programming environments, `END` may be optionally followed by the address of the first executable instruction, the "starting-execution address" of the program. This information is used by the loader to automatically start execution of the program after it is loaded.

6.1.3 Expressions

The operand field of an assembly language statement may contain an expression; the allowable expressions depend on the assembler. The following are valid expressions in almost any assembly language:

- A constant value.

- The current value of the `PLC` (e.g., `*`).

- A previously defined symbol.

- Two or more items above combined by arithmetic operators + and –.

Some assemblers, including Motorola's 68000 assemblers, also support multiplication, division, logical, and shift operators, and allow parenthesization and recognize operator precedence much like a high-level language does. However, in more primitive assemblers, these features are not included, and expression evaluation is often strictly left to right, so that `P+Q*R` is evaluated as `(P+Q)*R`, not `P+(Q*R)` as we would expect in Pascal. For clarity and safety, it's best to write `Q*R+P` in this situation so that we obtain the same result in any case.

There is another very important distinction between expressions in assembly language and in high-level languages. An operand expression in a high-level assignment statement is evaluated at *run time*, while the operand expression in an assembly language statement is evaluated at *assembly time*. Compare the following two statements:

```
D0 := XX;        {Assign the value of variable XX to D0.}
MOVE.W XX,D0     Load D0 with contents of mem location XX.
```

Apparently, the effect of both statements is the same, if we say that the address of a variable is equivalent to its name. However, consider what happens if the operand is not a simple variable:

```
D0 := XX+2;      {Add 2 to value of variable XX, store in D0.}
MOVE.W XX+2,D0   Load D0 with contents of mem location XX+2.
```

In the high-level language statement, the value of variable XX is read when the program is run, and then 2 is added. In assembly language, the operand expression is evaluated when the program is assembled, *not* when the program is run. The run-time effect of MOVE.W XX+2,D0 is to load D0 with the contents of memory location XX+2, which has nothing to do with the contents of location XX.

When an assembler evaluates expressions and assigns values to symbols in an assembly language program, it must internally use a number of significant bits at least as large as the width of the largest possible operand. Since the 68000 can manipulate 32-bit data and, in some members of the 68000 family, 32-bit addresses, a 68000 assembler must use at least 32-bit arithmetic to evaluate expressions and keep track of symbol values.

6.1.4   Assembly-Time, Load-Time, and Run-Time Operations

Probably the most important concept for novice assembly language programmers to learn is the distinction between assembly-time, load-time, and run-time operations, so we'll discuss them one more time:

assembly-time operation
- *Assembly-time operations* are performed by the assembler program, only once, when the assembly language program is assembled. Operand expressions are always evaluated at assembly time. When you see the operators + and –, remember that the additions and subtractions are performed by the assembler, not when the program is run.

load-time operation
- *Load-time operations* are performed by the loader program, only once, when the object program is loaded into memory. All instructions, and data constants generated by DC, are deposited in memory at load time.

run-time operation
- *Run-time operations* are performed by the machine language program on the target machine each time the corresponding instructions are executed. For example, an ADD.W instruction performs a run-time addition.

Sometimes the jargon used by assembly language programmers blurs the distinction between assembly-time and run-time operations. From the assembler's viewpoint, a symbol such as CNT in Table 6–3 is equivalent to its value in the symbol table, $2022. However, when programmers talk about run-time operations, they often use a symbol to refer to the contents of the corresponding memory address. Thus, a program might contain the comment `CNT:=15` or `Address(CNT)=$2022` when what it should really say is `MEM[CNT]:=15` or `CNT=$2022`. The meaning of such a comment is usually clear from the context.

Like instructions, all of the data values generated by `DC` statements are loaded into memory by the loader only once, at *load time*. It is customary to initialize run-time constants at load time, such as `ICNT` in Table 6–3. However, a good programmer must resist the temptation to initialize *variables* at load time. For example, changing line 14 of Table 6–3 to

```
SUM     DC.W    0
```

apparently eliminates the need for the `CLR.W` instruction that sets `SUM` to zero. This would be true if the program were executed only once. However, if the program were restarted at address `$2000` a second time without reloading it, `SUM` would still have the value produced by the program's previous execution, not zero. Therefore, all variables must be initialized at *run time*.

serially reusable   A program that can be terminated at an arbitrary point and immediately restarted from the beginning without error is called *serially reusable*. Assuming that a program is usable to begin with, adherence to one simple rule guarantees that the program is serially reusable:

- No instruction may modify another instruction or any other memory location that was initialized at load time.

In particular, locations initialized by `DC` or similar pseudo-operations must not be modified by the program.

self-modifying code   Programs that modify their own instructions as they execute are called *self-modifying*. Self-modifying code was used in early computers that lacked indirect addressing; the only way to access a memory location whose address was computed at run time was to "plug" the address into an instruction. However, using self-modifying code in modern machines is completely unnecessary, highly unstructured, difficult to debug, and likely to lead to the programmer's dismissal, especially when someone tries to run the code from read-only memory!

6.2 THE TWO-PASS ASSEMBLER

Assembly language allows forward references whereby a symbol may be referenced before it is defined, as shown below:

```
INITN   DS.W    1
        ...
        MOVE.W  INITN,D0        Get initial value.
        BNE     NEXT            OK if nonzero.
        MOVE.W  #10,D0          If zero use default.
NEXT    MOVE.W  D0,CNT          Initialize count.
        ...
CNT     DS.W    1
```

Here, the machine instruction for MOVE.W INITN,D0 can be generated immediately, because the address INITN has already been defined. However, MOVE.W D0,CNT and BNE NEXT contain forward references; their operands are not defined until later in the program. By moving the definition of CNT to the beginning of the program, we could eliminate one forward reference, but this trick isn't applicable to the other one.

two-pass assembler

A *two-pass assembler* program resolves forward references by reading the source file twice. On the first pass, each line is scanned and the symbol definitions that are encountered are used to build the symbol table. On the second pass, the lines are scanned again, and this time the appropriate machine language instructions and data are placed in the object module, and a listing is made if requested. Since all symbols are defined by the end of Pass 1, references to them can be resolved in Pass 2 by simply searching the symbol table. (A *one-pass assembler* avoids the second pass by clever programming techniques that "fix up" forward references as the necessary symbol definitions are encountered.)

one-pass assembler

To build the symbol table, a two-pass assembler must be able to update the PLC properly after reading each line of the source program in Pass 1. If a source line contains a machine instruction, the assembler must determine the length of the instruction, even though the value of its operand(s) may not yet be known. Fortunately, the length of an instruction usually can be determined from only the opcode mnemonic and the addressing modes of its operands, if any. For example, in the 68000 RTS is always one word long, while the length of MOVE.W src,dst depends on the addressing modes specified for the src and dst operands; the length can vary from one to five words.

Unfortunately, in some cases the length of a 68000 instruction depends on the assembly-time value of its operand(s). For example, consider the instruction MOVE.L VAR,D0. This instruction can always be encoded in three words using long absolute addressing for VAR. However, if the assembly-time value of address VAR is in the top or bottom 32 Kbytes of the address space, the 68000's short absolute addressing mode allows the instruction to be encoded in only two words. Therefore, most 68000 assemblers minimize program size by looking at the assembly-time value of VAR and using the short mode if possible.

In the MOVE.L VAR,D0 example, VAR may be a forward reference. In this case, the assembly-time value of VAR is undefined when the MOVE.L VAR,D0 instruction is encountered during Pass 1, and so the assembler can't tell whether short absolute addressing will be possible. Different assemblers treat this case in different ways.

Motorola's resident assembler uses a default of long absolute mode for as-yet-undefined addresses encountered during Pass 1, but it gets confused if the address can be expressed in short absolute mode during Pass 2. The programmer

phase error

can avoid these assembler *phase errors* by explicitly using a .W or .L size suffix with absolute operands, for example, MOVE.L VAR.W,D0. Notice that the opcode suffix (in this case, .L) applies to the operation and operand size, while the operand suffix (.W) applies to the addressing mode.

Motorola's older cross macro assembler does not use an operand size suffix

TABLE 6–4   Forward references using EQU.

```
*            One level of forward referencing with EQU, OK for some assemblers.
START        ...
             ...
LEN     EQU     LAST-START     LAST is undefined at this point in Pass 1
*                              and therefore so is LEN.
LENGTH  DC.L    LEN            However, LEN is properly defined in Pass 2,
*                              in time to be used here.
             ...
LAST    EQU     *              Address just past program end.
        END
*
*            Two levels of forward referencing with EQU -- unacceptable.
START        ...
             ...
LENGTH  DC.L    LEN            LEN is undefined at this point in both
*                              Pass 1 and Pass 2 -- error.
LEN     EQU     LAST-START     LAST is undefined at this point in Pass 1,
*                              and therefore so is LEN.  LEN is defined
*                              here in Pass 2, but too late to use above.
             ...
LAST    EQU     *              Address just past program end.
        END
```

to distinguish long and short absolute addressing modes. Instead, it chooses short or long absolute addressing depending on whether it has most recently seen an ORG or an ORG.L directive. Therefore, a program that is limited in size to the top and bottom 32 Kbytes of the address space may use the ORG directive to force all absolute addressing forward references to use the short mode, while a program that lies outside this range must use the ORG.L directive if it contains any forward-referenced absolute addresses.

ORG.L

If a source line contains a pseudo-operation that affects the PLC, the assembler must determine the effect on the PLC during Pass 1. For example, on DC.B the PLC should be incremented by the number of operands, that is, the number of memory byte values being defined. In Pass 1 the number of operands is known even if their values aren't. On the other hand, an operand of ORG or DS.x must be already defined when the pseudo-operation is first encountered in Pass 1, because the effect on the PLC depends on the operand's value.

Although EQU doesn't affect the PLC, its operands generally should not contain forward references. "Smart" assemblers may tolerate one level of forward referencing as shown in Table 6–4. Others may produce an error message if any symbols are still undefined at the end of Pass 1.

A simple two-pass assembler for our Chapter 5 subset of the 68000 instruction set is outlined in Table 6–5. During Pass 1, each line is scanned and labels are entered into the symbol table. Each line is classified according to the type of pseudo-operation or machine instruction specified by the opcode field. In this simple assembler, almost all machine instructions are treated alike.

TABLE 6–5   Two-pass assembler program.

```
PROGRAM Assembler (input,output);
TYPE
   charCol = 1..128; {Column numbers in input line}
   byteVal = 0..255; wordVal = 0..65535; {Bytes and words}
   longVal = 0..4398046511103; {Longwords}
   string8 = ARRAY [1..8] OF char; {Up to 8-char labels}
   mnemonicType = (null,comment,org,equ,dcx,dsx,branch,others,aend);
VAR
   mnemonic: mnemonicType;  opword: wordVal;  PLC: longVal; opLen: 1..4;
   label8: string8;  inputLine: ARRAY [charCol] OF char;
   opExpr: charCol; {Points to start of operand expr. in inputLine}
   gotOper, gotLabel: boolean;
   symbols: ARRAY [1..200] OF string8; {Symbol Table: 8-char symbols}
   symVals: ARRAY [1..200] OF longVal; {Symbol Table: 32-bit values}
PROCEDURE Enter (symbol: string8; symVal: longVal);
   { Enter a symbol and its value into the symbol table.}
FUNCTION SymbolValue (symbol: string8): longVal;
   { Find a symbol in the symbol table and return its value.}
PROCEDURE GetLine;
   { Get next line of text from input file and put in inputLine.}
PROCEDURE RewindSourceFile;
   { Make GetLine restart at the first line of the source file.}
PROCEDURE ScanLine;
   { Scan inputLine and perform the following functions:
      1. Set gotOper := false; gotLabel := false.
      2. If the line begins with a *, set mnemonic := comment and exit.
      3. If a label is present, set gotLabel := true; label8 := (the label).
      4. If a valid mnemonic and operands are present, set mnemonic :=
         (the corresponding mnemonicType constant); if it is a machine
         instruction, set opword := (the proper opcode word value,
         including src and dst fields if any).
      5. If a nonregister operand is present, set gotOper := true;
         set opExpr := (the starting column number of the operand);
         and set opLen := the operand length in bytes.}
PROCEDURE GetNextOper;
   { Look at global variable opExpr, and update it to point to the
     start of the next nonregister operand expression, if any,
     in inputLine.  Update gotOper and opLen according to the result.}
FUNCTION OperValue: longVal;
   { Evaluate the next nonregister operand expression in inputLine and
     return its value.  The expression is assumed to begin in column
     opExpr or thereafter in inputLine.  The values of symbols that are
     encountered are looked up in the symbol table by SymbolValue.}
PROCEDURE PutObject(addr: longVal; data: longVal; length: 1..4);
   { Enter the value of data into the object file so that it will be
     placed in the memory byte, word, or longword (length = 1, 2, or 4)
     address addr when the object module is loaded.}
```

TABLE 6–5   (continued)

```
BEGIN
  PLC := 0;
  REPEAT  {Pass 1 processing}
    GetLine; ScanLine;
    IF gotLabel AND (mnemonic <> equ) THEN Enter(label8,PLC);
    CASE mnemonic OF
     null, comment, aend: ; {Do nothing}
     orgl: BEGIN PLC := OperValue; AbsAddrDefault := long; END;
      org: BEGIN PLC := OperValue; AbsAddrDefault := short; END;
      equ: Enter(label8,OperValue);
      dcx: BEGIN IF opLen > 1 THEN AlignPLC;
             WHILE gotOper DO BEGIN PLC := PLC + opLen; GetNextOper END;
           END;
      dsx: BEGIN IF opLen > 1 THEN AlignPLC;
             PLC := PLC + opLen*OperValue; END;
   branch: PLC := PLC + 2;
   others: BEGIN PLC := PLC + 2;
             WHILE gotOper DO BEGIN PLC := PLC + opLen; GetNextOper END;
           END;
    END;  {CASE on mnemonic}
  UNTIL mnemonic = aend;  {End Pass 1}
  RewindSourceFile; PLC := 0;
  REPEAT  {Pass 2 processing}
    GetLine; ScanLine;
    CASE mnemonic OF
     null,comment,equ,aend: ; {Do nothing}
     orgl: BEGIN PLC := OperValue; AbsAddrDefault := long;
      org: BEGIN PLC := OperValue; AbsAddrDefault := short;
      dcx: BEGIN IF opLen > 1 THEN AlignPLC;
             WHILE gotOper DO BEGIN
               PutObject(PLC, OperValue, opLen);
               PLC := PLC + opLen; GetNextOper;  END;
             END;
      dsx: BEGIN IF opLen > 1 THEN AlignPLC;
             PLC := PLC + opLen*OperValue; END;
   branch: BEGIN PutObject(PLC, opword DIV 256, 1);
             PutObject(PLC+1, (OperValue-(PLC+2)+256) MOD 256, 1);
             PLC := PLC + 2;  END;
   others: BEGIN PutObject(PLC,opword,2); PLC := PLC + 2;
             WHILE gotOper DO BEGIN
               PutObject(PLC, OperValue, opLen);
               PLC := PLC + opLen; GetNextOper;
             END;
           END;
    END;  {CASE on mnemonic}
  UNTIL mnemonic = aend;  {End Pass 2}
END.
```

Branches are special, because the assembler must calculate an offset from the target address given in the operand field. After each line is scanned, the PLC is updated by an appropriate amount based on the instruction type and, in the case of pseudo-operations, the number or value of operands. During Pass 2, the PLC is maintained in the same way, and the object module is generated.

The details of most of the procedures in Table 6–5 are beyond the scope of this text. For example, a discussion of efficient methods for structuring and managing symbol tables would easily fill a chapter. Also, Table 6–5 does not show how a typical assembler checks for errors. The most commonly detected errors in assembly language programs are listed below:

- **Multiple symbol definition**: In Pass 1, a symbol already in the symbol table was defined again.

- **Illegal opcode**: In Pass 1 or 2, an unrecognizable mnemonic was encountered in the opcode field.

- **Undefined symbol**: In Pass 2, the operand field contained a symbol not in the symbol table.

- **Addressing error**: In Pass 2, an instruction specified an inaccessible address (e.g., a relative branch more than 127 bytes away).

- **Syntax error**: In Pass 1 or 2, an illegal character or ill-formed expression was encountered (e.g., X+:Y).

- **Phase error**: The value of a symbol during Pass 2 is different from what it was during Pass 1. This occurs most often when forward references confuse the assembler into assuming that an instruction is one length during Pass 1 and a different length during Pass 2.

Of course, the assembler detects only errors in assembly language format; the message NO ERRORS DETECTED is no guarantee that the program will run properly when loaded!

6.3 OBJECT MODULES

object module
object program
object file

An *object module* (or *object program* or *object file*) specifies bit strings to be placed into the computer's memory by a loader program. Symbolic information that was present in the assembly language source program is no longer necessary, and so a simple, terse format may be used.

object record

A typical object module format is shown in Figure 6–2(a); an object module is a series of *object records*. Each record has the format of Figure 6–2(b), and contains instruction and data bytes to be loaded into sequential locations in memory. The ADDR field tells the loader the address at which to deposit the first byte, and the BC (byte count) field indicates how many bytes follow.

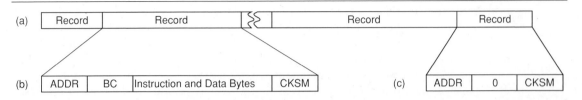

FIGURE 6–2   Object module format: (a) total program; (b) typical record;
(c) starting-execution-address record.

The ADDR field in a particular object module format may be two, three, or four bytes long, depending on the maximum address size that must be supported. The examples in this chapter show four bytes to accommodate a 32-bit address. Likewise, the BC field may be one or more bytes depending on the maximum record size that is desired. Since long programs can always be split into multiple records, we'll use the minimum of one byte for the BC field for examples in this chapter.

In some formats, if a record has a byte count of 0 as in Figure 6–2(c), its *starting-execution address* ADDR field is interpreted to be the *starting-execution address* of the program, the address to which the loader may jump after processing the last record.

checksum The CKSM (*checksum*) field at the end of a record is the two's-complement sum of all the bytes in the record including the ADDR and BC fields and ignoring overflow. This field may be checked by the loader to verify the integrity of the record. If any errors (tape dropouts, noise, etc.) occur when the record is written or read, the chances are 255/256 that the record's checksum will not match the one computed for the corrupted data.

Table 6–6 shows the object module for the source program that was given in Section 6.1. The bytes to be loaded in addresses $2000 through $2021 could have been put into one long record. However, a maximum record length of 16 was imposed for a more readable printed format.

Notice in Table 6–6 that a new record is started for the word at address $2026, so that nothing is loaded at addresses $2022 through $2025. This is done because the corresponding DS.W pseudo-operations in the source program merely reserve space; they do not cause any values to be stored in memory.

At this point, you may be wondering how object modules are actually stored

TABLE 6–6   Object program for the source program in Tables 6–1 and 6–3. Each line represents one record; all values are in hexadecimal.

ADDRESS	BC	DATA BYTES	CKSM
00002000	10	42 78 20 24 30 38 20 26 31 C0 20 22 D0 78 20 24	9B
00002010	10	31 C0 20 24 30 38 20 22 06 40 FF FF 66 EA 4E F8	F9
00002020	02	80 08	CA
00002026	02	00 11	59
00002000	00		20

as files on disk or tape. A common technique is to simply store a sequence of 8-bit bytes. For example, the object program in Table 6–6 would require a total of 66 bytes on the disk or tape: 20 for addresses, 5 for byte counts, 5 for checksums, and 36 for actual bytes to be loaded into memory.

With the above technique it is not possible to print an object file directly, since the 8-bit bytes have no relation to ASCII printing characters. An alternative often used in microcomputer systems is to store object modules as text files containing the actual printing characters that appear in Table 6–6. This format allows object modules to be printed directly, but also requires twice as much storage space since two characters are needed to represent one byte in hexadecimal. This format also makes the loader slightly more complicated, because each character pair must be converted into a byte value as it is read.

Object modules may be concatenated, for example, when several independently assembled program modules are joined to create a large program. It is possible for two or more records in an object module to store bytes at the same address. In this case, the record closest to the end of the module is the last to be processed and therefore has precedence. The last value loaded at a particular address overwrites previous ones. Likewise, if there are two or more starting-execution-address records, the last one takes precedence. For example, suppose the two records in Table 6–7 are appended to the object program in Table 6–6. If this were done, the program would start execution at location 2004 without initializing SUM, and CNT would be initialized to 13_{10} instead of 17_{10}. Such *patch*   perturbations are known as *patches*.

6.4 RELOCATING ASSEMBLERS AND LOADERS

load address   The *load address* of a program is the first address that it occupies in memory. Until now, we have assumed that the load address is fixed by an ORG pseudo-operation and is therefore known at assembly time. This allows the assembler *absolute address* to use known, *absolute* memory addresses in machine instructions and address *absolute code* constants; it generates *absolute code*. However, sometimes the load address of a program cannot be determined until just before the program is loaded. There are two major programming environments in which this problem occurs, and two different ways of dealing with it.

The Macintosh computer is a good example of the first environment, one in which a given application program may have to run on different machines with varying amounts of memory, and with other programs present in memory

TABLE 6–7   Additional records to patch object program.

ADDRESS	BC	DATA BYTES	CKSM
00002026	02	00 0D	55
00002004	00		24

position-
independent
code

at the same time. The load address cannot be fixed, because application programs could not coexist with each other or with the many different versions
of the Macintosh operating system if each program insisted on having a fixed
load address. Therefore, 68000 programs for the Macintosh are written using
position-independent code, so that the program can be loaded anywhere in memory and still run correctly. Special addressing modes and programming methods
for 68000 make this possible, as described in our Mac Notes.

The second environment is a large programming project, in which several
different modules of a program may be written by different people and at different times, and the length of each module is not known until it is completed.
Furthermore, as the program is debugged and maintained, the sizes of different
modules can shrink and expand. Somehow the memory available to the entire
program must be partitioned and load addresses must be assigned to individual
modules. This is the subject of this section.

One approach to partitioning memory is to make a worst-case estimate of
the length of each module and allow enough memory for it; then each module
contains a corresponding ORG statement. This method has two drawbacks. First,
the extra memory at the end of each module is wasted. Second, it is still possible
to underestimate the amount of memory needed by a module. This error is not
always obvious to the programmer, in which case the loader will place part of
one module on top of another, perhaps without even giving an error message.
Once the error is detected, more space must be allocated for the long module
and the load addresses of other modules must be adjusted accordingly.

relocatable
assembler
relocating loader
relocation
dictionary
relocatable code

Relocatable assemblers and *relocating loaders* avoid these problems by
allowing load addresses to be specified at load time. A relocatable assembler
keeps track of what must change in a program if the load address is changed,
and it passes a *relocation dictionary* containing this information to the relocating
loader, along with the assembled instructions. The assembled instructions and
relocation information together are called *relocatable code*.

6.4.1 Relocation

In order to generate relocatable code, a relocatable assembler must distinguish
between absolute and relocatable quantities:

absolute quantity

- The value of an *absolute* quantity (or symbol or expression) is independent
  of where the program is loaded.

relocatable
quantity

- The value of a *relocatable* quantity (or symbol or expression) depends on
  where the program is loaded.

A fairly standard set of rules for distinguishing between absolute and relocatable
quantities is given below:

- A numeric constant is absolute.
- The PLC is relocatable.

- A symbol appearing in the label field of a non-EQU statement is relocatable.

- A symbol appearing in the label field of an EQU statement has the same type as the value in the operand field.

- An expression involving only absolute constants and symbols yields an absolute value.

- If REL is a relocatable symbol and ABS is an absolute constant, symbol, or expression, then the following expression forms yield relocatable values: REL, REL+ABS, ABS+REL, REL-ABS.

- The difference of two relocatable symbols (REL-REL) is absolute. (The offset between two addresses stays constant when the program is moved.)

- The following expression forms are not allowed: REL+REL, ABS-REL, REL*REL, REL*ABS, ABS*REL. Here * is any operator but + or -.

The standard 68000 resident assembler generates relocatable code. For example, Table 6–8 shows the assembler listing for a program including relocation information (some of the machine instructions in this program are not introduced until Chapter 8). The assembler generates instructions and data as if the program will be loaded at memory address given in the ORG addr pseudo-operation. However, it also appends to the object module a list of all the locations containing relocatable quantities, values that must be adjusted if the program is loaded *load displacement* elsewhere. At load time, the programmer specifies a constant called the *load displacement*, which the loader adds to the load address of the relocatable object module and to all relocatable quantities as they are loaded.

All of the quantities marked with an "R" in Table 6–8 are relocatable. The load module for this program has a list of nine hex addresses (0000001C, 20, 24, 28, 38, 40, 44, 4A, 4E) that contain 16-bit relocatable quantities. If a load displacement of $2000 is specified at load time, then the load address is $2000, the starting address is $2018, and the loader adds $2000 to all relocatable quantities (e.g., word $2024 stores the value $2004).

Three symbols in Table 6–8 show typical uses of absolute quantities in a relocatable program:

- The difference between two addresses is absolute (LENGTH).

- A symbol equated with a numeric constant used for counting or similar purposes is absolute (NBITS).

- A fixed address outside the program is independent of the load address and hence absolute (SYSOVF).

TABLE 6–8   Relocatable assembler listing for a 68000 subroutine to divide a 64-bit unsigned integer by a 32-bit unsigned integer.

LN#	PLC	CONTENTS	LABEL	OPCODE	OPERAND	COMMENTS
1	00000000			ORG	0	Start at address 0.
2	00000000		NBITS	EQU	32	32-bit division.
3	00000000		DVND	DS.L	2	Quadword dividend (input).
4	00000008		DVSR	DS.L	1	Longword divisor (input).
5	0000000C		QUOT	DS.L	1	Longword quotient (result).
6	00000010		REM	DS.L	1	Longword remainder (result).
7	00000014		CNT	DS.W	1	Bit count (local variable).
8	00000016	003A	PRGLEN	DC.W	LENGTH	Length of program.
9	00000018	31FC 0020	DIVIDEL	MOVE.W	#NBITS,CNT	Initialize count.
	0000001C	0014R				
10	0000001E	2038 0000R		MOVE.L	DVND,D0	Put dividend into D0,D1.
11	00000022	2238 0004R		MOVE.L	DVND+4,D1	Put dividend into D0,D1.
12	00000026	B0B8 0008R		CMP.L	DVSR,D0	Will quotient fit?
13	0000002A	6504		BCS.S	DIVLUP	Branch if not.
14	0000002C	4EF8 1800		JMP	SYSOVF	Else report error.
15	00000030	E389	DIVLUP	LSL.L	#1,D1	Left shift D0,D1 with LSB:=0.
16	00000032	E390		ROXL.L	#1,D0	A carry here from MSB means
17	00000034	6506		BCS.S	QUOT1	dividend surely > DVSR.
18	00000036	B0B8 0008R		CMP.L	DVSR,D0	Compare high dividend & DVSR.
19	0000003A	6506		BCS.S	QUOTOK	Quotient bit = 0 if lower.
20	0000003C	5281	QUOT1	ADD.L	#1,D1	Else set quotient bit to 1.
21	0000003E	90B8 0008R		SUB.L	DVSR,D0	And update dividend.
22	00000042	5378 0014R	QUOTOK	SUB.W	#1,CNT	Decrement iteration count.
23	00000046	6EE8		BGT.S	DIVLUP	Continue until done.
24	00000048	21C0 0010R		MOVE.L	D0,REM	Store remainder.
25	0000004C	21C1 000CR		MOVE.L	D1,QUOT	Store quotient.
26	00000050	4E75		RTS		Return.
27	00000052		SYSOVF	EQU	$1800	System overflow report addr.
28	00000052		ENDADR	EQU	*	
29	00000052		LENGTH	EQU	ENDADR-DIVIDEL	
30	00000052			END	DIVIDEL	

SYMBOL TABLE:

SYMBOL	VALUE	SYMBOL	VALUE	SYMBOL	VALUE	SYMBOL	VALUE
CNT	00000014R	DIVIDEL	00000018R	DIVLUP	00000030R	DVND	00000000R
DVSR	00000008R	ENDADR	00000052R	LENGTH	0000003A	NBITS	00000020
PRGLEN	00000016	QUOT	0000000CR	QUOT1	0000003CR	QUOTOK	00000042R
REM	00000010R	SYSOVF	00001800				

6.4.2 Linking

The program in Table 6–8 communicates with another program using a known absolute address ($1800); however, this technique is usually impractical in the development of large programs. Just as one does not know the final load address of a module at assembly time, one also does not know the addresses of global

TABLE 6–9   Program with an external reference.

```
        XREF    PTIME           PTIME subroutine is defined elsewhere.
MAIN    ...
        JSR     PTIME           Print current time of day.
        ...
```

variables and subroutines. Therefore, a relocatable assembler provides one more facility—the ability to define symbolic external references that are resolved at load time.

XREF

XDEF

entry symbol

The XREF (external reference) pseudo-operation gives a list of symbols whose definitions are outside the current assembly language program module. The XDEF (external definition) pseudo-operation gives a list of symbols that are defined in the current module but whose definitions are also required by other program modules. Such symbols are often called *entry symbols.*A set of modules that make use of XDEF and XREF are shown in Tables 6–9, 6–10, and 6–11. Notice that XDEF and XREF may refer to either global data addresses (HOUR, MINUTE) or instruction addresses (PTIME).

external expression

Like absolute and relocatable expressions, *external expressions* must conform to a specific format. The following expression forms yield external values, where EXT is an externally defined symbol: EXT, EXT+ABS, ABS+EXT, EXT-ABS. All other forms involving EXT yield undefined values.

Since external symbol references are not resolved until load time, the re-

TABLE 6–10   Program with external references and entry symbols.

```
*       This routine prints the current time of day on a terminal.
        XREF    HOUR,MINUTE     HOUR and MINUTE are defined elsewhere.
        XDEF    PTIME           PTIME may be called by other programs.
PTIME   MOVE.B  HOUR,D1
        ...
        MOVE.B  MINUTE,D1
        ...
        RTS                     Return to calling program.
```

TABLE 6–11   Program with entry symbols.

```
*       The operating system runs this subroutine once per minute
*          to update the time of day.
        XDEF    HOUR,MINUTE     Global variables.
TIMER   ADD.B   #1,MINUTE
        ...
        MOVE.B  HOUR,D2
        ...
        RTS                     Return.
HOUR    DS.B    1
MINUTE  DS.B    1
```

Mac Note

Macintosh assemblers generate "relocatable" code, but not in the traditional way discussed in this section. Macintosh programs are relocatable because they adhere to a set of rules that makes them *position independent*—they can be located anywhere in memory with no changes at all.

A typical Macintosh assembler considers *all* code and data addresses to be relocatable quantities, but it distinguishes between code and data as we've shown previously. Code addresses are normally referenced using PC-relative addressing with displacements that are independent of the program's load address. Likewise, data addresses are normally referenced using based addressing with A5 and fixed displacements from the base of the applciation global space. When a Macintosh program contains just a single object module, the linker doesn't have to adjust any of these displacements.

When a Macintosh program contains multiple object modules, the linker does have some real work to do. Like other linkers, a Macintosh linker must resolve all of the external references and entry symbols in the object modules. In addition, it must combine the code and data portions of all the modules to produce a single contiguous code module that can be loaded in the application heap and a single contiguous data module that can be allocated in the application global space (relative to A5). As a result, most A5-relative displacements must be adjusted.

Note that the total size of the combined data module cannot exceed 32 Kbytes, because the 68000's based addressing mode supports only 16-bit displacements. Likewise, the total size of a single code module cannot exceed 32 Kbytes, because the 68000's relative addressing mode supports only 16-bit displacements.

code segment

jump table

To support programs whose code is larger than 32 Kbytes, the Macintosh linker allows code from multiple modules to be combined and placed in multiple *code segments*, each of which contains less than 32 Kbytes. Intersegment jumps are supported by a *jump table* which the linker builds and places in the application global space, where it may be accessed by any of the code modules.

Thus, when a Macintosh linker resolves jump instructions with external code destinations such as the JSR PTIME instruction in Table 6–6, it first determines if the destination label (PTIME) has been placed in the same segment as the calling instruction. If so, it computes the displacement between the destination label and the calling instruction and modifies the calling instruction to use relative addressing with this displacement. If the destination and caller are in different segments, the linker modifies the calling instruction to use based addressing relative to A5 and to jump to a location in the jump table built by the linker. The jump table contains an absolute jump to the destination label.

It is ironic that even though the 68000 architecture has a full 32-bit unsegmented address space, its lack of 32-bit displacements in based and relative addressing modes forced the Macintosh software designers to use 32-Kbyte segments for position-independent code. The 68020 architecture added addressing modes with 32-bit displacements, but for compatibility reasons Macintosh software designers will probably always be stuck with 32-Kbyte segments.

locatable assembler must append still more information to the object module: (1) a table of all external symbols and the object module locations whose values depend on the external symbols, and (2) a table of all entry symbols and their values. The relocating loader then processes all of the object modules of a large program together, building its own table of external and entry symbols. Since

Mac Note

A program that is assembled with a Macintosh assembler is not automatically guaranteed to be position independent. It is the programmer's responsibility to ensure that all code references use PC-relative addressing, and that all references to data in the application global area are made relative to A5. For example, the following code is *not* position independent, nor is it relocatable by the Macintosh linker:

```
START    ...
         MOVEA.L  ATHERE,A0      ;Load A0 with address of subroutine.
         JSR      (A0)           ;Jump to it.
         ...
ATHERE   DC.L     THERE          ;Address of subroutine.
         ...
THERE    MOVE     D0,D1          ;First instruction of subroutine.
         ...
```

In this code, location **ATHERE** contains the *offset* (say, $00000234) from the beginning of the code module to the first instruction of the subroutine **THERE**. Unlike Motorola's linker, the Macintosh linker does *not* add the module's load address to this value. Thus, at run time, location **ATHERE** still contains the relative offset (say, $00000234), and the JSR instruction jumps to an absolute address ($00000234) that is nowhere near the intended target (unless the load address of the code module happened to be exactly $00000000, which is highly unlikely).

the lengths of the object modules are now known, they can be optimally packed into memory without wasting space. Errors such as undefined and doubly defined external symbols may be detected. The loader may automatically search a library of standard functions (such as mathematics, input/output, general utilities) when undefined symbols are detected. In any case, all of the locations that depend on external symbols are adjusted by adding the value of the external symbol.

linking loader
link editor
linker

A loader that resolves external references, relocates object modules, and loads them is called a *linking loader*. In some systems, a separate program called a *link editor* or *linker* resolves external references and concatenates object modules into one contiguous relocatable object module, without loading it. The new, large object module can then be loaded anywhere in memory by a simple relocating loader that performs no linking.

6.5 MACROS

It is sometimes necessary to use a particular sequence of instructions in many different places in a program. For example, suppose we want to transfer an 8-bit value in the low-order byte of register D0 of the 68000 to the low-order byte of register A0, setting the high-order bytes of A0 to zero. The following instruction sequence does this, assuming that a one-word temporary variable **TEMPA** has been reserved by the statement **TEMPA DS.W 1** elsewhere in the program.

```
MOVE.B   D0,TEMPA+1    Save D0 in low-order byte of TEMPA.
CLR.B    TEMPA         Clear high-order byte of TEMPA.
MOVEA.W  TEMPA,A0      Load 16-bit value TEMPA into A0.
```

macro assembler

macro instruction (macro)

Although space must be allocated for `TEMPA` only once, the above instruction sequence must be replicated each time that D0 is to be transferred to A0. A *macro assembler* eliminates this drudgery by allowing the programmer to define *macro instructions (macros)* that are equivalent to longer sequences. A macro assembler performs all the functions of a standard assembler, plus it handles macros. Exact macro formats and features vary widely, but all macro assemblers perform the basic functions described below. Our examples are compatible with Motorola's cross macro assembler and resident assembler for the 68000.

`MACRO`
`ENDM`
macro definition

Two new pseudo-operations, `MACRO` and `ENDM`, allow the programmer to define a new mnemonic that takes the place of an entire instruction sequence. In the example above, the programmer may place the following *macro definition* at the beginning of the program:

```
MOVD0A0 MACRO
        MOVE.B  D0,TEMPA+1      Save D0 in low-order byte of TEMPA.
        CLR.B   TEMPA           Clear high-order byte of TEMPA.
        MOVEA.W TEMPA,A0        Load 16-bit value TEMPA into A0.
        ENDM
```

Without actually generating any machine instructions, this macro defines the mnemonic `MOVD0A0` to stand for the three-instruction sequence that copies the low-order byte of D0 to A0. Later in the program, the statements

```
        MOVE.B  J,D0
        MOVD0A0
```

macro call
macro expansion
macro parameter
formal parameter

may be used to transfer the 8-bit variable J to A0. The macro assembler *textually* replaces the `MOVD0A0` line with the three-line sequence that we defined earlier in the program. The `MOVD0A0` line is a *macro call* and the textual replacement is a *macro expansion*.

The usefulness of macros is further enhanced by the use of *parameters*. A macro definition may contain *formal parameters*; in the example below, \1 is a formal parameter:

```
MOVXA0  MACRO
        MOVE.B  \1,D0           Put variable into D0.
        MOVE.B  D0,TEMPA+1      Save D0 in low-order byte of TEMPA.
        CLR.B   TEMPA           Clear high-order byte of TEMPA.
        MOVEA.W TEMPA,A0        Load 16-bit value TEMPA into A0.
        ENDM
```

actual parameter

A call of the `MOVXA0` macro specifies *actual parameters* that are substituted for the formal parameters when the macro is expanded. Thus, the line

```
        MOVXA0  J
```

generates instructions to transfer J to A0; in fact, it generates exactly the same machine instructions as the previous two-line sequence using `MOVD0A0`.

\0, \1, ..., \9

In Motorola's 68000 assemblers, a macro definition can have at most ten formal parameters, with the reserved names \0, \1, ..., \9. The general form of a macro definition, with or without parameters, is

```
NAME    MACRO
        ...
        ...                        Macro body
        ...
        ENDM
```

Such a macro may be called by the statement

```
NAME    AP1,AP2,...,APN
```

When the macro is expanded, each appearance of a formal parameter \i (1 ≤ i ≤ 9) in the macro body is textually replaced by the corresponding actual parameter AP*i*. Each actual parameter may be a simple label, an expression, or a complex text string. If the actual parameter contains characters, such as spaces or commas, that could confuse the assembler, then it is enclosed in angle brackets. For example, the following macro definition and call could be made:

```
DEFSTRN MACRO
        DC.B    '\1',0
        ENDM
        ...
        DEFSTRN <One for you, two for me>
```

\0   Formal parameter \0 is special. It is used only in the operation size field in macro definitions and macro calls and allows the programmer to write a macro that can work on bytes, words, or longwords. For example, we could define a macro that ANDs two memory bytes, words, or longwords:

```
ANDM    MACRO
        MOVE.\0  \1,D0
        AND.\0   \2,D0
        MOVE.\0  D0,\1
        ENDM
```

To AND memory words LOCA and LOCB, we call ANDM as follows:

```
ANDM.W  LOCA,LOCB
```

Instead of using predefined parameter names, some macro assemblers, including the Macintosh's, require the formal parameter names to be listed on the first line of the macro definition. This makes the macro body somewhat easier to read and debug, because names can be chosen that have something to do with the function being performed, for example:

```
*         Extract high byte of SRCREG, put into DSTREG.
HIBYTE  MACRO    SRCREG,DSTREG,TMPLONG
        MOVE.L   SRCREG,TMPLONG      Use temporary longword
        MOVE.B   TMPLONG,DSTREG         in memory.
        ENDM
```

However, to be faithful to Motorola, we'll stick with their assemblers' more cryptic notation in this chapter and in the rest of the book.

nested macro call   Macro calls may be *nested*, that is, the body of a macro definition may contain a call to another macro. For example, we could have defined `MOVXA0` as follows:

```
MOVXA0  MACRO
        MOVE.B  \1,D0       Move \1 into D0.
        MOVD0A0             Move D0 to A0.
        ENDM
```

SET

A number of extra pseudo-operations are provided in macro assemblers. One such instruction is `SET`, which is the same as `EQU` except that it allows a symbol to be redefined without causing an error message. To see how this might be used, consider the following problem. A programmer wishes to reserve one contiguous block of memory for all variables; however, the variable definitions are to appear throughout the program, near the routines that use them. To accomplish this, the programmer reserves the memory and defines a macro at the beginning of the program as follows:

```
VARBLK  DS.B    100         Allocate 100 bytes for variables.
VAREND  EQU     *
NEXTV   SET     VARBLK
*
RESERV  MACRO               Reserve \2 bytes for variable \1.
\1      EQU     NEXTV       Enter \1 into symbol table.
NEXTV   SET     NEXTV+\2    Bump NEXTV to next available address.
        ENDM
```

Later in the program, three 1-byte variables and one 2-byte variable may be declared as follows:

```
        RESERV HOUR,1
        RESERV MINUTE,1
        RESERV SECOND,1
        RESERV DATE,2
```

conditional assembly

Macro assemblers also contain *conditional assembly* pseudo-operations that cause subsequent statements to be assembled only if a specified condition is true. The condition is tested at *assembly time*, not run time. For example, the following version of `RESERV` generates an "error message" if the available data area has been exceeded.

```
RESERV  MACRO
        IFGT    NEXTV+\2-VAREND
**  WARNING!! OUT OF VARIABLE SPACE! **
        ENDC
        IFLE    NEXTV+\2-VAREND
\1      EQU     NEXTV
NEXTV   SET     NEXTV+\2
        ENDC
        ENDM
```

IFGT
ENDC
IFLE

Here, `IFGT expr` causes subsequent statements until `ENDC` to be processed if expr>0, and skips them otherwise. Likewise, `IFLE expr` processes the statements if expr<=0.

Sometimes it is necessary to use a label within a macro body, as in the example below:

```
TST24Z   MACRO  VAR          Test high 24 bits of a longword for 0.
         MOVE.W VAR,D0        Test high-order word.
         BNE    \@            VAR not 0 if high-order word not 0.
         MOVE.B VAR+2,D0      Test next byte.
\@       EQU    *             Addr just past end of macro expansion.
*                            Z is now 1 if high 24 bits are 0.
         ENDM
```

\@   If we used a label like `L1` instead of `\@` above, we'd have a problem—since the same label (`L1`) is used every time the macro is called, a multiple symbol definition error occurs the second time that the macro is called. However, the label `\@` is special. Instead of entering `\@` into the symbol table, the assembler enters `@nnn`, where `nnn` is a decimal number from 001 to 999. The assembler generates a new number for each macro call, so each label is unique.

Different macro assemblers handle label definition problems in different ways. Some allow the programmer to declare symbols within a macro as either local or global. Some have a facility for automatically generating unique symbols (e.g., `L00001`, `L00002`, etc.). The most primitive macro assemblers simply require the programmer to make up and pass a unique label as a parameter on each macro invocation.

A macro assembler is a very powerful software tool. In fact, in principle it is possible to write a set of macros for a macro assembler for one machine so that it will recognize the mnemonics of a completely different machine and generate object code for it. The most powerful macro assemblers allow operations such as defining new macros within a macro call and concatenating strings to create unique symbols.

6.6 STRUCTURED ASSEMBLY LANGUAGE

Block-structured high-level languages such as Pascal derive their power and convenience from many features not found in "unstructured" assembly languages:

- The compiler translates each high-level statement into a sequence of machine instructions to perform a desired action, including run-time evaluation of arithmetic and logical expressions.

- The language allows programs and statements to be partitioned into a natural, hierarchical block structure.

- Using block structure, the compiler applies scope rules to variable names and other identifiers so that naming conventions are simplified.

- The language provides high-level statements such as `WHILE`, `REPEAT`, and `FOR` to simplify the control of loops.

TABLE 6–12   Structured assembly language version of DIVIDE program.

```
LABEL divaddr, endaddr;
VAR dvnd, dvsr, quot, rem : long;
proglength : DATAWORD endaddr-divaddr;
PROCEDURE DivideL;
  CONST nbits = 32; sysovfl = $1800;
  VAR cnt : word;
  BEGIN
    divaddr: {Define starting address of procedure code.}
    move dvnd,d0; move dvnd+4,d1.L; {Put dividend into D0,D1.}
    cmp dvsr,d0;   {Will quotient fit?}
    IF CC THEN jmp sysovf;
    clr quot; move dvnd,d1; {Set up operands for division.}
    lda dvnd;  ldb dvnd+1; {a,b := dvnd}
    move #nbits,cnt;   {# of bits in division, iterations of loop.}
    REPEAT
      lsl #1,d1.L; roxl #1,d0.L {Left shift D0,D1.}
      IF CS THEN   {High dvnd > dvsr,   set quotient bit}
        BEGIN add #1,d1.L; sub dvsr,d0 END {and update dividend.}
      ELSE {Trial subtraction needed.}
        BEGIN
          cmp dvsr,d0;
          IF CC THEN   {High dvnd >= dvsr,  set quotient bit}
            BEGIN add #1,d1.L; sub dvsr,d0 END {and update dividend.}
        END;
      sub #1,cnt;
    UNTIL LE; {Repeat for all bits.}
    move d0,rem; move d1,quot; {Save remainder and quotient.}
    rts; {Return.}
    endaddr: {Define last address of procedure code.}
  END;
```

- The language requires each variable or constant to belong to a predefined "type," and it enforces compatibility of types in program statements.

- The language provides a facility for user-defined structured data types.

- The user may write the source program in a free format using separators and comments to improve readability.

*structured
assembly
language*

SCAL

A *structured assembly language* provides all these features except the first—it still translates an assembly language statement into just one machine instruction.

Table 6–12 recodes the DIVIDE program from Table 6–8 into a hypothetical structured assembly language for the 68000, which we'll call *SCAL (Structured-Coding Assembly Language)*. The SCAL program looks like Pascal, but it generates almost the same machine instructions as the unstructured assembly language version.

SCAL programs use spaces, newlines, colons, semicolons, and curly brackets just as Pascal does to format and comment programs. The meanings of reserved words are similar to those in Pascal:

- PROCEDURE: indicates the beginning of a procedure block, beginning a new scope for variable names and other identifiers. Parameters are not shown, but could be supported in a fancier version of SCAL using a stack-oriented passing convention.

- VAR: reserves storage for variables of indicated types; SCAL knows the length of standard types such as byte, word, and long. Variables have scope limited to the block in which they are declared. VAR replaces DS.x from unstructured assembly language.

- DATA: at load time, stores a sequence of bytes, words, or longwords with the specified values, replacing DC.x from unstructured assembly language.

- CONST: at assembly time, equates an identifier with a specified constant or constant expression, replacing EQU from unstructured assembly language. Constants have scope limited to the block in which they are defined.

- LABEL: declares an identifier to be a statement or data label in the current scope. If a label is not declared by LABEL, then its scope is limited to the procedure in which it is defined. In Table 6–12, endaddr and divaddr must be declared in order to be used in the DATA statement, which occurs outside the procedure in which they are defined.

- BEGIN, END: delimit compound statements, including procedure bodies, as in Pascal.

Like Pascal, SCAL contains both simple and structured statements. Standard assembly language instructions such as move #nbits,cnt are the simple statements in SCAL. Notice that size suffixes such as .L are missing from most of SCAL's simple statements. This is possible because SCAL knows a declared type for most operands and can therefore assemble an instruction with the corresponding size, or point out an error if there is a mismatch in sizes. Registers in the 68000, of course, can be used as bytes, words, or longwords. Therefore, SCAL normally determines size from a declared, nonregister operand. If all the operands of an instruction are registers or constants, then a size suffix is needed (e.g., lsl #1,d1.L).

Structured statements in SCAL include compound statements, IF, REPEAT, and WHILE. Table 6–13 shows the unstructured equivalents of SCAL's conditional and repetitive statements. While Pascal statements can test conditions that are arbitrary boolean expressions, SCAL requires *condition* to be one that is tested by a 68000 conditional branch instruction. The condition is specified by the last two letters in the branch mnemonic (see Table 8–9). A condition test must be preceded by a machine instruction that sets the condition bits for the test. Thus, in Table 6–12 the SCAL statements

```
tst dvsr;   {Check for divide-by-zero.}
IF EQ THEN jmp sysovf;
```

TABLE 6–13   Comparison of SCAL structured statements and unstructured assembly language equivalents.

SCAL Structured Statement	Assembly Language Equivalent	
IF *condition* THEN *statement*		B(NOT *condition*) *labelA* *statement*
	labelA:	. . .

IF *condition*
   THEN *statement1*
   ELSE *statement2*
		B(NOT *condition*) *labelA*
		statement1
		BRA *labelB*

	labelA: *labelB*:	*statement2* . . .
REPEAT *statement list* UNTIL *condition*	*labelA*:	*statement list* B(NOT *condition*) *labelA*
WHILE *condition* DO *statement*		BRA *labelB*
	labelA: *labelB*:	*statement* B(*condition*) *labelA*

generate machine instructions corresponding to the assembly language instructions that were shown in Table 6–8:

```
        CMP.L   DVSR,D0
        BCS.S   DIVOK              NOT CC == CS
        JMP     SYSOVF
DIVOK   . . .
```

In a program with complicated loops, the structured statements allow the flow of control to be expressed much more clearly than by a maze of conditional branches. Occasionally the structured statements may produce code that is slightly longer than code with intertwined branches. For example, the program in Table 6–12 replicates two instructions (add #1,d1.L and sub dvsr,d0) that appeared only once in the unstructured assembly language version. However, the benefits of type checking and structure should be worth the slight increase in length using SCAL.

This section has furnished only a brief introduction to structured assembly language. Like their unstructured counterparts, structured assembly languages have instructions and features that vary widely. Motorola's resident assembler for the 68000 supports structured statements directly, while the MPW assembler for the Macintosh has a set of macros that implement structured statements. Among the assemblers for other processors in this book, Intel's standard assembler for the 8086 family is the most structured. Like SCAL, it "types" its operands very strongly according to size and other characteristics, but does not incorporate the features of scope and structured statements.

REFERENCES

Although there is no universally accepted standard assembly language, an IEEE Standards Committee has made an effort to establish one, as described in *Standard for Microprocessor Assembly Language*, IEEE Standard 694-1985.

The most accurate description of the assembly language for a particular computer is usually found in the software supplier's documentation. Motorola's cross macro assembler is described in Motorola publication M68KXASM/D3, *M68000 Cross Macro Assembler Reference Manual*, and the resident assembler is described in publication M68KMASM/D10, *M68000 Family Resident Structured Assembler Reference Manual*. The MPW assembler and its documentation is available from the Apple Programmer's and Developer's Association (Renton, WA 98055), while the MDS assembler is now supported by Consulair Corp. (Portola Valley, CA 94025).

If you get just one book on the Macintosh programming environment, make it *Macintosh Revealed, Volume 1: Unlocking the Toolbox* by Stephen Chernicoff (Hayden, 1987, 2nd ed.). It has an excellent description of the Macintosh run-time environment and the operating-system services available to application programs. Chernicoff has also written a companion volume, *Macintosh Revealed, Volume 2: Programming with the Toolbox* (Hayden, 1987, 2nd ed.) for advanced programmers.

If you've followed our discussion of microcomputer architecture and programming so far, then you would probably find Scott Kronick's introductory *MPW and Assembly Language Programming for the Macintosh* (Hayden, 1987) to be totally worthless technically. On the other hand, if you're confused and ready to give up on assembly language programming, then you might at least get some pleasure from Kronick's nontechnical "fear and loathing" sidebars; San Francisco gossip columnist Herb Caen has called one of Kronick's articles "one of the funniest pieces of stuff I've read in years."

More scholarly, general treatments of assemblers, loaders, and macro processors can be found in Peter Calingaert's *Program Translation Fundamentals* (Computer Science Press, 1988) and in D. W. Barron's little book *Assemblers and Loaders* (MacDonald/Elsevier, 1969). Jim Peterson has written sample assembler and loader programs in the MIX assembly language in his *Computer Organization and Assembly Language Programming* (Academic Press, 1978).

Structured assembly languages have existed for some time. Niklaus Wirth described such a language for the IBM 360 family in "PL/360, A Programming Language for the 360 Computers" (*Journal of the ACM*, January 1968). Probably the earliest structured assembly language for a microprocessor is PLZ/ASM, which Zilog designed for the Z8000 as described in "PLZ: A Family of System Programming Languages for Microprocessors" by Charlie Bass (*Computer*, March 1978).

E X E R C I S E S

6.1 Delete line 010 of Table 6–3 and reassemble the program by hand, showing the effects on the `LN#`, `PLC`, and `CONTENT` columns and on the symbol table.

6.2 Find all the assembly-time errors in the 68000 program below.

```
        ORG     2000H
INIT    MOVE    #0,D0           Initialize variables.
        MOVE.B  D0,V1
        MOVE.B  D0,L1
                                Now do some computation.
LOOP    MOVE.B  V3,A0           Get value of V3.
        MOVE.L  A0,V2           Save it as a longword.
        ADD     D0
        BEQ     L1
        MOVE.B  D0,V3
L1      MOVE.B  D0,V1
        BMI     LOOP            Continue until positive.
        BEQ     SYSOVF
        RET                     Done, return.
V1      DB.S    1
V3      DB.S    1
L1      DC.B    0D
SYSOVF  EQU     1990
        END
```

6.3 If an operand expression has the value -12_{10}, what value should be returned by the function `OperandValue` in Table 6–5?

6.4 Explain how the `branchInstr` case in Pass 2 of Table 6–5 computes the two's-complement offset value for a branch instruction.

6.5 Suppose that the object module produced by a 68000 relocatable assembler is stored as a sequence of ASCII printing characters, as suggested in Section 6.3. Write a complete specification for the object module format, including the list of addresses containing relocatable quantities and the list of external and entry symbols.

6.6 Why is it highly unlikely for the load address of a 68000 code module to be 00000000?

6.7 Can `IF` pseudo-operations be nested? How can the assembler match up `ENDC`s with the appropriate `IF`s?

6.8 Define an `ELSEIF` pseudo-operation that allows an `IF` pseudo-operation to assemble one set of statements or another. How can the assembler match up `ELSEIF`s and `ENDC`s with the appropriate `IF`s? How does this affect nesting of `IF`s?

6.9 Using the instruction execution times that were derived in Exercise 5.11, write a macro `DELAY` with a single parameter `T`, such that the expanded code delays exactly `T` microseconds. (Since few instructions are needed, you can derive their execution times now even if you didn't work Exercise 5.11.) Assume that `T` is interpreted as a 16-bit two's-complement number, and generate no delay if `T` is zero or negative. The expanded code should have less than 20 instructions for any value of `T`. Define all new pseudo-operations (e.g., `IFEQ`) and assembly-time operators (e.g., `DIV`, `MOD`) that you find necessary to write the macro.

C H A P T E R 7

Addressing

address

In order to do useful work, a computer must process data stored in memory. Data-processing instructions contain or imply *addresses* that locate the desired data. The length in bits of an address implies the maximum amount of memory that can be accessed by the processor; for example, a 16-bit address implies a 64-Kbyte memory. According to the designers of the PDP-11 family,[1]

> The biggest (and most common) mistake that can be made in a computer design is that of not providing enough address bits for memory addressing and management. It is clear that another address bit is required every two or three years, since memory prices decline about 30 percent yearly, and users tend to buy constant price successor systems.

The architects of the 68000 family were well aware of this phenomenom, so they provided for 32-bit addresses throughout the 68000 instruction-set design, even though only 24 of those bits were made available on the external pins of the MC68000 chip. Later family members, the MC68020 and MC68030, provide all 32 address bits externally, allowing over 4 billion bytes of physical memory to be directly accessed by the processor chip.

7.1 GENERAL CONCEPTS

Although the simplest way to specify an address is to store it as part of the instruction, the address manipulations required in typical applications suggest additional addressing modes that are more efficient or appropriate. The purposes of some of these addressing modes are to:

---

[1]C. G. Bell and J. C. Mudge, "The Evolution of the PDP-11," in *Computer Engineering: A DEC View of Hardware Systems Design*, by C. G. Bell, J. C. Mudge, and J. E. McNamara (Digital Press, 1978), pp. 381–382.

- Allow an instruction to access a memory location whose address is computed at run time, allowing efficient access of arrays, lists, and all kinds of data structures.

- Manipulate addresses in a way appropriate for the most commonly used data structures, such as stacks and one-dimensional arrays.

- Specify a full memory address with a smaller number of bits, thereby making instructions shorter.

- Compute addresses relative to instruction position so that a program may be loaded anywhere in memory without changing it.

No processor has all addressing modes, but the 68000 has most of them, as discussed in this chapter. The additional addressing modes of the MC68020 and MC68030 are described in Section 14.8. Throughout this chapter and the rest of this book, we'll use "68020" to refer to concepts that apply to both the MC68020 and MC68030.

7.1.1 Address Size and Register Size

In a typical processor, the size in bits of an address and the size of a register are not necessarily equal, but they are related. Table 7–1 lists these sizes for popular processors. Address size is usually the same as or twice the register size. Thus, addresses can be stored in registers or register pairs, and the same registers and instructions can be used for data and addresses.

TABLE 7–1   Address and register characteristics of popular processors.

Processor Family	Register Size (bits)	Address Size (bits)
DEC PDP-11	16	16
DEC VAX-11	32	32
Intel 8051	8	8 or 16
Intel 8080, Z80	8	16
Intel 8086, 80286	16	16[1]
Intel 80386	16 or 32[2]	16 or 32[2]
Motorola 6800, 6809	8	16
Motorola 68000	32	32[3]
National 32032	32	32
Zilog Z8000	16	31[4]
Zilog Z80	8 and 16	16

Notes: 1. On-chip memory management extends this to 20 bits in the 8086 and 80186, and to 24 bits in the 80286.
   2. Register size and address size are dynamically selectable.
   3. Only 24 bits are provided to the external memory address bus in the MC68000 and MC68010; all 32 bits are available in the MC68020 and MC68030.
   4. Only 23 bits used in initial chip design.

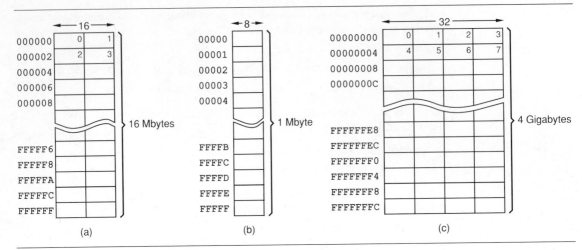

FIGURE 7–1   Arrangement of physical memory in different members of the 68000 family:
(a) MC68000 and MC68010; (b) MC68008; (c) MC68020 and MC68030.

7.1.2   Address Size and Memory Size

The 68000 architecture provides for 32-bit addresses, so that program counter, address registers, and all address arithmetic use 32 significant bits. However, in some members of the 68000 processor family, not all of the address bits are brought out to the processor chip's external pins. With these chips, the physical memory size is limited by the number of address bits physically available, rather than by the 68000 architecture itself.

The width of the data path to physical memory may also vary across a processor family. This data path width does not affect the size of instructions or data or the capacity of the memory as seen by a programmer, but it usually does affect the execution speed of programs. Figure 7–1 summarizes the physical memory arrangements used in the 68000 family.

access

The MC68000 and MC68010 processors provide 24 address bits, accessing a memory of up to 2^{24} bytes. As shown in Figure 7–1(a), the data path to this memory is 16 bits wide, so the processor can *access* (read or write) a 16-bit word in one memory cycle. To access only a single byte, the processor uses special control signals to disable access to the unused byte in the word. For example, when the processor writes a byte at an even address, it does not disturb the low-order (odd) byte in the word. Conversely, to access a longword, the processor must go to the memory twice, accessing first the high-order word and then the low-order word of the longword.

The MC68008 processor, intended for low-cost applications, provides only 20 address bits to access a 1-Mbyte physical memory as shown in Figure 7–1(b). Furthermore, the processor has only an 8-bit data path to the physical memory. Therefore, accesses to memory words or longwords require two or four memory cycles to access the component bytes. This arrangement reduces the number of memory and bus interface chips that are needed to implement a small memory system, while incurring a performance penalty of slower access to instructions and word and longword operands.

The MC68020 and MC68030 processors provide all 32 address bits at external pins, and so a memory of up to 2^{32} bytes (4 Gigabytes) may be addressed as in shown in Figure 7–1(c). Furthermore, a 68020's physical memory is 32 bits wide. Thus, the processor can access an aligned longword—one whose address is a multiple of 4—in one memory cycle. This arrangement provides faster fetching of instructions and longword data than in the other 68000 processors, at the expense of a wider and typically costlier memory. To access only a single word or byte, a 68020 processor uses special control signals to select only the desired portion of the longword.

7.1.3 Address Aliasing

The fact that some 68000 processors use 32-bit addresses internally but only deliver the low-order address bits to the memory system creates some interesting "aliasing" problems. For example, in the MC68000 or MC68010, the 256 different 32-bit addresses, $00123456, $01123456, $02123456, ..., through $FF123456, all access the same location in physical memory. In the 68020, on the other hand, each of these addresses refers to a different physical location. Thus, it is possible to write a program that runs correctly on one processor but not on the other.

For example, any MC68000 program that used the 8 high-order bits of address registers and pointer variables for something other than high-order address bits will fail when run on a 68020. To avoid these portability problems, 32-bit address values in the MC68000 and MC68010 should always be less than or equal to $007FFFFF or greater than or equal to $FF800000. Stated another way, the high-order 9 bits of a 32-bit address in the MC68000 or MC68010 must be all 0's or all 1's.

7.1.4 Alignment

aligned operand

All instructions in the 68000 are an integer number of words (an even number of bytes) long. On the other hand, the instructions may specify operands that are one, two, or four bytes long (bytes, words, and longwords). In general, the 68000 requires instructions and word and longword operands to be *aligned* on word boundaries. That is, an instruction or word or longword operand always starts at an even address, and its bytes are assembled with the more significant bytes in the lower-numbered memory locations. An attempt to access a word or longword at an odd address causes an "address error" trap.

Some processors allow nonaligned words and longwords to be accessed. This feature is a convenience for the programmer, who no longer needs to be concerned about alignment, but it potentially reduces processor performance in two ways. The first performance penalty occurs only when accessing nonaligned words: an extra memory access must be made to build the full word. The second penalty, claim some hardware designers, is more subtle: the extra memory bus interface circuitry used in the processor to rearrange nonaligned words complicates the processor hardware and ultimately reduces the maximum bus speed for all memory accesses. The 68020 can access nonaligned *operands* (not instructions), but alignment of word and longword operands is still recommended for fastest performance.

7.1.5 Addressing Modes

effective address

The purpose of addressing modes is to provide an *effective address* for an instruction's operand. In a data manipulation instruction, the effective address is the address of the data being manipulated. In a jump instruction, it is the address of the instruction being jumped to.

Most of the addressing modes described in this chapter are available in the 68000 processor, and we'll give 68000 program examples. However, for your interest and edification we'll also discuss a few modes that are not available on the 68000, and we'll describe all the extra modes available on the 68020 in Section 14.8.

direct addressing

Addressing modes may be classified as direct and indirect. In a *direct addressing* addressing mode, the effective address is taken directly from the instruction, or computed by combining a value in the instruction with a value in a register. In an *indirect* (or *deferred*) *addressing* mode, the address calculation yields the address of a memory location that contains the ultimate effective address, called an *indirect address*.

indirect addressing

deferred addressing

indirect address

EA field

In the 68000, an effective address is specified by a 6-bit *EA field* in the first word of an instruction (the opcode word). The format of the EA field is shown in Figure 7–2; MOVE instructions have two EA fields, one for each operand. The EA field specifies an operand using 3 bits for an addressing mode (*mode*) and 3 bits for a register (*reg*) to be used in the address calculation. Some addressing modes require additional information, contained in *extension words* following the opcode word.

mode

reg

extension word

The addressing modes and their encoding in the 68000 are modeled after those of the PDP-11, a popular minicomputer that used a 6-bit EA field to specify one of eight addressing modes and one of eight registers. However, the encoding used in the 68000 is much more clever because it allows access to 16 general registers and 12 addressing modes with only 3-bit mode and register-number

```
 11   9 8    6         5    3 2    0
 ┌─────┬──────┐        ┌──────┬──────┐
 │ reg │ mode │        │ mode │ reg  │
 └─────┴──────┘        └──────┴──────┘
      (a)                    (b)
```

FIGURE 7–2   Effective-address (EA) fields for 68000 operands: (a) dst operand of MOVE instructions; (b) all other EA fields.

fields (8 combinations each). In conjunction with the reg field, the eight mode combinations are used as follows:

0 reg specifies a data register (D0–D7) that contains the operand.

1 reg specifies an address register (A0–A7) that contains the operand.

2–6 reg specifies an address register that is used to compute the effective address of an operand in memory.

7 reg specifies one of five addressing modes that do not use the general registers (e.g., immediate, absolute); three combinations are left over for future expansion.

The assembly language notation for addressing modes used by different computers varies widely. Even for the 68000 itself, the notation for some modes varies depending on which assembler is used. The addressing modes of the 68000 and Motorola's resident assembler notation for them are shown in Table 7–2 and discussed in detail in subsequent subsections.

The 68000 has a "consistent" instruction set because any instruction that specifies an operand in memory may do so using any addressing mode that makes sense; but see Section 8.4.1 to find out what "makes sense."

7.2 SINGLE-COMPONENT ADDRESSING MODES

The simplest addressing modes specify an effective address with a single value in the instruction or in a register. Multicomponent addressing modes, described later, combine a value in the instruction with the contents of one or more registers to obtain the effective address.

In the figures in this chapter, "Opcode" denotes the instruction fields that contain the opcode and other information such as addressing mode and operand size. For generality, most figures in this chapter do not show the width of operands, since most instructions can manipulate 8-, 16-, or 32-bit data. Effective addresses are logically 32 bits wide, but different processor models have differing numbers of external pins to address memory physically, as explained previously. Consult Table 7–2 for a summary of the addressing modes discussed in this and the next section.

7.2.1 Register Direct

register direct addressing

In *register direct addressing*, an operand is contained in one of the processor's registers, D0–D7 or A0–A7 in the 68000. Figure 7–3 shows the encoding of a typical instruction using this mode. Since the 68000 has 16 registers but only 3 bits in the reg portion of an EA field, two different modes are required to address

TABLE 7–2   Addressing modes and assembly language notation for the 68000.

Name	mode	reg	Notation	Operand	Extension Words
Data-register direct	0	0–7	Dn	Dn	0
Address-register direct	1	0–7	An	An	0
Immediate	7	4	#data	data	1 or 2
Absolute long	7	1	addr32 or addr.L	MEM[addr32] or MEM[addr]	2
Absolute short	7	0	addr16 or addr.W	MEM[addr16] or MEM[addr]	1
Address-register indirect	2	0–7	(An)	MEM[An]	0
Auto-increment (by 1, 2 or 4)	3	0–7	(An)+	MEM[An], then An := An + operand size	0
Auto-decrement (by 1, 2, or 4)	4	0–7	-(An)	An := An - operand size, then MEM[An]	0
Indexed short	5	0–7	addr16(An)	MEM[addr16+An]	1
Based	5	0–7	disp16(An)	MEM[An+disp16]	1
Based indexed (short)	6	0–7	disp8(An,Xn)	MEM[An+XnLow+disp8]	1
Based indexed (long)	6	0–7	disp8(An,Xn.L)	MEM[An+Xn+disp8]	1
Relative	7	2	raddr16(PC)	MEM[(raddr16-PLC)+PC]	1
Relative indexed (short)	7	3	raddr8(PC,Xn)	MEM[(raddr8-PLC)+PC+XnLow]	1
Relative indexed (long)	7	3	raddr8(PC,Xn.L)	MEM[(raddr8-PLC)+PC+Xn]	1

Notes: Dn denotes a data register: D0–D7.
An denotes an address register: A0–A7 or SP (same as A7).
data is an 8-, 16-, or 32-bit value as needed for the operation size.
MEM[x] is the 8-, 16-, or 32-bit value beginning at memory address x, as needed for the operation size.
addr16 is a 16-bit absolute address, one that the assembler determines to be in the bottom or top 32 Kbytes of the 4-gigabyte address space. addr32 is any other, 32-bit absolute memory address.
addr.L and addr.W are forms used to force the Motorola resident assembler to use absolute long or short mode, respectively, for any absolute address addr. These forms are not recognized by the Motorola cross macro assembler, which uses ORG and ORG.L to set the default absolute addressing mode as explained in Section 6.2.
Xn denotes an index register: D0–D7, A0–A7, or SP (same as A7).
XnLow denotes the 32-bit value obtained by sign extending the contents of the 16 low-order bits of index register Xn.
disp8 and disp16 are 8- and 16-bit values that are sign extended to 32 bits before being used in the effective address calculation.
raddr8 and raddr16 are "relative addresses," ones that are within 128 and 32,768 bytes of the instruction. The instruction contains an 8- or 16-bit displacement (raddr-PLC, where PLC is the address of the extension word) that is sign extended to 32 bits and then added to the PC to obtain the effective address of the operand when the instruction is executed.
The "(PC)" syntax for relative addressing is not used by the Motorola cross macro assembler, which uses a special directive "RORG" to determine when to use relative addressing, as explained in Section 7.3.4.

data register direct addressing

address register direct addressing

all 16 registers. In *data register direct addressing*, the mode field is 0 and reg specifies a data register, D0–D7. In *address register direct addressing*, the mode field is 1 and reg specifies an address register, A0–A7.

Longword operations on 68000 registers obviously must use the entire register. However, as suggested by the dotted lines in the 68000's programming

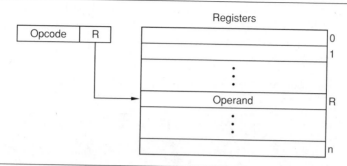

FIGURE 7–3   Register direct addressing.

model (Figure 5–4 on page 139), word operations use the 16 low-order bits of
the register and byte operations use the 8 low-order bits.

Byte and word operations on *data* registers do not use or affect the higher-
order bits of the register. In fact, the high-order bits of a data register cannot be
read or written at all by word or byte instructions, except by a byte or word sign-
extending instruction (EXT) and a word-swapping instruction (SWAP). Therefore,
if a program needs to change only the high-order byte of a register, it must store
the entire 32-bit register into memory, change the appropriate byte in memory,
and then reload the 32-bit register from memory.

Byte operations are not allowed on the *address* registers, but word operations are. When used as a destination operand, the entire 32-bit contents of an
address register is affected regardless of the operation size suffix of the instruc-

sign extension   tion. If the operation size is "word," then the source operand is *sign extended*
to 32 bits before being used. Thus, the instruction MOVEA.W #$1234,A0 sets
A0 to $00001234, while MOVEA.W #$8234,A0 sets A0 to $FFFF8234. This
is consistent with the 68000's notion of 16-bit "short" absolute addresses in the
bottom or top 32 Kbytes of the address space.

All processors must have register mode in some form, otherwise it would
be impossible to do anything with the registers! However, some operations make
no sense with register mode, for example JMP reg—a program can't jump to a
register.

In assembly language programs, registers are usually identified by reserved
identifiers (D0, A5, SP, etc.). Some assemblers, including the MPW assembler
for the Macintosh, allow any identifier to be EQU'ed to a register identifier. A
few, including Motorola's System V/68 assembler, require a special prefix to
distinguish register identifiers from other symbols (e.g., %A1, %D5, %CCR, etc.)

7.2.2   Absolute

absolute   The simplest way to specify a full memory address is to include it as part of
addressing   the instruction using *absolute addressing*, as shown in Figure 7–4. Absolute
                    mode gives the flexibility of specifying any location in the address space of the

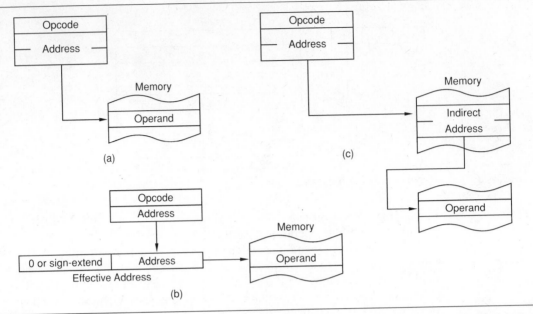

FIGURE 7-4   Absolute addressing modes: (a) long absolute; (b) short absolute; (c) absolute indirect.

computer. We used absolute addressing in our first 68000 assembly language program, Table 5–5 on page 148.

Absolute mode takes many instruction bits in a computer with a large address space—32 bits in the 68000. In order to reduce this number, many computers provide a "short absolute" addressing mode that gives direct access to a limited part of the entire address space. As shown in Figure 7–4(b), an instruction using this mode contains only the low-order address bits, since the high-order bits of the address are set to some default value.

In particular, the 68000 has two distinct absolute addressing modes. In *absolute long addressing*, the instruction has two extension words that contain a full 32-bit memory address, as shown in Figure 7–5(a).

absolute long addressing

absolute short addressing

In *absolute short addressing*, the instruction has only a single extension word from which a full address is derived as shown in Figure 7–5(b). The MSB of the 16-bit value is extended to create a 32-bit number, yielding an absolute address in either the bottom 32 Kbytes (MSB = 0) or the top 32 Kbytes (MSB = 1) of the 4-gigabyte address space. This allows part of the address space to be accessed by shorter instructions. We used this mode for many of the instructions in the 68000 programming examples in Chapters 5 and 6.

For operands that specify absolute addressing, Motorola's assemblers attempt to determine whether the short mode or long mode is appropriate, as explained in Section 6.2. With the resident assembler, the program may use an *operand suffix* (not opcode suffix) of .W or .L to force short or long mode,

operand suffix

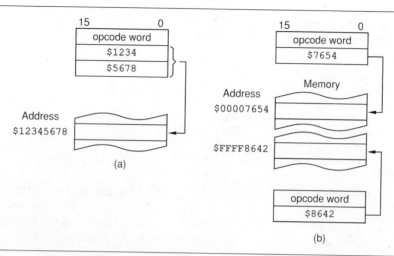

FIGURE 7–5   Absolute addressing in the 68000: (a) absolute long; (b) absolute short.

respectively. With the cross macro assembler, the ORG and ORG.L directives establish the default absolute addressing mode.

opcode suffix

The selection of long or short absolute addressing is independent of the size of an instruction's operand, which is determined by the *opcode suffix*. Regardless of the operand's size—byte, word, or longword—the instruction contains the address of the most significant byte of the operand.

In the 68000, absolute long addressing is obtained when mode is 7 and reg is 1 in the EA field. Absolute short addressing is obtained when mode is 7 and reg is 0. Note that in both cases, the reg field does not specify a register at all; rather, it specifies a "submode" that does not use any of the general registers in the addressing computation.

absolute indirect addressing

Because of its simplicity and flexibility, an absolute addressing mode is provided in almost all computers. An *absolute indirect addressing* mode is provided in a few processors, including the 68020. As shown in Figure 7–4(c), this mode simply uses the contents of the specified absolute address as the effective address. Details are provided in Section 14.8.

Mac Note

To preserve position independence, Macintosh programs do not normally use absolute addressing. Therefore, most Macintosh assemblers use PC-relative or based addressing as the default for symbolic operands that do not specify another addressing mode.

Nevertheless, Macintosh assemblers also provide a way to specify absolute addressing if you really insist, for example, to access an input/output port at a fixed absolute address (although this is dangerous, since different Macintosh models have their I/O ports at different addresses). The MPW and MDS assemblers use the notation (addr).W and (addr).L to specify absolute short and absolute long addressing, respectively.

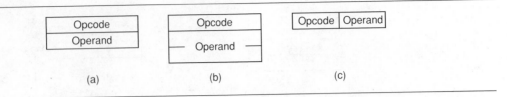

FIGURE 7–6   Immediate addressing formats: (a) immediate operand same length as opcode word; (b) double-length immediate; (c) short immediate.

7.2.3   Immediate

immediate addressing
literal

Immediate addressing allows a constant (or *literal*) to be specified as part of the instruction. As shown in Figure 7–6(a,b), an immediate operand is fetched from one or two extension words in memory immediately following the opcode word. The programs in the previous chapters illustrated some of the many uses of immediate operands:

- Constants to initialize variables (as in Table 6–8 on page 197).

- Constants to combine with variables by arithmetic or logical operations (as in Table 6–8 and in Table 5–6 on page 152).

- Offsets to add to address registers in order to move pointers to successive items or fields in a data structure (as in Table 5–10 on page 161).

- Constants to compare against variables for list and string terminations, branching conditions, and so on.

In many processors, another important use of immediate addressing is to put address constants into registers for later use by other addressing modes. For example, in the 68000 we could have used the instructions MOVEA.L #STKE,SP and MOVEA.L #MASKS,A0 instead of the corresponding LEA instructions in Table 5–12 on page 166. However, there are no MOVEA counterparts to LEA instructions that use the multicomponent addressing mode of the next section, such as LEA addr(An),Am. Therefore, consistency dictates using the LEA instruction in all cases. Also see Exercise 7.1 to discover a subtle difference between the LEA addr,An and MOVEA.L #addr,An instructions.

Except for address constants, most immediate operands tend to be small signed integers, often requiring only a few bits to represent. Therefore, the 68000 provides a very short immediate mode for some instructions as shown in Figure 7–6(c). For example, MOVEQ.L #n,dst can be used when n is between −128 and +127; the instruction encodes n as an 8-bit two's-complement number in the low-order byte of the opcode word, avoiding an extra immediate word altogether.

For destination operands it makes no sense to use immediate mode, since the destination result would overwrite the immediate operand in the instruction stream (e.g., MOVE.W D0,#1234). In the 68000, it also makes no sense to use

Mac Note

In the Macintosh environment, **LEA** *must* be used to load address "constants" into registers, because such "constants" aren't really constant. Consider the following Macintosh program which builds a 256-byte table containing the number of 1's in each 8-bit binary number:

```
ONETBL  DS.B    256             ;When BLDTBL finishes running, ONETBL[I]
                                ;  (0<=I<=255) will contain the number of
                                ;  1's in the binary representation of I.
MASKS   DC.B    1,2,4,8,$10,$20,$40,$80
                                ;Table of masks for 1's counting.
MASKE   EQU     *               ;Address just after table.

BLDTBL  LEA     ONETBL(A5),A2   ;Get address of first table entry.
        CLR.W   D0              ;D0 contains value of I (initially 0).
                                ;Now count the number of 1's in I.
BCNT1S  CLR.W   D1              ;Initialize '1' count.
        LEA     MASKS,A0        ;Point to 1-bit masks
        LEA     MASKE,A1        ;  and end of masks.
BLOOP   MOVE.B  (A0),D2         ;Get next bit mask.
        AND.B   D0,D2           ;Is there a '1' there?
        BEQ     BNO1            ;Skip if not.
        ADD.W   #1,D1           ;Else increment '1' count.
BNO1    ADDA.W  #1,A0           ;Point to next mask.
        CMPA.L  A1,A0           ;Past last mask?
        BNE     BLOOP           ;Continue if not. .
        MOVE.W  D1,(A2)         ;Fill table location I.
        ADDA.L  #1,A2           ;Bump A2 to next table entry.
        ADD.W   #1,D0           ;Next value of I.
        CMP.W   #256,D0         ;Finished all 256 entries?
        BNE     BCNT1S          ;No, do some more.
        _ExitToShell            ;Yes, all done.
```

The first **LEA** instruction in the program performs a run-time calculation of absolute address of the **ONETBL** array relative to A5, so that address-register indirect addressing can be used later in the program to initialize the elements of **ONETBL**. The calculation must be done at run-time because the **ONETBL** array is not allocated in the Macintosh's application global space until just before the program is run.

Later, two **LEA** instructions in the 1's-counting loop load A0 and A1 with the starting and ending addresses of the mask table, which is stored in the program's code module along with its instructions. Because **MASKS** and **MASKE** are code symbols, the Macintosh assembler uses PC-relative addressing in the **LEA** instructions, which perform the run-time calculations of the mask table's absolute starting and ending addresses accordingly. Once again, the calculation must be done at run-time because the program's load address is not determined until just before the Macintosh operating system runs it.

For both **data** address constants (**ONETBL**) and **code** address constants (**MASKS** and **MASKE**), immediate addressing cannot provide the correct absolute address at run time in the Macintosh environment.

---

immediate mode for the destination of a **JMP** or **JSR** instruction—this would mean that the target address is the next word of the instruction stream, which would have been the case anyway.

Immediate addressing is not really a necessary architectural feature, since constants can always be stored in arbitrary memory locations and accessed like other data using absolute addressing. For example, instead of "ADD.W #1,D1" we could write

```
ADD.W    ONE,D1
...
ONE      DC.W     1
```

However, immediate addressing reduces program size and speeds up program execution by eliminating out-of-sequence addresses for constants. Just as important, it gives the programmer one less set of bookkeeping details to worry about, such as thinking up unique names for all those constants!

In the 68000, immediate addressing is obtained when mode is 7 and reg is 4 in the EA field. The immediate operand occupies the one word following the opcode word for byte and word operations, two words for longword operations. For byte operations, the low-order byte of the immediate word contains the operand and the high-order byte is unused.

7.2.4   Register Indirect

register indirect addressing

In *register indirect addressing*, a register contains the effective address of an operand, as shown in Figure 7–7(a). A few processors, such as the 8080, Z80, and Z8000, have addresses that are twice the width of their registers. In these

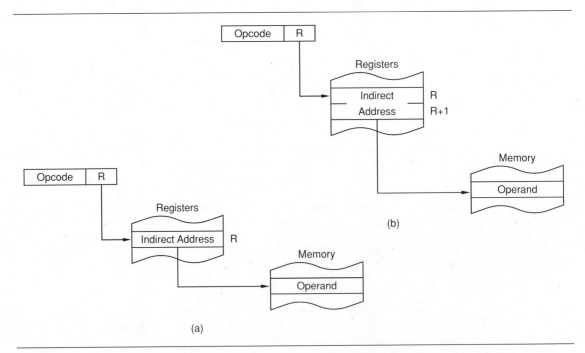

FIGURE 7–7   Register indirect addressing: (a) address size equals register size; (b) address size twice the register size.

machines, a register pair is used to form a full effective address in register indirect mode as shown in Figure 7–7(b).

All contemporary computers have register indirect mode in some form. This allows memory addresses to be computed during program execution rather than being fixed when the program is assembled. For example, compare the program in Table 5–9 with the one in Table 5–10 (see page 160). Execution-time address computation is required for many common operations, such as passing data structures to subroutines and accessing arbitrary data in arrays, stacks, queues, linked lists, and other data structures.

address-register indirect addressing

In the 68000, *address-register indirect addressing* is obtained when mode is 2 in the EA field. As the name implies, only address registers, not data registers, may be specified in this mode. However, there is a sneaky way to use data registers for indirect addressing in the 68020, divulged in Section 14.8.

7.2.5 Auto-Increment and Auto-Decrement

Register indirect addressing is often used to step through tables and lists of data, successively accessing each data item and bumping the register to point to the next one, as in the array initialization program in Table 5–10 on page 161. An *auto-increment addressing* mode computes an effective address the same as register indirect and then automatically increments the register by the operand size as shown in Figure 7–8. Thus, in Table 5–10, the sequence

auto-increment addressing

```
ILOOP    CLR.B    (A0)              Set component to zero.
         ADDA.W   #1,A0             Point to next component.
```

can be replaced by

```
ILOOP    CLR.B    (A0)+             Clear component and bump X to next.
```

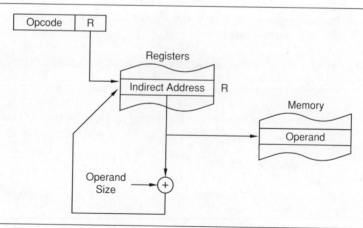

FIGURE 7–8   Auto-increment addressing.

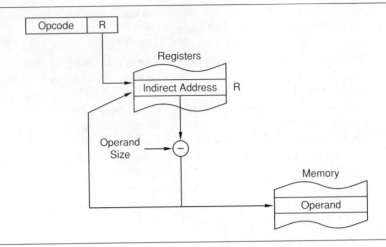

FIGURE 7–9   Auto-decrement addressing.

For another example, refer to Table 5–12 on page 166. Here, the instruction `MOVE.B (A0),D2` at label `BLOOP` becomes `MOVE.B (A0)+,D2`, and the instruction `ADDA.W #1,A0` may be eliminated.

The amount added to the register on auto-increment depends on the operand size. In a byte-addressable machine such as the 68000, the register must be incremented by 1 to point to the next byte, by 2 to point to the next word, or by 4 to point to the next double word. The operand size can be deduced from the instruction opcode, for example, `MOVE.B`, `MOVE.W`, or `MOVE.L`.

auto-decrement addressing

Auto-decrement addressing is similar to auto-increment mode; it subtracts the operand size from the address register as shown in Figure 7–9. However, it performs the subtraction *before* using the register contents as the effective address, not after. In combination with auto-increment mode, this allows any address register to be efficiently used as the stack pointer for a stack with the following characteristics:

- The stack pointer always points directly at the top stack item.

- The stack grows by decrementing the stack pointer.

With these conventions, auto-decrement mode of the 68000 can be used to push the contents of D0 onto a stack using A0 as a stack pointer as follows:

```
MOVE.W   D0,-(A0)
```

The item at top of the stack can be accessed using register indirect addressing. For example,

```
MOVE.W   (A0),D1
```

copies the item at the top of the stack into D1. Finally, an item may be popped using auto-increment addressing. For example,

```
ADD.W     (A0)+,D2
```

pops the item at the top of the stack and adds it to D2. Notice how the assembly language notation emphasizes auto-*pre*-decrement and auto-*post*-increment.

In the 68000, auto-increment addressing is obtained when mode is 3 in the EA field, while auto-decrement is obtained when mode is 4. Any address register may be specified in the reg field. In particular, if reg is 7, then register A7 (SP) is selected, and so we can do pushes and pops on the same stack that is used for subroutine return addresses. However, if the operand size is "byte," the processor automatically increments A7 by 2 to keep the system stack pointer aligned on a word boundary; the low-order byte of the word is unused.

Table 7–3 presents an example of a program using auto-increment and auto-decrement addressing. This is a 68000 assembly language version of the Pascal sorting program in Table 3–6 on page 63. It uses a feature of the 68000 that wasn't introduced in Chapter 5, namely, the ability to test the relations <, <=, >, and >= on two's-complement integers using the branch instructions BLT, BLE, BGT, and BGE, respectively.

The program in Table 7–3 uses A0 and A1 as pointers into two stacks that contain numbers sorted in ascending and descending order. Auto-increment and auto-decrement addressing are used to manipulate the stacks. The program calls five subroutines for input/output: READ reads an input number and leaves its value in D0; WRNUM prints the value of the integer in D0; and WRMSG1, WRMSG2, and WRMSG3 print messages.

7.3 MULTICOMPONENT ADDRESSING MODES

7.3.1 Indexed

indexed addressing

base address

index

index register

An *indexed addressing* mode combines two components by adding, and is the appropriate addressing mode for accessing arrays and tables. As shown in Figure 7–10, a fixed *base address* is specified as part of the instruction, as in absolute addressing. Then an *index* in a specified *index register* is added to the base address to form an effective address. When indexed mode is used to access an array, the base address in the instruction corresponds to the base address of the array, while the value in the index register corresponds to the index of the array component.

The 68000 was not designed with an explicit indexed addressing mode. However, we can use mode 5 to perform indexed addressing when the base address is in the bottom or the top 32 Kbytes of the 68000's address space; we listed this as the *indexed short addressing* mode in Table 7–2. As shown in Figure 7–11, in this mode the instruction contains a 16-bit extension word that

indexed short addressing

TABLE 7–3 Sorting program using stacks.

```
*
MAXLEN    EQU      200
SIZE      EQU      201
MINNUM    EQU      -99
MAXNUM    EQU      99
NNUMS     DS.W     1
STACKL    DS.W     SIZE
STKEL     EQU      *-2
STACKH    DS.W     SIZE
STKEH     EQU      *-2
SORT      LEA      STKEL,A0
          LEA      STKEH,A1
          MOVE.W   #MINNUM-1,(A0)
          MOVE.W   #MAXNUM+1,(A1)
          MOVE.W   #1,NNUMS
          JSR      WRMSG1
          JSR      READ
WHILE1    CMP.W    #MINNUM,D0
          BLT      WHILE4
          CMP.W    #MAXNUM,D0
          BGT      WHILE4
WHILE2    CMP.W    (A0),D0
          BGE      WHILE3
          MOVE.W   (A0)+,-(A1)
          BRA      WHILE2
WHILE3    CMP.W    (A1),D0
          BLE      OUT3
          MOVE.W   (A1)+,-(A0)
          BRA      WHILE3
OUT3      MOVE.W   D0,-(A0)
          JSR      WRNUM
          ADD.W    #1,NNUMS
IF1       CMP.W    #MAXLEN,NNUMS
          BGT      ELSE1
THEN1     JSR      READ
          BRA      IFEND1
ELSE1     JSR      WRMSG2
          MOVE.W   #MINNUM-1,D0
IFEND1    BRA      WHILE1
*
WHILE4    CMPA.W   #STKEL,A0
          BEQ      OUT4
          MOVE.W   (A0)+,-(A1)+
          BRA      WHILE4
OUT4      JSR      WRMSG3
WHILE5    CMPA.W   #STKEH,A1
          BEQ      OUT5
          MOVE.W   (A1)+,D0
          JSR      WRNUM
          BRA      WHILE5
OUT5      RTS
```

```
PROCEDURE StackSort; {Based on Table 3-6}
CONST maxLen = 200;
   stackSize = 201;
   minNum = -99;
   maxNum = 99;
VAR nNums,inNum : word; spL,spH : address;
   {Reg. usage: D0 = inNum; A0 = spL; A1 = spH}
   stackL, stackH :
      ARRAY [1..stackSize] OF word;
BEGIN
   spL := MemAddress(stackL[stackSize]);
   spH := MemAddress(stackH[stackSize]);
   MEM[spL] := minNum - 1;
   MEM[spH] := maxNum + 1;
   nNums := 1;
   writeln('Input sequence: ');
   read(inNum);
   WHILE inNum >= minNum

           AND inNum <= maxNum DO
      BEGIN
        WHILE inNum < MEM[spL] DO
          {Top of stackL --> stackH.}
            PushH(PopL);

        WHILE inNum > MEM[spH] DO
          {Top of stackH --> stackL.}
            PushL(PopH);

        PushL(inNum);
        write(inNum);
        nNums := nNums + 1;
        IF nNums <= maxLen THEN

          read(inNum)
        ELSE BEGIN
            writeln('*** Too many inputs');
            inNum := minNum - 1;
          END;
      END; {Inputs are now sorted.}
   WHILE spL <>
        MemAddress(stackL[stackSize]) DO
      {Move everything into stackH.}
        PushH(PopL);
   writeln; write('Sorted sequence: ');
   WHILE spH <>
        MemAddress(stackH[stackSize]) DO
      {Print contents of stackH.}
        write(PopH);

END;  {Return to caller.}
```

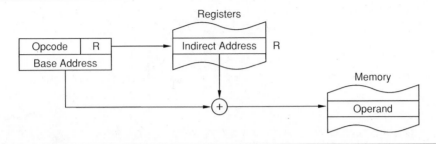

FIGURE 7–10   Indexed addressing computation.

is sign extended to yield a 32-bit base address in the bottom or top 32 Kbytes of the address space, and the index register is one of the address registers, A0–A7.

Most computers have indexed addressing modes that allow the base address to be anywhere in the address space, and that allow the index register to be any general register. However, we'll live with the 68000's indexed short mode in the examples in this section, and then compare it with the 68000's full-length "based" and "based indexed" modes later.

Suppose a Pascal program defines an array as follows:

```
VAR aname : ARRAY [first..last] OF baseType;
```

A corresponding assembly language program must reserve storage for the array, a total of $(last - first + 1) \cdot n$ bytes where n is the size in bytes of `baseType`. In typical Pascal implementations on microprocessors, n is 1, 2, and 4 for types

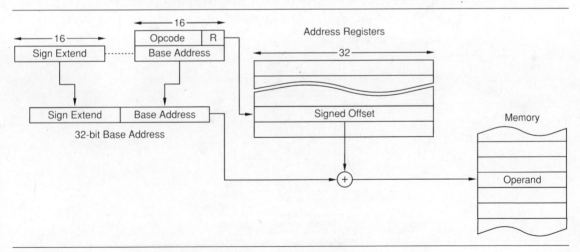

FIGURE 7–11   Indexed short addressing mode in the 68000.

Address
(hex)

Memory

1700	clist[1]
1701	clist[2]
1702	clist[3]
1703	clist[4]

FIGURE 7–12   Storage allocation for array CLIST[1..4].

char, integer, and real, respectively. A 4-byte array for the 68000 may be declared as follows:

```
        ORG     $1700
FIRST   EQU     1                   CONST first = 1;
LAST    EQU     4                     last = 4;
CLIST   DS.B    LAST-FIRST+1        VAR clist: ARRAY [first..last]
*                                             OF char;
```

In the assembly language program, the symbol CLIST is equated with the address of the first component of the array. Memory locations are used as shown in Figure 7–12. Thus, the symbol CLIST is equivalent to the number $1700.

address polynomial

The address of component *i* in an array is given by a formula called the *address polynomial*. For the array clist[1..4] the address polynomial is

$$\text{Address}(\text{clist}[i]) = \text{CLIST} + i - 1.$$

The address polynomial must take into account the index of the first component (first) and the length of each component (*n*) of an array. As shown in Figure 7–13, if the address of component aname[first] is ANAME, then the

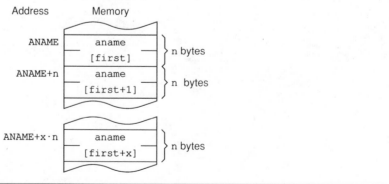

Address   Memory

ANAME   aname
             [first]   } n bytes

ANAME+n   aname
             [first+1]   } n bytes

ANAME+x·n   aname
             [first+x]   } n bytes

FIGURE 7–13   Addressing a one-dimensional array.

Mac Note

In the Macintosh environment, the address an of array component `aname[i]` is normally computed as the sum of *three* numbers:

(1) The base address of the application global space, contained in A5.

(2) The offset from the base address of the application global space to the effective base address of the array.

(3) The offset from the effective base address of the array to array component `aname[i]` (which is $i \cdot n$).

Although it is possible to do this with just the operations that we've introduced so far, it is much more convenient to use based indexed addressing. So we'll defer our discussion of array accessing in the Macintosh until Section 7.3.3.

address of `aname[first+x]` is $\text{ANAME} + x \cdot n$, where n is still the length of each component. Letting $i = \text{first} + x$ we get the general address polynomial:

$$\begin{aligned}
\text{Address(aname}[i]) &= \text{ANAME} + (i - \text{first}) \cdot n \\
&= (\text{ANAME} - \text{first} \cdot n) + i \cdot n \\
&= \text{EffectiveBaseAddress(aname)} + i \cdot n
\end{aligned}$$

effective base address

The *effective base address* of a one-dimensional array is the address assigned to component 0 if there is one. As shown by the parenthesization above, the effective base address is the constant part of the address polynomial. In the variable part of the address polynomial, the multiplication of the index i by the component size n is called *index scaling*.

index scaling

For the `clist` array, the general address polynomial yields:

$$\begin{aligned}
\text{Address(clist}[i]) &= \text{EffectiveBaseAddress(clist)} + i \cdot 1 \\
&= (\text{CLIST} - 1) + i
\end{aligned}$$

Thus, component i of the `clist` array can be read into register D1 of the 68000 by the following instruction sequence, assuming that the array is in the bottom or top 32 Kbytes of memory and that I is a 16-bit integer variable in memory:

```
LEA     CLIST-1,A0      Get effective base address.
ADDA.W  I,A0            Add component number.
MOVE.B  (A0),D1         Read clist[i].
```

The expression CLIST-1 has the value $16FF and is the effective base address of the array. We can also read `clist[i]` using the indexed short addressing mode on the 68000:

```
MOVEA.W I,A0            Get component number.
MOVE.B  CLIST-1(A0),D1  Read clist[i].
```

Figure 7–14 shows the operation of this instruction sequence, assuming that it starts at address $2000 and I is stored at address $2100.

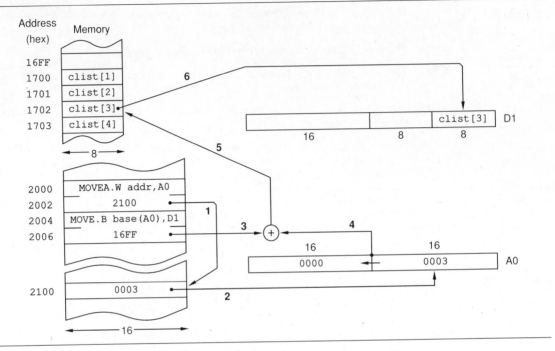

FIGURE 7–14   Indexed instruction execution.

Index scaling must always be done at run time, since the index i isn't known until then. For example, we could declare a 10-word array for the 68000 and access component i as shown in Table 7–4. The `MULS.W src,Dn` instruction multiplies the 16 low-order bits of data register Dn by the `src` operand and leaves the 32-bit result in Dn. This approach can be used for array items of any size if the constant `WRDSIZE` is defined to equal the item size.

A subroutine that uses indexed addressing to access an array is shown in Table 7–5. The program finds prime numbers without performing multiplication or division, by tabulating the multiples of known primes in an array.

TABLE 7–4   Index scaling for an array of words.

```
FRST     EQU    1                         CONST first = 1;
LST      EQU    10                              last = 10;
WRDSIZE  EQU    2                         {Size of items in WORDS array.}
WORDS    DS.B   (LST-FRST+1)*WRDSIZE      VAR words: ARRAY [first..last] OF word;
EWORDS   EQU    WORDS-(WRDSIZE*FRST)         {Define effective base address.}

         ...
         MOVE.W   I,D0                   Read i.
         MULS.W   #WRDSIZE,D0            Multiply by item size to scale.
         MOVEA.W  D0,A0                  Put into A0 to use as index.
         MOVE.W   EWORDS(A0),D1          D1 := words[i].
```

TABLE 7–5   Subroutine to find primes using an array and indexed addressing.

```
*
*
*            This subroutine finds and prints all prime numbers between
*        2 and NPRIME using the 'Sieve of Eratosthenes.' It declares
*        a boolean array PRIME[2..NPRIME], whose components indicate
*        whether or not each number between 2 and NPRIME is prime.
*        For simplicity, one byte is used for each component, with
*        0 = false, 1 = true.
*            The program begins by setting all components true; every
*        integer is potentially a prime. Then it marks the multiples
*        of the first prime (2) as being nonprimes. Then it looks for
*        the next prime and marks off its multiples. This continues
*        until we've marked the multiples of all primes less than
*        PLIMIT, approximately the square root of NPRIME. Now only
*        primes are left marked true, and they are printed.
*
```

			`PROCEDURE FindPrimes;`
`NPRIME`	`EQU`	`1000`	`CONST nPrime = 1000;`
`PLIMIT`	`EQU`	`32`	`    pLimit = 32;`
`PRIME`	`DS.B`	`NPRIME-1`	`VAR prime : ARRAY [2..nPrime] OF boolean;`
`*`			`    {reg} A1, A2 : word; {reg} D1 : byte;`
	`DS.W`	`0`	`BEGIN`
`FNDPRM`	`MOVEA.W`	`#2,A1`	`    FOR A1 := 2 TO nPrime DO`
`SETEM`	`MOVE.B`	`#1,PRIME-2(A1)`	`        prime[A1] := true;`
	`ADDA.W`	`#1,A1`	`        {Set the entire array true.}`
	`CMPA.W`	`#NPRIME,A1`	
	`BLE`	`SETEM`	
	`MOVEA.W`	`#2,A2`	`    A2 := 2; {First known prime.}`
`*`			`    REPEAT {Check integers 2 to pLimit.}`
`MARKEM`	`MOVE.B`	`PRIME-2(A2),D1`	`        IF prime[A2] THEN`
	`BEQ`	`NOTPRM`	`            BEGIN`
	`MOVEA.W`	`A2,A1`	`                A1 := A2 + A2; {Mark multiples...}`
	`ADDA.W`	`A2,A1`	`                REPEAT   {...of A2 as not prime.}`
`CLRLUP`	`CLR.B`	`PRIME-2(A1)`	`                    prime[A1] := false;`
	`ADDA.W`	`A2,A1`	`                    A1 := A1 + A2;`
	`CMPA.W`	`#NPRIME,A1`	`                UNTIL A1 > nPrime;`
	`BLE`	`CLRLUP`	`            END;`
`NOTPRM`	`ADDA.W`	`#1,A2`	`        A2 := A2 + 1;`
	`CMPA.W`	`#PLIMIT,A2`	`    UNTIL A2 > pLimit;`
	`BLE`	`MARKEM`	
	`JSR`	`WRMSG1`	`    write('Here are primes from 2 to ');`
	`MOVEA.W`	`#NPRIME,A1`	`    A1 := nPrime;`
	`JSR`	`PRINTA1`	`    writeln(A1); {Print the number in A1.}`
	`MOVEA.W`	`#2,A1`	`    FOR A1 := 2 TO nPrime DO`
`PRTLUP`	`MOVE.B`	`PRIME-2(A1),D1`	`        {Print all the primes.}`
	`BEQ`	`NEXTP`	`        IF prime[A1] THEN`
	`JSR`	`PRINTA1`	`            writeln(A1);`
`NEXTP`	`ADDA.W`	`#1,A1`	
	`CMPA.W`	`#NPRIME,A1`	
	`BLE`	`PRTLUP`	
	`RTS`		`END; {All done, return to caller}`

	Column			
Row	1	2	3	4
1	1700	1701	1702	1703
2	1704	1705	1706	1707
3	1708	1709	170A	170B

Legend: Addr.

FIGURE 7–15   Row-major storage of `matrix[1..3,1..4]`.

multidimensional array

Address polynomials can also be developed for *multidimensional arrays*. For example, Figure 7–15 shows the row-major storage allocation for a 3×4 array of bytes. The address polynomial is

$$\text{Address}(\texttt{matrix}[x.y]) = \texttt{MATRIX} + (x-1) \cdot 4 + (y-1)$$

Given a general two-dimensional array declaration,

```
VAR aname [xf..xl,yf..yl] OF baseType;
```

the address polynomial takes into account the effective base address of the array (the address of component `[0,0]`), the number of components in each row (`yl-yf+1`), and the size of each component (n):

$$\text{Address}(\texttt{aname}[x.y])$$
$$= \texttt{ANAME} + ((x - \texttt{xf}) \cdot (\texttt{yl} - \texttt{yf} + 1) + (y - \texttt{yf})) \cdot n$$
$$= (\texttt{ANAME} - (\texttt{xf} \cdot (\texttt{yl} - \texttt{yf} + 1) + \texttt{yf}) \cdot n) + (x \cdot (\texttt{yl} - \texttt{yf} + 1) + y) \cdot n$$
$$= \text{EffectiveBaseAddress}(\texttt{aname}) + (x \cdot (\texttt{yl} - \texttt{yf} + 1) + y) \cdot n$$

The quantity ($\texttt{ANAME} - (\texttt{xf} \cdot (\texttt{yl} - \texttt{yf} + 1) + \texttt{yf}) \cdot n$) is the effective base address of the array; this quantity is stored in the indexed instruction and the remaining quantity is computed at run time as shown below for an 8×4 array of words on the 68000:

```
MAT     DS.B      4*8*2          VAR mat: ARRAY [1..8,1..4] OF word;
EMAT    EQU       MAT-(4+1)*2    {Define effective base address}
X       DS.W      1                x, y : integer;
Y       DS.W      1
        ...
        MOVE.W    D1,X           Read x.
        MULS      #4,D1          Multiply by length of row (4).
        ADD.W     Y,D1           Add column number.
        MULS      #2,D1          Multiply by 2 to scale words.
        MOVEA.W   D1,A1          Put into addr reg to use as index.
        MOVE.W    EMAT(A1),D2    D2 := boxes[x,y].
```

addressing by indirection

In general, multiplication is needed to compute addresses in a multidimensional array. However, in processors that don't have fast multiplication instructions, multiplication can be avoided by a technique called *addressing by indirection*, which uses an auxiliary table of row addresses. Instead of computing

TABLE 7–6   Multidimensional array addressing by indirection.

```
           ORG       $2000
X          DS.W      1                       VAR x, y : integer;
Y          DS.W      1
ROW1       DS.B      10                           cell : ARRAY [3..7,10..19] OF byte;
ROW2       DS.B      10
ROW3       DS.B      10
ROW4       DS.B      10
ROW5       DS.B      10
ROWTB      DC.W      ROW1,ROW2,ROW3,ROW4,ROW5
RBASE      EQU       ROWTB-6
CBASE      EQU       -10
           ...
           MOVEA.W   X,A1                    Read x and multiply
           ADDA.W    X,A1                      by size of ROWTB components (2).
           MOVEA.W   RBASE(A1),A1            Get base address of row.
           ADDA.W    Y,A1                    Add column number.
           MOVE.B    CBASE(A1),D1            D1 := cell[x,y].
```

the starting address of a row as the effective base address plus $x \cdot (yl - yf + 1) \cdot n$, we simply look it up by using the row number as an index into the row address table. The column number is then added to the row address to obtain the address of the desired component. This technique is illustrated in Table 7–6 for a 5×10 array of bytes in the 68000.

Most contemporary machines have at least one indexed addressing mode. Some machines have an "indexed indirect" mode; this mode has two varieties:

*preindexed
indirect
addressing*

- *Preindexed indirect addressing.* The index is added to the base address to point to a memory word containing an indirect address that is used as the effective address.

*postindexed
indirect
addressing*

- *Postindexed indirect addressing.* The base address points to a memory word containing an indirect address; the index is added to the indirect address to obtain the effective address.

The 68020 has both of these modes, as described in Section 14.8.

7.3.2   Based

*base address
index
offset
displacement*

Based addressing is similar to indexed addressing, and often confused with it. A *base address* is just that—an *address*. An *index*, *offset*, or *displacement* is an integer that is added to one address to obtain a different address. In this text, we use "displacement" when referring to a specific instruction field that contains such an integer, "index" when referring to the contents of an index register or the result of an indexing computation, and "offset" when speaking in general.

*based addressing
base register*

In indexed addressing, the instruction contains a base address and an index register contains an offset. *Based addressing* is just the opposite—the instruction contains an offset and an address register (or *base register*) contains a base

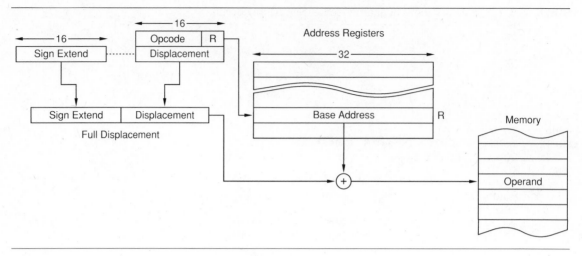

FIGURE 7–16   Based addressing in the 68000.

address. If offsets and base addresses are the same length, the two modes are indistinguishable—one addressing mode in the processor hardware suffices for both based and indexed addressing applications. Two different hardware modes are necessary only when offsets and base addresses have different lengths.

Figure 7–16 shows the calculation performed by based addressing in the 68000 (mode 5). The instruction contains a 16-bit signed displacement and an address register contains a 32-bit base address. Before the addition, the displacement is sign extended to a 32-bit signed integer. The 68020 also has a based addressing mode with a full 32-bit displacement, as described in Section 14.8.

Indexed addressing is used when the base address of a data structure is known at assembly time, but an arbitrary component must be accessed when the program is run, as in most array manipulation problems. Based addressing is used when the relative position of an item in a data structure is known at assembly time, but the starting address of the structure is not. Typical applications of based addressing include:

- Accessing data in a parameter area whose base address is passed to a subroutine (see Section 9.3).

- Accessing items in a stack frame; the base register becomes a stack-frame pointer (see Section 9.3).

- Accessing data in a position-independent program, when the base register is loaded with the starting address of the data area, as in the Macintosh environment (see Section 7.4).

- Accessing a particular field of a record in a linked list, by loading the base register with the starting address of the record.

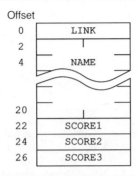

Offset	
0	LINK
2	
4	NAME
20	
22	SCORE1
24	SCORE2
26	SCORE3

FIGURE 7–17   Student information record format.

For an example of the last application, suppose we maintained a list of student records, where each record contains a link, a name, and three exam scores in the format shown in Figure 7–17. Now suppose that a number of such records have been chained together in a linked list, so that the LINK field of each record contains the memory address of the next one, and a a LINK of nil (0) indicates the end of the list. Finally, let there be a pointer variable HEAD that contains the address of the first record. Then the 68000 program fragment in Table 7–7 may be used to set the score fields of all records to an initial value. At each iteration of the loop, A0 contains the base address of a record and the displacements SCORE1, SCORE2, and SCORE3 are used to access the score fields.

If you're familiar with Pascal records, you can see how the Pascal statements in Table 7–7 have straightforward assembly language counterparts using based addressing. If you don't quite understand Pascal records, then further study of Figure 7–17 and Table 7–7 and a rereading of Section 3.3 should make you a lot more comfortable with the subject.

At this point we can reveal, if you haven't already guessed it, that based mode and indexed short mode in the 68000 are exactly the same. The mode number is the same, the assembly language syntax is the same, and the assembled instructions are bit by bit the same! (Compare Figure 7–16 with Figure 7–11.) "Indexed short" is just a mode that we invented to cover up the fact that the 68000 doesn't have a general indexed mode that works with long (32-bit) base addresses and arbitrary index registers. Instead, *real* 68000 programmers are expected to used "based indexed mode," described in the next section.

7.3.3   Based Indexed

based indexed addressing

The address calculation for *based indexed addressing* is shown in Figure 7–18. This mode adds together a base register (which contains a base address) and an index register (which contains the index of an item) to form the effective address.

TABLE 7–7   List initialization subroutine.

```
*                                    CONST
ISCR     EQU      -999                 initScore = -999;
*                                    TYPE
*                                      siLink = ^studentInfo;
*                                      studentInfo = RECORD
LINK     EQU      0                      link: siLink;
NAME     EQU      4                      name: ARRAY [1..20] OF char;
SCORE1   EQU      24                     score1: integer;
SCORE2   EQU      26                     score2: integer;
SCORE3   EQU      28                     score2: integer;
*                                    END;
NIL      EQU      0                  {End-of-list value.}
*                                    VAR {reg A0} next: siLink;
HEAD     DS.L     1                      head: siLink;
*                                      ...
SCOREI   MOVEA.L  HEAD,A0            next := head;
SCLOOP   CMPA.L   #NIL,A0            WHILE next <> nil DO
         BEQ      OUT                  BEGIN
         MOVE.W   #ISCR,SCORE1(A0)       next^.score1 := initScore;
         MOVE.W   #ISCR,SCORE2(A0)       next^.score2 := initScore;
         MOVE.W   #ISCR,SCORE3(A0)       next^.score3 := initScore;
         MOVEA.L  LINK(A0),A0            next := next^.link;
         BRA      SCLOOP               END;
OUT      ...
```

Based indexed addressing allows run-time computation of both the base address of a data structure and the offset to an item in it. For example, after a program computes the base address of a table or array, it may load it into a base register and then access arbitrary components whose indices are also computed at run time.

Two versions of the based indexed addressing calculation for the 68000

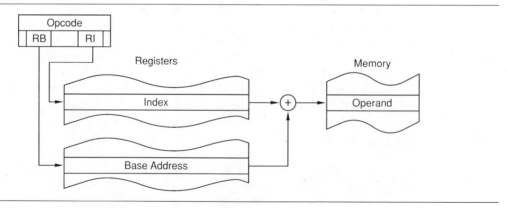

FIGURE 7–18   Based indexed addressing computation.

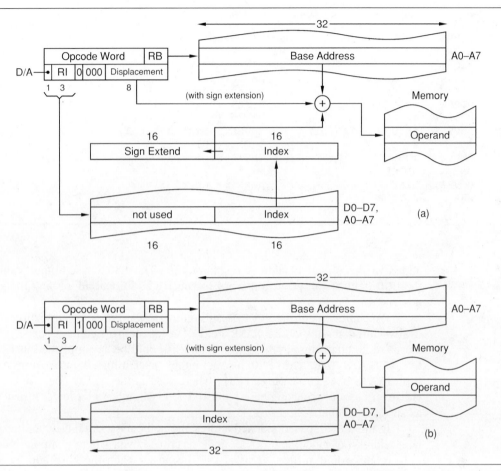

FIGURE 7–19   Based indexed addressing in the 68000: (a) 16-bit index mode; (b) 32-bit index mode.

are shown in Figure 7–19. In this mode, the base address is 32 bits wide and is contained in one of the address registers. The index register is specified in an extension word following the instruction. As shown in Figure 7–19(a), four bits are available in the extension word to specify the index register, so the index register can be any address or data register.

An additional bit in the extension word indicates how the index value is to be obtained from the index register. If this bit is 0, as in Figure 7–19(a), then the low-order word of the index register is sign extended to form the 32-bit index; this is called *based indexed short addressing*. If this bit is 1, as in Figure 7–19(b), then the entire 32-bit index register is used as the index; this is called *based indexed long addressing*. The 68000 further embellishes both based indexed modes by treating the low-order byte of the index word as a *short displacement*, a signed integer in the range −128 to +127 that is also

based indexed short addressing

based indexed long addressing

short displacement

TABLE 7–8   List initialization including name field.

```
SCOREI   MOVEA.L  HEAD,A0           next := head;
SCLOOP   CMPA.L   #NIL,A0           WHILE next <> nil DO
         BEQ      OUT                 BEGIN
         CLR.W    SCORE1(A0)            next^.score1 := 0;
         CLR.W    SCORE2(A0)            next^.score2 := 0;
         CLR.W    SCORE3(A0)            next^.score3 := 0;
         MOVE.W   #1,D1                 D1 := 1;
NLOOP    MOVE.B   #$20,NAME(A0,D1)      REPEAT next^.name[D1] := ' ';
         ADD.W    #1,D1                   D1 := D1 + 1;
         CMP.W    #20,D1                UNTIL D1 = 20;
         BNE      NLOOP
         MOVEA.L  LINK(A0),A0           next := next^.link;
         BRA      SCLOOP              END;
OUT      ...
```

added in the effective address computation. The 68020 uses other values in the 000 field of the extension word to specify additional addressing modes, as described in Section 14.8.

We can augment the SCOREI subroutine in the previous subsection so that it also initializes the entire NAME field of a list item to contain spaces. Since there are 20 characters in the NAME field, this could be accomplished just before the MOVEA.W LINK(A0),A0 instruction by executing 20 instructions of the form MOVE.B #$20,NAME+i(A0), where $20 is the ASCII code for a space. However, a sequence using based indexed addressing has a lot fewer instructions, as shown in Table 7–8.

In the 68000, based indexed addressing is the most often used multicomponent addressing mode, and is the mode of choice even where a simple indexed-only mode would suffice. This is true because, when the base address of an array is fixed, we can still load that base address into an address register (typically using LEA) and then use the fixed contents of that register with based indexed mode to access the array. Keeping the base address in a register avoids the need to carry long address constants in every instruction that accesses the array and, because the 68000 has so many address registers, it is not a serious inconvenience to allocate an address register for this purpose.

The 68000's short-index variety of based addressing improves the size and speed of programs that deal with small data structures, ones with indices between −32768 and +32767. Such "short" index values may be stored and manipulated as words instead of longwords. In fact, standard 68000 assembly language uses short-index mode as the default; as shown in Table 7–2, a suffix of ".L" is needed to select the long-index mode.

Table 7–9 recodes our prime numbers program using based indexed addressing. In this version, the PRIME array may be positioned anywhere in memory, since its full 32-bit address is loaded into A0. Also, we are now free to use data registers (such as D2 and D3) as index registers.

TABLE 7–9   Prime numbers program recoded with based indexed addressing.

```
*                                       PROCEDURE FindPrimes;
NPRIME   EQU     1000                   CONST nPrime = 1000;
PLIMIT   EQU     32                         pLimit = 32;
PRIME    DS.B    NPRIME-2+1             VAR prime: ARRAY [2..nPrime] OF boolean;
PRIMEBA  EQU     PRIME-2                   {reg} D2, D3: word; {reg} D1: byte;
*                                       BEGIN
FNDPRM   MOVE.W  #2,D2                      FOR D2 := 2 TO nPrime DO
         LEA     PRIMEBA,A0
SETEM    MOVE.B  #1,0(A0,D2)                  prime[D2] := true;
         ADD.W   #1,D2                        {Set the entire array true.}
         CMP.W   #NPRIME,D2
         BLE     SETEM
         MOVE.W  #2,D3                   D3 := 2; {First known prime.}
*                                       REPEAT {Check integers 2 to pLimit.}
MARKEM   MOVE.B  0(A0,D3),D1              IF prime[D3] THEN
         BEQ     NOTPRM                      BEGIN
         MOVE.W  D3,D2                         D2 := D3 + D3; {Mark multiples...}
         ADD.W   D3,D2                         REPEAT  {...of D3 as not prime.}
CLRLUP   CLR.B   0(A0,D2)                        prime[D2] := false;
         ADD.W   D3,D2                           D2 := D2 + D3;
         CMP.W   #NPRIME,D2                    UNTIL D2 > nPrime;
         BLE     CLRLUP                      END;
NOTPRM   ADD.W   #1,D3                     D3 := D3 + 1;
         CMP.W   #PLIMIT,D3             UNTIL D3 > pLimit;
         BLE     MARKEM
         JSR     WRMSG1                 write('Here are primes from 2 to ');
         MOVE.W  #NPRIME,D2             D2 := nPrime;
         JSR     PRINTD2                writeln(D2); {Print the number in D2.}
         MOVE.W  #2,D2                  FOR D2 := 2 TO nPrime DO
PRTLUP   MOVE.B  0(A0,D2),D1               {Print all the primes.}
         BEQ     NEXTP                     IF prime[D2] THEN
         JSR     PRINTD2                      writeln(D2);
NEXTP    ADD.W   #1,D2
         CMP.W   #NPRIME,D2
         BLE     PRTLUP
         RTS                            {All done, return to caller}
         END     FNDPRM                END;
```

7.3.4   Relative

PC-relative addressing

Modes that compute an effective address as the sum of a fixed displacement in the instruction and the current value of the program counter fall into the category of *(PC-) relative addressing*. A relative addressing mode often uses a small displacement, 8 or 16 bits wide, to specify an address nearby the current instruction, avoiding extra bits needed for a full absolute address.

The 68000 does not allow relative mode to be used to specify an operand that might be altered, for example, the destination of a MOVE instruction. The architects of the 68000 intended for a program to stand by itself as a "read-only" unit; a program should not be modified by its own instructions.

Mac Note

Based indexed addressing is normally used to access array elements in the Macintosh environment. In a Macintosh program, the effective base address of an array *must* be computed at run time and deposited in an address register, since this address is not determined until the program is loaded and runs. Thereafter, array components may be accessed with based indexed addressing.

In the example program of Table 7–9, only one instruction, the **LEA** at the beginning of the program, must be changed for the Macintosh environment:

```
                          ; PROCEDURE FindPrimes;
NPRIME   EQU    1000      ; CONST nPrime = 1000;
PLIMIT   EQU    32        ;    pLimit = 32;
PRIME    DS.B   NPRIME-2+1 ; VAR prime: ARRAY [2..nPrime] OF boolean;
PRIMEBA  EQU    PRIME-2   ;    {reg} D2, D3 : word; {reg} D1 : byte;
                          ; BEGIN
FNDPRM   MOVE.W #2,D2     ;    FOR D2 := 2 TO nPrime DO
         LEA    PRIMEBA(A5),A0;
         . . .            ;        . . .
```

At assembly time, the symbol **PRIME** is equated to an offset from the base address of the application global space, which is contained in A5 at run time. Thus, the sum of **PRIME** and the base address is the starting address of the block of memory allocated for the **prime** array. Since the index of the first array component is 2, **PRIME-2** (or **PRIMEBA**) is an offset to hypothetical component 0 of the array. Thus, the sum of **PRIMEBA** and the run-time value of A5 is the effective base address of the **prime** array. This is precisely what is computed by the **LEA** instruction above.

Arrays of constants stored in the code module of a Macintosh program can also be accessed with based indexed addressing. For example, consider the following subroutine which clears bit i of a byte x, where i and x are contained in registers D0 and D1, respectively:

```
CLRBIT   LEA    CMASKS,A0     ;Address of 1-bit-zero masks.
         AND.W  #$0007,D0     ;Force bit number to be <= 7.
         AND.B  0(A0,D0),D1   ;Clear bit (D0).
         RTS                  ;Done.
;                 Each mask below has a single 0, in bit i (0<=i<=7).
CMASKS   DC.B   $FE,$FD,$FB,$F7,$EF,$DF,$BF,$7F
```

In this case, the Macintosh assembler recognizes **CMASKS** to be a **code** symbol, and so it assembles an **LEA** instruction that uses PC-relative addressing to compute the run-time address of the mask table.

The most common use of relative addressing is in **branch** (or **jump**) instructions. Although the GOTO statement does not appear too often in well-structured programs in high-level languages, the corresponding **branch** primitive is essential for creating control structures in the corresponding machine language programs. The statements controlled by structured statements in Pascal and other high-level language programs are usually short. It follows that the branch instructions in the corresponding machine language programs usually jump to "nearby" addresses. For example, the targets of over 80% of all branch instructions were within 127 bytes of the instruction itself in one study

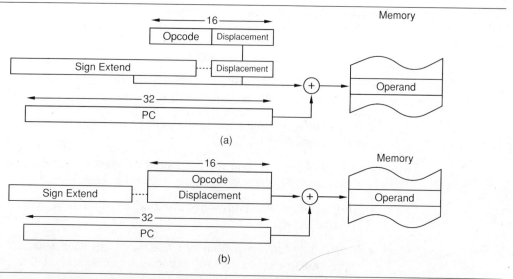

FIGURE 7–20   Relative address calculations in the 68000: (a) short mode for branch instructions; (b) word mode for long branches and general addressing.

of Intel 8080 programs. Therefore, short relative addressing allows most branch instructions to be specified in a small number of bits.

Figure 7–20(a) shows the address calculation used in the 68000's "short branch" instructions. The opcode word contains an 8-bit displacement that is sign extended to 32 bits and then added to the PC to obtain the effective address. When PC is added, it is already pointing to the next instruction. Thus, the branch instruction can have a target address that is within +126 to −128 bytes of the next instruction.

The 68000 also has a relative addressing mode with a 16-bit signed displacment, shown in Figure 7–20(b). In this case, the displacement is contained in an extension word following the opcode word, and is once again sign extended to 32 bits before adding to the PC. This mode is used in the 68000's "long branch" instructions, and is also available as a general addressing mode as shown in Table 7–2, when mode is 7 and reg is 2.

As also shown in Table 7–2, Motorola's resident assembler for the 68000 uses a "PC" identifier in its notations for general relative addressing modes. Thus, each relative addressing mode in the 68000 is similar to a based addressing counterpart, in its assembler format as well as its machine implementation. In relative modes, PC is used instead of one of A0–A7 as the base register.

Motorola's cross macro assembler for the 68000 does not have any special notation for relative modes; in fact, it can't distinguish relative from absolute and based modes just by looking at the format of an operand expression. Instead, it provides a special "RORG" directive in place of ORG for defining *relative symbols*, and it automatically chooses between relative addressing and the other

RORG
relative symbol

relative expression
absolute expression

modes depending on whether the operand is a *relative expression* or an *absolute expression*, which it distinguishes using the following rules:

- A numeric constant is absolute.

- The PLC is absolute if an ORG or ORG.L occurred most recently; it is relative if an RORG occurred most recently.

- A symbol appearing in the label field of a non-EQU statement has the value and type of the PLC.

- A symbol appearing in the label field of an EQU statement has the value and type of the expression in the operand field.

- An expression involving only absolute constants and symbols yields an absolute value.

- If REL is a relative symbol and ABS is an absolute constant, symbol, or expression, then the following expression forms yield relative values: REL, REL+ABS, ABS+REL, REL-ABS.

- The difference of two relative symbols (REL-REL) is absolute. (The offset between two addresses stays constant when the program is moved.)

- The following expression forms are not allowed: REL+REL, ABS-REL, REL*REL, REL*ABS, ABS*REL. Here * is any operator but + or -.

With either assembler, instructions that use relative addressing specify an operand address relative to the beginning of the program rather than a relative displacement from the current instruction. The assembler computes the required displacement as the difference between the given address expression (raddr16) and the address of the displacement word. If the displacement cannot be expressed in 16 bits, the assembler gives an "out-of-range" error message. It also gives an error message if relative addressing has been specified for a destination operand that might be altered—remember, operands accessed by relative addressing are considered "read-only" in the 68000.

When the processor hardware accesses a memory address that was specified with relative addressing, it activates a memory control signal that indicates that the address is in "program space" rather than "data space." This is important in systems with memory mapping and management units (MMUs) that treat program memory and data memory differently. The 68020 has additional relative addressing modes that provide 32-bit branch and relative operand displacements, as described in Section 14.8.

7.3.5 Relative Indexed

relative indexed addressing

Relative indexed addressing is a variant of relative addressing obtained in the 68000 when mode is 7 and reg is 3. Relative indexed works just like based

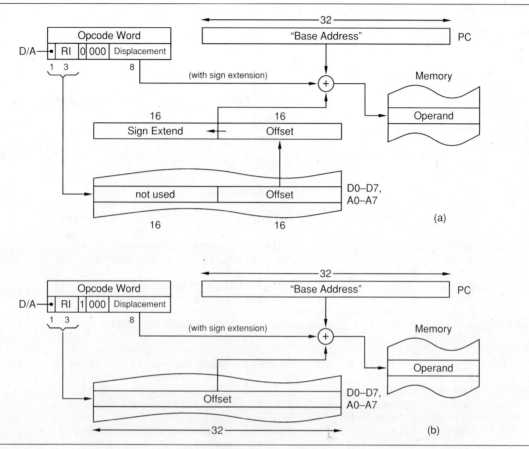

FIGURE 7–21   Relative indexed addressing in the 68000: (a) 16-bit index mode; (b) 32-bit index mode.

indexed addressing, except that the PC is used as the base register. This allows a program to access a nearby table of read-only data or jump targets.

Instructions using relative indexed addressing mode use the same extension word format as in based indexed addressing, as shown in Figure 7–21. An 8-bit displacement gives the distance to the table from the current PC, and an index register contains an additional offset to a particular item in the table. As in based indexed addressing, any register may serve as an index register, and either a long index or a short index may be used. As in relative mode, operands accessed by relative indexed addressing are considered to be unalterable. Motorola's assemblers for the 68000 distinguish between relative indexed and based indexed addressing either with a "PC" identifier or by the type of the operand expression, as discussed in the previous subsection.

Table 7–10 shows how relative indexed addressing could be used in the

TABLE 7–10   Assembly language equivalent of a Pascal CASE statement.

```
MINCASE EQU     5               CONST mincase = 5;
MAXCASE EQU     15                    maxcase = 15;
*                               VAR D1: mincase..maxcase;
        ...                         ...
        JMP     CASEIT          CASE D1 OF
FIRSTC  ...                         5,7 : BEGIN  {Write a subroutine for
        ...                               ...     each case's code.}
        RTS                             END;
NEXTC   ...                         6 : BEGIN
        ...                               ...
        RTS                             END;
        ...                         ...
LASTC   ...                         15 : BEGIN
        ...                               ...
        RTS                             END;
*
CASETBL DC.L    FIRSTC          {Table of starting addresses for
        DC.L    NEXTC            the subroutines for the cases.}
        DC.L    FIRSTC
        ...                     {Size of table should be
        DC.L    LASTC               maxcase-mincase+1 longwords.}
        IFNE    (*-CASETBL)-(4*(MAXCASE-MINCASE+1))
*** ERROR -- SIZE OF CASE TABLE INCORRECT FOR NUMBER OF CASES ***
        ENDC
*
CASEIT  CMP.W   #MINCASE,D1     {Make sure case number is in range.}
        BLT     CASEOUT         {Do nothing if case out of range.}
        CMP.W   #MAXCASE,D1
        BGT     CASEOUT         {OK, offset so first case index is 0.}
        SUB.W   #MINCASE,D1
        MULU.W  #4,D1           {Scale for longword table entries.}
        MOVE.L  CASETBL(PC,D1),A0   {Get subroutine starting address.}
        JSR     (A0)            {Call it.}
CASEOUT ...                     {Continue here when done with case.}
```

assembly language equivalent of a Pascal CASE statement. The assembly language program has a subroutine corresponding to each Pascal case, and it selects and executes one of them based on a case number passed in register D1. A small table (CASETBL) establishes the correspondence between case numbers and subroutines. If the same code is supposed to be executed for several cases, then the corresponding subroutine is written only once, while its address is referenced in the case table once for each case.

In the approach of Table 7–10, the individual case subroutines may be located anywhere in memory. However, the case table must start within 128 bytes of the instruction that references it (MOVE.L CASETBL(PC,D1),A0), because the 68000's relative indexed addressing mode has only an 8-bit displacement field. The 68020 has relative addressing modes with 16- and 32-bit displacement fields, which eliminate this restriction.

Mac Note

Assembly language coding of CASE statements in the Macintosh enviroment is complicated by the fact that code addresses are not known until run time, and therefore absolute addresses cannot be stored in the case table. One possible Macintosh implementation of the case table and code of Table 7–10 is shown below.

```
CASETBL  DC.W     FIRSTC-CASETBL    Table of offsets from start of table
         DC.W     NEXTC-CASETBL       to the subroutines for the cases.
         DC.W     FIRSTC-CASETBL
         ...                        Size of table should be
         DC.W     LASTC-CASETBL       maxcase-mincase+1 words.
*
CASEIT   CMP.W    #MINCASE,D1        Make sure case number is in range.
         BLT      CASEOUT           Do nothing if case out of range.
         CMP.W    #MAXCASE,D1
         BGT      CASEOUT           OK, offset so first case index is 0.
         SUB.W    #MINCASE,D1
         ADD.W    D1,D1             Scale for word table entries.
         MOVE.W   CASETBL(D1),D0    Get offset to start of subroutine.
         JSR      CASETBL(D0)       Call it.
CASEOUT  ...                        Continue here when done with case.
```

Both the MOVE and the JSR instructions use relative indexed addressing. (Although these instructions contain no PC identifier, the Macintosh assembler generates relative indexed addressing because CASETBL is a code symbol.)

In this implementation, the MOVE instruction finds an offset word in the case table and puts it into A0. The JSR instruction calls a subroutine whose starting address is computed as the sum of the current PC, the offset word in A0, and the offset from the current PC to CASETBL. Note that this last offset, like the offset from the MOVE instruction to CASETBL in this and the previous example, must be less than 128 bytes, because the 68000's relative indexed addressing mode has only an 8-bit displacement field.

Since the Macintosh environment requires code to be partitioned into 32-Kbyte segments, the case table itself contains only 16-bit offsets (defined by DC.W), and the subroutines for the individual cases must be in the same segment as the case table. However, other environments could store the case subroutines anywhere in the 68000's address space, by using a table of longword offsets and changing the last three instructions above:

```
         MULU.W   #4,D1             {Scale for longword table entries.}
         MOVE.L   CASETBL(D1),D0    {Get offset to start of subroutine.}
         JSR      CASETBL(D0.L)     {Call it.}
```

7.3.6   Paged

paged addressing
page

page number
page address

As shown in Figure 7–22(a) for a 64-Kbyte memory, *paged addressing* partitions memory into a number of equal-length *pages*. A 16-bit absolute address can now be split into two components as shown in Figure 7–22(b). In this example, an 8-bit *page number* indicates which of 256 pages contains a byte. An 8-bit *page address* gives the location of the byte within a 256-byte page.

Paged addressing has nothing to do with the physical organization or packaging of the memory system. It is simply used to specify an address in a smaller number of bits than the single-component addressing modes in the previous sec-

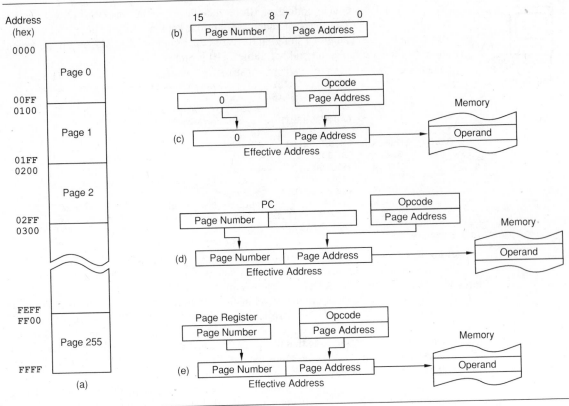

FIGURE 7-22   Paged addressing scheme: (a) address space partitioning; (b) address values; (c) base-page addressing; (d) current-page addressing; (e) page-register addressing.

tion. In paged addressing, an instruction contains only a page address as shown in Figure 7–22(c,d,e); the page number is obtained in some way implied by the instruction to create a long absolute address:

base-page addressing
- *Base-page addressing.* The page number is set to zero, yielding absolute addresses in page 0 (the *base page*) of memory.

current-page addressing
current page
- *Current-page addressing.* The page number is set equal to the high-order bits of the program counter (PC), yielding an address in the same page as the instruction itself (the *current page*).

page-register addressing
page register
- *Page-register addressing.* The page number is found in a *page register* that the program has previously loaded with the desired page number.

The 68000 does not have any paged addressing modes, but a few processors that do are listed in Table 7–11. (Because of its special status as the ancient minicomputer on which this author learned assembly language programming, the

TABLE 7–11   Paged addressing modes.

Computer	Memory Address Bits	Page Address Bits	Page Number Bits	Addressing Mode
HP 2116	15	10	5	Bit in instruction selects current or base page
Motorola 6809	16	8	8	8-bit page register DPR implied by instruction
Intel 8051				
(program memory)	16	8	8	MOVEP instruction reads from table in current page
(internal data mem.)	8	3	5	2-bit page register selects page 0, 1, 2, or 3

Hewlett-Packard 2116 is gratuitously included in the table.) Although paging reduces the address size for many instructions, it is still necessary at times to specify a full address. Therefore, machines with paging always have other addressing modes such as absolute and register indirect.

7.4 POSITION-INDEPENDENT CODE

load address   The *load address* of a program is the first address that it occupies in memory. As we discussed in Section 6.4, it is difficult to determine load addresses at the outset of a large programming project. Relocating assemblers and linking loaders allow the load address to be specified later, at load time. In dedicated programming applications these two tools are sufficient. However, they don't provide a total solution for commercial application programs that are used in computers with a variety of different memory configurations (such as the Macintosh family), or for programs that might have to occupy different areas of memory depending on what other programs are loaded at the same time (as in the Macintosh MultiFinder environment).

Theoretically, we could relink and relocate an application program each time that we load it, but this is inconvenient and time consuming. (Would you like to wait an extra 30 seconds, even 10 seconds, every time you start up your favorite text editor?) Instead, we prefer a program to work correctly with *any* load address, without any load-time patching of address references in the object
*statically position   module. A program that does this is called *statically position independent*.
independent*
A situation where static position independence is not just convenient, but essential, occurs when software modules are placed in read-only memory (ROM) chips. When a program is "burned" into a ROM chip, it is committed forever; we can make no adjustments to data or instructions, even if we know what adjustments are needed. For example, suppose that we're selling a 32-Kbyte ROM containing a set of IEEE floating-point math subroutines for the 68000. The "load address" of such a ROM is fixed when our customer plugs the ROM into the computer's memory circuit board—different sockets correspond to different load addresses. The problem is that different customers will almost certainly

want to plug the ROM into different sockets, due to varying system configurations. We need a program that works correctly with *any* load address.

In some application environments, it is also useful to be able to move a program in memory after its execution has already begun. No, this doesn't mean that programmers are unplugging and rearranging ROMs while their programs are running! More likely, this occurs when programs run under the control of a multi-user operating system that dynamically swaps jobs in and out of available read/write memory as needed. After a program is temporarily suspended, it may be reloaded into an area of memory different from where it started. A program that can be moved around in this way is called *dynamically relocatable* or *dynamically position independent*.

dynamically relocatable
dynamically position independent

The key characteristic of position-independent code is that it does not contain any absolute addresses. Two addressing modes can provide position independence: relative and based.

In relative addressing modes, a displacement gives the *difference* between the instruction address and the effective address. Therefore, the instruction and operand can be picked up as a unit and moved to a different part of memory without changing the displacement value stored in the instruction. The effective address is recomputed as a function of the current PC each time the instruction is executed, so instructions that use this mode are dynamically position independent. Recall, however, that the 68000 can use relative addressing only for unalterable (read-only) operands. Thus, this mode's usefulness in the 68000 is limited to jumps and to instructions that access read-only constants and tables.

Based addressing may be used in 68000 programs to perform position-independent read/write variable access. With this technique, the program must somehow compute its own load address when it starts running, and place this value in a base register. For example, the instruction `LEA START(PC),A0` computes the address of label `START` as a function of the current PC and places it in base register A0.

In the Macintosh environment, the read/write variables are stored in an area of memory different from the program itself. Before running a program, the operating system places a base address of this variable data area in base register A5.

In either case, once the load address is in a base register, all references to variable data within the program may be specified by based addressing with offsets from the base register. Since the load address is computed only once, at load time, instructions that use this mode are only statically position independent.

Adherence to the following rules will create programs that are statically position independent:

- The values of all address constants must be computed relative to the load address or the PC when the program is executed, rather than being specified using immediate addressing. Only nonaddress constant values, like those used for initializing counters, making data comparisons, and so on, may be accessed by immediate addressing.

- Other local data accesses must use based addressing referenced to the load address of the data area or must use PC-relative addressing. Absolute addressing is not allowed.

- All local jumps and subroutine calls must use PC-relative addressing.

- Absolute addresses may be used only to refer to absolute locations outside the position-independent program (for example, in a call to an operating system utility).

The static position independence rules are easier to follow in some processors, including the 68000, than in others. In general, statically position-independent code is difficult to write for processors without PC-relative addressing or a straightforward way to load the PC into a base register. While the ability to write statically position-independent code is a useful processor feature for some applications, many processors seem to get by without it.

Dynamic position independence can be achieved in simple programs by means of PC-relative addressing alone. However, in a program that manipulates address values such as pointers, dynamic position independence requires extensive use of based addressing. Each time that the program is moved, a new base address must be placed in a base register, and all data references must be made relative to the base register, using based or based indexed addressing. Still, dynamic position independence rules are difficult to enforce manually; for example, see Exercise 7.13. Therefore, dynamic position independence is normally achieved only in processors that have a special base register that the processor implicitly uses for *all* memory references (e.g., the Intel 80x86 family), and in processors that have external memory mapping and management units.

7.5 MEMORY MAPPING AND MANAGEMENT

memory mapping and management unit (MMU)

Memory mapping and management units (MMUs) are hardware devices that may be added to computer systems for any or all of the following reasons:

(1) To increase the amount of main memory in the system beyond that provided by the basic processor architecture.

(2) To partition a large amount of main memory in a way that allows several programs to share the memory without accidently or maliciously interfering with one another.

(3) To give programs the illusion that they have more main memory available to them than is physically provided for them in the computer.

memory mapping
memory management

It is convenient to think of *memory mapping* as performing the first function above, and *memory management* as performing the second; we'll introduce the two topics separately. However, as the discussion develops, we'll see that there

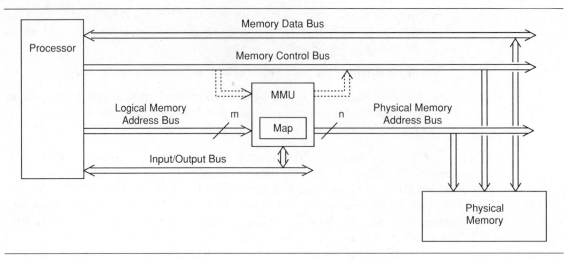

FIGURE 7–23   Placement of an MMU in a computer system.

virtual memory

is actually a fair amount of overlap between the two areas in practice. A combination of the first two functions above is used to achieve the third, called *virtual memory* and discussed in the last subsection.

7.5.1 Memory Mapping

As we indicated at the beginning of this chapter, one of the most common mistakes in computer processor design is the failure to provide enough address bits for a large memory. The industry's investment in software for small-address-space processors, such as the 6809 and the 8080, makes it desirable for computer architects to find ways to increase the usable address space of the existing machines, rather than ask programmers to rewrite all the software for a different, large-address-space machine. Therefore, memory mapping units have been designed and built to increase the amount of main memory that can be attached to processors with relatively small address spaces.

The typical placement of an MMU in a computer system is shown in Figure 7–23. The MMU intercepts each m-bit address from the processor and translates it into an n-bit address for the memory, where $n \geq m$. The m-bit address from the processor is called the *logical address* (sometimes *virtual address*), while the n-bit address is called the *physical address*. The logical-to-physical translation is controlled by a "map" in the MMU as explained shortly.

logical address
virtual address
physical address

The MMU is also connected to the processor's input/output (I/O) bus. The processor can read and write entries in the MMU's translation map using ordinary I/O instructions, as if the map consisted of a set of I/O ports. The interface is a little trickier if the computer uses memory-mapped I/O, in which case a special default mapping may be needed to access the MMU's "I/O ports."

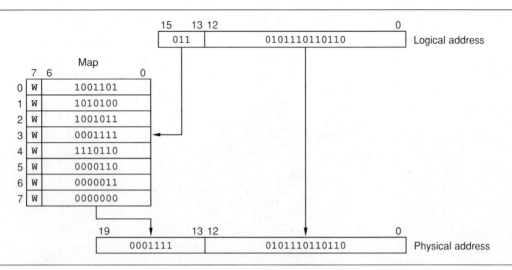

FIGURE 7–24   Simple logical-to-physical MMU translation map.

In any case, the processor controls the translation process since it can change the map from time to time as required.

With memory mapping, a program can still only access as much physical memory at one time as the basic processor architecture allows, for example, 64 Kbytes in a 6809, or up to 256 Kbytes (through four different mapping registers) in the 8086. However, by changing the map a program can access different "chunks" of the physical memory at different times. Thus, a program that manipulates a very large data structure could partition the data structure into chunks of 64 Kbytes or less, and explicitly change the map in order to access different chunks of the data structure.

Another common use of memory mapping is in multi-user operating systems. Each user's program may use the entire logical address space of the machine (say, 64 Kbytes), yet the operating system may allocate a different chunk of physical memory for each user. In this case, it is the operating system's responsibility to set up the map appropriately as each user's program is run. In this kind of application, the memory management function discussed in the next subsection is also very important; it provides "protection" to keep different users' programs from interfering with one another.

An example of a simple MMU map is shown in Figure 7–24, which assumes that $m = 16$ and $n = 20$. The MMU maps the 64-Kbyte logical address space of the processor into 1 Mbyte of physical address space. The 13 low-order bits of the logical address are passed through (or around) the MMU without modification. The three high-order bits are used as an index into the map, which has eight rows. A 7-bit number in the selected row is prefixed to the 13 low-order logical address bits to form a 20-bit physical address.

As shown in Figure 7–25, the MMU has the effect of dividing both the log-

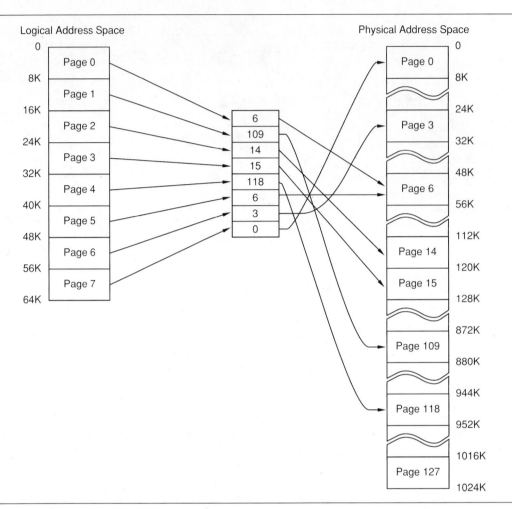

FIGURE 7–25 Logical-to-physical page mapping created by MMU.

page

ical and the physical address spaces into 8-Kbyte *pages*. At any time, addresses in each logical page are mapped into corresponding addresses in a physical page designated by a map entry. Conceptually, nothing prevents two or more logical pages from being mapped into the same physical page, but this isn't normally done. In any case, a program can access only a fraction of the entire physical memory at any time. To access a physical page that no logical page currently maps into, the program must change the map.

More sophisticated MMUs may allow a logical page to use less than a full page of physical memory and may also offer a finer choice of boundaries for physical pages. In this way, a program need not use a maximum-size physical page if it doesn't need it, improving the memory utilization in the computer.

7.5.2 Memory Management

Memory management allows several different programs (or "tasks" or "processes") to use the same physical memory without interfering with each other. For example, consider the MMU that we described in the previous subsection. One megabyte of physical memory could store a 64-Kbyte operating system and 15 independent user programs of 64 Kbytes each. Before running a particular program, the processor could set up the MMU to map the 64-Kbyte logical address space of the processor into 64 Kbytes of physical memory reserved for that program. Programs could not interfere with each other because each could access only its own 64-Kbyte portion of the physical memory, as determined by the map.

In fact, a program could even be protected from interfering with itself. For example, Figure 7–24 shows an extra bit, called W, that is available in each map entry. With appropriate circuitry inside the MMU and some simple modifications *write protection* to the control signals in the memory bus, this bit can be used to *write-protect* selected pages. In this way, when the W bit is set for a particular logical page, the processor cannot inadvertently overwrite instructions or data in that page.

A more sophisticated MMU could provide other forms of access control, *execute only* such as *execute-only* pages containing instructions that the processor may execute but not read as data. In a multi-user system, this would allow one user to execute another user's proprietary program with no possibility of copying it.

invalid Another useful access mode is *invalid*. For example, if a program requires only 24 Kbytes of memory, pages above 24K bytes in the memory map could be marked invalid so that physical memory would not have to be assigned to them.

An MMU can enforce its access rules using an interrupt or trap input to the processor. (Interrupts and traps are explained in Chapter 11.) If a program violates the rules, the MMU causes an interrupt that transfers control to an operating system routine that aborts or otherwise chastises the offending program.

At this point, readers who enjoy thwarting operating systems will have said to themselves, "Why can't my program simply change the map to gain access to another program's physical pages?" Indeed, this is a very real possibility unless precautions are taken in the system's hardware and software design. Several different approaches have been used in practice, but most rely on the idea of having at least two separate maps in the MMU, one for the operating system and one or more for user programs. In addition, the processor hardware is usually designed to have two modes of operation, user and supervisor. This is the technique used in the 68000.

supervisor mode In *supervisor mode*, the MMU's supervisor map is selected and the pro-
user mode cessor may execute any instruction in its instruction set. In *user mode*, a user map is selected and the processor may not execute any instruction from a pre-
privileged defined set of *privileged instructions*. These are instructions whose execution
instruction might compromise the integrity of the operating system.

The set of privileged instructions typically includes all I/O instructions.

The operating system always runs user programs in user mode, so privileged instructions cannot be executed. Therefore, if the MMU is controlled by I/O instructions, user programs cannot access the maps.

In systems like the 68000 that use memory-mapped I/O (Section 10.2.2), there are no I/O instructions to privilege, and the MMU "I/O ports" reside in the same physical address space as the rest of the memory. In this case, all that is needed is to ensure that the MMU I/O port addresses are never accessible through a page in the user map. A user program may be given access to other I/O ports, but never to the MMU's.

Several problems must still be overcome to make memory management useful:

- How can the memory management hardware and software be initialized?

When power is first applied to a computer, the MMU maps are blank or contain garbage. Therefore, the hardware must ensure that the processor "comes up" in supervisor mode and that some default logical-to-physical mapping is in effect. In this way, the processor can run a "bootstrap" program from read-only memory in the default page(s) to set up the maps.

- If user programs don't have access to the operating system's pages and they can't change the processor operating mode or the map, then how can they transfer control to the operating system?

Once again, a hardware solution is required. The processor must provide special instructions, such as software interrupts or traps (Section 11.3), that automatically invoke supervisor mode and jump to a subroutine in the operating system's address space, as determined by the supervisor map.

- What happens with interrupts?

The hardware should automatically switch to the supervisor mode and use the supervisor map when an interrupt takes place. Thus, all interrupts are handled (at least initially) by service routines in the operating system's address space.

- Memory management imposes many restrictions for memory access, privileged instructions, and so on. What happens when a program violates one of the rules?

protection violation

The processor and MMU hardware should detect all such *protection violations*. When a violation occurs, a high-priority interrupt or trap should occur. Like other interrupt service routines, the handler for this interrupt or trap should be in the operating system's address space.

- What happens if the stack pointer is not pointing into a valid stack area when an interrupt or trap occurs? At best, wouldn't the return address and processor status be lost? At worst, wouldn't the processor generate protection violation traps forever as it tries to push into nonexistent or protected memory?

The operating system can't do much to force users to write correct programs, and so a hardware solution is required. The processor should have *two* stack pointers, one for the user and the other for the operating system. In user mode, the processor always uses the user stack pointer, and the user has no way of messing up the supervisor stack pointer. In supervisor mode, the processor always uses the supervisor stack pointer; interrupt and trap information is pushed onto the supervisor stack. Therefore, the operating system need only ensure that it leaves its own stack pointer in a valid state each time that it returns control to a user program.

In the 68000, the user stack pointer is called A7 and the supervisor stack pointer is called A7'. Machine instructions that specify A7 access either A7 or A7' depending on the current mode, user or supervisor. In addition, a pair of privileged instructions, MOVE An, USP and MOVE USP, An, allow the operating system to access the user stack pointer in supervisor mode.

- How can data be moved between different programs' logical address spaces in applications that require data sharing?

The operating system can always set up its own map to read and write data in any physical pages that it wants to. Therefore, user programs can call the operating system to do interprogram transfers under operating system control.

- What about direct-memory access (DMA) transfers?

In one approach, the hardware is arranged to bypass the MMU during DMA transfers, so that DMA interfaces must deal with physical addresses. In another approach, there is at least one additional map in the MMU for DMA transfers, which the hardware selects automatically; in this case, the DMA interfaces deal with logical addresses only.

The solutions offered above are not unique. Also, many other issues must be considered in the design and use of memory management units and operating systems. Since a complete discussion is beyond the scope of this text, you should consult the references if you wish to pursue this topic further.

7.5.3 Virtual Memory

virtual memory

Like the federal government with its virtual money, some computers can pretend to operate with what they don't have—a large physical memory. *Virtual memory* techniques use a combination of memory mapping and memory management to give a program the illusion that it has access to a physical memory whose size can be as large as the entire logical address space of the processor, even though the main memory attached to the processor may be much smaller. In 68000 systems, the virtual memory available to a program could be as large as 4 gigabytes, while the main memory attached to the processor may be a few megabytes or even less.

present bit (P)

The management portion of an MMU helps to create virtual memory by providing a *present bit (P)* in each map entry. The P bit indicates whether each logical page is physically present in main memory. An accessible page that is not present in main memory is stored elsewhere, usually on a disk subsystem that has a much larger capacity, lower cost per bit, and slower access time than main memory.

The mapping portion of an MMU is also an essential ingredient in virtual memory systems. Since the number of logical pages is larger than the number of physical pages, there cannot be a fixed one-to-one mapping between logical and physical pages. Furthermore, a particular logical page may be stored in different physical pages during a program's execution, as it makes several trips back and forth to disk as the operating system decides which logical pages should reside in main memory at any given time. So, in a virtual memory system the MMU's map is frequently updated.

In a virtual memory environment, programs run at full speed, blithely assuming that all of their pages are physically present in main memory. However, when a program accesses a page that is not present (as indicated by the P bit), the *memory exception trap* MMU forces the processor to take a special *memory exception trap*. The memory exception trap is special because it may occur *in the middle of* an instruction (e.g., while fetching the source operand of a double-operand instruction), and because it must preserve enough information to allow the processor to continue the instruction later, after the operating system has brought the missing page into main memory. Virtual memory is most often used by *multiprogramming operating systems*, which can run one user's program while waiting for the missing page(s) of another's to be brought into main memory.

multiprogramming operating system

instruction continuation

The *instruction continuation* capability needed to support virtual memory is so tricky that it was not provided in the original MC68000 processor; only later did the 68010 and 68020 add this feature. To give you an idea of the complexity of restarting an instruction in the middle, the 68020 must save 46 words of internal state information on the stack when a memory exception occurs in the middle of an instruction's execution, as detailed in Section 14.10.

We have only touched upon the most basic concepts of virtual memory and operating system support. We'll revisit these topics again in our discussions of the 68010 and 68020 in Chapter 14, but a complete discussion is beyond the scope of this text. Once again, you are encouraged to study the references for more information.

R E F E R E N C E S

Bell and Mudge's view that a large address space is essential for an extensible, long-lived computer architecture is widely supported. For example, see the papers by the architects of the Zilog Z8000 and the Motorola 68000 that appear in the February 1979 issue of *Computer* (Vol. 12, No. 2).

On the other hand, different architects disagree on the importance of different addressing modes. For example, the architects of the 68000 felt that providing auto-increment and auto-decrement modes was the best way to manipulate stacks and also to provide primitives for moving and searching contiguous blocks of data. The architects of the Intel 8086 family, on the other hand, decided to omit the extra addressing modes and instead provide specialized PUSH, POP, and block move and compare instructions.

In another example of disagreement, addressing modes such as relative and based that support position-independent code were "one of the highest priority design goals" for the architects of the Motorola 6809 ("A Microprocessor for the Revolution: The 6809," by Terry Ritter and Joel Boney, *Byte*, Jan. 1979, Vol. 4, No. 1, pp. 14–42); these ideas were carried forward into the 68000 architecture. Other architects have downplayed the importance of 6809- and 68000-style static position-independent code in favor of memory mapping and management schemes that allow dynamic position independence. The difference of opinion occurs mainly because the different architects are focusing on different applications; 68000-type static position-independent code is very useful for "canned" software such as Macintosh applications, whereas dynamic position independence is needed in large multiprogramming systems that may move a program around in physical memory while it is still executing.

We have barely touched on the issues of memory mapping and management and their relationship to operating systems. A discussion of memory mapping and management schemes from the overall system architecture point of view may be found in *Introduction to Computer Architecture*, edited by Harold Stone (SRA, 1980, 2nd ed.), as well as in Stone's latest book, *High-Performance Computer Architecture* (Addison-Wesley, 1987). Treatments of this subject from the operating system designer's point of view can be found in *Operating Systems: Design and Implementation* by Andrew S. Tanenbaum (Prentice-Hall, 1987) and in *Operating System Concepts* by J. L. Peterson and A. Silberschatz (Addison-Wesley, 1985, 2nd ed.).

EXERCISES

7.1 The instructions LEA addr,An and MOVEA.L #addr,An are almost equivalent, but not quite. How does the assembler determine the size of the addr constant in each instruction? How can this lead to subtle bugs in one case?

7.2 Write a MOVEA instruction that is the equivalent of LEA (Am),An.

7.3 Rewrite the program in Table 7–5 without indexed addressing, using auto-increment addressing instead.

7.4 Many assemblers do not allow parentheses in operand expressions, and give all operators equal precedence (i.e., an expression is evaluated strictly from left to right). Rewrite the declaration of the WORDS array in Section 7.3.1 for such an assembler.

7.5 The effective base address of a two-dimensional array as defined in Section 7.3.1 is not really the address of component [0,0]. Explain.

7.6 What factors limit the maximum value of `NPRIME` that may be used in Table 7–5?

7.7 What is the effect on the program on Table 7–4 if all appearances of `D0` are replaced with `D1`?

Life

7.8 Write an assembly language program that simulates Conway's *Life*. The simulation takes place on a rectangular array of cells, each of which may contain an organism. Except for borders each cell has eight cells immediately adjacent to it, and so each organism may have up to eight neighbors. The survival and reproduction of organisms from generation to generation depend on the number of neighbors according to four simple rules:

(1) If an organism has no neighbors or only one neighbor, it dies of loneliness.

(2) If an organism has two or three neighbors, it survives to the next generation.

(3) If an organism has four or more neighbors, it dies of overcrowding.

(4) An organism is born in any empty cell that has exactly three neighbors.

All changes occur simultaneously; the fate of an organism depends on the current generation irrespective of what may happen to its neighbors in the next generation. Therefore, the game may be simulated in the program using two $m \times n$ arrays of bytes, `CURG` and `TEMPG`. Each array component contains the ASCII code for the letter "O" if the cell contains an organism, an ASCII space otherwise.

For each cell in `CURG`, the program examines the neighbors and puts the next generation outcome in the corresponding cell in `TEMPG`. (Border processing may be simplified by using an $m + 2 \times n + 2$ array in which the borders have been initialized to always contain spaces.) After processing all cells in `CURG`, the program can copy `TEMPG` into `CURG`, or simply swap the roles of `CURG` and `TEMPG`.

The array size $m \times n$ may correspond to the size of a CRT screen (e.g., 24×80). In Chapter 10, we shall continue the assignment by specifying a means of displaying the generations of Life on a CRT screen.

7.9 Rewrite the 1's-counting subroutine of Table 5–12 on page 166. The new version should contain a 256-byte table, `N1S[0..255]`, initialized at load time, where `N1S[i]` contains the number of 1's in the binary representation of `i`. The `BCNT1S` subroutine should simply look up the number of 1's in its input number, using indexed addressing.

7.10 Modify the binary-to-ASCII conversion subroutine of Exercise 5.22 so that the result characters are not stored in fixed memory locations. Instead, when the subroutine is called, the `A0` register is assumed to contain the base address of a 3-byte array `ASC[0..2]` in which the result characters are to be stored.

7.11 In many processors, it is difficult to write position-independent code because it is difficult for a program to determine the current value of the PC. In the 68000, the value of the PC is easily accessed using PC-relative addressing modes. However, just to make things difficult, suppose we got rid of the PC-relative addressing modes. Write a subroutine `MOVEPCA6` that computes and puts into A6 the address of the instruction following a `JSR MOVEPCA6` instruction.

7.12 Explain why the code below is statically position independent.

```
        ORG    0
FOP     DS.B   20                  Storage for FOP[1..20] of bytes.
I       DS.W   1                   Storage for an index into FOP.
        ...
        LEA    FOP-1(PC),A0        Effective base address of FOP.
        MOVE.W I,D0
        MOVE.B 0(D0,A0),D1         D1 := FOP[I].
```

7.13 Explain why the above code is *not* dynamically position independent.

7.14 Write a program that uses addressing by indirection to access a multidimensional array in the Macintosh environment. Assume that the array itself is stored in the application global space, but that the auxiliary table of "row addresses" is stored with the code. Instead of absolute row addresses, what information should be stored in this table?

7.15 One of the key decisions in the design of a memory-mapping scheme is the choice of page size. Discuss at least two factors in favor of a large page size, and two in favor of a small page size.

CHAPTER 8

Operations

What operations are absolutely necessary for a processor to be able to compute anything that is computable? Over 30 years ago, Van der Pol showed that it is theoretically possible to build a functional processor with just one instruction.[1] Although the logic circuits needed to implement a one-instruction processor may be simple compared with the 68000-transistor MC68000, the programs for such a machine would be overly large, complex, and slow.

Instead of minimizing the size of instruction sets, modern computer architects have tried to provide a "complete set" of instructions that support a variety of data types (integer, floating-point, boolean, character string, array, etc.) and program structures (conditional tests, loops, procedures, etc.). In a paper describing trade-offs in the design of the Zilog Z8000, architect Bernard Peuto said,[2]

> A large number of opcodes is very important: having a given instruction implemented in hardware saves bytes and improves speed. But usually one needs to concentrate more on the completeness of the operations available on a particular data type than on adding more and more esoteric instructions.

The feasibility of implementing a "complete set" of instructions is obviously limited by the capabilities of integrated circuit technology at any given time. In their original description of the 68000 architecture, forward-looking architects Skip Stritter and Tom Gunter said,[3]

---

[1] W. L. Van der Pol, "The Essential Types of Operations in an Automatic Computer," *Nachrichtentechnische Fachberichte*, vol. 4, pp. 144–145, 1956. For a more accessible discussion of single-instruction computers, see Chapter 5 of Daniel Tabak's *RISC Architecture* (Wiley, 1987).

[2] B. L. Peuto, "Architecture of a New Microprocessor," *Computer*, February 1979 (Vol. 12, No. 2, pp. 10–21).

[3] E. Stritter and T. Gunter, "A Microprocessor for a Changing World: The Motorola 68000," *Computer*, February 1979 (Vol. 12, No. 2, pp. 43–52).

The single-chip MC68000 microprocessor is a partial implementation of the 68000 architecture. It implements as large a subset of the complete architecture as current technologies will allow.... One-eighth of the operation-code map is currently unimplemented. Some of this space is allocated in the architecture—for example, for floating-point and string operations. Some of the free space is unspecified and will be allocated for future architectural enhancement.

Even when the IC capabilities available to a computer architect are seemingly unlimited, there are subtle trade-offs among the size of encoded instructions and programs, the complexity of the computation performed by a single instruction, and the speed of primitive operations. In an article describing the design methods used in the MC68030, Thomas L. Johnson said,[4]

Microprocessors like the MC68030 normally do not attempt to limit the programmer/compiler to load/store architectures. However, they do incorporate many high-level constructs to assist high-level language compiler writers (features such as simple stacking primitives for procedure calls/returns).... Overall, the trade-offs between ... implementation philosophies are normally ones of circuit complexity and assignment of system features between the software and hardware elements.

And practical engineering and marketing issues, such as the desire to maintain (the appearance of) compatibility with previous products, ultimately constrain the instruction-set architecture of a new microprocessor.

With all of the design choices available to computer architects, it's not surprising that dozens of different microprocessor architectures appeared during the 1970s and early 1980s. Yet because of the practical engineering and marketing decisions made by microprocessor *users* in the 1980s, two families now dominate the 16- and 32-bit microprocessor marketplace—the Motorola 68000 family and the Intel 80x86 family. Likewise, a small number of architectures dominate the mainframe computer market.

Despite the differences in instruction-set architectures, there are many similarities among the operations performed by different processors, sometimes for historical reasons, but just as often for practical ones. For example, almost every microprocessor has a branch instruction that specifies the target address using an 8-bit offset from the current PC; this is a very frequently used instruction that can be encoded in a small number of bits.

This chapter discusses the operations available in typical computer processors, except for input/output, which is covered in Chapter 10. Although a "complete set" of operation types is covered, "esoteric" operations of non-68000 processors are not. However, we do describe *all* of the operations of

---

[4]"The RISC/CISC Melting Pot," in the April 1987 issue of *Byte* (Vol. 12, No. 4, pp. 153–160), part of a five-article special section on "Instruction Set Strategies."

the MC68000 processor in this chapter. Later members of the family are fully described in Chapter 14.

A representative mnemonic is given for each operation in this chapter; in most cases we use 68000 mnemonics. However, you are cautioned that different manufacturers use quite different mnemonics for the same operations, and identical mnemonics may have different meanings in different computers. For example, Chapters 15 and 16 give manufacturers' mnemonics for operations in the Motorola 6809 and Intel 8086 processors. Still, the user manuals published by the manufacturers are the best source of detailed information not covered in this book.

Many operations in this chapter are described by Pascal statements. In these descriptions we sometimes make use of the auxiliary procedures and functions that were introduced in Table 5–8 on page 156.

notation   Don't forget that, in this chapter and throughout this book, we use the designation "68000" to refer to instructions and features that are common to the entire 68000 family, and we use Motorola part numbers to refer to specific family members (MC68000, MC68008, MC68010, MC68012, MC68020, MC68030, MC68040, ...). The programming model for the MC68000 and MC68008 processors is shown in Figure 8–1. Other family members have a few more special registers and status bits, as we'll show in Section 14.2 for the MC68010 and MC68012 and in Section 14.7 for the MC68020 and MC68030.

8.1 INSTRUCTION FORMATS

The data manipulation operations in the next few sections can be classified by the number of operands; the most common are single-operand and double-operand

single-operand   instructions. *Single-operand instructions* have the following format:
instruction

```
Opcode    Operand     Description
------    -------     -----------
  OP       dst        dst := OP(dst);
```

destination   Such instructions generally read the value of a *destination operand* dst, perform
operand   some function on it, and store the result back into dst. Depending on the
dst   processor and the instruction, dst may be either a register or a memory location specified by one of the allowed addressing modes.

double-operand   *Double-operand instructions* in most processors have the following format:
instruction

```
  OP       dst,src     dst := OP(src,dst);
```

source operand   Such instructions generally read the values of dst and a *source operand* src,
src   combine them in some way, and store the result back into dst. Data movement instructions are a special case, simply copying the value of src into dst.

As a documentation convention, 68000 instructions have the order of src and dst reversed in assembly language programs:

```
  OP       src,dst     dst := OP(src,dst);
```

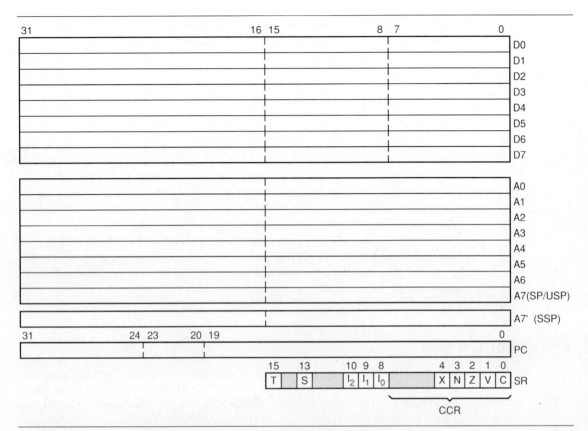

FIGURE 8–1   Programming model for the MC68000 and MC68008.

We'll stick with this convention in all of our discussions of the 68000.

The allowed identities of `src` and `dst` in a double-operand instruction depend on the processor architecture. In a one-address (accumulator-based) processor such as the 6809, `dst` is usually an accumulator and `src` is a register or memory location specified by an addressing mode:

```
OP        src           accum := OP(src,accum);
```

Here, the name of the `dst` operand need not appear in the operand field of the assembly language instruction; instead, it may be implied by the opcode mnemonic (e.g., `LDA src` to load accumulator A with `src`).

General-register processors such as the 68000 and 8086 have one-and-a-half-address instructions in which `dst` is one of the registers while `src` may be any register or memory location specified by an allowed addressing mode:

```
OP        src,reg       reg := OP(src,reg);
```

In the 68000, most one-and-a-half address instructions also have a reverse form in which `src` is a register and `dst` is a register or memory location:

```
OP        reg,dst       dst := OP(reg,dst);
```

The 68000 also has two-address instructions in which both `src` and `dst` may be memory locations specified by addressing modes; only in this case are memory-to-memory operations possible.

Most 16-bit and 32-bit processors support operations on 8-bit bytes as well as on 16-bit or 32-bit operands. Thus, typical data movement and manipulation instructions specify the length of the operand(s) as well as the operation. In assembly language, the operand length is usually indicated by a suffix on the instruction mnemonic. For example, `ADD.B`, `ADD.W`, and `ADD.L` instructions perform addition of bytes, words, and longwords in the 68000.

Normally, the `src` and `dst` operands in a double-operand instruction must have the same length. However, some instructions allow the `src` operand to be shorter than the `dst` operand, and automatically pad the `src` operand to the required size, for example, by extending the sign bit.

8.2 CONDITION BITS

A high percentage (up to 20%) of all instructions in typical computer programs are conditional branches, and so it's very important to optimize their length and execution efficiency. In some accumulator-based processors, a conditional branch instruction tests the value of the accumulator, and jumps according to a specified condition (e.g., zero/nonzero, positive/negative). The branch instruction contains a few bits to specify the condition, and a displacement field that locates the branch target relative to the current instruction. In a general-register processor, this scheme would require branch instructions to contain several additional bits to select which register to test. Luckily, conditional branches most often need to test a register or other operand that has just been manipulated. Processors with condition bits take advantage of this characteristic.

condition bit
condition code
condition flag

Condition bits (or *condition codes* or *condition flags*) are a collection of individual status bits that a processor automatically sets or clears according to the result of each instruction. For example, the 68000's Z bit, introduced in Chapter 5, is set to 1 when an operation produces a zero result, and cleared to 0 for a nonzero result.

conditional branch instruction

A *conditional branch instruction* tests the value of one or more condition bits and branches to a new location if the condition bits have a specified value. In Chapter 5 we introduced only the `branch if equal` (`BEQ`) and `branch if not equal` (`BNE`) instructions, which test condition bit Z. However, in the example programs in Chapter 7, we saw that there are other interesting conditions to test, such as greater than or less than zero. Additional condition bits are needed to indicate such relations.

processor status word (PSW)

The condition bits are part of the processor state that we defined in Chapter 5. In the programming model of a processor, they are often grouped together with other processor state information into a single n-bit register with a name such as *processor status word (PSW)*.

The number, naming, and meaning of condition bits vary on different processors, but the most popular set is found in the 68000, 6809, and 8086:

negative (N)

- *Negative (N)*. Equals the most significant (sign) bit of the result.

zero (Z)

- *Zero (Z)*. Set to 1 if all the bits of a result are zero, to 0 otherwise.

overflow (V)

- *Overflow (V)*. During arithmetic operations, set to 1 if two's-complement overflow occurs; set to 0 if no overflow occurs. When a program adds or subtracts n-bit *signed* numbers, V = 1 indicates that the true result is greater than $2^{n-1} - 1$ or less than -2^{n-1}. The expression N XOR V always gives the correct sign of a two's-complement result, since V = 1 indicates that N is wrong.

carry (C)

- *Carry (C)*. During addition operations, set equal to the carry out of the most significant bit (MSB) position. When a program adds n-bit *unsigned* numbers, C = 1 indicates that the true result is greater than $2^n - 1$. During subtraction operations, C is set to the *borrow* out of the MSB. When unsigned numbers are subtracted, C = 1 indicates that the true result is less than zero.

The condition bit settings are consistent with operand size. For example, the N bit equals bit 7 of the result after a byte operation, bit 15 after a word operation, or bit 31 after a longword operation. However, the exact rules for setting the condition bits still can vary for different instructions and different processors. Where there is a clear interpretation, all processors use the same rules; for example, all set V to 1 if ADD produces two's-complement overflow, to 0 otherwise. However, the rules are somewhat arbitrary for many instructions.

For example, how should the condition bits be set after a MOVE operation? Clearly, N and Z should be set according to the value just loaded. But what about C and V? In many processors, V is cleared to 0 and C is not affected. The reasons for this rule are subtle—clearing V assures that certain signed conditional branches will work properly, while preserving C is important in multiprecision operations.

Some processors, including the 8086, do not change any of the condition bits after a MOVE operation. Still others, including the 68000 and the 6809, use different rules depending on whether the destination is a memory location or a particular register. In general, one must carefully examine the user's manual for a processor to find the exact rules for condition bit setting.

Although the condition bits are affected by most data movement and manipulation instructions, sometimes it is necessary to test an operand that doesn't need to be moved or manipulated. The TST instruction is provided just for this purpose—TST dst reads its operand dst and sets the condition bits according to its value, and does nothing else.

Some processors have additional condition bits that aid in special operations:

parity (P)

- *Parity (P)*. Indicates that the result has even parity, that is, an even number of 1 bits.

half carry (H)

- *Half carry (H)*. Equals the carry between bits 3 and 4 of a byte during addition; used in binary-coded decimal (BCD) operations.

decimal adjust (D)

- *Decimal adjust (D)*. Indicates whether an addition or a subtraction occurred most recently; used in conjunction with H in BCD operations.

Most processors have instructions that manipulate the condition bits as a single unit. For example, the 8086 groups the condition bits together in a register called "FLAGS," and it has instructions that move FLAGS to and from the accumulator.

Occasionally it is also necessary to set a single condition bit to a particular, known value. Many processors have convenient instructions for doing this, for example:

```
CLRZ                Z := 0;
SETZ                Z := 1;
```

condition code register (CCR)

status register (SR)

The 68000's condition bits are contained in a special 8-bit register called the *condition code register (CCR)*, which is part of the *status register (SR)* shown in the 68000 programming model in Figure 8–1. Besides the "standard" condition bits, N, Z, V, and C, the 68000 has one more condition bit, not found in any other processor:

extend (X)

- *Extend (X)*. An extra carry bit, set in the same way as C, but not by all operations; used in multiprecision arithmetic.

The 68000 has several instructions that manipulate the CCR as a single unit:

```
MOVE.W   src,CCR      CCR := src; {Low byte of src only}
AND.B    #data,CCR    CCR := And(CCR,data);
OR.B     #data,CCR    CCR := Or(CCR,data);
EOR.B    #data,CCR    CCR := ExclusiveOr(CCR,data);
```

To read the CCR, a 68000 program must read the entire SR and extract the CCR information from the low byte:

```
MOVE.W   SR,dst       dst := SR; {Low byte of dst = CCR}
```

The 68000 does not provide explicit instructions for manipulating individual condition bits. Instead, we use the AND, OR, and EOR instructions listed above, with appropriate immediate values to affect only a single bit of CCR. For example, "AND.B #$FB,CCR" clears Z to 0. With a macro assembler, we can avoid memorizing constants like $FB by writing an appropriate set of macros, for example,

```
CLRZ    MACRO
        AND.B   #$FB,CCR
        ENDM
SETZ    MACRO
        OR.B    #$04,CCR
        ENDM
NOTZ    MACRO
        EOR.B   #$04,CCR
        ENDM
```

Tables in subsequent sections show which condition bits are affected by each 68000 instruction. Conditional branches that test the condition bits are described fully in Section 8.7.

8.3 PROCESSOR CONTROL AND STATUS BITS

Most processors have a small number of bits, typically part of the processor status word, that control certain general operating modes of the processor. Functions controlled by these bits include the following:

- Interrupt enabling. One or more bits may control the processor's ability to respond to external events called "interrupts," as described in Chapter 11.

- Instruction tracing. One or more bits may put the processor into a "single-step" mode where the programmer may examine the effects of instructions one at a time for debugging purposes.

- Special functions. One or more bits may control the enabling and disabling of special processing units, such as cache and memory management units.

privilege level

- Privilege level. One or more bits may set the current *privilege level* of the processor, where certain instructions and resources can be used only at high privilege levels. This allows the creation of multiprogramming operating-system environments in which user programs and the operating system are protected from each other.

In processors with privilege level, input/output instructions as well the instructions that modify the processor control bits themselves are generally privileged so that they can be executed only at high privilege levels.

The 68000's control and status bits are located in the upper byte of the status register (SR). They may be accessed with certain data movement and logical instructions that are introduced later in this chapter and summarized in Section 8.12.

processor priority level (PPL)

Bits 8–10 of SR are called the *processor priority level (PPL)* and determine whether or not interrupts are accepted, as described in Section 11.1. All 68000-family processors use PPL in the same way.

supervisor bit (S)
privileged
* instruction*

master bit (M)

trace bit (T)

The 68000 has two privilege levels, user and supervisor, controlled by the *supervisor bit (S)* in the SR. When S is 1, the 68000 is in supervisor mode, its higher privilege level; when S is 0, it is in user mode. Certain *privileged instructions* may be executed only in supervisor mode. Also, the processor chip indicates on its external signal pins whether it is currently running in user mode or supervisor mode, so that external memory management units can enforce access rights that depend on the current mode. The MC68020 and MC68030 SRs have a *master bit (M)* that selects between the "master stack pointer" and the "interrupt stack pointer" when S is 1, as described in Section 14.7.

In all 68000-family processors, instructions that affect the upper byte of SR are privileged—they cannot be executed in user mode. Still, a user program can set the S bit and force the processor into supervisor mode in a well-controlled manner by executing a TRAP instruction, as explained in Section 11.4.4. Also, interrupts force the processor into supervisor mode as described in Section 11.1.2.

Bit 15 of the SR in the MC68000 through MC68012 is called the *trace bit (T)*; it allows programs to be single stepped as described in Section 11.4.4. The MC68020 and MC68030 use two SR bits (14 and 15) to control single stepping.

8.4 DATA MOVES

data move

LD
ST

MOV

MOVE

By far the most frequently used instructions in typical computer processors are *data moves*—operations that move (actually, *copy*) data from one place to another in the registers and memory. In processors that support different lengths of data, such as bytes, words, and longwords, there are separate data movement instructions for each length. In most processors, data moves set the condition codes according to the value of the datum just moved.

The two most important data movement instructions are load (LD) and store (ST). Traditionally, LD and similar mnemonics denote operations that move data from memory to a processor register; ST denotes movement from a register to memory. However, there are many variations.

In the 8086, the assembly language mnemonic MOV is used for both directions of transfer, even though the instructions are encoded with different opcodes. The assembler deduces the intended transfer direction from the order of the operands. In the 8086, memory-to-memory moves are not allowed.

The 68000 uses the mnemonic MOVE for both directions of transfer, and it provides a full two-address instruction where both source and destination can be registers or memory locations. Therefore, memory-to-memory moves are possible.

Data movement instructions transfer data from source to destination. However, not all computers use the same convention for the direction of transfer in assembly language programs. Most have the following format:

```
MOV     dst,src     dst := src; {8086}
LD      dst,src     dst := src; {6809}
ST      src,dst     dst := src; {6809}
```

However, 68000 assembly language has the opposite format:

```
MOVE    src,dst    dst := src; {68000}
```

Most contemporary processors provide a means of pushing and popping data to or from a stack in just one instruction. Processors such as the 68000 and 6809 have auto-increment and auto-decrement as standard addressing modes; here PUSH and POP are just special cases of the regular data movement instructions, for example, MOVE src,-(SP) and MOVE (SP)+,dst, respectively. In these processors, any address register may be used as a stack pointer. The 8086 provides specialized instructions, PUSH and POP, that can only use the system stack pointer register for pushing and popping.

There are a number of other specialized data movement instructions in different processors. Most have instructions for moving the contents of the SR and other processor control and status registers to and from the general registers, accumulator, or stack. Some processors have an exchange (EXG) instruction that swaps the contents of two registers or a register and a memory location; a SWAP instruction swaps halves of an operand (e.g., swaps words in a longword operand). Some processors have load multiple (LDM) and store multiple (STM) instructions that allow a group of registers to be saved in memory or restored from memory in one instruction, useful in subroutines and interrupt routines. And some have instructions that can move entire blocks of data from one part of memory to another.

Table 8–1 summarizes the data movement instructions of the 68000. The first part of the table contains MOVE instructions, which we introduced and used in Section 5.5. These are general two-address instructions, since both src and dst may be specified.

MOVEQ

For MOVEs where dst is a data register and src is an immediate operand that can be expressed as an 8-bit two's-complement number, a one-word MOVEQ instruction may be used. This instruction is useful for loading small loop counters, array index constants, and other small signed integer values. It makes programs shorter and faster by replacing the three-word-long MOVE.L #data,dst that would otherwise have to be used. Most 68000 assemblers use this instruction automatically whenever possible, unless forced to use the long immediate form in specific cases by a MOVEI mnemonic.

MOVEI
LEA
PEA

The LEA and PEA instructions may be used to compute the absolute address of an operand at run time, using any addressing mode except register direct, auto-increment, or auto-decrement. LEA deposits the result in a specified address register, which can be used later to access the parameter using register indirect addressing. PEA pushes the result onto the SP stack, on which it is presumably passed to a subroutine for later retrieval and use. These instructions are extremely useful for passing VAR-type parameters to subroutines, as we'll see in Section 9.3.

MOVEM
register list mask

The MOVEM instructions load or store multiple registers in memory. MOVEM is a two-word instruction; the second word is a *register list mask* that specifies

TABLE 8–1   Data movement instructions in the 68000.

Mnemonic	Operands	Opcode Word	XNZVC	Description
MOVE.B	asrc,adst	0001ddddddssssss	-**00	Copy asrc to adst (byte)
MOVE.W	asrc,adst	0011ddddddssssss	-**00	Copy asrc to adst (word)
MOVE.L	asrc,adst	0010ddddddssssss	-**00	Copy asrc to adst (long)
MOVEA.W	asrc,An	0011aaa001ssssss	-----	Copy asrc to An (word)
MOVEA.L	asrc,An	0010aaa001ssssss	-----	Copy asrc to An (long)
MOVEQ.L	#qdata,Dn	0111rrr0qqqqqqqq	-**00	Copy qdata to Dn
LEA.L	csrc,An	0100aaa111ssssss	-----	Load An with effective address of csrc
PEA.L	csrc	0100100001ssssss	-----	Push effective address of csrc using SP
MOVEM.WL	regs,Mdst	010010001Ldddddd	-----	Store multiple registers
MOVEM.WL	Msrc,regs	010011001Lssssss	-----	Load multiple registers
SWAP.W	Dn	0100100001000rrr	-**00	Swap 16-bit halves of Dn
EXG.L	Dn,Dm	1100RRR101000rrr	-----	Exchange two data registers
EXG.L	An,Am	1100AAA101001aaa	-----	Exchange two address registers
EXG.L	Dn,An	1100rrr110001aaa	-----	Exchange data and address registers
MOVE.W	dsrc,CCR	0100010011ssssss	-----	Copy low byte of dsrc to CCR
MOVE.L	An,USP	0100111001100aaa	-----	Copy An to user SP (privileged operation)
MOVE.L	USP,An	0100111001101aaa	-----	Copy user SP to An (privileged operation)
MOVE.W	dsrc,SR	0100011011ssssss	-----	Copy dsrc to SR (privileged operation)
MOVE.W	SR,adst	0100000011dddddd	-----	Copy SR to adst
MOVEP.WL	Dn,dsp(An)	0000rrr11L001aaa	-----	Store peripheral data
MOVEP.WL	dsp(An),Dn	0000rrr10L001aaa	-----	Load peripheral data

Notes: See Table 8–2 for addressing mode restrictions.

Dm,Dn = one of the data registers, D0–D7. Am,An = one of the address registers, A0–A7.

data = immediate data appropriate for the size of the operation, stored in the byte, word, or longword following the instruction.

qdata = "quick" immediate operand, an 8-bit two's-complement number in the range −128 through +127.

dsp = 16-bit signed displacement for based addressing mode, contained in the word following the opcode word.

regs = a list of general registers.

ssssss = src field; dddddd = dst field; qqqqqqqq = qdata field.

aaa = An field; AAA = Am field; rrr = Dn field; RRR = Dm field.

L = size bit: 1 = long, 0 = word; LW = size field: 00 = byte, 01 = word, 10 = long.

Effects of instructions on condition code bits:

-: not affected.

1: always set to 1.

0: always cleared to 0.

*: set according to operation result as discussed in text.

U: undefined.

the registers to be moved, one per bit, so that any combination of the 16 general registers may be moved. Depending on the instruction's size suffix (.W or .L), either the low-order word or the entire 32-bit longword of each register is moved. In most cases, MOVEM moves to or from a block of memory beginning at the effective address of the Msrc or Mdst operand. However, the registers may be pushed onto or popped from a stack by specifying auto-decrement addressing for dst or auto-increment for src, respectively.

Bits 0 through 15 in MOVEM's register list mask correspond to the registers D0 through D7, and A0 through A7, respectively, except that the bit order is reversed in MOVEM.WL regs,-(An). In the assembly language instruction, ranges are denoted by dashes (D2-D5), and multiple register names and ranges are separated by slashes (A2/D2-D5/SP/D0). The order of registers in the assembly language instruction is irrelevant; registers are moved in the same order that they appear in the register list mask word—the low-order bit corresponds to the first register to be moved.

A typical use of MOVEM to save and restore registers in a subroutine is outlined below:

```
SUBR    MOVEM.L D0-D3/A0/A2,-(SP)      Save registers D0-D3,A0,A2.
        ...
        MOVEM.L (SP)+,D0-D3/A0/A2      Restore working registers.
        RTS                            Return to caller.
```

Of course, when registers or other data are saved and restored using the stack, the number and size of items pushed onto the stack must precisely match the number and size of items popped off the stack. Also, if any of the registers is being used to return a result to the caller, it should not be saved and restored; that is, the result must not be overwritten by the final MOVEM.

SWAP
EXG

The SWAP instruction simply swaps the 16-bit halves of a data register, setting the condition bits according to the 32-bit result. The EXG instruction swaps the contents of any two 32-bit registers, without affecting the condition bits.

A program can load any desired value into the CCR using the instruction MOVE.W dsrc,CCR. Even though the source operand is a word, its high-order byte is ignored and only the CCR, not the high-order byte of the SR, is affected. Two additional instructions allow the full SR to be accessed. However, the MOVE.W dsrc,SR instruction is privileged—the SR can be changed only in supervisor mode. Two more instructions access the user SP (USP) in supervisor mode.

The MOVEP instruction is used in conjunction with certain peripheral devices as explained in Section 10.2.3.

8.4.1 68000 Quirks

There are several important "irregularities" that you should keep in mind about the 68000's data movement and most other instructions:

- When the destination operand is an address register, the condition bits are not affected, except by CMPA instructions. According to the 68000's designers, the absolute numerical value of an address, even zero vs nonzero, is not deemed to have any significance; so why destroy the condition codes unnecessarily?

TABLE 8–2   Addressing mode restrictions in 68000-family processor and coprocessors.

Addressing Mode	EA field	Example	Source (_src)									Destination (_dst)							
			a	b	c	d	f	m	M	p	s	a	b	c	d	m	M	p	t
Data-register direct	0x	D1	X	X		X	X					X	X		X				X
Address-register direct	1x	A2	X									X							
Address-register indirect	2x	(A3)	X	X	X	X	X	X	X	X	X	X	X	X	X	X	X	X	X
Auto-increment	3x	(A4)+	X			X	X	X	X		X	X			X	X			X
Auto-decrement	4x	–(A5)	X			X	X	X			X	X			X	X	X		X
Based	5x	10(A6)	X	X	X	X	X	X	X	X	X	X	X	X	X	X	X	X	X
Based indexed	6x	20(A5,D4)	X	X	X	X	X	X	X	X	X	X	X	X	X	X	X	X	X
Absolute short	70	HERE.W	X	X	X	X	X	X	X	X	X	X	X	X	X	X	X	X	X
Absolute long	71	THERE.L	X	X	X	X	X	X	X	X	X	X	X	X	X	X	X	X	X
Relative	72	NEAR(PC)	X	X	X	X	X	X	X					X					X
Relative indexed	73	30(PC,D3)	X	X	X	X	X	X	X					X					X
Immediate	74	#1234	X			X	X	X											
Floating-point register	n/a	FP2					X												

Notes: Address-register direct is not allowed if the operand size is "byte."
  Source and destination types: a = any; b = bit; c = control; d = data; f = floating;
  m = memory; M = multiple; p = PMMU; s = silly; t = testable.

- In most data manipulation instructions, source operands may use any addressing mode except address register direct. Address registers are supposed to contain addresses, not data with arithmetic or bitwise significance.

- Destination operands may not use immediate or relative addressing modes. These modes access program memory, which should never be modified like data.

- Byte operations cannot be performed on address registers. Addresses are considered always to be word or longword quantities.

- Operations that treat their operands as bit patterns generally cannot be performed on address registers (SWAP, COM, etc.). Again, the 68000's designers considered an address to be an "entire" thing, not a number with individual bits or bytes to be torn apart.

- Although Motorola classifies SWAP as a "word" instruction, the condition bits are set according to the full 32-bit result.

Addressing mode irregularities are tabulated in Table 8–2. When we define a 68000 instruction, such as MOVE.B asrc,adst, this table specifies the allowable addressing modes for the source and destination operands—asrc can use only modes selected in the "Source a" column and adst can use only modes selected in the "Destination a" column. We refer to this table throughout this chapter and in Chapters 14 and 15 when defining instructions for 68000-family processors and coprocessors.

Most 68000 assemblers help the programmer work with the 68000's irregularities. First of all, the assembler will not assemble a nonexistent instruction—one with an illegal combination of operation, size, and addressing modes. Second, if the programmer does not specify a size suffix with the instruction mnemonic, the assembler fills in the proper size if only one exists, or uses a default of "word" otherwise (actually, the latter case is dangerous). Third, for certain instructions the assembler accepts a "generic" opcode mnemonic and assembles the proper instruction depending on the operands. For example, given a "MOVE" mnemonic, the assembler may produce MOVEA, MOVEQ, or one of a number of different MOVE instructions.

8.5 ADDITION AND SUBTRACTION

The basic arithmetic operation in any computer is binary addition. A typical ADD instruction has the following format:

```
ADD     src,dst      dst := dst + src + 0;
```

ADD

The ADD instruction adds two n-bit operands using n-bit binary addition with an initial carry of 0, stores an n-bit sum in dst, and sets the condition bits accordingly. This addition operation is appropriate for signed two's-complement numbers as well as unsigned numbers. For signed numbers, the N and V condition bits indicate the status of the result while, for unsigned numbers, the C bit indicates a carry out of the most significant bit position. The ADD instruction sets all of these bits; it is the programmer's responsibility to look at the appropriate condition bits for the type of numbers being added. Some examples of the condition bit settings are given in Table 8–3 using 8-bit numbers. The arithmetic weight of the carry bit is +256.

Most processors also have a subtraction operation that subtracts the source operand from the destination using two's-complement subtraction with an initial borrow of 0:

SUB

```
SUB     src,dst      dst := dst - src - 0;
```

In the typical hardware implementation of this operation, the result is obtained by adding the two's complement of src to dst; the two's complement of src is obtained by complementing the individual bits of src and adding 1. However, there is an important difference from normal addition in most processors—the condition bit C is set to 1 if SUB produces a *borrow*, and is cleared if there is no borrow. The borrow bit is the *complement* of the carry bit produced in the corresponding addition, as shown in Table 8–4 using 8-bit unsigned numbers. In 8-bit subtraction, the arithmetic weight of borrow is −256. Complete examples of the condition bit settings for subtraction are provided in Table 8–5.

Subtraction is a useful operation for comparing the values of two numbers. For example, X is less than Y if and only if X–Y is less than zero. Therefore, if SUB Y,X produces a negative result, then X is less than Y.

TABLE 8–3 Condition bit settings for addition.

Operation	N	Z	V	C	Signed Interpretation	Unsigned Interpretation
00000100 + 00000010					+4 + +2	4 + 2
00000110	0	0	0	0	+6	6
01010000 + 01110000					+80 + +112	80 + 112
11000000	1	0	1	0	−64, overflow	192
11010011 + 00101101					−45 + +45	211 + 45
00000000	0	1	0	1	0	0, carry 1
10010000 + 11000000					−112 + −64	144 + 192
01010000	0	0	1	1	+80, overflow	80, carry 1

CMP

A program usually doesn't need to store the difference after comparing two numbers. The compare (CMP) instruction subtracts two operands and sets the condition bits *without* storing the difference. CMP is used with conditional branch instructions as explained in Section 8.7. Like SUB, CMP sets C if the subtraction produces a borrow, not a carry. The format of the CMP instruction in a typical *non-68000* processor is as follows:

TABLE 8–4 Decimal subtractions and binary equivalents.

Decimal Subtraction	Binary Subtraction	Binary Addition
		1 (initial carry)
9 − 5	00001001 − 00000101	00001001 + 11111010
4	00000100, no borrow	00000100, carry 1, so borrow=0
		1 (initial carry)
2 − 13	00000010 − 00001101	00000010 + 11110010
245−256	11110101, borrow 1	11110101, carry 0, so borrow=1
		1 (initial carry)
7 − 7	00000111 − 00000111	00000111 + 11111000
0	00000000, no borrow	00000000, carry 1, so borrow=0

TABLE 8–5   Condition bit settings for subtraction.

Operation	N	Z	V	C	Signed Interpretation	Unsigned Interpretation
00000100					+4	4
− 00000010					− +2	− 2
00000010	0	0	0	0	+2	2
00000101					+5	5
− 00000111					− +7	− 7
11111110	1	0	0	1	−2	254, borrow 1
11111101					−3	253
− 11111101					− −3	− 253
00000010	0	1	0	0	0	0
10000001					−127	129
− 00000100					− +4	− 4
01111101	0	0	1	0	+125, overflow	125

```
        CMP      src,dst      Set condition bits using src-dst.
```

Thus, the instruction sequence

```
        CMP      P,Q          Set condition bits using P-Q.
        BGT      OUT          Branch if P-Q > 0.
```

performs the subtraction P−Q and branches if P > Q. However, the 68000 CMP instruction works differently, as we'll see shortly.

Table 8–6 summarizes the addition, subtraction, and related instructions in the 68000. There are seven variations of the ADD instruction, and for each variation there is a corresponding SUB instruction. Therefore, we'll describe only the ADDs, shown in the first part of the table.

ADD

The first two ADD instructions in Table 8–6 allow memory-to-register and register-to-memory adds of bytes, words, or longwords. If both operands are data registers, then the first encoding is used. On the other hand, if the destination operand is an address register, then the third instruction (ADDA) must be used.

ADDA

Notice that most of the addition instructions affect all of the condition bits, including X, while ADDA affects none of them.

ADDI
ADDQ

ADDI allows an immediate value to be added to any dst operand. This is particularly useful for adding immediate values to operands in memory. ADDQ is similar to ADDI, except the immediate value must be in the range 1–8, and is encoded in the opcode word itself, yielding a one-word-long instruction (plus any additional words required by the dst addressing mode).

Most 68000 assemblers allow the mnemonic "ADD" to be used for all of the above instructions. The assembler picks the best encoding based on the characteristics of the operands.

TABLE 8–6   Addition and subtraction instructions in the 68000.

Mnemonic	Operands	Opcode Word	XNZVC	Description
ADD.BWL	asrc,Dn	1101rrr0LWsssssss	★★★★★	Add asrc to Dn
ADD.BWL	Dn,mdst	1101rrr1LWddddddd	★★★★★	Add Dn to mdst
ADDA.WL	asrc,An	1101aaaL11sssssss	-----	Add asrc to An
ADDI.BWL	#data,adst	00000110LWddddddd	★★★★★	Add immediate data to adst
ADDQ.BWL	#qint,adst	0101qqq0LWddddddd	★★★★★	Add quick qint to adst
ADDX.BWL	Dm,Dn	1101rrr1LW000RRR	★★★★★	Add Dm and X to Dn
ADDX.BWL	-(Am),-(An)	1101aaa1LW001AAA	★★★★★	Add -(Am) and X to -(An)
SUB.BWL	asrc,Dn	1001rrr0LWssssss	★★★★★	Subtract asrc from Dn
SUB.BWL	Dn,mdst	1001rrr1LWddddddd	★★★★★	Subtract Dn from mdst
SUBA.WL	asrc,An	1001aaaL11sssssss	-----	Subtract asrc from An
SUBI.BWL	#data,adst	00000100LWddddddd	★★★★★	Subtract immediate data from adst
SUBQ.BWL	#qint,adst	0101qqq1LWddddddd	★★★★★	Subtract quick qint from adst
SUBX.BWL	Dm,Dn	1001rrr1LW000RRR	★★★★★	Subtract Dm and X from Dn
SUBX.BWL	-(Am),-(An)	1001aaa1LW001AAA	★★★★★	Subtract -(Am) and X from -(An)
CMP.BWL	asrc,Dn	1011rrr0LWssssss	-★★★★	Set CCR according to Dn - asrc
CMPA.WL	asrc,An	1011aaaL11sssssss	-★★★★	Set CCR according to An - asrc
CMPI.BWL	#data,adst	00001100LWddddddd	-★★★★	Set CCR according to adst - data
CMPM.BWL	(Am)+,(An)+	1011aaa1LW001AAA	-★★★★	Set CCR according to (An) - (Am)

Notes: qqq = qint field: 001–111=1–7, 000=8.
See Table 8–2 for addressing mode restrictions. Also see notes for Table 8–1.

ADDX

The ADDX instruction is used for multiprecision arithmetic. It operates like a normal ADD except that, instead of 0, it uses the X condition bit as the initial carry. Only two addressing mode variations are allowed with ADDX—register-to-register and memory-to-memory. The memory-to-memory version uses auto-decrement addressing for both operands. The idea is that multiprecision operands should be stored in memory with the less significant digits at the higher-numbered addresses, to be consistent with the 68000's memory-addressing convention (the rightmost byte of a word or longword has the highest address). Hence auto-decrement addressing is appropriate for processing a multiple-digit operand from least significant to most significant digit. For example, the code in Table 8–7 adds 96-bit operands, where each operand is stored in three longwords in memory.

There is a subtle difference between ADDX and ADD in the way they handle the Z bit. ADD sets or clears Z according to the result. ADDX clears Z for a nonzero result and leaves Z unchanged for a zero result. This allows multiprecision zero results to be detected easily. If a program sets Z to 1 before beginning a sequence of ADDX instructions, Z will still be 1 at the end of the sequence only if all of the results were zero.

SUB

The second part of Table 8–6 shows the SUB instructions corresponding to the ADDs. As we said before, each variation of SUB corresponds to a variation of ADD. However, keep in mind that during a SUB instruction the C and X bits

TABLE 8–7   Multiprecision addition of 96-bit operands.

```
DEFICIT DS.L    3                       Storage for this year's federal deficit.
NATDEBT DS.L    3                       Storage for the cumulative national debt.
        ...
        LEA.L   NATDEBT+12,A0   Address for auto-decrement access.
        LEA.L   DEFICIT+12,A1   Address for auto-decrement access.
        MOVE.W  #0,CCR          Clear X.
        ADDX.L  -(A1),-(A0)     Add DEFICIT to NATDEBT,
        ADDX.L  -(A1),-(A0)        one longword at a time.
        ADDX.L  -(A1),-(A0)
        ...
```

SUBX   are set to 1 for a borrow rather than for a carry. Also, SUBX handles the Z bit in the same way as ADDX.

The third part of Table 8–6 shows the four variations of the CMP instruction.
CMP   The CMP and CMPA instructions allow arbitrary src operands to be compared
CMPA   with data and address registers, respectively. CMPI compares immediate data
CMPI   with any destination operand, and is particularly useful for operands in memory.
CMPM compares two operands in memory, accessing both operands with auto-increment addressing. This instruction is particularly useful in loops that search strings of characters.

Each of the CMP instructions subtracts its first (src) operand from its second (dst):

```
        CMP     src,dst     Set condition bits using dst-src.
```

This is consistent with the SUB instruction, which subtracts its operands in the same order. However, it is inconsistent with the preferred reading of the CMP instruction, as shown by the following instruction sequence:

```
        CMP     P,Q         Set condition bits using Q-P.
        BGT     OUT         Branch if Q-P > 0.
```

In general, we would like the instructions "CMP P,Q; Brr OUT" to branch if P rr Q, where rr is any relation. Unfortunately, the 68000's behavior is just the opposite. This is a source of many bugs for 68000 assembly language programmers, especially programmers who are used to machines in which CMP works correctly.

8.6   SOME SINGLE-OPERAND INSTRUCTIONS

Because adding or subtracting 1 is such a common operation for maintaining counters and stepping through tables, most processors have short instructions
INC   that do this:
DEC

```
        INC     dst         dst := dst + 1;
        DEC     dst         dst := dst - 1;
```

Mac Note

All of the programs in this chapter are written to be easily adaptable to the Macintosh environment. Only the following changes are required:

(1) Add the **(A5)** notation for based address with respect to A5 for all instruction operands that are variables declared by DS. Such variables are stored in the application global space, whose base address is contained in A5 at run time.

(2) Do not initialize SP or allocate application memory for a return-address stack. The Macintosh operating system provides stack space and initializes SP.

(3) Return control to the operating system with the `_ExitToShell` macro.

(4) With the MPW assembler, use CODE and DATA directives to switch between `code` and `data` modules. DS directives should allocate space in the `data` module.

Any register may be the `dst` in these instructions; many processors can also increment and decrement memory locations.

In some processors, INC `dst` is not quite equivalent to ADD `dst,#1` for a subtle reason—ADD affects the C bit whereas INC does not. In these processors, INC can be used to increment the iteration counter in multiprecision arithmetic loops. Since C is not disturbed, it can hold an arithmetic carry value from the end of one iteration to the beginning of the next.

CLR
NOT
NEG

Three other single-operand instructions are clear (CLR), complement (NOT), and negate (NEG), defined as follows, where `b` is the length of the operand in bits and `2**b` is 2 to the power `b`:

```
CLR     dst         dst := 0;
COM     dst         dst := 2**b-1-dst;
NEG     dst         dst := ((2**b-1-dst)+1) mod 2**b;
```

CLR clears all of the bits of the destination operand to 0. NOT complements the individual bits of `dst`, that is, it takes the ones' complement. NEG negates `dst` by taking its two's complement—it complements the bits and then adds 1. The condition bits are set according to the result, but the rules for C and V vary among different processors. A consistent rule, used by the processors in this book, is to set C if there would be a borrow in the implied subtraction from 0 (i.e., if `dst` is anything but 0), and to set V only if `dst` is the "extra" negative number 10...0.

In processors that support arithmetic on two's-complement numbers with several widths, it is sometimes necessary to convert an operand to a larger size, for example, from a byte to a word. As we showed in Section 4.5.4, this is accomplished by filling the upper bits in the larger-size result with copies of the sign bit of the original operand. This operation is called "sign extension;" the corresponding instruction in the Motorola 6809 is called SEX.

SEX

TST

The 68000's versions of these instructions are listed in Table 8–8. The TST instruction, which sets CCR according to the value of its operand, is also included in this table.

TABLE 8–8   Single-operand instructions in the 68000.

Mnemonic	Operand	Opcode Word	XNZVC	Description
CLR.BWL	ddst	01000010LWdddddd	-0100	Clear all bits of ddst
NOT.BWL	ddst	01000110LWdddddd	-**00	Complement bits of ddst
NEG.BWL	ddst	01000100LWdddddd	*****	Negate ddst (2's complement)
NEGX.BWL	ddst	01000000LWdddddd	*****	Negate ddst and subtract X
EXT.W	Dn	0100100010000rrr	-**00	Sign extend low-order byte of Dn to word
EXT.L	Dn	0100100011000rrr	-**00	Sign extend low-order word of Dn to longword
TST.BWL	ddst	01001010LWdddddd	-**00	Set CCR according to ddst

Notes: See Table 8–2 for addressing mode restrictions. Also see notes for Table 8–1.

ADDQ
SUBQ

The 68000 does not have explicit INC and DEC instructions. Instead, the ADDQ and SUBQ instructions, introduced in the previous section, allow any integer from 1 to 8 to be added to or subtracted from any destination operand. Like other ADDs and SUBs, these instructions affect all of the condition bits. Therefore, they cannot be conveniently used in multiprecision arithmetic loops. However, the 68000 has several convenient loop control instructions that do not affect the condition bits, as we'll see in the next section.

8.7 PROGRAM CONTROL

Program control instructions have fundamental importance, since they are the primitives that allow conditional action and repetition in machine language programs. The simplest program control instruction is the unconditional jump (JMP). The JMP instruction in most processors allows an effective address to be specified by any of a variety of addressing modes. Unlike other instructions, which read or write an operand at the effective address, the JMP instruction simply loads the program counter (PC) with the effective address, thereby transferring control to the instruction stored there:

JMP

```
        JMP        dst           PC := effectiveAddress(dst);
```

Addressing modes such as register and immediate don't make any sense with the JMP instruction, and are never allowed. However, other addressing modes make JMP instruction very flexible. For example, absolute and relative modes can be used to perform jumps to fixed memory locations, while register indirect and indexed modes allow CASE-type statements to be coded by dynamically computing a target address using a register.

JSR

The jump to subroutine (JSR) instruction provides a means of calling a subroutine, the machine language equivalent of a Pascal procedure or function. Most contemporary processors dedicate one register as a stack pointer, and the JSR instruction saves a return address in the stack before jumping to the subroutine:

```
        JSR        dst           Push(PC); PC := effectiveAddress(dst);
```

```
 15        12 11        8 7                        0
   0110    | condition |      displacement        |
```

FIGURE 8–2   Format of short conditional branches in the 68000.

RTS

When the subroutine's execution is completed, control is given back to the calling program by a `return from subroutine` (RTS) instruction that pops the value off the top of the stack and loads it into the PC:

        RTS   PC := Pop;

In processors that don't have a stack, JSR deposits the return address in a specified register, and the return can be accomplished by a JMP instruction with register indirect addressing. Subroutines are discussed in detail in Chapter 9.

conditional jump instruction

    Conditional jump instructions test a specified condition and jump only if the condition is true. In processors without condition codes, typical conditions are "Accumulator zero" and "Accumulator negative." In processors with condition codes, the values of one or more condition bits are tested.

branch instruction

    Jumps that specify a target using PC-relative addressing are usually called *branch instructions*. As discussed in Section 7.3.4, typical branch instructions contain a short displacement to a target address "nearby" the current instruction. This reduces the size of the branch instruction and produces position independence. Because of their usefulness, conditional branches with short (1-byte) displacements are provided in most processors; their format in the 68000 is shown in Figure 8–2. The displacement is interpreted as a signed, two's-complement integer and added to the PC if the branch is taken. The 68000 and 6809 also have conditional branches with 16-bit displacements, and the 68020 even allows 32-bit displacements.

branch condition

    The standard branch conditions tested by most processors with condition codes are listed in Table 8–9. A branch condition may be based on a single bit or on a combination of bits, as shown in the table. Although the table contains 18 rows, there are only 16 distinct conditions because the pairs CC,HS and CS,LO are alternate mnemonics for the same conditions. The second through fourth columns of the table give the mnemonics and bit encodings used for each condition in 68000 machine instructions, which we'll use later.

BRA

    The first part of the table contains always-true (T) and always-false (F) conditions. The T condition is used in the `branch always` instruction (BRA), while the F condition produces the almost useless `branch never` instruction, which is unimplemented or undocumented in most processors. However, the F condition is useful in conjunction with the 68000's DBcc instruction, as we'll see later.

    The second part of the table lists branches that depend on a single condition bit. Processors with additional condition bits may have additional branches of this type.

TABLE 8–9   Branch conditions and their encodings in the 68000.

Type	Mnemonic	cc	CCCC	Branch If	Condition
Unconditional					
	BRA	T	0000	Always	true
	none	F	0001	Never	false
Single bit					
	BCC	CC	0100	Carry clear	$C = 0$
	BCS	CS	0101	Carry set	$C = 1$
	BNE	NE	0110	Not equal (to zero)	$Z = 0$
	BEQ	EQ	0111	Equal (to zero)	$Z = 1$
	BVC	VC	1000	Overflow clear	$V = 0$
	BVS	VS	1001	Overflow set	$V = 1$
	BPL	PL	1010	Plus	$N = 0$
	BMI	MI	1011	Minus	$N = 1$
Signed					
	BGE	GE	1100	Greater than or equal (to zero)	$(N \oplus V) = 0$
	BLT	LT	1101	Less than (zero)	$(N \oplus V) = 1$
	BGT	GT	1110	Greater than (zero)	$((N \oplus V) + Z) = 0$
	BLE	LE	1111	Less than or equal (to zero)	$((N \oplus V) + Z) = 1$
Unsigned					
	BHI	HI	0010	Higher	$(C + Z) = 0$
	BLS	LS	0011	Lower or the same	$(C + Z) = 1$
	BHS	HS	0100	Higher or the same	$C = 0$
	BLO	LO	0101	Lower	$C = 1$

Notes: + denotes logical OR; $\oplus$ denotes logical Exclusive OR.
For the signed branches, the expression $N \oplus V$ gives the sign of the true result, since V is 1 only if a comparison subtraction overflowed, producing the wrong sign.
cc = symbolic designation used in mnemonics of conditional branch, DBcc, Scc, and TRAPcc instructions. CCCC = 4-bit condition field in opcode word of conditional branch, DBcc, Scc, and TRAPcc instructions.

The third part of the table lists condition combinations and branches that test the value of a *signed* integer. If cc is one of the relations LT, GE, LE, GT, NE, EQ, then X cc Y if and only if X-Y cc 0. In the 68000, since the CMP Y,X instruction sets the condition bits according to X-Y, the following instruction sequence branches if and only if X cc Y:

```
CMP      Y,X          Set CCR using X-Y.
Bcc      LABEL        Branch if X cc Y.
```

The signed conditional branches also work correctly after data movement and TST instructions, branching if the just-accessed operand has the specified relationship with 0. This explains why data movement instructions clear V.

Condition combinations and branches in the last part of the table are used in comparisons of *unsigned* integers. In the 68000, a CMP Y,X instruction subtracts Y from X and sets C to 1 only if a borrow occurs, that is, only if X is less than Y when interpreted as an unsigned number. This observation produces the combinations of C and Z listed in the last four rows of the table.[5] Since these conditions use the borrow as reflected in the C bit, they normally make sense only after CMP instructions, and not after data movement instructions. For example, to compare unsigned operands X and Y, we write

```
CMP     Y,X            Set CCR using X-Y.
BHI     LABEL          Branch if X > Y (unsigned).
```

However, the following instruction sequence makes no sense:

```
MOVE    X,D1
BLO     LABEL          Branch if X < 0 (unsigned) ??
```

The MOVE instruction clears C and so the branch is never taken.

The BNE and BEQ instructions work properly with both signed and unsigned numbers. In fact, they test for bit-by-bit equality regardless of what a byte or word represents.

A frequently used construct in program loops is

```
LOOP    ...                    REPEAT
        ...                        ...
        SUB     #1,CNT             cnt := cnt - 1;
        BNE     LOOP               UNTIL cnt = 0;
```

The last two machine instructions in such a loop are combined in the **decrement and jump if not zero** (DJNZ) machine instruction, producing a slightly shorter loop:

```
LOOP    ...                    REPEAT
        ...                        ...
        DJNZ    CNT,LOOP           cnt := cnt - 1;
*                                  UNTIL cnt = 0;
```

Besides shortening the loop and speeding execution, this instruction has the advantage of not disturbing the condition codes, important in multiprecision arithmetic loops that pass a value in C from the end of one iteration to the beginning of the next. The 68000 does not implement DJNZ exactly as shown

DBcc

above. However, it has a family of looping instructions, DBcc, that can perform a DJNZ-like function as well as test conditions other than nonzero, as we'll soon see.

The 68000's program control instructions are summarized in Table 8–10.

JMP
JSR
RTS
RTR

The JMP and JSR instructions jump to a specified address. Before jumping, JSR pushes a return address onto the stack using A7 as the stack pointer (SP). The return address occupies two words on the stack. The RTS instruction returns from a subroutine by popping the return address off the stack. RTR pops a word off the stack and loads its low-order byte into CCR; then it pops a return address

---

[5]Disgustingly, Motorola's cross macro assembler doesn't recognize the BHS and BLO mnemonics; you have to memorize the proper equivalence with BCC and BCS.

TABLE 8–10   Program control instructions in the 68000.

Mnemonic	Operands	Opcode Word	XNZVC	Description
JMP	cdst	0100111011dddddd	-----	Jump to cdst
JSR	cdst	0100111010dddddd	-----	Jump to subroutine at cdst
RTS		0100111001110101	-----	Return from subroutine
RTR		0100111001110111	★★★★★	Pop CCR, then return
BRA	addr16	01100000oooooooo	-----	Branch to addr16
BSR	addr16	01100001oooooooo	-----	Branch to subroutine at addr16
Bcc	addr16	0110CCCCoooooooo	-----	Branch to addr16 if cc is true
DBcc	Dn,addr16	0101CCCC11001rrr	-----	Conditional loop primitive
Scc	adst	0101CCCC11dddddd	-----	Set dst according to cc
LINK	An,#disp	0100111001010aaa	-----	Link subroutine
UNLK	An	0100111001011aaa	-----	Clean up subroutine linkage

Notes: See Table 8–2 for addressing mode restrictions. Also see notes for Table 8–1.
      disp = displacement, ranging from −32768 to +32767, in the word following the opcode
          word.
      addr16 = branch target, an address within 32 Kbytes of the instruction.
      cc = condition, any of those listed in Table 8–9.
      CCCC = condition field, encoded as in Table 8–9.
      oooooooo = branch displacement field, a two's-complement number that must be even.

from the stack just like RTS. This is useful in subroutines that save the status of their caller.

BRA
BSR

short branch instruction

The BRA instruction jumps to a nearby address using a special form of relative addressing, as shown in Figure 8–3. The BSR instruction is similar, except it performs subroutine jump—it saves the current PC on the stack before jumping. Each instruction has two variants. A *short branch instruction* is one word long and contains an 8-bit displacement field that is interpreted as a two's-complement number and must be even. Thus the instruction specifies a target address within −128 to −2 or +2 to +126 bytes of the word following the instruction. A *long branch instruction* contains an 8-bit displacement of 0, and a second word contains a 16-bit displacement (−32768 to +32766 bytes), which also must be even.

long branch instruction

.S

Given the target address (addr16) for a particular branch instruction, the assembler computes the required displacement and decides whether to use the long or short format. If the addr16 expression contains a forward reference, then the assembler uses a long displacement. However, a suffix of ".S" attached to the branch mnemonic forces the assembler to use a short displacement.

The third group in Table 8–10 contains conditional instructions. Including BRA but excluding the mysterious "branch never," the 68000 has 15 distinct conditional branches of the form Bcc addr16 with the mnemonics and conditions shown in Table 8–9. The conditional branches contain an 8- or 16-bit displacement and use the same relative addressing mode as BRA and BSR.

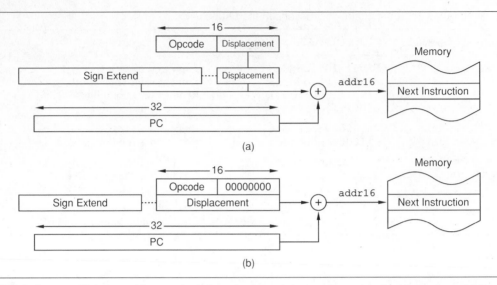

(b)

FIGURE 8–3   Relative address calculations for branch instructions: (a) short branches; (b) long branches.

DBcc

The DBcc Dn,addr16 instruction is a powerful loop control primitive with three parameters: a termination condition cc, a counter register Dn, and an address addr16. The instruction performs the following operations:

(1) The condition bit combination specified by cc is tested, where cc may be any of the branch conditions from Table 8–9. If the condition is true, then DBcc terminates and control passes to the next sequential instruction.

(2) If the tested condition was false, then the low-order word of data register Dn is decremented by 1.

(3) If the result of decrementing the low-order word of Dn was −1, then DBcc terminates and control passes to the next sequential instruction. Otherwise, a relative branch to address addr16 is taken by adding a 16-bit signed displacement in the instruction to the current value of the PC.

Thus, the DBcc instruction may be used to create a loop that terminates on either a specified condition or the exhaustion of an iteration count. Example programs using DBF and DBEQ will be shown in the next subsection. Some assemblers accept "DBRA" as an alternate mnemonic for DBF.

DBRA

Scc

The Scc dst instruction tests the same cc conditions as DBcc. It sets the specified dst byte to $FF if the condition is true; otherwise it sets dst to $00. This instruction is typically used to set a boolean variable according to the result of an expression evaluation, where true and false are encoded as $FF and $00 respectively.

*stack-frame
  pointer (FP)*
LINK

The last part of Table 8–10 shows the LINK and UNLK instructions. These instructions simplify stack-oriented subroutine calling conventions that use an address register An as a *stack-frame pointer (FP)*. The LINK An, #disp instruction performs three operations:

(1) It pushes the old FP (current 32-bit value of An) onto the stack.

(2) It creates a new FP by loading An with the updated SP.

(3) It reserves space on the stack for local variables by adding disp (usually negative) to SP.

UNLK

The UNLK An instruction undoes the effects of LINK:

(1) It loads SP with the contents of An, thereby deallocating the stack space that was occupied by local variables.

(2) It pops a 32-bit word from the stack and loads it into An, thereby restoring the old FP.

We'll give an example program using LINK and UNLK in Section 9.3.6.

8.7.1 Example Programs

The program in Table 7–3 on page 226 used *signed* conditional branches to sort numbers in the range −99 through +99. The program in Table 8–11, adapted from Table 3–7 on page 67, uses *unsigned* conditional branches (BLS) to check the head and tail pointers of a queue against a buffer limit. Unsigned conditional branches are appropriate because head and tail contain absolute memory addresses, which are unsigned integers. A very common programming error is to use signed conditional branches in this situation. When this is done, the program fails if numbers of opposite sign are compared, quite a mysterious problem to debug. In this example, a problem occurs only if the queue buffer happens to lie precisely in the middle of the 68000's memory address space.

The program in Table 8–11 also shows the correspondence between Pascal statements and assembly language instructions, and it illustrates many of the instructions that we've covered so far in this chapter. It can use BSR instead of JSR to call local subroutines because they are known to be located within 32 Kbytes of the current instructions. However, utility routines like READ and WRITELN might be located anywhere in memory, and so they are called with JSR. Notice that the main program contains an assembly language construct that cannot be modeled in standard Pascal without using GOTO, a good example where a Pascal loop "EXIT" statement would have been handy.

DBF

Table 8–12 shows a subroutine for counting the number of "1" bits in a byte. Its main loop, BLOOP, must be executed eight times and the loop count is maintained and tested using a DBF instruction. DBF D3, BLOOP decrements the loop count in D3 on each pass through the loop, and falls through to the RTS instruction when the loop count reaches −1.

TABLE 8–11   Word queueing program for the 68000.

```
*       This program enqueues a sequence of words. Each word is a
*       sequence of characters terminated by a space. The sequence
*       is terminated by a period. Each time a '!' is received, the
*       program dequeues and prints a word. The '!' is not printed.
*                               PROGRAM WordQueue;
QLEN    EQU     200             CONST qlen = 200;
ENDCHR  EQU     $2E               endChar = '.';
SPACE   EQU     $20               space = ' ';
DMPCHR  EQU     $21               dumpChar = '!';
*                               VAR inChar : char; {Uses register D0}
QUEUE   DS.B    QLEN              queue : ARRAY [0..qlen-1] OF char;
QENDA   EQU     *-1               {Define address of last queue item.}
HEAD    DS.L    1                 head, tail, A0, A1 : address;
TAIL    DS.L    1                 {A0,A1 = address registers}
STACK   DS.L    50                {Space for return address stack.}
STACKE  EQU     *
*
ENQ     MOVEA.L TAIL,A0         PROCEDURE Enqueue(D0 : char);
        MOVE.B  D0,(A0)         BEGIN
        ADDA.L  #1,A0             MEM[tail] := D0;
        LEA.L   QENDA,A1          A0 := tail + 1;
        CMPA.L  A1,A0             A1 := Addr(queue[qlen-1]) {Last address}
        BLS.S   ENQ2              IF A0 > A1
        LEA.L   QUEUE,A0            THEN
ENQ2    CMPA.L  HEAD,A0               A0 := Addr(queue[0]); {First address}
        BEQ.S   ENQOUT          IF A0 <> head THEN
        MOVE.L  A0,TAIL               tail := A0;
ENQOUT  RTS                       {Lose characters on overflow.}
*                               END; {Enqueue}
                                FUNCTION Dequeue : char; {Result in D0, }
DEQ     MOVEA.L HEAD,A0         BEGIN      { Z-bit = 1 if queue empty.}
        CMPA.L  TAIL,A0           A0 := head;
        BEQ.S   DEQOUT            IF A0 <> tail THEN
        MOVE.B  D0,(A0)             BEGIN   A := MEM[A0];
        ADDA.L  #1,A0               A0 := A0 + 1;
        LEA.L   QENDA,A1            A1 := Addr(queue[qlen-1]) {Last address}
        CMPA.L  A1,A0               IF A0 > A1
        BLS.S   DEQ2
        LEA.L   QUEUE,A0              A0 := Addr(queue[0]);
DEQ2    MOVE.L  A0,HEAD             head := A0;
        AND.B   #$FB,CCR           Z := 0;
*                                 END
*                               ELSE Z := 1; {Z-bit = 1 from BEQ}
DEQOUT  RTS                     END; {Dequeue}
```

DBEQ   An application for DBcc with a nontrivial condition is shown in Table 8–13. In this example, combining two conditional tests into one instruction speeds up the subroutine significantly. Since DBcc allows only a one-word count, the maximum buffer size in this example is 64 Kbytes.

TABLE 8–11   (continued)

```
WORDQ   LEA.L   STACKE,SP       BEGIN {Main Program}
        LEA.L   QUEUE,A0
        MOVE.L  A0,HEAD            head := Addr(queue[0]);
        MOVE.L  A0,TAIL            tail := Addr(queue[0]);
        JSR     READ              read(inChar);  {Get char, returned in D0.}
WHILE1  CMP.B   #ENDCHR,D0        WHILE inChar <> endChar DO
        BEQ.S   ENDW1               BEGIN
IF1     CMP.B   #DMPCHR,D0          IF inChar <> dumpChar THEN
        BEQ.S   ELSE1
        BSR     ENQ                    Enqueue(inChar)
        BRA.S   ENDIF1           ELSE BEGIN
*                                     WHILE true DO {GOTOs needed.}
ELSE1   BSR     DEQ                   BEGIN  D0 := Dequeue;
        BEQ.S   L10                     IF Z = 1 {queue empty}
        CMP.B   #SPACE,D0                 THEN GOTO 10;
        BEQ.S   L10                     IF D0 = space THEN GOTO 10;
        JSR     WRCHAR                  write(D0); {Print char in D0.}
        BRA     ELSE1                 END;
L10     JSR     WRITELN           10: writeln; {Start new line.}
*                                     END;
ENDIF1  JSR     READ              read(inChar); {Get next char.}
        BRA     WHILE1            END;
ENDW1   JMP     $8008        {Return to operating system.}
        END                 END. {Main Program}
```

8.8 LOGICAL INSTRUCTIONS

logical instruction   *Logical instructions* treat a data word as an array of bits, and handle each bit independently. An instruction that we've already covered, NOT, can be consid-
AND   ered a logical instruction because it complements the bits in a word, bit by bit.
OR   The most commonly used logical instructions on two operands are AND, OR, and
EOR   EOR (exclusive OR):

TABLE 8–12   Ones-counting subroutine using DBF.

```
*       Count number of '1' bits in a byte. Enter with byte in D0,
*       exit with A0, D2, and D3 destroyed and bit count in D1.
*
BCNT1S  CLR.W   D1              Initialize '1' count.
        MOVE.L  #7,D3           Init bit number -- go from 7 down to 0.
        LEA.L   MASKS,A0        Get address of bit-mask table.
BLOOP   MOVE.B  0(A0,D3),D2     Get next bit mask.
        AND.B   D0,D2           Is there a '1' there?
        BEQ.S   BNEXT           Skip if not.
        ADDQ.W  #1,D1           Else increment '1' count.
BNEXT   DBF     D3,BLOOP        Get next bit number; done?
        RTS                     Yes, return.
MASKS   DC.B    $1,$2,$4,$8,$10,$20,$40,$80
```

TABLE 8–13 String search subroutine.

```
*         Find the first occurrence in BUFFER of a character passed
*         in D0.  Return with Z = 0 if character not found, or with
*         Z = 1 and A0 pointing just past character if found.
*
SEARCH    LEA.L    BUFFER,A0     Point to start of buffer.
          MOVE.W   #BUFSIZ,D1    Get size of buffer.
          BRA      IN            Check for BUFSIZ = 0.
SLOOP     CMP.B    (A0)+,D0      Got a match?
IN        DBEQ     D1,SLOOP      Fall through on match or D1 = -1.
          RTS                    Return, Z = 1 if character found.
*
BUFSIZ    EQU      1000          Declare size of buffer (must be <64K).
BUFFER    DS.B     BUFSIZ        Reserve storage for buffer.
```

```
AND   dst,src        dst := And(dst,src);
OR    dst,src        dst := Or(dst,src);
EOR   dst,src        dst := ExclusiveOr(dst,src);
```

The function tables for various logical operations are given in Table 8–14. Most computers have AND, OR, and EOR instructions.

Logical instructions are most often used for extracting and combining fields that are packed into different data words. For example, suppose that the 4-bit field F1 appears in bits 11-8 of a data word P, and the 7-bit field F2 appears in the low-order bits of Q, as shown in Figure 8–4. The other bits of each word contain unknown values, not zeroes. The fields can be combined into one word T by the following 68000 instruction sequence:

TABLE 8–14 Function table for logical operations.

X	Y	NOT X	X AND Y	X OR Y	X EOR Y
0	0	1	0	0	0
0	1	1	0	1	1
1	0	0	0	1	1
1	1	0	1	1	0

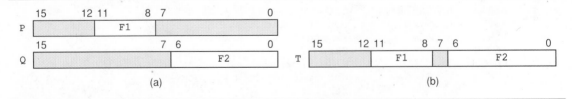

FIGURE 8–4 Packed data fields: (a) P and Q; (b) desired result T.

```
MOVE.W   P,D0
AND.W    #$0F00,D0      Clear all but bits 11-8.
MOVE.W   Q,D1
AND.W    #$007F,D1      Clear all but bits 6-0.
OR.W     D1,D0          Combine words.
MOVE.W   D0,T
```

mask   The hexadecimal constants $0F00 and $007F are called *masks*; they have ones in the fields to be extracted and zeroes elsewhere. The AND instructions clear the unused bits in P and Q to zero so that the desired fields can be combined by OR. General operations on packed data fields also require shifting fields left or right in a word; this will be covered in Section 8.9.

Logical instructions set the condition bits according to the results of their operation. Sometimes it's desirable to test a field of a word using a mask and the AND operation, setting the condition codes but not storing the result anywhere. The 6809 and 8086 have instructions that accomplish this, but the 68000 does not.

In programs that pack many boolean flags into a data word, it is desirable to address individual bits of a word. The standard logical instructions can do this using masks with a single 1 or 0 bit. For example, the instructions

```
AND.W    #$7FFF,dst
OR.W     #$8000,dst
EOR.W    #$8000,dst
```

bit manipulation   respectively clear, set, and complement the most significant bit of a dst operand.
instruction   However, the *bit manipulation instructions* provided in the 68000 and some other processors perform these functions more efficiently:

```
BCLR     bnum,dst       dst[bnum] := 0;
BSET     bnum,dst       dst[bnum] := 1;
BCHG     bnum,dst       dst[bnum] := Not(dst[bnum]);
BTST     bnum,dst       Z := Not(dst[bnum]);
```

static vs dynamic   These instructions manipulate a specified bit bnum in the dst word. Bit ma-
bit number   nipulation instructions are classified as *static* or *dynamic* depending on whether the instruction contains the bit number or specifies a register that contains the bit number.

Instructions that perform logical operations in the 68000 are summarized in Table 8–15. As shown in the first part of the table, logical operations can be performed register or memory to register, or immediate to register or memory. The AND and OR operations can also be performed register to memory. A register-to-memory version of Exclusive OR is not provided because the 68000's designers ran out of instruction opcodes, and Exclusive OR is used very infrequently in typical programs. However, all of the logical instructions are available in byte, word, and longword versions. Each instruction sets N and Z according to the result, clears V and C, and leaves X undisturbed.

AND to CCR   Instructions in the second part of Table 8–15 perform logical operations on
OR to CCR   the CCR, as we showed previously in Section 8.2. The AND instruction clears one or more CCR bits, OR sets bits, and EOR complements bits.

TABLE 8–15   Logical instructions in the 68000.

Mnemonic	Operands	Opcode Word	XNZVC	Description
AND.BWL	dsrc,Dn	1100rrr0LWssssss	-**00	AND dsrc to Dn
AND.BWL	Dn,mdst	1100rrr1LWdddddd	-**00	AND Dn to mdst
ANDI.BWL	#data,ddst	00000010LWdddddd	-**00	AND immediate data to ddst
OR.BWL	dsrc,Dn	1000rrr0LWssssss	-**00	OR dsrc to Dn
OR.BWL	Dn,mdst	1000rrr1LWdddddd	-**00	OR Dn to mdst
ORI.BWL	#data,ddst	00000000LWdddddd	-**00	OR immediate data to ddst
EOR.BWL	Dn,ddst	1011rrr1LWdddddd	-**00	Exclusive OR Dn to ddst
EORI.BWL	#data,ddst	00001010LWdddddd	-**00	Exclusive OR immediate data to ddst
ANDI.B	#data,CCR	0000001000111100	*****	AND immediate data to CCR
ORI.B	#data,CCR	0000000000111100	*****	OR immediate data to CCR
EORI.B	#data,CCR	0000101000111100	*****	Exclusive OR immediate data to CCR
ANDI.W	#data,SR	0000001001111100	*****	AND immediate data to SR (privileged)
ORI.W	#data,SR	0000000001111100	*****	OR immediate data to SR (privileged)
EORI.W	#data,SR	0000101001111100	*****	Exclusive OR immediate data to SR (priv.)
BCLR.L	#bnum,Dm	0000100010000RRR	--*--	Clear bit bnum of Dm
BSET.L	#bnum,Dm	0000100011000RRR	--*--	Set bit bnum of Dm
BCHG.L	#bnum,Dm	0000100001000RRR	--*--	Complement bit bnum of Dm
BTST.L	#bnum,Dm	0000100000000RRR	--*--	Test bit bnum of Dm
BCLR.B	#bnum,mdst	0000100010dddddd	--*--	Clear bit bnum of mdst
BSET.B	#bnum,mdst	0000100011dddddd	--*--	Set bit bnum of mdst
BCHG.B	#bnum,mdst	0000100001dddddd	--*--	Complement bit bnum of mdst
BTST.B	#bnum,tdst	0000100000dddddd	--*--	Test bit bnum of tdst
BCLR.L	Dn,Dm	0000rrr110000RRR	--*--	Clear bit Dn of Dm
BSET.L	Dn,Dm	0000rrr111000RRR	--*--	Set bit Dn of Dm
BCHG.L	Dn,Dm	0000rrr101000RRR	--*--	Complement bit Dn of Dm
BTST.L	Dn,Dm	0000rrr100000RRR	--*--	Test bit Dn of Dm
BCLR.B	Dn,mdst	0000rrr110dddddd	--*--	Clear bit Dn of mdst
BSET.B	Dn,mdst	0000rrr111dddddd	--*--	Set bit Dn of mdst
BCHG.B	Dn,mdst	0000rrr101dddddd	--*--	Complement bit Dn of mdst
BTST.B	Dn,tdst	0000rrr100dddddd	--*--	Test bit Dn of tdst

Notes: bnum = bit number, stored in the word following the instruction.
   See Table 8–2 for addressing mode restrictions. A further restriction is that a data register
   may not be used as the destination of BTST.B. Also see notes for Table 8–1.

EOR to CCR   The third part of Table 8–15 contains instructions that set, clear, and complement bits anywhere in the SR. Since these instructions may affect the processor control bits in the high-order byte of SR, they are privileged—they can be executed only in supervisor mode.

As shown in the last four parts of Table 8–15, the 68000 has four variations of each of the four bit manipulation instructions introduced earlier in this section:

- Static, data register (longword) destination. The bit number bnum is contained in the low-order five bits of the word following the instruction.

- Static, memory (byte) destination. The bit number bnum is contained in the low-order three bits of the word following the instruction.

- Dynamic, data register (longword) destination. The bit number is contained in the low-order five bits of a data register Dm.

- Dynamic, memory (byte) destination. The bit number is contained in the low-order three bits of a data register Dm.

All of the bit manipulation instructions test the specified bit *before* clearing, setting, or complementing it, and set the Z bit in the CCR to 1 if the bit was 0, otherwise to 0.

The 68020 has even more powerful instructions for clearing, setting, complementing, testing, inserting, and extracting multiple-bit fields. We describe these instructions in Section 14.9.3.

8.9 ROTATES AND SHIFTS

Rotate and shift operations manipulate the contents of one data word (or byte or longword), moving the bits of the word one or more positions to the right or left. All processors can shift and rotate the contents of registers, and many can also perform these operations on memory locations.

We use Pascal in this section to describe precisely the effects of rotate and shift instructions. We use the same type definitions as in Section 4.8:

```
TYPE
   bit = 0..1;
   word = ARRAY [0..highbit] OF bit;
```

where highbit is chosen according to the operand size; highbit = 7, 15, and 31 for bytes, words, and longwords, respectively. Furthermore, we define two Bshl Pascal shift functions, Bshl and Bshr, that operate as shown in Figure 8–5. Bshr They shift the contents of a binary word W left or right one position, fill the vacated position with the bit value Cin, and place the lost bit in bit variable Cout.

The 68000 has a comprehensive set of rotate and shift operations on registers and memory locations. The rotates and shifts of most other processors are

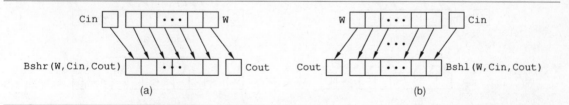

FIGURE 8–5   Pascal bit-shifting functions: (a) Bshr(W: word; Cin: bit; VAR Cout: bit): word; (b) Bshl(W: word; Cin: bit; VAR Cout: bit): word.

TABLE 8–16   Definitions of rotate and shift operations in the 68000.

Operation	Mnemonic	Definition
Rotate left	`ROL dst`	`dst := Bshl(dst,dst[highbit],C);`
Rotate right	`ROR dst`	`dst := Bshr(dst,dst[0],C);`
Rotate with X left	`ROXL dst`	`dst := Bshl(dst,X,C); X := C;`
Rotate with X right	`ROXR dst`	`dst := Bshr(dst,X,C); X := C;`
Logical shift left	`LSL dst`	`dst := Bshl(dst,0,C); X := C;`
Logical shift right	`LSR dst`	`dst := Bshr(dst,0,C); X := C;`
Arithmetic shift left	`ASL dst`	`dst := Bshl(dst,0,C); X := C;`
Arithmetic shift right	`ASR dst`	`dst := Bshr(dst,dst[highbit],C); X := C;`

a subset of what's available in the 68000, so we'll concentrate on the 68000's capabilities. All of the rotates and shifts in the 68000 can be defined in terms of the primitives in Figure 8–5, as shown in Table 8–16. We'll refer back to this table throughout this section.

8.9.1 Rotate Instructions

rotation
circular shift
cyclical shift

The name *rotation* is generally used if no bits are lost in the operation. Rotation operations are sometimes called *circular shifts* or *cyclical shifts*. The 68000's rotation instructions are described in Pascal in the first two parts of Table 8–16, and Figure 8–6 shows the effects of these operations. Simple left and right rotations move each bit of dst one position, filling the vacated position with the bit that "falls off" the other end. Rotations with extend employ the X condition bit; the vacated position is loaded with the value of X, and X and C are both loaded with the bit that falls off the other end. In all of these instructions, the N and Z condition bits are set in the obvious manner, and V is cleared to 0.

Each of the 68000's rotate instructions is actually available in three different "flavors," as shown in Table 8–17. The first form allows a memory word to be rotated by a single bit position. The second form allows a data register to be rotated by 1 to 8 positions, where an n-bit rotation is equivalent to performing

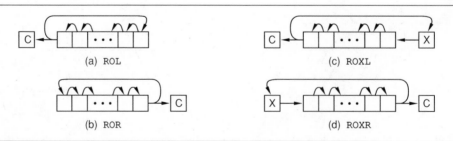

(a) ROL   (c) ROXL

(b) ROR   (d) ROXR

FIGURE 8–6   Rotation operations: (a) left; (b) right; (c) left with extend; (d) right with extend.

TABLE 8–17   Rotate and shift instructions in the 68000.

Mnemonic	Operands	Opcode Word	XNZVC	Description
ROL.W	mdst	1110011111dddddd	-**0*	Rotate mdst left
ROL.BWL	#cnt,Dn	1110ccc1LW011rrr	-**0*	Rotate Dn left cnt bits
ROL.BWL	Dm,Dn	1110RRR1LW111rrr	-**0*	Rotate Dn left Dm bits
ROR.W	mdst	1110011011dddddd	-**0*	Rotate mdst right
ROR.BWL	#cnt,Dn	1110ccc0LW011rrr	-**0*	Rotate Dn right cnt bits
ROR.BWL	Dm,Dn	1110RRR0LW111rrr	-**0*	Rotate Dn right Dm bits
ROXL.W	mdst	1110010111dddddd	***0*	Rotate mdst with X left
ROXL.BWL	#cnt,Dn	1110ccc1LW010rrr	***0*	Rotate Dn with X left cnt bits
ROXL.BWL	Dm,Dn	1110RRR1LW110rrr	***0*	Rotate Dn with X left Dm bits
ROXR.W	mdst	1110010011dddddd	***0*	Rotate mdst with X right
ROXR.BWL	#cnt,Dn	1110ccc0LW010rrr	***0*	Rotate Dn with X right cnt bits
ROXR.BWL	Dm,Dn	1110RRR0LW110rrr	***0*	Rotate Dn with X right Dm bits
LSL.W	mdst	1110001111dddddd	***0*	Logical shift mdst left
LSL.BWL	#cnt,Dn	1110ccc1LW001rrr	***0*	Logical shift Dn left cnt bits
LSL.BWL	Dm,Dn	1110RRR1LW101rrr	***0*	Logical shift Dn left Dm bits
LSR.W	mdst	1110001011dddddd	***0*	Logical shift mdst right
LSR.BWL	#cnt,Dn	1110ccc0LW001rrr	***0*	Logical shift Dn right cnt bits
LSR.BWL	Dm,Dn	1110RRR0LW101rrr	***0*	Logical shift Dn right Dm bits
ASL.W	mdst	1110000111dddddd	*****	Arithmetic shift mdst left
ASL.BWL	#cnt,Dn	1110ccc1LW000rrr	*****	Arithmetic shift Dn left cnt bits
ASL.BWL	Dm,Dn	1110RRR1LW100rrr	*****	Arithmetic shift Dn left Dm bits
ASR.W	mdst	1110000011dddddd	***0*	Arithmetic shift mdst right
ASR.BWL	#cnt,Dn	1110ccc0LW000rrr	***0*	Arithmetic shift Dn right cnt bits
ASR.BWL	Dm,Dn	1110RRR0LW100rrr	***0*	Arithmetic shift Dn right Dm bits

Notes: See Table 8–2 for addressing mode restrictions. Also see notes for Table 8–1.
 ccc = cnt field: 001–111 = 1–7, 000 = 8.
 Condition bit settings for *'ed cases:
     N—set if the most significant bit of the result is 1; cleared otherwise.
     Z—set if the result is zero; cleared otherwise.
     V—set if sign bit changed during ASL operation; cleared otherwise.
     C—set equal to last bit shifted out of the operand; cleared if shift count is zero.
     X—set equal to last bit shifted out of the operand; not affected if shift count is zero.

a single-bit rotation n times. And the third form allows a data register to be rotated by a variable number of positions n, where the value of n is contained in the six low-order bits of another data register.

Multiprecision rotations can be programmed using X as a link. For example, suppose that D0,D1 are a pair of 32-bit registers containing a 64-bit operand, high-order longword in D0. The equivalent of a "rotate left with extend" can be performed on the 64-bit operand by two 32-bit rotates:

```
ROXL.L  #1,D1     D1 := Bshl(D1,X,C); X := C {old D1[31]};
ROXL.L  #1,D0     D0 := Bshl(D0,X,C); X := C {old D0[31]};
```

A rotation of D0,D1 *without* extend is a little trickier to code, as we'll see in the next subsection.

FIGURE 8–7   Logical shifts: (a) left; (b) right.

8.9.2 Logical Shift Instructions

logical shift

The name *logical shift* is normally applied to shift operations that force a 0 into the vacated bit position. The value of the bit shifted off the end is usually saved in C, and the old value of C is lost. The other condition bits are set in much the same way as rotations. The 68000's one-bit logical left and right shifts were defined in the third part of Table 8–16 and are illustrated in Figure 8–7. Like the rotates, each logical shift instruction is available in three forms as shown in the third part of Table 8–17.

Now we return to the problem of performing a rotation without carry on a 64-bit operand in D0,D1. In the following instruction sequence, LSL is used to shift D1 left and force a 0 into its LSB; then if the left rotation of D0 produces a carry, the LSB of D1 is set to 1.

```
        LSL.L   #1,D1    D1 := Bshl(D1,0,C); X := C {old D1[31]};
        ROXL.L  #1,D0    D0 := Bshl(D0,X,C); X := C {old D0[31]};
        BCC.S   LSB0     IF C = 1 THEN
        BSET.L  #0,D1       D1[0] := 1;
LSB0    ...              {Now X and C equal LSB of new D0,D1.}
```

Although this instruction sequence sets X, N, V, and C in a way that is consistent with the byte, word, and longword versions of ROL, it does not set Z according to the 64-bit result. Exercise 8.21 seeks an instruction sequence that does.

packed data

Rotations and logical shifts are useful for manipulating *packed data*, that is, data words that have two or more independent values stored in different fields. To illustrate this concept, Figure 8–8(a) shows a 16-bit data word P with four fields F1, F2, F3, and F4. A packed format like this is ideal for a program

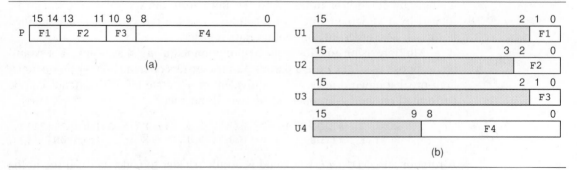

FIGURE 8–8   Four fields: (a) packed format; (b) unpacked format.

TABLE 8–18   "Ad hoc" packing and unpacking subroutines for the word format of Figure 8–8.

```
*           This subroutine unpacks four values in a packed word P,
*           placing them in registers D1, D2, D3, D4.
*
UNPACK  MOVE.W  P,D0            Get packed word.
        CLR.W   D1              Prepare D1 to receive F1.
        ROXL.W  #1,D0           Shift MSB of D0 through X
        ROXL.W  #1,D1              to LSB of D1.
        ROXL.W  #1,D0           Repeat, so
        ROXL.W  #1,D1              D1 now has F1, right-justified.
*
        MOVE.W  P,D2            Get packed word again.
        LSL.W   #2,D2           Left-justify F2, clearing out F1.
        LSR.W   #8,D2           Shift right 13 bits to
        LSR.W   #5,D2              right-justify F2 in D2.
*
        MOVE.W  P,D3            Get packed word again.
        AND.W   #$0600,D3       Clear all fields except F3.
        ROL.W   #7,D3           Rotate into proper position
*
        MOVE.W  P,D4            Get packed word again.
        AND.W   #$01FF,D4       Clear all fields except F4.
        RTS                     Unpacked values are now in D1-D4.

*           This subroutine packs the four values in registers
*           D1, D2, D3, D4 into a packed word P.  The unused bits in
*           each register are assumed to be 0.
*
PACK    ROR.W   #2,D1           Rotate F1 into position.
        MOVE.W  D1,D0           Move into D0 to merge with other fields.
        ROR.W   #5,D2           Rotate F2 into position.
        OR.W    D2,D0           Merge with F1.
        ROR.W   #7,D3           Rotate F3 into position.
        OR.W    D3,D0           Merge with F1 and F2.
        OR.W    D4,D0           Merge F4 with F1, F2, and F3.
        MOVE.W  D0,P            Save packed word.
        RTS                     Done, return.
```

unpacked data

that must store many data records. It takes a lot less storage to pack each record into one word than to use four full words in the *unpacked data* format of Figure 8–8(b). However, when a particular record is processed, it may be necessary to copy the packed values into an unpacked format, process them, and then repack the new values. Table 8–18 shows subroutines that do this using a combination of rotates, shifts, and logical operations in the 68000.

The UNPACK routine in Table 8–18 purposely uses a different approach for extracting each field, just to illustrate the different instructions and techniques that are available. However, such code, with imbedded constants and instructions that change depending on the data structure's format, is difficult to write, understand, and maintain. A better approach to packing and unpacking data is

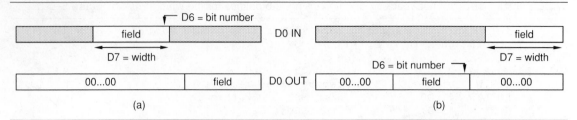

FIGURE 8–9   Input parameters and output results for packing and unpacking subroutines: (a) EXBITS; (b) POSBITS.

to write general subroutines that can extract and insert bit fields of any size and position in a register, and macros to invoke them with a particular set of parameters, as shown in Table 8–19 and Figure 8–9. Then the format of a packed data word can be defined with EQU statements, and packing and unpacking can be accomplished by a sequence of subroutine calls with the appropriate symbolic parameters, as shown in Table 8–20.

The 68020 takes packing and unpacking one step further by providing machine instructions that insert and extract bit fields. The parameters of 68020 bit field instructions may be either constants that are part of the instructions or variables contained in registers, as in our subroutines. We'll describe these instructions fully in Section 14.9.3.

8.9.3   Arithmetic Shift Instructions

arithmetic shift   *Arithmetic shifts* treat their operands as signed, two's-complement numbers. They operate in such a way that a 1-bit left shift is equivalent to multiplication by two and a 1-bit right shift is equivalent to division by two. Thus, arithmetic left and right shifts are defined as shown in the fourth part of Table 8–16 and illustrated in Figure 8–10. Like other rotates and shifts, each arithmetic shift instruction is available in three forms as shown in the last part of Table 8–17.

LSL   Notice that the LSL and ASL operations appear to be equivalent, at least
ASL   so far as Table 8–16 is concerned. However, there is a difference in the setting of the condition bits. LSL always clears V to 0, while ASL sets V according to an interpretation of arithmetic overflow: V is set to 1 if the operation caused the sign bit of dst to change, to 0 otherwise.

ASR   In the ASR operation, arithmetic overflow is impossible, so V is always

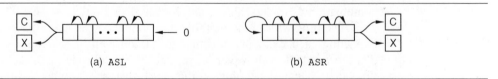

(a) ASL   (b) ASR

FIGURE 8–10   Arithmetic shifts: (a) left; (b) right.

TABLE 8–19   General subroutines and macros for extracting and inserting bit fields.

```
*
*         Subroutine to extract a bit field from D0.
*
*         D6.B = bit position of LSB of field.
*         D7.B = width of field (destroyed).
*         D0.L = result.
*
EXBITS  ADD.B   D6,D7        Compute number of bits to the left of field
        NEG.B   D7              = 32 - ( (LSB bit #) + (field width) ).
        ADD.B   #32,D7
        LSL.L   D7,D0        OK, left-justify the field.
        ADD.B   D6,D7        Add number of bits originally to right of field.
        LSR.L   D7,D0        OK, right-justify field.
        RTS                  All done.
*
*         Macro that uses the above subroutine to extract a packed field.
*         Usage:   EXTRACT.BWL SRC,LSB,WIDTH,DST
*
EXTRACT MACRO                \0 = SIZE, \1 = SRC, \2 = LSB, \3 = WIDTH, \4 = DST
        MOVE.\0  \1,D0       Get packed data.
        MOVE.B   #\2,D6      LSB of desired field.
        MOVE.B   #\3,D7      Width of desired field.
        BSR      EXBITS      Extract field.
        MOVE.\0  D0,\4       Store in destination.
        ENDM


*
*         Subroutine to position a right-justified bit field in D0.
*
*         D6.B = desired bit position of LSB of field.
*         D7.B = width of field (destroyed).
*         D0.L = result.
*
POSBITS NEG.B   D7           Compute number of bits to the left of field.
        ADD.B   #32,D7          = 32 - (field width)
        LSL.L   D7,D0        OK, left-justify the field.
        SUB.B   D6,D7        Compute number of bits needed to left of field.
        LSR.L   D7,D0        OK, move into position.
        RTS                  All done.
*
*         Macro that uses the above subroutine to insert a packed field.
*         Usage:   INSERT.BWL SRC,LSB,WIDTH,DST
*
INSERT  MACRO                \0 = SIZE, \1 = SRC, \2 = LSB, \3 = WIDTH, \4 = DST
        MOVE.\0  \1,D0       Get right-justified data.
        MOVE.B   #\2,D6      Desired LSB of field.
        MOVE.B   #\3,D7      Width of field.
        BSR      POSBITS     Position field and zero-out unused bits.
        OR.\0    D0,\4       Merge into destination.
        ENDM
```

TABLE 8–20 Well-structured versions of PACK and UNPACK for the word format of Figure 8–8.

```
*                           Define fields of packed data word.
F1LSB    EQU       14
F1WID    EQU       2
F2LSB    EQU       11
F2WID    EQU       3
F3LSB    EQU       9
F3WID    EQU       2
F4LSB    EQU       0
F4WID    EQU       9
*                           Pack F1-F4 from D1-D4 into P.
PACK     CLR.W     P
         INSERT.W  D1,F1LSB,F1WID,P
         INSERT.W  D2,F2LSB,F2WID,P
         INSERT.W  D3,F3LSB,F3WID,P
         INSERT.W  D4,F4LSB,F4WID,P
         RTS
*                           Unpack F1-F4 from P into D1-D4.
UNPACK   EXTRACT.W P,F1LSB,F1WID,D1
         EXTRACT.W P,F2LSB,F2WID,D2
         EXTRACT.W P,F3LSB,F3WID,D3
         EXTRACT.W P,F4LSB,F4WID,D4
         RTS
```

cleared. However, one problem with ASR is that it truncates in the "wrong" direction when its operand is negative, so that $-1 \div 2$ equals -1, not 0.

Multiprecision arithmetic shifts can be programmed by combining single-precision arithmetic shifts with rotates or logical shifts, using X as a link. For example, the following instruction sequence arithmetically right shifts a 64-bit register pair D0,D1:

```
ASR.L  #1,D0    D0:=Bshr(D0,D0[31],C); X:=C {old D0[0]};
ROXR.L #1,D1    D1:=Bshr(D1,X,C); X:=C {old D1[0]};
```

Unfortunately, multibit shifts cannot generally be used efficiently to code multibit multiprecision operations needed in floating-point and other algorithms, since there is only a 1-bit link (X) between words.

8.10 MULTIPLICATION AND DIVISION

Most processors have instructions for performing either signed or unsigned multiplication or both. Multiplication generally uses one of the algorithms given in Section 4.8, so that multiplying two words gives a longword product. Overflow is impossible since the product of two n-bit words is always representable in a $2n$-bit longword.

In processors with only unsigned multiplication instructions, a program can perform signed multiplication by testing the signs of the operands, negating the

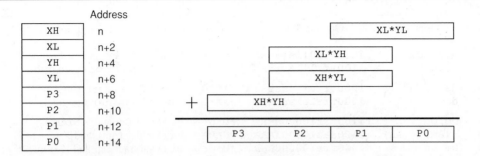

FIGURE 8–11   Variables and operations in 32-bit by 32-bit multiplication program.

negative operands, performing an unsigned multiplication, and finally negating the product if the signs were opposite.

Multiprecision unsigned operands can be multiplied using short unsigned multiplication as a primitive. For example, consider multiplying two longword operands X and Y to produce a quadword product. If we split each operand into two words, $X = XH.XL$ and $Y = YH.YL$, we may write the operation as follows:

$$X \cdot Y = (XL + 2^{16} \cdot XH) \cdot (YL + 2^{16} \cdot YH)$$
$$= XL \cdot YL + 2^{16} \cdot (XL \cdot YH + XH \cdot YL) + 2^{16} \cdot XH \cdot YH$$

Thus, a longword multiplication may be accomplished by four word multiplications and three quadword additions.

A division instruction is also provided in most processors. Again, either signed or unsigned division or both may be provided. As in the algorithms in Section 4.9, a typical division instruction divides a longword dividend by a single-word divisor, producing single-word quotient and remainder. The overflow bit is set if the divisor is zero or if the quotient requires more than one word to represent. Signed division is performed so that the remainder has the same sign as the dividend.

Like multiplication, signed division can be performed using unsigned division as a primitive. However, there is no obvious way to perform multiprecision division using a shorter division instruction as a primitive.

The 68000 has both unsigned and signed multiplication instructions, listed in the first part of Table 8–21. These instructions multiply the low-order word of a data register Dn by a one-word source operand, and leave the 32-bit result in Dn. Table 8–22 shows how a 32-bit by 32-bit unsigned multiplication with a
MULU   64-bit result can be accomplished with MULU and the equation at the beginning of this section. The operations and variable storage for this program follow the 68000 family's convention of storing the more significant words in lower-numbered addresses, as shown in Figure 8–11. In contrast with this program,
MULS   performing multiprecision signed or unsigned multiplication using MULS (*signed multiplication*) as a primitive would be much more difficult.

TABLE 8–21   Multiplication, division, and decimal instructions in the 68000.

Mnemonic	Operands	Opcode Word	XNZVC	Description
MULU.W	dsrc,Dn	1100rrr011ssssss	–**00	Multiply Dn by dsrc (unsigned)
MULS.W	dsrc,Dn	1100rrr111ssssss	–**00	Multiply Dn by dsrc (signed)
DIVU.W	dsrc,Dn	1000rrr011ssssss	–***0	Divide Dn by dsrc (unsigned)
DIVS.W	dsrc,Dn	1000rrr111ssssss	–***0	Divide Dn by dsrc (signed)
ABCD.B	Dm,Dn	1100rrr100000RRR	*U*U*	BCD add Dm and X to Dn
ABCD.B	–(Am),–(An)	1100aaa100001AAA	*U*U*	BCD add –(Am) and X to –(An)
SBCD.B	Dm,Dn	1000rrr100000RRR	*U*U*	BCD subtract Dm and X from Dn
SBCD.B	–(Am),–(An)	1000aaa100001AAA	*U*U*	BCD subtract –(Am) and X from –(An)
NBCD.B	ddst	0100100000dddddd	*U*U*	BCD negate ddst and subtract X

Notes: See Table 8–2 for addressing mode restrictions. Also see notes for Table 8–1.
   In the multiply operations, the low-order word of Dn is multiplied by the source operand and the 32-bit result is stored in Dn. Condition bits are set according to the 32-bit result.
   In the division operations, the quotient is stored in the low-order word of Dn and the remainder (same sign as quotient) is stored in the high-order word. N and Z are set according to the value of the quotient. Normally V is cleared; however, if the quotient cannot be expressed in 16 bits, Dn is not changed, V is set, and the values of N and Z are undefined. Division by zero causes a trap.
   In the BCD operations, X and C are set according to the decimal carry generated by the operation, Z is set according to the result byte, and N and V are undefined.

The 68000's unsigned and signed division instructions are listed in the second part of Table 8–21. Each instruction takes its 32-bit dividend from a data register Dn and its 16-bit divisor from its one-word source operand. At the end of the division, the quotient and remainder are stored in Dn, in the low-order and high-order words, respectively.

Two special conditions may occur during division. If the divisor is zero, then a "divide-by-0" trap occurs, which interrupts the execution of the current instruction stream and calls a special "trap handler" routine, as described in Section 11.4.4. It is the programmer's responsibility to provide a divide-by-0 trap handler routine if this event may occur.

The second special condition occurs if the divisor is much smaller than the dividend, and as a result the quotient requires more than 16 bits to represent. In this case, the V bit is set and the operands are not changed.

8.11 DECIMAL ARITHMETIC

Two binary-coded decimal (BCD) digits may be packed into a byte, with the high-order digit on the left; decimal numbers with any desired number of digits may then be represented by strings of bytes. A few microprocessors, including the 68000, have instructions that directly add packed-BCD numbers, as we'll see later.

DAA

Most microprocessors perform BCD operations using a a half-carry flag H and a decimal adjust (DAA) instruction along with normal binary addition

TABLE 8–22   Multiprecision unsigned multiplication subroutine for 68000.

```
XH        DS.W    1            High-order word of X.
XL        DS.W    1            Low-order word of X.
YH        DS.W    1            High-order word of Y.
YL        DS.W    1            Low-order word of Y.
*         Note: Do not change the storage order of the following words!
P3        DS.W    1            High-order word of product.
P2        DS.W    1            Next lower-order word of product.
P1        DS.W    1            Next lower-order word of product.
P0        DS.W    1            Low-order word of product.

*         Multiply XH,XL by YH,YL and store product in P3,P2,P1,P0.
*
LONGMUL   CLR.L   P3           P3,P2 := 0;
          MOVE.W  XL,D0
          MULU.W  YL,D0        D0.L := XL*YL;
          MOVE.L  D0,P1        P1,P0 := XL*YL;
          MOVE.W  XL,D0
          MULU.W  YH,D0        D0.L := XL*YH;
          ADD.L   D0,P2        P2,P1 := 0,P1 + XL*YH; {N.B.: Carry impossible}
          MOVE.W  YL,D0
          MULU.W  XH,D0        D0.L := XH*YL;
          ADD.L   D0,P2        P2,P1 := P2,P1 + XH*YL; {N.B.: Carry possible}
          BCC.S   NOCARRY
          MOVE.W  #1,P3        P3 := carry from above operation;
NOCARRY   MOVE.W  XH,D0
          MULU    YH,D0        D0.L := XH*YH;
          ADD.L   D0,P3        P3,P2 := P3,P2 + XH*YH;
          RTS                  {Done, return.}
```

of bytes. For example, suppose two 2-digit numbers PH,PL and QH,QL are stored in bytes P and Q. Then P and Q may be combined by normal binary addition to produce a sum S as shown in Figure 8–12. During the addition, the C bit is set to the carry out of bit 7 and the H bit is set to the carry between bits 3 and 4. The DAA instruction examines the states of C and H and restores the binary sum to valid packed BCD, using the following rules:

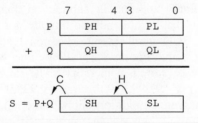

FIGURE 8–12   BCD interpretation of a sum of two bytes.

TABLE 8–23   Examples of decimal addition using binary addition and DAA.

	Example 1		Example 2		Example 3		Example 4	
P	0100 0110	46	0011 1001	39	0101 1000	58	1001 0111	97
Q	0101 0010	52	0100 0101	45	0111 1001	79	0110 1000	68
S = P+Q	1001 1000	98	0111 1110	7E	1101 0001	D1	1111 1111	FF
C, H	0 0		0 0		0 1		0 0	
DAA	1001 1000	98	1000 0100	84	0011 0111	137	0110 0101	165
C, H	0 0		0 1		1 1		1 1	

(1) If H is 1, then PL plus QL exceeded 15; SL is a valid BCD digit, but it is off by 6. This error is corrected by adding 6 to SL; no correction of SH is required since a carry has already occurred.

(2) If SL is between 10 and 15, it is not a valid BCD digit. This error is corrected by adding 6 to SL, setting H to 1, and adding 1 to SH to reflect the carry that should have occurred; this operation sets the C bit if SH was 15 before 1 was added.

(3) If C is now 1, then PH plus QH exceeded 15; SH is a valid BCD digit but it is off by 6. This error is corrected by adding 6 to SH.

(4) If SH is between 10 and 15, it is corrected by adding 6 to SH and setting C to 1 to reflect the carry that should have occurred.

Table 8–23 provides some examples of how DAA works. Notice that, if the sum of the two 2-digit numbers exceeds 99, then the C bit will be set, so that multiprecision BCD addition can be accomplished with normal add with carry instructions.

Packed-BCD numbers may also be subtracted, but the correction rules are different from those for addition (and left as an exercise for the reader). Some processors have an extra condition bit D to indicate whether an addition or subtraction occurred most recently, so that the DAA instruction can operate according to the appropriate rules. The 8086 simply has two DAA-type instructions, one that performs the correction steps for addition, the other for subtraction.

The 68000 has special add BCD and subtract BCD instructions that combine a binary addition or subtraction and BCD adjustment into a single instruction, so that extra condition bits are not required.

Signed BCD numbers may be conveniently represented in the signed-magnitude system. Figure 8–13 shows one way that signed-magnitude BCD numbers may be stored in memory. The range of numbers allowed with this representation is −9,999,999 through +9,999,999. In order to carry out the rules for signed-magnitude addition and subtraction, a program must first check the operands' signs. When P and Q are added, there are four separate cases (and instruction sequences) implied by the signs of P and Q.

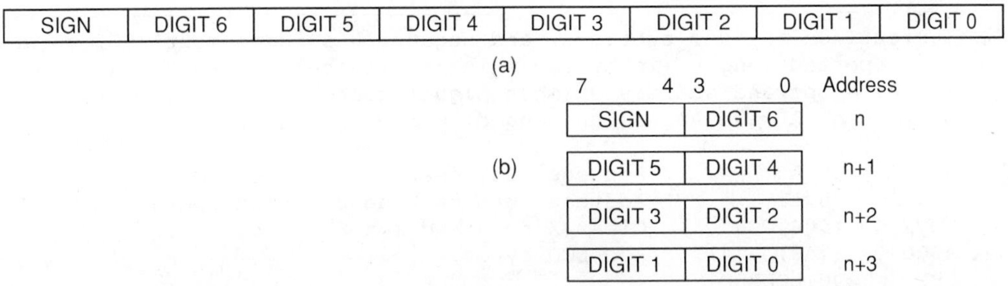

SIGN	DIGIT 6	DIGIT 5	DIGIT 4	DIGIT 3	DIGIT 2	DIGIT 1	DIGIT 0

(a)

```
         7     4 3     0   Address
        ┌────────┬────────┐
        │  SIGN  │ DIGIT 6│    n
        ├────────┼────────┤
(b)     │ DIGIT 5│ DIGIT 4│   n+1
        ├────────┼────────┤
        │ DIGIT 3│ DIGIT 2│   n+2
        ├────────┼────────┤
        │ DIGIT 1│ DIGIT 0│   n+3
        └────────┴────────┘
```

FIGURE 8–13   Representation of a signed BCD number, seven digits plus sign: (a) conventional representation; (b) memory addresses.

Signed BCD numbers can be added more easily if they are represented in the 10's-complement number system. Also, for a given number of bytes, the number range is slightly larger; the four bytes in Figure 8–13 can store 10's-complement BCD numbers in the range −50,000,000 through +49,999,999. Subtraction may be performed by negating the subtrahend and then adding. We present examples using the 68000 in the next subsection.

The last part of Table 8–21 lists the 68000's decimal instructions. These instructions operate much like the ADDX, SUBX, and NEGX instructions for multi-precision binary arithmetic, except that they only accept byte operands and they automatically perform a decimal adjustment on each result byte.

The 68000's decimal instructions are compatible with 10's-complement packed-BCD operands that have an even number of digits (and therefore occupy a whole number of bytes) and that are stored in memory with their more significant digits at lower-numbered addresses, as in Figure 8–13. For example, Table 8–24 shows general subroutines and macros for manipulating BCD operands in this format. Each subroutine is passed the size and addresses of its operands, and begins by adjusting the addresses to point just past the operands, in preparation for auto-decrement addressing. Next, each subroutine sets up CCR so that the initial carry or borrow is 0 and Z is 1, ensuring a correct result. Finally, each subroutine executes a simple loop to process its BCD operands one byte at a time.

8.12 MISCELLANEOUS 68000 CONTROL INSTRUCTIONS

Although we introduced data movement and logical instructions for the CCR, SR, and USP previously, we've repeated them in the first three parts of Table 8–25, just so you can easily find them all in one place. The last part of the table lists the few remaining instructions of the 68000, most of which would fall into a category of "processor control."

TABLE 8–24 General subroutines and macros for manipulating BCD operands.

```
*           Subroutines to add, subtract, and negate 10's-complement BCD operands.
*           D0 = operand length (in bytes, which is (number of digits) / 2).
*           A0, A1 = operand addresses (most significant byte).
*           On return, A0 and A1 are unchanged, and D0 is -1.
*
BCDADDS ADD.L    D0,A0           Address just past source operand.
        ADD.L    D0,A1           Address just past destination operand.
        MOVE.W   #$04,CCR        Clear X to 0 and set Z to 1.
BCDADD1 ABCD.B   -(A0),-(A1)     Add BCD bytes.
        DBF      D0,BCDADD1
        RTS
*
BCDSUBS ADD.L    D0,A0           Address just past source operand.
        ADD.L    D0,A1           Address just past destination operand.
        MOVE.W   #$04,CCR        Clear X to 0 and set Z to 1.
BCDSUB1 SBCD.B   -(A0),-(A1)     Subtract BCD bytes.
        DBF      D0,BCDSUB1
        RTS
*
BCDNEGS ADD.L    D0,A0           Address just past destination operand.
        MOVE.W   #$04,CCR        Clear X to 0 and set Z to 1.
BCDNEG1 NBCD.B   -(A0)           Negate BCD bytes.
        DBF      D0,NEGSUB1
        RTS


*           Macros that uses the subroutines above to perform BCD operations.
*           Usage:  BCDADD SIZE,SRC,DST
*                   BCDSUB SIZE,SRC,DST
*                   BCDNEG SIZE,DST
*
BCDADD  MACRO                    \1 = SIZE (bytes), \2 = SRC, \3 = DST
        MOVE.L   #\1,D0          Get size of BCD operands.
        LEA.L    \2,A0           Address of source operand.
        LEA.L    \3,A1           Address of destination operand.
        BSR      BCDADDS         Add operands.
        ENDM
*
BCDSUB  MACRO                    \1 = SIZE (bytes), \2 = SRC, \3 = DST
        MOVE.L   #\1,D0          Get size of BCD operands.
        LEA.L    \2,A0           Address of source operand.
        LEA.L    \3,A1           Address of destination operand.
        BSR      BCDSUBS         Subtract operands.
        ENDM
*
BCDNEG  MACRO                    \1 = SIZE (bytes), \2 = DST
        MOVE.L   #\1,D0          Get size of BCD operands.
        LEA.L    \2,A0           Address of destination operand.
        BSR      BCDNEGS         Negate operand.
        ENDM
```

TABLE 8–25   Miscellaneous control instructions in the 68000.

Mnemonic	Operands	Opcode Word	XNZVC	Description
MOVE.W	dsrc,CCR	0100010011ssssss	-----	Copy low byte of dsrc to CCR
ANDI.B	#data,CCR	0000001000111100	*****	AND immediate data to CCR
ORI.B	#data,CCR	0000000000111100	*****	OR immediate data to CCR
EORI.B	#data,CCR	0000101000111100	*****	Exclusive OR immediate data to CCR
MOVE.W	dsrc,SR	0100011011ssssss	-----	Copy dsrc to SR (privileged operation)
MOVE.W	SR,ddst	0100000011dddddd	-----	Copy SR to ddst
ANDI.W	#data,SR	0000001001111100	*****	AND immediate data to SR (privileged)
ORI.W	#data,SR	0000000001111100	*****	OR immediate data to SR (privileged)
EORI.W	#data,SR	0000101001111100	*****	Exclusive OR immediate data to SR (priv.)
MOVE.L	An,USP	0100111001100aaa	-----	Copy An to user SP (privileged operation)
MOVE.L	USP,An	0100111001101aaa	-----	Copy user SP to An (privileged operation)
NOP		0100111001110001	-----	No operation
TAS.B	ddst	0100101011dddddd	-**00	Test ddst, then set MSB of ddst to 1
TRAP	#vector	010011100100vvvv	-----	Trap using specified vector
TRAPV		0100111001110110	-----	Trap if V is 1
CHK.W	dsrc,Dn	0100rrr110ssssss	-*UUU	Check and trap if Dn < 0 or Dn > dsrc
ILLEGAL		0100101011111100	-----	Cause an illegal instruction trap
BKPT	#number	0100100001001nnn	-----	Cause an illegal instruction trap
STOP	#data	0100111001110010	*****	Load SR with data and stop (privileged)
RESET		0100111001110000	-----	Assert reset signal to external devices (priv.)
RTE		0100111001110011	*****	Return from exception (privileged)

Notes: See Table 8–2 for addressing mode restrictions. Also see notes for Table 8–1.
    In the CHK instruction, N is set if Dn < 0, cleared if Dn > dsrc, and left undefined otherwise.
    Privileged instructions cause a trap if executed in user mode (when S = 0).
    vector = TRAP instruction vector number, 0–15; vvvv = vector field.
    number = 3-bit breakpoint number (0–7) for use by the trap handler; nnn = number field.

NOP   The NOP instruction does nothing. Sometimes NOP is used to insert a very short delay in a program, perhaps because of critical timing requirements in an input/output program. However, this is dangerous because NOP's delay depends on the processor speed—68000s running at higher clock speeds do nothing faster! More often, NOP is used during debugging to replace an unwanted instruction in the object code without reassembling or recompiling the entire program. Multiword instructions are replaced with multiple NOPs.

TAS   The TAS (test and set) instruction reads a 1-byte operand, sets the condition bits according to its value, and then stores the operand with its MSB set to 1. As trivial and perhaps useless as this may seem, TAS is an extremely important primitive for multiprocessor systems, where two or more processors share the same physical memory, as we'll show in Section 12.3.4.

TRAP   The TRAP instruction is like a subroutine call, but with a few very important differences:

(1) The current PC is pushed using A7', the supervisor stack pointer, instead of A7, the normal user stack pointer.

(2) The current SR is also pushed, again using A7'.

(3) Instead of determining a jump address using one of the normal addressing modes, TRAP uses its 4-bit vector number as an index into a table of subroutine starting addresses, or "trap vectors." The trap vector table itself is stored in a predetermined area in low memory, as explained in Section 11.4.4.

(4) Before starting the subroutine's execution, the processor sets the S bit and thereby enters supervisor mode.

Recall that in user mode, a program may not execute instructions that directly affect the high-order byte of SR, including the S bit. However, the TRAP instruction provides a well-controlled, indirect means for user programs to enter supervisor mode and execute operating-system subroutines that perform privileged operations. (Of course, for full protection there must be external memory management hardware that prevents sneaky user programs from modifying the trap vector table to point to their own bogus subroutines.)

TRAPV   The TRAPV instruction causes a trap using a predetermined trap vector, but only if the V bit is 1. This instruction can be used by programs that expect overflow never to occur, but that wish to abort and return control to an operating system if their expectation is wrong.

CHK   The CHK instruction is intended for similar applications, in this case for array bounds checking. If Dn contains a value that is going to be used as an index into an array of size [0..dsrc], then CHK.W dsrc,Dn causes a trap if the index is out of bounds for this array. Note that dsrc is a word operand, and it is compared with the low-order word of Dn. The 68020 also has a longword version CHK.L, as well as a new instruction CHK2 with a nonzero lower bound.

ILLEGAL   The ILLEGAL instruction causes an "illegal instruction" trap to occur. Actually, the 68000 has lots of illegal and unimplemented instructions, and executing any one of them causes an illegal instruction trap. What makes ILLEGAL different is that Motorola promises to keep this instruction illegal in all future 68000 family members. So if you really want to generate an illegal instruction trap, this is the best way to do it.

BKPT   The BKPT instruction also generates an illegal instruction trap, and is intended for use in program debugging. (Although any illegal opcodes could be used to perform this function, the BKPT opcodes have additional hardware functionality in the 68010 and 68020.) Suppose a programmer wishes to determine the state of a program just before a certain instruction is executed. By replacing the opcode word of that instruction with BKPT, an on-line debugger can regain control of the processor through the illegal-instruction trap handler, allowing the programmer to display and modify the program state (registers, variables, etc.). At the programmer's command, the debugger eventually restores the original opcode word at the breakpoint location and returns control to the suspended program.

The last three instructions in Table 8–25 are privileged. Executing these or any of the other privileged instructions in user mode (S = 0) causes a "privilege violation" trap to occur.

STOP

The STOP instruction loads SR with an immediate word value and then stops the processor, but usually only temporarily. The processor stops with the PC pointing to the next sequential instruction, but it does not fetch it. Instead, it just sits there, waiting for an external interrupt to occur. If and when the interrupt occurs, the processor performs normal interrupt handling as described in Section 11.1.2, and eventually returns to execute the instructions after the STOP. This instruction is useful in systems whose main memory is shared with other devices that require frequent memory access, such as high-speed disks or other processors, so that memory cycles are not wasted by a processor that is simply busy-waiting.

RESET

The RESET instruction asserts an external reset signal line that the hardware designer may or may not have hooked up to reset the system's input/output devices. The events that occur at reset are very device dependent and sometimes rather mysterious. In any case, RESET does not affect the 68000 processor state in any way, except to bump the PC as usual to the next sequential instruction, which is duly executed.

RTE

Finally, the RTE instruction is used to return control to the program that was executing just before a trap or interrupt took place. It pops a word off the supervisor stack and into the SR, thereby restoring, among other things, the mode that the processor was in before the trap. Then it pops a longword into the PC, so that program execution is resumed right where it left off.

REFERENCES

Information on computer operation types is widely scattered; most computer engineers and architects learn about different operation types through their experience on different computers. The purpose of this chapter has been to bring some of this information together in a reasonable, structured format.

A considerable amount of study has been devoted to the design of compact, efficient, and well-structured computer instruction sets. In "A Design Philosophy for Microcomputer Architectures" (*Computer*, Vol. 10, No. 2, February 1977), Dennis Allison makes the case (as have many others) for language-directed machine design—fitting the machine instructions and features to the high-level language (or languages) that will most frequently run on it. More recently, many architects have taken a somewhat contrary position, arguing that instruction sets should be made simpler so that processors can be designed to run faster.

RISC machine

The seminal paper on so-called *RISC machines* is "The Case for the Reduced Instruction Set Computer" by David A. Patterson and David R. Ditzel (*Computer Architecture News*, Vol. 8, No. 6, October 1980, pp. 25–33).

The detailed specification of condition bit settings has been more of an art than a science. Most contemporary microprocessors base their condition bits on those of the classic PDP-11 minicomputer, but the PDP-11 has problems of its own, as described in "The PDP-11: A Case Study of How *Not* to Design Condition Codes," by Robert Russell (*Proc. 5th Annual Symp. on Computer Architecture*, IEEE publ. no. 78CH1284-9C, April 1978). A discussion of the considerations that influenced the design of the 68000 condition bits appears in Appendix A of the *MC68000 16-bit Microprocessor User's Manual* by Motorola.

E X E R C I S E S

8.1 List all of the 68000 data movement and manipulation instructions that do not allow an address register to be used as the source operand. Why aren't address registers allowed in these instructions?

8.2 Show two ways of encoding an instruction that has the effect of `ADD.L #12345,D1` in the 68000. Which encoding does your assembler choose? How can you force the other encoding?

8.3 Show three ways of encoding an instruction that has the effect of `ADD.L #4,D2` in the 68000. Which encoding does your assembler choose? How can you force the other encodings?

8.4 Show two ways of encoding an instruction that has the effect of `OR.L #12345,D1` in the 68000. Which encoding does your assembler choose? How can you force the other encoding?

8.5 The encodings of the instructions `AND.B Dn,mdst` and `ABCD.B Dm,Dn` are very similar. In fact, based on these encodings, it appears that the encodings of `AND.B D1,D2` and `ABCD.B D2,D1` are identical. What's wrong?

8.6 Do the 68000 instructions `ADD.B #-20,D1` and `SUB.B #20,D1` produce the same results? Explain.

8.7 Find a 68000 instruction besides `ADDA` or `SUBA` that can be used to add a 16-bit signed immediate value to any address register. Describe how, if at all, this instruction differs from `ADDA` in length, execution time, and condition-code settings.

8.8 Find a 68000 instruction that adds an immediate value and an address or data register to any address register. What is the range of allowable immediate values?

8.9 What is the arithmetic weight of the `C` bit after a 16-bit unsigned addition? After a 16-bit unsigned subtraction?

8.10 Does the following 68000 instruction sequence correctly negate a 64-bit two's-complement integer `XH,XL`? Justify your answer.

```
        COM.W   XH
        NEG.W   XL
        BNE.S   SKIP
        ADD     #1,XH
SKIP    ...
```

8.11 How many bits does it take to store the current U.S. national debt, in cents, as a two's-complement integer?

8.12 The following 68000 subroutine for adding two 3-byte integers P2,P1,P0 and Q2,Q1,Q0 fails for some values of P and Q. Explain why and fix it.

```
MY3SUMS  MOVE.L  P0,D0      Add low-order longwords.
         ADD.L   Q0,D0
         MOVE.L  D0,S0      Save low-order sum.
         MOVE.L  P1,D0      Add middle longwords.
         BCC.S   SKIP1
         ADD.L   #1,D0      Add 1 to D0 if C=1 from previous add.
SKIP1    ADD.L   Q1,D0
         MOVE.L  D0,S1      Save longword of sum.
         MOVE.L  P2,D0      Add high-order longwords.
         BCC.S   SKIP2
         ADD.L   #1,D0      Add 1 to D0 if C=1 from previous add.
SKIP2    ADD.L   Q2,D0
         MOVE.L  D0,S2      Save high-order longword of sum.
         RTS                Done, return.
```

8.13 A programmer tried the following three different 68000 instruction sequences for testing the relation D0 < 200 (unsigned byte), and found that they did not all give the same results. Explain the differences.

```
CMP.B  #200,D0        SEQUENCE A
BLO    OK


SUB.B  #200,D0        SEQUENCE B
BCS    OK


ADD.B  #-200,D0       SEQUENCE C
BCS    OK
```

8.14 What should normally be the first instruction in a 68000 subroutine that ends with an RTR instruction?

8.15 With regard to the mysterious "branch never" instruction, what is the effect of a 68000 Bcc that uses F as the condition cc and is encoded using the corresponding value of CCCC in Table 8–9?

8.16 Modify the SORT program in Table 7–3 on page 226 so that it sorts unsigned numbers in the range 1 through 255, terminating on a 0 input.

8.17 Show how to translate the following Pascal CASE statement into assembly language by using a jump instruction with indirect addressing:

```
CASE select OF
  1:       statementA;
  2,3,8:   statementB;
  4,7:     statementC;
  5:       statementD;
  6:       statementE;
END;
```

8.18 Optimize the 68000 BCNT1S subroutine in Table 8–12 with the BTST instruction.

8.19 Rewrite the 68000 BCNT1S subroutine in Table 8–12 so that it counts ones by a series of eight rotations and tests.

threaded code   8.20   In *threaded code*, a contiguous sequence of subroutine calls is replaced by a table of subroutine starting addresses, for example:

```
*       NONTHREADED                 THREADED
*
*       Subr. calls:                A "thread":
FIRST   JSR    SUBR1        FIRST   DC.L    SUBR1
        JSR    SUBR2                DC.L    SUBR2
        JSR    SUBR3                DC.L    SUBR3
        JSR    SUBR1                DC.L    SUBR1
        JSR    SUBR3                DC.L    SUBR3
        ...                         ...
        JSR    SUBR27               DC.L    SUBR27
LAST    JMP    $8008        LAST    DC.L    $8008   Return to oper. sys.
*
*       Typical subroutine format:
SUBR1   ...                 SUBR1   ...             First instruction.
        ...                         ...             Do not disturb A4.
        ...                         ...
        RTS                         MOVE.L  (A4)+,A0  End subroutine.
*                                   JMP     (A0)
*       To get started:
MAIN    JMP    FIRST        MAIN    LEA.L   FIRST,A4  Start of thread.
                                    MOVE.L  (A4)+,A0
                                    JMP     (A0)
```

Explain what's going on here, and then comment on the speed and size of threaded code compared to non-threaded code.

8.21   Write a 68000 instruction sequence that performs a 1-bit left rotation of a 64-bit operand in D0,D1 (high-order word in D0), and finishes with *all* of the condition bits set according to the 64-bit result.

8.22   Write a 68000 subroutine that performs a mutiple-bit right rotation of a 64-bit operand in D0,D1 (high-order word in D0), where the shift count is contained in the low-order six bits of D2. All register values should be preserved by the subroutine (except D0 and D1, of course), and the subroutine should return with *all* of the condition bits set according to the 64-bit result. (*Hint:* It may be useful to end your subroutine with RTR.)

8.23   Write a precise Pascal simulation for each of the 68000's rotate and shift instructions, including the effects on all of the condition bits.

8.24   Rewrite the field extracting subroutines and macros in Table 8–19 so that the additions and subtractions are done at assembly time. Next, rewrite the macros to eliminate the subroutine calls. Which version of the new macros is better, the one with or the one without subroutine calls?

8.25   Considering the subroutineless macros that you wrote for the previous exercise, what is the main defect of the 68000's static shift and rotate instructions? How can you "improve" the macros using conditional assembly?

8.26   Compare the size and execution time of the "ad hoc" and "structured" approaches for packing and unpacking a data word given in Section 8.9.2. For each approach, describe an application where that approach is clearly preferred over the other.

8.27 Write an assembly language program that initializes a table `N1S[0..255]` of bytes, where `N1S[i]` contains the number of ones in the binary representation of `i`. Use a series of eight rotations and tests to compute the number of ones for each entry.

8.28 Modify the `FNDPRM` program in Table 7–5 on page 231 so that it finds all primes between 2 and 8000 still using only a 1000-byte `PRIME` array, by packing eight `boolean` array components per byte.

8.29 Write a 68000 assembly language subroutine that computes the prime factors of an unsigned integer `N`. Use the algorithm below, and not the `DIV` instruction.

```
PROCEDURE Factors (N : integer);
  VAR rem, quot, I : integer;
  BEGIN
    WHILE N >= 2 DO BEGIN
      I := 1
      REPEAT {Try dividing by integers from 2 to N.}
        I := I + 1;
        quot := 0; rem := N; { Divide N by I, yielding quotient  }
        WHILE rem >= I DO    {    quot and remainder rem.         }
          BEGIN rem := rem - I; quot := quot + 1 END;
      UNTIL rem = 0; {Try values of I until one divides N evenly.}
      writeln(I); {Output a prime factor.}
      N := quot;   {Set N to be the quotient last found.}
    END;
  END;
```

8.30 Repeat the previous exercise, using a 68000 `DIV` instruction where applicable.

8.31 Write a 68000 instruction sequence that multiplies two 32-bit *signed* operands in D0 and D1 and leaves the 64-bit result in D2 (high order) and D3 (low order).

8.32 Write a sequence of 68000 instructions that divides a 32-bit signed integer in D1 by 2, truncating both positive and negative numbers toward 0, so that $-1 \div 2 = 0$.

8.33 Translate one of the multiplication or division algorithms in Section 4.8 or 4.9 into a 68000 assembly language program for 64-bit operands.

8.34 Write a binary-to-ASCII conversion algorithm along the lines of Exercise 5.23 that uses division by 10 to form the decimal digits (see also Section 4.3). Use it in an assembly language binary-to-ASCII conversion routine for the 68000.

8.35 State the rule for detecting overflow when 10's-complement packed-BCD numbers are added.

8.36 Determine the rules for a decimal adjust instruction that corrects the result of a binary subtraction on a packed-BCD byte.

8.37 Write general subroutines and macros, in the style of Table 8–24, for manipulating signed-magnitude packed-BCD numbers.

8.38 Write general subroutines and macros, in the style of Table 8–24, for adding and subtracting 10's-complement packed-BCD numbers where the two operands may have different lengths, but each length is still an even number of digits.

CHAPTER 9

Subroutines and Parameters

subroutine
call

Subroutines are the key to the structure of programs in any language, high or low level. A *subroutine* is a sequence of instructions that is defined and stored only once in a program, but which may be invoked (or *called*) from one or more places in the program. Two examples of frequently used subroutines in a typical computer are the instruction sequences that write a character to and read a character from a terminal.

One advantage of using subroutines should be obvious: program size is reduced by storing a commonly used sequence only once. Instead of repeating the entire sequence each time that it is needed, only a single instruction or short sequence of instructions is needed to call the subroutine. Another advantage is crucial in the development of large programs: individual tasks can be defined and processed by subroutines with well-defined interfaces and interactions with the rest of the program. In this way, different programmers can work on different subroutines (i.e., tasks), and individual subroutines can be written, debugged, optimized, and modified, more or less independently from the rest of the program. Indeed, the development of a large program would be virtually impossible without a subroutine mechanism to decompose large tasks into a collection of smaller ones.

parameter

formal parameter
actual parameter

All of the advantages of subroutines are amplified by the use of parameters. A *parameter* is a "dummy variable" in the subroutine definition, simply a place-holder whose identity is bound to a real variable or value each time the subroutine is called. The dummy variable in the subroutine definition is called a *formal parameter*, while the variable or value used on a particular call is called an *actual parameter*. Since different actual parameters may be specified on each call of a subroutine, the same subroutine may be used to perform identical processing on many different sets of data. For example, the subroutine `PrintAvg(x,y)` could be defined to print the average of two formal parameters `x` and `y`. Calling `PrintAvg` with three different sets of actual parameters would print three different results: `PrintAvg(1,5)` prints 3; `PrintAvg(17,100)` prints 58.5; and if a = 26 and b = 58, `PrintAvg(a,b)` prints 42.

Early in Chapter 2, we showed Pascal programs with "subroutines" called procedures and functions. We have been using Pascal procedures and functions informally ever since. In the first part of this chapter, we discuss Pascal procedures and functions in more depth, both to obtain a better understanding of Pascal and to see how procedures and functions relate to assembly language subroutines. We emphasize both areas for a number of reasons:

- Familiarity with the structure of Pascal procedures and functions can help a programmer improve the structure of corresponding assembly language subroutines.

- Pascal procedures and functions can be useful documentation aids for assembly language programs.

- Assembly language parameter-passing conventions can explain some of the mysteries of the run-time environment of a high-level language. For example, why do the values of local variables in a Pascal procedure become undefined each time the procedure is exited? We'll find out in Section 9.3.6.

- A good understanding of both high-level and assembly language parameter-passing conventions is required when a programmer links together high-level and assembly language program modules to perform a task.

9.1 PROCEDURES AND FUNCTIONS IN PASCAL

9.1.1 Procedures

procedure
procedure and
function
declaration part

block
procedure
heading
identifier
parameter list

procedure
statement

A Pascal *procedure* is a program-defined sequence of statements that can be invoked by a single statement. A procedure is defined in the *procedure and function declaration part* of a program block as shown in Figure 9–1. The declaration consists of the reserved word **PROCEDURE** followed by a *procedure heading* and a *block*. The *block* in a procedure declaration consists of declarations and a statement part, the same as a program block. A *procedure heading* contains an *identifier* that names the procedure and is followed by a *parameter list*. The *parameter list* gives the names and types of zero or more formal parameters, as described in the next section. For now, we'll discuss only procedures with no parameters (and empty parameter lists).

A procedure may be invoked (called) by a *procedure statement* that simply gives its name and any actual parameters to be substituted for the formal parameters, as shown in Figure 9–2. In general, a procedure (or function) must be defined before being invoked. Unlike assembly language, Pascal has a syntax that allows programs to be compiled by a one-pass algorithm. Since labels, constants, types, variables, and procedures and functions must all be defined before they are used, there are no forward references. However, if two procedures call

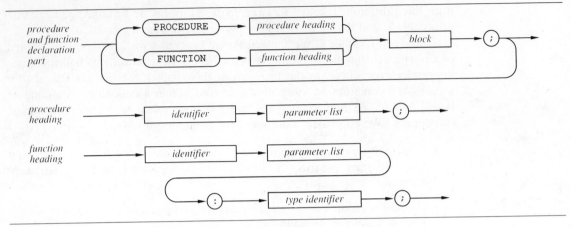

FIGURE 9–1   Procedure and function declaration part syntax diagram.

each other, then neither can be defined before being invoked. Pascal gets around this problem as described in Section 9.4.

The declarations in a procedure block define constants, variables, types, and additional procedures and functions that are all *local* to the current procedure. Such local items may not be referenced outside the scope of the current procedure; if items with the same names already exist outside, then they are redefined within the procedure without affecting their external definitions. If a procedure definition references an item not defined within the procedure, the item must have been defined outside.

Table 9–1 shows some examples of the scope rules. The global variables `common` and `maxi` are used within the scope of procedure `ProcA`. However, the global variable `maxi` is redefined within the scope of `ProcB`. The variable `temp`, which is local to `ProcA`, is erroneously used in `ProcB` and in the main program. Although the scope rules allow multiple uses of the same identifier, it is still best for clarity and correctness to use unique identifier names in different procedures.

The statement part of a procedure block indicates the actions performed each time that the procedure is invoked. All local variables have undefined values each time that the statement part is entered; they are not preserved between successive calls of the procedure.

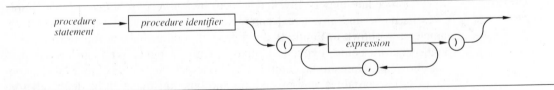

FIGURE 9–2   Procedure statement syntax.

TABLE 9–1   Examples of scope rules for procedures.

```
PROGRAM ScopeRules (input,output);

VAR common, maxi : integer;

PROCEDURE ProcA;
VAR temp, x : integer;
  BEGIN
    ...
    x := maxi;              {uses global 'maxi'}
    common := temp + x;   {global 'common', local 'temp', 'x'}
  END;

PROCEDURE ProcB;
VAR maxi, mini : integer; {'maxi' redefined locally}
  BEGIN
    ...
    mini := maxi;     {OK - 'mini' and 'maxi' both local}
    temp := 0; {error - 'temp' undefined in current scope}
    ...
  END;

BEGIN
  read(common,maxi);   {OK - initialize globals}
  temp := 10; {error - 'temp' undefined in current scope}
  ...
END.
```

Table 9–2 contains a program that removes spaces from input text. The program is rewritten in Table 9–3 using a procedure `SkipSpaces` to replace the innermost `REPEAT` statement. In the program body, the line "`SkipSpaces`" is the procedure statement; when it is encountered, the programmer-defined sequence (i.e., the `REPEAT` statement) is executed. The program actually became longer by using a procedure in this example, but there are still several advantages to using procedures in general:

TABLE 9–2   Pascal program to remove spaces from input text.

```
PROGRAM RemSpace (input,output);
{Remove spaces from input text terminated by a period.}

VAR inChar : char;

BEGIN
  REPEAT
    REPEAT read(inChar) UNTIL inChar <> ' ';
    write(inChar);
  UNTIL inChar = '.';
END.
```

TABLE 9–3   Removing spaces with a procedure.

```
PROGRAM RemSpaceProc (input,output);
{Remove spaces from input text terminated by a period.}

VAR inChar : char;

PROCEDURE SkipSpaces;
  BEGIN
    REPEAT read(inChar) UNTIL inChar <> ' ';
  END;

BEGIN
  REPEAT
    SkipSpaces;
    write(inChar);
  UNTIL inChar = '.';
END.
```

- A well-chosen procedure name contributes to program readability by concisely describing the operation being performed.

- Partitioning a program into a hierarchical structure of procedures with well-defined interfaces and interactions makes the program easier to design, debug, maintain, and modify.

- If a procedure is invoked more than once, program size is reduced compared with a structure that repeats the procedure body once for each invocation.

To illustrate the above ideas, Table 9–4 shows a more complex program for processing spaces. Instead of being discarded, strings of spaces are converted to the character "#" followed by a letter corresponding to the number of spaces in the string. Also, the main program uses a WHILE instead of a REPEAT statement, so that the terminating period is not printed. This example illustrates a number of concepts:

- The procedure has no parameters, but it communicates with the main program via the global variable inChar.

- The procedure has one local variable scnt, whose value it reinitializes each time that it is called.

- The procedure is called from two different places in the main program, the first place to "prime" the WHILE loop.

- The procedure may be modified to do a better job of space compression without changing the main program (see Exercise 9.1).

TABLE 9–4   Program to compress strings of spaces.

```
PROGRAM Compress (input,output);
{Compress a series of spaces in input text terminated by a period.}

VAR inChar : char;

PROCEDURE SkipSpaces;
   {A series of 1 to 26 spaces is translated into '#' followed by a
   character 'A' to 'Z'. Longer series are truncated to 26 spaces.}
   VAR scnt : integer;
   BEGIN
     scnt := -1;
     REPEAT
       read(inChar); scnt := scnt + 1;
     UNTIL inChar <> ' ';
     IF scnt > 26 THEN scnt := 26;
     IF scnt > 0 THEN write('#',chr(ord('A')-1+scnt));
   END;

BEGIN
  SkipSpaces;
  WHILE inChar <> '.' DO
    BEGIN
      write(inChar);
      SkipSpaces;
    END;
END.
```

9.1.2 Functions

function

function heading

A *function* is a programmer-defined sequence of statements that assigns a value to the function name (i.e., *returns* a value). A function is defined much like a procedure, as shown in Figure 9–1. The *function heading* is like a procedure heading, but it also must specify the *type* of the value returned by the function. The function name (*identifier*) must be assigned a value of this type within the function block. Like a procedure block, a function block may have its own local constants, types, variables, and subservient procedures and functions.

The main difference between procedures and functions is in the way that they are invoked. Whenever the function name and actual-parameter list appear in an expression in the calling program, the function statement part is executed, and the last value assigned to the function name in the function statement part is returned to the expression evaluation.

Table 9–5 shows a program that uses a function to read the next nonspace character of input text. The variable inChar is needed since the function is invoked *every* time the function name appears in an expression. The following main program, although syntactically correct, would read two nonspace characters per iteration but write only one of them:

TABLE 9–5   Removing spaces with a function.

```
PROGRAM RemSpaceFunc (input,output);
{Remove spaces from input text terminated by a period.}

VAR inChar : char;

FUNCTION NextNonspace : char;
  VAR tempChar : char;
  BEGIN
    REPEAT read(tempChar) UNTIL tempChar <> ' ';
    NextNonspace := tempChar;
  END;

BEGIN
  REPEAT
    inChar := NextNonspace;
    write(inChar);
  UNTIL inChar = '.';
END.
```

```
BEGIN
  REPEAT write(NextNonspace) UNTIL NextNonspace = '.';
END.
```

The local variable `tempChar` and the assignment statement in the function statement part in Table 9–5 are also necessary. The alternative function statement part,

```
BEGIN
  REPEAT read(NextNonspace) UNTIL NextNonspace <> ' ';
END;
```

would not use the value just assigned to `NextNonSpace` in the comparison. Instead, it would cause a recursive call of the function to itself (see Section 9.4). Unless recursive calls are desired, the function name must not appear in expressions in the function statement part.

9.2   PARAMETERS IN HIGH-LEVEL LANGUAGE PROGRAMS

9.2.1   Pascal Parameters

parameter list

Both procedures and functions in Pascal handle parameters in the same way. A procedure or function declaration indicates formal parameters in a *parameter list*, as shown by the syntax diagram in Figure 9–3. If there are no parameters, then the parameter list is empty, as in the examples in the previous section. If

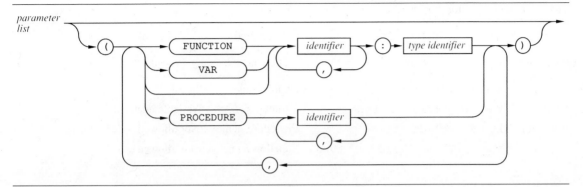

FIGURE 9–3   Parameter list syntax diagram.

there are one or more parameters, then each formal parameter is listed with its type as shown in the examples below:

```
PROCEDURE PrintAvg (x : real; y : real);
PROCEDURE FindChar (target : char; last : char; max : integer);
FUNCTION Xor (p : boolean; q : boolean) : boolean;
FUNCTION Power (x : real; n : integer) : real;
FUNCTION Prime (num : integer) : boolean;
```

If two or more formal parameters of the same type appear successively, the list may be abbreviated:

```
PROCEDURE PrintAvg (x,y : real);
PROCEDURE FindChar (target,last : char; max : integer);
FUNCTION Xor (p,q : boolean) : boolean;
```

Formal parameters may appear in any order and parameters of the same type need not be grouped together. However, when a procedure or function is called, the actual parameters must be listed in parentheses in the same order as in the definition:

```
VAR
   a,b : real; i,j,len : integer; f1,f2,f3 : boolean;
BEGIN
   ...
   PrintAvg(a,b);
   FindChar('t','.',len);
   f3 := Xor(f1,f2);
   a := Power(a*b,i+j);
   f1 := Prime(j+1);
   ...
```

TABLE 9–6 Kinds of parameters in Pascal.

Kind of Formal Parameter	Syntax	Required Actual Parameter	Effect of Assignment in Procedure
Value	`identifier : type`	Expression	Local
Variable	`VAR identifier : type`	Variable	Variable changed
Procedure	`PROCEDURE identifier`	Procedure name	Not allowed
Function	`FUNCTION identifier : type`	Function name	Not allowed

9.2.2 Value Parameters

value parameter

Pascal supports four kinds of parameters, listed in Table 9–6. The examples above have shown only *value parameters*. When a value parameter is specified, the actual parameter in the procedure call may be any expression whose result is the same type as the formal parameter. A constant or variable of this type is the simplest example of such an expression. When the procedure is called, the expression is evaluated and the resulting value is *copied* into a parameter area and passed to the procedure. Copying takes place even if the result is a large structured type such as an array. The procedure may modify the formal parameter via assignment statements, but this affects only the copy stored in the parameter area. For example, the program shown in Table 9–7 computes the value of n^2 for each n. When `Fact` is executed, the value of n is not disturbed even though the copy of n in the parameter area is eventually decremented to 1.

TABLE 9–7 Factorial and square program.

```
PROGRAM FactorialsAndSquares (input,output);

VAR n : integer;

FUNCTION Fact (i : integer) : real;
  VAR prod : real;
  BEGIN
    prod := 1;
    WHILE i > 1 DO
      BEGIN prod := prod*i; i := i - 1 END;
    Fact := prod;
  END;

BEGIN
  read(n);
  WHILE n > 0 DO      {Pass a copy of n to Fact}
    BEGIN writeln(n,Fact(n),n*n); read(n) END;
END.
```

TABLE 9–8 Program using a swapping procedure.

```
PROGRAM Swapping (input,output);

VAR a,b : integer;

PROCEDURE Swap (VAR x,y : integer);
  VAR t : integer;
  BEGIN
    t := x;
    x := y;
    y := t;
  END;

BEGIN
  a := 1;  b := 2;
  Swap(a,b);      {Pass the addresses of a,b to Swap}
  write(a,b);
END.
```

9.2.3 Variable Parameters

*variable
parameter*

Value parameters are the appropriate choice for passing inputs to a procedure or function. However, it is often necessary for a procedure to pass output results to the caller by using one or more parameters. A classic example of this requirement is the swapping procedure shown in Table 9–8. The Swap procedure declares *variable parameters* x and y. When a variable parameter is specified in a Pascal procedure or function, the actual parameter used in calls must be a *variable* of the corresponding type. The *address* of the variable, not a copy of its value, is passed to the procedure, and all statements in the procedure manipulate the variable directly. Thus, the program in Table 9–8 does actually swap the values of a and b and prints "2 1". If value parameters were used in the procedure definition, the program would print "1 2".

9.2.4 Procedure and Function Parameters

Pascal also allows procedure and function names to be passed as parameters. Table 9–9 presents a contrived example of a "using-procedure" that accepts the name of a "passed-procedure" as a parameter. Procedures and functions are seldom used as parameters in Pascal, but when they are, several precautions must be observed:

- If a passed-procedure has parameters, they may only be value parameters.

- Only a procedure or function name is passed, not its parameters; therefore the parameters must be "filled in" by the using-procedure.

TABLE 9–9 Program with procedures passed as parameters.

```
PROGRAM ArrayProcs (input,output);

CONST len = 80;
VAR charBuffer : ARRAY [1..len] OF char;

PROCEDURE DoBuff (PROCEDURE proc); {'using-procedure'}
  VAR i : integer;
  BEGIN
    FOR i := 1 TO len DO proc(i);
  END;

PROCEDURE Init (i : integer); {'passed-procedure'}
  BEGIN
    charBuffer[i] := ' ';
  END;

PROCEDURE Readc (i : integer); {'passed-procedure'}
  BEGIN
    read(charBuffer[i]);
  END;

PROCEDURE Printc (i : integer); {'passed-procedure'}
  BEGIN
    write(charBuffer[i]);
  END;

BEGIN
  DoBuff(Init);
  DoBuff(Printc); {Print a blank line.}
  writeln;
  DoBuff(Readc); {Read and print a line.}
  DoBuff(Printc);
END.
```

- The compiler does not necessarily check that the number of parameters required by passed-procedure equals the number of parameters assumed in the definition of the using-procedure.

9.2.5 Parameters in Other High-Level Languages

Algol Call by Value

Algol Call by Name

Replacement Rule

Parameter-passing conventions in other high-level languages may be similar to or different from Pascal's. For example, Algol has two methods. The *Algol Call by Value* method handles parameters just as Pascal handles value parameters. The *Algol Call by Name* method has no equivalent in Pascal. It is defined to have the same effect as a textual substitution of the actual parameters for the corresponding formal parameters in the subroutine; this is called the *Replacement Rule*. Although this method allows procedures like Swap to be written in the same way that Pascal would use variable parameters, it is still somewhat different.

For example, consider the effect of the replacement rule on the procedure body of `Swap` if `next` is an array of integers and we call `Swap(i,next[i])`:

```
BEGIN
  t := i;
  i := next[i];
  next[i] := t;
END;
```

Our intention is to swap the values of `i` and `next[i]`. But suppose that $i = 5$, `next[5]` = 4, and `next[4]` = 0. Then calling `Swap(i,next[i])` sets `i` to 4 (OK) while setting `next[4]` to 5 (wrong—we wanted to set `next[5]` to 5).

Fortran Call by Value

The *Fortran Call by Value* method is similar to using a Pascal value parameter, except that the (possibly modified) value in the parameter area is copied back into the original actual parameter when the subroutine is completed.

Call by Reference

PL/1 has a method called *Call by Reference* that is similar to using a Pascal variable parameter, except that it also allows an expression to be used as the actual parameter, temporarily allocating variable storage for the expression's value.

The C programming language provides only value parameters. However, the language allows the programmer to define pointer variables that contain the addresses of other variables and data structures, and to obtain the address of any variable simply by putting an ampersand (`&`) in front of its name. These facilities can be used anywhere, even in procedure definitions and calls. Thus, to obtain the effect of a Pascal variable parameter, a C procedure must use a pointer as the formal parameter, and pass the address of the variable as the parameter. The classic example, and source of hours of debug frustration for Pascal programmers learning C, is that to read an integer `x` in C, we say `read(&x)`, not `read(x)`.

The moral of the story is that a programmer must thoroughly understand the parameter-passing convention of a particular high-level language before writing any procedures that assign values to parameters. Fortunately for our purposes, Pascal variable and value parameters correspond nicely to the parameters most frequently used in assembly language subroutines. Value parameters correspond to numbers, characters, or other values passed to a subroutine, while variable parameters correspond to pointers or addresses. In the next section, we discuss how parameters are passed in assembly language subroutines.

9.3   ASSEMBLY LANGUAGE SUBROUTINES AND PARAMETERS

9.3.1   Subroutine Calling Methods

In order to execute subroutines, a processor must have a means for a program to save a return address when the subroutine is called, and a way for the subroutine to jump to the return address when the subroutine is finished. Theoretically, subroutine return addresses could be handled by ordinary instructions, as shown in Table 9–10 for the 68000. Here the programmer has set up a convention

TABLE 9–10   How to call subroutines in the 68000 without using JSR and RTS.

```
*            By convention, a subroutine return address is deposited in
*            the first two words of the subroutine.  The first executable
*            instruction begins in the third word of the subroutine.
*
MAIN         ...                      Main program.
             MOVE.L  #RET1,SUBR       Save return address.
             JMP     SUBR+4           Jump to subroutine.
RET1         ...                      Return here when subroutine finishes.
             ...
             MOVE.L  #RET2,SUBR       Save return address again.
             JMP     SUBR+4           Jump to subroutine.
RET2         ...                      Return here when subroutine finishes.
             ...
*
SUBR         DS.L    1                Allocate longword for return address.
             MOVE.W  D0,D2            First executable instruction.
             ...
             MOVEA.L SUBR,A0          Get return address from loc. SUBR.
             JMP     (A0)             Jump to address contained in A0.
```

for subroutine calling programs to save a return address in a longword at the beginning of the subroutine.

Because subroutines are used so often, all modern processors have special built-in instructions for calling subroutines and returning from them. Ancient minicomputer architectures such as the Hewlett-Packard 2116 actually had instructions that followed conventions similar to the one in Table 9–10. However, this convention has two major problems—it does not allow subroutines to be stored in read-only memory, and it does not allow subroutines to be called recursively (Section 9.4) or reentrantly (Section 12.4.2).

As we showed in Section 5.13, a pushdown stack is the natural data structure for saving subroutine return addresses. Therefore, most modern processors have a dedicated register (SP) that points into a stack of subroutine return addresses. The subroutine calling instructions (JSR or CALL) push return addresses onto the stack, and subroutine return instructions (RTS or RET) pop return addresses off the stack.

Some processors that don't have a hardware stack pointer, such as the IBM 370 family, have subroutine calling instructions that save the return address in a specified processor register. When subroutine calls are nested, it is up to the programmer to save the contents of this register in dedicated memory locations or in a stack.

9.3.2 Subroutine Parameters

In the previous section, we discussed several types of parameters used in Pascal procedures and functions. Table 9–11 shows the corresponding parameter types in assembly language subroutines.

Mac Note

In the Macintosh environment, the subroutine calling convention of Table 9–10 doesn't work, because return addresses like RET1 are not known at assembly time. You'd probably never want to use such a silly subroutine calling convention in the first place, but it is nevertheless instructive to adapt it to the Macintosh, just to reinforce your understanding of position-independent coding techniques.

In the Macintosh, if we tried to store return addresses in-line with the instructions (as in the original example) and access them with PC-relative addressing, we'd have two problems. First, most Macintosh assemblers don't give us an easy way to declare variables (as opposed to constants) in the code segment. Second, even if we did it, say, by using DC.L 0 and planning to overwrite the "constant" 0 with the return address, we would have no convenient way to *store* return addresses, since PC-relative addressing is not available for destination operands. For good reason, DS.L in the Macintosh normally allocates variables in the application global space, and that's where our return addresses should be stored.

Having settled that issue, we are left only with the problem of computing return addresses at run time. Here, an LEA instruction using PC-relative addressing works nicely. The complete example is recoded below.

```
MAIN      ...                       Main program.
          LEA.L    RET1,A0          Compute return address.
          MOVE.L   A0,SUBRET(A5)    Save it.
          JMP      SUBR             Jump to subroutine.
RET1      ...                       Return here when subroutine done.
          ...
          LEA.L    RET2,A0          Compute another return address.
          MOVE.L   A0,SUBRET(A5)    Save it.
          JMP      SUBR             Jump to subroutine.
RET2      ...                       Return here when subroutine done.
          ...
*
SUBRET    DS.L     1                Allocate longword for return address.
SUBR      MOVE.W   D0,D2            First executable instruction.
          ...
          MOVEA.L  SUBRET(A5),A0    Get return address from loc. SUBRET.
          JMP      (A0)             Jump to address contained in A0.
```

Note that the assembler automatically uses PC-relative addressing for operands RET1, RET2, and SUBR, because they are code symbols, while we have explicitly used based addressing to access variable SUBRET in the application global space.

TABLE 9–11   Parameters in Pascal and assembly language programs.

Pascal Parameter Type	Assembly Language Parameter Type
Value	Data value
Variable	Address of variable
Procedure or function name	Address of procedure or function

TABLE 9–12   Swapping subroutine using variable parameters.

```
*          Swap two 16-bit variables V0 and V1 whose addresses
*          are passed in address registers A0 and A1.
SWAP       MOVE.W   (A0),-(SP)        Push old V0 onto stack.
           MOVE.W   (A1),(A0)         Copy old V1 to V0.
           MOVE.W   (SP)+,(A1)        Pop old V0 from stack into V1.
           RTS
*
*          Main program -- swap the values of VARP and VARQ.
MAIN       ...
           LEA.L    VARP,A0           Address of VARP.
           LEA.L    VARQ,A1           Address of VARQ.
           JSR      SWAP
*          Values of VARP and VARQ are now swapped.
           ...
VARP       DS.W     1                 Reserve storage for VARP and VARQ.
VARQ       DS.W     1
```

input parameter

The parameter types specified in Pascal procedure and function definitions should be called *input parameters*, because they are passed from a calling program to a subroutine. However, subroutines can also pass results to a calling program. For example, a Pascal function returns one value to the calling program, while an assembly language subroutine can return many values. We'll

output parameter
output
result

call these values *output parameters*, *outputs*, or *results*.
To see the difference between variable parameters and value parameters, compare the 68000 swapping procedures in Tables 9–12 and 9–13. In the first example, the main program passes to the subroutine the addresses of the two variables; the subroutine accesses the variables by indirect addressing. In the second example, the main program passes copies of the variables to the subrou-

TABLE 9–13   Swapping subroutine using value parameters.

```
*          Swap two 16-bit values passed in registers D0 and D1.
SWAP       MOVE.W   D0,-(SP)          Push old value of D0 onto stack.
           MOVE.W   D1,D0             Copy old D1 to D0.
           MOVE.W   (SP)+,D1          Pop old D0 from stack into D1.
           RTS
*
*          Main program -- swap copies of the values of VARP and VARQ.
MAIN       ...
           MOVE.W   VARP,D0           Value of VARP.
           MOVE.W   VARQ,D1           Value of VARQ.
           JSR      SWAP
*          Copies of VARP and VARQ in D0 and D1 are
*          swapped, original VARP and VARQ untouched.
           ...
VARP       DS.W     1                 Reserve storage for VARP and VARQ.
VARQ       DS.W     1
```

Mac Note

Except as noted, all of the programs in this chapter are written to be easily adaptable to the Macintosh environment. Just about all that is needed is to add the (A5) notation for based addressing with respect to A5 for all instruction operands that are variables declared by DS. Such variables are stored in the application global space, whose base address is contained in A5 at run time. With the MPW assembler, it is also necessary to use CODE and DATA directives to switch between the code and data modules. (Refer to the Mac Note on page 184.)

tine, which the subroutine manipulates directly; the subroutine has no way to access the original variables themselves.

The 68000's LEA instruction is very useful for passing variable parameters. For example, suppose that a programmer wanted to swap VARP and SCORE[J], where SCORE[1..100] is an array of words. Then the following main program statements in Table 9–12 would do the trick:

```
LEA.L    VARP,A0         A0 now has address of VARP.
MOVE.W   J,D0            Get index of array item J.
MULU.W   #2,D0           Multiply by 2 for word offset.
LEA.L    SCORE-2,A1      Effective base address of array.
LEA.L    0(A1,D0),A1     A1 now has address of SCORE[J].
JSR      SWAP
```

Here the first two LEA instructions load the addresses of operands that are referenced with absolute addressing, and are equivalent to MOVEs with immediate addressing (e.g., MOVEA.L #VARP,A0). However, the third LEA instruction performs a run-time indexing computation—it adds the scaled index $2 \cdot J$ and the effective base address SCORE-2 and deposits the sum in A1. In the 68020, the 32-bit base addresses and index scaling available with based indexed addressing allow an even more efficient instruction sequence:

```
LEA.L    VARP,A0         A0 now has address of VARP.
MOVE.W   J,D0            Get index of array item J.
LEA.L    SCORE-2(D0*2),A1   A1 now has addr of SCORE[J].
JSR      SWAP
```

From these examples, it is apparent that all parameters in assembly language programs are really "values." With "variable" parameters, the "value" that is passed just happens to be the address of a variable. How parameters are classified doesn't make much difference, as long as the subroutine and calling program agree on how the parameters will be used.

9.3.3   Passing Parameters in Registers and Memory Locations

The simplest way for a program to pass parameters to a subroutine is to place them in the processor's registers. Likewise, the subroutine can return results to the calling program in the same way. This technique was used in the subroutines in the previous subsection and in Table 5–12 on page 166. Of course, the programmer must ensure that the calling program and the subroutine agree on which register contains each parameter. The register allocation for parameters is usually stated in a comment at the beginning of the subroutine. For example, subroutine WCNT1S in Table 5–12 states that the input parameter is passed in register D0 and the result in register D1.

If a processor does not have enough registers to hold all of the input or output parameters of a subroutine, then dedicated memory locations may be used instead. These memory locations are associated with the subroutine itself, not the calling program, so that each calling program places inputs and retrieves outputs in the same prearranged locations. For example, the 68000 DIVIDEL subroutine in Table 6–8 on page 197 expects the caller to place input parameters in locations DVND and DVSR, and it places outputs in locations QUOT and REM.

9.3.4 Parameter Areas

parameter area

It is also possible to associate memory locations for parameters with the calling program instead of the subroutine. In this case, the calling program places parameters in a preallocated *parameter area* and passes to the subroutine the base address of the parameter area. For example, Table 9–14 shows a new version of the DIVIDEL subroutine in which the calling program uses register A0 to pass the base address of the parameter area. Table 9–15 shows a program that calls this DIVIDEL subroutine. Notice how the parameter area is associated with the calling program, not the DIVIDEL subroutine. The calling program may use the same parameter area for other subroutines. If a main program calls many different subroutines, using a single parameter area saves memory compared with the alternative of allocating separate parameter variables for each subroutine. Of course, the parameter area must be big enough to hold the largest number of parameters used in any one subroutine.

Parameter areas are sometimes useful for subroutines that are stored in read-only memory (ROM). Since parameter values can't be stored into a ROM, it is more convenient to allocate storage for them with their calling programs in read/write memory (RAM).

Mac Note

In the Macintosh environment, the application global space may seem like a parameter area, because its contents are accessed with based addressing. However, this space as a whole contains *globals*, not subroutine parameters.

Still, it is quite reasonable to allocate parameter areas within the application global space for individual subroutine callers. For example, suppose that we assembled Table 9–15 in the Macintosh environment. Then both DIVPQ's local variables and the parameter area that it uses when calling DIVIDEL would be allocated by DS.L in the application global space. If the assembly-time offset PARMS is –$124, and the base address of the application global space (run-time A5) is $FA500, then the first instruction in the program (LEA.L PARMS(A5),A0) deposits $FA3DC into A0. This is the base address of the parameter area within the application global space.

TABLE 9–14   68000 DIVIDEL subroutine that uses a parameter area.

```
*        Input and output parameters are passed in an 8-word parameter
*        area.  The base address of the parameter area is passed to
*        the subroutine in register A0.  The offsets below define the
*        positions of each parameter in the parameter area.
*
HIDVND   EQU     0               High longword of quadword dividend (input).
LODVND   EQU     4               Low longword of dividend (input).
DVSR     EQU     8               Longword divisor (input).
QUOT     EQU     12              Longword quotient (result).
REM      EQU     16              Longword remainder (result).
*
DIVIDEL  MOVE.W  #32,CNT         Initialize count.
         MOVE.L  HIDVND(A0),D0   Keep high dividend and
         MOVE.L  LODVND(A0),D1     low dividend in registers.
         CMP.L   DVSR(A0),D0     Will quotient fit?
         BCS.S   DIVLUP          Branch if it will.
         JMP     SYSOVF          Else report overflow.
DIVLUP   LSL.L   #1,D1           Left shift dividend with LSB := 0.
         ROXL.L  #1,D0           A carry here from MSB means
         BCS.S   QUOT1             dividend surely > DVSR.
         CMP.L   DVSR(A0),D0     Else compare high DVND with DVSR.
         BCS.S   QUOTOK          Quotient bit = 0 if lower.
QUOT1    ADD.L   #1,D1           Else set quotient bit to 1.
         SUB.L   DVSR(A0),D0     And update dividend.
QUOTOK   SUB.W   #1,CNT          Decrement iteration count.
         BGT.S   DIVLUP          Continue until done.
         MOVE.L  D0,REM(A0)      Store remainder.
         MOVE.L  D1,QUOT(A0)     Store quotient.
         RTS                     Return.
CNT      DS.W    1               Bit count (local variable).
SYSOVF   EQU     $1800           System overflow report address.
```

TABLE 9–15   Program that calls DIVIDEL.

```
*        Compute PDIVQ := P DIV Q; PMODQ := P MOD Q;
*            where all are longword variables in memory.
DIVPQ    LEA.L   PARMS,A0        A0 points to parameter area.
         MOVE.L  P,LODVND(A0)    Pass low dividend.
         CLR.L   HIDVND(A0)      Clear high dividend.
         MOVE.L  Q,DVSR(A0)      Pass divisor.
         JSR     DIVIDEL         Do the division.
         MOVE.L  QUOT(A0),PDIVQ  Save the quotient.
         MOVE.L  REM(A0),PMODQ   Save the remainder.
         ...
P        DS.L    1               Storage for P, Q, PDIVQ, PMODQ
Q        DS.L    1                 (all longword variables).
PDIVQ    DS.L    1
PMODQ    DS.L    1
         ...
PARMS    DS.L    5               Storage for parameter area.
```

in-line parameter area

One special form of parameter area is called an *in-line parameter area*. Here the parameters are stored in the calling program immediately following the subroutine calling instruction (JSR). The "return address" stored by JSR is really the address of the first parameter. Before returning, the subroutine must bump this return address value past the parameter area; presumably, the subroutine knows exactly how many memory bytes to skip over. In-line parameter areas should only be used if the actual parameters for any given subroutine call are always constant, as in an output subroutine that prints a fixed message. If the actual parameters are variables, then the in-line parameter area must be modified each time that the subroutine is called, impossible in ROM and undesirable even in RAM because most memory management systems enforce write protection on program areas.

9.3.5   Static and Dynamic Allocation

static allocation

dynamic allocation

Storage allocation methods for subroutine parameters can be classified as static and dynamic. With *static allocation*, memory locations are reserved for the parameters of a particular subroutine or caller, and are unused at other times. Both versions of the DIVIDEL subroutine above use static allocation. With *dynamic allocation*, parameters are stored in the designated area during subroutine execution, but the storage is available for other uses the rest of the time. Passing parameters in registers as in Table 5–12 is the simplest form of dynamic allocation.

9.3.6   Stack-Oriented Parameter-Passing Conventions

stack-frame pointer (FP)

stack frame

Placing parameters in a pushdown stack is a form of dynamic allocation used both by assembly language programmers and by compilers for block-structured high-level languages such as Pascal and C. Parameters can generally use the same pushdown stack as return addresses, since most processors have instructions to push, pop, and access arbitrary data in the return-address stack.

Figure 9–4 shows a typical use of a return-address stack for passing parameters. The calling program reserves space on the stack for any output parameters and then pushes input parameters onto the stack. After the subroutine is called, the stack has the state shown in Figure 9–4(a). An address register is now used as a *stack-frame pointer (FP)*. The subroutine saves the old value of FP by pushing it onto the stack and then copies the value of SP into FP. The frame pointer provides a fixed reference for accessing parameters that does not change with SP as more items are pushed onto the stack. The region of the stack accessed during a subroutine's execution is called a *stack frame*.

As shown in Figure 9–4(b), local variables can also be pushed onto the stack during a subroutine's execution and accessed by offsets from FP. If a second (nested) subroutine is called, parameters are again pushed onto the stack and a new stack frame is created, as shown in Figure 9–4(c,d). As each subroutine returns, it "cleans up" the stack by:

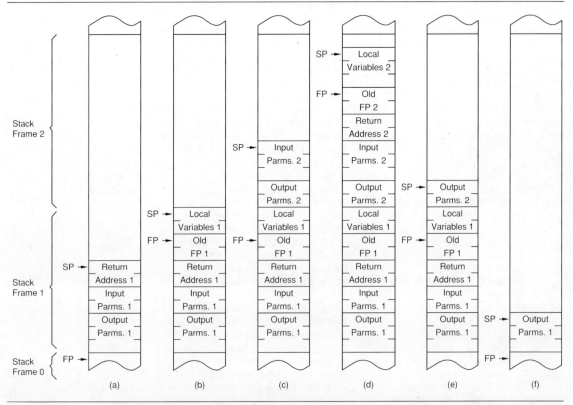

FIGURE 9–4   A pushdown stack with return address, parameters, and local variables: (a) just after calling SUBR1; (b) during execution of SUBR1; (c) just before a call to SUBR2; (d) during execution of SUBR2; (e) just after return from SUBR2; (f) just after return from SUBR1.

(1) Removing its local data by setting SP equal to FP.

(2) Restoring the old value of FP by popping it from the stack.

(3) Removing the input parameters from the stack and jumping to the return address, leaving only the output parameters on the stack.

The stack-oriented subroutine calling convention is illustrated by the version of the DIVIDEL subroutine shown in Table 9–16. Register A6 is used as the frame pointer, and the LINK and UNLK are used to establish and remove the frame-pointer linkage. A program that calls DIVIDEL is shown in Table 9–17. The state of the stack before the DIVIDEL subroutine is called is shown in Figure 9–5(a). The calling program reserves 10 bytes on the stack for REM, QUOT, and STATUS, and then pushes LODVND, HIDVND, and DVSR onto the stack [Figure 9–5(b)]. It calls DIVIDEL, which then pushes the old value of the frame pointer and CNT onto the stack as shown in Figure 9–5(c). Upon

TABLE 9–16   `DIVIDEL` subroutine that passes parameters on a stack.

```
*           The offsets below define positions of parameters and local
*           variables in the stack relative to a frame pointer (reg. A6).
CNT     EQU     -2          Local variable.
OLDFP   EQU     0           Old value of frame pointer.
RETADDR EQU     4           Return address.
DVSR    EQU     8           Longword divisor (input).
HIDVND  EQU     12          High-order longword dividend (input).
LODVND  EQU     16          High-order longword dividend (input).
REM     EQU     20          Longword remainder (result).
QUOT    EQU     24          Longword quotient (result).
STATUS  EQU     28          Word, 0 ==> OK, else overflow (result).
*
DIVIDEL LINK    A6,#-2      Save FP, allocate local var, and make new FP.
        MOVE.W  #32,CNT(A6) Store initial CNT.
        CLR.W   STATUS(A6)  Mark initial status OK.
        MOVE.L  HIDVND(A6),D0 Keep high dividend and
        MOVE.L  LODVND(A6),D1   low dividend in registers.
        CMP.L   DVSR(A6),D0 Will quotient fit in longword?
        BCS.S   DIVLUP      Branch if it will.
        MOVE.W  #1,STATUS(A6) Else report error.
        BRA.S   CLNSTK
DIVLUP  LSL.L   #1,D1       Left shift dividend with LSB := 0.
        ROXL.L  #1,D0       A carry here from MSB means
        BCS.S   QUOT1           dividend surely > DVSR.
        CMP.L   DVSR(A6),D0 Else compare high dividend with DVSR.
        BCS.S   QUOTOK      Quotient bit = 0 if lower.
QUOT1   ADD.L   #1,D1       Else set quotient bit to 1.
        SUB.L   DVSR(A6),D0 And update high dividend.
QUOTOK  SUB.W   #1,CNT(A6)  Decrement iteration count.
        BGT.S   DIVLUP      Continue until done.
        MOVE.L  D0,REM(A6)  Store remainder.
        MOVE.L  D1,QUOT(A6) Store quotient.
CLNSTK  UNLK    A6          Remove local variable and restore FP.
        MOVEA.L (SP)+,A0    Save return address in A0.
        ADDA.L  #REM-DVSR,SP Remove input parameters.
        JMP     (A0)        Return to caller.
```

Mac Note

Pascal programs in the Macintosh environment use the subroutine calling convention described in this subsection. The caller pushes parameters onto the stack in the same left-to-right order that they appear in the procedure or function definition.

Most of the Macintosh's low-level assembly language subroutines, such as the utilities in the Macintosh Toolbox, also use this convention. However, creating the A6 linkage using `LINK` and `UNLK` instructions is optional for these routines. If you study the calling convention closely, you'll see that it makes no difference to the caller whether the called subroutine maintains the A6 linkage. Linked stack frames are required only for nested Pascal procedures and functions, where inner procedures may have to follow the linkage in order to access variables declared in outer procedures.

TABLE 9–17   Program that calls stack-oriented `DIVIDEL`.

```
*        Compute PDIVQ := P DIV Q; PMODQ := P MOD Q;
*        where all are longword variables in memory.
DIVPQ    ADD.L    #-10,SP        Reserve space for output parameters.
         MOVE.L   P,-(SP)        Push low-order dividend.
         CLR.L    -(SP)          Push high-order dividend = 0.
         MOVE.L   Q,-(SP)        Push divisor.
         JSR      DIVIDEL        Do the division.
         MOVE.L   (SP)+,PMODQ    Pop remainder and store.
         MOVE.L   (SP)+,PDIVQ    Pop quotient and store.
         TST.W    (SP)+          Test status.
         BNE      DIVOVF         Branch on overflow.
         ...
P        DS.L     1             Storage for P, Q, PDIVQ, PMODQ
Q        DS.L     1                (all longword variables).
PDIVQ    DS.L     1
PMODQ    DS.L     1
```

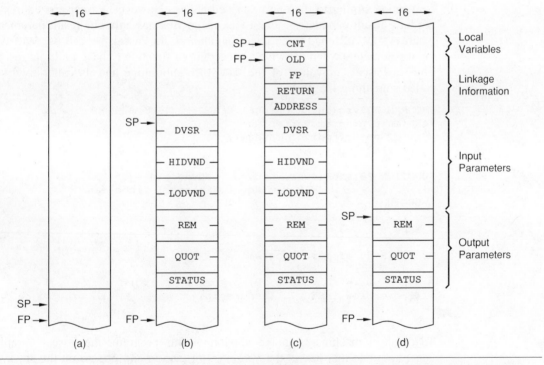

FIGURE 9–5   Stack contents during `DIVPQ` program: (a) at start; (b) just before calling `DIVIDEL`; (c) after first three instructions of `DIVIDEL`; (d) just after returning from `DIVIDEL`.

return, the stack is cleaned up, leaving only the output parameters REM, QUOT, and STATUS as shown in Figure 9–5(d).

The DIVIDEL subroutines in Table 9–14 and Table 9–16 both access parameters in a "parameter area," using based addressing with offsets from an address register. The major difference is that the parameter area for Table 9–14 is allocated statically when the program is assembled, while the parameter area for Table 9–16 is created dynamically on the stack each time that the subroutine is called. With static parameter areas, we need one for each subroutine; with a stack, we need only enough storage for the maximum number of parameters that are "active" when subroutines are nested. In a program with many subroutines, the stack convention could yield significant memory savings.

You may have noticed that the use of A6 as a frame pointer in this example is somewhat superfluous since SP doesn't change throughout the subroutine's execution; we could have used SP instead of A6 by adding 2 to all of the offsets. However, in more general subroutines, intermediate results of expression evaluations and other computations might be temporarily pushed onto and popped from the stack, so that parameter offsets from SP would be continually changing. In such a case, a fixed frame pointer (A6) is much easier to use than SP.

Procedures and functions in Pascal pass parameters using a stack-oriented convention similar to the one described above. However, Pascal procedures do not have result parameters, and a Pascal function has only one result parameter, whereas DIVIDEL had three result parameters. In Pascal, we can use VAR-type input parameters when we wish a procedure or function to have multiple results. Thus, a Pascal equivalent of the DIVIDEL subroutine and its caller might be coded something like this:

```
PROGRAM PDivpq(input,output);
VAR {Main program variables}
  p, q, pmodq, pdivq: integer;
  overflow: boolean;
...
FUNCTION PDivide(dvsr, hidvnd, lodvnd: integer;
                VAR rem, quot: integer) : boolean;
  BEGIN
    ... {Body of PDivide}
  END;
...
BEGIN {Body of main program}
  ...
  overflow := PDivide(q, 0, p, pmodq, pdivq)
  IF overflow THEN ... {handle it}
  ...
END.
```

To create a machine language version of this program, the Pascal compiler generates code that passes the *addresses* of pmodq and pdivq on the stack.

A corresponding assembly language version of the Pascal PDivide function is shown in Table 9–18 and its caller is shown in Table 9–19. The states of the stack during the execution of the function and its caller are shown in

TABLE 9–18   PDIVIDE subroutine that passes VAR parameters on a stack.

```
*          The offsets below define positions of parameters and local
*          variables in the stack relative to a frame pointer (reg. A6).
CNT       EQU      -2           Local variable.
OLDFP     EQU       0           Old value of frame pointer.
RETADDR   EQU       4           Return address.
DVSR      EQU       8           Longword divisor (input).
HIDVND    EQU      12           High-order longword dividend (input).
LODVND    EQU      16           High-order longword dividend (input).
AREM      EQU      20           Longword remainder (VAR input).
AQUOT     EQU      24           Longword quotient (VAR input).
STATUS    EQU      28           Word, 0 ==> OK, else overflow (result).
*
PDIVIDE   LINK     A6,#-2               Save FP, allocate local var, and make new FP.
          MOVE.W   #32,CNT(A6)          Store initial CNT.
          CLR.W    STATUS(A6)           Mark initial status OK.
          MOVE.L   HIDVND(A6),D0        Keep high dividend and
          MOVE.L   LODVND(A6),D1          low dividend in registers.
          CMP.L    DVSR(A6),D0          Will quotient fit in longword?
          BCS.S    DIVLUP               Branch if it will.
          MOVE.W   #1,STATUS(A6)        Else report error.
          BRA.S    CLNSTK
DIVLUP    LSL.L    #1,D1                Left shift dividend with LSB := 0.
          ROXL.L   #1,D0                A carry here from MSB means
          BCS.S    QUOT1                  dividend surely > DVSR.
          CMP.L    DVSR(A6),D0          Else compare high dividend with DVSR.
          BCS.S    QUOTOK               Quotient bit = 0 if lower.
QUOT1     ADD.L    #1,D1                Else set quotient bit to 1.
          SUB.L    DVSR(A6),D0          And update high dividend.
QUOTOK    SUB.W    #1,CNT(A6)           Decrement iteration count.
          BGT.S    DIVLUP               Continue until done.
          MOVE.L   AREM(A6),A0          Get address of remainder.
          MOVE.L   D0,(A0)              Store remainder.
          MOVE.L   AQUOT(A6),A0         Get address of quotient.
          MOVE.L   D1,(A1)              Store quotient.
CLNSTK    UNLK     A6                   Remove local variable and restore FP.
          MOVEA.L  (SP)+,A0             Save return address in A0.
          ADDA.L   #STATUS-DVSR,SP      Remove input parameters.
          JMP      (A0)                 Return to caller.
```

Figure 9–6. Coincidentally, the VAR parameters AREM and AQUOT, which contain the addresses of PMODQ and PDIVQ, happen to be the same size and occupy the same position on the stack as REM and QUOT in the previous version of this program. However, note that AREM and AQUOT are used quite differently, and as input parameters they are discarded when PDIVIDE finishes, as shown in Figure 9–6(d).

As in our assembly language examples, a Pascal procedure's local variables are stored on the stack along with parameters. This explains why the values of local variables are not preserved between successive invocations of the same

TABLE 9–19   Program that calls stack-oriented PDIVIDE with VAR parameters.

```
*         Compute PDIVQ := P DIV Q; PMODQ := P MOD Q;
*         where all are longword variables in memory.
PDIVPQ   ADD.L    #-2,SP        Reserve space for output parameter.
         PEA.L    PDIVQ         Push address of quotient.
         PEA.L    PMODQ         Push address of remainder.
         MOVE.L   P,-(SP)       Push low-order dividend.
         CLR.L    -(SP)         Push high-order dividend = 0.
         MOVE.L   Q,-(SP)       Push divisor.
         JSR      PDIVIDE       Do the division.
         TST.W    (SP)+         Test status.
         BNE      DIVOVF        Branch on overflow.
         ...
P        DS.L     1            Storage for P, Q, PDIVQ, PMODQ
Q        DS.L     1               (all longword variables).
PDIVQ    DS.L     1
PMODQ    DS.L     1
```

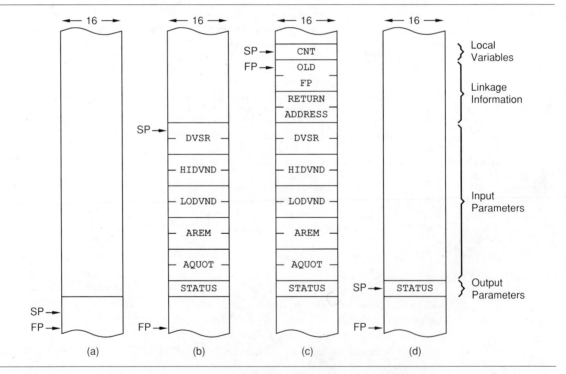

FIGURE 9–6   Stack contents during PDIVPQ program: (a) at start; (b) just before calling PDIVIDE; (c) during PDIVIDE; (d) just after returning from PDIVIDE.

procedure—the stack pointer may start at a different position on each invocation, so that the local variables as well as parameters could actually be stored in different memory locations on different invocations. For this reason, the frame pointer is especially important in the Pascal run-time environment. The linked list formed by the frame pointers of nested subroutines provides a means for inner procedures to access the parameters and local variables of outer procedures.

Stack-oriented parameter-passing conventions are so important in high-level languages that recent microprocessor architectures have provided new instructions and addressing modes to deal with them efficiently. The 68000's LINK and UNLK and the 68010 and 68020's RTD are instructions for allocating and de-allocating parameters on the stack. And the 68020 has a new family of "memory indirect" addressing modes that allow instructions to access VAR-type parameters whose addresses are on the stack, without having to copy those addresses into address registers as we did in the PDIVIDE subroutine in Table 9–18.

9.3.7 Another Example: Queue Manipulation Subroutines

To conclude this section, we give a set of 68000 subroutines that manipulate queues, including "prologues" that explain how the subroutines work. The subroutines operate on queues of words in a 68000 system with full 24-bit or 32-bit addresses. They may be easily modified for queues of bytes or longwords, and the queue descriptor table format and the subroutines may be optimized for 68000 systems with short (16-bit) addresses. A program that uses these subroutines is presented in Section 12.5. In keeping with the philosophy that programs should be self-documenting, we leave you to read Table 9–20. Also see Section 13.3 for a discussion of the documentation conventions used here.

9.4 RECURSION

9.4.1 Recursive Procedures and Functions

recursive   A procedure or function that calls itself is said to be *recursive*. The Pascal factorial function from Table 9–7 is redefined below as a recursive function:

```
FUNCTION Fact (i : integer) : real;
  BEGIN
    IF i <= 1 THEN Fact := 1 ELSE Fact := i * Fact(i-1);
  END;
```

basis part   Essential to this definition is a *basis part* that defines Fact(i) to be 1 for any i <= 1. For larger i, Fact(i) is defined to be the product of i and Fact(i-1). For example, in order to compute Fact(5), we must first compute Fact(4), which depends on Fact(3), which depends on Fact(2), which depends on Fact(1). The basis part ensures that we eventually reach a value of i for which Fact(i) does not depend on Fact(i-1), so that we can eventually terminate the recursive calls of Fact.

TABLE 9–20   Queue manipulation subroutines for the 68000.

```
*
* QUEUE MODULE
*
* This module contains three subroutines for manipulating queues
* of 16-bit words. A queue is defined by a queue descriptor table
* and a block of storage, as shown below.
*
*                                      QUEUE STORAGE BLOCK
*         --------------------         -------------
* QDTBL | QHEAD (longword) |   -------->| (word)    |
*       |------------------|   |        |-----------|
*       | QTAIL (longword) |   |        |           |
*       |------------------|   |        |   o o o   |
*       | QSTRT (longword) |----        |           |
*       |------------------|            |-----------|
*       | QEND  (longword) |----------->| (word)    |
*         --------------------          -------------
*
* Offsets in descriptor table:
*
QHEAD     EQU     0
QTAIL     EQU     4
QSTRT     EQU     8
QEND      EQU     12
*
* In this table, QSTRT and QEND are longword constants, initialized
* at load time, that give the starting and ending addresses of the
* memory buffer reserved for the queue itself.  QHEAD and QTAIL are
* are longwords reserved to store the queue head and tail (absolute
* memory addresses), and are manipulated by the subroutines.
*
* If a program defines several queues, it allocates a separate queue
* descriptor table and storage block for each one.  For example, the
* statements below define a 5-word queue Q1 and a 100-word queue Q2:
*
*Q1SIZE EQU     5               Size of Q1 (5 words).
*Q1BLK  DS.W    Q1SIZE-1        Storage block for Q1.
*Q1END  DS.W    1               Last location in Q1 storage block.
*Q1DT   DS.L    2               Q1 descriptor table -- QHEAD and QTAIL.
*       DC.L    Q1BLK,Q1END                          QSTRT and QEND.
*
*Q2SIZE EQU     100             Size of Q2 (100 words).
*Q2BLK  DS.W    Q2SIZE-1        Storage block for Q2.
*Q2END  DS.W    1               Last location in Q2 storage block.
*Q2DT   DS.L    2               Q2 descriptor table -- QHEAD and QTAIL.
*       DC.L    Q2BLK,Q2END                          QSTRT and QEND.
*
* Subroutines are provided to initialize a queue (QINIT), enqueue
* a word (QENQ), and dequeue a word (QDEQ).  Each subroutine must
* be passed the address of the descriptor table for the queue
* to be manipulated.
*
```

TABLE 9–20   (continued)

```
* SUBROUTINE QINIT -- Initialize a queue to be empty.
*
* INPUTS
*    #QDTBL -- The address of the queue descriptor table for the
*              queue to be initialized, passed in register A0.
* OUTPUTS, GLOBAL DATA, LOCAL DATA -- None
* FUNCTIONS
*    (1) Initialize the queue to empty by setting QHEAD and QTAIL
*        in QDTBL equal to the first address in the queue buffer.
* REGISTERS AFFECTED -- CCR
*
* TYPICAL CALLING SEQUENCE
*        LEA.L    Q1DT,A0
*        JSR      QINIT
*
QINIT    MOVE.L   QSTRT(A0),-(SP)  Put buffer starting address
         MOVE.L   (SP),QHEAD(A0)   into QHEAD and QTAIL.
         MOVE.L   (SP)+,QTAIL(A0)
         RTS                       Done, return.
*
* SUBROUTINE QENQ -- Enqueue one word into a queue.
*
* INPUTS
*    #QDTBL -- The address of the queue descriptor table for the
*              queue to be manipulated, passed in register A0.
*    QDATA  -- The word to be enqueued, passed in register D0.
* OUTPUTS
*    QFULL  -- 1 if the queue is full, else 0; passed in condition bit Z.
* GLOBAL DATA, LOCAL DATA -- None
* FUNCTIONS
*    (1) If the queue described by QDTBL is full, set QFULL to 1.
*    (2) If the queue is not full, enqueue QDATA and set QFULL to 0.
* REGISTERS AFFECTED -- CCR
*
* TYPICAL CALLING SEQUENCE
*        LEA.L    Q1DT,A0          Enqueue AWORD.
*        MOVE.W   AWORD,D0
*        JSR      QENQ
*        BEQ      OVFL             Branch if queue is full.
*
QENQ     MOVE.L   A1,-(SP)         Save A1.
         MOVEA.L  QTAIL(A0),A1     Get queue tail.
         MOVE.W   D0,(A1)+         Store QDATA at tail (no harm if full).
         CMPA.L   QEND(A0),A1      A1 points to next free location.
         BLS.S    QENQ1            Wrap-around?
         MOVEA.L  QSTRT(A0),A1     Reinitialize on wrap-around.
QENQ1    CMPA.L   QHEAD(A0),A1     Queue already full?
         BEQ.S    QENQ2            Return with Z = 1 if full.
         MOVE.L   A1,QTAIL(A0)     Else update tail.
         AND.B    #$FB,SR          Set Z := 0 since not full.
QENQ2    MOVEA.L  (SP)+,A1         Restore A1 (CCR not affected).
         RTS                       Return.
```

TABLE 9–20 (continued)

```
* SUBROUTINE QDEQ -- Dequeue one word from a queue.
*
* INPUTS
*    #QDTBL -- The address of the queue descriptor table for the
*              queue to be manipulated, passed in register A0.
* OUTPUTS
*    QEMPTY -- 1 if the queue is empty, else 0; passed in condition bit Z.
*    QDATA  -- The word dequeued, passed in register D0.
* GLOBAL DATA, LOCAL DATA -- None.
* FUNCTIONS
*    (1) If the queue described by QDTBL is empty, set QEMPTY to 1.
*    (2) If the queue isn't empty, dequeue QDATA and set QEMPTY to 0.
* REGISTERS AFFECTED -- D0, CCR
*
* TYPICAL CALLING SEQUENCE
*         LEA.L    Q1DT,A0          Dequeue a word into AWORD.
*         JSR      QDEQ
*         BEQ      UNDFL            Branch if queue is empty.
*         MOVE.W   D0,AWORD
*
QDEQ      MOVE.L   A1,-(SP)         Save A1.
          MOVEA.L  QHEAD(A0),A1     Get copy of head.
          CMPA.L   QTAIL(A0),A1     Queue empty?
          BEQ.S    QDEQ2            Return with Z = 1 if empty.
          MOVE.W   (A1)+,D0         Read QDATA word from queue.
          CMPA.L   QEND(A0),A1      A1 points to next queue item.
          BLS.S    QDEQ1            Wrap-around?
          MOVEA.L  QSTRT(A0),A1     Reinitialize head on wrap-around.
QDEQ1     MOVE.L   A1,QHEAD(A0)     Update real head in memory.
          AND.B    #$FB,SR          Set Z := 0 since not empty.
QDEQ2     MOVEA.L  (SP)+,A1         Restore A1 (CCR not affected).
          RTS                       Return.
```

simple recursion

indirect recursion

forward

The preceding example illustrates *simple recursion*, using a procedure that calls itself directly. It is also possible for a procedure to call one or more intermediate procedures that eventually call it. This is called *indirect recursion* and is illustrated in Table 9–21. Pascal syntax rules require a procedure to be defined before it is called, and each procedure in this example calls the other. Therefore, a special forward declaration is used to alert the compiler that the block defining ProcB is coming later. ProcB's parameter list is included in the forward declaration so that subsequent references to ProcB can be checked and compiled. Later, the body of ProcB is defined in the normal way, except that the parameter list is not repeated.

Block-structured languages such as Pascal and C allow all procedures and functions to be called recursively. Unstructured languages like Fortran usually do not permit recursion.

Our recursive definition of the factorial function may seem clever, but

Mac Note

The queue manipulation subroutines in Table 9–20 are not directly adaptable to the Macintosh environment in one respect—the queue descriptor tables contain both constants and variables in the same structure. Normally, Macintosh programs place constants in the code segment and variables in the data segment.

In MPW assembly language, we can put constants in the data segment as follows:

```
            DATA              Declare Q1 in data segment.
Q1SIZE  EQU    5              Size of Q1 (5 words).
Q1BLK   DS.W   Q1SIZE-1       Storage block for Q1.
Q1END   DS.W   1              Last location in Q1 storage block.
Q1DT    DS.L   2              Q1 descriptor table -- QHEAD and QTAIL.
        DC.L   Q1BLK,Q1END                         QSTRT and QEND.
        CODE              Continue instructions.
```

However, the assembler treats this as a special case, and the loader does not actually initialize constants in the data segment at load time, as it would constants in the code segment. Instead, the first executable instruction of the user's program must be a call (JSR) to the library routine _DataInit, which initializes the appropriate locations in the application global space using constants passed to it in its own separate code module.

The MDS assembler does not provide this facility, and so the programmer must write explicit code to initialize each queue descriptor table at run time. For example, the following declarations and code could be used for Q1:

```
Q1SIZE  EQU    5              Size of Q1 (5 words).
Q1BLK   DS.W   Q1SIZE-1       Storage block for Q1.
Q1END   DS.W   1              Last location in Q1 storage block.
Q1DT    DS.L   4              Q1 descriptor table.
        ...
Q1INIT  LEA.L  Q1DT(A5),A0    Address of Q1 descriptor table.
        LEA.L  Q1BLK(A5),A1   Starting address of Q1 storage block.
        MOVE.L A1,QHEAD(A0)   Put into QHEAD,
        MOVE.L A1,QTAIL(A0)     QTAIL,
        MOVE.L A1,QSTRT(A0)    and QSTRT.
        LEA.L  Q1END(A5),A1   Ending address of Q1 storage block.
        MOVE.L A1,QEND(A0)    Put into QEND.
        RTS              Done, return.
```

TABLE 9–21   A pair of procedures that use indirect recursion.

```
PROCEDURE ProcB(z : integer); forward;

PROCEDURE ProcA(x, y : integer);
  BEGIN
   ...
    ProcB(a); {Call ProcB}
   ...
  END;

PROCEDURE ProcB(z : integer);
  BEGIN
   ...
    ProcA(b,c); {Call ProcA}
   ...
  END;
```

the iterative solution in Table 9–7 may be more efficient. In general, problems that have easily-stated iterative solutions are best solved iteratively. Recursion should be reserved for problems that are most clearly stated recursively or that have no obvious iterative solution. An example of such a problem is given in the next subsection.

9.4.2 Recursive Subroutines

Recursion can be utilized in assembly language subroutines, but it places constraints on the subroutine-calling and parameter-passing conventions that may be used. Return addresses, parameters, and local variables may *not* be stored in dedicated, static locations, because they would be wiped out the first time that the subroutine recursively called itself. Instead, a new area for the return address, parameters, and local variables must be allocated on each recursive call, and deallocated on each return. Hence, a pushdown stack is the appropriate data structure for storing these items.

A subroutine that stores its return address and all parameters and local variables using a stack convention such as the one in Section 9.3.6 can be called recursively without error. This explains why Pascal procedures can call each other recursively and Fortran subprograms cannot; Fortran normally uses static memory allocation for parameters.

A pair of recursive subroutines can be used to analyze the game of NIM, a two-person game that begins with a heap of sticks. The players alternately remove sticks from the heap; the player who removes the last stick loses. The game is fully characterized by two parameters: NHEAP is the number of sticks initially in the heap, and NTAKE is the maximum number of sticks a player may take on each turn, the minimum being 1.

We would like to write a program that determines, given NHEAP and NTAKE, whether or not an intelligent first player (P1) can always win by making optimal moves. In order to formulate a recursive algorithm to make this determination, we first define a *winning position* for P1:

winning position

(1) If it is P1's turn and there are no sticks left, then the second player (P2) has just taken the last stick. This is a winning position for P1.

(2) If it is P1's turn and there is at least one winner among the new positions obtained by taking 1 to minimum(NTAKE, STICKSLEFT) sticks, then P1 can take the appropriate number of sticks and eventually win. This is a winning position for P1.

(3) If it is P2's turn and there are no sticks left, then P1 has just taken the last stick. This is *not* a winning position for P1.

(4) If it is P2's turn and at least one of the new positions obtained by taking 1 to minimum(NTAKE, STICKSLEFT) sticks is not a winner, P2 can take the appropriate number of sticks to prevent P1 from winning. This is *not* a winning position for P1.

Steps 1 and 3 above form the basis parts of two recursive subroutines, P1TURN and P2TURN, that call each other. Subroutine P1TURN determines, given NTAKE and STICKSLEFT, whether or not the current position is a winning position for P1, assuming it is P1's turn to move. Subroutine P2TURN does the same thing, assuming it is P2's turn. The subroutines are coded in 68000 assembly language in Table 9–22. Input and output parameters are passed in registers, and local variables are saved in the stack at the beginning of each subroutine and restored on exit. A program can initialize NTAKE to any desired value and call P1TURN with the initial heap size in register D1 to determine whether the game is a guaranteed win for an intelligent first player, as in the example below.

```
        MOVE.W   #5,NTAKE      Take 5 sticks maximum at a time.
        MOVE.W   #30,D1        Can P1 win starting with 30 sticks?
        JSR      P1TURN
        BEQ      IWIN
ILOSE   ...
IWIN    ...
```

Recursive programs often perform a tremendous amount of useful computation with relatively little memory. For example, the NIM subroutines are short, they have only one global variable (NTAKE), and they never have more than about 4·NHEAP words on the stack. Yet called with NHEAP = 30 and NTAKE = 5, the two subroutines are executed a total of 1,687,501 times. Try to figure out whether P1 won or lost that game yourself!

9.5 COROUTINES

9.5.1 General Structure

coroutine

So far, we have discussed subroutines only in the context of a master/slave relationship—a calling program (master) calls the subroutine (slave), which executes from beginning to end and returns to the calling program. In Pascal, subroutines (procedures and functions) are so subservient that they aren't even allowed to remember their own local data between successive calls. *Coroutines* replace this master/slave structure with a set of cooperating program modules with no identifiable master. Consider the following problem statement by R.W. Floyd:[1]

Read lines of text, until a completely blank line is found. Eliminate redundant blanks between the words. Print the text, thirty characters to a line, without breaking words between lines.

[1]"The Paradigms of Programming," *Comm. ACM* (August 1979, Vol. 22, No. 8, pp. 455–460).

TABLE 9–22   Recursive subroutines to analyze the game of NIM.

```
* Subroutine P1TURN determines if the current position
* is a winner for P1, given NTAKE (global variable) and
* STICKSLEFT (passed in register D1), assuming that it's
* P1's turn to move.  P1TURN saves registers D1 and D2 on
* entry and restores them on exit.  The result is returned
* in condition bit Z: 1 if a winning position, 0 otherwise.
*
P1TURN  MOVEM.W D1-D2,-(SP)      Save registers D1 and D2 on stack.
        TST.W   D1              Any sticks left?
        BEQ.S   WIN             Return with Z = 1 if none (P2 must have just
*                                   taken the last stick and so P1 just won).
        MOVE.W  NTAKE,D2        D2 := maximum # of sticks to take.
        BRA.S   P1L2            Jump into loop.
P1LOOP  JSR     P2TURN          Winning position for P1 after P2's move?
        BEQ.S   WIN             Yes, so mark this position a winner.
        SUB.W   #1,D2           Otherwise, try taking another stick.
        BEQ.S   LOSE            P1 loses if we've tried up to NTAKE sticks.
P1L2    SUB.W   #1,D1           Also loses if there are no more sticks.
        BGE.S   P1LOOP
*
LOSE    MOVEM.W (SP)+,D1-D2      Restore D1 and D2 from stack.
        AND.B   #$FB,CCR        Return with Z = 0 (not a winner for P1).
        RTS
WIN     MOVEM.W (SP)+,D1-D2      Restore D1 and D2 from stack.
        OR.B    #$04,CCR        Return with Z = 1 (a winner for P1).
        RTS
*
*
* Subroutine P2TURN determines if the current position
* is a winner for P1, given NTAKE (global variable) and
* STICKSLEFT (passed in register D1), assuming that it's
* P2's turn to move.  P2TURN saves registers D1 and D2 on
* entry and restores them on exit.  The result is returned
* in condition bit Z: 1 if a winning position, 0 otherwise.
* Exit code is shared with P1TURN.
*
P2TURN  MOVEM.W D1-D2,-(SP)      Save registers D1 and D2 on stack.
        TST.W   D1              Any sticks left?
        BEQ.S   LOSE            Return with Z = 0 if none (P1 must have
*                                   just taken the last stick and lost).
        MOVE.W  NTAKE,D2        D2 := maximum # of sticks to take.
        BRA.S   P2L2            Jump into loop.
P2LOOP  JSR     P1TURN          Does P1 have a losing position?
        BNE.S   LOSE            Found one, mark this a loser.
        SUB.W   #1,D2           Otherwise, try taking another stick.
        BEQ.S   WIN             P1 wins if we've tried up to NTAKE sticks.
P2L2    SUB.W   #1,D1           Also P1 wins if there are no more sticks.
        BGE.S   P2LOOP
        BRA.S   WIN
*
NTAKE   DS.W    1               Global var -- max # of sticks to take.
```

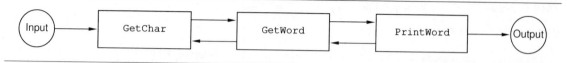

FIGURE 9-7   Three coroutines for text formatting.

According to Floyd, novice programmers take an unreasonably long time to solve this problem using typical programming languages. Even though both input and output are naturally expressed using levels of iteration, the input and output iterations do not mesh, which can make controlling the input and output an "undisciplined mess."

The problem can be solved naturally by decomposing it into three communicating coroutines for reading input characters, assembling them into words, and printing words, as shown in Figure 9–7. The GetChar coroutine reads input characters and detects blank lines. GetWord assembles words and discards spaces, getting individual characters from GetChar and passing complete words to PrintWord. The PrintWord coroutine formats words onto lines according to the line length limit.

9.5.2 Pascal Coroutines

COROUTINE
RESUME

In order to study coroutines in more detail, we shall make a hypothetical extension of the Pascal language. We use a new reserved word COROUTINE to define coroutines in the extended Pascal, and a reserved word RESUME to call a coroutine. When a coroutine is "resumed" for the first time, execution is started at its first statement. Once entered, a coroutine Cor1 may be temporarily suspended by the statement RESUME Cor2, which transfers control to Cor2, another coroutine. Now the statement RESUME Cor1 will leave Cor2 and continue execution of Cor1 at the point just after Cor1 called Cor2, not back at the beginning. Figure 9–8 illustrates this.

Table 9–23 defines the coroutines GetChar, GetWord, and PrintWord

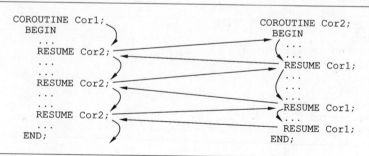

FIGURE 9-8   Two coroutines.

TABLE 9-23   Line-formatting program using coroutines.

```
PROGRAM Format (input,output);
{
   This program reads lines of input text until a completely
   blank line is found. It eliminates extra spaces between words
   and then packs them on output lines with a maximum line
   length of 30 characters, never breaking a word in the middle.
   Words longer than 30 characters are truncated.
}
CONST lineLength = 30;
VAR inChar : char; {Passes characters from GetChar to GetWord.}
    wordBuf : ARRAY [1..lineLength] OF char; {Buffer for accumulating
                  words and passing them from GetWord to PrintWord.}
    wordPnt : integer; {Index of last valid character in wordBuf.}
    blankLine : boolean; {Set true when a blank line is read.}

COROUTINE GetChar;
   BEGIN
     REPEAT {forever}
       blankLine := true;
       read(inChar);          {'read' sets eoln true...}
       WHILE NOT eoln DO      {...at the end of a line.}
         BEGIN
           blankLine := false;
           RESUME GetWord;
           read(inChar);
         END;
       inChar := ' ';  {A space is needed to flush the last word on a line.}
       RESUME GetWord;
     UNTIL false;
   END;

COROUTINE GetWord;
   BEGIN
     REPEAT {forever}
       wordPnt := 0;
       REPEAT {Skip spaces.}
         RESUME GetChar;
         IF blankLine THEN RESUME PrintWord;
       UNTIL inChar <> ' ';
       REPEAT
         IF wordPnt < lineLength THEN
           BEGIN
             wordPnt := wordPnt + 1;
             wordBuf[wordPnt] := inChar;
           END;
         RESUME GetChar;
       UNTIL inChar = ' ';
       RESUME PrintWord; {Got a word, go print it.}
     UNTIL false;
   END;
```

TABLE 9–23   (continued)

```
COROUTINE PrintWord;
  VAR column, i : integer;
  BEGIN
    column := 0;
    RESUME GetWord; {Get first word.}
    WHILE NOT blankLine DO
      BEGIN {Read and print a word.}
        {Will the word fit, including a separating space?}
        IF column = 0 THEN {Do nothing.}
        ELSE IF column + wordPnt + 1 <= lineLength THEN
          BEGIN write(' '); column := column + 1 END
        {Start a new line if word doesn't fit.}
        ELSE BEGIN writeln; column := 0 END;
        FOR i := 1 TO wordPnt DO {Print the current word.}
          BEGIN write(wordBuf[i]); column := column + 1 END;
        RESUME GetWord; {Get next word.}
      END;
    writeln; {Finish last line and return to Main.}
  END;
BEGIN {Main Program}
  Printword;
END.
```

for formatting text.[2] An important difference between coroutines and standard Pascal procedures is that coroutines must preserve the values of their local variables between successive calls. Thus `column` in `PrintWord` remembers the current output column number in order to handle the next word properly.

Each of the coroutines in Table 9–23 has been written independently as if the other coroutines were its subroutines. For example, `GetChar` reads characters and passes them to `GetWord`; it also translates an end-of-line condition into a space character for `GetWord`. Looking from another point of view, `GetWord` calls `GetChar` from two different places to get a character, totally unaware that `GetChar` may actually be resumed in either of two different places.

Coroutines `GetChar` and `GetWord` contain endless loops. However, a `blankLine` flag is passed up from `GetChar` to `PrintWord`, which returns control to the main program when all the lines have been processed.

9.5.3   Assembly Language Coroutines

*resumption
address*

In order to program coroutines in assembly language, we must save a *resumption address* for each coroutine. When `Cor1` resumes `Cor2`, it should save the current value of the program counter in a memory location `RES1` and jump to the address

---

[2]Since standard Pascal doesn't really support coroutines, we ignore a syntax error: these coroutine definitions contain forward references to each other.

TABLE 9–24 Assembly language instructions for linking two coroutines.

```
COR1    MOVE.L  (SP)+,RES2  Save Cor2's resumption addr in RES2.
        MOVE.L  RES1,-(SP)  Get Cor1's resumption address.
        RTS                 Return to it.
*
COR2    MOVE.L  (SP)+,RES1  Save Cor1's resumption addr in RES1.
        MOVE.L  RES2,-(SP)  Get Cor2's resumption address.
        RTS                 Return to it.
*
RES1    DS.L    1           Storage for Cor1's resumption addr.
RES2    DS.L    1           Storage for Cor2's resumption addr.
```

contained in a memory location RES2. Now Cor1 may be resumed by jumping to the address that was saved in RES1.

coroutine linkage

If a coroutine Cor1 in the 68000 calls Cor2 by JSR COR2 and vice versa, then instructions shown in Table 9–24 may be used to link the two coroutines. All that remains is for the values stored in RES1 and RES2 to be initialized when the program is started, to the address of the first executable instruction of each coroutine. Once this linkage is established, Cor1 can call Cor2 by executing JSR COR2 and vice versa.

The line-formatting coroutines in Table 9–24 have been coded for the 68000 in Table 9–25. A macro COLINK is defined at the end of the program to generate coroutine linkages. In general, the coroutine linkage instructions must take into account both the coroutine that is being suspended and the one that is being resumed. For example, GetWord can be resumed from both GetChar and PrintWord and so two different linkages are needed. However, notice that there is still only one resumption address for each coroutine.

9.5.4 Coroutine Applications

filter

Coroutines are most commonly used in programs that read inputs, transform them in some way, and produce outputs, as shown in Figure 9–9(a). Because of the analogy with electronics, such programs are often called *filters*; sometimes filters are cascaded. For example, the following filters might be applied to a text file to find spelling errors:

(1) Remove all punctuation and reformat the text so that each line contains only one word.

(2) Remove all words that consist of only upper-case letters (assuming that they are acronyms or mnemonics).

(3) Translate each upper-case letter into the corresponding lower-case letter.

(4) Look up each word in a dictionary and output all words that are not found.

TABLE 9–25   A 68000 version of the line-formatting program.

```
SPC      EQU      $20              ASCII space.
CR       EQU      $0D              ASCII carriage return.
LINELN   EQU      30               Maximum output line length.
WRDBUF   DS.B     LINELN           Word buffer.
BLANK    DS.B     1                Blank-line flag.
COLUMN   DS.W     1                Output column number.
STACK    DS.W     20               Stack area.
STACKE   EQU      *                Stack initialization address.
GCHRRES  DS.L     1                Resumption address for GetChar.
GWRDRES  DS.L     1                Resumption address for GetWord.
PWRDRES  DS.L     1                Resumption address for PrintWord.
*
COLINK   MACRO                     Coroutine linkages, \1 = FROM, \2 = TO.
         MOVE.L   (SP)+,\1
         MOVE.L   \2,-(SP)
         RTS
         ENDM
GETCHR   COLINK   GWRDRES,GCHRRES
GETWRDG  COLINK   GCHRRES,GWRDRES
GETWRDP  COLINK   PWRDRES,GWRDRES
PRTWRD   COLINK   GWRDRES,PWRDRES
*
*                 COROUTINE GetChar -- returns a character in D0.
GCHRIN   MOVE.B   #0FFH,BLANK      Assume we have a blank line.
GCHR1    JSR      READ             Read a character into D0.
         CMP.B    #CR,D0           Is it the end of line?
         BEQ.S    GCHR5
         CLR.B    BLANK            No, not a blank line.
GCHR2    JSR      GETWRDG          Give the character to GETWRD...
         BRA      GCHR1            ...and do some more.
GCHR5    MOVE.B   #SPC,D0          At end of line, force a space...
         JSR      GETWRDG          ...and give it to GETWRD.
         BRA      GCHRIN           Go read more lines.
*
*                 COROUTINE GetWord -- puts a word in WRDBUF[1..D1].
GWRDIN   CLR.W    D1               Set index before start of WRDBUF.
GWRD1    JSR      GETCHR           Get a character.
         TST.B    BLANK            Hit a blank line?
         BEQ.S    GWRD2            No, continue.
         JSR      PRTWRD           Yes, resume PRTWRD.
GWRD2    CMP.B    #SPC,D0          Skip over spaces.
         BEQ      GWRD1
GWRD3    CMP.W    #LINELN,D1       Is there room left in WRDBUF?
         BGE.S    GWRD4            No, ignore character.
         ADD.W    #1,D1            Yes, put the character in WRDBUF.
         MOVE.B   D0,0(A1,D1)
GWRD4    JSR      GETCHR           Get another character...
         CMP.B    #SPC,D0          ...and continue processing until a
         BNE      GWRD3                 space character is found.
         JSR      PRTWRD           Now we have a word, go print it...
         BRA      GWRDIN           ...and then get some more words.
```

TABLE 9–25   (continued)

```
*            COROUTINE PrintWord -- prints the word in WRDBUF[1..D1].
PWRDIN  CLR.W    COLUMN           Set output column to zero.
PWRD1   JSR      GETWRDP          Get a word.
        TST.B    BLANK            Hit a blank line?
        BNE.S    PWRD9            Yep, exit.
        TST.W    COLUMN           Nope, are we in the middle of a line?
        BEQ.S    PRTBUF           Print word now if we're at column zero.
*                                 Otherwise, will the word fit?
        MOVE.W   D1,D2            Get the word length
        ADD.W    COLUMN,D2        ...plus the number of characters so far.
        CMP.W    #LINELN-1,D2     Will word fit, including a space?
        BGT.S    PWRD5            Start a new line if it won't fit.
        MOVE.B   #SPC,D0          Otherwise output a space.
        JSR      WRITED0
        ADD.W    #1,COLUMN        Update column position...
        BRA.S    PRTBUF           ...and print the word.
PWRD5   JSR      WRITELN          Print CR and LF for a new line.
        CLR.W    COLUMN
PRTBUF  MOVE.W   #1,D2            Print the word in WRDBUF.
PRTB1   CMP.W    D1,D2            Any chars left?
        BGT      PWRD1            No, go process more words.
        MOVE.B   0(A1,D2),D0      Else print the character in D0.
        JSR      WRITED0
        ADD.W    #1,D2            Update character index...
        ADD.W    #1,COLUMN        ...and column position accordingly.
        BRA      PRTB1
PWRD9   JSR      WRITELN          Print CR and LF for a new line.
        RTS                       Return to main program.
*
MAIN    MOVEA.L  #STACKE,SP       Initialize SP.
        LEA.L    WRDBUF-1,A1      Effective base addressive of WRDBUF.
        LEA.L    GWRDIN,GWRDRES   Initialize coroutine linkages.
        LEA.L    GCHRIN,GCHRRES
        JSR      PWRDIN           Print words until blank line found.
        JMP      SYSRET           Return to operating system.
```

A program could be devised to perform these tasks one at a time, producing three temporary files that pass the results of one filter to the next, as shown in Figure 9–9(b). Alternatively, the program could be organized as four coroutines as shown in Figure 9–9(c). In the first case, the individual filters can be executed at different times and therefore can be fit individually into a small memory. In the second case, the coroutine structure avoids the extra file space and processing time associated with reading and writing temporary files, at the possible expense of requiring a larger program memory.

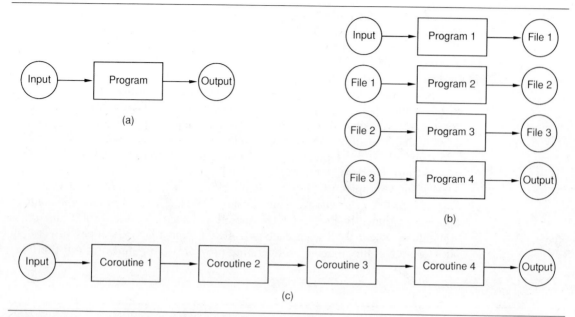

FIGURE 9–9   Filters and coroutines: (a) a simple filter; (b) a cascade of filters using intermediate files; (c) an equivalent coroutine structure.

R E F E R E N C E S

The history of subroutines, coroutines, and related concepts has been traced by Donald E. Knuth in *Fundamental Algorithms* (Addison-Wesley, 1973, 2nd ed., pp. 225–227). Instructions for calling subroutines were included in all of the early digital computers, although it was not until the 1960s that a pushdown stack was used to store return addresses [in the B 5000 (W. Lonergan and P. King, "Design of the B 5000 system," *Datamation*, Vol. 5, No. 7, May 1961, pp. 28–32; also in Bell and Newell's *Computer Structures*, McGraw-Hill, 1971)].

Techniques for passing parameters in high-level languages are thoroughly discussed in *Programming Language Structures* by E. I. Organick, A. I. Forsythe, and R. P. Plummer (Academic Press, 1978). The correspondence between parameter-passing conventions and run-time storage allocation and operations is explained in *Compiler Construction for Digital Computers* by David Gries (Wiley, 1971) and in *Principles of Compiler Design* by A. V. Aho and J. D. Ullman (Addison-Wesley, 1977).

The architecture of the B 5000 supported parameter passing on a stack; Algol and other related high-level languages have popularized the use of the stack. More recently, special instructions have been provided in new computer architectures to facilitate parameter passing on a stack (RET n in the 80x86 and LINK and UNLK in the 68000).

Recursive algorithms are discussed in *Recursive Programming Techniques* by D. W. Barron (American Elsevier, 1968). *Programming Language Structures* also contains an extensive discussion of recursion. A very readable introduction to the general idea of recursion, using examples in Pascal, is *Thinking Recursively* by Eric S. Roberts (Wiley, 1986).

Coroutines and their relationship to multipass algorithms are discussed in *Programming Language Structures* and in *Fundamental Algorithms*. The word "coroutine" was coined by M. E. Conway and appears in his paper, "Design of a Separable Transition-Diagram Compiler" (*Comm. ACM*, Vol. 6, No. 7, July 1963, pp. 396–408). However, Knuth has found the concept mentioned as early as 1954 in a UNIVAC "programming tip."

Many examples of filter programs are given in Kernighan and Plauger's *Software Tools in Pascal* (Addison-Wesley, 1981). The idea of cascading filters appears prominently in the UNIX operating system for the 68000 and other *pipe* computers, where such a cascade is called a *pipe*. UNIX's pipes effectively allow a user to link together cooperating programs (coroutines) at run time.

E X E R C I S E S

9.1   Fix the space-compressing program in Table 9–4 so that strings of one or two spaces are not translated, and strings of more than 26 spaces are translated into two or more "#x" codes.

9.2   What kind of parameters (value or variable) are used by the standard Pascal procedures **read** and **write**?

9.3   Explain what happens during the procedure call **Swap(i,next[i])** if Pascal variable parameters are used and if Fortran value parameters are used.

9.4   List the name, type, and passing convention for each input and output parameter of the subroutines in Chapters 5 through 9 of this book.

9.5   In tabular form, list the advantages and disadvantages of each parameter-passing convention discussed in Section 9.3.

9.6   Suppose that all subroutines in a program share a common parameter area. What problems does this create when subroutines are nested?

9.7   Describe how the number of different subroutines versus the number of different callers affects the choice of static parameter-passing methods (dedicated memory locations for each subroutine versus a parameter area for each caller).

9.8   Modify the DIVIDEL subroutine in Table 9–14 so that it can be stored in a read-only memory. (Hint: CNT.) Modify the calling program to work with the new subroutine.

9.9   Modify the DIVIDEL subroutine in Table 9–16 to use an in-line parameter area. Modify the calling program to work with the new subroutine.

9.10 Write one **LEA** instruction to replace the next-to-last instruction in Table 9–16.

9.11 Rewrite the entry and exit code in Table 9–16 without the 68000's **LINK** and **UNLK** instructions.

9.12 How would you classify the parameters used in the queue manipulation subroutines in Table 9–20?

9.13 Under what conditions could the two **AND.B #$FB,SR** instructions in Table 9–20 be eliminated without affecting the operation of the program?

9.14 Add a subroutine **QROOM** (and prologue) to the queue manipulation subroutines in Table 9–20 whose input parameters are a 16-bit unsigned integer **N** and the address of a queue descriptor table, and whose output is a single bit indicating whether the specified queue has room for **N** more bytes in it.

9.15 Show that it is not necessary to push and pop D1 and D2 in the NIM subroutines in Table 9–22, if D1 and D2 are instead incremented at appropriate places.

9.16 Write a Pascal version of the NIM subroutines in Table 9–22.

9.17 Install the NIM subroutines in Table 9–22 on your favorite 68000-based computer. Also write and run a main program that calls the subroutines for all values of **NTAKE** from 2 to 6 and **NHEAP** from 1 to 30 and prints the results (win or lose) for each possible starting configuration.

9.18 Augment the program in the previous exercise so that it counts and prints the number of times that **P1TURN** and **P2TURN** are called for each starting configuration.

9.19 Study the results of the previous exercise and propose a simple formula that determines whether a starting position is a guaranteed winner for an intelligent first player, given **NTAKE** and **NHEAP**. Try to prove informally that your formula is correct (or use mathematical induction if you are so inclined).

eight queens problem

9.20 The *eight queens problem* is a classic in computer science and mathematics. Its object is to place eight chess queens on an empty 8×8 chessboard so that no queen can capture any of the others. A queen can capture any piece in the same row, column, or diagonal. Therefore any solution must position each queen on a different row, column, and diagonal. There exist 92 different solutions (including symmetrical ones), which can be found by trial and error.

Your assignment is to write a program in Pascal or assembly language to generate all of the solutions to the problem. The main data structure in the program is an 8×8 **boolean** array that represents the chessboard. The heart of the program is a recursive procedure **try(col:integer)** that tries to place 9–col queens in columns **col** through 8 of the chessboard, printing solutions as they are found. It does this by finding all squares in column **col** that are not yet under attack. For each such square, it places a queen on the board and calls **try(col+1)**, unless **col = 8**, in which case it prints out a solution. The main program simply initializes the board array to contain no queens and calls **try(1)**.

9.21   The 1s-counting program in Exercise 7.9 requires a table N1S[0..255] of 256 integers where N1S[i] contains the number of 1s in the 8-bit binary representation of i. The Pascal program below uses a recursive procedure to initialize such an array. Translate this program into assembly language for the 68000.

```
PROGRAM CountOnesInNonnegativeNumbers (input,output);
VAR inNum, tmpNum, cnt : integer; N1S : ARRAY [0..255] OF integer;
PROCEDURE CntInit (weight, index, ones : integer);
  BEGIN
     IF weight = 256 THEN N1S[index] := ones
       ELSE BEGIN CntInit(weight*2,index,ones);
                  CntInit(weight*2,index+weight,ones+1) END;
  END;
BEGIN {Main program}
  CntInit(1,0,0); {Initialize N1S array.}
  read(inNum);
  WHILE inNum >= 0 DO  {Process nonnegative input numbers.}
    BEGIN
      cnt := 0; tmpnum := inNum;
      WHILE tmpNum > 0 DO
        BEGIN cnt := cnt + N1S[tmpNum MOD 256];
              tmpNum := tmpNum DIV 256          END;
      writeln('The number of ones in ',inNum,' is ',cnt);
      read(inNum);
    END;
END.  {All done, bye.}
```

recursive macro   9.22   A *recursive macro* is a macro that invokes itself. In a macro assembler that allows recursion, it is possible to write a recursive macro to initialize the N1S table from the previous exercise at load time. An example of such a macro and its invocation is shown below:

```
CINIT   MACRO   WT,CNT
        IFNE    WT,256
        CINIT   WT*2,CNT
        CINIT   WT*2,CNT+1
        ENDIF
        IFEQ    WT,256
        DS.B    CNT
        ENDIF
        ENDM
*
N1S     CINIT   1,0              Initialize table of 256 bytes.
```

Although the above code creates a table of 256 bytes, it does not have the property that N1S[I] equals the number of ones in the binary representation of I. Explain why, and write a recursive macro that initializes N1S properly.

9.23   Rewrite the program in Table 9–23 in standard Pascal as a main program that does the work of GetWord, and two procedures GetChar and PrintWord. Describe the changes required in the absence of coroutines.

9.24   Starting coroutines from a main program and later terminating them is often tricky. Explain why the main program in Table 9–23 calls PrintWord with a standard Pascal procedure statement instead of using RESUME.

9.25 Explain why the assembly language main program in Table 9–25 calls PWRDIN directly instead of going through the coroutine linkage. Also, why isn't PWRDRES initialized by the main program?

9.26 Another way to initialize the coroutine linkages in Table 9–25 is via statements like GWRDRES DC.L GWRDIN. What's wrong with this approach?

9.27 Insert a Translate coroutine between GetChar and GetWord in Table 9–23 that processes "escape" sequences of the form "!x". The processing for escape sequences depends on the character x:

1-9 Insert 1 to 9 "unpaddable" spaces into output stream. These spaces are treated like normal printing characters.

! Insert the character "!" into the output stream.

< Convert upper-case letters to lower case until further notice.

> Suspend conversion of upper-case letters until further notice.

u Convert the next character to lower case if it is a letter.

If x is not one of the above characters, ignore the "!x" sequence.

9.28 Translate the Translate coroutine above into 68000 assembly language.

9.29 Show how a resumption address stored at the top of the stack can be used to link two coroutines on the 68000. Explain why this technique breaks down when there are three or more coroutines.

9.30 Devise a coroutine linkage structure for the 68000 that allows each coroutine to have an independent stack accessed by SP, such that the resumption address of each suspended coroutine is always at the top of its own stack.

C H A P T E R   1 0

Input/Output

In previous chapters, we've indicated that basic computer organization hasn't changed drastically during the entire history of electronic computers, although technological improvements have definitely made computers faster, cheaper, more powerful, and smaller. Of the three major subsystems of a computer, input/output has experienced the biggest evolution, because of the explosion of computer applications and the hundreds of different devices that are now part of computer systems. Back in the 1950s, few computer architects would have predicted that some day more computers would be used in automobiles than in any other application, and that one of the most common output devices would be a fuel-injected carburetor!

Despite the proliferation of devices, fairly standard techniques are still used to connect typical devices to a computer system. For a programmer who understands the basic principles of input/output interfacing and programming, it is a relatively simple matter to learn the characteristics of any new device and program the computer to "talk to" it. This chapter describes these basic principles. The examples that we furnish in this chapter are somewhat stylized—the characteristics of input/output devices and interfaces for the 68000 and other computers vary widely.

10.1   I/O ORGANIZATION

10.1.1   Buses

In Section 1.3, we showed the basic organization of a computer as consisting of processor, memory, and input/output (I/O). The processor communicated with the I/O subsystem by means of an I/O bus. In Figure 10–1 we expand our view. Like a memory bus, the I/O bus contains data, address, and control lines. The address lines allow a program to select among different I/O devices connected to the system, while the data lines carry the actual data being transferred.

The size of the I/O bus need not match the size of the memory bus. For example, the 8086 memory bus has 20 address lines and 16 data lines, while its

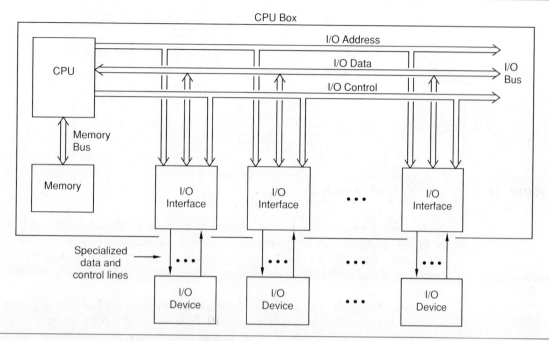

FIGURE 10–1   Input/output (I/O) subsystem.

I/O bus has 16 address lines and either 8 or 16 data lines (system dependent). Even if the I/O bus and the memory bus happen to share some lines (e.g., address), they are still logically independent. Numerically equal addresses on the two buses still refer to different entities, because a control signal from the processor distinguishes between memory and I/O operations. For example, I/O address 5 is totally independent from memory location 5.

10.1.2 Devices and Interfaces

peripheral device
I/O device
I/O interface
device interface

The I/O subsystem in Figure 10–1 contains both devices and interfaces. A *peripheral device* (or *I/O device*) performs some function for the computer. An *I/O interface* (or *device interface*) controls the operation of a peripheral device according to commands from the computer processor; it also converts computer data into whatever format is required by the device and vice versa. Also as shown in the figure, a peripheral device is often housed separately from the processor, while the interface is almost always packaged together with the processor and memory in one "CPU box."

There are many different peripheral devices that convert computer data into forms that are useful in the world outside the computer; such devices include displays, printers, plotters, digital-to-analog converters, mechanical relays, and fuel-injected carburetors. Many other devices convert data from the outside

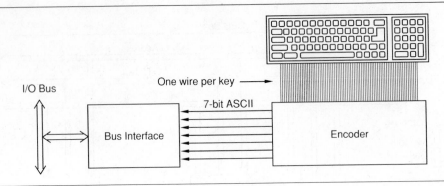

FIGURE 10–2   Keyboard and interface.

world into forms usable by the computer; examples include keyboards, text scanners, joysticks, analog-to-digital converters, mechanical switches, and crash detectors. The sole purpose of some devices is simply to store data for later retrieval; these are called *mass storage devices* and include magnetic disks and tapes.

mass storage device

Sometimes the dividing line between an interface and the device that it controls is fuzzy. For example, Figure 10–2 shows the circuitry associated with a simple mechanical keyboard. The encoder circuit converts a mechanical switch depression into a 7-bit number in the ASCII code. The bus interface can place this number on the I/O bus on demand by the processor. So it seems that the device interface consists of the Encoder and Bus Interface blocks. In a typical system, however, the encoder is packaged with the keyboard; then only a small number of wires are needed between the encoder (in the keyboard package) and the bus interface (in the CPU box). Most computer designers would say that the Encoder block is part of the keyboard, and the device interface consists of the Bus Interface block alone. Fortunately, the dividing line is unimportant to I/O programs that deal with the keyboard. More important is the "I/O programming model" that an I/O program sees, as discussed in the next subsection.

10.1.3 Ports

I/O port
I/O register
I/O programming model

An *I/O port* (or *I/O register*) is a part of a device interface, a group of bits accessed by the processor during I/O operations. The *I/O programming model* of a device describes all of the I/O ports associated with the device. The I/O programming model of the keyboard in Figure 10–2 contains just one 8-bit I/O port named KBDATA, as shown in Figure 10–3. The high-order bit of KBDATA is always 0. The low-order bits of KBDATA contain the output of the Encoder block in Figure 10–2, that is, the 7-bit ASCII code for the key that is currently being depressed, or 0000000 if no key is depressed.

To read data from the keyboard in Figure 10–2, a program must execute an instruction that transfers the contents of KBDATA into one of the processor

```
7  6                    0
0 | Key code (ASCII) |   KBDATA (read-only)
```

FIGURE 10–3   Programming model for a keyboard.

input port

registers. Once the data is in the processor, it can be manipulated like any other data. Although the interface "writes" keyboard data into KBDATA, the port is read-only from the point of view of the processor; any attempt by the processor to write data into KBDATA has no effect. Therefore, we can call KBDATA an *input port*.

output port

Figure 10–4(a) shows a very simple output device that interprets an 8-bit byte as two 4-bit BCD digits and displays the digits on two seven-segment displays. The I/O programming model consists of one 8-bit port DIGOUT, shown in Figure 10–4(b). To display two digits, the processor must transfer an 8-bit value into DIGOUT. In this case, DIGOUT is an *output port* and is write-only from the point of view of the processor; an attempt to read it produces an undefined value.

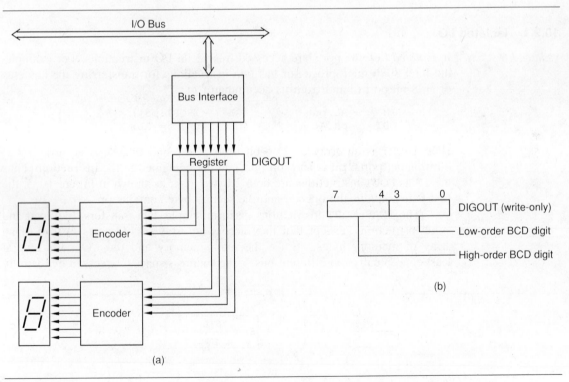

(a)

(b)

FIGURE 10–4   Seven-segment display: (a) device and interface; (b) programming model.

There is an important distinction between the input and output ports described above. In the case of the input port, KBDATA contains the instantaneous value of the encoder output; when a key is depressed or released, KBDATA changes immediately. KBDATA is not really a "register," since it has no memory; it simply "buffers" the output of the encoder onto the I/O data bus. On the other hand, the output port DIGOUT *is* a storage register. After the processor writes a value into DIGOUT, it does not change until the next write operation. The interface hardware is purposely designed this way. Otherwise the processor would have to write the same value continuously into DIGOUT to maintain the display.

The keyboard and display above are very simple examples of I/O interfaces and ports. Later we describe I/O interfaces with more complex ways of controlling I/O devices.

10.2   I/O PROGRAMMING

So far, we haven't said how I/O port data is transferred to and from processor registers. This section discusses two techniques that are used in different processors to perform I/O transfers.

10.2.1   Isolated I/O

isolated I/O   In *isolated I/O*, the ports are accessed by special I/O instructions. For example, the Intel 8086 microprocessor has two instructions for transferring the contents of an 8-bit port to and from its accumulator AL:

$$
\begin{array}{llll}
\text{IN} & \text{AL,pn} & & \text{AL := IPORT[pn];} \\
\text{OUT} & \text{pn,AL} & & \text{OPORT[pn] := AL;}
\end{array}
$$

Here `IPORT` is an array of 2^8 8-bit input ports, and `OPORT` is an array of 2^8 8-bit output ports; `pn` is an 8-bit port number contained in the instruction. Thus the `IN` and `OUT` instructions are both 2 bytes long; as shown in Figure 10–5, the first byte contains the opcode and the second byte contains `pn`.

The `IN` and `OUT` instructions perform simple data transfers, like load and store instructions, except that they access an array of I/O ports instead of an array of memory bytes. Since the main memory and the I/O ports are (at least conceptually) on different buses, the "address spaces" accessed by memory

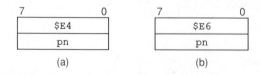

(a)   (b)

FIGURE 10–5   Format of 8086 I/O instructions: (a) IN AL,pn; (b) OUT pn,AL.

TABLE 10–1   Keyboard input and display output for the 8086.

```
*          Read two decimal digits from the keyboard and display them
*          on the seven-segment display. Ignore illegal characters.
*
KBDATA  EQU    5              Keyboard input port number.
DIGOUT  EQU    7              Seven-segment display port number.
*
*          First, a subroutine to read one decimal digit, convert it
*          to 4-bit BCD, and return the result in 8-bit accumulator AL.
RDDIG   IN     AL,KBDATA      Read current character.
        CMP    AL,0           Set condition bits (IN doesn't).
        JE     RDDIG          Loop until a key is pressed (jump if AL = 0).
        MOV    BL,AL          Got character, save in BL.
WAITUP  IN     AL,KBDATA      Keep reading into AL
        CMP    AL,0             and wait for the key to be released.
        JNE    WAITUP         Fall through when key is released (AL = 0).
        SUB    AL,30H         Adjust ASCII '0'-'9' to 0-9.
        JL     RDDIG          Was less than '0' if AL < 0; try again.
        CMP    AL,9           Else check top of range.
        JG     RDDIG          Invalid if AL > 9.
        RET                   Valid digit, return.
*
*          Now, the main program.
DIGDSP  CALL   RDDIG          Read high-order decimal digit into RL0.
        SHL    AL,1           Shift left 4 bits ...
        SHL    AL,1
        SHL    AL,1
        SHL    AL,1
        MOV    CL,AL          ... and save in CL.
        CALL   RDDIG          Read low-order decimal digit.
        OR     AL,CL          Merge with high-order digit.
        OUT    DIGOUT,AL      Send to seven-segment display.
        JMP    DIGDSP         Do another pair of digits.
        END    DIGDSP
```

reference and I/O instructions are different, even though they both may happen to recognize the same numerical addresses.

Like memory banks, I/O ports need not be installed at every address that is available for them. In fact, a typical small computer has far less than 2^{16} or even 2^8 I/O ports; 5 to 50 is a more typical range.

A simple 8086 program using isolated I/O is shown in Table 10–1. When reading this program, keep in mind that 8086 assembly language instructions have the format "OPCODE dst, src," the opposite of the 68000, and that AL, BL, and CL are 8-bit registers. The program reads a pair of decimal digits from the keyboard and displays them on the seven-segment displays until the next pair is typed.

The RDDIG subroutine reads from the keyboard, looking for decimal digits, characters in the range '0'..'9'. When it finds a valid decimal digit, it converts it to a 4-bit number that is returned in AL. The only way that RDDIG can determine when a key is typed is to read the KBDATA port continuously and wait for it to become nonzero. Once a key is pressed, the subroutine waits for it to be released before continuing. Otherwise, the next time that the subroutine was entered, it would mistake the first key depression for a new one.

The main program merges pairs of BCD digits from RDDIG and sends them to the 2-digit seven-segment display. Notice that only one OUT instruction is needed to store an 8-bit value into DIGOUT. Once the processor stores a value into DIGOUT, that value is displayed until the processor stores into DIGOUT again.

I/O timing

We should say something now about *I/O timing*, since I/O devices usually exist in an environment where time is significant. In the example above, the processor spends almost all of its time executing the first three instructions of the RDDIG subroutine, waiting for somebody to press a key. It normally spends only a small amount of time in the next three instructions waiting for the key to be released. Even less time is spent in the remainder of the subroutine and in the main program, since each instruction takes only about one microsecond (10^{-6} second) to execute, while keys are depressed at a maximum rate of about five per second. Because of this great disparity in speed, it is extremely unlikely that the program would miss any key depressions. In more time-critical applications, however, the programmer must analyze the I/O requirements and the program to determine whether the program can keep up with the I/O.

Also, you may be concerned about the computer wasting its time waiting for a key to be pressed by a slow human, when it could be doing some useful task like computing pi to one million digits. In Chapter 11, we show how interrupts avoid this shameful waste of computer time, so that I/O programs are activated only when an I/O event is known to have occurred.

10.2.2 Memory-Mapped I/O

memory-mapped I/O

In the previous subsection, we pointed out that I/O buses are very similar to memory buses, and that I/O instructions are similar to load and store instructions on memory. *Memory-mapped I/O* takes advantage of the similarity by eliminating the I/O bus and I/O instructions; this structure is used in all 68000 systems.

Figure 10–6 shows the hardware organization of a computer with memory-mapped I/O. Both the main memory and all I/O ports communicate with the processor using a shared Memory and I/O Bus. Each I/O port has an address in the main memory address space of the processor. An input port responds to any instruction that reads at its address; an output port responds to any instruction that writes at its address. Typically, the system designer reserves a portion of the total address space for I/O ports, for example, the top 4 Kbytes. However, theoretically a hardware designer can locate an I/O port at any address, as long as there is no memory at that address too.

Any processor can use memory-mapped I/O if the system hardware designer attaches I/O ports to the main memory bus. For example, if an 8086

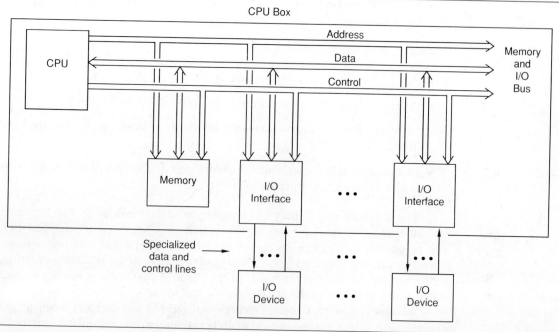

FIGURE 10–6   Memory-mapped I/O structure.

system designer decided to use memory-mapped I/O, then the I/O ports could be designed to connect to the memory bus, and the IN and OUT instructions would be replaced by the following ones:

```
MOV     AL,pn           AL := MEM[pn];  {IN}
MOV     pn,AL           MEM[pn]  := AL;  {OUT}
```

Here pn is a memory address in the range reserved for I/O ports, and the system hardware designer has simply fooled the processor into accessing I/O ports when it thinks that it is accessing memory bytes in that range.

Memory-mapped I/O is a necessity in processors that have no special I/O instructions. The PDP-11 was the first minicomputer to require memory-mapped I/O; following the PDP-11 architecture, the 68000 also requires it. Memory-mapped I/O has a number of advantages:

- No opcodes or processor circuits are used up for I/O instructions.

- All memory reference instructions, not just loads and stores to a restricted set of registers, may be used to manipulate I/O ports.

- The number of available I/O port addresses is virtually unlimited.

- The hardware bus structure is simplified.

- In special applications, the processor can fetch instructions from the I/O ports themselves.[1]

Of course, there are disadvantages too:

- Part of the memory address space is used up.

- Interfaces may need more circuitry to recognize longer addresses.

- Memory reference instructions may be longer or slower than optimized I/O instructions.

- In future systems, combining memory and I/O may make it difficult to achieve certain performance gains.[2]

The keyboard and display I/O program from the previous section has been rewritten in Table 10–2 for the 68000, which must use memory-mapped I/O. The program uses `MOVE.B` instead of the isolated-I/O `IN` and `OUT` instructions. There is only one improvement in the 68000 version: in the `RDDIG` subroutine, a `TST` instruction can test the value of the KBDATA port without having to load it first into a register, as the 8086 program had to do.

I/O port numbers

An observation that applies to both isolated I/O and memory-mapped I/O organizations is that the assignment of I/O port numbers is determined strictly by the whims of the hardware designer. Read and write operations on a particular port number are totally independent, unlike normal memory where a read returns the last value written. In particular, a hardware designer who likes to confuse novice programmers could have assigned the KBDATA input port and the DIGOUT output port exactly the same port number (e.g., 5). As long as the programmer doesn't get too upset over this apparent conflict, everything still works fine.

However, it is more traditional to assign identical port numbers only when the functions or meanings of input and output ports are related. In fact, when designing an output port, a meticulous hardware designer will provide an input port at the same address whose sole function is to read the data stored in the output port, as shown in Figure 10–7 for an improved seven-segment display port. Notice that, in this case, we use the same name for the input port and the output port. The combined input/output port behaves more like a memory location, so that a program can read the input port to verify the contents of the output port. This is especially important if one wants to write a program that tests the hardware, as well as being useful in some application programs.

[1] Why and how this is done is explained in an article by J. Lawrence Nichols, "The Overlooked Advantage of Memory-Mapped I/O," in *Computer* (May 1985, Vol. 18, No. 5, pp. 114–115). Nichols has patented the idea and explains it further in an article, "Intelligent Interface Speeds I/O Transfers," in *Microprocessor Report* (April 1988, vol. 2, no. 4, pp. 12–15, published by MicroDesign Resources, Palo Alto, CA).

[2] For example, see Bernard Peuto's article on the Z8000, "Architecture of a New Microprocessor," in *Computer*, Feb. 1979.

TABLE 10–2   Keyboard input and display output for the 68000.

```
*          Read two decimal digits from the keyboard and display them
*          on the seven-segment display. Ignore illegal characters.
*
KBDATA  EQU      $FFFFF005         Keyboard input port address.
DIGOUT  EQU      $FFFFF007         Seven-segment display port address.
*
*          First, a subroutine to read one decimal digit, convert
*          it to 4-bit BCD, and return the result in register D0.
RDDIG   MOVE.B   KBDATA,D0         Read current character.
        BEQ      RDDIG             Wait for a key to be pressed.
WAITUP  TST.B    KBDATA            Now the character is in D0,
        BNE      WAITUP              wait for the key to be released.
        SUB.B    #$30,D0           Now, was it a valid decimal digit?
        BLT      RDDIG             Not if it's less than ASCII '0' ...
        CMP.B    #9,D0
        BGT      RDDIG             ... or greater than ASCII '9'.
        RTS                        Valid digit, return.
*
*          Now, the main program.
DIGDSP  JSR      RDDIG             Read high-order decimal digit into A.
        LSL.B    #4,D0             Shift left 4 bits ...
        MOVE.B   D0,D1               ... and save in D1.
        JSR      RDDIG             Read low-order decimal digit.
        OR.B     D1,D0             Merge with high-order digit.
        MOVE.B   D0,DIGOUT         Send to seven-segment display.
        BRA      DIGDSP            Do another pair of digits.
        END      DIGDSP
```

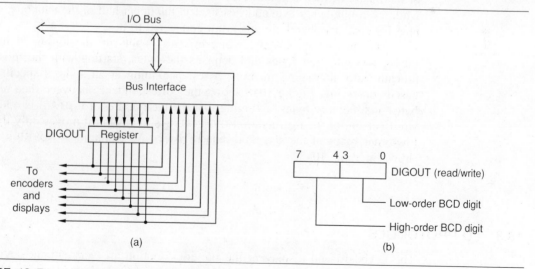

FIGURE 10–7   Input/output port with loopback: (a) interface arrangement; (b) programming model.

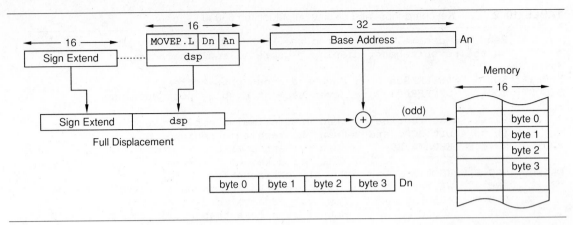

FIGURE 10–8   Data register bytes and memory bytes used by MOVEP.L instruction.

10.2.3   The 68000 MOVEP Instruction

MOVEP

The 68000's MOVEP instruction was specifically designed to facilitate access to peripheral circuits whose I/O programming models contain blocks of bytes at successive word addresses. Circuits that fall into this category include the Motorola MC68120 Intelligent Peripheral Controller and the MC68230 Parallel Interface and Timer. Any peripheral circuit whose data bus is only 8 bits wide falls into this category, since it is connected only to the upper or the lower half of the 68000's 16-bit data bus. For example, if it is connected to the lower half of the data bus, then odd-numbered byte addresses select the peripheral circuit, while even-numbered byte addresses select the upper half of the data bus, which may have no peripheral circuits at all connected to it.

The instruction MOVEP.L Dn,dsp(An) splits up the longword in data register Dn into four bytes and deposits the bytes, starting with the most significant, into alternating memory bytes, beginning at an address specified by based addressing. Figure 10–8 shows the correspondence between data register bytes and memory bytes, assuming that the base address (dsp+An) is odd. The word version of the instruction, MOVEP.W, is similar; but it moves only the two low-order bytes of the specified data register. An example of MOVEP's use is shown in Table 10–3.

10.3   I/O PROTOCOLS

The keyboard and display in the previous section are very simple devices to control. For proper operation, more complex I/O devices require additional hardware to implement some kind of "handshake" protocol.

TABLE 10–3   Code for moving a table from memory to a peripheral in the 68000.

```
*          This code reads a table of 4*N bytes beginning at memory address
*          MEMTBL and deposits them in 4*N alternating bytes beginning at
*          address PERIPH and ending at address PERIPH + 8*N - 2.
*

           MOVE.W   #N,D0            Get word count.
           LEA.L    MEMTBL,A0        Set up address of table.
           LEA.L    PERIPH,A1        Set up address of peripheral.
           BRA      IN               Check for N = 0.
TLOOP      MOVE.L   (A0)+,D1         Get word from table.
           MOVEP.L D1,0(A1)          Transfer to peripheral.
           ADDA.L   #8,A1            Get next peripheral address.
IN         DBF      D0,TLOOP         Done with N longwords?
           ...                       Fall through when done.
```

10.3.1 Input Operations

*handshake
  protocol*

The handshake protocol for a typical input device is shown in Figure 10–9. When the processor wants to read data, it sends a pulse on the START I/O control line. The device interface responds by initiating the input operation (an action that is device dependent), and by placing the logic value false on the READY line. When the operation is completed, the interface stores the input data in its DATA register, which really is a register with memory, unlike KBDATA in the previous section. At the same time, it sets READY to true. Therefore, the processor can test the value of READY and read the input data as soon as READY becomes true. The input data value is valid until the next operation begins.

Some processors with isolated I/O have special instructions for sending a START I/O control pulse and testing READY. For example, the Hewlett-Packard

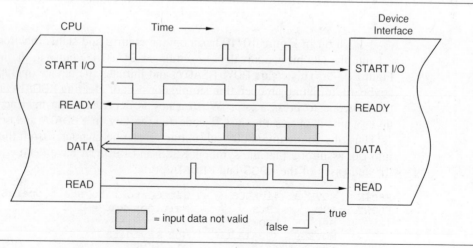

FIGURE 10–9   Handshake protocol for an input device.

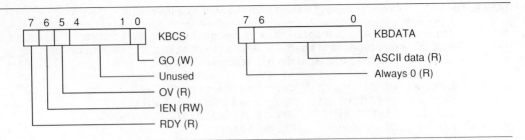

FIGURE 10–10 Programming model for a keyboard with control and status port.

control and status port

2116 minicomputer used the instructions STC pn and SFS pn for these two functions, where pn is the port number. However, most microcomputers and many minicomputers provide special *control and status ports* that accomplish these functions using normal input and output instructions, independent of whether memory-mapped or isolated I/O is used.

For example, Figure 10–10 shows the I/O programming model for a keyboard with a control and status port KBCS. This is actually both an input port and an output port; each bit has one of the following behaviors:

- *Read-only (R).* The value of the bit is set by the interface and can be read by the processor; writing a value into it has no effect.

- *Write-only (W).* The value of the bit can be written by the processor; reading returns an unpredictable value.

- *Read/write (RW).* The value of the bit can be read and written by the processor; reading generally returns the value last written.

- *Unused.* Writing this bit has no effect, and reading returns an unpredictable value.

Each bit in Figure 10–10 has a unique control and status function. Writing a 1 into the GO bit is equivalent to sending a START I/O pulse to the interface in Figure 10–9. This clears RDY (READY) and initiates the device operation. For a keyboard, initiating an operation simply consists of clearing KBDATA and waiting for someone to press a key. When a key is depressed, the interface cheers it up ...; no, it places the ASCII code for the key in KBDATA and sets RDY to 1. Thus, the following 68000 subroutine reads one character from the keyboard into D0, assuming that the symbols KBCS and KBDATA have been equated with the addresses of the KBCS and KBDATA ports:

```
KBDIN   MOVE.B  #1,KBCS         Set GO to 1 to start operation.
KBDWT   TST     KBCS            Wait for RDY = 1.
        BPL     KBDWT
        MOVE.B  KBDATA,D0       Get key data.
        AND.B   #$7F,D0         Clear MSB.
        RTS                     Return with 7-bit ASCII in D0.
```

TABLE 10–4   Reading a keyboard with overrun detection.

```
*                               Keyboard input subroutine.
KBDIN   BTST.B  #5,KBCS         Check for overrun.
        BNE     KBOUT           Exit with Z=0 on overrun.
        MOVE.B  #1,KBCS         Else set GO to 1 to request a key.
KBDWT   TST.B   KBCS            Wait for RDY=1.
        BPL     KBDWT
        MOVE.B  KBDATA,D0       Get key data.
        AND.B   #$7F,D0         Clear MSB.
        OR.B    #$04,CCR        Set Z:=1 for successful return.
KBOUT   RTS                     Return with 7-bit ASCII in A.
*
MAIN    ...                     Initialization.
        ...
LOOP    ...                     Main processing loop.
        JSR     KBDIN           Get the next character.
        BNE     MISSIT          Bomb out if we missed it.
        ...                     Otherwise process the character...
        JMP     LOOP            ...and go do some more.
MISSIT  ...                     Handle the error.
        ...
        END     MAIN
```

busy-wait loop   The instructions that wait for RDY to become 1 above are called a *busy-wait loop*. When the processor is busy-waiting for an I/O operation to be completed, no useful computation takes place. Busy-waiting can be minimized by overlapping I/O as discussed in the next subsection, or by using interrupts as described in the next chapter.

Two other bits are provided in KBCS. When set to 1, the IEN bit enables the keyboard to interrupt the processor as described in the next chapter. It is a read/write bit so that a program can easily determine whether the keyboard interrupt is currently enabled (useful in interrupt polling programs; see Section 11.2.3). The OV bit indicates an "overrun" condition; the interface sets it to 1 whenever the keyboard receives two characters in a row without an intervening read of KBDATA by the processor. It is automatically cleared when GO is set. Table 10–4 shows a program that makes use of the OV bit to detect overrun.

10.3.2 Overlapped I/O

Suppose that we are reading characters from a mechanical input device such as a document scanner. Because of the mechanical motion of the scanning head over the document, there is fixed delay from the time that each input character is requested until it is available. The three basic steps that we used for performing an input operation in the previous subsection were (1) request a byte, (2) wait for the byte, and (3) read the byte. These steps yield a document scanner input subroutine such as the following:

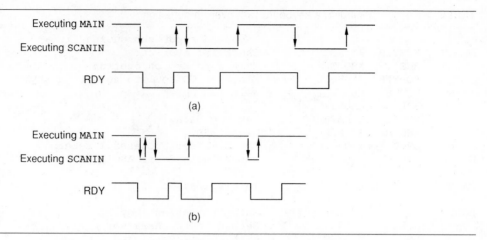

FIGURE 10–11   Input/output operations: (a) non-overlapped; (b) overlapped.

```
SCANIN    MOVE.B  #1,SCANCS     Set GO to move the scan head.
SCANWT    TST.B   SCANCS        Wait for the head to stop on
          BPL     SCANWT          the next character (RDY = 1).
          MOVE.B  SCANDATA,D0   Read the character.
          RTS                   Return 8-bit ASCII value in D0.
```

Figure 10–11(a) shows the time behavior of a main program that calls this subroutine. Each time that the main program calls SCANIN, the next byte is requested and the subroutine busy-waits for the whole time that the scan head is moving.

If we allow our program to think ahead, we can overlap I/O with computation to reduce or even eliminate busy-waiting. The scanner input subroutine below simply rearranges the basic steps into (1) wait for the current byte, (2) read the current byte, and (3) request the next byte:

```
SCANIN    TST.B   SCANCS        Wait for the scan head to stop on
          BPL     SCANIN          current character (RDY = 1).
          MOVE.B  SCANDATA,D0   Read the character.
          MOVE.B  #1,SCANCS     Start head moving for next char.
          RTS                   Return 8-bit ASCII value in D0.
```

Figure 10–11(b) shows the time behavior of the new subroutine. The first time that SCANIN is called, the scan head is already stopped over the first character; its ASCII value is read immediately and the head is started moving for the second character. By the time that SCANIN is called the second time, the scan head has moved almost halfway to the second character, and so the amount of busy-waiting is reduced. In fact, the main program performs so much computation between the second and third characters that there is no busy-waiting on the third call of SCANIN at all. Thus, the I/O operation (reading the next character) is always overlapped with computation that must take place before the main program can process the next character.

Overlapped I/O is useful for devices for which the processor must request a mechanical action for each I/O operation. Depending on the nature of the device and interface, it may be necessary to request the first I/O operation from the main program in order to "prime" the I/O subroutine.

10.3.3 Output Operations

The hardware handshake protocol that is used by a typical output device is shown in Figure 10–12. First the processor sends output data to the interface using the DATA bus and the WRITE control signal; the interface stores the data in an internal register. Then the processor issues a START I/O pulse. The interface immediately sets READY to false and sends its data to the device. Later it sets READY to true, when more data can be accepted.

The I/O programming model for a character output device such as a printer or CRT display is shown in Figure 10–13. The RDY bit indicates that the device can accept another character, while GO indicates that the character currently in

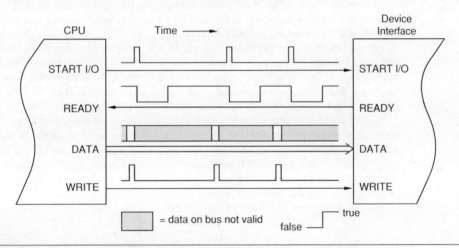

FIGURE 10–12   Handshake protocol for an output device.

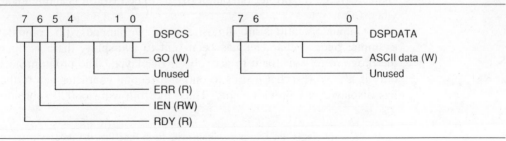

FIGURE 10–13   Programming model for a character output device.

Mac Note

Programmers in the Macintosh environment do not normally have direct access to I/O ports. The details of I/O port bits and protocols are hidden from 99.9% of Macintosh programmers. Instead, most programs perform all input and output using I/O drivers provided by the Macintosh operating system.

The main output device of a Macintosh application is the display screen. Unlike a CRT terminal, which is connected to a computer using a relatively low-speed serial interface, the Macintosh display is an integral part of the system and has a very high bandwidth interface to the processor. As explained in Section 11.5.3, the processor writes information into a block of main memory whose bits correspond to individual pixels on the display. The display hardware reads these memory locations continuously and draws corresponding images on the screen.

QuickDraw

DrawChar

The *QuickDraw* display driver routines provided by the Macintosh operating system handle all the details of dealing with the display interface. For example, a program may call the QuickDraw routine **DrawChar** to draw a character at the current cursor position. This routine creates the appropriate bit pattern in the display memory and advances the cursor. Other routines may be called to move the cursor to arbitrary positions, change text style, or draw arbitrary shapes.

Simarly, the detailed operation of Macintosh input devices is hidden from most programmers' view. The main input devices are the mouse and the keyboard. The Macintosh operating system is responsible for scanning input devices and noticing when events occur (keystrokes, mouse button changes, etc.). Thus, most Macintosh programs do not scan input device interfaces directly. Instead, they call the operating system routine

GetNextEvent

GetNextEvent, which returns a record indicating what type of input event, if any, has occurred since **GetNextEvent** was last called, along with other information relating to the event. For example, a keystroke event record gives the ASCII code of the key, while a mouse event record gives the position of the mouse.

The **GetNextEvent** facility has a major effect on the structure of Macintosh application programs. Instead of busy-waiting on input ports at arbitrary places in the program, the main program of a typical Macintosh application contains a loop, called

event loop

the *event loop*, that calls **GetNextEvent**. When an input event occurs, the program performs the processing and the output operations required by it, and then returns to the event loop to wait for something else to do.

DSPDATA should be displayed.[3] IEN allows interrupts as described in the next chapter, and ERR indicates that an error occurred while displaying the previous character (e.g., the printer ran out of paper). The ERR bit is automatically cleared when GO is set.

Output operations are almost always overlapped with computation. For example, once a character has been sent to a display, there is no reason for the program to wait for it to actually be displayed. The program needs to wait only if it is so fast that it tries to output a second character before the interface has displayed the previous one. Thus, the following 68000 subroutine can be

---

[3]In some interfaces, the GO bit is eliminated. Each time that the processor writes a character into DSPDATA, the interface automatically issues a "GO" command.

used to perform overlapped output of characters using the interface defined in Figure 10–13:

```
*          Display a character passed in D0.
CHROUT     TST.B    DSPCS        Has previous char been displayed?
           BPL      CHROUT       Wait until done.
           MOVE.B   D0,DSPDATA   Send new character to interface...
           MOVE.B   #1,DSPCS     ...and display it.
           RTS                   Done, return.
```

10.4 I/O DRIVERS

I/O driver

Most computer operating systems provide a set of subroutines for performing input and output operations using standard I/O devices. These subroutines are called *I/O drivers*. An I/O driver hides the details of a device and its hardware interface from the programmer and provides a clean software interface instead. In this section, we describe some simple I/O drivers, both to demonstrate the actual coding of the driver subroutines and to show typical software interfaces that I/O drivers present to application programs.

10.4.1 Terminal I/O

Input and output drivers for the keyboard and display of the previous section are coded in Table 10–5. There are two subroutines for reading characters from the keyboard: CHRIN reads a single character and returns it in register D0, while LINEIN reads a line of text terminated by a carriage return, storing the line in a buffer supplied by the calling program. There are also two subroutines for printing characters on the display: CHROUT prints a single character passed in A, while LINEOUT prints the contents of a buffer supplied by the calling program.

The keyboard and display are logically independent devices, even if they happen to be physically packaged together, as in a CRT terminal. Therefore, characters that are typed on the keyboard do not automatically appear on the display unless they are "echoed" by a program, as in the CHRIN subroutine.

Most displays move their cursor or printing mechanism to the beginning of the current line when they receive a carriage return (CR) character, but they do not start a new line. To save the user the trouble of typing a line feed character (LF) after each carriage return, the LINEIN subroutine automatically sends LF to the display after CR is received. Also, LINEOUT appends LF to each CR that it displays. The LF characters are not appended in CHRIN and CHROUT so that a user who so wishes can send or receive CR without echoing LF.

A main program that makes use of the LINEIN and LINEOUT drivers is shown in Table 10–6. The program reads an input line, reverses its order, and displays it. The DC.B assembler directive can take a character string as its operand, and stores the ASCII values of the characters in successive bytes of memory. Notice that the formats of input buffers and output buffers are

TABLE 10–5   Keyboard and display I/O drivers.

```
* KEYBOARD/DISPLAY INPUT/OUTPUT MODULE
*
* This module contains two subroutines, CHRIN and LINEIN, to
* read a single character or a line of text from a keyboard.
* It also contains two subroutines, CHROUT and LINEOUT, to
* print a single character or a line of text on a display.
*
* Control characters and I/O port addresses are defined below.
*
LF       EQU       $0A             Line feed character.
CR       EQU       $0D             Carriage return character.
KBCS     EQU       $FFFFF001       Keyboard control and status.
KBDATA   EQU       $FFFFF003       Keyboard data.
DSPCS    EQU       $FFFFF005       Display control and status.
DSPDATA  EQU       $FFFFF007       Display data.


*
* SUBROUTINE CHRIN -- Read one input character from a keyboard
*                     and echo it on the display.
*
* INPUTS, GLOBAL VARIABLES, LOCAL VARIABLES -- None.
*
* OUTPUTS
*     INCHAR -- The character just read, passed in D0.
*
* REGISTERS AFFECTED -- D0
*
CHRIN    MOVE.B   #1,KBCS          Request one character.
WTIN     TST.B    KBCS             Is it ready?
         BPL      WTIN             Wait for it.
         MOVE.B   KBDATA,D0        Get the character.
         AND.B    #$7F             Clear MSB.
         JSR      CHROUT           Echo the character on the display.
         RTS                       Done, return.


*
* SUBROUTINE CHROUT -- Print one character on a display.
*
* INPUTS
*     OUTCHAR -- The character to be displayed, passed in D0.
*
* OUTPUTS, GLOBAL VARIABLES, LOCAL VARIABLES -- None.
*
* REGISTERS AFFECTED -- None.
*
CHROUT   TST.B    DSPCS            Has previous character been displayed?
         BPL      CHROUT           Wait for completion.
         MOVE.B   D0,DSPDATA       Send the new character to interface.
         MOVE.B   #1,DSPCS         Display the character.
         RTS                       Done, return.
```

TABLE 10–5   (continued)

```
* SUBROUTINE LINEIN -- Read a line of text into a buffer.
*
* This subroutine reads a line of text from a terminal into a
* buffer with the format shown below.  The input line is ter-
* minated by a carriage return.  The first four bytes of the
* buffer are initialized by the calling program to contain the
* address of the last byte of the buffer.  This is used to
* prevent the subroutine from overwriting memory if the user
* types in too long a line.  The next four bytes of the buffer
* are reserved for the subroutine to store a variable BUFPNT
* that points to the last input character in the filled buffer.
* The remainder of the buffer is used to store input characters.
*
* BUFFER FORMAT       TXTBUF   |__           __|
*                              |__           __|
*                              |__    o-------+---------
*                              |_____|        |
*     BUFPNT  (TXTBUF+4)       |__           __|       |
*                              |__           __|       |
*                              |__    o-------+------  |
*                              |_____|      |  |
*           TXTBUF+8  |             |   |  |
*                              |             |   |  |
*                              |      o      |<-----  |
*                              |      o      |        |
*                              |      o      |        |
*                              |_____|<--------
*
* INPUTS   -- #TXTBUF -- longword pointer to TXTBUF, passed in A0.
* OUTPUTS -- TXTBUF+4 -- longword pointer to last character.
*            TXTBUF+8,... -- input characters.
* GLOBAL VARIABLES, LOCAL VARIABLES -- None.
* REGISTERS AFFECTED -- D0, A1
* NOTES    -- TXTBUF longword is not disturbed by LINEIN and
*             therefore may be initialized at load time.
*
LINEIN  MOVEA.L A0,A1          Put address of first byte of
        ADDA.L  #8,A1             character buffer into A1.
GETCHR  JSR     CHRIN          Read one character.
        MOVE.B  D0,(A1)        Store it.
        CMP.B   #CR,D0         Done if carriage return.
        BEQ.S   LINDUN
        CMPA.L  (A0),A1        Else is it OK to bump pointer?
        BCC     GETCHR         Not if at end of buffer.
        ADDA.L  #1,A1          Else bump pointer to next character.
        BRA     GETCHR         Get another character.
LINDUN  MOVEA.L A1,4(A0)       Save pointer to last character.
        MOVE.B  #LF,D0         Give the typist a new line
        JSR     CHROUT            (CHRIN has already echoed CR).
        RTS                    Done, return.
```

TABLE 10–5   (continued)

```
* SUBROUTINE LINEOUT -- Display text from a buffer.
*
* This subroutine displays text on a terminal from a buffer
* with the format shown below.  The first four bytes of the
* buffer contain the address of the last character to be
* displayed, and are followed by the characters themselves.
* The buffer may contain any number of characters and lines.
*
* BUFFER FORMAT      TXTBUF   |__            __|
*                            |__            __|
*                            |__    o-------+---------
*                            |_____|        |
*          TXTBUF+4          |               |        |
*                            |               |        |
*                            |       o       |        |
*                            |       o       |        |
*                            |       o       |        |
*                            |_____|<--------
*
* INPUTS   -- #TXTBUF -- a pointer to TXTBUF, passed in register A0
* OUTPUTS, GLOBAL VARIABLES, LOCAL VARIABLES -- None.
* REGISTERS AFFECTED -- D0, A1
* NOTES    -- Entire text buffer is not disturbed by LINEOUT
*             and therefore may be initialized at load time.
*
LINEOUT MOVEA.L A0,A1        Put address of first byte of
        ADDA.L  #3,A1          character buffer into A1.
PUTCHR  ADDA.L  #1,A1        Point to next character.
        MOVE.B  (A1),D0      Get it.
        JSR     CHROUT       Display it.
        CMP.B   #CR,D0       Character still in A --
        BNE.S   NOTCR          was it a carriage return?
        MOVE.B  #LF,D0       Always follow CR by a line feed.
        JSR     CHROUT
NOTCR   CMPA.L  (A0),A1      At the end?
        BCS     PUTCHR       Continue if not.
        RTS                  Else done, return.
```

similar, so that the contents of an input buffer filled by LINEIN can be printed if LINEOUT is passed the address of the *second* longword in the buffer. Also observe carefully which buffer pointers are initialized at load time by DC.L pseudo-operations, and which are loaded at run time.

10.4.2 Shared I/O Drivers

Quite often a computer has several identical devices connected to it, for example, several CRT terminals. Typically each device has its own interface; the interfaces are identical except that each one has a different set of port numbers. Instead of writing separate drivers for each device, it is possible to write an I/O driver that

TABLE 10–6   Main program that calls `LINEIN` and `LINEOUT`.

```
*         Read input lines and display them in reverse order.
*
INBUF     DC.L      INBUFE              Address of last byte in buffer.
INBUFP    DS.L      1                   Reserve space for buffer pointer...
INBUFT    DS.B      100                 ...and 100 characters of text.
INBUFE    EQU       *-1                 Define address of last byte.
STACK     DS.L      20                  Reserve space for return-address stack.
STACKE    EQU       *
*
MSG1      DC.L      MSG1E               Address of last byte in message.
          DC.B      'Please type an input line:'
MSG1E     DC.B      CR                  Last byte is carriage return.
*
MSG2      DC.L      MSG2E               Address of last byte in message.
          DC.B      'Your line in reverse is as follows:'
MSG2E     DC.B      CR                  Last byte is carriage return.
*
REVERSE   MOVEA.L   #STACKE,SP          Initialize stack pointer.
          MOVEA.L   #MSG1,A0            Prompt user for an input line.
          JSR       LINEOUT
          MOVEA.L   #INBUF,A0           Pass the address of input buffer.
          JSR       LINEIN              Get a line of input.
          MOVEA.L   #INBUFT,A0          Address of first input character.
          MOVEA.L   INBUFP,A1           Address of last input character.
          SUBA.L    #1,A1               Bump to char before carriage return.
SWAPEM    CMPA.L    A1,A0               Swap bytes until A0 >= A1.
          BHS       REVDUN
          MOVE.B    (A0),D0             Swap the bytes pointed to by A0 and A1.
          MOVE.B    (A1),(A0)
          MOVE.B    D0,(A1)
          ADDA.L    #1,A0               Bump A0 forward and A1 backward.
          SUBA.L    #1,A1
          BRA       SWAPEM              Repeat.
REVDUN    MOVEA.L   #MSG2,A0            Display the second message.
          JSR       LINEOUT
          MOVEA.L   #INBUFP,A0          Display the reversed input line.
          JSR       LINEOUT
          JMP       REVERSE             Run the program forever.
          END       REVERSE
```

can be shared by all devices of the same type. All that this requires is that the base address of the set of port numbers of the device be passed to the driver as a parameter. For example, Table 10–7 adapts the `CHRIN` and `CHROUT` subroutines from the previous example to work with any keyboard and display whose I/O ports have the same functions and relative numbering order. The address of the keyboard control and status register (`KBCSADR`) is passed to the subroutines in register A2, and the other ports are accessed using based addressing with fixed offsets from A2.

TABLE 10–7   Shared keyboard input and display output drivers.

```
* SUBROUTINE CHRINA -- Read one input character from a selected
*                      keyboard and echo it on the display.
*
* INPUTS -- KBCSADR -- Address of the keyboard control and status
*                      port, passed in register A2.
* GLOBAL VARIABLES, LOCAL VARIABLES  -- None.
* OUTPUTS -- INCHAR -- The character just read, passed in D0.
* REGISTERS AFFECTED -- D0
*
* Port addresses are defined relative to the address of KBCS.
OKBCS    EQU    0            Offset to keyboard control and status.
OKBDATA  EQU    2            Offset to keyboard data.
ODSPCS   EQU    4            Offset to display control and status.
ODSPDAT  EQU    6            Offset to display data.
*
CHRINA   MOVE.B #1,OKBCS(A2)      Request one character.
WTIN     TST.B  OKBCS(A2)         Is it ready?
         BPL    WTIN              Wait for it.
         MOVE.B OKBDATA(A2),D0    Get the character.
         AND.B  #$7F,D0           Clear MSB.
         JSR    CHROUTA           Echo the character on the display.
         RTS                      Done, return.
*
* SUBROUTINE CHROUTA -- Print one character on a selected display.
*
* INPUTS -- KBCSADR  -- Address of the keyboard control and status
*                       port, passed in register A2
*          OUTCHAR   -- The character to be displayed, passed in D0.
* OUTPUTS, GLOBAL VARIABLES, LOCAL VARIABLES -- None.
* REGISTERS AFFECTED -- None.
*
CHROUTA  TST.B  ODSPCS(A2)        Has previous character been displayed?
         BPL    CHROUTA           Wait for completion.
         MOVE.B D0,ODSPDAT(A2)    Send the new character to interface.
         MOVE.B #1,ODSPCS(A2)     Display the character.
         RTS                      Done, return.
```

The shared drivers in Table 10–7 are more general than the "dedicated" drivers given previously. In fact, a dedicated driver subroutine can be coded by calling CHROUTA with a particular value of A2:

```
*         Character output driver for terminal number 0.
CHROUT0 MOVE.L  A2,-(SP)        Save A2.
        MOVEA.L #$FFFFF001,A2   I/O base address for terminal 0.
        JSR     CHROUTA         Output the character in D0.
        MOVEA.L (SP)+,A2        Restore A2.
        RTS                     Done, return.
```

Shared drivers are easy to write in computers that use memory-mapped I/O, because all of the usual indirect and based addressing modes are available for dynamically computing a port address at run time. On the other hand, in some computers with isolated I/O, shared drivers are impossible to write without using self-modifying code. For example, in the Intel 8080 and MCS-48, the I/O port number is always specified as part of the instruction; there are no instructions that take the port number from a register. The 8086 solves the problem by providing two "flavors" of I/O instructions—one that specifies the port number as part of the instruction and another that takes the port number from a register.

REFERENCES

Detailed discussion of I/O system architecture from a hardware designer's point of view can be found in *Microprocessor-Based Design* by Michael Slater (Mayfield, 1987) and *Microcomputer Interfacing* by Harold S. Stone (Addison-Wesley, 1982). An introduction to microcomputer I/O hardware appears in J. Wakerly's article "Microprocessor Input/Output Architecture" (*Computer*, Vol. 10, No. 2, February 1977, pp. 26–33).

This chapter has only touched the surface of possible I/O driver organizations and I/O buffering schemes. A section in Jim Peterson's *Computer Organization and Assembly Language Programming* (Academic Press, 1978) shows how to perform overlapped I/O on blocks of data. A good discussion of several possible buffering schemes can be found in Knuth's *Fundamental Algorithms* (Addison-Wesley, 1973, 2nd ed.). Both of the above books use Knuth's hypothetical `MIX` computer for assembly language program examples.

EXERCISES

10.1 Devise a programming model for a one-digit seven-segment display, where the interface does not have an ENCODER block like the one in Figure 10–4(a). Instead, there is a single output port SEGS with a bit corresponding to each of the seven segments; a 1 lights the segment and a 0 extinguishes it. Draw a figure that shows the correspondence between bits of SEGS and segments. Then write a 68000 subroutine that uses SEGS to display a single BCD digit passed in D0.

10.2 Suppose you are in charge of the design of a microcomputer system that is to contain an input device whose sole function is to keep track of the current date, day, and time of day to the nearest millisecond. You are to specify a programming model for the device interface so that your hardware engineers can start building it and your programmers can start writing I/O drivers for it. All numbers are to be stored as unsigned binary integers. The I/O ports associated with the device must provide the capability of both initializing and reading the time information.

10.3 Repeat the previous exercise, using BCD representation for numbers where appropriate.

10.4   The keyboard input and display programs in Tables 10–1 and 10–2 use signed
conditional branches to determine whether or not each input character is in range.
Although these particular programs work with standard ASCII, unsigned branches
are a better choice for comparing characters in general. Explain why.

10.5   Show how to eliminate one CMP instruction in the RDDIG subroutine in Table
10–1 or 10–2 by performing the subtraction first.

10.6   Explain why there is a slight chance that overrun may go undetected in the KBDIN
subroutine in Table 10–4.

10.7   Rewrite the KBDIN subroutine in Table 10–4 to use overlapped I/O. Show how
it is now possible to ensure that overrun never goes undetected. Is overrun now
more or less likely to occur than in the original program?

10.8   Rewrite the RDDIG subroutine in Table 10–1 or 10–2 to reduce the amount of
busy-waiting by waiting for key release at the beginning of RDDIG. Explain the
differences in the two versions when keys are typed very quickly.

10.9   Modify the CHROUT subroutine in Table 10–5 so that it detects errors using the
ERR bit, in much the same way as KBDIN in Table 10–4.

10.10   Modify the CHROUT subroutine in Table 10–5 to work with an interface that eliminates the GO bit as described in footnote 1.

10.11   Most of the ASCII control characters (columns 0 and 1 in Appendix A) have
no effect when displayed or printed. Write a CHROUT driver that converts control
characters other than CR, LF, and BS into a two-character sequence, "&" followed
by the corresponding character in column 4 or 5 of the ASCII code chart. This
is reasonable because the control characters are generated on most keyboards by
holding down the control (CTRL) key and typing the corresponding column 4 or
5 character.

10.12   Write a LINEIN driver that allows simple editing of input lines typed on a CRT
terminal. Typing a backspace (CTRL-H) should remove the previous character
from the input buffer and echo a backspace, space, and another backspace, thereby
erasing the previous character and properly adjusting the display's cursor. Typing
a CTRL-C should remove all characters from the input buffer and start a new line
on the display. (Hints: Characters need not be physically removed from the input
buffer; it is sufficient to update the buffer pointer appropriately. Be sure that your
program doesn't allow backspacing beyond the beginning of the input buffer.)

10.13   Write a LINEIN driver that allows simple editing of input lines typed on an
ancient teleprinter. CTRL-C should operate the same as in the previous exercise.
Typing a delete character (DEL or RUB key) should echo a backslash (\) and the
previous character in the input buffer, and remove the character from the buffer.
Successive delete characters should echo and delete additional characters in the
input buffer, *without* echoing a backslash. After echoing the last deleted character
in a sequence of deletions, the driver should echo another backslash. (Note that
the program doesn't know that it has received the last delete character until it
receives something other than a delete character.) Since partial input lines with
many deletions are difficult to read, also provide a CTRL-R command that starts

a new line on the printer, prints the current (edited) input buffer contents, and allows the user to resume typing at the next character position.

10.14 Write a program that combines the keyboard and display I/O drivers from this chapter with the queue module from Chapter 9. Define four queues UCQ, LCQ, DQ, and OQ that can be manipulated by the queue module. Provide a main program that continuously reads characters from the keyboard using CHRIN. As each character is received, it should be enqueued in UCQ, LCQ, DQ, or OQ according to whether it is an upper-case letter, a lower-case letter, a decimal digit, or any other character. If the queue is full, the character should be discarded; each queue should hold 10 characters when full. If the character is a carriage return, it should not be enqueued; instead a maximum of six characters from each queue should be dequeued and displayed. The contents of each queue should be displayed on a separate line.

10.15 Write a set of I/O drivers for the timing device defined in Exercise 10.2. You will have to define a buffer format and write two subroutines for initializing the time from a buffer and loading a buffer with the current time information. Be sure to consider the problem of correctly reading the current time just as the second is changing from $m.999$ to $n.000$. It may be possible to get the answer $m.000$ or $n.999$ depending on the order in which the ports are read. At what other transitions can this kind of anomaly occur? How could the person who specified the hardware interface have avoided this?

10.16 Write a program to play Life as described in Exercise 7.8, where the Life array size corresponds to the size of a CRT screen. Write a subroutine DISPLAY that displays the current generation of Life in the CURG array by calling another subroutine COUT to display each character in the Life array. If the CRT terminal does not have automatic wrap-around at the end of a line, DISPLAY must send CR and LF characters after each line except the last. On the other hand, with automatic wrap-around, DISPLAY must not send the last character on the last line in order to keep the display from "rolling." Write a main program that initializes the Life array to a random population and computes and displays Life one generation at a time.

CHAPTER 11

Interrupts and Direct Memory Access

"We interrupt this program for a special announcement..."

interrupt system

This familiar phrase describes the basic function of an *interrupt system*—to notify a program each time an I/O operation has been completed. Instead of busy-waiting for operation completion, the processor runs an I/O program only when an I/O event is known to have occurred.

In the first two sections of this chapter, we discuss interrupt system structures and programming in general, and use the 68000 as a specific example. Some processors use interrupt-like "traps" to signal other events—these are described in the third section. The interrupt and trap mechanisms of the 68000 are summarized in the fourth section.

direct memory access (DMA) channel

With devices that generate a large number of low-level I/O events, *direct memory access (DMA) channels* can be used to reduce processor loading. A DMA channel allows the processor to issue a single high-level command (e.g., "read block of data from tape") to initiate an entire sequence of low-level I/O events (e.g., reading individual bytes). As described in the last section of this chapter, DMA does this by transferring data directly between an I/O device and memory without processor intervention.

11.1 BASIC INTERRUPT SYSTEM STRUCTURE AND PROGRAMMING

With a simple I/O system, the only way that the processor can determine that a device has completed an operation is to test continuously the READY flag in the device interface. However, in a computer with many I/O devices, such as terminals, printers, and disks, all devices must be kept running concurrently for maximum efficiency. The processor cannot afford to waste time busy-waiting for one device to complete an operation while other devices may already be ready for service. An interrupt system solves this problem by allowing any I/O device to initiate a service routine in the processor when it completes an I/O operation, freeing the processor to do other things when the I/O devices are busy.

interrupt request signal

    Using an interrupt system, each device can send an *interrupt request signal* to the processor when it completes an operation. The processor accepts an interrupt request by temporarily suspending the operation of the current program.

interrupt service routine

It then executes an *interrupt service routine* for the I/O operation that was just completed, perhaps initiating still another I/O operation. After "servicing the interrupt," the processor returns control to the interrupted program. Except for an increase in execution time, the fact that an interrupt occurred is transparent to the interrupted program. (Don't you sometimes wish that interruptions of your favorite TV program were just as transparent?)

    There are at least as many variations in interrupt system structure as there are processor organizations.[1] In this section we discuss some general ideas and describe a fairly simple interrupt system structure, a subset of the one used by the Motorola 68000. In succeeding sections we discuss other variations and in Section 11.4 we summarize the full 68000 interrupt system.

11.1.1 General Considerations

Interrupts are usually allowed to occur only between, not during, the execution of individual instructions. For example, the instruction MOVE.W D1, (A1)+ cannot be interrupted after storing D1 but before auto-incrementing A1. In the Pascal simulation of the 68000 in Table 5–2 on page 138, the presence of an interrupt would be tested by a procedure CheckForInterrupt called right after Execute in the main loop of the simulation program:

```
WHILE true DO {Basic instruction interpretation cycle}
  BEGIN
    Fetch;
    Execute;
    CheckForInterrupt;
  END;
```

The actions that take place in CheckForInterrupt "fool" the processor into executing the interrupt service routine, so that the next instruction fetched will be the first instruction of the interrupt service routine; we give details later.

    The processor normally has a means of disabling interrupts completely, typically by setting or clearing one of the processor status bits. When interrupts are allowed and one does occur, the following actions are taken:

  (1) The processor saves part of the current processor state and enters the interrupt service routine, which may save the rest of the processor state.

---

[1]Perhaps more, because modern LSI interrupt control circuits give computer system designers many choices among different interrupt structures, independent of the processor.

(2) The service routine determines the identity of the interrupting device interface.

(3) The service routine identifies and services the condition that caused the device interface to request an interrupt.

(4) The service routine restores the saved processor state, and the processor resumes the program that was interrupted.

processor state

In the first step above, *processor state* refers to the program counter (PC) and all of the registers in the programming model of the processor. When an interrupt takes place, the processor hardware must at least save the current value of the PC so that the interrupted program can later be resumed. The saved PC points to the instruction that would have been executed next if the interrupt hadn't occurred. The interrupt service routine must also save all registers whose values it might disturb. As a minimum, the condition bits should be saved; most service routines also save at least a few general-purpose registers which they then use to perform their task; and complex service routines may need to save all of the registers. When the service routine completes its work, it restores the saved register values and PC.

context switching

The act of saving PC, registers, and condition bits after an interrupt, or restoring them later, is called *context switching*. In systems with frequent interrupts, the speed of context switching can have a significant impact on system performance. Therefore, many processors have features to speed up context switching, such as instructions that load and store multiple registers. In fact, some processors, including the Motorola 6809, even save and restore the registers automatically on interrupt calls and returns.

The second step in the list above, identifying the interrupting device interface, can be accomplished in a number of different ways as described later. For the moment, we will assume that there is only one interrupting device interface so that the second step is not needed.

The third step, servicing the condition that caused the interrupt, is accomplished by normal instructions on I/O ports. The last step, resuming the interrupted program, is another context switch. This is often accomplished by a special instruction that restores the saved processor state; restoring the PC causes a jump back to the interrupted program.

interrupt latency

The time that elapses from the first appearance of a device's interrupt request signal until the processor begins to execute the first instruction of the interrupt service routine is called the *interrupt latency*. The maximum interrupt latency is the sum of two components:

(1) The execution time of the slowest machine instruction. If an interrupt request occurs as the processor is just starting to execute such an instruction, the processor cannot begin context switching until the instruction is completed.

(2) The time to perform a context switch. This number includes the time for the hardware to save the PC and any other registers that it saves automatically before jumping to the interrupt service routine.

Many people define interrupt latency also to include the execution time of the first few instructions of the interrupt service routine, the ones that save some or all of the remaining registers in the processor state. Thus, the interrupt latency is the time from the occurrence of the interrupt request signal until the service routine begins to identify and service the interrupting condition. In this case, the latency depends on the complexity of the interrupt service routine—simple routines may save only one or two registers, while complex ones may save all of them.

If a program temporarily disables interrupts, then the maximum interrupt latency is increased by the time that interrupts are disabled. Also, if a computer system includes coprocessors (such as the MC68881 floating-point unit) or other general-purpose resources whose state might be changed by an interrupt service routine, then the time for saving their state may also be considered to be part of interrupt latency.

11.1.2   A Simple Interrupt System

In this section we describe a small subset of the Motorola 68000 interrupt system; its full capabilities are discussed in Sections 11.2 through 11.4.

The 68000 processor has a 3-bit interrupt-request bus consisting of signals IPL2, IPL1, and IPL0, to which an external device can apply a 3-bit number (0–7) giving the current *interrupt-request priority level (IPL)*. At all times, the processor also has a current *processor priority level (PPL)*, a 3-bit number (0–7) contained in bits I_2, I_1, I_0 of the status register (SR). The processor will accept an interrupt request only if the IPL applied by a device is numerically greater than the PPL set by the running program, or if the IPL is 7.

interrupt-request priority level (IPL)

processor priority level (PPL)

For example, if PPL is currently 3, the processor will only accept interrupt requests with IPLs of 4, 5, 6, or 7. If PPL is 0, the processor will accept IPLs of 1 or greater. Since an IPL of 0 is never greater than PPL, external devices use an IPL of 0 to indicate that no interrupt request is pending. Therefore, there are only seven IPL values that indicate true interrupt requests (1–7). Note that an interrupt with an IPL of 7 will always be accepted, regardless of PPL (see Section 11.2.5).

In practice, more than one device interface may be capable of placing an interrupt request on the IPL bus. Different devices may use different priority levels, or there may be multiple devices at each priority level. In any case, the processor must somehow determine which device is requesting service at any time.

System configurations with multiple interrupting devices are discussed later. A simple system configuration with only one interrupting device is shown in Figure 11–1. In the remainder of this subsection, we assume that only one

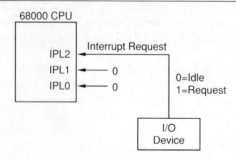

FIGURE 11–1   A 68000 interrupt system with one interrupting device at IPL = 4.

interface is connected to IPL in this way, and that it always uses the same IPL value (in this example, 4) when requesting interrupt service.

Figure 11–2 shows the state of a program just before an interrupt is accepted. When the processor accepts an interrupt request on IPL, it performs several actions automatically before fetching the next instruction. Figure 11–3 shows the results of these actions. The processor saves part of its state by pushing PC and SR onto the stack, using the supervisor stack pointer (SSP). It sets the PPL field ($I_2I_1I_0$) in SR to be equal to IPL, which prevents the current request on the IPL bus from causing further interrupts. It also sets the S bit in SR to 1, so that the interrupt service routine is executed in supervisor mode.

interrupt vector   Finally, the processor loads the PC with the 32-bit number contained in a longword *interrupt vector* stored in memory. The address of the interrupt vector is a function of the 3-bit value on IPL — if the IPL value is n, then the vector address is $\$00000060 + 4 \cdot n$. For example, if the IPL value is 4, then the vector address is $\$00000070$.

The longword stored at the vector address is the starting address of an interrupt service routine that has been written by a programmer. Even though the address of the vector (e.g., $\$00000070$) is fixed in the processor's hardware design, the interrupt service routine may be located anywhere in memory (e.g., at address $\$00123456$); the interrupt vector (`MEM[$00000070]` = $\$00123456$) determines the starting address.

After accepting an interrupt as described above, the processor returns to its normal instruction fetching and execution process. Since the PC has been loaded with the starting address of the interrupt service routine, the next instruction executed will be the first instruction of the interrupt service routine. The interrupt routine services whatever condition caused the interrupt, and causes the interface to remove its request from the IPL bus. Note that even before the IPL bus is cleared, the request is ignored because IPL is no longer greater than PPL (because the processor set PPL equal to IPL before entering the service routine).

register saving   An interrupt service routine must not disturb the values in any of the
and restoring   processor registers, since this would have unpredictable effects on the interrupted program. If the service routine needs registers for temporary storage, it must

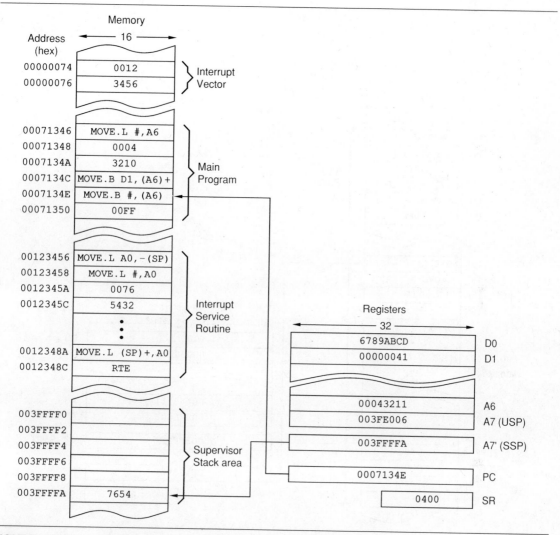

FIGURE 11–2   Program state just before interrupt is accepted.

push the current values of those registers onto the stack before using them, and then restore those values by popping them from the stack just before returning to the interrupted program.

RTE

The service routine returns to the interrupted program by executing an RTE (return from exception) instruction. RTE restores the original values of PC and SR by popping them off the stack. Therefore, just after RTE is executed, the program will once again have exactly the state shown in Figure 11–3(a), as if the interrupt had never occurred. Since the value of the PPL field in SR

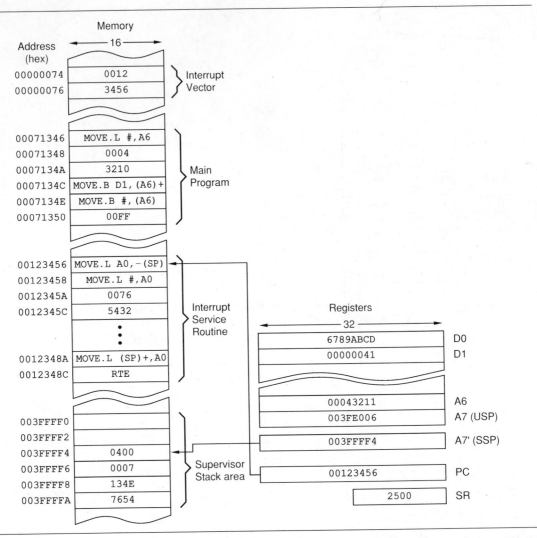

FIGURE 11-3 Program state just after interrupt is accepted.

is restored to its previous value when the saved SR is popped from the stack, further interrupts may now be accepted when requested on the IPL bus.

11.1.3 An I/O Program Using Interrupts

Table 11–1 is a 68000 program that uses interrupts to print text strings using the display interface that was defined in Figure 10–13 on page 371. The interface requests interrupts as shown in Figure 11–4. The RDY bit in the DSPCS control and status register is 1 whenever the display is ready to accept another character.

RDY

TABLE 11–1   Display output program using interrupts.

```
*              Subroutines STROUT and STRINT are used to print text
*         strings on the display.  A text string is defined to be a
*         sequence of non-NUL ASCII characters terminated by NUL (0).
*              To print a string, a program must call STROUT with the
*         address of the first character of the string in A0.  STROUT
*         turns on the display interrupts, prints the first character,
*         and returns to the calling program.  Successive characters
*         are printed by the interrupt service routine STRINT.
*              The global variable SBUSY, when nonzero, indicates that
*         a string is currently being printed.  Thus, when STROUT is
*         entered, it will not start printing a new string until it
*         finds that the previous string has been completely printed.
*         STRINT clears SBUSY after printing the last character.
*         However, the main program must also initialize SBUSY to 0
*         so that STROUT doesn't hang the first time that it is called.
*

          ORG     $00000070     IPL-4 interrupt vector address.
          DC.L    STRINT        Address of interrupt service routine.

          ORG     $00002000
*
*         Define display interface registers.
DSPCS     EQU     $FFFFF005     Display control and status port.
DSPDATA   EQU     $FFFFF007     Display data port.
*
*         Local and global variables.
SBUSY     DS.B    1             Nonzero when string is being displayed.
BUFPNT    DS.L    1             Pointer to character being displayed.
*
*
STROUT    TST.B   SBUSY         Is a previous string being
          BNE     STROUT           displayed?  Wait for it.
          MOVE.L  A0,BUFPNT     Save buffer pointer.
          MOVE.B  #$FF,SBUSY    Set SBUSY flag.
          MOVE.B  (A0),DSPDATA  Get first character and display it.
          MOVE.B  #$41,DSPCS    Set IEN and GO.
          RTS                   Done, return.
*
STRINT    MOVE.L  A0,-(SP)      Save A0.
          MOVEA.L BUFPNT,A0     Get buffer pointer.
          ADD.L   #1,BUFPNT     Bump pointer to next character.
          TST.B   (A0)          Check next character.
          BEQ.S   STRDUN        Quit if it's a NUL ($00).
          MOVE.B  (A0),DSPDATA  Otherwise display it.
          MOVE.B  #$41,DSPCS    Set IEN and GO.
          BRA.S   STRRET        Return to interrupted program.
STRDUN    CLR.B   DSPCS         Clear IEN.
          CLR.B   SBUSY         Clear SBUSY flag.
STRRET    MOVEA.L (SP)+,A0      Restore A0.
          RTE                   Return to interrupted program.
```

TABLE 11–1   (continued)

```
*       Main program.
MAIN    ...                             Initialization.
        CLR.B    SBUSY                  Clear SBUSY flag.
LOOP    ...                             Do some processing.
        LEA.L    MSG1,A0                Print the first message.
        JSR      STROUT
        ...                             Do some more processing.
        LEA.L    MSG2,A0                Print the second message.
        JSR      STROUT
        ...                             Do some more processing.
        JMP      LOOP
*
CR      EQU      $0D
LF      EQU      $0A
MSG1    DC.B     'The quick brown fox jumps over the lazy dog.'
        DC.B     CR,LF,0
MSG2    DC.B     'That was a pretty unimaginative message!'
        DC.B     CR,LF,0
        END
```

interrupt enable
bit (IEN)

The programmer sets the *interrupt enable bit (IEN)* to 1 if an interrupt is desired whenever the display is ready.

The AND gate (Section 1.2) in the display interface places a level-4 interrupt request on IPL whenever IEN and RDY are both 1. Thus, a request is made on IPL each time that a character printing operation is completed. This request is

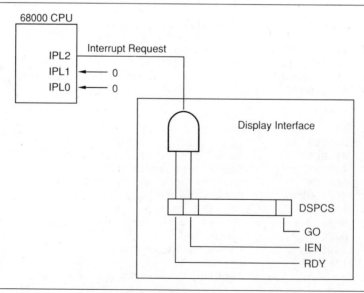

FIGURE 11–4   Display interface interrupt hardware.

removed each time that STRINT sends another character to the display (by setting GO, which clears RDY), or when STRINT finds that it has no more characters to send (and clears IEN).

The main program can display a string by calling STROUT with the string's address in A0. STROUT enables the display interrupt, prints the first character, and then returns control to the main program, which may continue to perform useful computation. The remainder of the string is displayed by the interrupt service routine STRINT, which uses the variable BUFPNT to keep track of which character is being displayed.

The time behavior of the interrupt program is shown in Figure 11–5. The global variable SBUSY indicates whether or not the current string has been completely printed, so that STROUT can automatically busy-wait for completion when a second string is requested too soon, as in Figure 11–5(b). Note that the RDY bit in the display control and status register is a hardware flag that indicates completion of a single character output operation, while SBUSY is a software flag that indicates completion of a higher-level software process, the printing of an entire string.

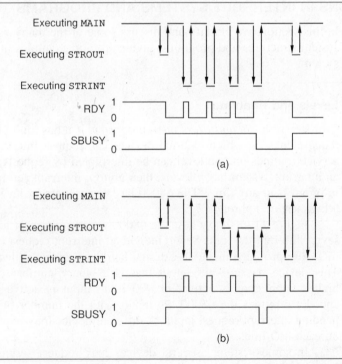

FIGURE 11–5   Time behavior of interrupt program: (a) first string fully printed before second is requested; (b) second string requested before first is fully printed.

Mac Note

event record
event queue

The Macintosh uses the 68000's interrupt system, but 99.9% of application programs in the Macintosh environment never have to deal with interrupts. Instead, the operating system contains service routines for all device interrupts.

Interrupts are enabled almost all the time. When an interrupt occurs, say from a keystroke or a mouse click, the interrupt service routine determines what type of I/O event just occurred and builds an *event record* describing it. The event record is placed on an internal *event queue*, which keeps track of I/O events in the order that they occur. Thus, while an application program performs a computation, the operating system can accumulate one or more events in the background.

When an application program needs further input from the user in order to continue, it calls the operating system routine `GetNextEvent`, which returns the record at the head of the event queue—the oldest unprocessed event. Since application programs spend most of their time waiting for user inputs, a typical main program is a loop that repeatedly calls `GetNextEvent`—this is the event loop described in the Mac Note on page 372.

When an application program is actually performing some significant work, the interrupt system allows input/output operations to continue in the background. Thus, when a text editor is scrolling its text display, the user can still type on the keyboard, and the typed-ahead keystrokes are saved in the event queue for subsequent processing by the text editor application program.

11.2   VARIATIONS IN INTERRUPT SYSTEMS AND PROGRAMS

In this section, we classify and discuss some of the many variations in interrupt system structures and programs, giving specific examples in the 68000 interrupt system.

11.2.1   Interrupt Levels and Enabling

multilevel
*   interrupt system*

A processor has a *multilevel interrupt system* if it has multiple levels or interrupt request lines on which external devices can request interrupts, and if interrupt service routines on one level can be interrupted by requests on another level. If an interrupt system has *n* levels, then up to *n* interrupt service routines could be in progress at any time. The 68000 has seven interrupt levels, corresponding to IPL values of 1 through 7.

priority encoder

Figure 11–6 shows how the 68000's seven interrupt levels can be used by seven different devices. Seven individual interrupt request inputs, IRQ1 through IRQ7, are provided using an external hardware device called a *priority encoder*. This device has a 3-bit output that is a binary number corresponding to its highest input that is active, or 000 if no input is active. Thus, the priority encoder provides the 68000 IPL inputs with the number of the highest priority pending interrupt request input. A different device may request interrupt service on each IRQ line.

In some systems, several devices may request service on the same IRQ line. This is absolutely necessary in 68000 systems that have more than seven interrupting devices, since only seven interrupt levels are available. When mul-

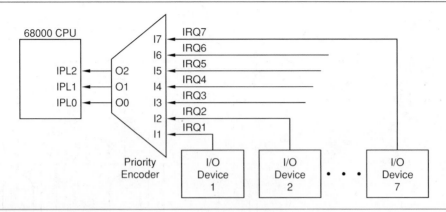

FIGURE 11–6   Seven-level interrupt hardware for the 68000.

tiple devices use the same IRQ line, then some method is needed to distinguish them, such as polling or vectoring as discussed later.

Actually, it is quite common to group together devices of similar characteristics or priority onto the same level or IRQ line in a multilevel interrupt system. For example, all the disks and tapes in a system could be placed on one level and all the high-speed communication links on another level. Then, for example, a lengthy disk interrupt service routine can be interrupted by a communication link so that input characters are not lost.

By setting the appropriate processor priority in PPL, the 68000 processor can accept interrupt requests on some levels while ignoring others. Thus a program can quickly disable all interrupts on a "low-priority" level (e.g., disks) while still allowing interrupts from a "high-priority" level (e.g., communication links). Selectively disabling interrupts on one or more levels is called *interrupt masking*.

interrupt masking

In addition to masking groups of interrupt levels, the processor can also disable interrupts from a specific device by manipulating the interrupt enable bit (IEN) in the device interface control and status register. Figure 11–7 illustrates this for the 68000 (AND and OR gates were introduced in Section 1.2). Three interfaces have interrupt request outputs connected to IRQ5. However, only two of the interfaces (1 and 3) have their IEN bits set to 1 and can request an interrupt when RDY is 1, and as shown, only interface 3 is actually requesting an interrupt at this time. If the processor masks interrupt requests on IRQ5 by setting PPL to 5 or greater, then even this request will be ignored (and remain pending) until the processor again sets PPL to 4 or less.

Generally when a processor accepts an interrupt on a particular level, it disables interrupts on that level until the current interrupt has been fully serviced. However, reenabling the level after partial service is possible any time after the current interrupt request signal is removed.

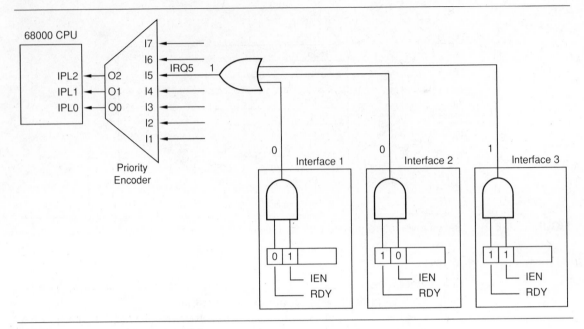

FIGURE 11–7   Interrupt enabling.

11.2.2 Interrupt Priority

interrupt priority

In a multilevel interrupt system, *interrupt priority* determines whether an interrupt service routine for one level can be interrupted by a request on another level. In a typical system, each interrupt line has a fixed priority. For example, in Figure 11–6 the priority runs from IRQ1 (lowest) to IRQ7 (highest); this priority is fixed by the hardware priority encoder device.

It is also possible for two or more devices to request interrupt service at exactly the same time. An unlikely way for this to happen is for two devices to actually complete their operations within one processor instruction cycle (less than a microsecond) of each other. A more likely way is for two or more devices to request interrupts during a longer interval of time in which the processor has masked interrupts. When the processor finally reenables interrupts, multiple requests will be pending. Interrupt priority governs the order in which these multiple requests are serviced.

When multiple interfaces request interrupts on the same interrupt request line, as in Figure 11–7, the processor must select one of the interfaces to service. The way in which the selection is made determines the interfaces' priority. One of two different techniques is generally used:

fixed priority

- *Fixed priority.* The interfaces are examined in a fixed priority order; the first one found to be requesting an interrupt is serviced.

round-robin
priority

- *Round-robin priority.* The interfaces are ordered, but the search for an interface needing service starts with the interface *after* the last one that was serviced; the search continues at the beginning of the list when the end is reached.

Round-robin priority is more "fair" than fixed priority because it prevents fast devices from monopolizing interrupt service at the expense of slower devices. It is also more "reliable" because it prevents a faulty high-priority device from locking out low-priority devices by interrupting continuously. As we'll see in the next subsection, round-robin priority is easy to implement in software polling programs.

When priority is resolved by hardware rather than software, fixed priority is often used because the circuits are simpler. For example, the interrupt system of the PDP-11 imposes a fixed priority on each device according to its physical distance on the I/O bus from the processor—closer devices have higher priority.

11.2.3   Interrupt Identification and Polling

interrupt polling

When a program knows that some device has interrupted, but it doesn't know which one, it can simply "go out and ask"! This is called *interrupt polling.*

The control and status registers of most device interfaces contain a bit or a group of bits that indicates whether an interrupt has been requested. For example, the keyboard and display interfaces in Figure 10–10 and Figure 10–13 request an interrupt whenever both RDY and IEN are 1. Even if both devices request interrupts using IRQ5, a program can determine which device, if any, has requested an interrupt at the current time by checking the RDY and IEN bits on both interfaces.

If multiple interrupt requests are made simultaneously, the order in which the interfaces are polled determines their priority. Table 11–2 shows a 68000 program with routines for both fixed-priority and round-robin polling. A "polling table" specifies the address of the control and status register and the starting address of the interrupt service routine for each device that can request interrupts on IRQ5. This example assumes that there are only three devices, but an arbitrary number of devices could be serviced using additional table entries.

The polling routine RPOLL checks the control and status registers for interrupt requests using the variable NEXTP to remember which interface was polled last, yielding round-robin priority. FPOLL forces NEXTP to point to the beginning of the table each time that it is entered, yielding fixed priority. Depending on the address value that the programmer uses to initialize the IRQ5 vector (MEM[$00000074]), IRQ5 interrupts are serviced by either FPOLL or RPOLL (FPOLL in this example).

11.2.4   Vectored Interrupts

Polling routines take time to execute and, in a system with many devices and frequent interrupts, the time spent polling can be significant. Therefore, many

TABLE 11–2   Interrupt polling programs for the 68000.

```
*              Subroutines FPOLL and RPOLL identify an interrupting device
*          by polling and transfer control to its interrupt service routine.
*          FPOLL uses fixed-priority polling, while RPOLL uses round-robin
*          polling.  A device is assumed to be interrupting if the RDY and IEN
*          bits (bits 7 and 6) in its control and status register are both 1.
*              One or more interrupting devices are listed in a polling table.
*          Each table entry contains two longwords: the address of the control
*          and status register of the device and the starting address of its
*          interrupt service routine.  The table is terminated by a zero word.
*

          ORG    $00000074      IRQ5 interrupt vector address.
          DC.L   FPOLL          Fixed-priority polling
*                                  (or RPOLL for round-robin polling).
          ORG    $00001000
*          Polling table.  Addresses of control and status registers
*          and service routines are assumed to be defined elsewhere.
POLLTB    DC.L   KBDCS,KBDINT    Keyboard.
          DC.L   DSPCS,DSPINT    Display.
          DC.L   PTRCS,PTRINT    Papertape reader.
          DC.L   0               End of table.
NEXTP     DS.L   1               Next to be polled.  For round-robin polling,
*                                  initialize to #POLLTB at run time.
*          Fixed-priority polling routine.
FPOLL     LEA.L  POLLTB,NEXTP    Start at beginning of POLLTB.
*                                Fall through to RPOLL.
*          Round-robin polling routine.
RPOLL     MOVEA.L NEXTP,A0       Address in table of next device to poll.
RNEXT     MOVEA.L (A0),A1        Get address of C&S reg for next device.
          TST.L   A1             Is it zero?
          BNE.S   RCHK           No, check C&S reg.
          LEA.L   POLLTB,A0      Yes, wrap-around to start of table.
          MOVEA.L (A0),A1        Get address of C&S reg.
RCHK      ADDA.L  #8,A0          Address of next entry in table.
          MOVE.B  (A1),D1        Check C&S reg -- bits 7 and 6 = 1?
          AND.B   #$C0,D1        Clear 6 low-order bits.
          CMP.B   #$C0,D1        D1 is now 11000000 if device interrupting.
          BEQ.S   RJMP           Jump to service routine if interrupting.
          CMPA.L  NEXTP,A0       Has next entry been checked before?
          BNE     RNEXT          No, check it.
ERROR     RTE                    False interrupt, return.
*
RJMP      MOVE.L  A0,NEXTP       Save address of next to be polled.
          MOVEA.L 4(A0),A0       Get address of service routine...
          JMP     (A0)           ...and jump to it.
```

computers have built-in hardware that automatically selects a different interrupt service routine for each different device. An interrupt system with this capability *vectored interrupt* is said to have *vectored interrupts*.

Vectored interrupt systems require a priority scheme (fixed or round robin)

interrupt vector number

interrupt acknowledge cycle

autovector

to be provided in hardware. In this way, when the processor accepts an interrupt, it can give a positive acknowledgment to the interrupting device interface with highest priority. When the interface receives this acknowledgment, it identifies itself in some way. In 68000 systems, it does this by sending an 8-bit *interrupt vector number* to the processor, using a special bus cycle called an *interrupt acknowledge cycle*. Note that there is no relationship between the interrupt vector number and any of the memory addresses used by the device's I/O ports.

During a 68000 interrupt acknowledge cycle, the interrupting device is not *required* to identify itself by sending an 8-bit interrupt vector number to the processor. If the device does not identify itself, then the processor assumes a vector number $v = 24 + i$, where i is the IPL for this interrupt. This *autovector* feature may be used in small systems to provide seven vectored interrupts with very little external hardware for priority arbitration. The choice of whether a device uses the autovector feature or supplies its own vector number belongs to the system hardware designer.[2]

In either case, the processor uses $4 \cdot v$ as the vector address; the longword stored at this address is the interrupt vector—the starting address of the interrupt service routine. The 68000 processor reserves the first 1024 bytes of memory for a table of 256 longword interrupt vectors.

11.2.5 Nonmaskable Interrupts

nonmaskable interrupt (NMI)

A *nonmaskable interrupt (NMI)* is one that cannot be masked by software; that is, it is always enabled. Most processors provide such an interrupt for handling supercritical events such as power failure or hardware errors.

The 6809 and 8086 have explicit NMI inputs; the 68000 does not. Instead, the 68000 designates IPL = 7 as a nonmaskable interrupt level. Therefore, when IPL is 7, an interrupt request will always be accepted, even if the PPL is 7. This is an exception to the general rule that IPL must be greater than PPL for an interrupt request to be accepted.

NMI inputs are generally "edge sensitive," so that an interrupt request will be recognized when the NMI input makes a transition from inactive to active. Therefore, the interrupt service routine must remove the condition that activated NMI before additional inactive-to-active transitions can be recognized.

The 68000 level-7 interrupt is no exception to the edge-sensitive rule. After all, consider what would happen if it weren't edge sensitive. Before entering the interrupt service routine, the processor sets PPL equal to IPL. At all other levels, this is sufficient to prevent the current request from reinterrupting its own service routine, because IPL must ordinarily be greater than PPL to be recognized. However, for IPL = 7, PPL = 7 does not prevent recognition of the nonmaskable interrupt request. Hence edge-sensitive behavior is required—a level-7 interrupt request will be recognized only on a transition from IPL < 7 to IPL = 7.

---

[2]The designer of a 68000-controlled fuel-injected carburetor would probably use autovectors.

watchdog timer   Nonmaskable interrupts are particularly useful for watchdog timers. A *watchdog timer* is an interrupt or reset that the hardware will generate after a predetermined interval *unless* software periodically performs a certain sequence of instructions. The sequence of instructions is normally set up so that it won't be executed unless the program is "sane." Thus, if the program goes insane, the watchdog timer will time out, causing a nonmaskable interrupt. The interrupt service routine is then supposed to evaluate the situation and restart the program along a sane course. Because a *nonmaskable* interrupt is used, an insane program usually cannot prevent the watchdog timer from having the desired effect.

11.3   TRAPS AND SOFTWARE INTERRUPTS

11.3.1   Traps

trap   Many processors can create hardware interrupt requests on the occurrence of certain internal processor events. Such interrupts are often called *traps* to distinguish them from I/O interrupts, and may occur on events such as the following:

- Exceptional conditions, such as division by zero or overflow or underflow on floating-point operations.

- Program faults, such as attempts to execute illegal or undefined instructions or attempts to access nonexistent or protected memory.

- Hardware faults, such as power failures and memory parity errors.

trap vector   When a trap event occurs, the processor pushes the PC and processor status onto the stack just as it does for an interrupt, and then jumps to a service routine whose starting address is contained in a predetermined *trap vector* location in memory. A typical processor provides different trap vectors for different conditions or groups of conditions.

11.3.2   Software Interrupts and Trap Instructions

Most processors have explicit instructions that affect the processor state in much the same way as an I/O interrupt or an internally caused trap. These instructions

software interrupt   are called *software interrupts*, *system calls*, or *trap instructions*.
system call   The 68000 has 16 trap instructions, TRAP #N, where N ranges from 0 to
trap instruction   15. When one of these instructions is executed, PC and SR are pushed onto the stack in the same way as during an IPL-requested hardware interrupt. Then control is transferred to a corresponding interrupt service routine whose 32-bit starting address is contained in interrupt vector number 32+N. For example, the starting address for the TRAP #14 service routine is contained in the longword at address $000000B8. The service routine does its thing and then returns control to the calling program by executing an RTE instruction.

Trap instructions are very important in computers with memory mapping and management and multiprogramming operating systems. For reliable operation, the operating system (OS) in such a computer normally runs in supervisor mode and the region of memory used by the OS is normally protected from direct access by user programs. A user program may not even be able to do a subroutine jump to an OS utility routine—otherwise it could conceivably crash the system by jumping into the middle of the routine.

Instead, trap instructions provide a well-controlled means for a user program to gain access to the operating system and other supervisor-mode resources. Like interrupts, traps in the 68000 automatically cause a change to supervisor mode. When the OS is accessed only through a predetermined trap service routine, it can dependably validate the requests and privilege of the user programs that request service. Programs running in user mode cannot simply set the 68000's S bit and jump into OS routines at a place of their own choosing. Also, since the OS has its own private stack pointer (SSP), a malicious user program cannot trick the OS into doing something foolish by placing bogus state information on the stack.

Besides providing the necessary switch to supervisor mode, trap instructions are useful for calling OS utilities for two other reasons. They are efficient because they are generally shorter in length than subroutine jumps. And they are convenient because they do not require the calling program to know the addresses of OS utilities in memory at assembly time, load time, or even run time; the starting addresses are stored in trap vectors. Thus, the same application program can run with many different software releases of an operating system, even though the OS code that implements a given utility may have been changed and moved.

Even though there are only a few trap instructions in the 68000, a program can call a larger number of different OS utility routines by placing a one-word utility code after the TRAP instruction. When the service routine is entered, the value of the PC saved on the stack will point to the utility-code word. The service routine can use this word as an index into its own internal table of utility routine addresses, and it can add 2 to the saved PC on the stack so that the one-word code is skipped on the return.

Alternatively, the utility code may be passed in a processor register, say D0. Upon entry, the trap service routine would simply read the value in D0 to determine which utility routine to execute. Other parameters may be passed in other registers, as in normal subroutine calling conventions.

11.4 SUMMARY OF 68000 INTERRUPT SYSTEM AND TRAPS

exception   Motorola classifies interrupts, traps, and reset as *exceptions*. In this section, we summarize the 68000's exceptions, concluding with the particularly exceptional bus error, address error, and reset conditions.

11.4.1   Exception Vectors

exception vector table

vector base register (VBR)

The 68000's *exception vector table* starts at memory address 0 and contains 256 longwords. In the 68010 and 68020, this table may be located elsewhere in memory, as determined by a new 32-bit register, the *vector base register (VBR)*. Each entry in the exception vector table contains the starting address of a routine that handles an exception—an interrupt, trap, or reset.

Vectors 0 through 63 are assigned for system use—reset, traps, and interrupt autovectors—while vectors 64 through 255 are available for user devices, as shown in Table 11–3. The entry for the reset exception contains two longwords, the initial values of SSP and PC after a processor reset. All other entries contain a single longword, the starting address of a service routine for an interrupt or trap.

11.4.2   Interrupt Handling

The 68000 has a seven-level, vectored, priority interrupt system. External hardware creates interrupt requests by supplying a 3-bit interrupt priority level (IPL) to the processor. An IPL of 0 indicates that no interrupt is pending, while values of 1 to 7 indicate that at least one interrupt is pending.

Like other processors, the 68000 checks for and accepts interrupts only between instructions. It compares the IPL with the current processor priority level (PPL) contained in SR bits 10–8. In general, if IPL is greater than PPL, the processor acknowledges the interrupt and initiates interrupt processing. Otherwise the processor continues program execution. IPL values 1 through 6 give rise to "normal" interrupts with level 6 having the highest priority. IPL values 0 and 7 are special:

- An IPL of 0 can never be greater than the processor priority and is therefore used to indicate that no interrupt is pending.

- An IPL of 7 is acknowledged even if the processor priority is 7. Therefore interrupt level 7 is nonmaskable.

Once the 68000 processor has decided to acknowledge an interrupt request, it performs several steps:

(1) The processor makes an internal copy of SR.

(2) The processor sets the PPL bits in SR equal to IPL to prevent further interrupts at the same or lower levels.

(3) The processor enters supervisor mode by setting the S bit in SR to 1. It also clears the T bit in SR to inhibit tracing.

(4) The processor pushes PC onto the stack. Then it pushes its internal copy of the old SR onto the stack. Since the processor is in supervisor mode, these operations use the supervisor stack pointer (SSP).

TABLE 11–3   Exception vector assignments in the 68000.

Number	Address (hex)	Cause
0	00000000	Reset (initial SSP)
1	00000004	Reset (initial PC)
2	00000008	Bus error
3	0000000C	Address error
4	00000010	Illegal instructions and BKPT
5	00000014	Zero divide
6	00000018	CHK2,[1] CHK instructions
7	0000001C	cpTRAPcc,[1] TRAPcc,[1] TRAPV instructions
8	00000020	Privilege violation
9	00000024	Trace
10	00000028	Unimplemented instruction (line 1010)
11	0000002C	Unimplemented instruction (line 1111)
12	00000030	Unassigned, reserved
13	00000034	Coprocessor protocol violation[1]
14	00000038	Format error[2]
15	0000003C	Uninitialized interrupt vector[3]
16–23	00000040–0000005C	Unassigned, reserved
24	00000060	Spurious interrupt
25	00000064	Level 1 autovector
26	00000068	Level 2 autovector
27	0000006C	Level 3 autovector
28	00000070	Level 4 autovector
29	00000074	Level 5 autovector
30	00000078	Level 6 autovector
31	0000007C	Level 7 autovector
32–47	00000080–000000BC	TRAP #0–15 instructions
48–54	000000C0–000000D8	Floating-point coprocessor errors[4]
55	000000DC	Unassigned, reserved
56–58	000000E0–000000E8	Memory management unit errors[4]
59–63	000000EC–000000FC	Unassigned, reserved
64–255	00000100–000003FC	User device interrupts

Notes: 1. Generated by 68020 only.
2. Generated by 68010 and 68020 only.
3. Generated by 68000-family peripheral chips that have an "interrupt vector register," if that register has not been initialized to specify which user-device interrupt vector (64–255) that the peripheral chip should use.
4. Generated by Motorola's external floating-point and MMU chips, usually in conjunction with a 68020.

(5) The processor gives the device interface an opportunity to identify itself: the device may place an 8-bit interrupt vector number on the data bus. The same external hardware, if any, that resolved among multiple interrupt requests to generate IPL must also decide which interface gets to put its vector number on the data bus. If the external hardware asserts the

Bus Error input, the processor uses vector number 24 (*spurious interrupt*). If no vector number is provided, then the processor uses an autovector corresponding to the IPL: $v = 24 + \text{IPL}$.

(6) The processor uses the 8-bit vector number v as an index into the exception vector table; it fetches a longword from address $4 \cdot v$.

(7) The processor jumps to the interrupt service routine by loading PC with the longword that it fetched from the vector table.

Programs normally terminate interrupt processing by executing an RTE instruction, which restores SR and PC by popping their saved values from the supervisor (SSP) stack. The interrupted program continues at the location and in the state determined by the restored values.

11.4.3   Pascal Simulation of 68000 Interrupt Handling

A Pascal simulation of how the 68000 checks for and handles interrupt requests is presented in Table 11–4. This simulation is meant to work in conjunction with the instruction execution procedures in Table 5–8 on page 156. The procedure CheckForInterrupt shows how interrupt requests are checked after the execution of each instruction. The procedure ReturnFromInterrupt shows the actions performed by the 68000 RTE instruction. The auxiliary function and procedure SRword and RestoreSR pack and unpack the individual SR bits to and from a 16-bit word format that matches the one shown in the 68000 programming model (Figure 5–4 on page 139).

11.4.4   Traps

A trap in the 68000 causes the same kind of processing as an interrupt: the processor changes to supervisor mode, pushes PC and SR, and jumps to a service routine whose starting address is read from the exception vector table. The 68000 handles traps from many different sources; their vector numbers and causes are listed below.

2 *Bus error.* External hardware, such as a memory management unit, asserted the Bus Error input signal during a memory access.

3 *Address error.* The processor attempted to access a word or longword at an odd address.

4 *Illegal instruction.* The processor attempted to execute an instruction with an illegal combination of opcode and addressing mode, as determined by decoding the opcode word. Note that an illegal opcode word for one 68000-family processor may be defined and legal in another 68000-family processor. For example, opcode words $06C0–$06CF (the RTM instruction) are legal only in the MC68020.

TABLE 11–4   Pascal simulation of 68000 interrupt handling.

```
FUNCTION SRword: word; {Build up SR word from individual bits.}
  BEGIN SRword :=
        ((((((((((T*4+S)*32+PPL)*16)+X)*2)+N)*2)+Z)*2)+V)S ()*2+C END;

PROCEDURE RestoreSR(w: word); {Restore SR bits from word w.}
    T := Bits(15,15,w); S := Bits(13,13,w); PPL := Bits(10,8,w);
    X := Bits(4,4,w); N := Bits(3,3,w); Z := Bits(2,2,w);
    V := Bits(1,1,w); C := Bits(0,0,w);
    IF S = 0 THEN {Returning to user mode -- shadow USP into REG[A7].}
       BEGIN SSP := REG[A7]; REG[A7] := USP END;
END;


PROCEDURE CheckForInterrupt;
VAR devnum: 0..255;
  BEGIN
    IF IPL > PPL THEN BEGIN
      IF Autovector THEN devnum := 24 + IPL
      ELSE devnum := ReadDevnumFromDevice;
      PushWord(Bits(15,0,PC)); PushWord(Bits(31,16,PC));
      PushWord(SRword);
      IF S = 0 THEN {Entering supervisor mode -- shadow SSP into REG[A7].}
         BEGIN USP := REG[A7]; REG[A7] := SSP END;
      S := 1; T := 0; PPL := IPL; {Update new SR as required.}
      {Set up PC to start interrupt service routine.}
      PC := 65536*ReadWord(4*devnum) + ReadWord(4*devnum+2);
    END;

PROCEDURE ReturnFromInterrupt;
  BEGIN
    RestoreSR(PopWord); {Restore SR.}
    PC := PopWord*65536 + PopWord; {Restore PC.}
  END;
```

5 *Zero divide.* A DIVU or DIVS instruction had a zero divisor.

6,7 *Conditional trap instruction.* The processor executed a CHK or TRAPV instruction in which the conditions for a trap were satisfied.

8 *Privilege violation.* The processor attempted to execute a privileged instruction in user mode. This trap allows an operating system to gain control if a user program attempts to thwart it.

9 *Trace.* The T bit was 1 at the beginning of an instruction's execution. This feature may be used by a debugger to single step a program as follows. The debugger executes an RTE to the user program such that the SR value restored from the stack has the T bit set. The processor then executes one instruction of the user program and returns control to the debugger via the trace trap handler.

A-line opcode

10 *Unimplemented instruction.* The processor attempted to execute an instruction with bits 15–12 of the opcode word equal to 1010, a so-called *A-line opcode.* Motorola has not defined instructions for these opcodes, but has not publicly guaranteed that they won't in some future processor. Nevertheless, certain software systems (most notably the Macintosh operating system) use these opcodes to create a system call instruction with a 12-bit utility code imbedded in the opcode word.

F-line opcode

11 *Unimplemented instruction.* The processor attempted to execute an instruction with bits 15–12 of the opcode word equal to 1111, a so-called *F-line opcode.* These opcodes are used in advanced 68000 processors for additional instructions such as floating-point arithmetic. Users of older processors may write trap handlers to emulate the new instructions.

32–47 *Unconditional trap instruction.* The processor executed **TRAP #N**, where N ranges from 0 to 15. These instructions are normally used to call operating system utilities.

Bus and address error traps are taken immediately, as soon as an offending memory access occurs, possibly in the middle of an instruction's execution. Privilege violation and illegal and unimplemented instruction traps take place when the offending instruction is fetched and decoded, but before execution begins and any damage is done; the saved PC is the address of the instruction that caused the trap. The remaining traps take place immediately after the execution of the instruction that caused them; the saved PC is the address of the next instruction.

11.4.5 Bus and Address Errors

Bus and address error traps are unusual in that they may occur in the middle of an instruction's execution. As a result, the saved PC is the address of neither the offending instruction nor its successor; it is an address "in the vicinity" of the offending instruction—one to five words beyond the start of it. Bus and address error traps are also different from other traps in that they push four words of diagnostic information onto the stack, in addition to PC and SR. If a second bus or address error occurs while this information is being saved, the processor gives up and halts; only a hardware reset will restart it.

Figure 11–8 shows the state of the supervisor stack after a bus or address error. Here, the instruction register (IR) value is the first word of the instruction that caused the error; and the effective address register (EAR) value is the address that was being accessed when the error occurred (also see Figure 5–3 on page 137). The last word provides additional information about the type of memory access: read or write, instruction or not, and function.

Note that an **RTE** instruction should not be executed when the stack has the state shown in Figure 11–8. The trap handler is expected to "clean up" the stack by removing the four words of diagnostic information. It must also determine

Mac Note

Programs written in the Macintosh environment call operating system utilities using traps generated by the A-line unimplemented instruction opcodes.

Such trap instructions have one of the formats shown in the figure. Bits 15–12 are always set to 1010, the A-line opcode. Bit 11 distinguishes between two types of traps. *Operating system traps* perform low-level operations such as file I/O and memory allocation. *Toolbox traps* call QuickDraw and other routines that deal with the user interface.

15				12 11 10	8 7	0
1	0	1	0	0	flags	trap number

"Operating System" format

15				12 11 10 9 8		0
1	0	1	0	1	flags	trap number

"Toolbox" format

Whenever an A-line opcode is encountered, the processor traps through vector 10 and executes the trap handler, which is part of the Macintosh operating system. Using the return address on the stack, the trap handler locates the A-line opcode in the calling program and decodes its low-order 12 bits to determine what to do next. Depending on the format, 8 or 9 bits are used as an index into a table of utility routines, and the remaining bits are flags that give the handler additional information on how to complete the requested operation.

Typical Macintosh programming systems, such as the MPW and MDS assemblers, provide macro packages, such as `Traps.a`, that define mnemonics for all of the traps. For example, the macro `_DrawChar` expands into `DC.W $A883`, an A-line opcode word that specifies Toolbox trap number `$83`.

whether to return control to the offending program at all and, if so, where? The offending instruction was not completely executed, and the saved PC may not even point to the beginning of an instruction. In all likelihood, the offending program must be aborted.

The Bus Error input of the 68000 processor is intended to be used by external memory management units (MMUs) to signal protection violations and abort the offending instructions (and programs); it serves this purpose well. There was also some effort by early 68000 system designers to use the Bus Error input to

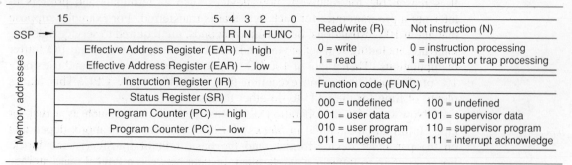

FIGURE 11–8 Format of information saved during bus or address error trap.

support virtual memory operations. If an external MMU determined that an address was "not present" in physical memory, it could try to abort the current instruction by asserting Bus Error, bring the missing information into physical memory, and reexecute the offending instruction later.

Using the saved information in Figure 11–8, a very smart program (one that could decode and backward-simulate all 68000 instructions) could usually figure out what the exact processor state was at the time that the bus error occurred, but not always. For example, suppose a bus error occurs while the processor is reading an operand of the instruction `CMPM.B (A0)+,(A0)+`. It is impossible to determine from the saved information whether the processor was reading the first or second operand when the error occurred. Thus, even if the situation that caused the error is corrected, it is impossible to determine reliably the proper program state for reexecuting the offending instruction. As a result, general-purpose implementations of virtual memory had to wait for the 68010 and 68020 processors, which support instruction continuation after bus errors by storing more internal processor information on the stack, as discussed in Section 14.1.

11.4.6   Reset

Though classified as an exception, the reset condition is handled differently from interrupts and traps. When a reset signal is applied to the 68000, the processor is placed in supervisor mode with processor priority 7. No assumptions are made about the validity of the processor registers, and so the processor does *not* save the old PC and SR. Instead, it immediately loads SSP with a value fetched from vector table entry 0, and loads PC with a value fetched from vector table entry 1. Then it begins instruction execution at the address contained in PC.

11.5   DIRECT MEMORY ACCESS

11.5.1   Motivation

It is reasonable for relatively slow devices such as terminals and printers to interrupt a program once for each byte that is transferred. For example, suppose that about 100 instructions, or 100 microseconds, are required to service a device interrupt, including register saving and restoring, device service, and I/O buffer manipulations. Then a rate of 100 I/O transfers (interrupts) per second uses only 1% of the total instruction execution time available to the CPU. This leaves plenty of time for the CPU to do other things.

block

Now consider the operation of a mass storage device such as a disk or tape. Information is stored in *blocks* of 128 to 2048 bytes or more, depending on the particular device format, and the basic unit of transfer is one block. For a program to transfer a single block of data between a typical mass storage device and memory, it must first initiate a mechanical operation (such as moving *access latency*

the tape) to bring the selected block under a read/write head. The time spent waiting for this operation to be completed is called *access latency*. Average access latency for a disk ranges from about 8 to 250 milliseconds; a long tape can have an access latency of minutes. In any case, it seems reasonable to use an interrupt to signal the appearance of the selected block under the read/write head, to avoid a long period of busy-waiting.

Once the selected block appears under the read/write head, interrupts lose their usefulness. For example, in a single-density, 5.25" minifloppy disk, data bits pass under the read/write head at the rate of one byte per 64 microseconds. It is unlikely that an interrupt service routine could do all of the required operations in 64 microseconds and return to the interrupted program before the next byte appeared. More likely, a very tight, efficient busy-wait loop would be required to perform the transfer.

With a double-density minifloppy disk, the programming problem becomes even more difficult, with a byte appearing every 32 or 16 microseconds. And with a typical "hard" disk, a programmed transfer is impossible on most CPUs, since a byte appears every 8 microseconds or less. At this point, we must look for another approach.

direct memory access (DMA) channel

A *direct memory access (DMA) channel* is a special hardware arrangement that allows a device interface to quickly transfer data directly to or from main memory without processor intervention. Ordinarily, the CPU is the "master" of the memory bus—it provides the address and control signals for each transfer that takes place. However, a DMA channel can temporarily become bus master as required to control the transfer of I/O data directly between a device and main memory.

cycle stealing

For example, suppose a hard disk has a transfer rate of one byte per 8 microseconds and the main memory cycle time is 0.5 microseconds. Then a DMA channel can "steal" one memory cycle out of every 16 to transfer disk data, still leaving available 15 out of every 16 memory cycles for the CPU's use.

Because a DMA channel transfers data directly between a device and memory, it has no effect on the processor state (assuming that the DMA transfer is not writing new information over the current program or its data!). The only effect on program operation is that instructions occasionally take a little longer to execute, because they must wait for a "slow" memory access. In the disk example above, the CPU is slowed down by no more than about 7%. The actual slowdown may be less, because sometimes DMA may steal cycles that the CPU didn't need anyway. For example, the DMA channel might transfer I/O data while the CPU is executing a multiply, divide, or other instruction whose execution time is not limited by memory speed.

11.5.2 DMA Channel Programming

As with other I/O interfaces, the programming models for DMA channels vary by device and computer. However, we can point out some common requirements

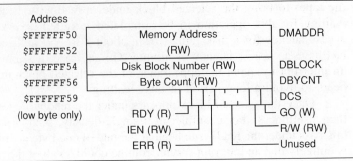

FIGURE 11-9   Programming model for a disk DMA channel.

of all DMA channels for mass storage devices such as disks. To perform a transfer, the channel must first be told the direction of transfer: disk to memory (read) or memory to disk (write). For a read, it must be told where to get the data on the disk and where to put it in main memory, and vice versa for a write. It must also be told how many bytes to transfer.

A stylized programming model for a disk DMA channel for the 68000 is shown in Figure 11–9. The control and status register (DCS) contains the RDY, IEN, ERR, and GO bits typical of other device interfaces. In addition, it contains a bit R/W for selecting the direction of transfer (1 = read, 0 = write). When IEN is 1, the DMA channel interrupts when an entire block transfer has been completed, not once per byte.

A 32-bit register DMADDR gives the starting address in main memory for the transfer. A 16-bit register DBLOCK gives the starting block number on the disk for the transfer. Depending on the type of disk, DBLOCK may be subdivided into fields with information such as drive number, surface number, track number, and sector number. For large disks, a wider register or multiple registers might be required. In any case, DBLOCK addresses only full blocks on the disk, not individual bytes. The size of a block depends on the disk; we'll use a size of 256 bytes in this example.

Register DBYCNT indicates the number of bytes to be transferred between the disk and main memory. Typically, DBYCNT is set equal to the block size, so that exactly one block is transferred at a time. If DBYCNT specifies a larger number of bytes, then the DMA channel will automatically increment the block number in DBLOCK to access the next sequential block(s). A disk or tape physically can only read or write a full block at a time; if DBYCNT is not a multiple of the block size, then the DMA channel must compensate. For example, on read operations the channel still reads the entire last block from the device, but only stores in main memory the bytes actually required by DBYCNT. On write operations, it pads the end of the last block with zeroes to reach a multiple of the block size.

A program that uses DMA to read complete blocks of data from a disk is shown in Table 11–5. It reads one block at a time from the disk, using DMA

TABLE 11-5   Disk input program using DMA.

```
BLKSIZ  EQU     256             Disk block size.
*                               Addresses of disk interface registers.
DMADDR  EQU     $FFFFFF50       Main memory address (longword).
DBLOCK  EQU     $FFFFFF54       Block number (word).
DBYCNT  EQU     $FFFFFF56       Number of bytes to transfer (word).
DCS     EQU     $FFFFFF59       Control and status (byte).
*
BLOCKN  DS.W    1               Program variable -- disk block #.
DSKBUF  DS.B    BLKSIZ          Buffer for one disk block.
*
DISKIO  ...                     Begin program.
        ...
LOOP    ...                     Process one block per iteration.
*                               Determine block number, put in BLOCKN.
        ...
*                               Now ready to get a block from the disk.
        LEA.L   DSKBUF,DMADDR   Address of memory buffer for transfer.
        MOVE.L  BLOCKN,DBLOCK   Disk block number.
        MOVE.L  #BLKSIZ,DBYCNT  Block and buffer size.
        MOVE.B  #$03,DCS        Set disk for read and go.
*                               If possible, do other work while waiting.
        ...
*                               Now we need the buffer contents --
WTDSK   MOVE.B  DCS,D0             has the reading finished?
        BPL     WTDSK           Wait until ready.
        AND.B   #$20,D0         Check error bit.
        BNE     DERROR          Handle errors if set.
*                               Now process the buffer...
        ..
        JMP     LOOP            ...and go do some more.
DERROR  ...                     Handle disk errors.
```

to dump each block into a 256-byte memory buffer DSKBUF. After requesting a block, the program continues with other computation; when it is ready to process the block, it must busy-wait on the RDY bit in DCS. After processing the block, the program decides which block to process next and repeats.

As the program stands, it can't begin reading a second block from the disk while still processing a first, because the DMA transfer could overwrite the contents of DSKBUF with the second block before the program has finished

double buffering   processing the first. However, a technique called *double buffering* allows this kind of overlap to take place. We provide two buffers: the DMA fills an I/O buffer while the program accesses data in a work buffer. After each program iteration and DMA transfer are completed, the program copies the contents of the I/O buffer into the work buffer for the next iteration and initiates another transfer. Alternatively, the copying operation could be eliminated by simply swapping the roles of the two buffers after each iteration. Either way, the I/O device can be kept busy continuously if computation is faster than I/O.

Interrupts are often used instead of busy-waiting for DMA completion in multiblock transfers. An interrupt indicates the completion of each DMA block transfer, and the interrupt service routine initiates the next DMA block transfer. After the last block has been transferred, the service routine signals completion to the main program using a software flag. Operation is similar to that of the display output program in Table 11–1, except that interrupts occur once per block instead of once per character.

11.5.3   Memory-Mapped Displays

memory-mapped display

An important application of DMA in many computers is the *memory-mapped display*. In this arrangement, a DMA channel is designed to access a block of memory in which each byte corresponds to a character position on a cathode-ray-tube display (CRT). To send a character to a particular position on the display, a program simply writes the ASCII value of the character into the corresponding location in the memory buffer. The DMA channel automatically accesses each byte in the buffer about 60 times per second, sending each ASCII character to video circuits that form the corresponding graphic symbol on the CRT, typically a high-resolution video monitor. In home-computer applications that do not require high resolution, an ordinary television is used instead of a monitor.

Memory-mapped displays are also used in computer graphics. In this case, each bit in each byte in the display buffer corresponds to a dot on the display that can be either on or off (bright or dark). A program creates an image on the display by setting up appropriate bits in the display buffer. Note that higher-resolution displays require larger buffers than do low-resolution displays. For example, a 512×512 display requires 2^{18} bits or 32 Kbytes of memory. Additional features, such as grey scale and color, require more than one bit of information for each dot (or *picture element*, *pixel*), and multiply the memory requirements by a corresponding factor.

picture element
pixel

Memory-mapped displays in different computers have varying degrees of sophistication. For example, the address of the display buffer may be fixed by the hardware, or it may be programmable—the user selects among two or more buffers by issuing I/O commands to the DMA interface. In another example, scrolling text may require a program to move up all the data in the display buffer to make room for a new line at the end, or it may only require a pointer and one line in the buffer to be updated. In the second case, the DMA starts the display in the middle of the buffer at a location designated by a "top-of-display" pointer, and wraps back to the beginning when it hits the buffer end.

Small computers with memory-mapped displays include the Apple II family, the Macintosh family, and the IBM PC and compatibles. In conjunction with a built-in keyboard, the memory-mapped display takes the place of the separate CRT terminal that would otherwise be used to communicate with the machine. In fact, most "smart" CRT terminals such as the DEC VT-100 family and compatibles actually contain a microprocessor with a memory-mapped display interface.

REFERENCES

The possibility of overlapping computation with input/output was recognized in early computer designs, but was not immediately pursued. As explained in the classic Burks, Goldstine, and von Neumann paper (in C. G. Bell and A. Newell's *Computer Structures: Readings and Examples* (McGraw-Hill, 1971), pp. 117–118), "Simultaneous operation of the computer and the input–output organ requires additional temporary storage and introduces a synchronizing problem, and hence it is not being considered for the first model."

Interrupt systems provided the needed synchronization mechanism in machines such as the Univac 1103 (circa 1953), Lincoln Laboratory's TX-2 (circa 1957), and Manchester University's Atlas (circa 1960) (*Computer Structures*, pp. 45, 274, 277). DMA channels were provided in the Atlas and in the IBM 7094 computer (circa 1960) (*Computer Structures*, pp. 523–524). The Atlas computer also introduced the idea of "extracodes" upon which modern software interrupt and system call instructions are based (*Computer Structures*, pp. 274–277).

General discussions of the hardware structure of modern interrupt systems and DMA channels can be found in several texts, including *Computer Architecture and Organization* by John Hayes (McGraw-Hill, 1988, 2nd ed.), *Computer Organization* by V. C. Hamacher, Z. G. Vranesic, and S. G. Zaky (McGraw-Hill, 1984, 2nd ed.), and *Digital Systems: Hardware Organization and Design* by F. J. Hill and G. R. Peterson (Wiley, 1987, 3rd ed.). The best source of information on interrupt systems and DMA channels for specific processors is of course the manufacturers' literature.

EXERCISES

11.1   Modify the `CheckForInterrupt` procedure in Table 11–4 to handle level-7 interrupt requests properly.

11.2   Write a program that uses interrupts to measure and print the time between successive hits on a pushbutton. Three I/O devices are needed:

   (1) A real-time clock should be used to produce interrupts at regular intervals; its interrupt service routine should increment a variable `TIME` in memory.

   (2) A keyboard or similar input device should be used for button hits, producing an interrupt each time that the button is hit. A variable `LHIT` can be used to keep track of the time of the latest button hit.

   (3) A CRT or other display output device should be used to print a message indicating the elapsed time after each time that the button is hit. The message should be formatted as a string and printed under interrupt control as in Table 11–1.

   Note: A single button hit that occurs while the message is being printed must not be lost. If two or more hits occur during this time, the second and successive ones may be lost. *Further note:* If a real-time clock is not available, then one can be simulated by a main program loop that busy-waits for approximately 1 millisecond (as determined by instruction execution times) and then increments **TIME**. The time lost servicing interrupts is negligible for the purposes of this exercise.

11.3　Modify the above program so that the button can be hit several times while a message is being printed, without losing information. In order to do this, provide a queue for elapsed time values. Each time that the button is hit, the elapsed time value should be put into the queue. The main program continuously checks to see if the output routine is idle; whenever the output routine is idle, the main program checks the queue for a value to print.

11.4　Suppose that an operating system for the 68000 has 200 different utility routines that are to be accessed by user programs with the **TRAP #0** instruction. The user programs must pass a "utility ID" to the vector-32 trap handler to select a particular utility routine. Discuss the pros and cons of passing this parameter in a data register versus passing it "in-line" in the word following the **TRAP** instruction.

11.5　Write a service routine for the **TRAP** instruction on the 68000 that assumes that the **TRAP** is followed by a one-word code that designates a particular operating system utility routine to be called. The service routine should "fudge" the saved PC on the stack so that the utility routine can return using an **RTI**, and then use the one-word code as an index into a table of utility routine starting addresses.

11.6　Modify the 68000 instruction execution simulation procedure given in Table 5–8 on page 156 to handle address error traps and to execute the **TRAP #N** instruction.

11.7　Describe a simple program bug that causes a 68000 processor to halt.

11.8　Rewrite the DMA input program in Table 11–5 to use double buffering so that the contents of the I/O buffer are copied into the work buffer upon the completion of each DMA operation.

11.9　Rewrite the DMA input program in Table 11–5 to use double buffering so that the roles of the I/O buffer and the work buffer are swapped upon the completion of each DMA operation. Be sure to show how the main program selects the proper buffer to access.

CHAPTER 12

Processes and Concurrency

Even though a typical microcomputer executes only one instruction at a time, it must still manage several interrelated activities during a short period of time. For example, almost all application programs involve user input, computation, and user output. Interactive programs must display recent results, compute new results using current information, and scan for new inputs, all simultaneously as far as a user is concerned. Yet the processor is working on only one of these tasks during any given instruction execution cycle.

In the previous chapter, we saw how interrupts allow I/O operations to be overlapped with computation. In a more general case, several different computational tasks as well as several I/O tasks could be worked on concurrently. Concurrency is achieved in single-processor systems by means of interrupts, which allow one task to be suspended temporarily so that another may run.. In multiprocessor systems, an even greater degree of concurrency is achieved with multiple processors, each of which is executing its own private instruction stream at any given instant.

When we try to do more than one thing at a time, even in a computer system, it's easy to become confused. Therefore, to handle concurrent tasks correctly, we need a sound, abstract understanding of what concurrency in a computer system really means, and we need to couple that understanding with practical knowledge of techniques for writing concurrent programs. This chapter addresses these needs by defining the abstract ideas of processes and concurrency, by explaining the anomolous timing-dependent behaviors that can occur in concurrent programs, and by presenting methods for structuring concurrent programs and their data.

TABLE 12–1   Legal conditions of a process P.

Activity	Wakefulness	Description
Active	Awake	CPU is executing P's instructions.
Active	Asleep	CPU is executing instructions for some other process; but P may still be awakened by an interrupt or other event.
Inactive	Asleep	CPU is executing instructions for some other process and interrupts for P cannot occur; P may be awakened only by another process explicitly reactivating it.

12.1 INTERRUPT PROCESSES

12.1.1 Processes

process

The abstract concept of a "process" is a convenient aid to understanding and discussing the behavior of programs in an interrupt environment. A *process* may be loosely defined as a program in execution. The state of a process includes the processor (CPU) state and the values of the program's variables stored in memory. Thus we can say that a process is a discrete progression in time of discernible changing states. The minimum grain of time is the processor's instruction interpretation cycle.

active

inactive
terminated
awake
asleep

In an interrupt environment, it is convenient to think of a program as containing a set of processes that are activated, suspended, resumed, and terminated during the program's execution. A process is *active* if one or more of its instructions have been executed, and one or more instructions have yet to be executed; otherwise it is *inactive* (or *terminated*). An active process is *awake* if its instructions are currently being executed by the processor; otherwise it is *asleep*. An inactive process can be considered to be always asleep. Table 12–1 summarizes the possible conditions of processes.

suspend
put to sleep
resume
awaken

For example, consider the display output program that was shown in Table 11–1. It contains two processes, the main program (MPP) and the string printing process (SPP). Periodically MPP activates SPP by calling STROUT. After sending one character to the display, STROUT *suspends* (or *puts to sleep*) SPP and returns control to MPP. Thereafter, SPP is periodically *resumed* (or *awakened*) by display interrupts, which are serviced by STRINT. SPP is put to sleep when STRINT returns to the interrupted program, and terminated when the last character of a line has been printed.

In Figure 11–5, the state of variable SBUSY corresponds to the active (1) or inactive (0) state of SPP, whereas MPP is always active. The asleep and awake states of the processes can be derived from the execution trace. SPP is awake when the processor is executing STROUT or STRINT, and asleep at other times; MPP is awake whenever SPP is asleep, and vice versa.

Because interrupts can occur at arbitrary times, it may be possible at any time for an awake process to be put to sleep and a sleeping process to be awakened. This gives rise to the single most important characteristic of process behavior:

- Within a given process, instruction are executed in the order in which they were written, but instructions from other processes may intervene.

At the very lowest level, this behavior imposes the requirement that all registers in the processor state be saved and restored by interrupt service routines. But there may also be effects at higher levels, in particular when two or more processes share instructions or data, as we'll see later.

12.1.2 A Simplifying Restriction

Multiple processes usually operate under the control of an operating system or executive. Some operating systems allow processes to be dynamically created and destroyed as suggested above, while others require all processes to be created at system initialization. In the latter case, processes are always active; they can only be awakened and put to sleep, not activated or terminated. We can use this idea in the MPP/SPP example by saying SPP never really terminates itself; even after printing the last character of a line, SPP simply puts itself to sleep. But now we must recognize that there are two distinct ways in which SPP could be reawakened after putting itself to sleep: by an interrupt or by an explicit command from another process.

We shall use the above ideas to simplify the discussions in the remainder of this chapter. We shall consider a process to be always active, but progressing through times of wakefulness and sleep. There are three basic situations in which a process can wake up or go to sleep:

(1) An awake process goes to sleep when an arbitrary device interrupt occurs, and is awakened when the interrupt service routine returns control to it.

(2) A sleeping process is awakened by its own device interrupt, and it executes its interrupt service routine. The process goes to sleep when it returns control to the interrupted program. Before going to sleep, it may or may not arrange to be reawakened later by its device interrupt.

(3) A sleeping process may be awakened by an explicit command from another process (e.g., a command to begin printing a line of text). It goes to sleep by returning control to the calling process, but before doing so it usually arranges to be reawakened later by its device interrupt.

12.2 CONCURRENCY

For the most efficient use of computer resources, computation and I/O should be overlapped whenever possible. The display output program in Table 11–1 on page 389 made good use of concurrency by using an interrupt process to complete output operations initiated by the main program process.

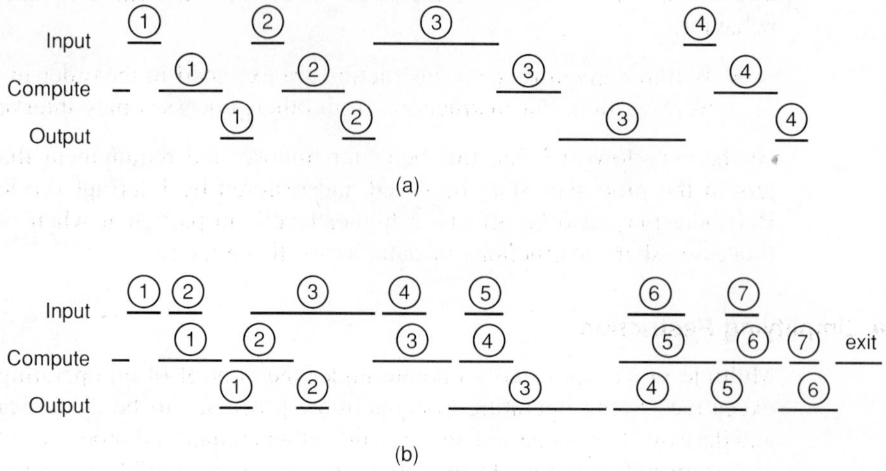

FIGURE 12–1   Input/output concurrency: (a) no interrupts and no overlap; (b) interrupts and overlap.

12.2.1 Multiple Interrupt Processes

A typical program requires input operations as well as output operations. The general outline for such a program is as follows:

(1) Read a set of inputs.

(2) Compute with the inputs to produce a set of outputs.

(3) Write the set of outputs.

(4) If there are more inputs, return to step 1, else terminate.

We can consider input, computation, and output to be three separate processes. Without interrupts, however, a program would be forced to execute each step separately, with no time overlap, as shown in Figure 12–1(a). The circled numbers identify each set of data as it is read from the input device, processed by the CPU, and written to the output device.

A more desirable behavior, achieved by using interrupts, is shown in Figure 12–1(b). The main program must still wait for the first set of inputs. However, the input process can begin to read the second set of inputs as soon as the computation process has received the first set. When the computation process becomes ready for the second set of inputs, they are already available. From this point on, most of the computation is overlapped with input and output. Occasionally the computation process must wait for a slow input operation (third set) or output operation (third set also) to complete. After finding that the last (seventh) set of inputs is empty, the computation process must wait for the current output operation to complete before returning control to the operating system.

TABLE 12–2   Program to reverse lines of input text.

```
PROGRAM ReverseLines (input, output);
VAR inputBuffer, outputBuffer : ARRAY [1..100] OF char;
  inputAvailable, outputPrinted, working : boolean;

PROCESS LineIn;
  IOVAR kbdData : char;  kbdIEN, kbdReady, kbdGo : boolean;
  BEGIN
    WHILE true DO {forever}
      BEGIN
        inputAvailable := false;  ClearInputBuffer;
        REPEAT {Enable interrupt, request keystroke, clear ready.}
          kbdIEN := true; kbdGo := true; kbdReady := false;
          SLEEP UNTIL kbdReady = true; {Wait for keyboard interrupt.}
          PutInInputBuffer(kbdData);
        UNTIL kbdData = terminator;
        kbdIEN := false; inputAvailable := true; SLEEP;
      END; {WHILE}
  END; {LineIn}

PROCESS LineOut;
  IOVAR dspData : char;  dspIEN, dspReady, dspGo : boolean;
  BEGIN
    WHILE true DO {forever}
      BEGIN
        outputPrinted := false;
        WHILE CharsLeftToBePrinted DO {If there's an output char...}
          BEGIN  {...send char to display data register,...}
            dspData := GetNextOutputChar;
            {...enable interrupt, start display, and clear ready.}
            dspIEN := true; dspGo := true; dspReady := false;
            SLEEP UNTIL dspReady = true; {Wait for display interrupt.}
          END;
        dspIEN := false; outputPrinted := true; SLEEP;
      END; {WHILE}
  END; {LineOut}
```

A program that achieves the behavior in Figure 12–1(b) is outlined in Table 12–2 in pseudo-Pascal. The program defines three processes to read lines of input text, reverse the order of the characters in each line, and print the reversed lines. The new reserved word PROCESS begins the definition of a process, and SLEEP and WAKEUP explicitly suspend and resume processes. A process can "SLEEP" until explicitly awakened by another process via WAKEUP, or it can "SLEEP UNTIL" a specified condition becomes true (e.g., an interrupt request).

PROCESS
SLEEP
WAKEUP
SLEEP UNTIL

IOVAR

Another new reserved word, IOVAR, is used to declare I/O ports. The program simulates the bits in the control and status ports of a keyboard and display by boolean IOVARs, and the data ports by char IOVARs. The device interfaces read IOVARs and change their values when I/O events occur (e.g.,

TABLE 12–2   (continued)

```
PROCESS MainLoop;
  LABEL 10; VAR workBuffer : ARRAY [1..100] OF char;
  BEGIN
    WAKEUP LineIn;   {Request LineIn to read the first line...}
    WHILE true DO                 {...and put it in inputBuffer.}
      BEGIN
        SLEEP UNTIL inputAvailable;  {Wait for an input line.}
        IF InputBufferEmpty THEN GOTO 10;  {Exit on blank line.}
        workBuffer := inputBuffer;  {Copy input line...}
        WAKEUP LineIn;   {...and start reading next line.}
        ReverseWorkBuffer; {Reverse characters in work buffer.}
        SLEEP UNTIL outputPrinted; {Wait for a chance to print.};
        outputBuffer := workBuffer; {Copy line...}
        WAKEUP LineOut;   {...and start printing it.}
      END;
  10: SLEEP UNTIL outputPrinted; {Wait for last line to be printed.}
    working := false;   SLEEP {forever};
  END;

BEGIN  {Main program.}
  working := true; outputPrinted := true;   {Initialization.}
  WAKEUP MainLoop; WHILE working DO ; {Wait for MainLoop to finish.}
END .
```

the keyboard interface sets `kbdReady` to `true` when a character is received). Several procedure and function definitions have been left to your imagination.

The main program simply wakes up process `MainLoop` and busy-waits for `MainLoop` to finish all of its operations. `MainLoop` performs the three-step loop (input, compute, output) and goes to sleep whenever the input process or output process has not completed its operation by the time that `MainLoop` is ready to initiate the next input or output operation.

12.2.2   Implementation Details

The processes in Table 12–2 are closely related to coroutines. When a process is resumed after sleeping, its computation should proceed where it left off, just like a coroutine that is resumed after calling another coroutine. In an assembly language version of the program, we could provide a variable that stores the resumption (or "wake-up") address for each process.

Another alternative is to simulate the more general coroutine structure using subroutines. For example, Table 12–3 shows how the `LineOut` process can be coded using two procedures. Instead of using a `WAKEUP LineOut` statement to print a line, a main program would simply invoke the procedure `StartLineOut`. The interrupt system then calls the procedure `DspIntr` each time that a display interrupt occurs. These two procedures have precisely the same structure as the 68000 subroutines `STROUT` and `STRINT` in Table 11–1.

TABLE 12–3   Procedure version of `LineOut` process.

```
PROCEDURE StartLineOut; {Display interrupt initialization routine.}
  BEGIN
    outputPrinted := false;  dspData := GetNextOutputChar;
    {Enable interrupt, start display, and clear ready.}
    dspIEN := true; dspGo := true; dspReady := false;
  END;

PROCEDURE DspIntr; {Called by interrupt system when
                (dspIEN = true) AND (dspReady = true) }
  BEGIN  {Display interrupt service routine.}
    IF CharsLeftToBePrinted THEN
      BEGIN {Send character to display data register,...}
        dspData := GetNextOutputChar;
        {...enable interrupt, start display, and clear ready.}
        dspIEN := true; dspGo := true; dspReady := false;
      END;
    ELSE BEGIN dspIEN := false; outputPrinted := true END;
  END;
```

12.2.3 Waking and Sleeping

Regardless of whether coroutines or subroutines are used to code processes, we need ways to wake up processes and put them to sleep. We presume that the entire program is operating under the control of an operating system or executive, so that the main program is awakened for the first time when the executive runs it, and put to its final rest when control is finally returned to the executive.

In Table 12–2, MainLoop can wake up the interrupt process LineIn or LineOut by calling a subroutine that enables the device interrupt, requests the first I/O operation, and returns control to MainLoop. Subsequently LineIn and LineOut are reawakened periodically by interrupts; each puts itself to sleep by requesting another I/O operation and returning control to the interrupted program. When LineIn or LineOut eventually returns control to the interrupted program *without* requesting another I/O operation, it can only be reawakened explicitly by another process.

That leaves us with the question of how MainLoop can put itself to sleep, since it has no interrupts of its own. If there is an operating system, MainLoop can temporarily return control to it, allowing the operating system to schedule other useful work while MainLoop is asleep. In the absence of such an executive, MainLoop can simply enter a busy-waiting loop. In either case, MainLoop must rely on some other process to wake it up. For example, suppose MainLoop uses a global boolean variable mainWaitingForInput to indicate that it has gone to sleep waiting for input. Then each time that LineIn finishes reading a line, it can inspect mainWaitingForInput to determine whether MainLoop should be reawakened. A typical sequence of events might be as follows, assuming that computation for a line proceeds much faster than input:

(1) MainLoop finds that `inputAvailable` is false. Therefore, it sets `mainWaitingForInput` to true and puts itself to sleep.

(2) LineIn wakes up, reads a character, and goes back to sleep; this step is repeated zero or more times.

(3) LineIn wakes up and reads the last character of a line, and therefore sets `inputAvailable` to true. Then it checks `mainWaitingForInput` and finds the value true; it wakes up MainLoop and puts itself to sleep.

(4) MainLoop wakes up, copies the new input line, and wakes up LineIn.

(5) MainLoop continues and eventually returns to step 1.

12.3   TIMING-DEPENDENT PROCESS BEHAVIOR

12.3.1   Deadlocks and Critical Sections

The method suggested above for suspending and resuming MainLoop seems reasonable, but it contains a timing-dependent error. Consider the following sequence of operations that could occur if computation and input for one line take about the same length of time:

(1) MainLoop finds that `inputAvailable` is false. Therefore, it sets `mainWaitingForInput` to true and is about to put itself to sleep when all of a sudden ...

(2) LineIn wakes up and reads the last character of a line, and so it sets `inputAvailable` to true. Then it checks `mainWaitingForInput`, finds the value true, wakes up MainLoop, and puts itself to sleep.

(3) MainLoop wakes up and immediately puts itself to sleep as planned.

(4) Both MainLoop and LineIn are now asleep, waiting to be reawakened by each other, and both sleep peacefully forever.

deadlock

This situation is called a *deadlock*; two processes are deadlocked if neither can continue until the other continues. A similar deadlock can occur between MainLoop and LineOut.

critical section

The sequence of instructions in MainLoop that test `inputAvailable` and update `mainWaitingForInput` is called a "critical section." A *critical section* of a process is a set of instructions that access variables shared with one or more additional processes, such that the results of execution may vary unpredictably if the variables are accessed by another process during the critical section's execution.

mutual exclusion

To avoid deadlocks and other timing-dependent errors, a critical section, once entered, must be allowed to execute to completion without any instructions from other processes intervening. This is sometimes called *mutual exclusion*.

We can provide mutual exclusion in a critical section in an assembly language program by disabling the processor interrupt system at the beginning of the critical section, and reenabling it at the end.

12.3.2 Detecting Critical Sections

We have defined critical sections, but we have not supplied any rules on how to detect them. In general, finding critical sections requires a careful analysis of a program and its environment. For example, the last two instructions of `LineIn` might appear to be a critical section according to the following scenario:

(1) `LineIn` is awakened and reads the last character of an input line. Therefore, it sets `inputAvailable` to `true`, and it is about to put itself to sleep when ...

(2) `MainLoop` wakes up, finds that `inputAvailable` is `true`, copies the input line, and wakes up `LineIn`.

(3) `LineIn` wakes up and immediately puts itself to sleep as planned, without reading another line.

However, in most environments this can't happen, because `LineIn` is awakened by an interrupt and `MainLoop` can be resumed only after the `LineIn` interrupt service routine has run to completion. In other environments, the scenario could be possible, for example, if `LineIn` and `MainLoop` actually run simultaneously on two different processors that share variables in a common main memory.

It might appear that the best course of action is to disable interrupts whenever a critical section possibly exists. However, this must be done with discretion for two reasons:

(1) Disabling interrupts for a long period of time can have an adverse effect on I/O system performance, resulting in lost inputs and delayed outputs.

(2) Disabling interrupts at the wrong place can lead to deadlocks.

Disabling interrupts for a short period of time usually does not cause inputs to be lost, since most device interfaces keep an interrupt request pending until it is serviced. However, if a second input appears while the interrupt for a first input is still pending, then a typical interface will lose one of the inputs and fail to issue a second interrupt request after the first has been serviced.

To illustrate the deadlock problem, suppose that we disabled the interrupt system in `MainLoop` in Table 12–2 before the first `SLEEP` statement and reenabled it after checking `InputBufferEmpty`. Then if `MainLoop` ever goes to sleep waiting for input, it will do so with interrupts disabled. It can never be reawakened, because input interrupts are required to do so.

Thus, we must reiterate that correct structuring and coding of a program with multiple processes requires a careful analysis of the program and its environment. Formal methods for detecting and avoiding deadlocks are discussed in most operating system books (see References).

12.3.3 Locking and Semaphores

locking

semaphore

Another way to guard critical sections is by *locking* shared resources so that only one process at a time may access them. This can be done by providing a flag or *semaphore* for each resource that indicates when the resource is in use. A process that wishes to access a shared resource uses the semaphore as follows:

(1) The process checks the current value of the semaphore. If the semaphore is zero, the process may proceed to the next step. A nonzero value indicates that some other process is accessing the shared resource. In this case, the current process should go to sleep until the other process sets the semaphore to zero.

(2) The process may now access the resource, excluding other processes by setting the semaphore to a nonzero value.

(3) After accessing the resource, the process releases it by setting the semaphore to zero.

A process that goes to sleep waiting for a semaphore must have some confidence that it will eventually be awakened, either by an interrupt or by an operating system that keeps track of semaphores and waiting processes. If a process "sleeps" by simply busy-waiting and if the interrupt system is off, then we've created not only mutual exclusion, but also a deadlock! A problem occurs in coding the above semaphore operations in assembly language. Consider the following 68000 code:

```
CHECK    TST.B    SEMAPH       Want SEMAPH=0 ==> resource available.
         BNE      CHECK        Busy-wait for it.
         MOVE.B   #1,SEMAPH    Set semaphore to 1.
         ...                   Use resource.
         CLR.B    SEMAPH       Release resource for others.
```

Now suppose that each of two different processes has a copy of this code for accessing a shared resource using the semaphore SEMAPH. An unfortunate sequence of events is depicted in Figure 12–2. Process A finds SEMAPH = 0, but before setting it to 1, is interrupted. Process B gains access to the resource, since it finds that SEMAPH is still 0. Now if control gets back to process A before process B releases the shared resource, then both processes will have simultaneous access to the resource. One way that this could happen is if process B goes to sleep while waiting for an I/O event to occur.

The solution to the problem is to make testing and setting the semaphore an indivisible operation. To do this, many processors provide a test and set (TSET) instruction that reads the value of an operand in memory, sets the

TSET

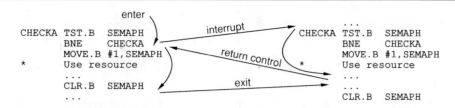

FIGURE 12–2   A failed semaphore check.

BSET

condition bits accordingly, and sets the memory value to 1, all in one instruction. In the 68000, the `BSET` instruction tests and sets a single bit of a memory byte in a single instruction which, like all single instructions, cannot be interrupted in the middle. Thus, in the 68000, we can recode our shared resource check as follows:

```
CHECK  BSET.B  #0,SEMAPH   Want (SEMAPH bit 0)=0 ==> resource
       BNE     CHECK           available; busy-wait for it.
       ...                 Resource available, got it, use it.
       BCLR.B  #0,SEMAPH   Release it for others.
```

In this code, the `BSET` instruction always sets bit 0 of `SEMAPH` to 1, even if it is already 1. Therefore, the shared resource always either becomes or remains locked during the execution of `BSET`. Control falls through the conditional branch instruction and a new process gains control of the resource only if bit 0 of `SEMAPH` was 0 before it was set to 1.

12.3.4 Multiple Processors

Many high-performance computers have multiple processors that communicate through a shared memory. A typical multiprocessor system architecture is shown in Figure 12–3. Each processor has a "local memory" that contains its instructions and private data. However, each processor is also connected to a "system bus," where it can access a shared memory. Since each processor spends most of its time accessing instructions and data in its local memory, the system bus and shared memory can easily handle each processor's occasional requests for shared data. If two processors should attempt to access the shared memory simultaneously, one is delayed briefly while the other gains access. From the point of view of the delayed processor, the memory temporarily looks "slow," as if its bus were tied up with a DMA cycle. Instruction execution, though delayed slightly, proceeds normally.

Each memory access to a typical memory system, including the shared memory in Figure 12–3, is either a read or a write. An instruction like `BSET` must perform *two* memory accesses on its data operand. The first access is a read to test the operand, and the second is a write to store the updated value. As a result, semaphore operations that use the `BSET` instruction may fail in a

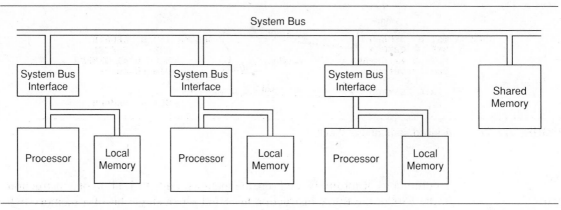

System Bus

FIGURE 12–3   A multiprocessor system architecture.

multiprocessor environment. If two processors are executing BSET at the same time, their read and write cycles may overlap:

(1) Processor 1 begins to execute BSET—it reads SEMAPH from the shared memory, finding a value of 0.

(2) Processor 2 simultaneously begins to execute BSET—it reads SEMAPH from the shared memory, also finding a value of 0.

(3) Processor 1 completes BSET, writing $01 into SEMAPH.

(4) Processor 2 completes BSET, writing $01 into SEMAPH.

(5) Both processors use the shared resource (disaster!).

To solve this problem, the system hardware must somehow provide an indivisible "read–modify–write" memory sequence that can be used in semaphore operations.

TAS

The 68000 solves this problem with the TAS instruction, which tests a byte and then sets its MSB to 1. During the execution of TAS, the 68000 processor chip asserts a bus control signal to indicate that no other processors may access the memory until TAS has completed both its read and its write. It is the responsibility of the system hardware designer to ensure that integrity of this read–modify–write bus cycle is preserved.

As you probably have gathered by now, there is a lot more to process management than meets the eye. A complete discussion of process communication and synchronization is beyond the scope of this text, but a large body of literature exists on the subject (see References). An example of an assembly language program with three processes is presented in Section 12.5.

TABLE 12-4　　　　Interrupt service routine for time-of-day clock.

```
{ The time-of-day clock is driven from the 60-Hz AC power line,
  producing an interrupt every 1/60th second if its IEN bit is 1.
  The interrupt service routine uses these 'ticks' to keep track
  of the current time of day to the nearest 1/60th second, using
  global variables tick, second, minute, and hour.
}
PROCEDURE TimerIntr; {Called by interrupt system if
                     (timerIEN = true) AND (timerReady = true)}
  BEGIN {Timer interrupt service routine.}
    tick := tick + 1;
    IF tick = 60 THEN
      BEGIN tick := 0; second := second + 1;
      IF second = 60 THEN
        BEGIN second := 0; minute := minute + 1;
          IF minute = 60 THEN
            BEGIN minute := 0; hour := hour + 1;
              IF hour = 24 THEN
                BEGIN hour := 0; IncrementDayAndDate END;
            END;
        END;
      END;  {Now request next timer tick.}
    timerIEN := true; timerGo := true; timerReady := false;
  END;
```

12.4 SHARED DATA AND INSTRUCTIONS

In a multiple process (interrupt) environment, it is possible for two or more processes to share the same data or variables. Special precautions must be taken in programs with this behavior.

12.4.1 Shared Variables and Data Structures

In the previous section, we studied a program with three processes that used variables in memory to synchronize their operations. Critical sections appeared when both processes could access a shared variable simultaneously, leading to the possibility of deadlocks.

Critical sections can also appear in more innocent-looking applications of shared data than process synchronization and, although the results may not be as severe as a deadlock, errors can nonetheless occur. For example, consider the Pascal outline of the interrupt service routine for a time-of-day clock, shown in Table 12–4. Suppose that a main program reads the current time of day by a statement sequence such as the following:

```
sec1 := second;
min1 := minute;
hour1 := hour;
```

An error can occur if a timer interrupt takes place in the middle of this sequence. For example, suppose that the current time is 7:05:59, we have just executed the first statement above, and the timer interrupt occurs. Then when the processor has finished the above sequence, it will have recorded the time as being 7:06:59. Even larger errors can occur at times like 7:59:59. In order to prevent such errors, timer interrupts must be disabled whenever a program reads the time.

locking

The time variables above form a simple data structure. Turning off interrupts or otherwise preventing multiple processes from accessing a data structure is called *locking* the data structure. There are three ways for errors to occur when two or more processes simultaneously access an unlocked data structure:

(1) If the data structure is not locked for reading, then one process could interrupt and update the data structure while another process is reading it. The reading process could see inconsistent information.

(2) If the data structure is not locked for updating, then one process could interrupt and read the data structure while another process is updating it. Again the reading process could see inconsistent information.

(3) If the data structure is not locked for updating, then two processes could try to update the data structure at the same time, possibly destroying the data structure's integrity.

Note that no errors occur if two processes simply *read* a data structure simultaneously. We've already seen one way that case 1 above can occur. An example of case 2 is for the timer interrupt service routine itself to be interrupted by another process that reads the time, possibly yielding the time 7:05:00 during the transition from 7:05:59 to 7:06:00. Although some process reads the wrong time in cases 1 and 2, at least the integrity of the data structure is not affected.

To illustrate case 3 above, suppose that a user program initializes the current time of day with the following instruction sequence:

```
read(hour1,min1,sec1);
hour   := hour1;
minute := min1;
second := sec1;
```

Now suppose that the current time of day as indicated by hour, minute, second is 1:59:59 and a user tries to reinitialize the time to 3:00:00 (e.g., to go onto daylight-saving time). If a timer interrupt occurs between the second and third lines above, then the time will be incorrectly initialized to 4:00:00.

Worse errors can occur with more complicated data structures. For example, it is usually disastrous to interrupt a process that updates a linked list in order to perform another updating operation on the same list. This can often produce unwanted circular lists, dismembered sublists with no pointers to them, and all sorts of other horrors.

In a few rare instances, it may be possible for two processes to update the same data structure simultaneously without error. For example, consider the case of two processes that access a queue, where one puts data into the queue and the other removes it. If the queue is implemented with `head` and `tail` pointers as suggested in Section 3.4, then you can convince yourself that the integrity of the queue will be preserved, since one process can only update the `head` and the other only the `tail`.[1] However, to be safe, one should always lock data structures that might be accessed by multiple processes.

12.4.2 Shared Instructions (Reentrant Programs)

reentrant
subroutine

Consider a subroutine that is invoked from two or more different processes. After being invoked from one process it might be "reentered" from a second process before the first has finished executing it. A subroutine that still produces correct results when reentered in this way is called *reentrant*.

For example, suppose that a main program and one or more interrupt routines make use of a `DIVIDEL` subroutine in the 68000. Suppose that the main program has called `DIVIDEL` and, in the middle of its execution, an interrupt from an output device occurs. And suppose that the interrupt service routine makes use of a binary-to-ASCII conversion algorithm that computes digits by successive divisions by 10. Then the interrupt routine will reenter `DIVIDEL` and execute it to completion before resuming `DIVIDEL` in the main program process.

There is nothing inherently harmful about a sequence of instructions being executed "simultaneously" by two different processes. Since instructions in a non-self-modifying program are "read only," the instruction sequence is the same for both processes. Each process may create a different set of values in the processor registers as instructions are executed, but this is no problem if the interrupting process follows the usual practice of pushing the registers onto a stack and popping them on exit. The problems occur when instructions refer to variables in fixed locations in memory.

For example, consider the 68000 `DIVIDEL` program that was shown in Table 6–8 on page 197. Four parameters are passed to the subroutine in fixed memory locations (DVND, DVSR, REM, QUOT), and another location is used to store a local variable (CNT). If the subroutine is suspended by an interrupt, the values of the registers and the return address will be preserved on the stack and properly restored on return. However, if `DIVIDEL` is called again from the interrupt service routine, the old values of the parameters and local variable will be lost forever. Figure 12–4 shows what happens. The computation remaining to be done in the first call of `DIVIDEL` will be resumed with incorrect data, and the results will be wrong. In general, whenever a subroutine uses fixed

---

[1] The worst that can happen is for the dequeueing process to think that the queue is empty just as the enqueueing process is putting data into it, or vice versa. However, the integrity of the queue is preserved, so that the dequeueing process will discover the newly enqueued data the next time that it checks the queue, as if the enqueueing process had operated just a little while later in the first place.

37	DVND		96	DVND		96	DVND
8	DVSR		10	DVSR		10	DVSR
–	QUOT		–	QUOT		9	QUOT
–	REM		–	REM		6	REM
5	CNT		5	CNT		0	CNT
(a)			(b)			(c)	

FIGURE 12–4   Effects on parameters when nonreentrant `DIVIDEL` subroutine is reentered: (a) dividing 37 by 8 just before interrupt; (b) dividing 96 by 10 on second entry of `DIVIDEL`; (c) on return from interrupt.

memory locations for parameters or local variables, it is doomed to fail if it is ever reentered.

Table 9–16 on page 332 showed a `DIVIDEL` subroutine that works properly when reentered; it *is* reentrant. Since all parameters and local variables are placed on the stack, a new set is allocated for each invocation of the subroutine. Figure 12–5 traces the stack contents during the execution of a program using this version of `DIVIDEL`. The values of the parameters and the local variable for the first invocation of `DIVIDEL` are preserved on the stack during the interrupt service routine and again during the second, reentrant invocation of `DIVIDEL`.

The `DIVIDEL` program shown in Table 9–14 on page 329 passes parameters in a parameter area. It is *almost* reentrant if each calling process uses a different parameter area. The local variable `CNT` still is a problem, because it is shared by all callers. The problem can be solved by storing `CNT` in a spare processor register (D2) or on the stack, or by requiring the calling program to allocate a word in the parameter area for it.

The queue manipulation subroutines in Table 9–20 on page 338 are reentrant because there are no local variables and the parameters are all passed in registers.

Using only registers and a stack for all parameters and local variables is the best way to create reentrant subroutines. In this way, space for parameters and local variables is allocated dynamically, only as much as needed at any time. Subroutines that use the stack convention described in Section 9.3.6 are reentrant if each invocation of the subroutine always runs to completion before any higher-level invocations are resumed. This is usually the case in a single-user interrupt environment. In some environments, such as multi-user systems, programs can be suspended and resumed at arbitrary points in their execution. In this case, a separate stack area must be provided for each process.

Reentrant programs are important in systems programming, especially in multiple-user environments where a process is associated with each user; typical applications include the following:

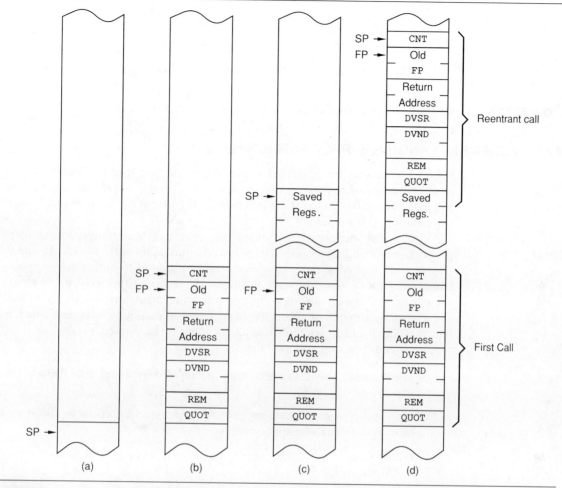

FIGURE 12–5   Stack contents using reentrant `DIVIDEL` while: (a) executing `MAIN`; (b) executing `DIVIDEL` from `MAIN`; (c) executing `INTSVC`; (d) executing `DIVIDEL` from `INTSVC`.

- Utility programs such as binary-to-ASCII conversion must be reentrant because they can be called by different users (processes) at the same time.

- If a large, commonly used program such as a compiler or text editor is reentrant, it needs to be stored in memory only once; different users may use it simultaneously, each with a separate data area.

- A group of identical I/O devices (say, CRT terminals) can share a reentrant interrupt service routine, using a separate buffer area and configuration table for each copy of the device.

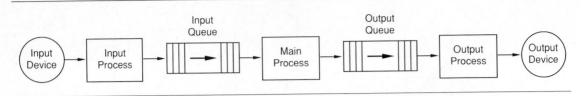

FIGURE 12–6   Structure of a program that uses queues to buffer input and output.

12.5 ASSEMBLY LANGUAGE PROGRAM EXAMPLE

Figure 12–6 shows the general structure of a program that brings together many of the concepts of multiple processes, critical sections, and shared instructions and data. The program has three processes that perform the three steps of input, computation, and output.

Input and output are performed one character at a time, and the main program reads and writes one character at a time. In order to smooth input, output, and processing time variations, queues are used to buffer the input and output characters. In this way, the input device can stay busy by "looking ahead" and filling up the input queue when the main program is slow, and likewise during bursts of speed the main program can dump lots of characters into the output queue without waiting for them to be printed. Thus, the three processes could be outlined as follows:

(1) Input Process: gets characters from the input device and puts them in the input queue.

(2) Main Process: gets characters from the input queue, processes them, and places results in the output queue.

(3) Output Process: gets characters from the output queue and sends them to the output device.

A 68000 assembly language version of the program is shown in Table 12–5. Two queues (IQ and OQ) are declared according to the specifications of the queue module in Table 9–20; the queue module's subroutines QINIT, QENQ, and QDEQ are utilized accordingly. The main program initializes the two queues, marks the output process as waiting for data to appear in OQ, and wakes up the input process to request the first character. Then it enters a computation loop that reads and writes characters as necessary.

The input process is awakened for the first time by the subroutine IWAKE, which requests one character from the input device. Subsequently the input process is awakened by input device interrupts. The interrupt service routine ISVC puts each input character into IQ.

If the input device is very fast or MAIN is very slow, then ISVC may eventually find that IQ has become full. In this case, the input process saves the current input character in a variable SAVEIN, sets variable WAITIQ to 1 to

TABLE 12-5   Assembly language program that uses queues to buffer input and output.

```
OQ        DS.B    10                  Output queue.
OQDT      DS.L    2                   Output queue descriptor table.
          DC.L    OQ,OQ+9
IQ        DS.B    10                  Input queue.
IQDT      DS.L    2                   Input queue descriptor table.
          DC.L    IQ,IQ+9
WAITOQ    DS.B    1                   Nonzero when output process is waiting
*                                       for a character to appear in {\qq OQ}.
WAITIQ    DS.B    1                   Nonzero when input process is waiting
*                                       for space in IQ.
SAVEIN    DS.B    1                   Save input character when waiting
STACK     DS.L    20                    for room in IQ.
STACKE    EQU     *                   Return address stack.
*
MAIN      LEA.L   STACKE,A7           Initialize return-address stack.
          LEA.L   OQDT,A0             Initialize output queue...
          JSR     QINIT
          LEA.L   IQDT,A0             ...and input queue.
          JSR     QINIT
          MOVE.B  #1,WAITOQ           Mark output process waiting for char.
          JSR     IWAKE               Wake up input and request first char.
LOOP      JSR     INCHR               Main processing loop.
          ...
          JSR     INCHR               Read and write as many characters
          ...                           as desired.
          JSR     OUTCHR
          ...
          JSR     INCHR
          ...
          JSR     OUTCHR
          ...
          JMP     LOOP                Repeat the processing loop.
*
*                                     Come here when all done processing.
EXIT      JSR     INOFF               Turn off input interrupts.
WTOUT     TST.B   WAITOQ              Busy-wait until last char printed.
          BEQ     WTOUT
          JMP     $1800               Return to operating system.
```

show that it is waiting for space in IQ, and goes to sleep *without* requesting another input. Later, when MAIN removes a character from IQ, it puts the saved character SAVEIN into IQ and reawakens the input process by calling IWAKE again.

A similar situation occurs in the output process. OUTCHR calls OWAKE to print the first character from OQ. Subsequent characters are removed from OQ and printed by the output interrupt service routine OSVC. If OQ is empty, then OSVC sets WAITOQ to 1 and goes to sleep without printing another character. Later,

TABLE 12–5   (continued)

```
*           Subroutine to get one input character from input queue.
INCHR   LEA.L   IQDT,A0     Get a character from the input queue.
        JSR     INTSOFF     *** Critical section -- interrupts off.
        JSR     QDEQ
        MOVE.W  SR,D6       Save queue status (Z bit in CCR).
        MOVE.B  D0,D5       Save input char.
        TST.B   WAITIQ      Input queue must have room for
        BEQ.S   INCH4         at least one more character now,
        MOVE.B  SAVEIN,D0     so if input process was waiting on
        LEA.L   IQDT,A0       queue full, then
        JSR     QENQ          enqueue the saved character...
        BEQ.S   WHAAAT        (impossible error if queue full)
        JSR     IWAKE         ...and wake up the input process.
INCH4   JSR     INTSON      *** End critical sec. -- interrupts on.
        MOVE.B  D5,D0       Restore input char.
        BTST.L  #2,D6       Check saved Z -- did we really get a char?
        BNE     INCHR       Branch and try again if we didn't.
        RTS                 Else return.
WHAAAT  JMP     $1800       Impossible error, return to operating system.
*
*           Subroutine to put one output character into output queue.
OUTCHR  MOVE.B  D0,D5       Save output character.
        LEA.L   OQDT,A0     Try to enqueue it.
        JSR     INTSOFF     *** Critical section -- interrupts off.
        JSR     QENQ
        MOVE.W  SR,D6       Save queue status (Z bit in CCR).
        TST.B   WAITOQ      Output queue must have...
        BEQ.S   OUTCH4        ...at least one character in it now...
        JSR     OWAKE         ...so wake up output if it was waiting.
OUTCH4  JSR     INTSON      *** End critical sec. -- interrupts on.
        MOVE.B  D5,D0       Restore output char.
        BTST.L  #2,D6       Check saved Z -- did we really enqueue char?
        BNE     OUTCHR      Branch and try again if we didn't.
        RTS                 Else return.

*           Subroutine to turn off all interrupts (except NMI -- level 7).
INTSOFF OR.W    #$700,SR    Set PPL field of SR to 7.
        RTS

*           Subroutine to enable interrupts at all levels.
INTSON  AND.W   #$F8FF,SR   Set PPL field of SR to 0.
        RTS
```

when MAIN puts another character into OQ, it reawakens the output process by calling OWAKE again.

MAIN calls two subroutines, INCHR and OUTCHR, to handle the details of reading and writing each character by manipulating the queues and waking up sleeping processes. For example, INCHR attempts to dequeue a character from IQ. If it is unsuccessful, it simply busy-waits for a character to appear. In any

TABLE 12–5 (continued)

```
*            Device-dependent declarations and subroutines.
ICS      EQU      $FFFFF001      Input device control and status reg.
IDATA    EQU      $FFFFF003      Input device data register.
OCS      EQU      $FFFFF011      Output device control and status reg.
ODATA    EQU      $FFFFF013      Output device data register.
*
*            Wake up input process and request one character.
IWAKE    CLR.B    WAITIQ         Mark the input process not waiting.
         MOVE.B   #$41,ICS       Set IEN and GO...
         RTS                     ...thereby requesting a character.
*
*            Interrupt service routine for input device.
ISVC     MOVEM.L  D0/A0,-(SP)    Save working registers.
         MOVE.B   IDATA,D0       Get character.
         MOVE.B   D0,SAVEIN      Save it for possible later use.
         LEA.L    IQDT,A0        Put into input queue.
         JSR      QENQ
         BEQ.S    IQFUL          Queue full?
         MOVE.B   #$41,ICS       No, set IEN and GO to request next char.
ISVCRET  MOVEM.L  (SP)+,D0/A0    Restore working registers.
         RTE                     Return to interrupted program.
IQFUL    JSR      INOFF          Disable interrupts from input device.
         MOVE.B   #1,WAITIQ      Put the input process to sleep...
         BRA      ISVCRET        ...until there's room in IQ.
*
INOFF    CLR.B    ICS            Subroutine to turn off input device.
         RTS
*
*            Wake up output process and print one character.
OWAKE    CLR.B    WAITOQ         Mark the output process not waiting.
         LEA.L    OQDT,A0        Get a character from the output queue.
         JSR      QDEQ
         BEQ      WHAAAT         Queue empty?? Impossible!
         MOVE.B   D0,ODATA       Output the character.
         MOVE.B   #$41,OCS       Set IEN and GO.
         RTS
*
*            Interrupt service routine for output device.
OSVC     MOVEM.L  D0/A0,-(SP)    Save working registers.
         LEA.L    OQDT,A0        Get another character to print.
         JSR      QDEQ
         BEQ.S    OQMT           Go to sleep if none left.
         MOVE.B   D0,ODATA       Else output the character.
         MOVE.B   #$41,OCS       Set IEN and GO.
         BRA      ISVCRET        Return to interrupted program.
OQMT     CLR.B    OCS            Turn off output device.
         MOVE.B   #1,WAITOQ      Put the output process to sleep...
         BRA      ISVCRET        ...until there's a character in OQ.
```

case, after `INCHR` calls `QDEQ` there must be at least one free byte in `IQ`, so that the input process can now be awakened if it was waiting for space in `IQ`.

Most of the instructions in `INCHR` are in a critical section. The `INTSOFF` subroutine sets the PPL field in SR to 7 to disable interrupts; `INTSON` later sets PPL to 0 to reenable interrupts. Consider the following sequence of events that could occur if interrupts were not disabled:

(1) `IQ` is full and `MAIN` calls `INCHR`.

(2) `INCHR` calls `QDEQ`, leaving space in `IQ` for one more character.

(3) An input device interrupt occurs and makes `IQ` full again.

(4) Another input device interrupt occurs; since `IQ` is full, the input character is saved in `SAVEIN`, input interrupts are disabled, and `WAITIQ` is set to 1.

(5) `INCHR` is finally resumed, and finds that `WAITIQ` is 1.

(6) Thinking that there must now be room in `IQ`, `INCHR` tries to enqueue the saved character and the "impossible" error occurs.[2]

Another reason for a critical section in `INCHR` is that it shares a data structure, `IQ`, with another process, the input process. If an input interrupt occurs while `INCHR` is executing `QDEQ`, then both processes will be manipulating the data structure simultaneously. Whether or not a timing-dependent error occurs in this situation depends on the internal workings of the `QDEQ` and `QENQ` subroutines, as we've explained before. Disabling interrupts in `INCHR` ensures that each process gets exclusive access to `IQ`.

With all the potential timing-dependent errors, one may be tempted to disable interrupts for most of the time. But this can cause problems too. For example, if we moved the `MOVE.W D7,SR` instruction in `INCHR` down three lines, then interrupts will be disabled for the entire `INCHR` subroutine, even if `INCHR` is busy-waiting for a character to appear in `IQ`. In this case, it will busy-wait forever, because the input interrupt can't put a character into the queue.

The `OUTCHR` procedure has a structure similar to `INCHR`'s, and it also contains a critical section.

Notice the order in which software flags are set and cleared in the wake-up and interrupt service routines. Two useful rules of thumb apply here:

- Any software action indicating that interrupts are being *enabled* (such as clearing `WAITIQ`) should be taken *before* the corresponding hardware action (e.g., `ICS:=$41`), lest an interrupt take place before the software has been "told" that such an event is possible.

---

[2]In this situation, one might propose that the critical section could be eliminated by modifying the program's attitude—instead of giving up, let it try again! If we replace the instruction `BEQ WHAAAT` with `BEQ INCH4`, then if the queue is full, no harm is done and the wake-up operation is tried again later. However, this kind of solution doesn't work in general.

TABLE 12–6   Subroutines for nested disabling and enabling of interrupts.

```
INTSOFF MOVE.W  SR,D7        Save current value of SR, including PPL.
        OR.W    #$700,SR     Set PPL field in SR to 7.
        RTS

INTSON  MOVE.W  D7,SR        Restore previous PPL into SR.
        RTS
```

- Conversely, any software action indicating that interrupts are being *disabled* (such as setting WAITIQ) should be taken *after* the corresponding hardware action (e.g., ICS:=0), lest one last interrupt slip in with the software "thinking" that interrupts are off.

interrupt system disabling and enabling

Another potential pitfall is the way in which the interrupt system is disabled and reenabled in subroutines like INCHR and OUTCHR. For example, suppose that the main program performs some time-critical operation during which it must disable interrupts below a certain priority level, say level 4. If during that time the main program calls INCHR or OUTCHR, it will suddenly find that the interrupts are enabled at all levels. The problem is that INCHR and OUTCHR turn off the interrupt system by setting PPL to 7, and then unconditionally enable all levels by setting PPL to 0 without checking what the value of PPL was to begin with. This problem can be solved by modifying the INTSOFF and INTSON subroutines to save and restore the current value of PPL, as coded in Table 12–6. The INTSOFF subroutine saves the current SR, including PPL, in register D7, so that the INTSON subroutine can later restore it. Of course, the value in D7 must be preserved between the call of INTSOFF and the corresponding call of INTSON. For example, if the QDEQ subroutine called by the INCHR subroutine in Table 12–5 did not preserve D7, then INCHR would have to save D7 on the stack before calling QDEQ, and restore it before calling INTSON.

As a final note, we should point out again that the implementations of the queue manipulation subroutines in Table 9–20 on page 338 are fully reentrant. This means that the main computation loop in Table 12–6 could declare additional queues and manipulate them using QENQ and QDEQ. No errors will occur, even if QENQ and QDEQ are reentered by the interrupt service routines that use them.

The timing-dependent errors that can occur in multiple processes may seem rather obscure, which may encourage naive programmers to treat them lightly. Unfortunately, such errors are often difficult to predict before they are observed and, once observed, they are difficult to reproduce for the purposes of analysis and correction. As discussed in the References, modern operating systems and high-level languages for concurrent processing provide facilities and impose restrictions that make it possible to write concurrent programs with predictable behavior.

REFERENCES

Most systems programming and all operating systems books discuss issues of process management. Two good systems programming references are *Software System Principles* by Peter Freeman (SRA, 1975) and *Systems Programming* by John J. Donovan (McGraw-Hill, 1972). And two very good operating systems references are *Operating System Concepts* by J. L. Peterson and A. Silberschatz (Addison-Wesley, 1985, 2nd ed.) and *Operating Systems: Design and Implementation* by A. S. Tanenbaum (Prentice-Hall, 1987).

The concepts of processes and concurrency and the methods for interprocess communication are crucial to modern operating system design. A detailed and enlightening discussion of processes and concurrency can be found in Per Brinch Hansen's book *Operating System Principles* (Prentice-Hall, 1973). Brinch Hansen has also devised an extension of Pascal, called Concurrent Pascal, on which he bases "a method for writing concurrent computer programs of high quality," as described in his book, *The Architecture of Concurrent Programs* (Prentice-Hall, 1977). A more recent little book that is totally devoted to interprocessor communication is M. Ben-Ari's *Principles of Concurrent Programming* (Prentice-Hall International, 1982).

One of the oldest and most widely used languages that supports concurrent processes is PL/I; for example, see Mark Elson's *Concepts of Programming Languages* (SRA, 1973). In PL/I, the reserved word **TASK** declares that a procedure may be executed concurrently with the calling program, and **EVENT** variables are used as completion flags to synchronize processes. A process may use a **WAIT** statement to relinquish control to the operating system until a specified **EVENT** variable has been set to 1.

EXERCISES

12.1 Modify the program in Exercise 11.2 so that the button can be hit several times while a message is being printed, without losing information. In order to do this, provide a queue for elapsed time values. Each time that the button is hit, the elapsed time value should be put into the queue.

In this implementation, the main program after initialization should have just one instruction, **SELF JMP SELF**. The output routines and the pushbutton routines are treated as two separate processes communicating through a queue. The output process sleeps if the current message has been printed and the queue is empty. The pushbutton process wakes up output whenever it puts a value into a previously empty queue.

Study and comment on the possibility of critical sections when the processes access the common queue data structure. Use a long message (say, 70 characters) and a slow output device (say, 30 characters per second) to test your program's behavior for multiple hits.

12.2   Write reentrant interrupt display output routines similar to those in Table 11–1 on page 389 that can be shared among several identical display devices. A caller of each routine should use register A2 to pass it the base address of a "configuration table" that contains information unique to each display device: (a) the address of the DSPCS register; (b) BUFPNT; (c) SBUSY.

12.3   Modify the polling routines in Table 11–2 so that the polling table contains *three* 16-bit numbers for each device. The third number would normally be the base address of a software "configuration table," such as the one used in the previous exercise. The polling routines should load this third number into the register A2 before jumping to the specified interrupt service routine.

12.4   Describe how a deadlock could occur between the MainLoop and LineOut processes in Table 12–2.

12.5   Translate the ReverseLines program in Table 12–2 into an assembly language program for the 68000. Explain how you implement the WAKEUP and SLEEP primitives, and indicate where you disable interrupts to guard critical sections.

12.6   Translate the processes in Table 12–2 into assembly language subroutines and a main program for the 68000. Use a coroutine-like mechanism for saving process resumption addresses. Provide a simple operating system that does something interesting when MainLoop is asleep (for example, flashing the lights on the front panel if your computer has one).

12.7   Which is a more stringent requirement for a subroutine, recursion or reentrancy? In other words, answer these two questions:

  (1) Are all recursive subroutines guaranteed to run without error if reentered by another process?

  (2) Are all reentrant subroutines guaranteed to run without error if they call themselves?

  Use examples to illustrate your answers.

12.8   Suppose that the statement WAKEUP LineOut near the end of the MainLoop process in Table 12–2 merely schedules LineOut to be executed soon, but does not necessarily cause it to be run immediately. Instead, MainLoop can keep running for a while. What potential problems does this introduce and how can they be solved?

12.9   Suppose that a multiprocessor system with the structure shown in Section 12.3.4 handles multiple users, each with a CRT terminal. Each user's input process may run on any processor in the system. In order to show their bosses how heavily the system is used (and thus justify the purchase of a bigger system), the system programmers have placed in the shared memory a longword variable KEYCOUNT that is incremented every time an input process accepts a user's keystroke. Write an instruction sequence that updates KEYCOUNT correctly, even if two processors attempt to increment it simultaneously. (*Warning:* The read–modify–write cycle performed by ADDQ.L #1,KEYCOUNT is *not* indivisible.)

12.10 Redefine the queue descriptor table format in Table 9–20 on page 338 to contain a semaphore QSEM. Rewrite QINIT to initialize QSEM properly, and rewrite the QENQ and QDEQ procedures using TAS to ensure that QHEAD and QTAIL are always updated properly reliably when multiple 68000 processors can enqueue or dequeue items in the same queue.

12.11 Suppose that a queue module were developed that dequeues items by shifting down all of the items in a memory buffer, as suggested in Exercise 3.16. How does this affect the reentrant behavior discussed at the end of Section 12.4.1?

12.12 Suppose that we use the input and output routines in Table 12–5 with a CRT terminal. Since we cannot prevent a user from typing too fast, in the ISVC routine we may cause inputs to be lost if we disable interrupts. Show how to replace the code at IQFUL with code that warns the user of the impending disaster by ringing the bell at the terminal. Consider and explain your solution carefully, because it is easy to design an incorrect solution with deadlocks and other problems.

12.13 Write a program that plays Life as described in Exercises 7.8 and 10.16, using interrupt-driven I/O. The program should contain three processes:

(1) *Input process:* Accepts hexadecimal characters (0–9, A–F) typed at an ASCII keyboard. The input process converts each digit into a binary number from 0 to 15 and places the number in an input queue.

(2) *Output process:* Removes characters from an output queue and prints them on a CRT screen.

(3) *Main program process:* Initializes Life array, queues, and I/O routines, and then looks for work in the input queue. Each time that it finds a number in the input queue, it computes this number of generations of Life and then calls DISPLAY to display the current generation. DISPLAY outputs individual characters by placing them in the output queue.

When the output queue becomes full, DISPLAY must wait for characters to be sent to the CRT before putting more in the queue. For maximum efficiency, the output queue should have room for at least one screen full of characters. The input queue should have room for only five characters. If a character is typed and the input queue is full, the program should discard the character and place a "BEL" character in the output queue to warn the user that an input has been lost. Comment on the presence or absence of potential deadlock situations in your program.

CHAPTER 13

Program Development

Novice programmers are often preoccupied with what initially seems to be the most difficult aspect of writing programs: translating ideas into a programming language, or "coding." However, this activity is only one stage in a complete programming project, which has at least seven definable components:

- Requirements analysis
- Specification
- Design
- Documentation
- Coding
- Testing and debugging
- Maintenance

development cycle   The first five stages above take place during the traditional *development cycle* of a programming project. Figure 13–1 shows that coding is just a small part of the development cycle. But even more significant is a breakdown of programming effort expended over the entire lifetime of a large program. As shown in Figure 13–2, once a large program is in operation, maintaining it may actually require more effort than the original development cycle. The high cost of program maintenance underscores the need for an effective development cycle to reduce or simplify maintenance requirements.

In this chapter, we make some general comments on the stages of program development, and give particulars as they apply to assembly language programming. A complete discussion of applicable software engineering techniques is beyond the scope of this text, but a large body of literature exists on the subject (see References).

At this point, you may not be too interested in the problems of medium-to-large programming projects because most of the programs that you've encountered so far might be classified as "toy programs." The purpose of this

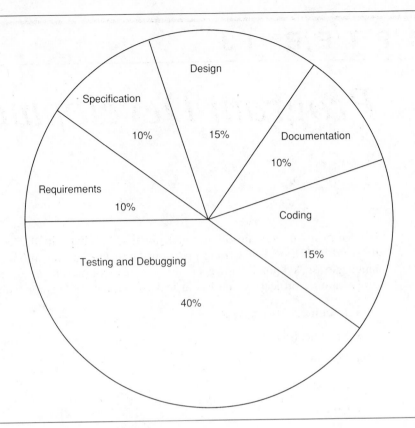

FIGURE 13–1   Development effort for a typical program.

chapter is to give you an appreciation of "real-world" programming problems and practices to encourage you to form good programming habits now, before you are forced to learn them the hard way!

13.1   THE STAGES OF PROGRAM DEVELOPMENT

requirements analysis

Requirements analysis, present in some form in all problem-solving activities, defines the requirements for an acceptable solution to the problem. Most programmers don't get involved in this stage, because it usually takes place at a management level and involves issues such as general approach (should a computer be used at all?), staffing and other resources (will this project effectively utilize the talents of existing personnel?), project costs (can we afford to solve this problem?), and schedules (will the solution be ready soon enough to be useful?).

external specification

The inputs and outputs of a program and their relationship are defined by an *external specification*. For example, the specification for a text editor defines

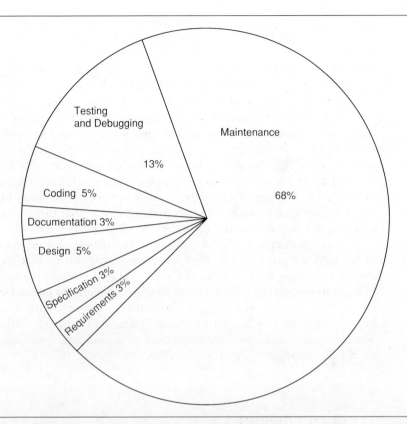

FIGURE 13–2   Total programming effort for a large program.

the format of the text files and it lists all of the editing commands and the effects of each. However, an external specification does not contain a description of *how* the program achieves these effects; this is part of design.

design   The structure of a program is defined during the *design* stage, remembering that "programs equal algorithms plus data structures." The design stage often decomposes the problem by outlining a solution in terms of a set of coop-

module   erating high-level program *modules*. This approach requires additional design
internal   and *internal specification*, since each module and its interaction with the others
specification   must be specified, and then the internal structure of each module must be designed. Depending on the module's complexity, additional decomposition into submodules might also take place.

documentation   Most *documentation* should be created during the specification and design stages. Concise yet complete documentation is needed to communicate specifications and design concepts among the current implementors and future users and maintainers of a program. To a lesser extent, documentation is needed in the coding stage to explain the details of program coding.

coding   In the *coding* stage, the design is translated into a programming language for a specific computer system. When coding begins, design usually stops, which is a good argument for not starting coding prematurely. Several studies have shown that design errors are more common than coding errors, so that a good design is essential to project success. Also, one is much more likely to reduce the size of a program or enhance its performance by design improvements in algorithms and data structures than by coding tricks or local optimizations.

debugging

    The word *debugging* usually suggests an activity in which the obvious errors in a program are eliminated so that the program runs without "blowing

testing

up." *Testing* refers to a more refined activity that verifies not only that the program runs, but also that it meets its external specifications. Testing requires a test plan, basically a set of input patterns and expected responses for verifying the behavior and operating limits of the program. Quite often the test plan is given as part of the original specification to ensure that the tests are not biased in a way that would obscure the errors in a known design.

maintenance

    Large programs require *maintenance* after they have been put into operation in the field for two reasons. First, there are usually errors that are not detected during the testing stage. Obviously, increased effort during the testing stage can reduce this maintenance requirement. Second, and almost inevitable, is that users of a system will call for changes and enhancements after the system has been put into operation. The cost of this maintenance is strongly influenced by the specification, design, and documentation of a program; therefore, maintenance must be considered early in the development cycle.

13.2   SPECIFICATION AND DESIGN

The external specification of a program comes directly from the results of requirements analysis, while internal specifications come later. During the development cycle, some looping between specification and design often occurs as shown in Figure 13–3. This looping may be required when attempts to design the program reveal ambiguities, contradictions, or other deficiencies in the external specification. But most of the looping occurs because of the "top-down" approach that is used in problem solving. When the solution to an original external specification is designed as a collection of cooperating modules, each module and its interfaces with its partners must be documented by internal specifications. Then the workings of each module must be designed. The whole process may be repeated many times as modules at each level are designed as collections of lower-level modules.

13.2.1   Program Structure

hierarchy chart

The partitioning of a program into modules can be illustrated and documented in a *hierarchy chart* that shows the relationships among modules. For example, consider the following external specification:

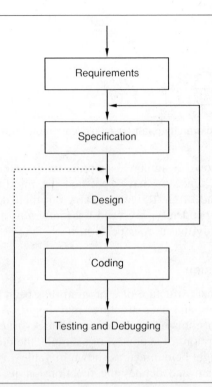

FIGURE 13–3   The program development cycle.

Write a program that multiplies pairs of 16-bit two's-complement integers to produce 32-bit results. The computer's input device consists of 16 toggle switches and a pushbutton; for each input number, the user enters a binary number using the switches and then pushes the pushbutton. The output device consists of 16 lights. After completing the multiplication, the program uses the lights to display the multiplier, multiplicand, high-order product, and low-order product, each for 10 seconds. The lights are turned off for 1 second after each number is displayed. The multiplication process is repeated until a pair of zeroes is entered.

Even this very simple program can be decomposed into a number of cooperating modules, as shown in Figure 13–4. The main program performs multiplication and calls three different subroutines for support:

- INSW: reads a 16-bit number from the switches.

- OUTDSP: displays a 16-bit number in the lights.

- DELAYN: delays for a specified number of seconds.

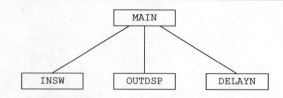

FIGURE 13–4 Preliminary hierarchy chart for multiplication program.

Top-down design breaks a program into smaller chunks that can be handled separately. Once we have specified the interfaces between MAIN and INSW, OUTDSP, and DELAYN, we can carry out their detailed design and coding more or less independently. We need not know *how* a particular module performs its function, only that it *does* perform it.

13.2.2 Detailed Module Design

Once the basic structure of a program has been determined, the detailed design of algorithms and data structures may begin. At this stage, it is convenient to outline algorithms using an informal block-structured language that allows English descriptions of actions. For example, the initial design of the multiplication program might be outlined as shown in Table 13–1. The pseudo-code shows the main program and defines the functions of its three supporting modules. Of

TABLE 13–1 Initial design of multiplication program.

```
PROGRAM Multiply;
VAR X, Y -- input numbers (each a 16-bit 2's-comp integer)
  PH, PL -- high-order and low-order product
    (PH and PL form a 32-bit 2's-complement integer)
FUNCTION INSW : word;
  This function reads a 16-bit word from the input switches
  and returns the 16-bit value to the caller.
PROCEDURE OUTDSP (num : word);
  This procedure displays a 16-bit word in the lights.
PROCEDURE DELAYN (N : unsigned integer);
  This procedure delays for N seconds, where N is a 16-bit
  value interpreted as an unsigned integer (0 <= N <= 65535).
  (Reminder: Don't forget to check for N = 0.)
BEGIN   Main program
  Read X and Y from the switches.
  WHILE (X <> 0) OR (Y <> 0) DO
    BEGIN
      Compute the double-length product PH,PL.
      Display X, Y, PH, and PL with appropriate delays.
      Read X and Y from the switches.
    END;
END.
```

course, we might not need so much preliminary design work to develop such a simple program. However, our purpose is to illustrate techniques that can be applied to larger programs, so we continue the example.

13.2.3 Design Iterations

After doing an initial design, we may determine that further decomposition is needed. For example, we may discover a sequence of steps that occurs often enough to warrant the definition of a new procedure:

```
PROCEDURE DISPLAY (num : word);
  This procedure displays a number in the lights with
  the delays required by the specification, that is:
    BEGIN  OUTDSP(num); DELAYN(10); OUTDSP(0); DELAYN(1)  END;
```

In addition, we may discover that our computer does not have a multiplication instruction and so we will have to use a 16×16-bit multiplication subroutine from a program library. We may also find that there is no hardware timer so that we will have to use busy-waiting to produce delays. Therefore, we will write a subroutine DLY1S that busy-waits for 1 second, and design DELAYN to delay N seconds by calling DLY1S N times. These changes result in the program structure shown in Figure 13–5. At this point, we can also refine the design so that the main program body reads as follows:

```
BEGIN  Main program
  X := INSW; Y := INSW;  (Read X and Y)
  WHILE (X <> 0) OR (Y <> 0) DO
    BEGIN
      PH,PL := X*Y;  (Call MULT16 for double-length product)
      DISPLAY(X); DISPLAY(Y);  (Display X and Y)
      DISPLAY(PH); DISPLAY(PL);  (Display product)
      X := INSW; Y := INSW;  (Read X and Y)
    END;
END.
```

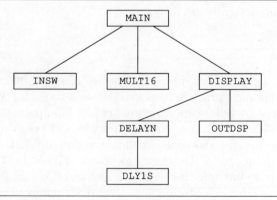

FIGURE 13–5   A second hierarchy chart for multiplication program.

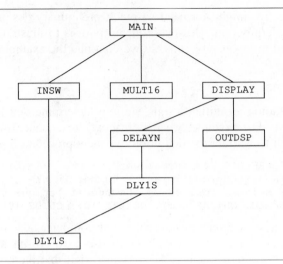

FIGURE 13–6   Final hierarchy chart for multiplication program.

Some design problems may not show up until coding or even testing, requiring another iteration of design and specification, as shown by the dotted line in Figure 13–3. For example, we may find that due to pushbutton "contact bounce," the INSW subroutine must wait 10 milliseconds before reading an input number from the switches. Therefore we provide another subroutine DLY10M to delay for 10 milliseconds. At the same time, we may find it convenient to obtain a 1-second delay in DLY1S by calling DLY10M 100 times, yielding the final program structure shown in Figure 13–6.

Large hierarchy charts may be partitioned according to the structure of the underlying modules themselves. The top-level diagram shows the relationship among high-level modules whose internal structures are defined in lower-level diagrams. This reflects block structure in Pascal and the principle of "top-down" program design in any language.

13.2.4   Data Structures

data module

So far we have shown the relationships among a main program and its subroutines, but data structures are also part of a program. Whenever a data structure is shared by two or more subroutines, it is important to specify exactly which subroutines may access the data structure and how. In a hierarchy chart, a *data module* may be shown as another module with dotted lines to the subroutines that may access it. Using this technique, Figure 13–7 shows the structure of a solution to the timer problem in Exercise 11.3.

Hierarchy charts and high-level descriptions of algorithms and data structures help a programmer to keep track of program structure during design, but

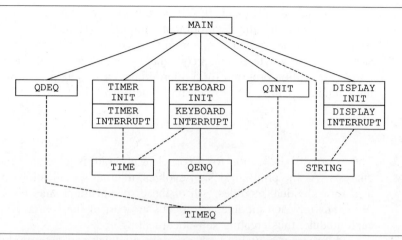

FIGURE 13–7   Hierarchy chart for the timer problem in Exercise 11.3.

the module specifications must be spelled out in much more detail in the program's documentation. In the next section, we describe exactly what information is required and how it can be formatted in a "prologue" for each module.

13.3 DOCUMENTATION

Documentation should not be generated at one fixed time during the program development cycle. Instead, documentation should be generated as appropriate throughout the project. Your only documentation experience so far may be writing comments for high-level and assembly language code, but the most important program documentation is generated long before the coding stage, during specification and design.

It is a common practice in industry to make all programs self-documenting, so that all documentation, including specifications and design, is contained in the same text file as the source code itself. Writing *self-documenting code* has several advantages over keeping separate handwritten or typed documentation:

self-documenting code

- It is easier to relate the documentation to the code.

- Efficient procedures can be instituted for maintaining all code and documentation on a development computer system.

- When the design (or code) is changed, it is convenient to make the appropriate documentation changes (otherwise there is a tendency for documentation to lag design).

- During revisions and maintenance, if the source code is available, then all the documentation is guaranteed to be available too (not lost in a paper shuffle).

The main disadvantage of self-documenting code is that it increases the size of the text files that the development computer system must handle. Including backup files, a development system may need 200 to 1000 bytes or more of disk storage for every byte of object code that is developed.[1] Thus, developing a 200-Kbyte application program for a microprocessor may require a minicomputer or midicomputer with a 200-Mbyte file system.

13.3.1   Prologues

prologue

The external specification for a complete program is generated by requirements analysis. As the program design evolves, internal specifications must be generated for individual modules. All of these specifications may be documented by *prologues* for each module. Prologues are part of the source code text file for each module, thus creating self-documenting code.

program module
data module

A program contains both program modules and data modules. *Program modules* contain subroutines and local data structures. Separate *data modules* are required only for data structures that are shared among several program modules.

13.3.2   Program Module Prologues

local data
global data

Figure 13–8 shows the structure of the text file for a program module that contains a number of subroutines. The module begins with a brief overview of its overall function. Then the global and local data structures that are used by the subroutines are defined, and local data structures declared. (If a data structure is used by only one subroutine, it may appear with that subroutine instead.) A data structure is *local* to a program module if it is accessed only by the module and its submodules, otherwise it is *global*. Finally, the module contains a prologue and source code for each subroutine.

Examples of program modules with prologues were given in Table 9–20 on page 338 and Table 10–5 on page 338. The module overview and definition of data structures do not follow a rigid format, but they must be present. Notice in both examples that it is possible to draw figures for data structures as part of the definition; this is easy to do with modern text editors. The prologue for each subroutine should contain the following information:

---

[1]For example, consider the queue module in Table 9–20 on page 338. It generates about 60 bytes of code and, with its modest documentation, the text contains about 4800 ASCII characters, a storage factor of 80 to 1. If we had drawn pretty boxes around the prologues, as is done by some programmers, the figure would be 100 to 1 or higher. Adding to this the storage for hierarchy charts, memos, and notes and double the figure for backups, we get a minimum factor of 300 to 1. To this must be added the storage for object modules and temporary files created during assembly, editing, and formatting. If multiple copies or generations of programs are kept in the file system by different programmers, the storage factor quickly reaches 1000 to 1 or higher. Obviously a powerful development system is required to manage effectively all of the files associated with a large programming project.

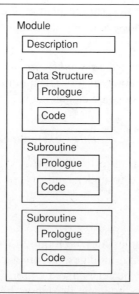

FIGURE 13–8   Structure of a program module's text file.

- *Name and short description:* the name of the subroutine and a one-line description of what it does.

- *Description:* a longer description of the subroutine, if needed. Areas worth mentioning include: purpose, assumptions about operating environment, functions performed and algorithms used, and expected ranges of inputs and outputs.

- *Inputs:* the input parameters of the subroutine and how they are passed.

- *Outputs:* the output parameters of the subroutine and how they are passed. Input and output parameters should be given descriptive names even if they are passed in registers.

- *Global data:* definitions of any global data structures that are accessed (except for those already defined in the module prologue).

- *Local data:* definitions and declarations of all local data structures (except for those already defined in the module prologue).[2]

---

[2]In defining local data, you usually need not be concerned with temporaries, but you must certainly define all variables and data structures whose values must be preserved between successive calls of the subroutine. For example, in Table 11–1 on page 389, SBUSY is a global variable accessed by both the main program and interrupt routines; BUFPNT is a local variable whose value must be preserved between successive calls of the interrupt routines.

- *Functions:* a description of how the inputs of the subroutine are used to produce outputs, and any dependence or side effects on local and global data.

- *Registers affected (assembly language prologues only):* a description of which processor registers are modified by the subroutine (if missing, assume all registers are changed, except that output parameters will be passed as specified).

- *Typical calling sequence:* example code for calling the subroutine.

- *Notes:* operating restrictions, tricks, and any other information a programmer may need to understand, fix, or enhance the subroutine.

13.3.3 Data Module Prologues

Separate data modules may be required for data structures that are accessed by two or more program modules. Figure 13–7 showed such an example. Another example is the text buffer in a text editor program. It must be accessed by input, output, and editing modules; the hierarchy chart is shown in Figure 13–9.

Prologues for data modules should give a precise definition of the data structures, including graphics or an easily understood pseudo-language to illustrate table layouts and pointers. Tables 9–20 and 10–5 illustrated the use of graphics for defining data structures.

In practice, separate data modules are often undesirable. Instead, a global data structure is *hidden* under a set of subroutines that access and manipulate the data structure. For example, consider the symbol table for an assembler. The assembler program must perform a number of different operations on the symbol table, such as inserting new symbols, looking up old ones, and sorting the symbol table. If the symbol table is defined as a global data structure, then the main program must know the table's structure in order to manipulate it.

A better program organization is shown in Figure 13–10. Here a module called SYMBOL ROUTINES contains the symbol table and several submodules that perform the required functions. Since the main program accesses the symbol table only through this module, it is possible to change the organization of the

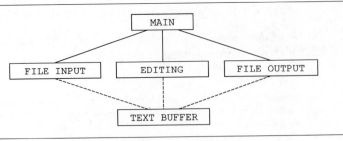

FIGURE 13–9   Hierarchy chart for a text editor.

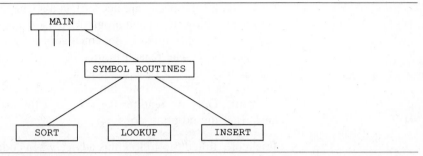

FIGURE 13–10   Partial hierarchy chart for an assembler.

symbol table (e.g., from contiguous table to linked list) without requiring any changes in the main program. SYMBOL ROUTINES hides the details of the symbol table's structure from the main program.

13.3.4   Ownership of Global Data Structures

ownership

A data structure is *owned* by the module in which it is declared (i.e., in which memory is allocated for it). The data structure is local to the declaring module, and global to lower-level modules. Thus, a low-level program module may have no local data structures, but its subroutines still must manipulate global data structures declared at a higher level. An example is the queue module in Table 9–20. It doesn't own any queues itself, but it can manipulate queues having the defined structure.

The definition of a global data structure should appear not only in the module that owns it, but also in every module that uses it. However, it is tedious to retype long data structure definitions for every module. Worse, it is impossible to ensure consistency when a definition appears in many different places. To eliminate these problems, sophisticated program development systems provide *include* *processing*. In such a system, each global data structure is defined in a separate text file. Then the programmer may simply type "#include *filename*" (or a similar directive) in each prologue that is to include the data structure's definition. The include processor automatically inserts the text from the specified file. Thus, any changes in the definition of a data structure are automatically propagated to all the prologues that use it. However, it is still the programmer's responsibility to make any required coding changes.

include
processing

13.3.5   Documenting Code

In their excellent little book, *The Elements of Programming Style*, Kernighan and Plauger give sound advice for documenting code in a high-level language:

The best documentation for a computer program is a clean structure.
It also helps if the code is well formatted, with good mnemonic iden-

tifiers and labels (if any are needed), and a smattering of enlightening comments. Flowcharts and program descriptions are of secondary importance; the only reliable documentation of a computer program is the code itself. The reason is simple — whenever there are multiple representations of a program, the chance for discrepancy exists. If the code is in error, artistic flowcharts and detailed comments are to no avail. Only by reading the code can the programmer know for sure what the program does.

It is more difficult to follow this advice when coding in assembly language. In fact, the main purpose of comments in assembly language code is to relate the code to a higher-level description of what's going on.

Two different styles of documenting assembly language code have been used in this book. The first (and most popular) style is to use English language sentences and phrases to document individual statements or small groups of statements. You should not feel obliged to comment every line when you use this style. You should assume that anyone who reads your program understands the effects of each instruction in the programming language. Avoid comments like

```
        ADD.W   #1,D0              Add 1 to D0.
```

A more descriptive comment might be

```
        ADD.W   #1,D0              Increment the iteration count.
```

If the reason for incrementing D0 is completely obvious, then there should be no comment at all. According to Kernighan and Plauger, "Anything that contributes no new information, but merely echoes code, is superfluous."

The second style is to use statements in a high-level language to document groups of assembly language statements. Any readable language or pseudo-language may be used; we've used Pascal (with occasional liberties) throughout this book. Good assembly language programmers formulate their initial designs using such a language anyway. This style of documentation simply retains the original design, explicitly showing the correspondence between the high-level formulation and the resulting assembly language code. The emphasis is not on syntactic correctness of the high-level description, but on readability and accuracy in describing what the assembly language program does.

13.4 CODING

13.4.1 Coding Rules

Coding is probably the best understood aspect of programming; in fact, coding a well-designed program is a fairly mechanical operation. The most important thing to know about coding is that good code must be built upon good design.

A programmer cannot expect to make significant improvements in program performance by clever coding—the best improvements are made in design.

In *The Elements of Programming Style*, Kernighan and Plauger discuss the merits and pitfalls of dozens of programs, from which they compile a list of rules of programming style. Many of these rules are especially applicable to coding:

- Write clearly — don't be too clever.

- Say what you mean, simply and directly.

- Let the machine do the dirty work.

- Write first in an easy-to-understand pseudo-language; then translate into whatever language you have to use.

- Don't stop with your first draft.

- Choose a data representation that makes the program simple.

- Don't patch bad code — rewrite it.

- Make sure input cannot violate the limits of the program.

- Identify bad input; recover if possible.

- Make sure all variables are initialized before use.

- Watch out for off-by-one errors.

- Take care to branch the right way on equality.

- Make sure your program "does nothing" gracefully.

- Make it right before you make it faster.

- Make it clear before you make it faster.

- Keep it right when you make it faster.

- Don't diddle code to make it faster — find a better algorithm.

- Make sure comments and code agree.

- Don't just echo the code with comments — make every comment count.

- Don't comment bad code — rewrite it.

- Use variable names that mean something.

- Use statement labels that mean something.

The examples in Kernighan and Plauger's book clearly demonstrate the validity of these rules. All of the assembly language and Pascal programs in this book have been coded with these rules in mind, although there are undoubtedly a few violations. (*Exercise*: Find some of them!)

The most important rules are the ones that advise you to keep things simple and avoid tricky code. Having said this, we must now face reality—most programmers love to write tricky code. After all, it makes the job more interesting, it gives programmers an ego boost to show how clever they are, and in many cases it even provides job security (no one else can maintain the code!).

There *are* legitimate uses for tricky code. Occasionally it is necessary to squeeze the last drop of performance out of a program or squeeze the last possible byte of code into a computer's memory. Such needs may stem from anything from poor planning and design to simple economics—a potential cost savings in 100,000 copies of a computer system or program can pay for a lot of extra development work and still leave a profit. Therefore, the next subsection will describe a number of coding "tricks," pointing out their pitfalls as appropriate. However, we remind you that good design techniques can improve a program's potential performance long before coding has begun.[3]

13.4.2 Coding Tricks

The purpose of most coding tricks is to produce faster programs. Since a typical program spends most of its time executing loops, speeding up critical loops can improve a program's performance more than any other coding changes. In short loops, the speed improvement obtained by eliminating just a few instructions can be substantial. We shall discuss several methods for speeding up loops:

- Eliminating unnecessary instructions.

- Optimizing register usage within loops.

- Moving unconditional branches to outside the loop.

- Exploiting special cases (dangerous).

- Moving instructions with invariant results to outside the loop.

- Collapsing multiple conditional tests into one.

If a programmer mechanically translates a high-level language statement into assembly language, there will often be unnecessary instructions. For example, consider the following IF statement, which computes the maximum of two integers i and j:

```
IF i > j THEN max := i ELSE max := j;
```

---

[3]Design and coding techniques are discussed in the References at the end of this chapter. Apparently the difference between tricks and techniques is that tricks aren't normally dignified in textbooks (except this one!).

This statement may be written in assembly language according to an equivalent primitive sequence as suggested in Section 2.8:

```
        MOVE.W   I,D0
        CMP.W    J,D0
        BGT.S    LABELA
        MOVE.W   J,MAX
        BRA.S    LABELB
LABELA  MOVE.W   I,MAX
LABELB  ...
```

However, a shorter and faster sequence can be written that is just as easy, perhaps easier, to understand:

```
        MOVE.W   I,D0
        CMP.W    J,D0
        BGT.S    LABELA
        MOVE.W   J,D0
LABELA  MOVE.W   D0,MAX
```

Another general technique is to optimize the use of registers within loops. Since instructions that operate on registers are generally shorter and faster than ones that operate on memory, the most frequently used variables and constants should be kept in registers during loops.

Unconditional branches that occur within loops can often be moved to outside the loop, reducing the number of instructions in the loop. For example, look at the loop in Table 7–7 on page 236, and then read the recoded version of it below:

```
SCOREI  MOVEA.L  HEAD,A0            next := head;
        BRA.S    LOOPIN             REPEAT
SCLOOP  MOVE.W   #ISCR,SCORE1(A0)     next^.score1 := initScore;
        MOVE.W   #ISCR,SCORE2(A0)     next^.score2 := initScore;
        MOVE.W   #ISCR,SCORE3(A0)     next^.score3 := initScore;
        MOVEA.L  LINK(A0),A0          next := next^.link;
LOOPIN  CMPA.L   #NIL,A0            UNTIL next = nil;
        BNE      SCLOOP
OUT     ...
```

The general idea here is to structure the loop so that the unconditional branch back to the beginning of the loop is replaced by a conditional branch that we needed somewhere in the loop anyway.

The loop above contains two more areas for potential improvement. The first improvement is to move instructions or pieces of instructions with invariant results to outside the loop. Such instructions are often assignments of a constant value to a variable; the assignment needs to be done only once before entering the loop, not over and over as the loop is executed. In our example, the immediate

TABLE 13–2   Subroutine that searches a buffer for a character.

```
*        Find the first occurrence in BUFFER of a character
*        passed in D0.  Return with Z = 1 if character not found,
*        or with Z = 0 and A0 pointing to character if found.
SEARCH   LEA.L    BUFFER,A0        Point to start of buffer.
         LEA.L    BUFEND,A1        Address just past end of buffer.
SLOOP    CMP.B    (A0)+,D0         Match?
         BEQ.S    OUT              Exit if match found.
         CMPA.L   A1,A0            At end?
         BNE      SLOOP            No, look some more.
         RTS                       No match, return with Z = 1.
OUT      ADDA.L   #-1,A0           Adjust A0 to point to matched char.
         AND.B    #$FB,CCR         Set Z := 0 for match.
         RTS                       Done, return.
*
BUFFER   DS.B     1000             Reserve 1000-byte buffer.
BUFEND   EQU      *                Define address just past buffer.
```

value ISCR appears in three MOVE instructions inside the loop; the program is faster and shorter if we put ISCR in a register only once, outside the loop:

```
SCOREI   MOVEA.L  HEAD,A0             next := head;
         MOVE.W   #ISCR,D1            D1 := initScore;
         BRA.S    LOOPIN              REPEAT
SCLOOP   MOVE.W   D1,SCORE1(A0)         next^.score1 := D1;
         MOVE.W   D1,SCORE2(A0)         next^.score2 := D1;
         MOVE.W   D1,SCORE3(A0)         next^.score3 := D1;
         MOVEA.L  LINK(A0),A0           next := next^.link;
LOOPIN   CMPA.L   #NIL,A0             UNTIL next = nil
         BNE      SCLOOP
OUT      ...
```

The second "improvement" takes advantage of a fortuitous combination of instructions and data. The CMPA.W #NIL,A0 instruction appears to be redundant because NIL is defined to be 0 and the Z bit almost always detects this value. In particular, the Z bit will already be set if A0 was just loaded with 0 by the preceding MOVEA instruction. Or will it? Since the destination of the MOVEA is an *address* register, the condition bits are not affected! Thus, the CMPA instruction is absolutely necessary. However, we can still speed up the comparison by loading a spare register with #NIL outside the loop so that we can use a register-to-register instruction inside the loop.

Perhaps the most clever method for speeding up a loop is to collapse multiple conditional tests into one. For example, consider the subroutine in Table 13–2 that searches a buffer for a character. It appears that we have done the best coding that we possibly can, even using auto-increment addressing to save an instruction inside the loop. Both conditional tests inside the loop seem necessary—one to find the character and one to stop the loop if the character isn't found. However, we can eliminate one of the tests by ensuring that we will *always* find the character, deciding outside the loop whether we found the

TABLE 13–3   Optimized buffer-search subroutine.

```
*        Find the first occurrence in BUFFER of a character
*        passed in D0.  Return with Z = 1 if character not found,
*        or with Z = 0 and A0 pointing to character if found.
SEARCH   LEA.L   BUFFER,A0      Point to start of buffer.
         LEA.L   EXTRA,A1       Address of extra character at buffer end.
         MOVE.B  D0,(A1)        Store char to stop us for sure.
SLOOP    CMP.B   (A0)+,D0       Match?
         BNE     SLOOP          No, continue.
         ADDA.L  #-1,A0         Yes, point to matched character.
         CMPA.L  A1,A0          Stopped at end of buffer?
         RTS                    Return, Z = 0 if match, Z = 1 if no match.
*
BUFFER   DS.B    1000           Reserve 1000-byte buffer.
EXTRA    DS.B    1              Extra byte for termination.
```

character inside the buffer or just past the buffer's end. In this example, we can double the speed of the loop as shown in Table 13–3.

Many high-level language compilers automatically perform code optimizations such as eliminating redundant instructions and removing invariant computations from loops. ("Let the machine do the dirty work.") A programmer's best advice for coding in both high-level and assembly languages is to "make it right before you make it faster."

13.5 TESTING AND DEBUGGING

The purpose of testing and debugging is to make a program meet its specifications. *Testing* is an activity that detects the existence of errors in a program. *Debugging* finds the causes of detected errors and then repairs them. As shown in the pie chart in Figure 13–1, testing and debugging form the largest single component in the program development process.

testing
debugging

13.5.1 Development Approach

Even after starting with a good design, many novice programmers have a haphazard approach to the remainder of program development. They code the entire program and then run it the first time with their fingers crossed. Every programmer should have the joy of seeing a large program perform perfectly on its first run, but for most this is a once-in-a-lifetime experience. More often, a program with such a daring first test either does nothing or "blows up."

A more sensible method for developing a large program is to code, test, and debug it in small chunks. One of two approaches may be used:

bottom-up
development

- *Bottom-up development.* The lowest-level modules are coded, tested, and debugged first. These modules, which are now known to be working, may be employed in developing higher-level modules. For example, in developing the multiplication program in Section 13.2, a programmer could code and test the INSW, OUTSW, and DELAYN subroutines before coding the main program. However, a simple "throwaway" main program must be written to test each subroutine.

top-down development

stub

- *Top-down development.* The highest-level modules are coded, tested, and debugged first. In order to test them, the lower-level modules that have not yet been coded must be replaced by *stubs* that match their input/output specifications, but with much less functionality. For example, in developing the multiplication program, a programmer could test the main program's input, output, and control, but use a stub for multiplication. The stub would return the values of X and Y in PH, PL instead of actually computing the product X · Y.

There are advantages and disadvantages to both approaches. In bottom-up development, fundamental errors in the design of top-level modules may not be caught until late in the project. In top-down development, problems with program size or performance may not become apparent until critical low-level modules are developed. Both approaches require additional code to be written for testing. In practice, it is often best to use a combination of the two approaches, developing both high-level and critical low-level modules first, and using stubs for less critical modules to be developed later.[4]

unit testing

system integration and test

In large programming projects the need to partition the testing and debugging problem is well recognized. About half of the total testing and debugging effort is devoted to ensuring that individual modules meet their internal specifications; this activity is sometimes called *unit testing*. The remaining effort is spent on *system integration and test*, in which the modules are linked together and the external specifications of the program are checked.

13.5.2 Testing

Testing detects the presence of bugs, while debugging locates known bugs and eliminates them. Debugging and testing a program or module usually requires several iterations. Each round of debugging allows the programmer to test for more subtle bugs.

The first tests that are applied to a program may be simple ones, because most programs contain obvious bugs at the outset. An example of a simple test is, "If I give the program an input, does it produce an output, any output at all?" Once we get the program to produce *some* output, we can check whether we get the *correct* output under all circumstances.

---

[4]However, when using this approach, always remember the famous cartoon of the bridge whose construction was started at both ends, but failed to meet in the middle.

The next group of tests should ensure that the program behaves properly for typical inputs and boundary conditions. Ideally the "typical inputs" and expected behavior should be defined in the program's original external specification, so that the programmer cannot subconsciously avoid cases that aren't handled properly by the actual design and code. A good prologue defines a module's inputs and behavior well enough that the prologue itself provides the list of test inputs.

Boundary conditions should be tested from both sides. First the program must produce correct outputs for inputs just inside the allowed range. But it may also need to detect the presence of inputs outside the allowed range. Even if it doesn't detect bad inputs, the program should at least behave reasonably when it receives them.

13.5.3 Debugging

Finding a bug in a program requires the same common-sense approach as any other kind of troubleshooting. By applying a series of tests, a programmer may determine in what areas the bug might be and in what areas it cannot be, eventually narrowing the area of search until the bug is found.[5] The logic of debugging is the same as the logic of program design—breaking a problem into smaller and smaller pieces until it is solved. The main question is, "What tools can be used to break the problem into smaller pieces?"

defensive program design

The most effective debugging tools are created during design and coding. A program should be designed and coded *defensively*. The range of inputs should be checked and the occurrence of "impossible" cases should be flagged rather than ignored. Quite often the erroneous values produced by bugs will be caught by these checks before they have propagated too far, making bug detection trivial and isolation simple.

In addition, a programmer can provide facilities for tracing the program's execution, printing the program's state at key points, and allowing the program to be initialized, started, and stopped in the middle. It may seem inefficient to write a lot of extra code that will eventually be thrown away, but it can lead to substantial savings in debugging time. In fact, up to half of a good programmer's code may be "throwaway" code written for debugging purposes only.

on-line debugger

In many high-level language programming systems and in most assembly language programming systems, many of the facilities mentioned above can be obtained without writing any extra code. An *on-line debugger* is an interactive

---

[5] An episode of the original *Star Trek* TV series gave an excellent example of debugging principles. Captain Kirk is lost on a planet below, and the following conversation takes place on the bridge of the *Enterprise*. Sulu (panicked): "Mr. Spock, our sensors are unable to pinpoint the captain." Spock (impatient): "I suggest, Mr. Sulu, that if you cannot determine where the captain *is*, then you determine where he *is not*." Sulu (shocked): "You mean, search the entire planet?? Why, that could take years!" Spock (icily): "Then you had better start immediately."

system program for debugging a user's assembly language program; it provides a number of useful facilities:

breakpoint

symbolic debugger

in-circuit emulator

- *Single stepping.* The user program may be executed one instruction at a time, with control returning to the debugger after each step.

- *Running.* The user program may be started at an arbitrary address and run at full speed.

- *Running with breakpoints.* The user may specify a list of addresses, called *breakpoints*, such that control is returned to the debugger whenever an instruction is executed at one of these addresses.

- *Memory examining and changing.* The contents of memory may be examined and altered.

- *Register examining and changing.* The last values that the processor registers had during program execution may be examined and altered.

- *Symbolic references.* Some debuggers, called *symbolic debuggers*, keep a copy of the assembler symbol table so the user can specify memory addresses by assembly-time symbols instead of by absolute numbers.

Debuggers are usually found only on program development systems. A small, dedicated microcomputer system in a cash register or automobile does not have or need a debugger. A debugger is needed only during the development of the application programs, not during system operation.

Dedicated systems are often developed with the aid of an *in-circuit emulator*. The in-circuit emulator replaces the dedicated system's microprocessor with a plug and cable to a development system. The development system has more memory, peripherals, and programs, so that the application programs and debugger can run there during development.

Using a debugger and an accurate assembly listing, you can very quickly debug a program, even one with no built-in debugging facilities. The algorithm for a typical debugging session might go something like this:

(1) Run the program with a set of test inputs and observe the effects of the bug(s).

(2) Make an educated guess of where the bug is located (e.g., main program, multiplication subroutine, output subroutine). Check the assembly listing—if you suddenly see the bug staring you in the face, you're done. Otherwise, set a breakpoint just before the program enters the suspected area. If the suspected area is large, set the breakpoint somewhere near the middle.

(3) Run the program again. If the breakpoint is not reached, the bug obviously occurs earlier in the program; remove the breakpoint and return to step 2.

(4) Otherwise, if the breakpoint is reached, examine processor registers, stack, and important variables and subroutine parameters to see whether they have the correct values. If the bug has already occurred, once again remove the breakpoint and return to step 2.

(5) Otherwise, if the bug has not yet occurred, single step the program, observing whether branches are taken in the expected direction and also observing the states of registers and memory at key points. If the bug pops out, you're done. Otherwise, if this gets too confusing or the bug remains hidden, return to step 1 or 2.

Once you locate a bug, you can fix it. However, Kernighan and Plauger have stated a wise rule: "Don't stop at one bug." When you locate one bug, you should always suspect that there are others lurking nearby, and you should check the nearby code carefully. Also, you must be very careful not to introduce new bugs when fixing the old ones.

Sometimes there is a long turnaround time for editing, assembling, and reloading a program, so that it's important to catch as many bugs as possible in each debugging session. When small bugs are found, it is often possible to test a different area of the program or to "patch" one or two instructions, so you can continue debugging. If the patch involves deleting instructions, you can replace them with NOPs. If the fix requires instructions to be added, you can overwrite an instruction with a subroutine jump to a patch in an unused area of memory; the patch contains the overwritten instruction, the instructions to be added, and a return. You must carefully observe instruction lengths in this kind of patching (e.g., a one-word MOVE D1,D2 cannot be overwritten by a two-word JSR PATCH).

common bugs   Experience has demonstrated the existence of some common bugs for beginning assembly language programmers:

- Failing to initialize SP at the beginning of the program.

- Putting data in-line with instructions. You must keep data separate from the code to be executed.

- Altering constants. Anything declared with a DC pseudo-operation must not be altered.

- Incorrect use of assembly-time and run-time constants. The following examples are possible ways to try to load D0 with the ASCII code for "J".

```
        ORG     $1234
LETJ    EQU     $4A           Define LETJ to be same as $4A.
ZLETJ   DC.B    $4A           Stores $4A at mem. address $1234.
        . . .
        MOVE.B  LETJ,D0       Wrong, loads D0 with MEM[$4A].
        MOVE.B  #ZLETJ,D0     Wrong, loads D0 with $34.
        MOVE.B  #LETJ,D0      Correct.
        MOVE.B  ZLETJ,D0      Correct.
```

- Incorrect manipulation of the stack pointer. If your program jumps off into never-never land, it is probably a result of executing an `RTS` at the end of a subroutine that pushed more items onto the stack than it popped, or vice versa. Beware of constructs like the following, which fails if the branch is taken:

```
SUBR    MOVE.L  D1,-(SP)     Save D1.
        ...
        BEQ     DONE         Exit on special case.
        ...                  Else continue.
        MOVE.L  (SP)+,D1     Restore D1.
DONE    RTS                  Return to caller.
```

- In the same vein, note that subroutines must always return via `RTS`, not by a jump directly to some address in the main program.

- Off-by-one errors. A loop may execute one too many or one too few times if the loop counter is initialized improperly, or if the wrong type of branch is used (e.g., `BLT` vs `BLE`).

- Failure at boundary conditions. A program may work fine for most inputs, but fail for the minimum (often 0) or maximum case.

- Backwards operands. It is easy to swap the source and destination of a double-operand instruction accidentally, especially if you have experience with a machine that uses that opposite order from the one you're using.

- Backwards `CMP`. You always have to watch out for this one on the 68000, unless you have an assembler that lets you write the operands in their natural order. Even then, you have to make sure you're using the "good" assembler or option.

- Wrong operand size. With most 68000 opcodes, if you don't write a size suffix, the assembler defaults to "word." That's not always what you need.

- Wrong address or index register size. With absolute and indexed addressing, the assembler uses a default address constant or index register size if you don't attach a size suffix to the operand. Again, the default may not be what you need.

- Improper use of the `ORG` pseudo-operation. Occasionally a programmer `ORG`s for data and then re-`ORG`s at a convenient, higher address for instructions, without leaving enough room for the data just declared. This doesn't cause any assembler errors, but it will cause run-time errors.

- Improper base for constants. Forgetting the "$" or other specifier for hexadecimal and other constants is an innocent error that can have strange effects.

- Incorrect format of assembler expressions. Operand expressions may sometimes yield unexpected results without creating assembler errors. For example, the statement EBASE EQU BASE-2*FIRST may yield a value of (BASE-2)*FIRST or BASE-(2*FIRST) depending on whether or not the operators have equal precedence. The statement CON EQU 3 + 5 will yield the value 3 if the assembler interprets the space after "3" as beginning the comment field. Be on the lookout for values in the "Contents" column of the assembler listing that don't match up with what was apparently specified in the "Operand" column.

- Inconsistent definition of variables and constants. It's easy to make a small change in a data structure that affects other data or instructions, and forget to update the dependent items. Therefore, it's best to define data structures defensively, so that either the dependent changes will be made automatically or the inconsistencies generate assembler errors. For example, see the definitions of QENDA and STACKE in Table 8–11 on page 286, or the CASETBL definition in Table 7–10 on page 244.

We close this section with some useful rules for debugging:

- Program defensively.

- Don't stop with one bug.

- Record all bugs as they are observed.

- Record all patches as they are created.

REFERENCES

The best source of practical advice on program design, documentation, coding, and debugging is *The Elements of Programming Style* by Brian W. Kernighan and P. J. Plauger (McGraw-Hill, 1978, 2nd ed.). Pascal programmers can also benefit from the "style clinics" scattered throughout *An Introduction to Programming and Problem Solving with Pascal* by G. M. Schneider, S. W. Weingart, and D. M. Perlman (Wiley, 1982, 2nd ed.). *Advanced Programming and Problem Solving with Pascal* by G. M. Schneider and S. C. Bruell (Wiley, 1987, 2nd ed.) devotes a chapter to debugging, testing, and formal verification techniques.

A number of good books have been published on the specific subject of software engineering. The classic is *The Mythical Man-Month* by Fred P. Brooks (Addison-Wesley, 1975). This short, entertaining, and easy-to-read book is a collection of thought-provoking essays on the nature and management of computer programming projects, and is required reading for anyone who participates in the development of large programs. In it, Brooks gives specific advice for program specification, design, documentation, coding, testing, and debugging, and he discusses the general problems of large program management.

Another useful book is *Principles of Software Engineering and Design* by Zelkowitz, Shaw, and Gannon (Prentice-Hall, 1979). The central thesis of this book is prominently displayed on its front cover, which we've adapted here as Figure 13–2. The book also covers the stages of program development outlined in this chapter in much more detail. A more recent book that also covers the stages of program development in depth is *Software Engineering Environments, Concepts and Technology* by Robert N. Charette (Intertext/McGraw-Hill, 1986)

A less recent but still interesting book for programmers and managers alike is *The Psychology of Computer Programming* by Gerald M. Weinberg (Van Nostrand Reinhold, 1971). It investigates the actual behavior and thought processes of programmers as they carry out their daily activities, and relates them to the stages of program development.

E X E R C I S E S

13.1   Design the program specified in Exercise 10.14. Your design should include a hierarchy chart, an outline of the code for all program modules except the queue module, and definitions of all data structures.

13.2   Write a prologue for the `DIVIDE` subroutine in Table 9–14 on page 329.

13.3   Write a prologue for the polling subroutines in Table 11–2 on page 396.

13.4   Recode the program in Table 7–3 on page 226 so that all of the unconditional branches that now appear inside loops are moved to outside the loops.

13.5   Show what additional comments should be included if a programmer changes the tenth line in the `QENQ` subroutine in Table 9–20 on page 338 to read as follows:

```
*       AND.B   #$FB,CCR        Set Z := 0 since not full.
```

13.6   A comparison instruction usually has three possible outcomes: less than, equal, or greater than. Quite often, only two of these outcomes are of interest, the third being "impossible." For example, in a loop that decrements a counter from some positive value and terminates when the counter reaches zero, the counter should never be negative. Nevertheless, defensive programming requires that `BLE DONE` rather than `BEQ DONE` be used to test for termination, to limit the effects of a bug that somehow makes the counter negative (otherwise the program could enter a very long or endless loop). Find at least four different Pascal or assembly language programs in this book in which this principle was followed. Also find at least four programs in which this principle was violated and show how to fix them.

CHAPTER 14

Advanced 68000-Family Processors

Since the introduction of the 68000 architecture in the late 1970s, Motorola has introduced several microprocessor chips that extend the architecture and improve the performance of the original MC68000 microprocessor. The first extensions, the MC68010 and MC68012, make it possible to implement virtual memory and virtual machines in a 68000 system. The next extensions, the MC68020 and MC68030, greatly increase processing speed and add new addressing modes and instructions. Differences among 68000-family processors are summarized in Table 14–1.

By and large, each new processor retains 100% object-code compatibility with its predecessors. For example, any program written for the MC68000 can run on an MC68010 or MC68020 processor without changes to the object code— the new processors retain all of the instructions of the MC68000 as a subset of their extended instruction sets.

The instruction sets of the MC68010 and MC68012 are identical. The only difference between these processors is in their IC packages—the MC68010 provides external pins for 24 address bits, while the MC68012 provides 31. Thus, the MC68012 can access 2 Gigabytes of physical memory, while the MC68010 is limited to 16 Mbytes as in the original MC68000. In the remainder

68010

of this chapter, and throughout this book, we use *68010* to refer to features that apply to both the MC68010 and the MC68012 processors.

Likewise, the instruction sets of the MC68020 and MC68030 are identical (with one exception). Compared with the MC68020, the MC68030 has an integrated MMU and additional performace-enhancing circuitry such as a data

68020

cache. We use *68020* to refer to features that apply to both the MC68020 and the MC68030 processors.

TABLE 14–1 Differences among 68000 family members.

Feature	MC68000/08	MC68010/12	MC68020/30
Memory data bus width (bits)	16/8	16	8, 16, or 32
Memory address bus width (bits)	24/20	24/31	32
Internal data bus size (bits)	16	16	32
Word alignment of instructions	required	required	required
Word alignment of data	required	required	not required
Virtual machine support	no	yes	yes
Virtual memory support	no	yes	yes
Stack pointers	A7, A7'	A7, A7'	A7, A7', A7"
Additional control registers	none	SFC,DFC,VBR	SFC,DFC,VBR,CACR,CAAR
Additional bits in SR	none	none	T0,T1,M
Additional addressing modes	none	none	see Section 14.8
Additional instructions	none	see Section 14.2	see Section 14.9
Instruction continuation after bus error	no	yes	yes
On-chip memory management unit	no	no	no/yes
Instruction cache	none	3-word loops	64 longwords
Data cache	none	none	none/64 longwords

14.1 VIRTUAL MEMORY AND VIRTUAL MACHINE SUPPORT

The most important extension in the 68010 architecture is its support of virtual memory; this extension is also carried forward to the 68020 architecture. As discussed in Section 7.5.3, virtual memory requires an MMU to translate logical addresses into physical (main memory) addresses, with the capability of interrupting normal instruction processing if a logical address belongs to page that is not present in main memory. The processor in turn must be capable of suspending the execution of an instruction that causes such an interruption, and resuming the instruction later, after the required page has been brought into main memory.

Most 68000-family processors, including the 68010, do not contain memory mapping and management circuits. Instead, they expect external circuits to be placed between the processor's address outputs and the main memory's address inputs to perform the logical-to-physical address mapping, as we showed in Figure 7–23 on page 250. In order to support virtual memory, the mapping circuits must have a way to inform the processor that a requested logical address is not present in main memory, or that the operation being performed at this address is not allowed and should be aborted. Most 68000-family processor

Bus Error (BERR)

chips have a *Bus Error (BERR)* input for just this purpose.

In the MC68000 chip, a signal applied to the BERR input causes the execution of the current instruction to be aborted, and the processor immediately takes a bus error trap through vector 2, as we explained in Section 11.4.5. However, the processor does keep not track of exactly how far the offending instruction had progressed when the trap is taken. Thus, even if the trap handler repairs the condition that caused the bus error (such as the destination address being "not present"), it doesn't know whether to restart the offending instruction from the beginning or to undo its partial effects somehow before restarting.

In the 68010, a bus error trap does not cause instructions to be aborted, but merely suspended. To suspend an instruction, the processor saves additional internal state information on the stack while handling the trap, as we show in Section 14.4. At the end of the software trap handler, the 68010's RTE recognizes the saved state information, restores it, and resumes execution in the middle of the suspended instruction.

virtual machine

Besides virtual memory, the 68010 supports *virtual machine* operation. Suppose that a 68000 or 68010 application program, APP, uses both user and supervisor mode, and "thinks" that it has complete control of the processor and its environment. Such a program can run in user mode on a virtual machine in the 68010, under the control of a higher-level operating system, OS/VM. Any attempt by APP to access privileged resources will cause a trap and return control to OS/VM, which decides whether to grant access (as in debugging), and perhaps emulates resources that are not physically present in the system. The major changes made to the 68010 for virtual machine support are in the handling of the high-order byte of the SR, as discussed in the next section.

14.2 68010 PROGRAMMING MODEL AND CONTROL OPERATIONS

As shown in Figure 14–1(a), the registers visible in user mode in the 68010 are the same as in the original 68000, with one important exception. The user can no longer read the high byte of SR, because the 68000's MOVE SR,dst instruction is privileged in the 68010. This is necessary for virtual machine support—an application program APP that thinks it is running in supervisor mode must not be allowed to read the high-order byte of SR and find out otherwise. The privileged-instruction trap that takes place when MOVE SR,dst is executed allows the virtual-machine operating system OS/VM to "fool" APP into thinking that it is running in supervisor mode.

For user programs that are only interested in the state of the low-order byte of SR, the 68010 provides the new MOVE CCR,dst instruction. It copies only the low-order byte of SR to the dst operand, and sets the high-order byte of dst to zero, without causing a trap. However, this creates a bit of a dilemma—which instruction should be used in new programs? If the new instruction is executed on an older 68000-family processor, it causes an illegal-instruction trap and, if the old instruction is executed on a 68010, it causes a privilege trap. Either way, appropriate trap routines must be provided if the program is to run properly on both processors.

The additional registers accessible in supervisor mode in the 68010 are shown in Figure 14–1(b). As in the MC68000, a supervisor stack pointer (A7', SSP) is used in supervisor mode, and the high-order bits of SR are accessible. In addition, three new registers support virtual machine operations and memory protection schemes, as we'll show.

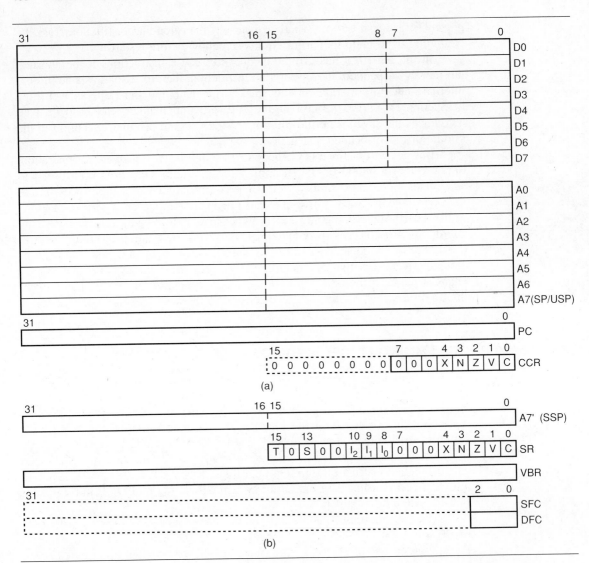

FIGURE 14–1 Programming model of the 68010: (a) user registers; (b) supervisor registers.

vector base register (VBR)

The *vector base register (VBR)* contains the base address of the exception vector table in the 68010. The MC68000 processor reserves the first 1024 bytes of memory for a table of starting addresses for routines that handle interrupts and traps, as discussed in Chapter 11. The 68010 allows the exception vector table to start at any address, as specified by VBR. Thus, different virtual machines may have different tables and hence different exception handlers. At reset, the processor automatically sets VBR to zero so that initially the exception vectors, including the reset vector itself, are taken from low memory as in the MC68000.

TABLE 14–2   Bus function codes.

FC2	FC1	FC0	Access Type
0	0	0	Undefined, reserved
0	0	1	User data
0	1	0	User program
0	1	1	Undefined, reserved
1	0	0	Undefined, reserved
1	0	1	Supervisor data
1	1	0	Supervisor program
1	1	1	Interrupt acknowledge

Notes: *Program references* are defined as either instruction fetches or operand fetches that use
PC-relative addressing modes. All other memory accesses are *data references*.

*function code
FC2–0*

address space

To support external memory-mapping and management circuits, the 68010 chip has three *function code* output signals, FC2, FC1, FC0, which indicate the type of each bus access, as shown in Table 14–2.[1] These outputs may be decoded by an MMU that selects a different memory mapping depending on whether the processor is in user or supervisor mode, and whether it is accessing code or data. Each valid function code selects a different *address space*.

With an MMU of the type just described, it is sometimes necessary to move information between two address spaces. For example, when a user program calls an operating system utility routine that runs in supervisor mode, the utility routine may need to copy parameters from user memory or return results there. The 68010's SFC and DFC registers are used along with the new MOVES instruction to do this, as described shortly.

*MOVEC
control register
opcode extension
    word*

The data movement instructions that deal with the new registers in the 68010's programming model are listed in Table 14–3. The MOVEC instructions allow any of the *control registers* to be loaded or stored. Rather than use up scarce opcode space, these infrequently used instructions use an *opcode extension word* to specify the general register and the control register to be used, as shown in Figure 14–2(a).

The MOVES instruction transfers a register operand to or from an arbitrary memory address space. In this case, a second opcode word specifies a general register and the direction of transfer, as shown in Figure 14–2(c). For memory source operands, the three low-order bits of SFC are placed on the processor's FC2–FC0 outputs during the memory read. Similarly, for memory source operands, the three low-order bits of DFC are placed on FC2–FC0 during the memory write. Thus, MOVES gives an operating system the capability of reading or writing information in an address space. To preserve operating system integrity, both MOVEC and MOVES are privileged instructions.

[1]The MC68000 has these outputs as well, but they aren't very useful without other 68010 features like instruction continuation and the SFC and DFC registers.

TABLE 14–3 Control data movement instructions in the 68010.

Mnemonic	Operands	Opcode Word(s)	XNZVC	Description
MOVE.W	CCR,dst	0100001011dddddd	-----	Copy 0,CCR to dst
MOVE.W	SR,dst	0100000011dddddd	-----	Copy SR to dst (privileged operation)
MOVEC.L	Rc,Rn	0100111001111010 Annncccccccccccc	-----	Copy control register Rc to Rn (privileged)
MOVEC.L	Rn,Rc	0100111001111011 Annncccccccccccc	-----	Copy Rn to control register Rc (privileged)
MOVES.BWL	ssrc,Rn	00001110LWsssssss Annn000000000000	-----	Copy ssrc [SFC] to Rn (privileged operation)
MOVES.BWL	Rn,sdst	00001110LWdddddd Annn100000000000	-----	Copy Rn to sdst [DFC] (privileged operation)

Notes: Privileged instructions cause a trap if executed in user mode (when S = 0).
 dst = destination operand, cannot use address register direct, immediate, or relative addressing modes.
 ssrc = "memory alterable" source operand, cannot use register direct, immediate, or relative addressing modes.
 sdst = "memory alterable" destination operand, cannot use register direct, immediate, or relative addressing modes.
 Rn = one of the general registers, D0–D7 or A0–A7.
 Rc = one of the control registers, USP, ISP, MSP, VBR, SFC, or DFC.
 ssssss = ssrc field; dddddd = dst or sdst field; LW = size field: 00 = byte, 01 = word, 10 = long.
 In opcode extension words, A = D/A bit (1 = address register, 0 = data register); nnn = Rn field; cccccccccccc = Rc field; also see Figure 14–2.

14.3 68010 EXTENDED OPERATIONS

RTD

All of the 68010's changes that we've discussed so far were made to support virtual memory and virtual machine operation. However, the designers apparently couldn't resist the temptation to add just one more general-purpose instruction. Listed in Table 14–4, RTD pops a longword off the stack and into PC to perform a subroutine return; then it adds a 16-bit signed displacement to SP. Normally, the displacement is positive, so RTD deallocates input parameters that were placed

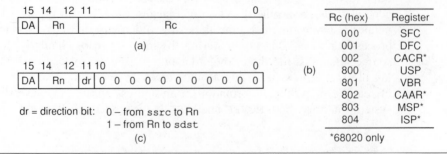

FIGURE 14–2 Opcode extension words: (a) MOVEC; (b) Rc field encoding; (c) MOVES.

TABLE 14-4   Additional instructions in the 68010.

Mnemonic	Operands	Opcode Word	XNZVC	Description
RTD	#disp	0100111001110100	-----	Return from subroutine and add `disp` to SP
BKPT	#number	0100100001001nnn	-----	Execute breakpoint bus cycle, then trap

Notes: `disp` = displacement, ranging from −32768 to +32767, in the word following the opcode.
`number` = 3-bit breakpoint number (0–7) for use by the trap handler; nnn = `number` field.

on the stack in the subroutine-calling convention of Section 9.3.6. (Perhaps Motorola's marketing department requested RTD so that they could promote the 68010 as featuring "improved high-level language support"!)

The 68010's designers also increased the functionality of the 68000's BKPT instruction for better support of in-circuit emulators and hardware debuggers. *breakpoint* Besides causing an illegal instruction trap, BKPT executes a special *breakpoint* *acknowledge* *acknowledge cycle* on the 68010 memory bus. This allows the debugging hard- *cycle* ware to notice that a breakpoint has been reached and perform any special hardware operations that might be required for proper debugger operation (for example, disabling memory mapping or slowing down the clock).

14.4 68010 EXCEPTION HANDLING

The 68010 uses a different format than the original 68000 for the information that it pushes onto the supervisor stack while handling exceptions. The original 68000 format for interrupts and traps other than bus errors and address errors is shown in Figure 14–3(a). The 68010 pushes an additional word giving the format of the stacked information and the vector offset of the exception, as shown in Figure 14–3(b,c). The 0000 field in the stacked information is called

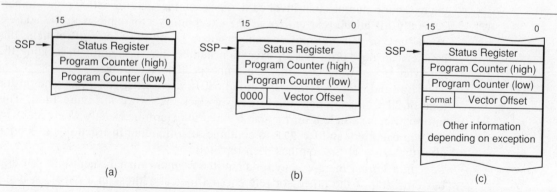

FIGURE 14-3   Exception stack formats: (a) MC68000 and MC68008 interrupts and most traps; (b) 68010 interrupts and most traps; (c) general format for all 68010 and 68020 exceptions.

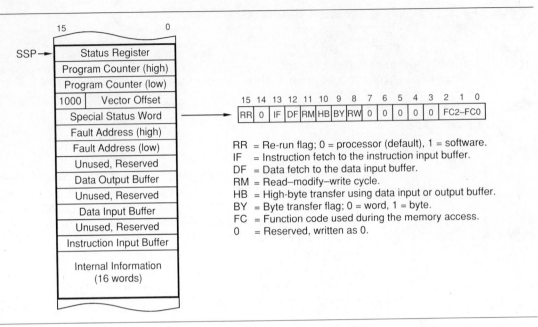

FIGURE 14–4   Supervisor stack format for 68010 bus error and address error traps.

format code
vector offset   the *format code*; the only other valid format code in the 68010 is 1000. The *vector offset* field is the vector number of the exception multiplied by 4.

The format code field allows the 68010 and later 68000-family processors to push different information onto the supervisor stack depending on the type of exception. The RTE instruction may then examine the format code to determine how many words to pop from the stack, and what to do with them.

The vector offset field allows a "generic" exception handler to determine the exception number that invoked it. For example, careful 68000 programmers generally fill all unused entries in the exception vector table with the address of an "unexpected interrupt or trap" handler. Using the vector offset field, this handler can now print out an exception number that is helpful in locating the hardware or software bugs that cause unexpected exceptions.

Bus and address error traps in the 68010 use format code 1000 and push a total of 29 words (!) onto the supervisor stack, as shown in Figure 14–4. This information is sufficient for the trap handler to determine exactly where and why the trap occurred, and for RTE to continue the offending instruction's execution after the cause of the trap has been repaired.

In a virtual memory environment, the memory management unit causes a bus error trap if the processor references a logical address in a page that is not currently present in physical memory. The bus error trap handler in turn passes to the operating system the 29 words of information on the supervisor stack, along with the other context information (such as general-register contents) of the suspended process. The operating system arranges to put the missing page into physical memory and, in the meantime, allows other processes to run. Once the missing page is in main memory, the operating system restores the saved context of the suspended process, puts the 29 saved words back onto the top of the supervisor stack, and executes an RTE. The processor happily continues, retrying the memory access that caused the original trap and completing the suspended instruction. Processing then continues normally.

The 68010's RTE instruction is a bit more careful than the original 68000's. Before restoring PC and other processor state information, RTE checks the format code on the stack to make sure that it is one of the two allowed values. Also, if the format code is 1000, RTE checks some of the saved "internal information" on the stack for validity. If any of these checks fail, RTE causes a "format error exception" (vector number 14).

14.5   STRING OPERATIONS AND 68010 LOOP MODE

Programs that manipulate text strings and other linear blocks of data often must copy a string from one part of memory to another, compare two strings for equality, or search a string for the first occurrence of a particular character. Many processors, including the Intel 80x86 family, provide specialized *string instructions* to perform these operations efficiently.

string instruction

String instructions specify information such as the maximum string length, the starting addresses of source and destination strings, and the operation to be performed. After fetching and decoding the instruction, the processor iteratively reads and writes as many operand bytes as needed to complete the operation. A big speed advantage of string instructions is that, since the processor controls the iteration internally, only operand accesses are made to memory. No time is wasted fetching instructions as in an explicit programmed loop to perform the same operation.

Unfortunately, string instructions have disadvantages too. Depending on how they are encoded, they may use up valuable opcode space, and in any case they complicate the processor's instruction execution logic. They must be designed to be interruptible in the middle and restartable; otherwise operations on long strings would increase interrupt latency too much. Probably the biggest disadvantage of string manipulation instructions is that they usually aren't general—they never seem to have quite the behavior and options that the assembly language programmer or compiler would like them to have.

After weighing the alternatives, the architects of the 68000 family took a different approach to providing efficient string operations. The designers of the MC68000 argued that the availability of auto-increment and auto-decrement addressing modes with all data manipulation instructions, combined with the powerful DBcc loop control instruction, give a programmer the ability to create very short, fast string processing loops that are tailored to an individual program's

TABLE 14–5   Loopable instructions in the 68010.

Operations			Allowable Addressing Modes (src, dst or dst)		
MOVE.BWL			(Am),(An) (Am)+,(An) -(Am),(An) Rm,(An)	(Am),(An)+ (Am)+,(An)+ -(Am),(An)+ Rm,(An)+	(Am),-(An) (Am)+,-(An) -(Am),-(An)
ADD.BWL OR.BWL	AND.BWL SUB.BWL	CMP.BWL	(Am),Dn	(An)+,Dn	-(An),Dn
ADDA.WL	CMPA.WL	SUBA.WL	(Am),An	(An)+,An	-(An),An
ADD.BWL OR.BWL	AND.BWL SUB.BWL	CMP.BWL	Dn,(Am)	Dn,(An)+	Dn,-(An)
ABCD.B ADDX.BWL	SBCD.B SUBX.BWL		-(Am),-(An)		
CMPM.BWL			(Am)+,(An)+		
CLR.BWL NOT.BWL	NEG.BWL TST.BWL	NEGX.BWL NBCD.BWL	(An)	(An)+	-(An)
ASL.W LSR.W ROXL.W	ASR.W ROL.W ROXR.W	LSL.W ROR.W	#1,(An)	#1,(An)+	#1,-(An)

requirements. To fill a gap in the 68000 architecture—its lack of memory-to-memory operations except MOVE—they also provided the CMPM (Am)+, (An)+ instruction as a primitive for string comparison loops.

The designers of the MC68010 and MC68012 took this concept one step further, in hardware. If a 68010 processor encounters a two-instruction loop consisting of a *loopable instruction* and DBcc, then it enters *loop mode*. In loop mode, the 68010 remembers the loopable instruction and DBcc internally and fetches only operands until the loop is completed. Such a loop has the following format:

loopable instruction loop mode

```
LOOP    <loopable instruction>
        DBcc    Dn,LOOP
NEXT    ...
```

Thus, if the loopable instruction is MOVE.B (A0)+, (A1)+, then only source and destination operand accesses, not instruction fetches, will occur until the loop terminates and the instruction at location NEXT is fetched. A complete list of loopable instructions is given in Table 14–5.

As an example of loop-mode operation, consider the task of copying a 0-terminated string with maximum length STRLEN from SRCBUF to DSTBUF. The following instruction sequence does the trick:

```
            LEA.L    SRCBUF,A0
            LEA.L    DSTBUF,A1
            MOVE.W   #STRLEN,D0
            BRA.S    COPYIN
COPYSTR MOVE.B   (A0)+,(A1)+
COPYIN  DBNE     D0,FINDCHAR
```

The last two instructions are executed in loop mode. Using timing figures from Motorola's *M68000 Programmer's Reference Manual* (5th ed.), each iteration of this loop in the 68010 requires two memory accesses spanning a total of 14 processor clock cycles. In the original 68000, the same loop requires five memory accesses spanning 22 processor clock cycles, a 50% longer execution time.[2] The string search subroutine in Table 8–13 on page 288 also benefits from loop mode in the 68010 (see Exercise 14.3).

14.6 MC68020 AND MC68030 EXTENSIONS

compatibility

The 68020 extends the programming model, addressing modes, operations, and performance of the original 68000 processor. Like the 68010, the 68020 is upward compatible at the object code level with the older members of the 68000 family. That is, any program written for one of the older processors can run on a 68020 processor without changes to the object code—the 68020 retains all of the instructions of the older 68000-family processors as a subset of its extended instruction set.

In the reverse direction, many application programs written for the 68020 can run on older 68000-family processors, with a little help. All 68000-family processors fully decode the 16-bit opcode word of each instruction that they execute, and trap on illegal or unimplemented instructions. Thus, an older 68000-family processor that attempts to execute a 68020 instruction will trap; the "little help" mentioned above could be a trap handler that decodes the offending instruction and emulates the corresponding 68020 operation.

Unfortunately, this approach does not apply to the extended addressing modes of the 68020, which are described in Section 14.8. Older 68000-family processors do not check for illegal addressing modes. When presented with a 68020 addressing mode, an older 68000 processor ignores the E and scale fields in the first extension word, and thus uses the wrong effective address. Worse, for extended modes with base or outer displacement words, the processor may go "out to lunch" as it erroneously interprets the displacement words as instructions.

Like the 68010, the 68020 supports virtual memory and virtual machine operations.

---

[2]If you look at the memory accesses in the loop, you'll count only four—the two instruction fetches and the two operands of MOVE. The fifth memory access is a "prefetch" of the instruction word following DBNE. The processor throws this word away when it discovers that it must branch to the location specified by DBNE.

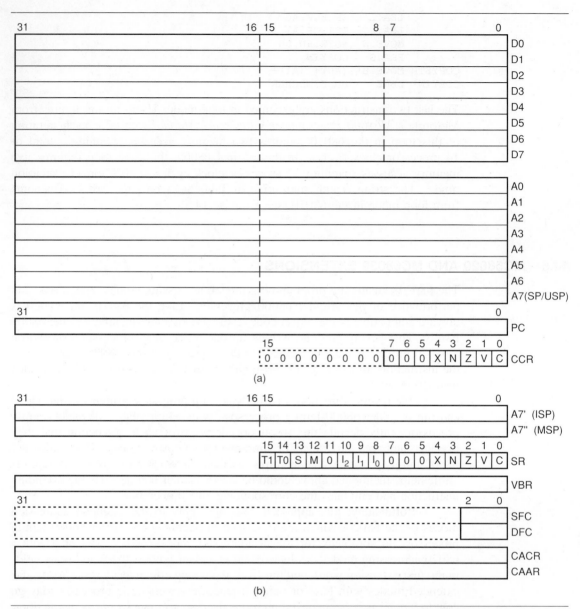

FIGURE 14–5   Programming model of the 68020: (a) user registers; (b) supervisor registers.

14.7 68020 PROGRAMMING MODEL

As shown in Figure 14–5(a), the registers visible in user mode in the 68020 are the same as in the original 68000, with the same important exception as in the 68010. The user can no longer read the high byte of SR, because the

TABLE 14–6   Trace bits in the 68020.

T1	T0	Tracing Function
0	0	No tracing
0	1	Trace on change of flow (BRA, JMP, JSR, etc.)
1	0	Trace all instructions
1	1	Undefined, reserved

MOVE SR, dst instruction is privileged in the 68020. Like the 68010, the 68020 provides the unprivileged MOVE CCR, dst instruction that reads only the low-order byte of SR.

The additional registers accessible in supervisor mode in the 68020 are shown in Figure 14–5(b). Two different stack pointers are accessible in supervisor mode. The *interrupt stack pointer (A7', ISP)* corresponds to the supervisor stack pointer (SSP) in older 68000-family processors, and is the default stack pointer in supervisor mode. The *master stack pointer (A7", MSP)* is an extra stack pointer that is used in supervisor mode when the *master (M)* bit in SR is 1. The purpose of MSP is to allow task and context information to be separated from interrupt I/O information in sophisticated multitasking operating systems.

interrupt stack pointer (A7', ISP)

master stack pointer (A7", MSP)

master (M)

If a 68020 program never sets M to 1, then only ISP is used in supervisor mode; this is the default at system reset. Operating systems that wish to use MSP may do so by explicitly setting M to 1. When the 68020 handles an exception—an interrupt or a trap—it pushes context information onto the supervisor stack currently selected by M. If the exception is an interrupt, however, the 68020 also saves a second copy of the context onto the ISP stack and then clears M to 0. In this way, interrupt processing always uses the ISP stack.

Besides the addition of the M bit, the only other change to SR in the 68020 is the replacement of the trace bit T with two bits *T1* and *T0*. The pair of bits provide two modes of tracing, as shown in Table 14–6. The new "trace on change of flow" mode allows for faster execution of traced programs, since the program stops only for branches, jumps, traps, calls, and returns, and not for sequentially executed instructions.

T1, T0

The 68020's vector base register (VBR) is used as in the 68010 to set the base address of the interrupt vector table. Likewise, the 68020's SFC and DFC registers are used as in the 68010 by MOVES instructions to move operands from one address space to another.

cache control register (CACR)

cache address register (CAAR)

The *cache control register (CACR)* and the *cache address register (CAAR)* allow software to manipulate the state of the on-chip instruction cache in the MC68020 and the on-chip instruction and data cache in the MC68030. The meanings of the bits in these registers differ slightly between the two processors, as we'll see in our cache discussions in Sections 15.1 and 15.2.

	15	14	13	12	11	10	9	8	7	6	5	4	3	2	1	0
(a)	DA		RI		WL	0	0	0					Displacement			

	15	14	13	12	11	10	9	8	7	6	5	4	3	2	1	0
(b)	DA		RI		WL	scale		E=0					Displacement			

	15	14	13	12	11	10	9	8	7	6	5	4	3	2	1	0
	DA		RI		WL	scale		E=1	BS	IS	BDsize		0		I/IS	
(c)	Base Displacement (0, 1, or 2 Words)															
	Outer Displacement (0, 1, or 2 Words)															

FIGURE 14–6 Extension word formats: (a) MC68000/08/10/12; (b) 68020 brief format; (c) 68020 full format.

14.8 68020 EXTENDED ADDRESSING MODES

The 68020 extends the addressing modes of the original 68000 architecture. The extensions add index scaling and 16- and 32-bit displacement options to the original based indexed and relative indexed modes, and include new memory indirect indexed modes with a full complement of options. As we'll show throughout this section, the extended modes are often very useful for obtaining one-step access to items in complex data structures.

The extended modes are encoded using the 000 field in the extension word of based indexed and relative indexed modes. The leftover mode–reg combinations (mode = 7, reg = 5–7) in the EA fields of the original 68000 remain unused and are still available for future use by Motorola.

Figure 14–6(a,b) compares the extension word formats of the original 68000 and the 68020, and Table 14–7 lists the meaning and encoding of the fields in the first extension word. The scale field determines a scale factor that is applied to the index register before adding to the base address, as discussed in Section 14.8.3. However, if the scale field is 00, then the scale factor is 1, and the unmodified index register value is added to the base register, just as in the original 68000 mode with the same encoding [Figure 14–6(a)].

full-format extension word

When the E bit of the extension word is 1, the 68020 interprets the word as a *full-format extension word* as shown in Figure 14–6(c). Instead of using its low byte for an 8-bit displacement, the full-format extension word contains additional fields that select an extended addressing mode and optional displacements, contained in one to four additional extension words, which are added during the addressing computation. Like the original 8-bit displacements, any 16-bit displacements that are specified are sign-extended to 32 bits before being added.

The meanings of full-format extension word fields are given in Table 14–7, and the addressing modes available through the various combinations of IS and I/IS are listed in Table 14–8. Using a full-format extension word, it is possible

TABLE 14–7   Extension word field encodings.

Field	Description	Values
DA	Index register type	0 = Dn 1 = An
RI	Index register number	0–7 = D0–D7 or A0–A7
WL	Word/longword index size	0 = sign-extended word 1 = longword
scale	Scale factor	00 = 1 01 = 2 10 = 4 11 = 8
E	Extension word format	0 = brief format 1 = full format
BS	Base suppress	0 = base register added 1 = base register not added
IS	Index suppress	0 = evaluate and add index operand 1 = do not evaluate or add index operand
BDsize	Base displacement size	00 = reserved, not allowed 01 = null displacement 10 = word displacement 11 = longword displacement
I/IS	Index/indirect selection	See next table

TABLE 14–8   Addressing modes selected by IS and I/IS.

IS	I/IS	Mode	Discussed in
0	000	Extended Based Indexed	Section 14.8.4
0	001	Memory indirect preindexed with null displacement	Section 14.8.5
0	010	Memory indirect preindexed with word displacement	Section 14.8.5
0	011	Memory indirect preindexed with longword displacement	Section 14.8.5
0	100	Reserved	
0	101	Memory indirect postindexed with null displacement	Section 14.8.6
0	110	Memory indirect postindexed with word displacement	Section 14.8.6
0	111	Memory indirect postindexed with longword displacement	Section 14.8.6
1	000	Extended Based	Section 14.8.1
1	001	Memory indirect with null displacement	Section 14.8.2
1	010	Memory indirect with word displacement	Section 14.8.2
1	011	Memory indirect with longword displacement	Section 14.8.2
1	100–111	Reserved	

to construct an address specifier, including displacement words, that contains up to five extension words. Thus a MOVE instruction with full-format extensions for both src and dst operands can be up to 11 words long, the longest 68020 instruction.

14.8.1   Extended Based

extended based addressing

Based addressing in the 68000 uses a 32-bit address register for the base address and a 16-bit displacement in the instruction that are added to form the effective address of the operand. In the 68020, *extended based addressing* performs the same calculation using a 32-bit displacement in the instruction.

As shown in Figure 14–7, this mode requires three extension words. The first extension word is in full format with the "base suppress" (BS) bit set to 0, the "index suppress" (IS) bit set to 1, the "base displacement size" (BDsize) field set to 11 (longword displacement), and the I/IS field set to 000. Because IS is set, the addressing computation ignores the index fields (DA, RI, WL, and scale), and adds only the base register and the longword displacement to form the effective address. Remember that the base register is a 32-bit address register whose number is given in the RB field of the first instruction word. The longword *base displacement* is contained in the second and third extension words.

base displacement

Extended based addressing is useful for accessing items in very large data structures. For example, suppose that we defined the following Pascal record type:

```
TYPE pixel = 0..255; {picture elements, one byte each}
     illustration = RECORD
       picture: PACKED ARRAY [0..383, 0..511] OF pixel;
       caption: PACKED ARRAY [1..80] of char;
       number: integer;
       options: ARRAY [1..10] OF integer;
     END;
```

In assembly language, we might define the offsets to the individual fields in such a record as shown in Table 14–9. Here we have used two macros, RSTART and

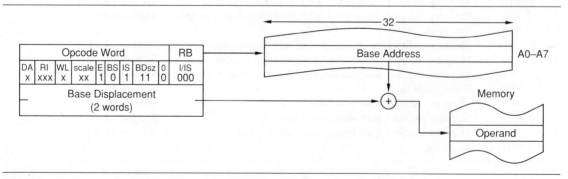

FIGURE 14–7   Based addressing with 32-bit displacement.

TABLE 14–9   Assembly language macros and statements for defining a record format.

```
*           Use this macro before defining fields of a record.
RSTART   MACRO
OFFSET   SET    0
         ENDM
*           Use this macro to define each field, \1 = NAME, \2 = SIZE (bytes).
FIELD    MACRO
\1       EQU    OFFSET
OFFSET   SET    OFFSET+(\2)
         ENDM
*           Now define fields of an ILLUSTRATION record
         RSTART
         FIELD  PICTURE,384*512   picture: PACKED ARRAY [0..383, 0..511] OF pixel;
         FIELD  CAPTION,80        caption: PACKED ARRAY [1..80] of char;
         FIELD  NUMBER,2          number: integer;
         FIELD  OPTIONS,20        options: ARRAY [1..10] OF integer;
```

FIELD, to help us define field offsets from the beginning of a record without making clerical errors, by keeping track of the total offset. For example, the third call of FIELD defines the symbol NUMBER to be the offset from the beginning of a record to the number field or $0 + (384 \cdot 512) + 80 = 196.688$.

The NUMBER offset is greater than the 32,767 maximum positive offset that can be used in 68000 based addressing. However, a 32-bit displacement may be used in the 68020 to access the number field in a single instruction, assuming that A0 contains the base address of an illustration record:

```
    MOVE.W  NUMBER.L(A0),D1      Get number field, put in D1.
```

The ".L" suffix forces the assembler to use a 32-bit displacement for NUMBER. This suffix may be optional depending on the assembler and defaults in effect when it encounters the instruction.

Other addressing modes may be obtained by changing the BS and BDsize fields in Figure 14–7, but the resulting modes aren't very useful:

- BDsize = 10 (16-bit displacement). This addressing mode has the same effect as the 68000's standard based addressing mode, except that the instruction is one word longer.

- BDsize = 01 (null displacement). This mode is just an expensive version of address register indirect addressing.

- BS = 1 (base suppress). With BDsize set to 11 or 01, this mode is equivalent to long or short absolute addressing, but again the instruction is one word longer than the standard absolute addressing modes.

- BDsize = 01, BS = 1 (null displacement, base suppress). The effective address of this mode is zero. Granted, the instruction is no longer than one using short absolute addressing with an address of zero, but this seems like a lot of trouble to go through just to generate a zero!

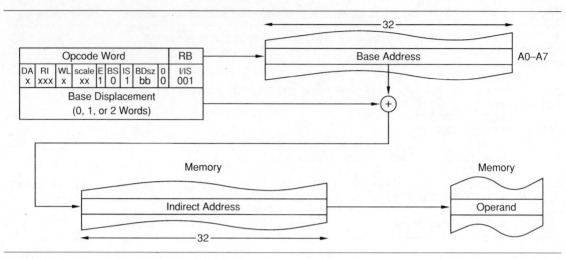

FIGURE 14–8 Memory indirect addressing.

14.8.2 Memory Indirect

The designers of the original 68000 had a certain philosophy about address registers—with plenty of address registers, the 68000 allows the addresses of frequently used variables and data structures to be put into registers once, so that address-register indirect and based addressing can then be used to access the data efficiently. Since typical operations on many data structures require addresses to be changed on each iteration of a loop, it makes even more sense to keep changeable addresses in registers. However, the designers of the 68020 apparently felt that there are some situations (in which an address is used only once or the processor has run out of address registers) where it makes sense to use a changeable address without putting it into a register. "Memory indirect" is the first of several 68020 addressing modes that support this idea by keeping and using changeable addresses in memory.

memory indirect addressing

In 68020 *memory indirect addressing*, the contents of a base register and a displacement are added and point to a memory location containing a 32-bit *indirect address* that is fetched and used as the effective address of the operand, as shown in Figure 14–8.[3] In assembly language programs, square brackets are used to specify the extra fetch that occurs in memory indirect addressing:

indirect address notation

[...]

```
MOVE.W (basedisp,An),D0    ;based addressing
MOVE.W ([basedisp,An]),D0  ;memory indirect addressing
```

nomenclature

[3]Motorola documentation uses slightly different nomenclature, where the sum of the base register and displacement is called the "indirect memory address," and the value stored there (which we call the "indirect address") is called the "value at indirect memory address." We use a different nomenclature because ours is traditional and we believe that it's important to have a concise name for the thing that we call the "indirect address."

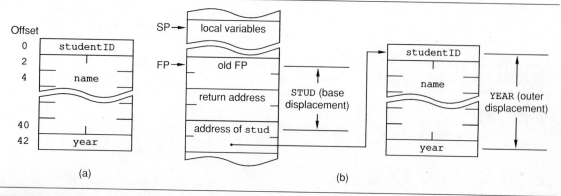

FIGURE 14–9   Student record: (a) memory layout; (b) a record passed as a parameter to a procedure.

The base displacement in this mode may be either 16 bits or 32 bits. As in extended based addressing, a suffix of ".L" forces a 32-bit displacement:

```
MOVE.W ([basedisp.L,An]),D0   ;memory indirect, long
```

To see how memory indirect addressing might be useful, consider the following Pascal record definition:

```
TYPE studrec = RECORD
                 studentID : integer;
                 name : ARRAY [1..40] OF char;
                 year : integer;
               END;
```

Figure 14–9(a) shows how such a record might be laid out in memory. Now suppose that a Pascal procedure is passed such a record as a VAR parameter:

```
PROCEDURE UpdateStudent(VAR stud: studrec);
```

Within this procedure, we may wish to access the studentID field of the stud record:

```
ID := stud.studentID;
```

What machine language instruction(s) should the compiler generate to perform this operation? To answer this question, we must recall how Pascal parameters are passed on the stack, as we discussed in Section 9.3.6 and as we show in Figure 14–9(b) for the UpdateStudent procedure. Since stud is a VAR parameter, the address of stud is passed on the stack at a fixed offset STUD from the location referenced by frame pointer FP during the execution of UpdateStudent. If we assume that FP is in fact A6, the following 68000 instructions may be used to read the nextID field:

```
MOVE.L   STUD(A6),A0        ;Address of record stud
MOVE.W   (A0),ID            ;Get studentID field
```

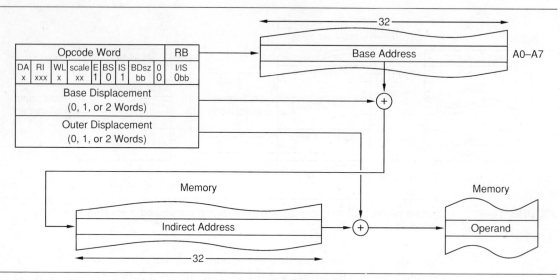

FIGURE 14–10   Memory indirect with displacement addressing.

With the 68020, we can accomplish the same thing in assembly language using memory indirect addressing and no temporary register A0:

```
MOVE.W  ([STUD,A6]),ID
```

The preceding example made good use of the fact that the `studentID` field of a `studrec` record has an offset of zero from the beginning of the record. What about accessing other fields? Well, the 68020 has a mode for them too. In *memory indirect with displacement addressing*, a 16- or 32-bit *outer displacement* is added to the indirect address to form the effective address of the operand, as shown in Figure 14–10. The notation "bb" in the BDsize and I/IS fields indicates that these bits determine the base displacement and outer displacement sizes, which are not shown explicitly in the figure.

For example, suppose that our Pascal procedure accesses the `year` field in Figure 14–9(b):

```
yr := stud.year;
```

The corresponding operation may be accomplished with just a single 68020 instruction:

```
MOVE.W  ([STUD,A6],YEAR),YR
```

As in extended based addressing, other addressing modes may be obtained by changing the BS and BDsize fields in Figure 14–10. In addition, the I/IS field gives us three choices of outer displacement—word, longword, or none. Most of the resulting modes are useful; a few of the more interesting ones are listed here:

memory indirect with displacement addressing

outer displacement

- BS = 1, I/IS = 001 (base suppress, null outer displacement). The resulting mode is equivalent to the "generic" absolute indirect addressing mode found in many computers, illustrated in Figure 7–4(c) on page 218. Either a long or a short pointer to the indirect address may be used, depending on the value in the BDsize field, but the indirect address itself is always a longword.

- BS = 0, BDsize = 01, I/IS = 001 (base register used, null base displacement, null outer displacement). The best name for this mode is "address register indirect indirect," since it adds one level of indirection to standard address register indirect addressing.

- BS = 1, BDsize = 01 (base suppress, null base displacement). This mode might be called "memory based." It is equivalent to the 68000's standard based addressing mode except that the base address is stored in a memory location instead of a base register. A word or longword displacement may by selected using the I/IS field.

14.8.3   Index Scaling

index
offset

scaled indexed
addressing

The *index* of an item in an array is simply its item number. The *offset* to the item in memory from the effective base address of the array equals the index only if the size of each item is one byte. Otherwise, the index must be multiplied by the item size, in bytes, to obtain the offset. *Scaled indexed addressing* performs this multiplication as part of the addressing mode computation.

Index scaling is available in all of the 68020's addressing modes that contain an extension word. As shown in Figure 14–11, the 2-bit scale field selects one of four possible scale factors, 1, 2, 4, or 8, corresponding to item sizes of byte, word, longword, and quadword. The DA, RI, and WL fields select a

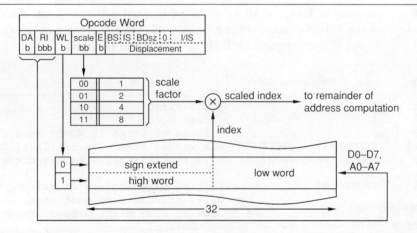

FIGURE 14–11   Scaled index computation in the 68020.

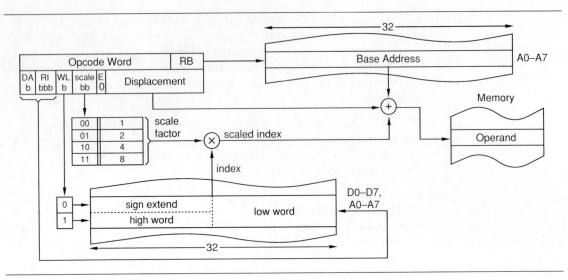

FIGURE 14–12 Based indexed addressing with 8-bit displacement and index scaling.

(sign-extended) word or longword index register that is multiplied by the selected scale factor. Because the available scale factors are powers of 2, multiplication is fast, accomplished by a simple shift. Note that the result of the multiplication is *not* stored back into the index register during the scaling computation.

Index scaling is applied to the 68000's standard based indexed addressing as shown in Figure 14–12. The scaled index from Figure 14–11 is simply added with the base register and the displacement to form the effective address of the operand. The assembly language notation for index scaling simply appends "*scale*" to the index register identifier, where *scale* is 1, 2, 4, or 8.

The scaling code that we showed earlier in Table 7–4 on page 230 is recoded in Table 14–10 using based indexed addressing and taking advantage of the 68020's index scaling facility. However, for item sizes other than 1, 2, 4, and 8, the approach of Table 7–4 must still be used.

TABLE 14–10 Index scaling in the 68020.

```
FRST     EQU     1                      CONST first = 1;
LST      EQU     10                         last = 10;
WRDSIZE  EQU     2                         {Size of items in WORDS array.}
WORDS    DS.B    (LST-FRST+1)*WRDSIZE   VAR words: ARRAY [first..last] OF word;
EWORDS   EQU     WORDS-(WRDSIZE*FRST)      {Define effective base address.}
         . . .
         LEA     EWORDS,A0           Get effective base address of array;
                                        typically this is done just once.
         . . .                       The following code might appear inside a loop.
         MOVE.W  I,D0                   Read i.
         MOVE.W  0(A0,D0.W*WRDSIZE),D1  D1 := words[i].
```

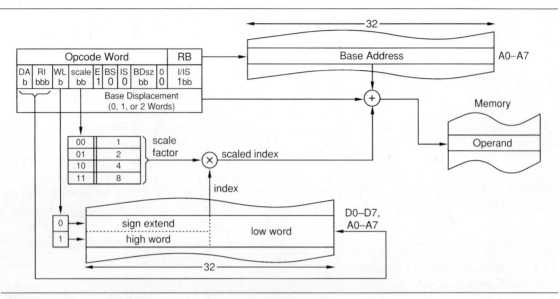

FIGURE 14–13   Extended based indexed addressing with 16- and 32-bit indices and index scaling.

14.8.4   Extended Based Indexed

extended based indexed addressing

A scaled index may be included in the extended based addressing calculations of Section 14.8.1, resulting in *extended based indexed addressing*, as shown in Figure 14–13.

Table 14–10 showed an example of based indexed addressing with scaling and a base displacement of 0. For an example where a larger base displacement would be useful, let's revisit the illustration record type that we defined in Table 14–9. To initialize the caption field to contain all spaces (byte value $20), we could execute the following loop, assuming that A0 contains the base address of an illustration record:

```
         MOVE.W  #1,D1                   FOR D1 := 1 UNTIL 80 DO
CLOOP    MOVE.B  #$20,CAPTION-1(A0,D1)     A0^.caption[D1] := ' ';
         ADD.W   #1,D1
         CMP.W   #80,D1
         BNE     CLOOP
```

Here each element of the caption array is accessed in a single instruction, where CAPTION-1 is the effective base address of the array in the record, A0 contains base address of the record, and D1 contains the index of the current element.

With array elements whose size is 2, 4, or 8 bytes, we can use index scaling. For example, the following code clears the options array in an illustration record.

```
        MOVE.W  #1,D1                    FOR D1 := 1 UNTIL 10 DO
OLOOP   CLR.W   OPTIONS-2(A0,D1*2)         A0^.options[D1] := 0;
        ADD.W   #1,D1
        CMP.W   #10,D1
        BNE     OLOOP
```

data register indirect addressing

As you might expect, several different addressing modes can be obtained from extended based indexed mode, depending on the options selected in the BS, IS, and BDsize fields of the extension word. When the base register is suppressed and the base displacement is null, a particularly useful mode is obtained. This mode is useful because it is *simple*—the effective address is simply the contents of the specified index register. This gives us a way of accomplishing *data register indirect addressing* on the 68020. If you still want complexity, the remaining options let you scale the index register or use only its low-order word!

14.8.5 Memory Indirect Preindexed

memory indirect preindexed addressing

The memory indirect addressing mode that we described in Section 14.8.2 can be further embellished with a scaled index. Figure 14–14 shows the effective address computation for *memory indirect preindexed addressing*. The scaled index is added to the sum of the base register and the base displacement before fetching the indirect address. Thus, this mode is useful for accessing a table of indirect addresses, that is, a table of pointers.

For example, starting with the studrec type illustrated in Figure 14–9(a), we might define a pointer type that can reference student records:

```
TYPE studrecPointer = ^studrec;
```

Then we can define an array of pointers to keep track of students by "seat number" in a 100-seat lecture hall:

```
VAR seat : ARRAY [1..100] OF studrecPointer;
```

Each array item is a pointer to the record describing the student sitting in the seat with that number. To find out the year of the student sitting in the seat whose number is in register D1, we could execute the 68020 instruction,

```
MOVE.W  [(SEAT-4,D1*4),YEAR],YR     yr := seat[D1]^.year;
```

This instruction assumes that the seat array has its item 1 stored at address SEAT, so its effective base address is SEAT-4. In this example of memory indirect preindexed addressing, the base register is not used and the BS (base suppress) bit is set; we leave it to you, in Exercise 14.9, to come up with an example where a base register *is* used.

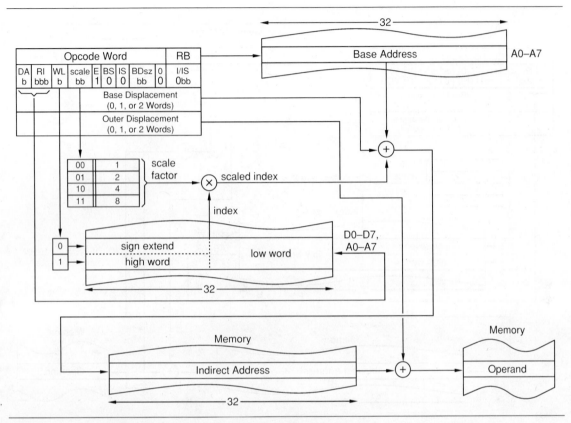

FIGURE 14–14   Memory indirect preindexed addressing.

14.8.6 Memory Indirect Postindexed

memory indirect
postindexed
addressing

A scaled index may be added *after* the indirect address is fetched in *memory indirect postindexed addressing*; the effective address calculation for this mode is shown in Figure 14–15.

In the `studrec` examples of the previous subsections, we can use memory indirect postindexed addressing to access an array within a record. If A6 is the frame pointer FP in Figure 14–9(b), then the `UpdateStudent` procedure could execute the following code to clear the `name` array in the record *stud* that is passed to it:

```
        MOVE.W  #1,D1               FOR D1 := 1 UNTIL 40 DO
NLOOP   MOVE.B  #$20,[(STUD,A6),D1,NAME-1]
        ADD.W   #1,D1                   stud.name[D1] := ' ';
        CMP.W   #40,D1
        BNE     NLOOP
```

At this point, we might begin to argue the usefulness of complex addressing modes. Though the code above is "elegant," an optimizing compiler probably

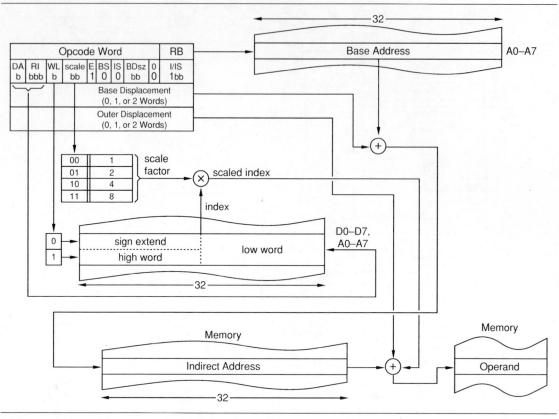

FIGURE 14–15 Memory indirect postindexed addressing.

should not generate it. Putting a complex addressing mode inside a loop may slow down the program's execution, especially if part of the addressing mode computation is the same each time through the loop. In this example, computing the base address of the `name` array once, outside the loop, would be faster:

```
        LEA      [(STUD,A6),NAME-1],A0   A0 := Addr(stud.name[0]);
        MOVE.W   #1,D1                   FOR D1 := 1 UNTIL 40 DO
NLOOP   MOVE.B   #$20,0(A0,D1)              MemByte[A0+D1] := ' ';
        ADD.W    #1,D1
        CMP.W    #40,D1
        BNE      NLOOP
```

Although we could probably conjure up an example where both a preindex and a postindex could be used together, the 68020 addressing modes only allow one or the other, not both.

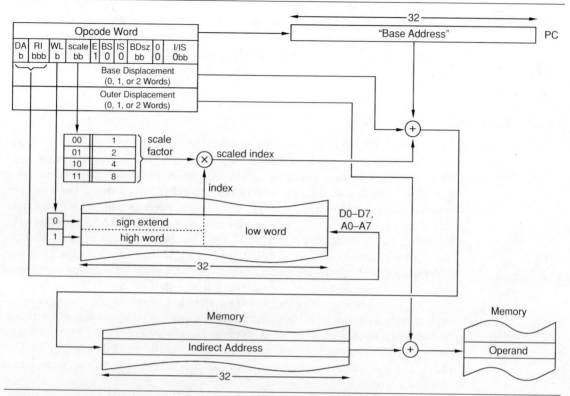

FIGURE 14–16   PC-relative memory indirect preindexed addressing.

14.8.7 PC-Relative Extended Modes

Had enough? No, you haven't! For every addressing mode in the preceding subsections, there is a corresponding PC-relative mode! These modes are obtained from the standard 68000's PC-relative and relative-indexed modes by using nonzero values in the scale or E fields of the first extension word.

PC-relative modes simply use the PC instead of a base register in the addressing computation. For example, Figure 14–16 shows the PC-relative version of memory indirect preindexed addressing. In assembly language programs, PC-relative addressing is indicated by using the identifier "PC" instead of an address register name.

PC-relative
memory indirect
preindexed
addressing
ZPC

Assembly language programs may use the identifier "ZPC" instead of "PC" to create an addressing mode that is derived from the standard 68000's relative or relative-indexed mode, but in which the BS (base suppress) bit in the full-format extension word has been set. In this case, the PC will not be included in the effective address computation. The result of the computation is therefore an absolute address—exactly the same absolute address that would be generated by the corresponding based mode with BS set. However, with ZPC, when the processor hardware accesses the absolute address in memory, the processor's function code output signals indicate that the address is in program space rather than data space (see Table 14–2). This is important in systems with memory mapping and management units (MMUs) that treat program memory and data memory differently.

14.8.8   Summary

All of the 68020 addressing modes and the Motorola resident assembler's notations for them are summarized in Table 14–11 in a way that is independent of their machine language encodings. The assembler picks the shortest encoding based on address and displacement values and other information. For example, register indirect addressing " (reg) " may be encoded as address register indirect if reg is an address register, or index register indirect addressing otherwise. Likewise, based addressing " (bd, An) " may be encoded in the original 68000's based mode (one extension word) if bd fits in 16 bits, or in extended based addressing (three extension words) otherwise. As usual, the programmer may force a particular address or displacement size with ".W" and ".L" suffixes.

For consistency with older 68000 assemblers, most 68020 assemblers accept some variations in addressing mode notation. For example, absolute addresses may be written with or without enclosing parentheses. Also, in many cases, base displacements may be written outside the parentheses that enclose the rest of the address expression, for example, bd(An, Xn.WL*SC) for based indexed addressing.

Many more addressing modes than are shown in Table 14–11 can be obtained from the based indexed, memory indirect, and relative modes by suppressing the base register, index register, base displacement, and outer displacement, individually or in combination. The architects of the 68020 would make no claim that all or even most of these modes are useful. Rather, they are all provided for consistency's sake, both in the internal encoding and processing of addressing modes in 68020 chips, and in the automatic translation of high-level language constructs into machine language by compilers.

14.9   68020 EXTENDED OPERATIONS

14.9.1   Data Movement

The data movement instructions that deal with the new registers in the 68020's programming model are listed in Table 14–12. These are the same as the 68010's extended instructions, which were shown in Table 14–3. The only difference is that the MOVEC instructions have more control registers with which they can be used.

TABLE 14–11   Assembly language notation for all 68020 addressing modes.

Name	Notation	Operand
Data-register direct	`Dn`	`Dn`
Address-register direct	`An`	`An`
Immediate	`#data`	`data`
Absolute	`(addr.WL)` or `addr.WL`	`MEM[addr]`
Address-register indirect	`(An)`	`MEM[An]`
Index-register indirect	`(Xn.WL)`	`MEM[Xn]`
Auto-increment	`(An)+`	`MEM[An]`, then
(by 1, 2 or 4)		`An := An + operand size`
Auto-decrement	`-(An)`	`An := An - operand size,`
(by 1, 2, or 4)		`then MEM[An]`
Indexed	`(addr.WL,Xn*SC)`	`MEM[addr+Xn*SC]`
	or `addr.WL(Xn*SC)`	
Based	`(bd.WL,An)` or `bd.WL(An)`	`MEM[bd+An]`
Based indexed	`(disp.WL,An,Xn.WL*SC)`	`MEM[disp+An+Xn*SC]`
	or `disp.WL(An,Xn.WL*SC)`	
Memory indirect	`([addr.WL])`	`MEM[MEML[addr]]`
Memory indirect with	`([bd.WL,An],od.WL)`	`MEM[MEML[bd+An]+od]`
base displacement		
Mem. indir. preindexed	`([bd.WL,An,Xn.WL*SC],od.WL)`	`MEM[MEML[bd+An+Xn*SC]+od]`
Mem. indir. postindexed	`([bd.WL,An],Xn.WL*SC,od.WL)`	`MEM[MEML[bd+An]+Xn*SC+od]`
Relative	`(ra.WL,PC)`	`MEM[(ra-PLC)+PC]`
Relative indexed	`(ra.WL,PC,Xn.WL*SC)`	`MEM[(ra-PLC)+PC+Xn*SC]`
Relative indirect	`([ra.WL,PC],od.WL)`	`MEM[MEML[(ra-PLC)+PC]+od]`
Rel. indirect preindexed	`([ra.WL,PC,Xn.WL*SC],od.WL)`	`MEM[MEML[(ra-PLC)+PC+Xn*SC]+od]`
Rel. indirect postindexed	`([ra.WL,PC],Xn.WL*SC,od.WL)`	`MEM[MEML[(ra-PLC)+PC]+Xn*SC+od]`

Notes: `Dn` denotes a data register: D0–D7.

`An` denotes an address register: A0–A7 or SP (same as A7).

`data` is an 8-, 16-, or 32-bit value as needed for the operation size.

`MEM[x]` is the 8-, 16-, or 32-bit value beginning at memory address x, as needed for the operation size; `MEML[x]` is always a 32-bit value.

`addr.WL` represents an absolute address `addr`, with optional ".W" or ".L" suffix to force the assembler to use a 16-bit or 32-bit address value.

`bd.WL`, `od.WL`, and `disp.WL` represent base displacements with optional suffix to force the assembler into submission. `disp.WL` may also be assembled with an 8-bit displacement.

`Xn.WL` represents an index register (D0–D7, A0–A7, SP) with optional suffix to select the short or long indexed mode. `Xn` denotes the corresponding, possibly sign-extended, 32-bit value.

`ra.WL` represents a relative address `ra` with optional suffix to force a 16-bit or 32-bit displacement.

14.9.2   Extended Displacements, Operand Sizes, and Types

Although the 68000 family uses full 32-bit addressing to access a 4-gigabyte memory address space, some operations in the original family members were restricted to a 64-Kbyte region of memory because displacement fields were limited to 16 bits. As we learned in Section 14.8, the 68020 partially fixes this problem by allowing 32-bit displacements in based and PC-relative addressing

TABLE 14–12 Control data movement instructions in the 68020.

Mnemonic	Operands	Opcode Word(s)	XNZVC	Description
MOVE.W	CCR,dst	0100001011dddddd	-----	Copy 0,CCR to dst
MOVE.W	SR,dst	0100000011dddddd	-----	Copy SR to dst (privileged operation)
MOVEC.L	Rc,Rn	0100111001111010 Annncccccccccccc	-----	Copy control register Rc to Rn (privileged)
MOVEC.L	Rn,Rc	0100111001111011 Annncccccccccccc	-----	Copy Rn to control register Rc (privileged)
MOVES.BWL	ssrc,Rn	00001110LWssssss Annn000000000000	-----	Copy ssrc [SFC] to Rn (privileged operation)
MOVES.BWL	Rn,sdst	00001110LWdddddd Annn100000000000	-----	Copy Rn to sdst [DFC] (privileged operation)

Notes: Privileged instructions cause a trap if executed in user mode (when S = 0).
   dst = destination operand, cannot use address register direct, immediate, or relative address-ing modes.
   ssrc = "memory alterable" source operand, cannot use register direct, immediate, or relative addressing modes.
   sdst = "memory alterable" destination operand, cannot use register direct, immediate, or relative addressing modes.
   Rn = one of the general registers, D0–D7 or A0–A7.
   Rc = one of the control registers, USP, ISP, MSP, VBR, SFC, DFC, CACR, or CAAR.
   ssssss = ssrc field; dddddd = dst or sdst field; LW = size field: 00 = byte, 01 = word, 10 = long.
   In opcode extension words, A = D/A bit (1 = address register, 0 = data register); nnn = Rn field; cccccccccccc = Rc field; also see Figure 14–2.

modes. The rest of the fix is found in the 68020's provision for 32-bit displace-ments and operands in the instructions summarized in Table 14–13 and discussed in this subsection.

BRA
Bcc
BSR

    The 68020's relative branches, BRA, Bcc, and BSR, can have a 32-bit dis-placement field. Since all 68000 processors must have their instructions aligned on word boundaries, an odd branch displacement is never needed. Therefore, the 68020 can interpret an 8-bit displacement of $FF in a branch instruction to mean that the real, 32-bit displacement is stored in the two words following the instruction, as shown in Figure 14–17.

LINK

    As we showed in Section 9.3.6, the LINK instruction is used by stack-

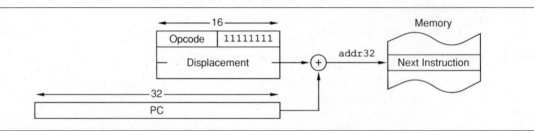

FIGURE 14–17 A 68020 branch instruction with 32-bit displacement.

TABLE 14-13   Instructions with extended displacements, operand sizes, and types in the 68020.

Mnemonic	Operands	Opcode Word(s)	XNZVC	Description
BRA	addr32	01100000oooooooo	-----	Branch to `addr32`
BSR	addr32	01100001oooooooo	-----	Branch to subroutine at `addr32`
Bcc	addr32	0110CCCCoooooooo	-----	Branch to `addr32` if cc is true
LINK	An,#disp	0100100000001aaa	-----	Link subroutine (long displacement)
CHK.L	dsrc,Dn	0100rrr100ssssss	-*UUU	Check and trap if Dn < 0 or Dn > `dsrc`
MULU.L	dsrc,Dl	0100110000ssssss 0LLL000000000hhh	-***0	Dl := Dl × `dsrc` (unsigned, long prod.)
MULU.L	dsrc,Dh:Dl	0100110000ssssss 0LLL010000000hhh	-**00	Dh:Dl := Dl × `dsrc` (unsigned, quad prod.)
MULS.L	dsrc,Dl	0100110000ssssss 0LLL100000000hhh	-***0	Dl := Dl × `dsrc` (signed, long prod.)
MULS.L	dsrc,Dh:Dl	0100110000ssssss 0LLL110000000hhh	-**00	Dh:Dl := Dl × `dsrc` (signed, quad prod.)
DIVU.L	dsrc,Dq	0100110001ssssss 0qqq000000000qqq	-***0	Dq := Dq ÷ `dsrc` (unsigned)
DIVU.L	dsrc,Dr:Dq	0100110001ssssss 0qqq010000000rrr	-***0	Dq := Dr:Dq ÷ `dsrc`; Dr := rem. (unsigned)
DIVUL.L	dsrc,Dr:Dq	0100110001ssssss 0qqq000000000rrr	-***0	Dq := Dq ÷ `dsrc`; Dr := rem. (unsigned)
DIVS.L	dsrc,Dq	0100110001ssssss 0qqq100000000qqq	-***0	Dq := Dq ÷ `dsrc` (signed)
DIVS.L	dsrc,Dr:Dq	0100110001ssssss 0qqq110000000rrr	-***0	Dq := Dr:Dq ÷ `dsrc`; Dr := rem. (signed)
DIVSL.L	dsrc,Dr:Dq	0100110001ssssss 0qqq100000000rrr	-***0	Dq := Dq ÷ `dsrc`; Dr := rem. (signed)
EXTB.L	Dn	0100100111000rrr	-**00	Sign extend low byte of Dn to longword
CMPI.BWL	#data,tdst	00001100LWdddddd	-****	Set CCR according to `tdst-data`
TST.BWL	tdst	01001010LWdddddd	-**00	Set CCR according to `tdst`

Notes: `addr32` = branch target, an address anywhere in the 4-gigabyte address space.

`disp` = displacement, a 32-bit two's-complement number in the longword following the opcode word.

cc = condition, any of those listed in Table 8–9 on page 281.

CCCC = condition field, encoded as in Table 8–9 on page 281.

oooooooo = branch displacement field, a two's-complement number that is even or $FF.

In opcode extension words, LLL = Dl field; hhh = Dl field; qqq = Dq field; rrr = Dr field; also see Figure 14–18.

Also see notes for Table 8–1 on page 270.

oriented subroutine-calling conventions to allocate space for local variables on the stack. For subroutines with local data structures that occupy more than 32 Kbytes of stack space, such as large arrays, the 68020 has a version of LINK with a 32-bit displacement. Also in support of large data structures, the 68020 has a

CHK   version of the CHK instruction in which the upper bound is a 32-bit longword.

        A few of the 68000's arithmetic instructions have been extended in the

MULU.L   68020 to support larger operand sizes. Two new multiplication instructions,

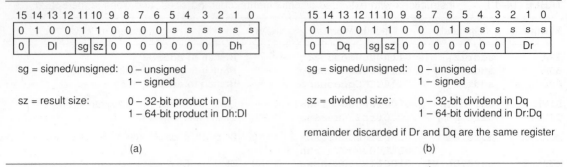

FIGURE 14–18   Extended multiply and divide instruction formats in the 68020: (a) `MULU.L` and `MULS.L`; (b) `DIVU.L`, `DIVUL.L`, `DIVS.L`, and `DIVSL.L`.

`MULS.L`

`MULU.L` and `MULS.L`, multiply two 32-bit operands and produce either a 32-bit or a 64-bit result. An opcode extension word is used to specify the size of the result, the type of operation (signed or unsigned), and the register(s) in which to store the result, as shown in Figure 14–18(a). As you know, the product of two 32-bit operands may require up to 64 bits to store. When `MULU.L` or `MULS.L` specifies a 32-bit result, the V bit is set if the result doesn't fit in 32 bits.

The division instructions have also been extended in the 68020, with encoding and options shown in Figure 14–18(b). The new instructions divide a 32- or 64-bit dividend Dq or Dr:Dq by a 32-bit divisor `dsrc` and produce a 32-bit quotient and a 32-bit remainder. The remainder is optional; if the Dr and Dq fields specify the same register, the remainder is discarded. Like the `DIVS.W`

`DIVS.L`

instruction, `DIVS.L` divides signed operands in such a way that the remainder has the same sign as the dividend. Also like the original word-division instructions, all of the long-division instructions set V if the quotient would require more than 32 bits to express, and cause a trap if the divisor is zero.

`EXTB.L`

A new sign-extension instruction, `EXTB.L`, has been added to sign-extend a byte into a longword. Previously, this operation required more than one instruction to accomplish. (How many? That would give away the answer to Exercise 14.14!)

`CMPI`
`TST`

Two instructions, `CMPI` and `TST`, have been enhanced in the 68020 to allow their destination operand to use PC-relative addressing. At first glance, you might agree with the original 68000 designers' intent of forbidding relative addressing with these instructions. After all, operands accessed by relative addressing are supposed to be *constants*. A `TST` or `CMPI` with a constant should always yield the same result, and so it makes no sense to execute this instruction in the first place.

Or does it? What the original 68000 designers forgot was that in relative indexed mode, the *index* is a variable, and so a `TST` or `CMPI` with an item in an *array* of constants can easily yield different results with different indices. (For some reason, they did not make this mistake with `BTST`; perhaps they remembered that `BTST`'s bit number may be a variable.) So `TST` and `CMPI`

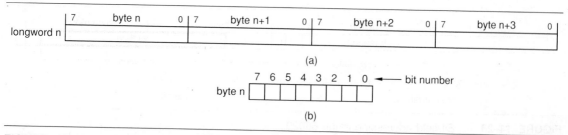

FIGURE 14–19   Numbering inconsistency in the 68000 family: (a) a Big Endian for bytes; (b) a Little Endian for bits.

with relative addressing may be useful instructions in some kinds of table-based case-handling code.

14.9.3   Bit Field Instructions

bit field

The 68020 has a powerful and complete set of *bit field* instructions that manipulate fields of 1 to 32 bits aligned on arbitrary bit boundaries anywhere in memory. But before we look at the detailed operation of these instructions, we must first revisit ideas of bit and byte numbering in memory.

As we showed in Section 5.1.1, 68000-family processors are Big Endians in the way that they number the bytes in a word or longword—the least significant byte has the biggest address, as in Figure 14–19(a). However, the original 68000-family processors are Little Endians when it comes to numbering the bits in a byte—the least significant bit has the littlest bit number, as in Figure 14–19(b). The inconsistent numbering plans are more than just a documentation quirk—the processor specifically uses Big-Endian byte numbering to execute all byte-size instructions, and uses Little-Endian bit numbering for bit manipulation instructions (BSET, BCLR, etc.).

The inconsistency between bit and byte numbering created no problem in the original 68000. However, when the designers of the 68020 decided to support a new data type—bit fields that start at arbitrary bit positions in arbitrary bytes in memory—they found that it would be extremely awkward to formulate meaningful bit addresses using a combination of the existing bit and byte numbering conventions. So they made what was probably the best decision under the circumstances—for the purposes of bit-field instructions only, they threw out the original 68000 bit numbering scheme and started over.

Figure 14–20 shows the bit-field addressing scheme in the 68020, which is pure Big Endian for both bits and bytes. Pure Big Endians imagine all 2^{32} memory bytes to be laid out in a single row and numbered from left to right as shown in the figure. Conventional memory addressing is used to determine the *base byte* of a bit field anywhere in this row of 2^{32} bytes. The actual beginning of the field, called the *base bit*, is located using a *field offset* from the leftmost bit (bit 7) of the base byte. A field may be 1 to 32 bits wide, with the additional bits appearing to the right of the base bit.

base byte
base bit
field offset

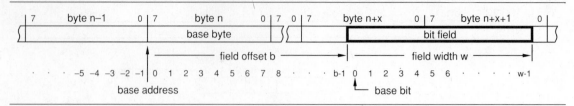

FIGURE 14–20   Bit-field addressing in the 68020.

The 68000's conventional Little-Endian bit numbers, shown above the bytes in Figure 14–20 for reference, are not equal to field offsets. For example, a field offset of 0 selects bit 7 in the base byte, an offset of 5 selects bit 2 in the base byte, and an offset of $b = 8 \cdot x + i$, where $0 \le i \le 7$, selects bit $7 - i$ in a byte x bytes to the right of the base byte.

Bit-field instructions contain extension words, shown in Figure 14–21, that may specify field offsets in one of two ways. The extension word may contain a 5-bit offset field that is interpreted as an unsigned number giving a field offset from 0 to 31; the field begins 0 to 31 bits to the right of bit 7 of the base byte. Or it may specify one of the data registers D0–D7 whose contents are interpreted as a 32-bit two's-complement number; the field may begin up to 2^{31} bits to the left or $2^{31} - 1$ bits to the right of bit 7 of the base byte.

Likewise, the extension word may contain a 5-bit width field, where 00000 corresponds to a width of 32 and other combinations correspond to their normal unsigned values. Or it may specify one of the data registers D0–D7 whose five low-order bits are interpreted in the same way.

Now that we understand how bit fields are defined and specified, we can discuss the bit-field instructions themselves, which are listed in Table 14–14. Each instruction specifies a bit field using the three parameters discussed previously: a base-byte address that is determined with a normal addressing mode (`bsrc` or `bdst`), a field offset (`off`), and a field width (`wid`). If `bsrc` or `bdst` specifies a data register, the base byte is the most significant byte of the register. The field offset and width may be independently specified as immediate values or data registers.

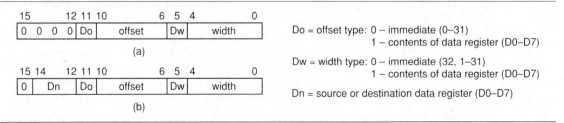

FIGURE 14–21   Bit-field instruction extension word formats: (a) `BFCLR, BFSET, BFCHG, BFTST`; (b) `BFINS, BFEXTU, BFEXTS, BFFFO`.

TABLE 14–14   Bit-field instructions in the 68020.

Mnemonic	Operands	Opcode Word	XNZVC	Description
BFCLR	bdst{off:wd}	1110110011dddddd	-**00	Test and clear bit field
BFSET	bdst{off:wd}	1110111011dddddd	-**00	Test and set bit field
BFCHG	bdst{off:wd}	1110101011dddddd	-**00	Test and complement bit field
BFTST	bsrc{off:wd}	1110111011ssssss	-**00	Test bit field
BFINS	Dn,bdst{off:wd}	1110111111dddddd	-**00	Insert low-order bits of Dn into bit field
BFEXTU	bsrc{off:wd},Dn	1110100111dddddd	-**00	Extract and zero-extend bit field into Dn
BFEXTS	bsrc{off:wd},Dn	1110101111dddddd	-**00	Extract and sign-extend bit field into Dn
BFFFO	bsrc{off:wd},Dn	1110101111dddddd	-**00	Find first 1 in bit field, put offset in Dn

Notes: All bit-field instructions have an opcode extension word in the format of Figure 14–21.
     bsrc = "bit field" source operand, cannot use address register direct, auto-increment, auto-
         decrement, or immediate addressing modes.
     bdst = "bit field" destination operand, cannot use address register direct, auto-increment,
         auto-decrement, immediate, or relative addressing modes.
     Condition bit settings:
         X: not affected.
         Z: set to 1 if all of the bits of the field are 0, else cleared.
         N: set equal to the leftmost bit of the field.
         V,C: always cleared to 0.
     Also see notes for Table 8–1 on page 270.

Instructions in the first group of Table 14–14 are analogous to the bit-manipulation instructions of the original 68000 instruction set, except that they operate on bit fields. Like the bit-manipulation instructions, they set the condition bits according to the value of the destination bit field *before* the operation (set, clear, or complement) is performed. The N and Z bits reflect the value of the field only, not the byte or bytes that contain it.

Instructions in the second group of Table 14–14 are used to move bit fields to and from registers. An n-bit field is always stored in the n low-order bits of a register. The BFINS instruction inserts a bit field from a register into memory. Two other instructions are provided for extracting a bit field from memory, depending on whether the bit field is considered to be a signed quantity. BFEXTU is used for unsigned bit fields; it fills the unused $32 - n$ bits of the destination register with zeroes. BFEXTS treats bit fields as signed quantities; it fills the unused $32 - n$ bits of the destination register with copies of the leftmost bit of the field. All three of these instructions set the N and Z condition bits according to the value of the inserted or extracted field after the operation is performed.

The last instruction in Table 14–14, BFFFO, searches for the first 1 in a bit field, starting with the leftmost bit. The result, left in Dn, is the offset to the first 1 bit if found, or the offset to the bit just to the right of the field if no 1 is found. BFFFO sets the condition bits according to the value of the specified bit field.

BFINS

BFEXTU

BFEXTS

BFFFO

TABLE 14–15   Additional data manipulation and program control instructions in the 68020.

Mnemonic	Operands	Opcode Word(s)	XNZVC	Description
CMP2.BWL	csrc,Rn	00000LW011ssssss Annn000000000000	–U*U*	Compare register with bounds pair
CAS.BWL	Dc,Du,mdst	00001BL011dddddd 0000000uuu000ccc	–****	Compare and swap operand
CAS2.WL	Dc1:Dc2,Du1:Du2,(Rn1):(Rn2) 	000011L011111100 Annn000uuu000ccc Annn000uuu000ccc	–****	Compare and swap two operands
PACK	Dm,Dn,#adj	1000rrr101000RRR	-----	Pack low nibbles of two bytes into one
PACK	-(Am),-(An),#adj	1000aaa101001AAA	-----	Pack low nibbles of two bytes into one
UNPK	Dm,Dn,#adj	1000rrr110000RRR	-----	Unpack nibbles of a byte into two
UNPK	-(Am),-(An),#adj	1000aaa110001AAA	-----	Unpack nibbles of a byte into two
RTD	#disp	0100111001110100	-----	Return from subr. and add disp to SP
CALLM	#argcnt,cdst	0000011011dddddd	-----	Call module
RTM	Rn	000001101100arrr	*****	Return from module

Notes: csrc, cdst = "control" source or destination operand, cannot use register direct, auto-
   increment, auto-decrement, or immediate addressing modes.
   Rn, Rn1, Rn2 = one of the general registers, D0–D7 or A0–A7.
   Dc, Du, Dc1, Du1, Dc2, Du2 = one of the data registers, D0–D7.
   adj = 16-bit adjustment value, stored in the word following the opcode word.
   BL = size field: 01 = byte, 10 = word, 11 = long.
   disp = displacement, ranging from −32768 through +32767, in the word following the
   opcode.
   rrr = Rn field; a = Rn type: 0 = data register, 1 = address register.
   argcnt = argument byte count in the range 0–255, stored in the low byte of the word
   following the opcode word.
   In opcode extension words, A = D/A bit (1 = address register, 0 = data register); nnn = Rn,
   Rn1, or Rn2 field; uuu = Du, Du1, or Du2 field; ccc = Dc, Dc1, or Dc2 field; also
   see Figure 14–22.
   Also see notes for Table 8–1 on page 270.

14.9.4   Other Data Manipulation and Program Control Instructions

CMP2

The few remaining data manipulation and program control instructions of the 68020 are listed in Table 14–15. The CMP2 instruction is used for general array bounds checking. It has two source operands, a pair of bytes, words, or longwords stored in memory starting at the address specified by the instruction's source effective address field. The destination operand is a data or address register, specified in an extension word that follows the opcode word, as shown in Figure 14–22(a).

The first of CMP2's two source operands is the *lower bound* and the second is the *upper bound*. Comparing the destination register Rn with both bounds, CMP2 sets C if Rn is "out of bounds"—less than the lower bound or greater than the upper bound—and clears C otherwise. It also sets Z if Rn equals either bound, and clears Z otherwise. Thus, an assembly language programmer or a compiler

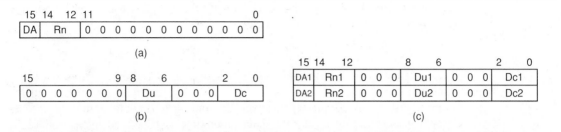

FIGURE 14–22   Extension word formats: (a) `CMP2`; (b) `CAS`; (c) `CAS2`.

can use `CMP2` to check the validity of each access to an array conveniently and efficiently as a program runs:

```
BUF      DS.B     LAST-FIRST+1        VAR buf[first..last] : char;
BUFBNDS  DC.W     FIRST,LAST
I        DS.W     1                           i: integer;
         ...                         BEGIN
         MOVE.W   I,D1                  buf[i] := ' ';
         CMP2.W   BUFBNDS,D1
         BCS      BNDERR
         MOVE.B   #$20,BUF-FIRST(D1)
         ...
BNDERR   ...                          {Handle array bounds errors.}
```

If `CMP2` has an operation-size suffix of byte or word and the destination is an address register, then the source operands are sign extended to 32 bits and compared with the full address register. If the destination is a data register, then the comparison is limited to the low-order byte or word of the data register.

The operands of `CMP2` may be either signed or unsigned values, depending on the program application, and for this reason `CMP2`'s internal operation is a little tricky. Suppose a `CMP2.B` instruction has a lower bound of 10000001_2, an upper bound of 00000001_2, and a destination operand of 00000000_2. Should the operands be treated as signed values (-127, $+1$, $+0$) or unsigned values (129, 1, 0)? The answer lies in the relationship between the upper and lower bounds. If they are treated as unsigned values, the range that they define is meaningless (lower bound = 129, upper bound = 1). Therefore, they must be treated as signed values, and the destination operand (0) is in bounds.

In general, if the lower bound of `CMP2` is unsigned-greater than the upper bound, the operands are treated as signed numbers; otherwise they are treated as unsigned numbers. Note that if, the upper and lower bounds are equal, the distinction is irrelevant; there is only a single in-bounds value, equal to the common upper and lower bound.

The second part of Table 14–15 contains "compare and swap" instructions that are useful primitives for updating data structures in a multiprocessor environment. Consider the operation of updating a very simple data structure—a global variable that keeps track of the total number of user keystrokes that have been received by the system. Each process that handles user input might have an instruction such as the following:

```
ADDQ.L  #1,KEYCOUNT    Increment keystroke count.
```

Even if there are multiple processes that update KEYCOUNT in this way in an interrupt environment, there is no problem since the update is completed in a single instruction. Suppose, however, that our system contains multiple processors communicating through a shared memory, as discussed in Section 12.3.4, and that each input process may run on a different processor. In order to execute the ADDQ.L #1,KEYCOUNT instruction, a processor must read KEYCOUNT, add 1, and write the result. If two processors execute this instruction at the same time, they may both read KEYCOUNT before either has updated it, increment it, and write the same value back; the resulting count is off by 1.

CAS

The update problem may be solved with a traditional semaphore that locks KEYCOUNT using the TAS instruction, as in the solution to Exercise 12.9. However, the 68020 provides another alternative. The CAS Dc,Du,mdst instruction compares the value in a memory location mdst with a "compare operand" in a data register Dc and sets the condition codes accordingly. If the mdst and Dc are equal, then an "update operand" in a data register Du is written into mdst. Otherwise, the (unequal) value of mdst is written into Dc. The access to mdst is performed using an indivisible read–modify–write cycle. Thus, CAS allows a memory location mdst to be safely updated in an arbitrary way, not just incremented, using the following algorithm:

(1) Copy the current value of mdst into a data register Dc.

(2) Compute an updated value from Dc and place the result in a data register Du.

(3) Execute CAS Dc,Du,mdst. Note that the hardware prevents any other processor from accessing mdst while this instruction is being executed.

(4) If the Z bit is 1, the update was successful; exit. Otherwise, another process on this processor (via interrupt) or another processor (via shared memory) must have updated mdst before CAS was executed. Return to step 2 and try again. (We don't have to go to step 1 because CAS updates Dc if the comparison is unsuccessful.)

For the KEYCOUNT problem, this algorithm translates into the following code:

```
STEP1    MOVE.L   KEYCOUNT,D1     Put current value into "Dc".
STEP2    MOVE.L   D1,D2           Put updated value
         ADDQ.L   #1,D2             into "Du".
STEP3    CAS.L    D1,D2,KEYCOUNT  Compare and update.
STEP4    BNE      STEP2           Try again if unsuccessful.
         ...                      Fall through if successful.
```

The CAS-based update algorithm works very efficiently as long as the time that it takes to execute step 2 is short compared with average interval between the various processors' attempts to update `mdst`. Most of the time, the update will be successful on the first try; occasionally, one or a few more attempts will be needed before steps 2–4 complete without interference. Even in the worst case—a bunch of processors doing nothing but trying to increment `mdst` continuously—CAS works with reasonable efficiency (see Exercise 14.18).

Notice in the third column of Table 14–15 that, although CAS has three operands, only `mdst` is specified in the opcode word. An extension word is used to specify the `Dc` and `Du` operands, as shown in Figure 14–22(b).

CAS2

Now suppose that the users of our multiprocessor system are such prolific typists that a 32-bit integer is not sufficient to count their keystrokes over a long period of time. The 68020 provides another instruction, CAS2, which reliably updates *two* destination operands in memory. Thus, we could provide a quadword keystroke counter, and update it as two longword operands using CAS2.

The operation of CAS2 is analogous with CAS, with the compare and update operands replaced by register pairs `Dc1:Dc2` and `Du1:Du2`, and the arbitrary memory destination `mdst` replaced with a pair of memory destination operands accessible only by register indirect addressing `(Rn1):(Rn2)`. All of the operands are specified in two extension words, shown in Figure 14–22(c).

In order to execute CAS2 as an indivisible operation, the 68020 has a means of performing an indivisible read1–read2–modify–write1–write2 cycle on the pair of memory operands (which may be at arbitrary, unrelated memory locations). The individual steps in the execution of CAS2 are listed below:

(1) Compare `Dc1` with `(Rn1)`, and set condition codes accordingly. If unequal ($Z = 0$), go to step 4.

(2) Compare `Dc2` with `(Rn2)`, and set condition codes accordingly. If unequal ($Z = 0$), go to step 4.

(3) Copy `Du1` to `(Rn1)`, copy `Du2` to `(Rn2)`, and exit.

(4) Copy `(Rn1)` to `Dc1`, copy `(Rn2)` to `Dc2`, and exit.

To maintain a quadword keystroke count, we use CAS2 in the following code:

```
STEP1    LEA.L    KEYCNTLO,A1        Address of current value.
         MOVE.L   (A1),D1            Put current value into "Dc1".
         LEA.L    KEYCNTHI,A2        Address of current value.
         MOVE.L   (A2),D2            Put current value into "Dc2".
STEP2    MOVE.L   D1,D3              Put updated value into "Du1"
         MOVE.L   D2,D4                 and "Du2".
         ADDQ.L   #1,D3              Double-longword add.
         BCC.S    STEP3
         ADDQ.L   #1,D4              Carry into high longword.
STEP3    CAS2.L   D1:D2,D3:D4,(A1):(A2)    Compare and update.
STEP4    BNE      STEP2              Try again if unsuccessful.
         ...                         Fall through if successful.
```

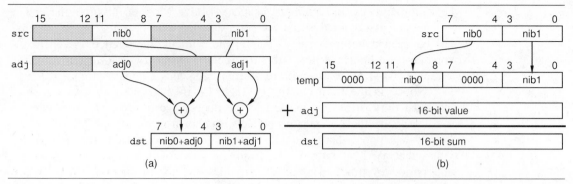

FIGURE 14–23 Operations performed by (a) PACK src,dst,#adj; (b) UNPK src,dst,#adj.

The 68020's designers intended the major applications of CAS and CAS2 to occur in sophisticated multiprocessor operating systems, for updating data structures more complex than simple counters. For example, in such an environment, CAS can be used to update the head or tail pointer of a queue reliably (Exercise 14.19), and CAS2 can be used to insert or delete items reliably in a two-way linked list (Exercise 14.21).

PACK
UNPK

Shown in the third part of Table 14–15, PACK and UNPK are two instructions for converting between nibble and byte data, as might be required between BCD operands and their ASCII equivalents. Figure 14–23 shows the effects of both instructions. Like the ABCD and SBCD, the operands of each instruction may be data registers or may be memory locations accessed with auto-decrement addressing. PACK may be used to convert a pair of ASCII digits into a byte with two BCD digits (Exercise 14.22), while UNPK may be used to perform the opposite transformation (Exercise 14.24).

RTD

The 68020's RTD subroutine return instruction is the same as the 68010's—it pops a return address from the stack and then deallocates parameters by adding a displacement to SP. CALLM and RTM are explained in Section 14.9.7.

14.9.5 Traps

The 68020 has a few new trap instructions, as shown in Table 14–16. Refer to Table 11–3 on page 401 for the exception vector assignments for these instructions.

CHK2
TRAPcc

The CHK2 instruction performs the same comparisons as CMP2, but also generates a trap if the destination register is out of bounds. A TRAPcc instruction generates a trap if the specified condition cc is true. With the right condition, TRAPcc may be used to determine whether a program is running on a 68020 or an earlier processor (see Exercise 14.25).

BKPT

The functionality of the 68020's BKPT instruction is increased, compared with the 68010. In addition to running a breakpoint acknowledge bus cycle, the processor allows a debugging device (typically a hardware emulator or logic

TABLE 14–16   New trap instructions in the 68020.

Mnemonic	Operands	Opcode Word	XNZVC	Description
CHK2.BWL	csrc,Rn	00000LW011ssssss	-U*U*	Compare register with bounds pair
TRAPcc		0101CCCC11111100	-----	Trap if condition true
TRAPcc.W	#tdata	0101CCCC11111010	-----	Trap if condition true
TRAPcc.L	#tdata	0101CCCC11111011	-----	Trap if condition true
BKPT	#number	0100100001001nnn	-----	Execute breakpoint cycle

Notes: csrc = "control" source operand, cannot use register direct, auto-increment, auto-decrement,
          or immediate addressing modes.
    Rn = one of the general registers, D0–D7 or A0–A7.
    tdata = 16- or 32-bit immediate data for use by the trap handler, stored in the word(s)
          following the opcode word.
    cc = condition, any of those listed in Table 8–9 on page 281.
    CCCC = condition field, encoded as in Table 8–9 on page 281.
    number = 3-bit breakpoint number (0–7) for use by the trap handler and the debug hardware;
        nnn = number field.

analyzer) optionally to place an instruction opcode word on the bus. The processor reads this word and executes it instead of the original BKPT instruction; no trap is generated. On the other hand, if an opcode word is not placed on the bus, then the processor takes an illegal instruction trap, just as it does for BKPT instructions in earlier 68000-family processors. The idea is to let the debugging hardware decide whether to return control to the debugger (via the illegal instruction trap) or to execute the original instruction opcode word (supplied by the debugging hardware) each time that a BKPT instruction is encountered. For example, the hardware could be set up to return control to the debugger only after the N th occurrence of a particular breakpoint.

14.9.6 Coprocessor Instructions

As technological improvements in integrated circuits make it possible to design bigger and better processors, and as the performance requirements of computer applications demand them, computer architects must expand the features and instruction sets of existing processors. Even before technology makes bigger chips easier to build, new features may be added using one or more chips external *coprocessor*   to the processor. Such chips, called *coprocessors*, contain their own feature-specific registers and execute the instructions that deal with the new features. However, the main processor is still responsible for fetching and executing the majority of instructions; it only passes the new instructions (and possibly their operands) to a coprocessor as they are encountered.

Later, when the technology has improved, features originally provided by a coprocessor may be integrated in the same chip with the main processor. For example, one or both of two coprocessors, the MC68851 paged memory management unit (PMMU) and the MC68881 floating-point unit (FPU), may be attached to the MC68020 processor. However, the PMMU functions are

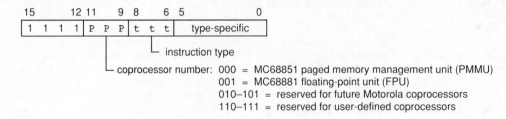

FIGURE 14–24   Format of 68020 coprocessor instructions (F-line opcodes).

integrated with the main processor in the MC68030 chip, and both the PMMU and the FPU could be integrated in the MC68040.

The architects of the original MC68000 provided for the evolution of 68000-family features by reserving one-eighth of its total opcode space, so-called A-line and F-line opcodes (Section 11.4.4), for future expansion of the instruction set. The A-line opcodes cause unimplemented-instruction traps in all 68000-family processors introduced so far. The F-line opcodes also cause unimplemented-instruction traps in 68000-family processors introduced prior to the MC68020. However, in the MC68020 and later processors, F-line opcodes

coprocessor instruction

are used for *coprocessor instructions*. When a 68020 processor encounters an F-line opcode, it instructs a coprocessor to execute the instruction. Only if an appropriate coprocessor is not present does an F-line opcode cause an unimplemented-instruction trap.

Figure 14–24 shows how the F-line opcodes are used for coprocessor instructions. A 68020 can have up to eight different coprocessors attached to it, and three bits indicate which one the instruction uses. So far, Motorola has introduced only two coprocessors, the PMMU and the FPU (coprocessor numbers 000 and 001). Three more bits distinguish among different types of coprocessor instructions, discussed in this subsection, and the remaining bits are used differently depending on coprocessor and instruction type.

Table 14–17 lists the coprocessor instructions that are decoded by the 68020. In this subsection, we discuss these general coprocessor instructions and the mechanisms by which they are executed. The specific capabilities and instructions of the FPU and PMMU coprocessors are discussed in Sections 15.3 and 15.4, respectively.

cpGEN
EA field

The first instruction in Table 14–17, cpGEN, is the most general coprocessor instruction. It contains a 6-bit *EA field*, eeeeee, that may be used to specify a source or destination operand for the instruction, and it contains an opcode

coprocessor command word

extension word (the *coprocessor command word*) that is passed to the coprocessor to specify the exact operation to be performed. The opcode extension word may be followed by additional extension words as required by the addressing mode in the EA field or as otherwise required by the coprocessor.

The actual mnemonic and encoding used for a cpGEN-type instruction depends on the coprocessor. The "cp" prefix is generally replaced by a prefix

TABLE 14-17   Coprocessor instructions in the 68020.

Mnemonic	Operands	Opcode Word	XNZVC	Description
cpGEN	various	1111PPP000eeeeee xxxxxxxxxxxxxxxx	*****	Coprocessor general function
cpBcc.W	addr16	1111PPP010CCCCCC	-----	Branch on coprocessor condition
cpBcc.L	addr32	1111PPP011CCCCCC	-----	Branch on coprocessor condition
cpScc	dst	1111PPP001dddddd 0000000000CCCCCC	-----	Set on coprocessor condition
cpDBcc	Dn,addr16	1111PPP001001rrr 0000000000CCCCCC	-----	Conditional loop primitive
cpTRAPcc		1111PPP001111100 0000000000CCCCCC	-----	Trap if coprocessor condition true
cpTRAPcc.W	#tdata	1111PPP001111010 0000000000CCCCCC	-----	Trap if coprocessor condition true
cpTRAPcc.L	#tdata	1111PPP001111010 0000000000CCCCCC	-----	Trap if coprocessor condition true
cpSAVE	Mdst	1111PPP100dddddd	-----	Coprocessor save (privileged operation)
cpRESTORE	Msrc	1111PPP101ssssss	-----	Coprocessor restore (privileged operation)

Notes: cp = coprocessor identifier, for example, "F" for MC68881 floating-point processor or "P"
for MC68851 paged memory management unit.
cc = coprocessor condition, specific to each different coprocessor.
addr16 = branch target, an address within 32 Kbytes of the instruction.
addr32 = branch target, an address anywhere in the 4-gigabyte address space.
tdata = 16- or 32-bit immediate data for use by the trap handler, stored in the word(s)
following the opcode and extension words.
PPP = coprocessor number, for example, 000 for the MC68851 PMMU or 001 for the
MC68881 FPU.
eeeeee = effective address (EA) field for source or destination operand.
CCCCCC = condition field, specific to each different coprocessor.
xxxxxxxxxxxxxxxx = command word passed to the coprocessor.
Also see notes for Table 8-1 on page 270.

corresponding to the coprocessor number, and "GEN" is replaced by a descriptive
mnemonic for the operation. For example, MC68881 FPU instructions based on
cpGEN include FADD, FMUL, FMOVE, FMOVEM, and FTST. To be more specific,
the instruction FMUL.D src,FPn is a floating-point multiplication of a double-
precision source operand and destination, a floating-point register. It is encoded
as shown in Figure 14-25. The source operand is specified in the EA field of
the cpGEN opcode word. The destination register (FPn), operation type (FMUL),
and operation size (double-precision, .D) are all specified in the coprocessor
command word. During the execution of FMUL.D src,FPn, the main 68020
processor is responsible for:

(1) decoding the cpGEN opcode;

(2) passing the command word to the coprocessor; and

(3) fetching the src operand when the coprocessor requests it.

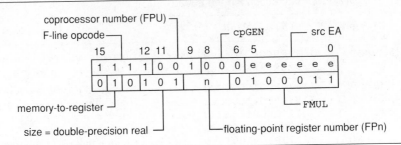

FIGURE 14–25 Encoding of FMUL.D src,FPn using cpGEN.

The coprocessor is responsible for:

(1) decoding the command word;

(2) requesting the main processor to fetch the src operand, and reading it from the main processor when it becomes available;

(3) performing a double-precision floating-point multiplication on the src operand and an internal register FPn; and

(4) saving the result in FPn and setting internal condition codes accordingly.

Once the main processor has satisfied the coprocessor's requests for the operands of a cpGEN instruction, it need not wait for the coprocessor to completely execute that instruction. Some coprocessor instructions, such as floating-point sine and cosine, take a long time to execute, and so the main processor can continue its own execution of non-coprocessor instructions while the coprocessor works on its own instruction in parallel. If the main processor encounters a second coprocessor instruction before the first has completed, the coprocessor gives the hardware interface a "busy" status, and only then does the main processor have to wait for the previous coprocessor instruction to complete.

The second part of Table 14–17 contains coprocessor conditional instructions. The operation of cpBcc, cpScc, cpDBcc, and cpTRAPcc is analogous to that of the similarly named 68020 instructions, except that a coprocessor condition is tested. To execute one of these instructions, the 68020 processor first transfers the opcode word to the coprocessor, which decodes its low-order bits (the CCCCC field) and evaluates the specified internal condition, such as a condition code or an error flag. The coprocessor returns a value of true or false to the 68020, which then completes the instruction's execution by branching, setting, decrementing, or trapping as required.

Instructions in the third part of Table 14–17 relate to context switching. A coprocessor's state must be considered part of the total processor state in an interrupt or other multiple-process environment. Each coprocessor has a user-visible programming model whose registers must be preserved during a context switch; the coprocessor has instructions for saving and restoring these registers.

cpBcc
cpScc
cpDBcc
cpTRAPcc

For example, the FPU has `FMOVEM` instructions that are similar in operation to the main processor's `MOVEM` instruction. These instructions, like most other coprocessor instructions, use the `cpGEN` format.

As we've mentioned, some coprocessor instructions take a long time to execute. If the main processor is interrupted or otherwise needs to perform a context switch while the coprocessor is executing one of these, it might have to wait a long time for the coprocessor instruction to complete. However, the instructions in the third part of Table 14–17 allow a slow coprocessor instruction to be suspended in the middle, so that the context switch can occur immediately.

cpSAVE

The `cpSAVE Mdst` instruction causes the coprocessor to suspend any operation that it was performing, save its internal state at the effective address specified by `Mdst`, and enter an idle state. A `cpMOVEM` instruction may then be used to save the registers in the coprocessor's programming model. Later, another `cpMOVEM` may be used to restore the saved coprocessor registers. This

cpRESTORE

would be followed by `cpRESTORE Msrc`, which loads the coprocessor's saved internal state from the effective address specified by `Msrc` and continues operation from that state.

The exact sequence of operations performed by a coprocessor instruction depends largely on the coprocessor and instruction type. However, the basic operations are taken from a well-defined set of primitives that are implemented by the 68020 main processor hardware; these primitives may generally be used by any coprocessor and instruction type. Some of the more commonly used primitives are listed below:

- Transfer opcode word. The coprocessor gets a copy of the coprocessor instruction's opcode word from the main processor, in order to decode type-specific information in the low-order bits.

- Transfer from instruction stream. The coprocessor reads up to 256 bytes of additional information from the instruction stream.

- Transfer multiple coprocessor registers. One or more coprocessor registers are transferred to or from the effective address specified by the EA field in the opcode word.

- Evaluate and transfer effective address. The main processor evaluates the effective address specified in the EA field of the opcode word and transfers the 32-bit value to the coprocessor.

- Evaluate effective address and transfer data. The main processor evaluates the effective address specified in the EA field of the opcode word and transfers an operand at this address to or from the coprocessor. The coprocessor specifies allowable addressing modes as well as the operand size (0–255 bytes) and direction of transfer.

- Write to previously evaluated effective address. The coprocessor transfers an operand to the main processor, which writes it to the most recently evaluated effective address.

- Take address and transfer data. The coprocessor transfers an address to the main processor; the main processor transfers data between this address and the coprocessor.

- Transfer to/from top of stack. The main processor transfers data between the coprocessor and the currently active main processor stack.

- Transfer single main processor register. The main processor transfers one of the general registers, D0–D7 or A0–A7, to or from the coprocessor.

- Transfer main processor control register. The main processor transfers one of the control registers (defined in Figure 14–2) to or from the coprocessor.

- Transfer multiple main processor registers. The main processor transfers zero or more general registers to or from the coprocessor, as specified by a register select mask supplied by the coprocessor.

- Supervisor check. The main processor indicates whether it is operating in supervisor state, to enable the coprocessor to decide whether to execute a privileged instruction.

- True/false. The coprocessor returns a true/false indication to the main processor during the execution of a conditional instruction.

Each coprocessor instruction invokes these and other primitives in a prescribed sequence in order to evaluate, read, and write operands.

14.9.7 MC68020 Module Call and Return

The module call and return instructions are implemented only in the MC68020, not in the MC68030. Some industry observers believe that Motorola implemented these instructions at the request of a particular large customer, but subsequently decided that they were not worth retaining in the family architecture. Nevertheless, we'll discuss them here because they introduce important architectural concepts—multiple privilege levels and call gates—first implemented on a mainframe computer in the 1960s in the Multics operating system, and more recently implemented in microprocessors by Intel, the 80286 and 80386.

In a traditional subroutine call, one subroutine directly calls another using an address that is assembled or compiled into a JSR instruction, as shown in *module call* Figure 14–26(a). In an MC68020 *module call*, the CALLM instruction specifies CALLM the address of a *module descriptor* that contains the actual starting address of *module descriptor* the module code, as shown in Figure 14–26(b).

From this point of view, a module call is nothing more than an indirect subroutine call. Because the actual starting address of the subroutine is stored in only one place, in the module descriptor, an operating system that dynamically relocates the subroutine in memory has only that one pointer to update. Users of the relocated subroutine need to know only the address of the module descriptor, which remains fixed.

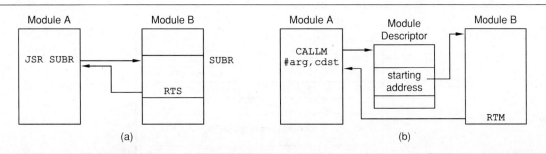

FIGURE 14–26   Subroutine calls: (a) traditional, using `JSR` and `RTS`; (b) module call, using `CALLM` and `RTM`.

What we've described so far can be accomplished in the 68020 by an ordinary `JSR` instruction using memory indirect addressing. But wait, there's more! Figure 14–27 shows general format of a module descriptor specified by a `CALLM` instruction. We'll describe the function of each of its fields in due course. For the moment, let us assume that the *opt* and *type* fields in the first longword are 0, in which case the *access level* and *module stack pointer* fields are not used.

opt

type

access level

module stack pointer

module entry word pointer

module entry word

module data area pointer

The second longword of the module descriptor is the *module entry word pointer*, the starting address of the module. However, this is not quite the starting *execution* address. As shown in Figure 14–28, the first word of the module's code, called the *module entry word*, looks like an opcode extension word; it specifies a data or address register Rn that the processor will load with the *module data area pointer* (taken from the module descriptor) when the `CALLM` instruction is executed. The module's executable instruction stream begins in the *second* word of the module.

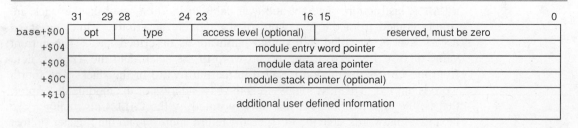

FIGURE 14–27   Module descriptor format.

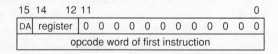

FIGURE 14–28   Module entry word format.

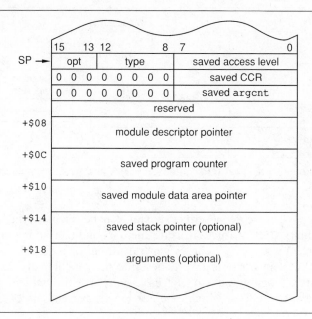

FIGURE 14–29   Stack format after execution of a CALLM instruction.

The data area pointer is stored in the descriptor so that the base address of a data area can be specified at run time, not at assembly or compile time. This is similar to Macintosh environment's use of A5 as the run-time base address of the application global space.

Figure 14–29 shows all of the information that is placed on the stack by a CALLM instruction. The opt and type fields in the first word on the stack are simply copied from the first word of the module descriptor, while the saved access level is provided by external hardware as described later. The current value of CCR is saved in the second word of the stack, and the argcnt field from the CALLM instruction is saved in the third word of the stack. The fourth word is unused. The next longword is the base address of the module descriptor, that is, the effective address that was specified by the CALLM instruction. The next two longwords save the PC (i.e., the return address) and the register Rn that was specified in the module entry word (i.e., the old module data area pointer). When opt and type are 0, as we presently assume, SP is not saved and the next longword is not used; the old value of SP can be easily determined from its present value.

Additional words on the stack contain arguments (parameters), but they are not put there by CALLM. A program must push parameters (or their addresses) onto the stack before using CALLM, as in the following example, similar to the stack-oriented divide routines of Section 9.3.6:

```
MDIVPQ  PEA     PDIVQ       Push address of quotient.
        PEA     PMODQ       Push address of remainder.
        MOVE.L  P,-(SP)     Push low-order dividend.
        CLR.L   -(SP)       Push high-order dividend = 0.
        MOVE.L  Q,-(SP)     Push divisor.
        CALLM   #20,MDIVIDE Do the division.
        ...
P       DS.L    1           Storage for P, Q, PDIVQ, PMODQ
Q       DS.L    1              (all longword variables).
PDIVQ   DS.L    1
PMODQ   DS.L    1
```

RTM
 A module's code ends with the RTM instruction, which restores PC, CCR, Rn, SP, and the externally maintained access level using the information in the stack frame of Figure 14–29. It also removes all of the arguments from the stack, using the saved argument count. As in subroutine-calling conventions using LINK, UNLK, and RTD, it is the programmer's responsibility to ensure that the number of parameters actually pushed and the argcnt specified by CALLM are consistent.

 What we have described so far is a subroutine-calling mechanism that could have been implemented with a short sequence of existing 68000 instructions, and the usefulness of CALLM and RTM seems doubtful. But wait, there's still more!

 We've previously discussed the notion of privilege in the 68000 family; programs operating in supervisor mode can execute any instruction and access any resource, while programs operating in user mode have limited capabilities. Sophisticated system environments can benefit from a finer degree of control over privilege, with a greater number of privilege levels. For example, suppose that a software system is designed with the hierarchy shown in Figure 14–30. The operating-system "kernel" at the heart of the system is most privileged, performing input/output, process scheduling and dispatching, and memory management. The file system makes I/O requests to the kernel in order to read and write files as requested by an application subsystem at the next level (e.g., a database manager). Finally, users write programs to perform specific tasks using an application subsystem (e.g., search the database and report all accounts that are over 30 days in arrears).

 In such an environment, it is desirable to segregate program modules according to their trustworthiness. For example, the operating-system kernel may have a subroutine that starts a DMA transfer from a specified disk block to a specified buffer in memory. This subroutine would normally be used by the kernel itself (to get virtual memory pages from disk) and by the file system (to read user files, a block at a time). While the kernel and the file system can be trusted to know what they're doing, a user or application program using the disk-read subroutine could accidently crash the system by transferring data to the wrong place. Worse, it could compromise system security by surreptitiously replacing system password tables with its own. Thus, the system should be designed so that the disk-read subroutine (level 0, most privileged) can be called

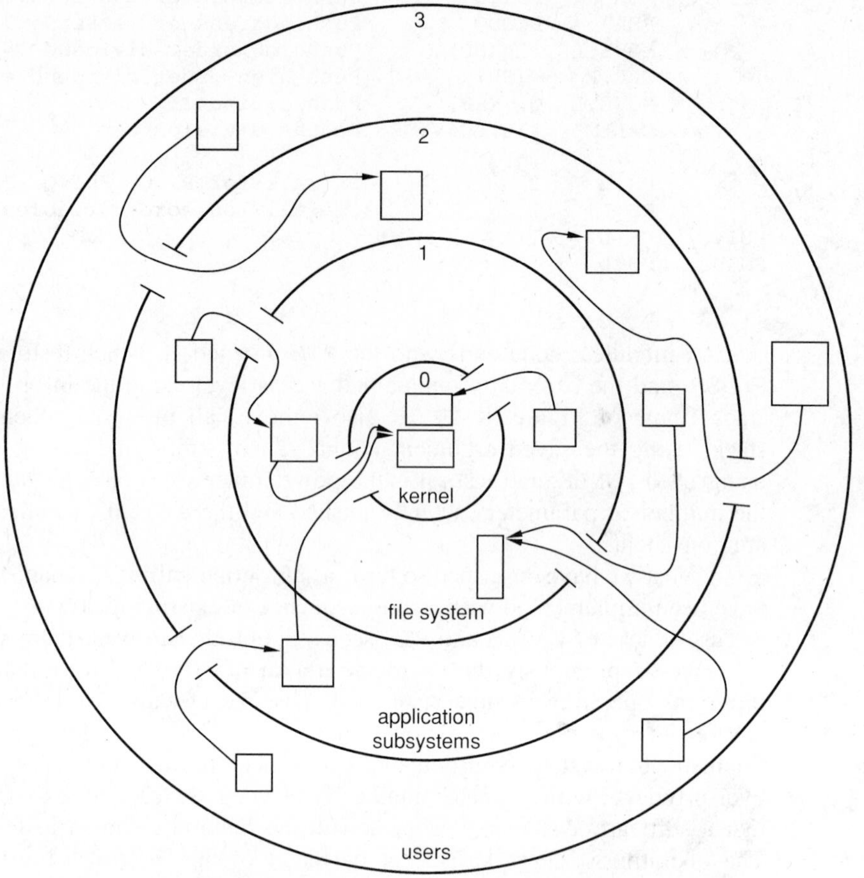

FIGURE 14–30 Hierarchical system environment with four levels of privilege (0 = most privileged).

by the kernel or the file system (privilege level ≤ 1), but not by applications or users (privilege level > 1).

current access level (CAL)

Using special external hardware, the MC68020 can support up to 256 privilege levels. An 8-bit external register contains the *current access level (CAL)*. Programs can request a change in privilege level by executing a CALLM instruction with a descriptor whose type field is 00001. In this case, the processor passes the value of the descriptor's access level field to the external hardware, which must determine whether the change in privilege level should be allowed. If the change is allowed, the external hardware passes the old value of CAL to the processor to save on the stack, along with a status code of "OK," and the processor completes the execution of CALLM. If the change is not allowed, the external hardware passes a "not OK" status to the processor, which then takes a format error exception.

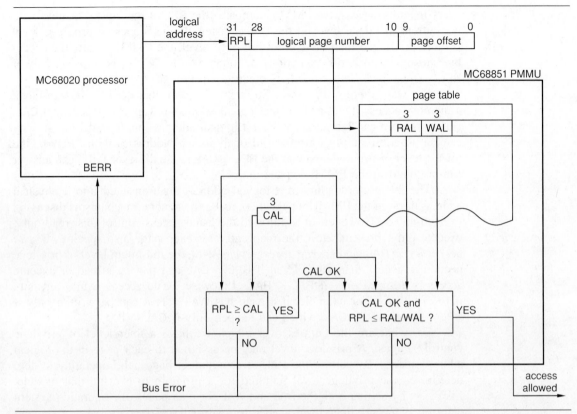

FIGURE 14–31   Access-level checking operations in MC68851 PMMU.

In this scheme, most of the intelligence—deciding whether to grant access at a particular privilege level—is relegated to the external hardware. Motorola provides this hardware in the MC68851 paged memory management unit (PMMU). The PMMU supports up to eight privilege levels, much less than the 256 possible, but more than adequate for practical system environments.

All 68000 processors provide coarse control over privilege level with user and supervisor modes, which disable and enable the execution of privileged instructions. We've said that the module call and return mechanism allows a finer degree of privilege level control. The question is, control over what? Again, the PMMU provides the answer.

requested privilege level (RPL)

Recall that an MMU translates from logical addresses to physical addresses, and causes a bus error exception when a requested access to a particular logical address is illegal. The MC68851 PMMU associates a *requested privilege level (RPL)* with every logical address that it receives from the CPU. When the PMMU is programmed to support eight privilege levels, the RPL is contained in the three high-order bits of each 32-bit logical address, as shown in Figure 14–31. During every memory access, the PMMU compares the RPL of the logical address with the current privilege level in the CAL register. If the requested privilege level is more privileged than the current privilege level, the PMMU aborts the access by causing a bus error exception. In other words, access is allowed only if RPL ≥ CAL, since higher numbers mean *less* privilege.

But wait, there's *still* more. So far, we've seen that the PMMU can block a memory access if the RPL of the logical address is less privileged than CAL. But a program can fabricate any 32-bit logical address that it wants to. So why can't a program simply formulate all of its logical addresses with RPL = 7, the lowest level of privilege, so that the RPL ≥ CAL test will never fail? The answer can be found in the PMMU's page map.

read access level (RAL)
write access level (WAL)

The 29 low-order bits of a logical address are translated into a physical address through the PMMU's page map, using the general mechanisms discussed in Section 7.5. However, in addition to the usual access-control bits (read only, execute only, present, etc.), the map entry for each page also specifies a *read access level (RAL)* and a *write access level (WAL)*, the minimum level of privilege needed to access that page. Even if RPL ≥ CAL test passes, a read or execute access is allowed only if RPL ≤ RAL. Likewise, write access is allowed only if RPL ≤ WAL. For example, if a page has WAL = 1, it can be written only if RPL ≤ 1 and RPL ≥ CAL, which can happen only if CAL ≤ 1.

So, what are the entities over which we have a finer level of privilege control? Pages. A privilege level may be assigned to each page in the logical address space. By setting the RAL of a module's pages, the operating system determines the privilege level required for a program to execute that module. Likewise, by setting both the RAL and WAL for data pages, the operating system determines the privilege level needed to read or write the data.

call gate

A program with a low level of privilege may access more-privileged resources by executing a CALLM instruction with a descriptor that provides for a higher level of privilege. Such a descriptor is known as a *call gate*. Access provided through a call gate is very structured and safe, since the calling program can, at most, pass parameters and transfer control to the entry point of the more-privileged module. The called module accesses the privileged resources and puts results in the address space of the caller (which it can always access, because the caller is *less* privileged). The RTM instruction, executed at the end of the called module, restores the original, low privilege level of the caller.

The MC68020 and the MC68851 PMMU contain several mechanisms to prevent a calling program from using bogus module descriptors or otherwise "fooling" a privileged module into doing something dangerous. For example, when CALLM causes a change in privilege level, it normally copies parameters from the caller's stack to a private stack belonging to the module, pointed to by the module stack pointer field in the descriptor. (Copying does not take place if the opt field of the module descriptor is 100.) In this way, the called module is not affected by problems in the caller's stack (such as odd SP or insufficient space). For a full description of the module call mechanism and applications, refer to Motorola's MC68020 and MC68851 user manuals.

TABLE 14-18   Exception stack formats in the 68020.

Name	Format Code	Size (words)	Causes	Additional Saved Information
Normal 4-word	0000	4	Interrupts and most traps	None
Normal 6-word	0010	6	CHK, CHK2, cpTRAPcc, TRAPcc, TRAPV, trace, zero divide, coprocessor postinstruction exceptions	Instruction address
Throwaway	0001	4	Interrupts (on interrupt stack)	None
Short bus cycle fault	1010	16	Address and bus errors at the beginning of an instruction	Special status word, internal buffers and registers
Long bus cycle fault	1011	46	Address and bus errors in the middle of an instruction	Special status word, more internal buffers and registers
Coprocessor midinstruction	1001	10	Errors in the middle of coprocessor intructions	Instruction address, internal registers

14.10   68020 EXCEPTION HANDLING

Like the 68010, the 68020 uses a different format than the original 68000 for the information pushed onto the supervisor stack while handling exceptions, as shown in Figure 14–3(c). The 68020 has six different formats for this information, as summarized in Table 14–18.

normal 4-word format

normal 6-word format

The *normal 4-word format* is identical to the one used by the 68010 for interrupts and most traps. However, some traps use the *normal 6-word format* in the 68020, different from the 4-word format that they use in the 68010. The extra two words contain the address of the instruction that caused the exception. This is often different from the saved PC, which for many traps is the address of the instruction *after* the one that caused the exception.

Recall from Section 14.7 that the 68020 has two stack pointers, MSP and ISP, that are used in supervisor mode depending on the state of the M bit in SR. If M is 0, then the ISP stack is used to handle exceptions. If M is 1, then the MSP stack is used to handle exceptions, at least initially. In this case, however, if the exception is an interrupt, a second copy of the processor state information

throwaway format

is pushed onto the ISP stack using the *throwaway format*, and M is cleared to zero. This allows an operating system easily to maintain separate stacks for its own I/O-related interrupt processes and user process management activities.

short bus cycle fault format

The 68020 has two different formats for saving the processor state when a bus error or address error occurs. If the error occurs at the beginning of an instruction's execution, before the processor state has been affected, then the *short bus cycle fault format* is used. This format contains "only" 16 words, enough information for the trap handler to determine the cause of the fault and

*long bus cycle
fault format*

for the processor to restart the offending instruction after the cause of the fault has been repaired. However, if an error occurs in the middle of an instruction, then the 46-word *long bus cycle fault format* is used. It doesn't take this much information for the trap handler to determine the cause of the fault, but all of it is necessary for the processor to resume the offending instruction successfully in the middle, due to the 68020's complex internal structure.[4]

*coprocessor
midinstruction
format*

Coprocessors attached to the 68020 can generate traps. A trap generated at the beginning of a coprocessor instruction's execution, such as the one generated when the coprocessor is given an illegal command, uses the normal 4-word stack format. A trap generated at the end of a coprocessor instruction's execution, such as the one caused by `cpTRAPcc`, uses the normal 6-word stack format. All others use the *coprocessor midinstruction format*, which contains 10 words. The "internal registers" in this format are registers of the 68020, not the coprocessor, which must be restored in order for the 68020 to resume communication with the coprocessor in the middle of a coprocessor instruction. The internal state of the coprocessor itself is not saved automatically by any of these traps; the trap handler must use the `cpSAVE` coprocessor instruction to do this.

R E F E R E N C E S

Features of the MC68010 and MC68012 are described in Motorola's standard 68000-family reference manuals, such as *M68000 8-/16-/32-Bit Microprocessors Programmer's Reference Manual* (Prentice-Hall, 1986). The MC68020 is covered in the somewhat thicker *MC68020 32-Bit Microprocessor User's Manual* (Prentice-Hall, 1985, 2nd ed.), and the MC68030 is described in the very thick *MC68030 Enhanced 32-Bit Microprocessor User's Manual* (Motorola, 1987, publ. no. MC68030UM/AD).

Reference manuals make for rather dry reading, of course. More interesting discussions of 68000-family processor architectures can be found in articles written by the designers themselves. For example, "The Motorola MC68020," by Doug MacGregor, Dave Mothersole, and Bill Moyer (IEEE *Micro*, Vol. 4., No. 4, August 1984, pp. 101–118), focuses on the chip's primary design goals—compatibility and performance—as well as describes its basic architecture. The internal architecture of the MC68030 is described in "The RISC/CISC Melting Pot," by Thomas L. Johnson (*Byte*, Vol. 12, No. 4, April 1987, pp. 153–160).

Not much has been written about the 68020 architecture by outsiders yet. However, Donald Krantz and David Stanley give an entertaining account of how

---

[4]The 68020 processor has a three-stage instruction pipeline that at any instant contains up to three instructions that are partially fetched, decoded, and executed. Theoretically, the 68020 could "unwind" the pipeline when a bus cycle fault occurs, and save only information concerning the offending instruction; this is the approach used in many mainframe computers. However, this is tricky, and so the 68020 takes the simpler approach of saving the entire pipeline state.

SFC, DFC, and the MOVES instruction might have been invented, in their slightly silly *68000 Assembly Language* (Addison-Wesley, 1986). (I say "silly" because the book suggests that we should write programs in assembly language because "most of us can't afford the compilers that generate such good code" [p. 124].)

E X E R C I S E S

14.1 Like all 68000-family processors, the MC68012 internally uses 32 address bits (0–31). However, it provides only 31 of these bits on external pins; bit 30 is missing because of "packaging limitations." Sketch the usable address space of the MC68012 with respect to the full 4-Gigabyte address space. Why do you suppose Motorola omitted address bit 30 instead of 31?

14.2 Rewrite the last three lines of Table 9–16 on page 332 using a 68010 and 68020 instruction.

14.3 Using the timing charts in the *M68000 Programmer's Reference Manual*, determine the execution time in clock ticks of one iteration of the loop in Table 8–13 on page 288 in the MC68000 and in the MC68010.

14.4 Expand the analysis of the previous exercise to develop formulas, for both processor chips, that give the total subroutine execution time as a function of if and where a match occurs.

14.5 If a Pascal procedure A calls procedure B, show how procedure B can use the MC68020's memory indirect addressing modes to access procedure A's local variables, assuming the stack environment of Figure 9–4 on page 331.

14.6 In Section 14.8.4, we showed how extended based indexed addressing could be used to access items in an array at the end of a very long record. Under what circumstances would this mode be useful for accessing items in an array that was passed on the stack as a value parameter to a Pascal subroutine?

14.7 Show how to encode "index register indirect" addressing in the MC68020.

14.8 Show how to encode the general indexed addressing mode addr(Xn.WL*SCALE) in the MC68020. What is the maximum number of extension words required? Under what circumstances can this mode be encoded with a single extension word?

14.9 Write a Pascal program fragment for which the corresponding assembly language code could reasonably be expected to use memory indirect preindexed addressing, with a nonzero base register, base displacement, and index register. Draw a figure that shows how your data structure is defined and accessed.

14.10 Optimize the program fragment at the end of Section 14.8.6 even further using the DBF instruction.

14.11 Find a 68000 program control instruction whose functionality in the 68020 could have been extended to 32 bits in two different ways, but wasn't. Discuss the potential usefulness and the implementation issues for each area of extension.

14.12 We said in Section 14.9.2 that `MULU/S.L dsrc,Dl` sets V if its result "doesn't fit" in 32 bits. State the exact rules that `MULU.L` and `MULS.L` should use for setting the V bit.

14.13 What happens if you execute `DIVU.L` or `DIVS.L` with Dr = Dq and sz = 1?

14.14 Without the 68020's `EXTB` instruction, how do you sign extend a byte into a word?

14.15 Design a bit-field addressing scheme that is consistent with the bit and byte numbering plans used in the original 68000 architecture. Compare your scheme with the one that is actually used in the 68020.

14.16 Compare the effects of the 68020 bit-field instruction `BFCLR dst{#3,#1}` with the effects of the bit manipulation instruction `BCLR.B #3,dst`.

14.17 Believe it or not, the functionality of the 68020's `NOP` instruction has been enhanced, compared with `NOP` in the MC68000. How? [You'll have to dig up an old MC68000 *User's Manual* (3rd ed. or earlier) and compare it with the MC68020 *User's Manual* for the answer.]

14.18 Suppose that N 68020 processors access a shared memory, and each processor does nothing but attempt to increment a variable `BUSYCNT` in this memory continuously. Prove that, if the processors all use the `CAS`-based update algorithm in Section 14.9.4, then the average number of times that each processor has to execute the `CAS` loop for a successful update is no greater than N.

14.19 Rewrite the `QENQ` and `QDEQ` procedures in Table 9–20 on page 338 using `CAS` so that they work reliably when multiple 68020 processors can enqueue or dequeue items in the same queue.

14.20 Compare the performance of the preceding exercise's approach to updating queue pointers with that of Exercise 12.10.

14.21 Write 68020 subroutines for inserting and deleting items in a two-way linked list, using `CAS2` to ensure that pointers are updated properly even if multiple processors can access the same list. Draw figures illustrating the data structures, and list the input and output parameters of each subroutine.

14.22 Assume that a 10-byte buffer `DECSTR` contains 10 ASCII characters known to be decimal digits, between '0' and '9'. Write a 68020 subroutine using `PACK` to fill a 5-byte buffer `DECNUM` with the corresponding unsigned packed-BCD number.

14.23 Repeat the previous exercise, with validity checking for `DECSTR`. The subroutine should return with Z = 0 and `DECNUM` untouched if any character in `DECSTR` is not a decimal digit. Otherwise, it works as before and returns with Z = 1.

14.24 Write a subroutine using `UNPK` to fill a 10-byte buffer `DECSTR` with the ASCII representation of an unsigned packed-BCD number in a 5-byte buffer `DECNUM`.

14.25 Find an instruction that does nothing (a `NOP`) when executed on the 68020, but causes an illegal instruction trap when executed on earlier 68000 processors.

CHAPTER 15

68000-Family System Elements

As you know by now, a computer system contains more than just a processor. In this chapter we describe some of the other elements that are used in 68000-based computer systems—cache memories, floating-point coprocessors, memory mapping and management units, and two simple peripheral interfaces.

For 20 years, advances in integrated circuit technology have steadily increased the size and complexity of the circuits that can be fabricated on a single chip. Given this increased capability, the manufacturers of processor ICs can include various system elements on the same chip with the processor. For example, cache memories, traditionally implemented in discrete logic separate from the processor, are part of the MC68020 and MC68030 chips, as described in the first two sections of this chapter. A floating-point coprocessor, now implemented as the MC68881 chip and described in the third section, may be included on-chip in the MC68040. A final example is the MC68851 paged memory mapping and management unit for the MC68020, described in the fourth section. A subset of its functions are included on-chip in the MC68030, as described in the fifth section.

The elements that we've mentioned so far are all oriented toward large, high-performance computer systems. But there are also peripheral circuits that can be found in almost any system. Two of the most commonly used peripheral chips are described in the last two sections of this chapter—the MC6850 serial communication chip and the MC68230 parallel interface and timer chip. In the future, we can expect to see similar functions included in single-chip microcomputers based on the 68000 processor architecture.

15.1   MC68020 ON-CHIP INSTRUCTION CACHE

The instruction execution speed of a high-performance computer is almost always limited by the rate at which the processor can fetch instructions and data from main memory, for two reasons:

(1) In a microprocessor, operations that use only on-chip resources such as registers can be completed very quickly, while operations that use off-chip resources such as main memory are necessarily slower because of the added delay of the circuits that send and receive off-chip signals.

(2) Even though microprocessor and memory chips use the same integrated circuit technology, a main memory *system* is typically slower than the processor, because of the timing and electrical buffering requirements for connecting a large number of memory chips. Also, the large size of a main memory system often precludes the use of faster (and costlier) chips.

One economical way to speed up the operation of a microprocessor system might be to build its main memory in two sections. The bulk of the memory could be designed in the conventional manner with relatively slow and inexpensive memory chips. But a small section could be designed using the fastest (and probably costliest) available memory chips. To optimize performance, programmers would assemble or compile their programs so that the most frequently used subroutines and data were located in the fast memory, and the remainder in slow memory.

Because 10% of the code in a typical program accounts for 90% of the execution time, the scheme proposed above might be possible. However, it's not too practical in most programming environments. For example, the crucial sections of code and data may be scattered, making it inefficient to locate program pieces in memory as suggested. It may not even be possible to determine which sections of code are the most frequently used in the first place. Worst of all, the run-time characteristics of a particular program may be data dependent; for example, the most frequently used instructions of a text editor program may depend on user options set during the editing session.

The idea of providing a small, fast memory for frequently used instructions and data would be more appealing if the definition of "frequently used" could be determined automatically by hardware, as a program is running, without requiring the program to be reassembled or recompiled to take advantage of it. Such a memory can be designed, in fact, as we'll now describe.

15.1.1   Cache Basics

cache

A *cache* is a high-speed memory containing recently or frequently used information. As shown in Figure 15–1, the cache is placed between the processor and main memory. It may contain instructions or data or both. However, the cache does not occupy a fixed set of addresses in the memory address space.

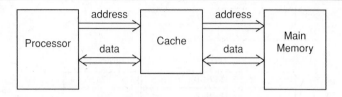

FIGURE 15–1   Placement of an instruction and data cache in a computer system.

Instead, it duplicates what is stored at a small set of main memory addresses. The cache size is much smaller than main memory, so ideally it contains only frequently used information.

If a system contains both a memory-mapping and management unit (MMU) and a cache, then there are two possible places to put the cache. If it is placed between the processor and the MMU, as in Figure 15–2(a), then the cache receives logical addresses and is called a *logical cache*. If it is placed between the MMU and main memory, as in Figure 15–2(b), then it receives physical addresses and is called a *physical cache*. The caches in the MC68020 and MC68030 are logical caches.

logical cache

physical cache

Each entry in a cache is called a *line*. As shown in Figure 15–3, each line has two parts—an *information* field (instruction or data) and a *tag* field (the main memory address that the information came from). The number of bytes in the information field, called the *line size*, is often equal to the width of the physical memory, but it can be larger.

line
information
tag
line size

When the processor needs to access memory, it first checks all of the tag fields to see if the requested address is duplicated in the cache. If the address is

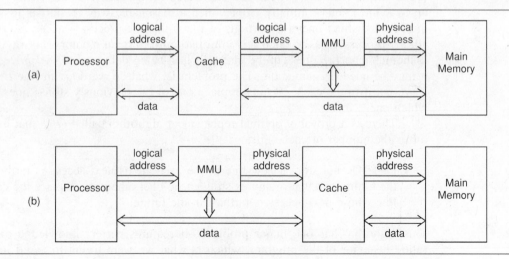

FIGURE 15–2   Cache placement with an MMU: (a) logical cache; (b) physical cache.

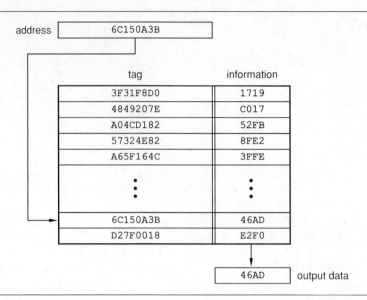

FIGURE 15–3   Cache structure.

hit   present (a *hit*), the access (read or write) is performed on the cache, a very fast
miss   operation. If the requested address is not present (a *miss*), then main memory
                 must be consulted to complete the access, a relatively slow operation. The
hit ratio   *hit ratio* is the fraction of the total memory accesses that are cache hits. To
                 maximize system performance, the hit ratio must be maximized.

Since the cache is smaller than main memory, a mechanism is needed to decide which addresses should be duplicated in the cache. If the cache holds up to L lines and is initially empty, then a reasonable way to start is to store the first L distinct lines (or portions of lines) that the processor accesses. After all, the processor has to fetch this information from main memory anyway, and it shouldn't hurt to put it in the cache as it is being delivered to the processor; it may be needed again soon. The problem is, what do we do with line $L + 1$? If we put it in the cache, it must replace one of the previously stored lines, but which one?

OPT   There is a provably optimal replacement algorithm called *OPT* that maximizes the number of cache hits:

- OPT: Do not store a new line in the cache if its next access is farther in the future than that of any existing cache line; otherwise, replace the cache line whose next access is farthest in the future.

This algorithm has one major problem—it requires perfect knowledge of the future behavior of the program, which is what we were trying to avoid in the first place!

Undaunted, the clever hardware engineer thinks, "Well, I don't know anything about the future, but my investment advisors keep telling me that past
performance is a good indicator of the future. Why not run OPT backwards?"
least recently used   This kind of thinking leads to the *least recently used (LRU)* replacement algo-
(LRU)   rithm:

- LRU: Replace the cache line whose last access was farthest in the past.

Surprisingly, this simple turnabout works quite well and has been used in a wide
variety of system applications. To implement the LRU algorithm, a cache has
age counter   one or more bits associated with each line to implement an *age counter*. Each
time that a line is used, its age counter is cleared. Periodically, the hardware
increments all of the age counters (which "stick" at the maximum count value).
The LRU algorithm replaces the line with the highest age count.

So far, we have assumed that a cache has L lines, each of which can
store information from any location in main memory. Such a cache is called a
fully associative   *fully associative cache*, because its memory is an *associative memory*, sometimes
cache   called a *content addressable memory (CAM)*. A row of information in an ordinary
associative   RAM is selected by a numerical address; a row of information in a CAM is
memory   selected by tag value. When an input tag is presented to a CAM, the CAM
content   hardware quickly compares it with all of the stored tags and produces as output
addressable   either the corresponding information or a *no match* signal. This is precisely the
memory (CAM)   behavior that is required for a cache to work as we've described it.
no match

15.1.2 Direct-Mapped and Set-Associative Caches

To be usable as a cache memory, a CAM must of course be fast. For high-speed
operation, a CAM needs a separate tag comparator for each row of memory; thus,
fast CAMs require much more chip area per bit and are much more expensive
than other forms of memory. For this reason, computer architects have devised
less expensive cache structures that require little or no associative memory, as
we'll now describe.

direct-mapped   Figure 15–4 shows a *direct-mapped cache* of 2^n bytes. The cache contains
cache 2^l lines, each of which contains a tag and 2^b information bytes, where $l + b = n$.
A main memory address contains three fields: p-bit page, l-bit line, and b-bit
byte. The byte at main memory address A can be stored at only one place in
the cache, in the line and byte selected by the $l + b$ low-order bits of A. The tag
field of the selected line stores the p high-order bits of A.

When access to a particular main memory address is requested, the cache
hardware uses the line number as an index to select the corresponding line in
the cache. It compares the tag for that line with the page number and, if they
match, it accesses the selected byte in the line. Otherwise, the requested address
is not in the cache. In this case, the replacement decision is easy—the selected
line *must* be replaced. Its tag is replaced with the new page number and its
information bytes are loaded from main memory.

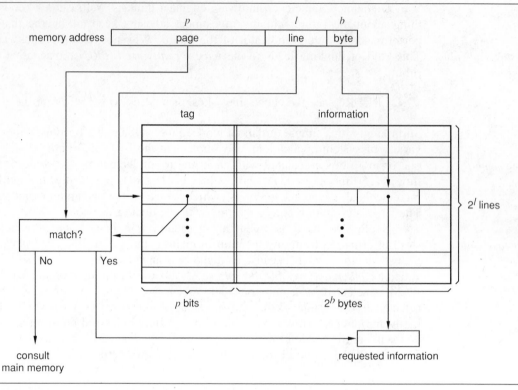

FIGURE 15–4   Direct-mapped cache structure.

Of course, a cache can transfer more than one byte at a time to or from the processor or main memory. For example, if the processor tries to read a longword and all the bytes of that longword are stored in the same cache line, then the cache delivers all four bytes to the processor in one step. Likewise, when the cache reads information from main memory, it does so using the maximum possible data bus width and transfer rate.

While a direct-mapped cache has a relatively inexpensive hardware implementation, it gives a poorer hit ratio than a fully associative cache of the same size because it has only one possible place to duplicate each memory address. Thus, if two frequently used memory addresses have identical low-order bits, they will compete for the same cache line and keep bumping each other out of the cache, causing misses. In very large direct-mapped caches (8 Kbytes or more), the problem is not too severe, because the probability of two addresses having the same low-order bits is small. But in small caches (1 Kbyte or less), the problem can be quite severe.

S-way set
  associative
  cache

set size

An *S*-way *set associative cache* provides *S* different lines that can duplicate memory addresses with identical low-order bits; *S* is called the *set size* and is typically on the order of 2–16. Set associative cache operation can be visualized as being similar to Figure 15–4, but with the tag and information fields replicated horizontally *S* times. When access to a particular main memory address is requested, the cache hardware uses the low-order address bits to select a set of lines in the cache. It quickly compares *all* of the tags in the set with the page number and, if one matches, it accesses the selected byte in the corresponding information field. Otherwise, the requested address is not in the cache and one of the lines must be replaced, typically using the LRU algorithm.

15.1.3　Write Operations

write policy

When a write operation is requested by the processor, what happens depends on the *write policy* of the cache:

write back

- *Write back.* The information is written into the cache and the cache bytes are marked as "modified." Before replacing a line containing modified bytes, the cache hardware writes the modified bytes back to main memory.

write through

- *Write through.* The information is immediately written into both the cache and main memory.

write around

- *Write around.* If a line containing the information is present in the cache, the processor uses either the write-back or write-through policy. However, if the access is a miss, the processor writes the information directly in main memory without updating the cache.

The write-back policy adds complexity to the cache hardware, but typically has the best performance because it eliminates all but one main memory access when the same location is written many times in succession. However, this policy is not appropriate if I/O devices or other processors concurrently access main memory, because they may read "stale" information that has been updated in the cache but not in main memory. The write-through policy guarantees that main memory and cache contents are always consistent.

The write-around policy is used to prevent occasional write misses to "random" addresses from replacing existing lines in the cache. This policy is especially useful in direct-mapped caches with large line sizes, because it prevents large amounts of "good" information from being replaced by a single write miss. The theory is that, if an address is going to be written frequently, it will also be read occasionally, which will bring it into the cache; if a write is a one-time operation, then the cache is not disturbed.

15.1.4　MC68020 Instruction Cache

Now that you know all about caches, the MC68020's on-chip instruction cache is easy to describe. It is a 256-byte direct-mapped logical cache with a line size of four bytes that is used only for instruction fetches. The MC68020 cache is never used for data accesses, even if they occur in program space (which is

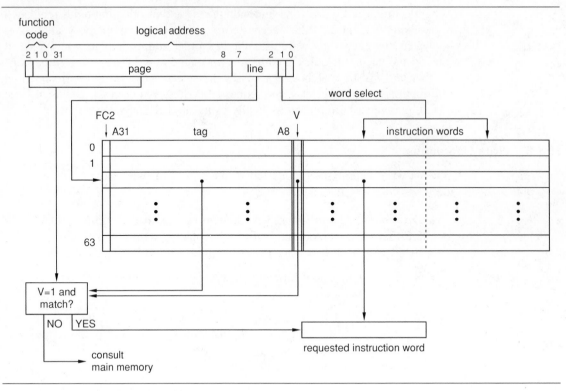

FIGURE 15–5   Instruction cache structure in the MC68020.

possible using the MOVES instruction). Since writes are never performed on the cache, there is no write policy.

As shown in Figure 15–5, the tag field contains the 24 high-order address bits and a mode bit *FC2*. The FC2 bit is one of the processor's function code bits (Section 14.2) and is treated like another address bit; it distinguishes between user-mode and supervisor-mode accesses, which are considered to be in different address spaces. Each line also contains a *valid (V)* bit, which is used to invalidate cache lines that have not been loaded; a tag match can occur only if V = 1.

FC2

valid (V)

cache control register (CACR)
cache address register (CAAR)

The *cache control register (CACR)* and the *cache address register (CAAR)*, part of the MC68020's programming model, are used to enable and maintain the cache, mostly during debugging. Their formats are shown in Figure 15–6 and the functions of their individual fields are listed below:

enable cache (E)

- The *enable cache (E)* bit, when 1, allows the cache to be used. If E is 0, the processor bypasses the cache and accesses main memory directly.

freeze cache (F)

- The *freeze cache (F)* bit, when 1, prevents misses from replacing existing cache lines. Instructions already in the cache continue to be accessed in the cache.

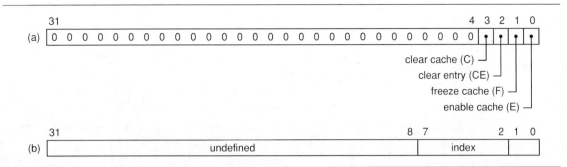

FIGURE 15–6   Formats of MC68020 cache registers: (a) control (CACR); (b) address (CAAR).

clear entry (CE)   • The *clear entry (CE)* bit may be set to 1 to clear the V bit of the cache line whose index is contained in CAAR.

index   • The *index* field contains the index of a cache line that is to be cleared.

clear cache (C)   • The *clear cache (C)* bit may be set to 1 to clear the V bits of all cache lines. An operating system may use this function to clear user instructions from the cache during a context switch. The cache must be cleared if there is an MMU between the cache and main memory, because another user process may access different physical memory locations using the same logical (cached) addresses.

The performance gains provided by the cache are significant. Even if the fastest possible chips are used for main memory, the processor still runs about 25% faster when instructions are found in the cache than when they are not. If main memory is slower, the relative improvement is even greater. In any case, the overall performance improvement also depends on the cache's hit ratio. For a long sequence of "straight-line" code, the hit ratio will be 0. Conversely, a short loop with many iterations and no interruptions may give a hit ratio close to 1. Industry experience suggests that MC68020 processors running "typical" applications have instruction cache hit ratios on the order of 40%–70%.

15.2   MC68030 ON-CHIP INSTRUCTION AND DATA CACHES

The MC68030 has separate on-chip logical caches for instructions and data. Since the MC68030 also has an on-chip MMU, the caches theoretically could have been designed as physical caches. However, the designers decided to implement logical caches to obtain the best possible performance. When the processor produces a logical address, it gives it to both the MMU and the appropriate cache simultaneously. In this way, cached information becomes available as soon as possible, without the delay of an MMU translation.

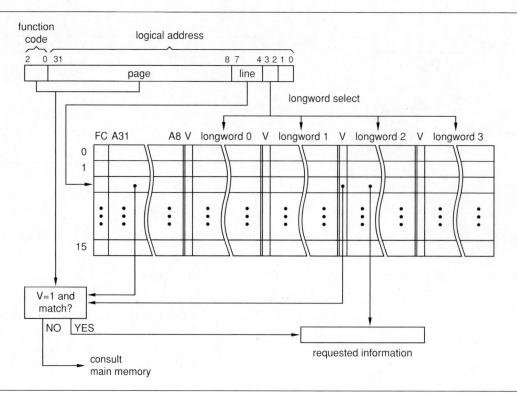

FIGURE 15–7   Instruction cache and data cache structure in the MC68030.

Each cache contains 256 bytes and is organized as a direct-mapped cache with 16 lines of 16 bytes each. As shown in Figure 15–7, each line has tag field and four longword entries. An individual valid bit V is associated with each entry, so that a line may be only partially loaded.

Tag matching is performed on address bits A31–A8 and on a function code field FC. In the instruction cache, the FC field contains just one function code bit, FC2, to distinguish between user and supervisor address spaces. As in the MC68020, the MC68030 instruction cache is never used for data accesses, even if they occur in program space. Data accesses, except accesses to CPU space, use the data cache, whose FC field contains all three function code bits, FC0–FC2, to distinguish among various combinations of user, supervisor, program, and data address spaces. Accesses to CPU space never use the cache.

In either cache, a miss occurs when the tag field does not match or the V bit of a selected longword is 0. When a read operation produces a miss, the cache loads the requested information from main memory, a longword read operation. The information is given to the processor and stored in the appropriate cache entry, whose V bit is now set to 1. If the tag field did not match, the tag field of the affected line is updated and the other V bits in that line are cleared. If an

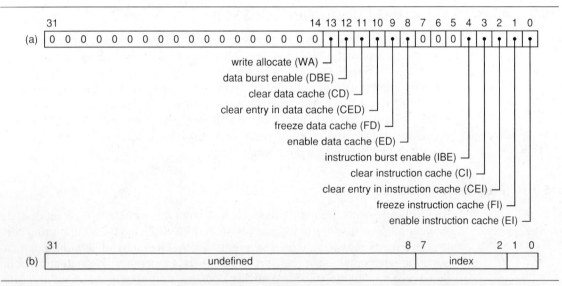

FIGURE 15-8   Formats of MC68030 cache registers: (a) control (CACR); (b) address (CAAR).

operand crosses a longword boundary, its two halves are handled independently; each may be a hit or a miss and is handled appropriately.

During a read miss, the cache may optionally fill the entire cache line from main memory using four longword read operations in a special *burst mode*. This feature improves the performance of systems with certain types of memory chips that can read from consecutive addresses faster than they can from "random" addresses. Burst-mode filling is enabled for the instruction cache by the *instruction burst enable (IBE)* bit in the CACR, and for the data cache by the *data burst enable (DBE)* bit.

The data cache uses a write-through policy for write operations that result in a hit. When a miss occurs, the write policy depends on the state of the *write allocation (WA)* bit in the CACR. If WA = 0, a write-around policy is used—main memory is updated but the cache is not affected. If WA = 1, main memory is updated and the cache is also affected. The effect on the cache depends on the type of write operand. If the operand is an aligned longword, it is stored in the cache, the corresponding tag is updated, the V bit for the stored longword is set, and the other three V bits in the affected line are cleared. If the operand is a byte or a word or nonaligned, the corresponding tag(s) are not affected, but the corresponding V bit(s) are cleared.

Shown in Figure 15–8, the MC68030's *cache control register (CACR)* and the *cache address register (CAAR)* have fields and functions similar to those of the MC68020's. The IBE, DBE, and WA bits were explained already. The remaining bits in CACR are counterparts of the C, CE, F, and E bits in the MC68020 CACR. The index field of CAAR selects a line and longword whose V bit is to be cleared, also as in the MC68020.

burst mode

instruction burst enable (IBE)
data burst enable (DBE)

write allocation (WA)

cache control register (CACR)
cache address register (CAAR)

15.3 MC68881 FLOATING-POINT COPROCESSOR

MC68881

Motorola's *MC68881* chip is a coprocessor with registers and instructions for performing arithmetic using the IEEE floating-point arithmetic standard that we introduced in Section 4.11.3. The MC68881 is normally connected to a 68020 main processor; it communicates with the 68020 and executes instructions using the primitives that we discussed in Section 14.9.6. It can also be used in non-68020 systems that have hardware or software that emulates the 68020-defined coprocessor interface. Throughout this section, we'll refer to the MC68881 as simply the *FPU (floating-point unit)*.

floating-point unit (FPU)

15.3.1 Programming Model

floating-point data registers (FP0–FP7)

extended-precision format

The FPU augments the main processor's programming model with a set of eight general-purpose floating-point data registers (FP0–FP7) and three supporting control and status registers, shown in Figure 15–9. Operands of floating-point instructions are contained in registers FP0–FP7 and in memory. Each floating-point data register is 80 bits wide and always contains a number in *extended-precision format* with sign, 15-bit exponent, and 64-bit mantissa; memory operands can be in other formats, as explained in the next subsection.

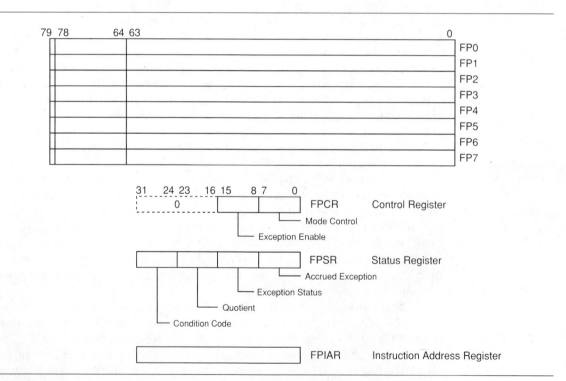

FIGURE 15–9   Programming model of the MC68881 floating-point unit (FPU).

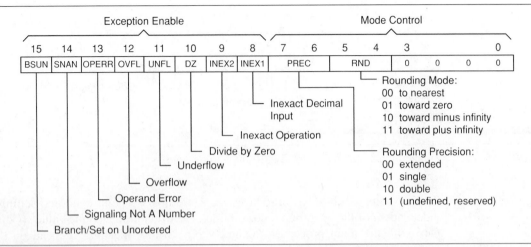

FIGURE 15–10   Control bits in the floating-point control register (FPCR).

floating-point control register (FPCR)
rounding precision

The low-order word of the *floating-point control register (FPCR)* controls certain options; the high-order word is not used. As detailed in Figure 15–10, bits 6 and 7 control *rounding precision*. The FPU initially computes all results to extended precision (64-bit mantissa). However, if a less precise rounding mode (double or single) is selected, the FPU rounds the extended-precision result to a lesser number of mantissa bits (53 or 24) before storing it. This doesn't save any time, but it allows the MC68881 to emulate and produce the same results as less capable FPUs that cannot perform extended-precision arithmetic.

rounding mode

Bits 4 and 5 of FPCR determine the *rounding mode*, the method by which the FPU rounds results that cannot be expressed exactly within the selected precision. For example, the result of the operation $1 \div 3$ is 0.010101..., and cannot be expressed exactly in any finite number of bits; rounding takes place in every precision.

Although the low-order byte of FPCR allows many different combinations of rounding precision and mode, bits 4–7 must be set to zero for compatibility with the IEEE floating-point standard.

floating-point exception

The second byte of FPCR contains one bit for each of eight classes of *floating-point exceptions*. If a bit is 1 and a corresponding exception occurs, a trap will be taken using a specific vector number in the range 48–54 (seven different vectors, INEX1 and INEX2 use the same one). A program must contain a handler for each of these traps, just as it does for the other 68000-family traps that we discussed in Section 11.4.4.

floating-point status register (FPSR)
condition code byte

The *floating-point status register (FPSR)* contains result codes that are modified by most floating-point instructions. Shown in Figure 15–11, the *condition code byte* contains four bits that are set according to the value in a floating-point register at the end of an instruction's execution. Naturally, these bits are distinct from similarly named bits in the main processor's CCR. Also, a given

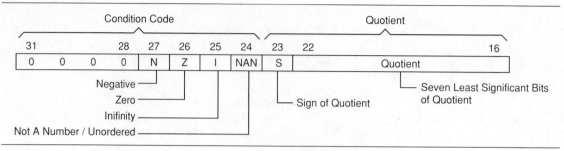

FIGURE 15–11   Floating-point status register (FPSR) high-order word.

floating-point result always produces the same floating-point condition settings, independent of the operation (add, subtract, etc.) that produced the value. (Compare with the main processor's C and V bits, whose meanings depend on the instruction that set them.)

negative (N)
zero (Z)
infinity (I)

Negative (N) and *zero (Z)* conditions occur in the obvious way. The *infinity (I)* bit is set on overflow, for example, when multiplying two numbers whose product is larger than can be expressed in the selected precision. Not only is the I bit set; the result stored is plus or minus infinity, which the IEEE floating-point standard represents with an exponent field of all 1's and a mantissa of 0.

not-a-number (NAN)

The *not-a-number (NAN)* bit is set by operations that have no definite mathematical interpretation, such as infinity divided by infinity. As with infinity conditions, the result itself also reflects the condition; a not-a-number result is represented with an exponent field of all 1's and a non-0 mantissa.

quotient byte

The FPSR *quotient byte* in Figure 15–11 is set at the completion of the FMOD and FREM instructions, and contains the seven least significant bits and the sign of the quotient. This information may be used to speed the evaluation of certain functions.

exception status byte

The *exception status byte*, shown in Figure 15–12, is cleared at the start of most floating-point operations, and its individual bits are set if an exception occurs during the operation. However, operations that can never generate a floating-point exception do not affect this byte at all. Also shown in the figure,

accrued exception status byte

the *accrued exception status byte* is *not* cleared at the start of every operation. Instead, its bits are set as logical combinations of bits in the exception status byte, and they remain set during a sequence of instructions until the program explicitly clears them by writing to the FPSR. In this way, a program can perform a lengthy floating-point computation and check only once, at the end, to see if any exceptions occurred.

floating-point instruction address register (FPIAR)

Each time that the FPU starts to execute an instruction that might cause a floating-point exception, it loads the *floating-point instruction address register (FPIAR)* with the 32-bit address of that instruction. This is especially important for long (time-consuming) floating-point operations. Since the main processor may continue to execute its own instructions in parallel with the coprocessor, its PC may be considerably advanced beyond the floating-point instruction when a

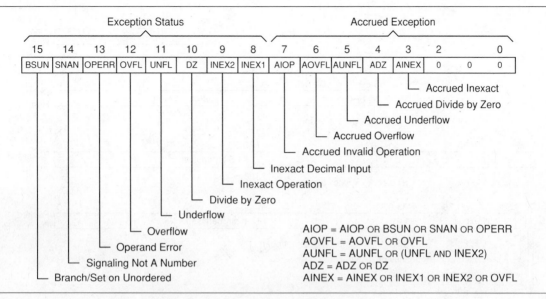

FIGURE 15–12   Floating-point status register (FPSR) low-order word.

trap finally occurs. The saved PC on the main processor stack does not locate the offending floating-point instruction, but FPIAR shows the trap handler precisely which instruction caused the exception. Note that FPIAR is not affected by instructions that cannot cause an exception.

15.3.2 Data Types

The MC68881 FPU recognizes seven different data types for operands that are stored in memory. As shown in Figure 15–13, the first three types are ordinary two's-complement integers of size byte, word, and longword. These are exactly the same types processed by the 68000's integer arithmetic instructions. How-

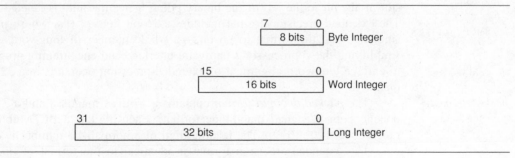

FIGURE 15–13   Ordinary integer data types for MC68881 memory operands.

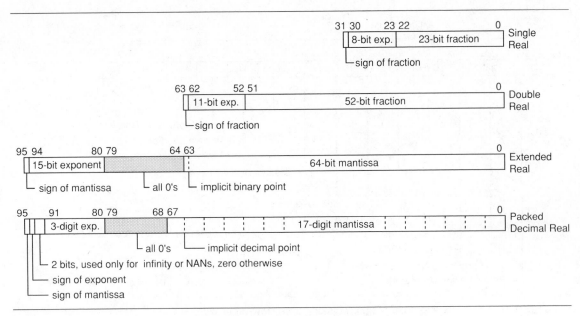

FIGURE 15–14   Real data types for MC68881 memory operands.

ever, integer operands are converted to extended-precision floating-point format before being used by the FPU.

single-precision binary real format

The remaining types, shown in Figure 15–14, are floating-point (real) formats. The first of these is the IEEE standard *single-precision binary real format* and was described in Section 4.11.3. Recall that the mantissa of a normalized number in this format has the form 1.xxxxxx, where "1" is the so-called hidden bit. Only the bits to the right of the binary point are explicitly stored, and are labeled the *fraction* field in the figure.

fraction

double-precision format

extended-precision format

mantissa

The other formats in Figure 15–14 are also prescribed or allowed by the IEEE floating-point standard. The *double-precision format* is similar in structure to single precision, with more exponent and fraction bits. The *extended-precision format*, besides having more bits, differs from the previous formats by explicitly storing the bit to the left of the binary point; hence the field is labeled *mantissa*. The extended-precision format includes a 16-bit field of 0's, whose purpose is simply to pad the format to 96 bits—a whole number of longwords—thereby simplifying the coprocessor's hardware interface and encouraging programmers to enforce longword alignment of extended-precision operands in a 32-bit-wide memory.

packed decimal format

The *packed decimal format* contains a 17-digit mantissa and a 3-digit exponent, both in signed magnitude format. Each digit is a BCD nibble in the range 0000–1001 (0–9). The leading digit of a normalized number is nonzero.

The extended-precision format is identical to the format of operands in the FPU's data registers, except that the 16-bit field of 0's is absent from the registers. Memory operands in the other three real formats, as well as in the three integer formats, are always converted to extended precision before being loaded into data registers or used in floating-point operations. Conversely, extended-precision results in data registers are converted to one of the other formats, if specified, before being stored in memory. If the result cannot be represented exactly in the specified memory format, one or more of the bits in the exception byte may be set.

15.3.3 Instructions

Most of the MC68881 FPU's instructions use the cpGEN coprocessor format, which was described in Section 14.9.6. Among these, most have two operands and use a specific format for the command word after the cpGEN opcode word, as shown in Figure 15–15. For these instructions, the destination operand is always a floating-point data register FPn specified by the nnn field in the command word. The m bit in the command word specifies the type of source operand. If m = 0, the source is another floating-point data register specified by the sss field. If m = 1, the source is a "memory" operand. In this case, the source operand's effective address is given by the EA field in the opcode word, and its data format is given by the sss field as detailed in the figure. If the effective address is a 68000-processor data register, then the data format must fit in 32 bits—byte, word, longword, or single precision. The seven low-order bits of the command word contain a *subopcode* field that specifies the exact operation to be performed using the source and destination operands.

subopcode

Table 15–1 lists the FPU's data movement instructions. For each instruction, the third column gives the format of the word following the cpGEN opcode word; most are in the format shown in Figure 15–15. An opcode suffix on the

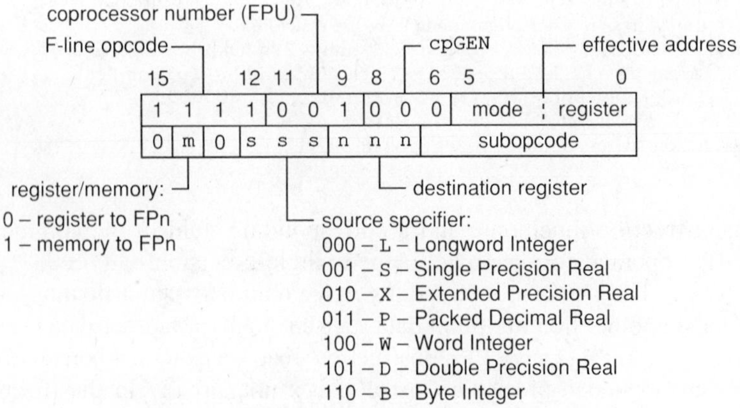

FIGURE 15–15   Format of most MC68881 double-operand instructions.

TABLE 15-1   Floating-point data movement instructions in the MC68881.

Mnemonic	Operands	Command Word	Description
FMOVE	fsrc,FPn	0m0sssnnn0000000	Move fsrc to floating-point data register
FMOVE	FPn,ddst	011dddnnnkkkkkkk	Move floating-point data register to ddst
FMOVECR.X	#data,FPn	010111nnnooooooo	Move constant ROM value
FMOVE.L	asrc,FPr	100rrr0000000000	Move asrc to floating-point control register
FMOVE.L	FPr,adst	101rrr0000000000	Move floating-point control register to adst
FMOVEM.X	Msrc,frlist	11010000LLLLLLLL	Move memory to multiple registers (static)
FMOVEM.X	frlist,Mdst	111a0000LLLLLLLL	Move multiple registers to memory (static)
FMOVEM.X	Msrc,Dn	11011000nnn0000	Move memory to multiple registers (dynamic)
FMOVEM.X	Dn,Mdst	111a1000nnn0000	Move multiple registers to memory (dynamic)
FMOVEM.X	Msrc,fcrlist	100RRR0000000000	Move multiple control registers
FMOVEM.X	fcrlist,Mdst	101RRR0000000000	Move multiple control registers
FGETEXP	fsrc,FPn	0m0sssnnn0011110	Get exponent
FGETMAN	fsrc,FPn	0m0sssnnn0011111	Get mantissa
FINT	fsrc,FPn	0m0sssnnn0000001	Integer part
FINTRZ	fsrc,FPn	0m0sssnnn0000011	Integer part, round to zero
FNOP		0000000000000000	No operation

Notes: Memory operands (fsrc or dst) may have any data format:
          .B – byte integer
          .W – word integer
          .L – longword integer
          .S – single-precision real
          .D – double-precision real
          .X – extended-precision real
          .P – packed-decimal real
  FPm, FPn = one of the floating-point data registers, FP0–FP7.
  FPr = one of the floating-point control registers, FPCR, FPSR, or FPIAR.
  frlist = a list of floating-point data registers;
  fcrlist = a list of floating-point control registers.
  Dn = one of the main processor data registers, D0–D7, whose low-order byte specifies a list
      a floating-point data registers.
  See Table 8–2 on page 272 for addressing mode restrictions. An additional restriction is that
      asrc can use address-register direct mode only if FPr is FPIAR).
  m = register/memory field; sss = source specifier field; nnn = FPn field. See Figure 15–15.
  rrr = FPr field; mmm = FPm field; RRR = fcrlist field; LLLLLLLL = fplist field.
  kkkkkkk = k-factor field, used only with FMOVE.P FPn,dst, else 0000000.
  ooooooo = offset to data in MC68881 constant ROM.
  a = 0 if the destination addressing mode is auto-decrement, else 1.

instruction mnemonic and a corresponding field in the command word specify the operand format (byte integer, single-precision real, etc.).

    The first two instructions move data between a floating-point data register and another floating-point data register, main processor data register, or memory.

FMOVE fsrc,FPn   The FMOVE fsrc,FPn instruction reads a source operand fsrc, converts it into extended-precision format if it's not already in that format, and deposits it in register FPn, setting the condition codes and exception bytes according to the result.

FMOVE FPn,dst   The FMOVE FPn,dst instruction makes a copy of the extended-precision value in register FPn, converts it to the specified data format, and copies the result to the destination `dst`, setting the exception bytes according to the result; however, the condition codes are not affected.

The 68000's standard immediate addressing mode is available for the `fsrc` operand of an `FMOVE fsrc,FPn` instruction. However, some immediate values are used so often that the FPU provides a more efficient way of loading them into a register. The *constant ROM* is a small, on-chip, read-only memory that contains 22 useful constants, such as 0, 1, *e*, and π. The `FMOVECR` instruction copies one of these constants into a register in extended-precision format. The `ooooooo` field in the command word specifies the location of the constant in the on-chip ROM.

constant ROM
FMOVECR

FMOVE.L

Two `FMOVE.L` instructions in Table 15–1 are used to load and store values in the three control and status registers, FPCR, FPSR, and FPIAR. These instructions do not affect the condition and exception bytes, unless the destination is the FPSR itself.

FMOVEM.X

Several flavors of `FMOVEM.X` instructions are available to move multiple floating-point data or control registers to and from memory. The image of a data register in memory is stored in the 96-bit extended-precision format. The list of data registers may be specified either statically in the command word (`frlist`) or dynamically in a main-processor register (Dn). A list of control registers may only be specified statically (`fcrlist`).

Individual components of a floating-point number may be extracted using instructions from the next-to-last group in Table 15–1. The `fsrc` operand of each instruction may be a floating-point data register or a "memory" operand in any format. The operand is converted to extended-precision format and the appropriate information is extracted, converted to an extended-precision floating-point number, and deposited in the destination register FPn.

FGETEXP

FGETMAN
FINT

FINTRZ

The `FGETEXP` instruction extracts the exponent field, for example, an integer in the range −126 through +127 when the source operand is in single-precision real format. `FGETMAN` extracts the mantissa field, a real number between 1.0 and 2.0 for all binary source formats. The `FINT` instruction rounds its operand using the current rounding mode and then extracts the integer part. `FINTRZ` is similar, except that it uses round-to-zero mode regardless of the mode currently selected in FPCR. All of these instructions affect the condition codes and the exception bytes.

FNOP

A floating-point no-operation instruction, `FNOP`, is included at the end of Table 15–1. It does not affect any floating-point registers, condition codes, or exception bytes. However, it is useful for synchronizing the operation of the FPU with a main processor. Recall from Section 14.9.6 that a 68020 main processor can continue to execute its own instructions while the FPU executes a lengthy instruction of its own, such as a floating-point sine or cosine. Only if the 68020 encounters a second FPU instruction before the first has completed does the FPU give a "busy" status, forcing the 68020 to wait for the previous FPU instruction to complete. The `FNOP` instruction can be used to force this synchronization to occur, even if no additional floating-point operations are required.

TABLE 15–2   Floating-point arithmetic instructions in the MC68881.

Mnemonic	Operands	Command Word	Description
FABS	fsrc,FPn	0m0sssnnn0011000	Absolute value
FNEG	fsrc,FPn	0m0sssnnn0011010	Negate
FSQRT	fsrc,FPn	0m0sssnnn0000100	Square root
FTST	fsrc	0m0sss0000111010	Test
FADD	fsrc,FPn	0m0sssnnn0100010	Add
FSUB	fsrc,FPn	0m0sssnnn0101000	Subtract (FPn − fsrc)
FCMP	fsrc,FPn	0m0sssnnn0111000	Compare (FPn − fsrc)
FMUL	fsrc,FPn	0m0sssnnn0100011	Multiply (FPn × fsrc)
FDIV	fsrc,FPn	0m0sssnnn0100000	Divide (FPn ÷ fsrc)
FMOD	fsrc,FPn	0m0sssnnn0100001	Modulo remainder (FPn ÷ fsrc)
FREM	fsrc,FPn	0m0sssnnn0100001	IEEE remainder (FPn ÷ fsrc)
FSGLDIV	fsrc,FPn	0m0sssnnn0100100	Divide (FPn ÷ fsrc)
FSGLMUL	fsrc,FPn	0m0sssnnn0100111	Multiply (FPn × fsrc)
FSCALE	fsrc,FPn	0m0sssnnn0100110	Scale exponent (FPn × 2^{fsrc})

Notes: See notes for Table 15–1.

That's enough of instructions that do almost nothing. In Table 15–2, we finally list some instructions that perform floating-point arithmetic operations. All of these instructions have the format of Figure 15–15, and they all affect the condition codes and the exception bytes.

FABS
FNEG
FSQRT
FTST

Instructions in the first group of Table 15–2 read their fsrc operand, convert it to extended precision if necessary, perform the specified operation, and store the result in register FPn. Listed next, the FTST instruction is similar, but it merely sets the condition codes and exception bytes without storing the result anywhere. The remaining instructions combine the fsrc operand with FPn; all except FCMP store the result back into FPn.

FCMP
FADD
FSUB
FCMP

The floating-point addition and subtraction instructions work as you might expect. In particular, FSUB and FCMP subtract their operands in the same order as the 68000's SUB and CMP, and so the same cautions about the sense of conditional branches following a comparison apply.

FMUL
FDIV

Floating-point multiplication and division instructions, FMUL and FDIV, are less complicated than the corresponding integer instructions, in that the source (after extension) and result operands are all the same size. For example, even though the product of two n-bit mantissas may require $2n$ bits to be represented exactly, during floating-point multiplication the extra low-order bits are rounded to create an n-bit mantissa for the result, and the INEX2 exception bit is set to alert any program that really cares about the slight loss of precision.

FMOD
FREM

Since the result of FDIV is the quotient only, two other instructions are available to obtain the remainder of a division. FMOD and FREM differ only in the rounding mode used during the calculation of the remainder—round-to-zero in FMOD and round-to-nearest in FREM.

TABLE 15–3   Floating-point transcendental instructions in the MC68881.

Mnemonic	Operands	Command Word	Description
FSIN	fsrc,FPn	0m0sssnnn0001110	Sine
FCOS	fsrc,FPn	0m0sssnnn0011101	Cosine
FTAN	fsrc,FPn	0m0sssnnn0001111	Tangent
FSINCOS	fsrc,FPm:FPn	0m0sssnnn0110mmm	Simultaneous sine and cosine
FACOS	fsrc,FPn	0m0sssnnn0011100	Arc cosine
FASIN	fsrc,FPn	0m0sssnnn0001100	Arc sine
FATAN	fsrc,FPn	0m0sssnnn0001010	Arc tangent
FSINH	fsrc,FPn	0m0sssnnn0000010	Hyperbolic sine
FCOSH	fsrc,FPn	0m0sssnnn0011001	Hyperbolic cosine
FTANH	fsrc,FPn	0m0sssnnn0001001	Hyperbolic tangent
FATANH	fsrc,FPn	0m0sssnnn0001101	Hyperbolic arc tangent
FETOX	fsrc,FPn	0m0sssnnn0010000	Exponential ($e^{\texttt{fsrc}}$)
FLOGN	fsrc,FPn	0m0sssnnn0010100	Log_e
FETOXM1	fsrc,FPn	0m0sssnnn0001000	Exponential ($e^{\texttt{fsrc}} - 1$)
FLOGNP1	fsrc,FPn	0m0sssnnn0000110	$\text{Log}_e(\texttt{fsrc} + 1)$
FTENTOX	fsrc,FPn	0m0sssnnn0010010	Exponential ($10^{\texttt{fsrc}}$)
FLOG10	fsrc,FPn	0m0sssnnn0010101	Log_{10}
FTWOTOX	fsrc,FPn	0m0sssnnn0010001	Exponential ($2^{\texttt{fsrc}}$)
FLOG2	fsrc,FPn	0m0sssnnn0010110	Log_2

Notes: See notes for Table 15–1.

FSGLMUL
FSGLDIV
FSCALE

Instructions in the last part of Table 15–2 are optimized versions of operations that can actually be performed by other instructions. FSGLMUL and FSGLDIV use only 24 bits of mantissa during their calculations and consequently execute faster than FMUL and FDIV in most cases. FSCALE multiplies a register by a power of 2 by simply adding to its exponent field, which is much faster than performing an actual multiplication.

The MC68881 FPU has a rich set of instructions that compute transcendental functions, as shown in Table 15–3. Each instruction reads a source operand fsrc, converts it to extended precision if necessary, computes the designated function, and deposits the result in register FPn. All of these instructions affect the condition codes and the exception bytes.

All of the instructions that we've studied so far use the cpGEN coprocessor instruction format. The MC68881 FPU versions of the remaining coprocessor instructions are listed in Table 15–4 and work as described in Section 14.9.6. Instructions in the first part of the table test conditions that are unique to the FPU, combinations of condition bits FPSR.

infinities
not-a-number
(NAN)

The relations defined between floating-point operands are not the same as the ones between integers, because the IEEE floating-point standard includes *infinities* and *not-a-number (NAN)* as possible operands. When two IEEE floating-point numbers are compared, their relation is not necessarily one of the usual

TABLE 15–4   Additional MC68881 instructions.

Mnemonic	Operands	Opcode Word	Description
FBcc.W	addr16	1111001010CCCCCC	Branch on floating-point condition
FBcc.L	addr32	1111001011CCCCCC	Branch on floating-point condition
FScc	dst	1111001001dddddd	Set on floating-point condition
		0000000000CCCCCC	
FDBcc	Dn,addr16	1111001001001rrr	Conditional loop primitive
		0000000000CCCCCC	
FTRAPcc		1111001001111100	Trap if floating-point condition true
		0000000000CCCCCC	
FTRAPcc.W	#tdata	1111001001111010	Trap if floating-point condition true
		0000000000CCCCCC	
FTRAPcc.L	#tdata	1111001001111011	Trap if floating-point condition true
		0000000000CCCCCC	
FSAVE	Mdst	1111001100dddddd	Save FPU internal state (privileged operation)
FRESTORE	Msrc	1111001101ssssss	Restore FPU internal state (privileged operation)

Notes: cc = floating-point condition, see next table.
      addr16 = branch target, an address within 32 Kbytes of the instruction.
      addr32 = branch target, an address anywhere in the 4-gigabyte address space.
      tdata = 16- or 32-bit immediate data for use by the trap handler, stored in the word(s)
          following the opcode and command words.
      CCCCCC = condition field, see next table.
      ssssss = Msrc field; dddddd = dst or Mdst field.
      Also see notes for Table 15–1.

three—greater than, less than, or equal. For example, the difference of two "+infinity" operands cannot be determined (which is more infinite than the other?), and so the difference is defined to be NAN. Likewise, the difference of NAN and any other number is also NAN. Thus, a fourth relation may exist between two operands—*unordered*. Floating-point conditions in the FPU must handle NAN results and comparisons of unordered operands.

unordered

Table 15–5 lists the floating-point conditions of the MC68881 FPU. The first part of the table contains so-called *IEEE nonaware conditions*; each one provides for the possibility of NAN results. These conditions are called "nonaware" because they are intended for use by programmers and compilers that are unfamiliar with the implications of NAN operands. Therefore, the FPU sets the *BSUN* (branch/set on unordered) exception bit if the NAN bit is 1 during the execution of an instruction that specifies a nonaware condition. The idea is that, since NANs are an unexpected problem, a trap should alert the programmer.

IEEE nonaware condition

BSUN

Listed in the second part of the table, *IEEE aware conditions* also consider NAN results; in fact, their boolean conditions are identical to the ones for nonaware conditions. The difference is that instructions using aware conditions never set the BSUN exception bit. An "aware" program is supposed to look for and handle NANs explicitly.

IEEE aware condition

The conditions in the last part of the table are provided for completeness, but are seldom used. The first two set BSUN if NAN is 1; the other two do not.

TABLE 15–5   Floating-point conditions and their encodings in the MC68881.

Type	cc	CCCCCC	Branch/Set/Trap If	Boolean Condition
IEEE nonaware				
	SEQ	010001	Signaling equal	Z
	SNE	011110	Signaling not equal	$\overline{Z}$
	GT	010010	Greater than	$\overline{(NAN + Z + N)}$
	NGT	011101	Not greater than	$NAN + Z + N$
	GE	010011	Greater than or equal	$Z + \overline{(NAN + N)}$
	NGE	011100	Not (greater than or equal)	$NAN + (N \cdot \overline{Z})$
	LT	010100	Less than	$N \cdot \overline{(NAN + Z)}$
	NLT	011011	Not less than	$NAN + Z + \overline{N}$
	LE	010101	Less than or equal	$Z + (N \cdot \overline{NAN})$
	NLE	011010	Not (less than or equal)	$NAN + \overline{(N + Z)}$
	GL	010110	Greater than or less than	$\overline{(NAN + Z)}$
	NGL	011001	Greater than or less than	$NAN + Z$
	GLE	010111	Greater, less, or equal	$\overline{NAN}$
	NGLE	011000	Not (greater, less, or equal)	NAN
IEEE aware				
	NE	001110	Not equal	$\overline{Z} + NAN$
	EQ	000001	Equal	$Z \cdot \overline{NAN}$
	OGT	000010	Ordered greater than	$\overline{(NAN + Z + N)}$
	ULE	001101	Unordered or less or equal	$NAN + Z + N$
	OGE	000011	Ordered greater than or equal	$Z + \overline{(NAN + N)}$
	ULT	001100	Unordered or less than	$NAN + (N \cdot \overline{Z})$
	OLT	000100	Ordered less than	$N \cdot \overline{(NAN + Z)}$
	UGE	001011	Unordered or greater or equal	$NAN + Z + \overline{N}$
	OLE	000101	Ordered less than or equal	$Z + (N \cdot \overline{NAN})$
	UGT	001010	Unordered or greater than	$NAN + \overline{(N + Z)}$
	OGL	000110	Ordered greater or less than	$\overline{(NAN + Z)}$
	UEQ	001001	Unordered or equal	$NAN + Z$
	OR	000111	Ordered	$\overline{NAN}$
	UN	001000	Unordered	NAN
Miscellaneous				
	SF	010000	Signaling false	0
	ST	011111	Signaling true	1
	F	000000	False	0
	T	001111	True	1

Notes: The logic expression listed under "Condition" must evaluate to 1 for the branch or trap to
be taken or for the destination operand to be set.
+ denotes logical OR; · denotes logical AND; an overbar denotes logical complementation.
cc = symbolic designation used in mnemonics of FBcc, FDBcc, FScc, and FTRAPcc
instructions.
CCCCCC = 6-bit field in the command word of conditional instructions.

15.3.4   Programming

Assembly language programs for a 68020 system containing an MC68881 FPU can be written in much the same way as for any other system. Most 68020 assemblers recognize the mnemonics for FPU instructions and operands. However, the programmer must remember that the FPU completes the execution of cpGEN-type instructions in parallel with 68020 instruction execution. As soon as such an FPU instruction has fetched all of its operands, it releases the 68020, which continues to fetch and execute its own instructions. If the 68020 tries to send another instruction to the FPU before the previous one has been completed, the FPU sends a busy signal back, and the 68020 waits until the FPU is ready.

This parallel execution has a number of implications for programming style. First, the overall performance of a program may be improved if 68020 instructions can be placed between FPU instructions, so that the FPU has as much time as possible to complete an operation without forcing the 68020 to busy-wait. Second, a program cannot guarantee that an FPU operation has been completed unless it successfully begins another one; FNOPs may be used for this purpose. Third, in a multiple-process environment, fast context switching may not always be possible because the FPU may be executing a slow instruction, which normally must be completed before the FPU registers can be saved.

FSAVE
FRESTORE

However, the FSAVE and FRESTORE instructions may be used to suspend and later restore such an instruction in the middle.

In addition, systems with FPUs must provide trap handlers for all of the new exceptions that might occur. Interface problems between the main processor and coprocessor can trigger trap 13, a coprocessor protocol violation. Exceptions generated by the floating-point operations themselves can trigger traps 48–54. And the handler for trap 7, normally invoked by TRAPcc or TRAPV, can now

FTRAPcc

also be invoked by FTRAPcc.

15.4   MC68851 PAGED MEMORY MANAGEMENT UNIT

We described the general applications and functions of memory mapping and management units (MMUs) in a computer system in Section 7.5. A memory mapping and management scheme was not specified as part of the original 68000 architecture, although Motorola announced a rather strange mapping scheme and a corresponding MMU chip, the *MC68451*, shortly after introducing the MC68000. The MC68451 never succeeded in the marketplace; instead, serious

MC68451

designers of 68000-based systems specified their own memory mapping and management schemes and designed corresponding hardware using standard MSI and LSI ICs; the original Sun workstations are the most successful examples of such systems.[1]

---

[1] In fairness to the designers, the MC68451 did use a pretty clever way of getting around the size and speed limitations of the IC technology of that time. But the resulting memory mapping algorithm and options, which we won't go into here, were just too inconvenient.

MC68851 paged
memory
management
unit (PMMU)

Later, Motorola announced a new mapping scheme and embodied it in the *MC68851 paged memory management unit (PMMU)*. Because of its high performance and its affinity with traditional memory mapping and management architectures, the PMMU was well accepted; for example, the PMMU was included in the design of the Macintosh II. Furthermore, Motorola guaranteed the PMMU's long-term survival in the 68000-family architecture by including a subset of the PMMU's functions on-chip in the MC68030. Future members of the 68000 family will almost certainly continue to include PMMU functions on-chip.

15.4.1 Basic Organization and Function

As we showed in Figure 7–23 on page 250, an MMU is placed on the address lines between the processor and memory, where it translates each logical address into a corresponding physical address. A typical MMU also has an I/O connection that the processor uses to program the MMU's map and control registers. An MC68851 PMMU's connection to an MC68020 processor and memory is shown in Figure 15–16. Instead of having an I/O connection to the main processor, the PMMU uses the MC68020 coprocessor interface. Thus, the main processor accesses and manages the PMMU's internal resources using coprocessor instructions.

page
page number
page offset

translation table

The basic address mapping performed by the PMMU is similar to what we described in Section 7.5 and is shown in Figure 15–17. Both the logical and the physical address spaces are divided into equal-sized *pages*. The high-order bits (*page number*) of a logical address select a map entry that contains a physical address and access rights for the page. The low-order bits (*page offset*) of the logical address are used directly in the physical address. As discussed later, the PMMU may optionally organize its map as a hierarchical set of *translation tables*. In this case, the page number field of a logical address in Figure 15–17

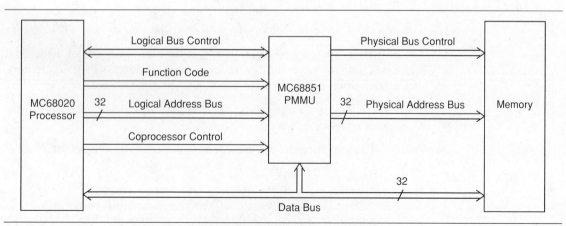

FIGURE 15–16   Placement of an MC68851 PMMU in an MC68020 system.

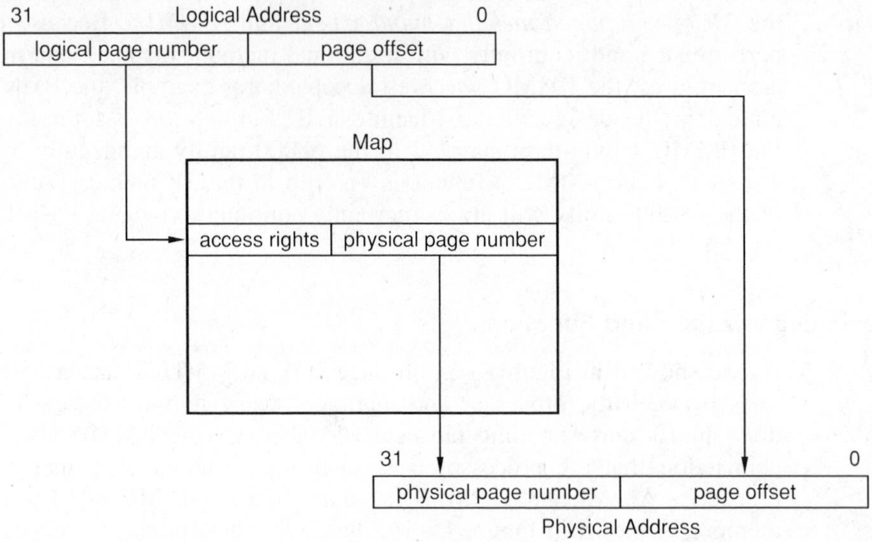

FIGURE 15–17   Logical-to-physical mapping performed by the MC68851 PMMU.

is subdivided into as many as four subfields, and as many as six tables may be consulted to determine the physical page number.

Early MMU designs for the 68000, including both the MC68451 chip and the Sun workstations, stored the entire map in the MMU chips. This approach places a hardware limit on the maximum size of the map and also tends to create a certain inflexibility in the use of map entries. To avoid these problems, the MC68851 PMMU stores its translation tables (map) in main memory itself, so that the map may be arbitrarily large. Thus, a basic processor-to-main-memory access might include the following steps:

(1) The processor issues a memory request over the logical bus.

(2) The PMMU extracts the page number from the high-order bits of the logical address. Using the page number, it determines the address in main memory of the translation table entry for the requested logical page.

(3) The PMMU issues a request over the physical bus to read the table entry from main memory.

(4) Based on information in the table entry, the PMMU checks the access rights for the requested page (e.g., write protection).

(5) If access is allowed, the PMMU uses additional information in the table entry to determine the physical address corresponding to the requested logical address. It issues a memory request over the physical bus, thereby satisfying the processor's original memory request.

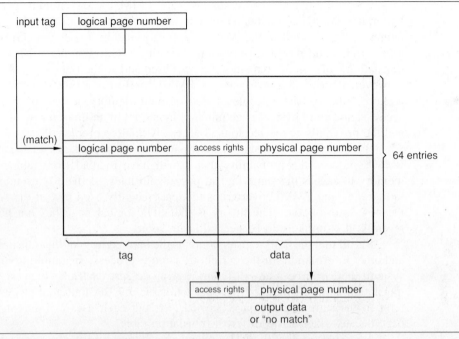

FIGURE 15–18   Address translation cache (ATC) in the MC68851 PMMU.

This may seem like a lot of steps per main-processor request, but the PMMU hardware can execute most of them quickly. The most time-consuming steps are the memory accesses over the physical bus. Notice that the steps above include *two* physical memory accesses for each logical access requested by the processor. Thus, it potentially takes the processor twice as long to access memory when using the PMMU.

When the translation tables are organized hierarchically, the performance penalty can be even worse. Six table entries may have to be fetched for each logical request, and each table entry may contain two longwords, requiring two physical memory accesses. Thus, 12 extra physical memory cycles might be needed to complete just one logical memory access.

address translation cache (ATC)

To reduce the performance penalty for fetching table entries in main memory, the PMMU chip contains a hardware-controlled *address translation cache (ATC)* that stores the results of up to 64 recent logical-to-physical translations. The basic structure of the ATC is shown in Figure 15–18. The ATC is an associative memory, like the fully associative instruction and data cache described in Section 15.1.1. In the ATC, each tag is a logical page number, and the corresponding data field contains a physical page number and access rights. When an input tag is presented to the ATC, the hardware quickly compares the input tag with all of the stored tags and produces as output either the corresponding data or a no-match signal.

Each time that the processor gives the PMMU a logical address for translation, the PMMU compares its logical page number with all of the logical page numbers (tags) stored in the ATC. If it finds a match, it uses the corresponding access rights and physical page number in the ATC to complete the access; the translation tables in main memory are not used and so the translation is very fast. However, if no match is found, the PMMU performs a (possibly hierarchical) lookup in the translation tables stored in main memory, a slow operation. The access rights and physical page number are stored in an unused row of the ATC, and the originally requested logical access is finally completed.

By storing new translation information in an unused row of the ATC, the PMMU reduces the probability that it will have to read from tables in main memory to access the same logical page again later. If there is no unused row in the ATC, the PMMU overwrites the least recently used row of the ATC with the new information. The theory is that, if a logical page has not been used recently, it is unlikely to be needed again soon.

Recall that the CRP register contains the base address of the translation table and other information for the current user-mode process. In a multiprogramming system, there can be many different user processes, each of which has its own translation table, pointed to by a different value in CRP. Different processes may refer to the same logical page, say $1234, but each uses a different physical page because each has a different translation table.

Now suppose that the ATC contains translation information for logical page $1234, and a context switch to a different user process occurs. By all rights, the ATC entry for page $1234 should be invalidated, because page $1234 in the new process is completely unrelated to the previous one and uses a different physical page. Many such entries may have to be invalidated after a context switch. Later, when the original user process is resumed, its original entry for page $1234 will be restored by reading the translation table in main memory.

The PMMU attempts to reduce the inefficiency of invalidating and restoring user-process ATC entries during context switches by maintaining a small, programmer-invisible list of the eight most recently used values of CRP. This
root pointer table (RPT)   list, indexed from 0 to 7, is called the *root pointer table (RPT)*. When the PMMU puts a translation entry into the ATC, it also includes the RPT index (0–7) corresponding to the CRP value and translation table that was used. The RPT index,
task alias   called the *task alias*, distinguishes among ATC entries from different processes that happen to have the same logical page number. Thus, ATC entries need not be invalidated during context switches, as long as there are eight or fewer user processes. If there are more than eight processes, the PMMU automatically invalidates the ATC entries of the least recently run process and reuses its task alias for the new process.

Figure 15–19 shows the precise format of entries in the ATC. The tag contains three fields in addition to the logical address:

function code (FC)   • The *function code (FC)* field is the function code value that was used by the processor during the memory access that created this ATC entry,

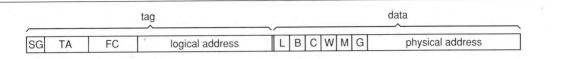

FIGURE 15–19   Detailed format of entries in the ATC.

distinguishing between user/supervisor and program/data address spaces. (Refer to Section 14.2 for a discussion of function codes.)

task alias (TA)
- The *task alias (TA)* field contains the task alias defined above.

shared global (SG)
- The *shared global (SG)* bit indicates sharing, as discussed later.

For a logical address from the processor to match an ATC entry, it must exactly match the entry's logical address and FC fields. In addition, either the current task alias must match the entry's TA field, or the entry's SG must be set.

The data portion of an ATC entry contains the physical memory address of the page and six bits of control information. When the translation tables are read and an ATC entry is created, the control bits are extracted from similarly named information fields, defined later. Subsequently, the control bits in the ATC are consulted and possibly updated each time that the ATC entry is used.

15.4.2 Programming Model

Even though the translation tables used by the PMMU are stored in main memory, the PMMU chip does contain several programmer-visible registers that control the mapping process. These registers are accessed using coprocessor instructions, and they form the PMMU's programming model shown in Figure 15–20.

For each logical-to-physical address translation, the PMMU uses one of three different translation tables, depending on the type of access. The memory address and other characteristics of each translation table are contained in a 64-bit PMMU register:

CPU root pointer (CRP)
- The *CPU root pointer (CRP)* register is used for normal memory accesses by a main processor running in user mode.

supervisor root pointer (SRP)
- The *supervisor root pointer (SRP)* register is used for memory accesses by a main processor running in supervisor mode.

DMA root pointer (DRP)
- The *DMA root pointer (DRP)* register is used for memory accesses by a DMA device. Such a device may share the logical address bus with the main processor.

Three more registers are used in various aspects of the translation process:

translation control (TC)
- The *translation control (TC)* register is used to specify the format of logical addresses—the sizes of page number and offset fields—and other options that affect logical-to-physical address translation.

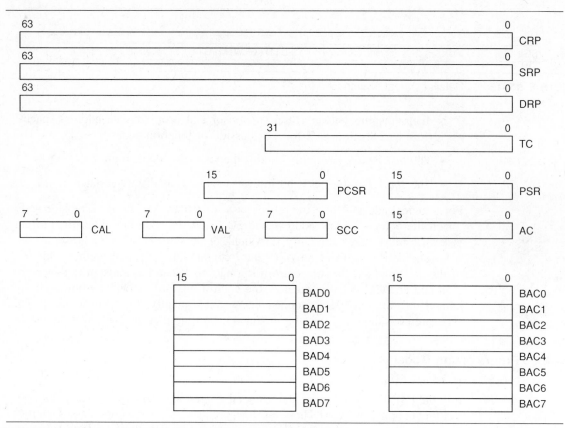

FIGURE 15–20   Programming model of the MC68851 PMMU.

PMMU cache status register (PCSR) lock warning

- The *PMMU cache status register (PCSR)* has fields that indicate when the ATC reuses an RPT task alias, and which one. It also has a *lock warning* bit that is set when all but one of the ATC entries are "locked" and cannot be replaced.

PMMU status register (PSR)

- The *PMMU status register (PSR)* can be loaded with information about a particular logical address. An operating system can use this information to determine the reason for a protection violation (write protect, supervisor only, etc.).

As explained in Section 14.9.7, the PMMU can be used along with the MC68020's module call and return instructions to support a finer level of privilege than just user and supervisor modes. Four PMMU registers are used in conjunction with this capability:

access control (AC)

- The *access control (AC)* register configures the PMMU's support of multiple privilege levels. The number of privilege levels provided within the main processor's user mode may be specified as 1, 2, 4, or 8, and the CALLM and RTM instructions may be enabled or disabled.

current access level (CAL)
- The *current access level (CAL)* register contains the privilege level, 0–7, of the currently executing module. Programs can request a change in this privilege level by executing a CALLM instruction with an appropriate module descriptor.

validate access level (VAL)
- The *validate access level (VAL)* register contains the privilege level of the caller of the current module. It is set equal to CAL during the execution of CALLM, before CAL is changed, and it is restored to its old value by RTM.

stack change control (SCC)
- The *stack change control (SCC)* register specifies whether the main processor should change stack pointers when calling a module at a more privileged level.

In addition to performing address translation, the PMMU aids program debugging by providing eight pairs of breakpoint registers that are used with the MC68020's BKPT instruction:

breakpoint acknowledge data (BAD0–7)
- The *breakpoint acknowledge data (BAD0–7)* registers hold opcode words that may be provided to the MC68020 processor during a breakpoint acknowledge bus cycle, as explained in Section 14.9.5.

breakpoint acknowledge control (BAC0–7)
- Eight *breakpoint acknowledge control (BAC0–7)* registers determine the PMMU's response to breakpoints. Each register contains an enable bit and an 8-bit breakpoint skip count.

When the MC68020 executes a BKPT #n instruction, the PMMU examines the corresponding control register BACn. If the enable bit is clear or the skip count is zero, the PMMU allows the CPU to take an illegal instruction trap. However, if the enable bit is set and the skip count is nonzero, the PMMU transfers the opcode word in register BADn to the processor, which uses it to continue instruction execution without trapping. The opcode word in register BADn is normally a copy of the original opcode word that the debugger replaced with the BKPT #n instruction. Thus, the debugger can allow an instruction to be executed up to 255 times before a trap is taken, by placing the desired number of nonbreak executions in the BACn skip count.

Additional details of the formats and functions for all of the PMMU registers are given in Motorola's MC68851 user manual (see References).

15.4.3 Address Translation

In Figure 7–24 on page 251, we showed an address translation map for a system with a 64-Kbyte logical address space divided into eight 8-Kbyte pages. Many computer systems use much smaller page sizes, such as 256 or 512 bytes, for two reasons:

internal
  fragmentation

(1) A smaller page size reduces *internal fragmentation*, memory waste that occurs when a process requires an amount of memory that is just slightly larger than a multiple of the page size. In our example, a 9-Kbyte process would have to be allocated two pages or 16 Kbytes, of which 7 Kbytes would be wasted.

(2) In a multiprogramming system, it is convenient to use a page size equal to the data block size of the disk that stores pages when they are not present in physical memory. Many disks have blocks as small as 256 bytes.

At the same time, the total memory space used by microprocessor systems is ever-increasing. It is not uncommon to find a 68020-based multiprogramming system with 16 Mbytes or more of physical memory, and several times that amount of logical address space. The maximum size of the 68020's logical address space is 2^{32} bytes, of course.

invalid

If we used a page size of 2^8 (256) bytes and performed the logical-to-physical mapping shown in Figure 15–17, the Map size would be $2^{32-8} = 2^{24}$, over 16 million entries. Of course, most systems do not have 2^{32} bytes of physical memory. Nevertheless, all 2^{24} map entries would be required, even if most of the logical pages were not used and therefore marked *invalid*. What we gain in page-size convenience, we certainly pay for in the size and maintenance overhead of a huge map.

translation tree

descriptor

table descriptor

The MC68851 PMMU provides the benefits of small pages, without the overhead of a huge map, by organizing its translation tables hierarchically in main memory. An example of a such a hierarchical map, called a *translation tree*, is shown in Figure 15–21. The root pointer (stored in SRP, CRP, or DRP) gives the base address of a 16-entry translation table at the first level of the hierarchy. Each entry in this table is called a *descriptor* and corresponds to a 2^{28}-byte region of the logical address space, as selected by logical address bits A31–A28. If one of these regions is not used, its descriptor is marked invalid. Otherwise, the first-level table contains a *table descriptor* that points to a second-level table.

In the example of Figure 15–21, there are four second-level tables, each of which partitions its 2^{28}-byte region of the logical address space into 256 1-Mbyte regions, as selected by address bits A27–A20. As in the first-level tables, each second-level descriptor either is marked invalid or contains a pointer to a table at the next level.

page table
page descriptor

Each third-level table (a *page table*) contains 4096 *page descriptors*, one of which is selected using address bits A19–A8. Each page descriptor either is marked invalid or contains the base address of the corresponding logical page in physical memory. In this example, the page size is 256 bytes, and so the eight low-order bits of logical and physical addresses are equal.

Translation trees, with their ability to have invalid descriptors in the first- and second-level tables, use a lot fewer page descriptors than the linear mapping scheme that we first described. For example, an invalid descriptor in the first-level table in Figure 15–21 ultimately saves 2^{20} page descriptors. The total

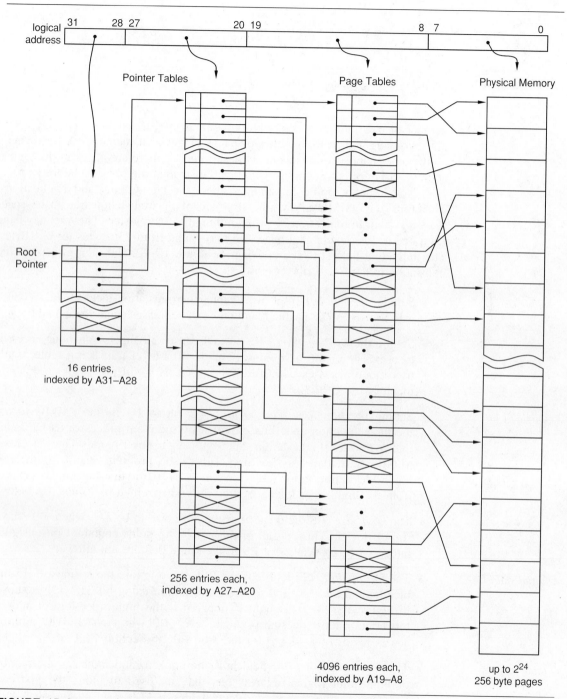

FIGURE 15–21   Hierarchical organization of translation tables in the MC68851.

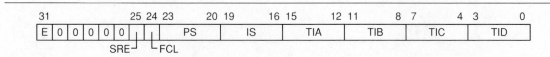

FIGURE 15–22   Format of the translation control (TC) register.

number of page and table descriptors required by a translation tree is typically not much larger than the number of pages in physical memory. A linear map, on the other hand, requires as many descriptors as there are pages in the logical address space, often orders of magnitude larger than the physical address space.

No single mapping hierarchy is best for all systems and applications. Therefore, the PMMU allows the structure of the translation tree to be specified at system initialization by programming the TC register. The tree may have from one to five levels, and page size may range from 256 bytes to 32 Kbytes. The individual fields in TC are shown in Figure 15–22, and their effects on the translation tree are described below.

enable (E)
- Setting the *enable (E)* bit to 1 enables the translation mechanism. When E is 0, translation is disabled, and physical addresses equal logical addresses.

SRP enable (SRE)
- Setting the *SRP enable (SRE)* bit to 1 causes all supervisor-mode accesses to use SRP as the base address of the first-level translation table, while user-mode accesses use CRP. When SRE is 0, all processor accesses to memory use CRP.

function code lookup (FCL)
- Setting the *function code lookup (FCL)* bit to 1 tells the PMMU to use the three function code bits provided by the main processor as the index into a first-level translation table with eight descriptors. Thus, accesses to different address spaces (user, supervisor, program, data) use different second-level translation tables. When FCL is 0, the first-level index is taken from the high-order logical address bits as specified by IS and TIA below.

page size (PS)
- The *page size (PS)* field specifies the page size to be 2^{PS}, where PS ranges from 8 to 15. This and all of the remaining fields contain 4-bit unsigned integers (0–15). Values of PS in the range 0–7 are not allowed.

initial shift (IS)
- The *initial shift (IS)* field tells the PMMU to ignore the leftmost 0–15 bits of a logical address, and to begin translation using bit $31 - IS$, as shown in Figure 15–23. This field is nonzero if the high-order logical address bits contain the requested privilege level (RPL) in a system with multiple access levels (e.g., IS = 3 for the 3-bit RPL in Section 14.9.7).

table index A (TIA)
- The *table index A (TIA)* field must be nonzero and indicates the number of high-order logical address bits that are used to index the first-level translation tables (or second-level tables if FCL = 1). Each such table contains 2^{TIA} descriptors.

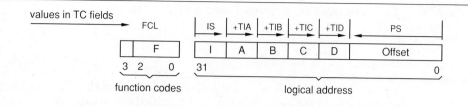

FIGURE 15–23   Positions of table index fields based on TC fields.

*table index B
(TIB)*
- The *table index B (TIB)* field indicates how many bits are used to index the second-level translation tables (or third-level tables if FCL = 1). If TIB is 0, translation ends at the previous level and TIC and TID must be 0. Otherwise, each table at this level contains 2^{TIB} descriptors.

*table index C
(TIC)*
- The *table index C (TIC)* field indicates how many bits are used to index the third-level translation tables (or fourth-level tables if FCL = 1). If TIC is 0, translation ends at the previous level and TID must be 0. Otherwise, each table at this level contains 2^{TIC} descriptors.

*table index D
(TID)*
- The *table index D (TID)* field indicates how many bits are used to index the fourth-level translation tables (or fifth-level tables if FCL = 1). If TID is 0, translation ends at the previous level. Otherwise, each table at this level contains 2^{TID} descriptors.

The sum of the values in IS, TIA, TIB, TIC, TID, and PS must be 32.

15.4.4   Root Pointers and Descriptors

table address

*descriptor type
(DT)*

With the basic structure of the translation tables now defined, we can look at the detailed formats of the root pointers and descriptors. Address translation always begins with one of the root pointers, SRP, CRP, or DRP, which have the format shown in Figure 15–24. The low-order longword of the register (*table address*) contains the base address in physical memory of the first-level translation table. This and all translation tables must be aligned on 16-byte boundaries.

The value in the *descriptor type (DT)* field identifies the type of descriptor as shown in Table 15–6. A DT value of 2 or 3 is normally used for root pointers.

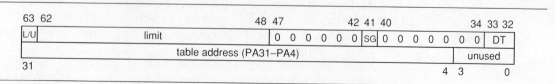

FIGURE 15–24   Format of root pointer registers, SRP, CRP, and DRP.

TABLE 15–6   Descriptor types in root pointers and translation tables.

DT	Type	Description
0	Invalid	All pages within the address range covered by this descriptor are considered invalid. The other fields of this descriptor are not used by the PMMU, and may be used by the operating system (for example, to store the reason that the descriptor is invalid—out of range, swapped out, etc.). This type is not allowed for root pointers.
1	Page	This type normally occurs in page tables. If it occurs in a pointer table or root pointer, then the next-level translation table for this descriptor does not exist. Instead, logical addresses are linearly mapped into a single contiguous region of physical memory.
2	Valid 4 byte	A next-level translation table exists and contains short-format descriptors.
3	Valid 8 byte	A next-level translation table exists and contains long-format descriptors.

shared global (SG)

  The *shared global (SG)* bit indicates sharing. If SG is 1 then the logical-to-physical mappings for all tasks using this root pointer are assumed to be identical. Therefore, the task alias can be ignored when entering or comparing translation information in the ATC. The SG bit is usually set in SRP and DRP, since supervisor and DMA mappings are normally identical for all tasks.

limit

L/U

  The *limit* and *L/U* fields may be used to limit the size of the first-level translation table (or linearly mapped region of memory, if DT = 1). If L/U is 0, then limit specifies a maximum value for the first-level table index. For example, suppose FCL = 0 and TIA = 4. Then the range of a first-level index is 0–15 and the first-level table normally has 16 descriptors, as in Figure 15–21. However, if only the first three descriptors are used, then the limit field may be set to 2, and the last 13 descriptors are never accessed and need not be stored in memory. A logical address with first-level index in the range 3–15 cannot be accessed.

  When L/U is 1, limit specifies a minimum value for the first-level table index. In the example with FCL = 0 and TIA = 4, setting L/U = 1 and limit = 10 would restrict the range of valid first-level index values to 10–15.

  If the first-level table is based on function code (FCL = 1), then it always has exactly eight entries and the L/U and limit fields are not used.

  Now we can discuss the formats of the descriptors in the translation tables themselves. All of the descriptors in a given table are the same size, either long or short, as determined by the DT field of root pointer or descriptor that located the table. When the translation tree is programmed to have N levels ($2 \leq N \leq 5$), tables at levels 1 through $N - 1$ of the tree normally contain table descriptors, while tables at level N normally contain page descriptors.

long-format table descriptor

  A *long-format table descriptor* contains two longwords and is shown in Figure 15–25(a). Its fields are defined below:

table address

  • The *table address* field contains the base address in physical memory of the next-level translation table.

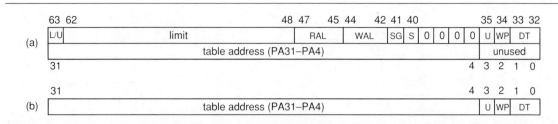

FIGURE 15–25   Table descriptors: (a) long (8-byte) format; (b) short (4-byte) format.

lower/upper (L/U)   • The *lower/upper (L/U)* bit controls whether limit contains a lower or an upper bound on valid index values for the next-level translation table.

limit   • The *limit* field contains a lower or upper bound on index values for the next-level translation table.

read access level (RAL)   • The *read access level (RAL)* field contains the minimum privilege level (maximum numeric value of CAL) that is allowed for read access to a page that is located with this descriptor.

write access level (WAL)   • The *write access level (WAL)* field contains the minimum privilege level (maximum numeric value of CAL) that is allowed for write access to a page that is located with this descriptor.

shared global (SG)   • The *shared global (SG)* bit, when 1, indicates that all pages that are located with this descriptor are shared.

supervisor (S)   • The *supervisor (S)* bit, when 1, indicates that pages located with this descriptor may be accessed only in supervisor mode.

used (U)   • The *used (U)* bit, initially cleared to 0 by software, is set to 1 by the PMMU when the PMMU uses the descriptor in a translation.

write protect (WP)   • The *write protect (WP)* bit, when 1, indicates that pages located by this descriptor absolutely may not be written, regardless of the privilege level and mode of the writing process.

descriptor type (DT)   • The *descriptor type (DT)* field selects one of types listed in Table 15–6.

Note that the DT field distinguishes among three basic types of descriptors— invalid, page, and table—at the *current* level of the table, but determines the descriptor size (long or short) at the *next* level of the table.

short-format table descriptor   A *short-format table descriptor* omits several of the long-format fields and contains just one longword, as shown in Figure 15–25(b). This format may be used if all of the following conditions are true:

(1) The next-level table is full size, not limited by L/U and limit.

(2) Access levels defined by RAL and WAL either are not used or are least privileged.

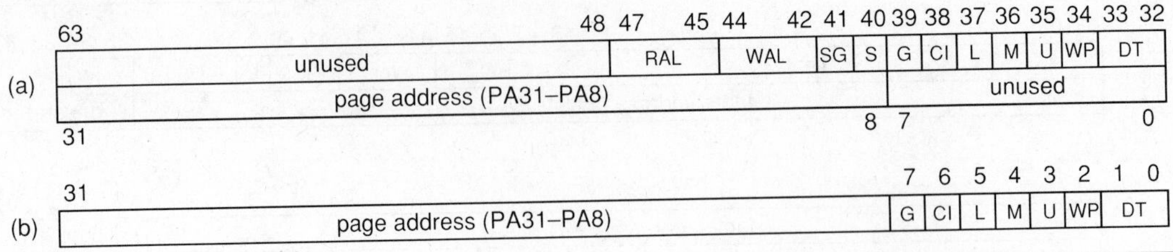

FIGURE 15–26   Page descriptors: (a) long (8-byte) format; (b) short (4-byte) format.

(3) Pages located through this descriptor may be accessed in any mode (S = 0).

(4) Pages located through this descriptor are not shared (SG = 0).

type-1 page descriptor

type-1 long-format page descriptor

Type-1 page descriptors are found at the last level of the translation tree. A *type-1 long-format page descriptor* has the format shown in Figure 15–26(a). Several of the fields have the same names as fields in table descriptors and have the same definitions. The DT field in a page descriptor always has the value 1. The additional fields are defined below:

page address

- The *page address* field contains the 24 high-order bits of the page's base address in physical memory. If the page size is $2^n \cdot 256$ bytes, then n low-order bits of this field are unused but treated as if they were 0, since pages begin on $(2^n \cdot 256)$-byte boundaries.

gate (G)

- The *gate (G)* bit, when 1, indicates that the page is allowed to contain module descriptors (call gates) for the MC68020 `CALLM` instruction.

cache inhibit (CI)

- The *cache inhibit (CI)* bit, when 1, indicates that data in this page should not be stored in a local instruction or data cache. (Such caches were discussed in Sections 15.1 and 15.2.)

lock (L)

- The *lock (L)* bit, when 1, indicates that once this descriptor is stored in the ATC, it should remain there indefinitely. The ATC's LRU replacement algorithm may not replace this descriptor with another one; it is removed only when all ATC entries with the same task alias are removed.

modified (M)

- The *modified (M)* bit, when 1, indicates that the processor has written to this page. The PMMU sets this bit when a write occurs.

type-1 short-format page descriptor

A *type-1 short-format page descriptor* has the format of Figure 15–26(b). It may be used when only a subset of the long-format fields are required.

In a system with virtual memory, the operating system uses M and U to help decide which old pages in physical memory should be replaced when it needs space for new pages that are currently stored only in the disk subsystem. A page that has not been used recently is a good candidate for replacement. On the other hand, a modified page may not be such a good candidate, because an

63 62	48 47	45 44	42 41	40	39	38	37	36	35	34	33	32
L/U	limit	RAL	WAL	SG	S	G	CI	L	M	U	WP	DT
page address (PA31–PA8)				unused								
31				8	7							0

FIGURE 15–27   Type-2 long-format page descriptors.

type-2 page descriptor

type-2 long-format page descriptor

type-2 short-format page descriptor

indirect descriptor

descriptor address

updated copy must be stored in the disk subsystem before the page is overwritten in physical memory by a new one.

We mentioned in Table 15–6 that a table descriptor may have its DT field equal to 1, in which case the next-level translation table for the descriptor does not exist. Instead, it is treated as a *type-2 page descriptor* that linearly maps a range of logical addresses into a single contiguous region of physical memory. The *type-2 long-format page descriptor* is shown in Figure 15–27. Like a long-format table descriptor, it has L/U and limit fields that restrict the range of next-level index values. Although there are no next-level table entries, the contiguously mapped region is limited to logical addresses whose next-level index field falls within the restricted range. The remaining fields of the descriptor are identical to those of a long-format page descriptor. A *type-2 short-format page descriptor* is identical to a type-1 short-format page descriptor. Type-2 descriptors are typically used for memory-resident programs and data that are loaded into memory at system initialization and never swapped out.

The PMMU normally expects to find valid or invalid page descriptors, with DT = 1 or DT = 0, at the last level of the translation tree. However, it also allows descriptors with DT = 2 or DT = 3, which are called *indirect descriptors* and have the format shown in Figure 15–28. The *descriptor address* field contains an indirect address, the address of a short (DT = 2) or long (DT = 3) page descriptor. Only one level of indirection is allowed.

Indirect descriptors are useful when a physical page is shared by multiple processes. Only one, "primary" page descriptor contains the physical address and control bits for the page, and all of the sharing processes access the primary descriptor through indirect descriptors. In this way, the operating system has only one set of control bits to deal with when making page allocation and swapping decisions.

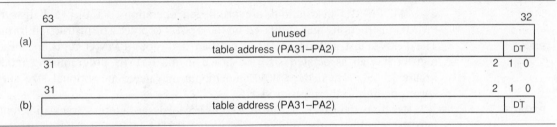

FIGURE 15–28   Indirect descriptors: (a) long (8-byte) format; (b) short (4-byte) format.

15.4.5 Protection

Each time that the processor presents a logical address to the PMMU for translation, the PMMU checks its access rights for possible protection violations. Because of the hierarchical structure of the translation tree, different access rights may be specified at different levels of the tree. For example, a first- or second-level table descriptor may specify write protection, while the page descriptor does not. The PMMU always enforces the safest or most restrictive protection that it encounters during a particular translation. The possible protection violations are listed below:

- *Invalid descriptor.* A descriptor with DT = 0 was encountered during translation.

- *Write protect.* During a write, one or more of the descriptors used in the translation had WP = 1.

- *Write access violation.* During a write, the current access level in CAL was less privileged than the WAL field of a descriptor used in the translation.

- *Read access violation.* During a read, the current access level in CAL was less privileged than the RAL field of a descriptor used in the translation.

- *Limit violation.* The limit field of a long descriptor was exceeded.

- *Supervisor only.* During a user-mode access, a long descriptor had its S bit set.

When any of these violations occur, the PMMU terminates the access with a bus error exception. It is the trap handler's responsibility to determine what went wrong, using exception information on the stack and the PTEST instruction described in the next subsection.

15.4.6 Instruction Set

Compared with the MC68881 FPU, the MC68851 PMMU has very few instructions. After all, the PMMU performs very little "computation;" instead, its functions are oriented toward the configuration and use of translation tables and breakpoint information.

All PMMU instructions are privileged operations. Table 15–7 lists the PMMU instructions that are based on the cpGEN coprocessor instruction format.

PMOVE The PMOVE instructions are used to load and store PMMU registers. Each register has an associated size as shown in the PMMU programming model, Figure 15–28. Thus, the PMOVE mnemonic may have an optional size suffix corresponding to the register size.

PLOADR Next in the table, PLOADR fc,fsrc loads an address translation entry into the ATC as if the processor had read the fsrc operand while asserting

PLOADW a bus function code of fc. PLOADW fc,fsrc does the same thing, but as

TABLE 15-7 General instructions of the MC68851 PMMU.

Mnemonic	Operands	Command Word	Description (all are privileged)
PMOVE	preg,adst	01pppp10000nnn00	Move PMMU register to adst
PMOVE	asrc,preg	01pppp00000nnn00	Move asrc to PMMU register
PLOADR	fc,psrc	00100010000fffff	Load entry for psrc into ATC (read)
PLOADW	fc,psrc	00100000000fffff	Load entry for psrc into ATC (write)
PFLUSHA		0010010000000000	Flush all ATC entries
PFLUSH	fc,#mask	0011000mmmmfffff	Flush ATC by function code only
PFLUSH	fc,#mask,psrc	0011100mmmmfffff	Flush by function code and effective address
PFLUSHS	fc,#mask	0011010mmmmfffff	Flush by function code, shared entries too
PFLUSHS	fc,#mask,psrc	0011110mmmmfffff	Flush by function code and address, shared
PFLUSHR	msrc	1010000000000000	Flush ATC and RPT entries matching msrc
PTESTR	fc,psrc,#lev	100LLL10000fffff	Test psrc for read access
PTESTW	fc,psrc,#lev	100LLL00000fffff	Test psrc for write access
PTESTR	fc,psrc,#lev,An	100LLL11aaafffff	Test psrc for read, An := descriptor
PTESTW	fc,psrc,#lev,An	100LLL01aaafffff	Test psrc for write, An := descriptor
PVALID	VAL,psrc	0010100000000000	Validate psrc as a pointer against VAL
PVALID	An,psrc	0010110000000aaa	Validate psrc as a pointer against An

Notes: preg = one of the registers in the PMMU's programming model.
  pppp specifies preg; values 0-15 specify TC, DRP, SRP, CRP, CAL, VAL, SCC, AC, PSR,
      PCSR, none, none, BADn, BACn, none, none.
  nnn = n if preg specifies BADn or BACn, else 000.
  See Table 8-2 on page 272 for addressing mode restrictions. An additional restriction is that
      asrc and adst may not use register direct mode if the operand is CRP, SRP, or DRP.
  fc = function code; fffff = function code field, in one of four formats:
      1bbbb - fc is a 4-bit function code value bbbb.
      01rrr - fc specifies a main processor data register Dn containing the function code.
      00000 - the main processor SFC register contains the function code.
      00001 - the main processor DFC register contains the function code.
  lev = depth to which the translation table is searched: 0 = search ATC only; 1-7 = ignore
      ATC and search up to lev levels of the translation table in memory.
  LLLL = lev field.
  mask = 4-bit function code mask value; mmmm = mask field.
  An = a main processor address register; aaa = An field.

if the processor had written fsrc. An operating system (OS) may use these instructions to force the translation information for an operand to be loaded into the ATC without actually reading or writing the operand. This might be done for diagnostic purposes or in order to prepare for a time-critical operation, such as a DMA transfer, during which extra accesses to main memory should not occur.

PFLUSH   The third group in Table 15-7 contains several flavors of PFLUSH instructions. These instructions are complementary to PLOAD in that they they *remove* (actually, invalidate) ATC entries. Although the PMMU hardware removes "old" ATC entries automatically, an OS may sometimes want to flush ATC entries explicitly for diagnostic or performance reasons.

With proper use of PFLUSH instructions, an OS can increase the probability that translation entries are found in the ATC without searching main memory, and thereby make programs run faster. For example, when a particular process terminates and returns control to the OS, the ATC entries of that process are no longer needed. Therefore, the OS can safely flush them, and free up valuable ATC space for active processes.[2]

PFLUSHA

The `PFLUSHA` instruction invalidates all of the entries in the ATC, while the remaining `PFLUSH` instructions invalidate only ATC entries whose function code field, ANDed with `mask`, matches `fc` ANDed with `mask`. The OS can use these instructions to free up ATC space selectively, for example, invalidating only ATC entries for data accesses, not code accesses.

Flushing can be done even more selectively, down to the page level. If `PFLUSH` specifies a `psrc` operand, an ATC entry will be invalidated only if its logical page number is the same as the logical page number of `psrc`.

The PMMU supports a sharing mechanism by which multiple logical pages may map into a single physical page. This mechanism is used in multiprogramming systems to avoid storing multiple copies of a shared program. Each process that uses the program, say, a text editor, has map entries that point to the single copy of the program code in memory, but each process also has a private stack and data area. In such an environment, it's usually not polite (or efficient) to flush the shared code pages when just one process terminates, because the other processes still need them. Therefore, the `PFLUSH` instruction described above does not invalidate ATC entries for shared pages. If such entries are to be invalidated, then `PFLUSHS` must be used.

PFLUSHS
PFLUSHR

When a particular user process is terminated, an OS can use the `PFLUSHR` instruction to invalidate ATC entries that came from the translation table of that process. The `msrc` operand is a quadword that is compared with the eight recently used values of CRP in the RPT. If a match is found, all unshared ATC entries that were created with this CRP (i.e., have the same task alias) are invalidated; shared entries are not affected.

PTESTR
PTESTW

An OS may use the `PTEST` instructions (`PTESTR` and `PTESTW`) in the fourth group of Table 15–7 to get information about the logical page in which an operand resides, without actually reading or writing the operand. For example, the OS may wish to determine whether the operand's page is currently resident in physical memory, or whether access is allowed at the current level of privilege. An operating system uses these instructions in the trap handler for bus error exceptions to determine the cause of the exception. The effects of `PTESTR` and `PTESTW` are almost identical, differing only in that one checks for read accessibility and the other checks for write accessibility.

---

[2]Of course, the PMMU hardware will eventually invalidate the ATC entries for a terminated process as the entries age, but probably not before unnecessarily invalidating entries for "less recently used" but still active processes. After all, if the terminated process had performed a burst of computation just before dying, then from the point of view of the ATC its entries would be very recently used and unlikely to be discarded soon.

```
15 14 13 12 11 10 9  8  7  6        3  2     0
┌──┬──┬──┬──┬──┬──┬──┬──┬──┬──┬──┬──┬──┬───────┐
│B │L │S │A │W │I │M │G │C │0 │0 │0 │0 │  N    │
└──┴──┴──┴──┴──┴──┴──┴──┴──┴──┴──┴──┴──┴───────┘
```

FIGURE 15-29   Format of the PMMU status register (PSR).

If the `lev` parameter is 0, `PTEST` gets its information from the ATC; otherwise, `lev` specifies the maximum number of levels (1–7) that may be searched to find the information in the translation tables in memory. If `PTEST` specifies an address register, An is loaded with the physical address of the last map entry, if any, that was successfully read from memory during the translation table search. In any case, `PTEST` sets or clears bits in PSR according to information derived during the address translation process. Figure 15–29 shows the layout of PSR and Table 15–8 lists the conditions that cause each bit to be set. The 3-bit N field is set to the number of levels actually searched in the translation tree. The PSR is affected only by `PTEST` instructions and `PMOVE`s to PSR.

PVALID

The `PVALID` instructions at the end of Table 15–7 are part of the PMMU's facility for supporting a finer level of privilege in user-mode programs. The first instruction compares the privilege level in the VAL register (the privilege level of a module's caller) with the *requested privilege level (RPL)* for the `psrc` operand. The RPL is contained in the high-order bits of `psrc`'s effective address. If `psrc`'s RPL specifies a greater privilege level than VAL, an MMU access level

requested privilege level (RPL)

TABLE 15-8   PMMU status bits and their meanings.

Bit	Condition	Set If
B	Bus error	A bus error occurred on the physical bus during a descriptor fetch or, if `lev` = 0, an entry was found in the ATC with its BERR bit set.
L	Limit violation	The limit field of a long descriptor was exceeded.
S	Supervisor only	A long descriptor had its S bit set but `fc` in the `PTEST` instruction did not indicate supervisor mode.
A	Access level violation	The RAL field (for `PTESTR`) or WAL field (for `PTESTW`) of a long descriptor indicated less privilege than CAL.
W	Write protected	The WP bit of a descriptor was set, or the WAL field (for `PTESTW`) of a long descriptor indicated less privilege than CAL. Set only by `PTESTW`.
I	Invalid	An invalid descriptor was encountered, B or L was set, or, if `lev` = 0, a descriptor for the specified address was not found in the ATC.
M	Modified	The page descriptor for the specified address had its M bit set.
G	Gate	The page descriptor for the specified address had its G bit set.
C	Globally shared	A long descriptor had its SG bit set.

Notes: Each bit is cleared if the listed condition is not true.

TABLE 15–9   Additional instructions of the MC68851 PMMU.

Mnemonic	Operands	Opcode Word	Description (all are privileged)
PBcc.W	addr16	1111001010CCCCCC	Branch on PMMU condition
PBcc.L	addr32	1111001011CCCCCC	Branch on PMMU condition
PScc	ddst	1111000001dddddd	Set on PMMU condition
		0000000000CCCCCC	
PDBcc	Dn,addr16	1111000001001rrr	Conditional loop primitive
		0000000000CCCCCC	
PTRAPcc		1111000001111100	Trap if PMMU condition true
		0000000000CCCCCC	
PTRAPcc.W	#tdata	1111000001111010	Trap if PMMU condition true
		0000000000CCCCCC	
PTRAPcc.L	#tdata	1111000001111011	Trap if PMMU condition true
		0000000000CCCCCC	
PSAVE	Mdst	1111000100dddddd	Save PMMU internal state
PRESTORE	Msrc	1111000101ssssss	Restore PMMU internal state

Notes: cc = PMMU condition, see next table.
  addr16 = branch target, an address within 32 Kbytes of the instruction.
  addr32 = branch target, an address anywhere in the 4-gigabyte address space.
  See Table 8–2 on page 272 for addressing mode restrictions.
  Dn = one of the main processor data registers, D0–D7.
  tdata = 16- or 32-bit immediate data for use by the trap handler, stored in the word(s)
     following the opcode and command words.
  CCCCCC = condition field, see next table.
  ssssss = Msrc field; dddddd = dst or Mdst field;

exception occurs; otherwise execution continues with the next instruction. Thus, a module can use this instruction to validate a pointer that has been passed to it, ensuring that the calling module has not fabricated a logical address containing a privilege level greater than what it is entitled to. The second PVALID instruction does the same thing, except that it compares psrc's privilege level with the privilege level indicated by the high-order bits of an address register An.

The remaining PMMU instructions are listed in Table 15–9 and work as described in Section 14.9.6. Instructions in the first part of the table test individual conditions bits in PSR, as detailed in Table 15–10.

PSAVE   The PSAVE instruction suspends any operation that the PMMU is currently performing and saves the PMMU's state on the stack. Unlike the FPU's version of this instruction, which saves only the programmer-invisible internal state, PSAVE stores both the PMMU's internal state and a subset of its programmer-visible registers. Since PSAVE is designed to be used during context switching, the registers saved are the ones likely to be modified by another process: SRP, CRP, PSR, CAL, and VAL. Additional internal state information and registers are saved depending on what the PMMU is doing:

- *Idle.* If no MMU operations are in progress and no breakpoints are enabled, 12 bytes of internal state information are saved.

TABLE 15–10   Testable conditions and their encodings in the MC68851 PMMU.

cc	CCCCCC	Branch/Set/Trap If	cc	CCCCCC	Branch/Set/Trap If
BS	000000	B set	BC	000001	B clear
LS	000010	L set	LC	000011	L clear
SS	000100	S set	SC	000101	S clear
AS	000110	A set	AC	000111	A clear
WS	001000	W set	WC	001001	W clear
IS	001010	I set	IC	001011	I clear
GS	001100	G set	GC	001101	G clear
CS	001110	C set	CC	001111	C clear

Notes: cc = symbolic designation used in mnemonics of PBcc, PDBcc, PScc, and PTRAPcc
        instructions.
       CCCCCC = 6-bit field in the command word of conditional instructions.

- *Mid-coprocessor*. If an MMU or module call operation is in progress and no breakpoints are enabled, 20 bytes of internal state information are saved.

- *Breakpoints enabled*. If one or more breakpoints are enabled, registers BAC0–7 and BAD0–7 and 20 bytes of internal state information are saved.

PRESTORE

In each case, the last word pushed onto the stack is a "format word" that indicates what was saved by PSAVE. The PRESTORE instruction uses this word to pop the information on the stack back into the appropriate registers.

15.5 MC68030 ON-CHIP MEMORY MANAGEMENT UNIT

The MC68030 has an on-chip MMU whose registers and functions are a subset of the ones provided by the MC68851 PMMU. Major omissions in the MC68030's MMU are summarized below:

- There is no root pointer table (RPT), and task aliases are not supported.

- Multiple access levels are not supported, and the MC68030 does not implement the module call and return instructions.

- Page sharing among multiple processes is not supported.

- ATC entries cannot be locked.

- Breakpoints are not supported.

- The ATC contains only 22 entries instead of 64. Since 64 entries would give better performance, where did the number "22" come from? Apparently, that's all of the room that was left on the MC68030 chip after all of its other features were laid out.

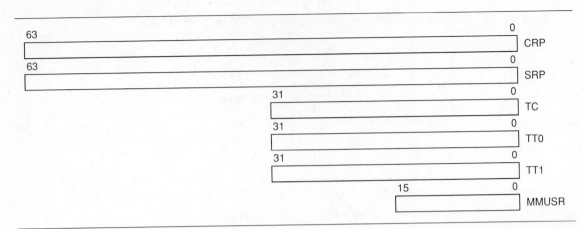

FIGURE 15–30   Programming model of the MC68030's on-chip MMU.

- Logical-to-physical address translation cannot be performed for external DMA devices, since the MC68030's external address bus contains only physical, not logical, addresses. DMA devices must use physical addresses.

Still, the MMU's address translation tables and descriptors are identical in format to the PMMU's, except for the fields relating to access levels, shared pages, and locked ATC entries, which are not used. Also, the MMU has one new feature— transparent translation of two independent blocks of logical address space into physical address space, without using the translation tables.

The MMU's programming model is shown in Figure 15–30. Compared with the PMMU's programming model, several differences are obvious:

- DRP is missing. Address translation for DMA transfers is not supported.

transparent translation registers (TT0, TT1)

- Two *transparent translation registers (TT0, TT1)* have been added. Each register specifies a block of 16 Mbytes or more of logical address space where the translation tables are ignored; instead, each logical address is used directly as a physical address.

- PCSR is missing. The features that PCSR helps to support on the PMMU (ATC locking, shared pages, task aliases) are not supported by the MMU.

MMU status register (MMUSR)

- PSR is now called the *MMU status register (MMUSR)*. The MMUSR has the same status bits as the PSR, except that it is missing the bits for features not supported by the MMU (modules, shared pages), and a bit has been added to support transparent translation.

- CAL, VAL, SCC, and AC are gone. Modules are not supported.

- BAC0–7, BAD0–7 are missing. Although the MC68030 can execute the BKPT #n instruction, skip counts are not supported as in the PMMU.

TABLE 15–11   MMU instructions in the MC68030.

Mnemonic	Operands	Command Word	Description (all are privileged)
PMOVE	preg,pdst	01pppp1100000000	Move MMU register to pdst
PMOVE	psrc,preg	01pppp0100000000	Move psrc to MMU register
PMOVEFD	psrc,preg	01pppp0000000000	Move psrc to MMU register, flush disable
PLOADR	fc,psrc	00100010000fffff	Load entry for psrc into ATC (read)
PLOADW	fc,psrc	00100000000fffff	Load entry for psrc into ATC (write)
PFLUSHA		0010010000000000	Flush all ATC entries
PFLUSH	fc,#mask	0011000mmmmfffff	Flush ATC by function code only
PFLUSH	fc,#mask,psrc	0011100mmmmfffff	Flush by function code and effective address
PTESTR	fc,psrc,#lev	100LLL10000fffff	Test psrc for read access
PTESTW	fc,psrc,#lev	100LLL00000fffff	Test psrc for write access
PTESTR	fc,psrc,#lev,An	100LLL11aaafffff	Test psrc for read, An := descriptor
PTESTW	fc,psrc,#lev,An	100LLL01aaafffff	Test psrc for write, An := descriptor

Notes: preg = one of the registers in the MMU's programming model.
      pppp specifies preg: 0000 = TC, 0010 = SRP, 0011 = CRP, 1000 = MMUSR.
      See Table 8–2 on page 272 for addressing mode restrictions.
      fc = function code; fffff = function code field, in one of four formats:
           10bbb – fc is a 3-bit function code value bbb.
           01rrr – fc specifies a main processor data register Dn containing the function code.
           00000 – fc specifies the main processor SFC register, which contains the function
               code.
           00001 – fc specifies the main processor DFC register, which contains the function
               code.
      lev = depth to which the translation table is searched: 0 = search ATC only; 1–7 = ignore
           ATC and search up to lev levels of the translation table in memory.
      LLLL = lev field.
      mask = 4-bit function code mask value; mmmm = mask field.
      An = a main processor address register; aaa = An field.

Instructions that are associated with the MC68030 PMMU are listed in Table 15–11. Each instruction uses a cpGEN-type opcode word with a coprocessor number of 0; that is, the opcode word is 1111000000ssssss. Missing from the list are the PMMU instructions that support modules (PVALID), shared pages (PFLUSHS), and the RPT (PFLUSHR). Also missing are all of the conditional instructions, and PSAVE and PRESTORE. During context switches, MMU registers must be saved and restored with individual PMOVE instructions.

15.6 MC6850 ASYNCHRONOUS COMMUNICATIONS INTERFACE ADAPTER

universal asynchronous receiver/ transmitter (UART)

Serial communication links are often used to connect computers to display terminals or to other computers, as explained in Appendix B. A specialized I/O interface is used to transmit and receive data on a serial communication link. Many manufacturers of integrated circuits offer a complete asynchronous serial interface on a single LSI chip, called a *universal asynchronous receiver/transmitter*

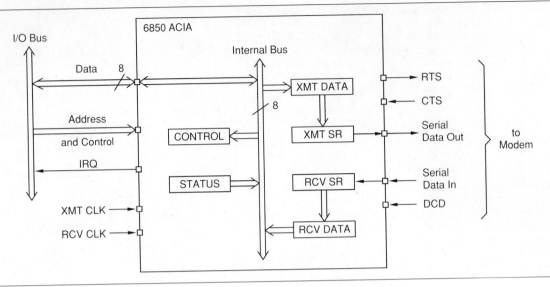

FIGURE 15–31   Simplified block diagram of the Motorola MC6850 ACIA.

(UART) or similar name. Most single-chip microcomputers have one or more built-in UARTs.

asynchronous communications interface adapter (ACIA)

The Motorola MC6850, which Motorola calls an *asynchronous communications interface adapter (ACIA)*, is a simple LSI serial I/O interface circuit that is often used in 68000 systems. A block diagram of the ACIA is shown in Figure 15–31. On one side, the ACIA can transmit data and receive data on an asynchronous, full-duplex serial link at speeds up to 19.2 Kbps or more. On the other side, the ACIA connects to a processor's I/O bus.

As shown in Figure 15–32, the I/O programming model of the ACIA has two 8-bit input ports and two 8-bit output ports. In a typical system configuration, the STATUS input port and the CONTROL output port have the same memory address or port number (e.g., $010040 for the console ACIA in the Motorola MC68000 Educational Computer Board). Likewise, the RCV DATA input port and the XMT DATA output port have the same port number, usually near the STATUS/CONTROL port number (e.g., $010042). Characteristics of the ports are described in the following subsections.

15.6.1   Control Port

CONTROL reset

In order to use the ACIA to send and receive serial data, a program must first set up the operating mode of the ACIA in the *CONTROL* port. Sending a byte of $03 to the ACIA CONTROL port *resets* the ACIA, clearing out any previous operating mode and disabling the ACIA from sending or receiving data until a new mode is set up. The new mode is established by sending an appropriate bit pattern to CONTROL, as detailed in Figure 15–32 and explained below.

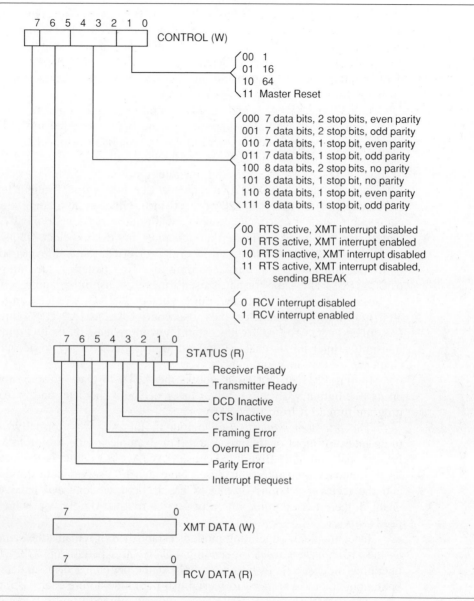

FIGURE 15–32   I/O programming model of the Motorola MC6850 ACIA.

The transmitting and receiving bit rates of the ACIA are established by a combination of external clock inputs (*XMT CLK* and *RCV CLK* in Figure 15–31) and a programmable divider ratio. The ACIA transmits serial data at a bit rate equal to the incoming XMT CLK frequency divided by 1, 16, or 64, according

XMT CLK
RCV CLK

to the bit pattern loaded into bits 1–0 of CONTROL. While receiving, the ACIA uses a bit-sampling procedure described in Appendix B. The sampling rate for this procedure is equal to the RCV CLK frequency, and the number of samples per bit equals 1, 16, or 64 as determined by bits 1–0 of CONTROL. The same divider ratio is used for transmitting and receiving. In practice, only divider ratios of 16 and 64 are useful for receiving.

Usually the XMT CLK and RCV CLK inputs are both connected to the same clock source. For example, suppose they are both connected to a 153.6 KHz clock. Then a programmed divider ratio of 16 would allow the ACIA to transmit and receive at 9600 bps, while a ratio of 64 would allow it to operate at 2400 bps. To operate the ACIA at a different bit rate, the user would have to modify the hardware to connect the XMT CLK and RCV CLK inputs to a different frequency, for example, 19.2 KHz for 1200 or 300 bps. Older systems may make these connections with a mechanical switch, while newer systems typically have an output port to control hardware that generates any desired clock frequencies.

The ACIA can transmit and receive 7 or 8 data bits, an even, odd, or no parity bit, and 1 or 2 stop bits, according to a 3-bit pattern loaded into bits 4–2 of CONTROL. The same format is used for both transmitting and receiving.

Bits 6–5 of CONTROL determine whether the ACIA requests an interrupt after transmitting a character; they also control the ACIA's RTS output signal (described later). The ACIA places an interrupt request on its IRQ output if the transmitter interrupt is enabled and the transmitter is ready to accept another character for transmission.

Setting bit 7 of CONTROL allows the ACIA to place an interrupt request on its IRQ output when the receiver has received a character and is ready for a program to read it from RCV DATA.

interrupt request (IRQ)

The *interrupt request (IRQ)* output of the ACIA is normally connected to an interrupt input of the processor. For example, in the Motorola MC68000 Educational Computer Board, the console ACIA's IRQ output is connected to the level-5 autovectored interrupt input. Note that IRQ serves both the transmitter and the receiver sections of the ACIA. If both sections can have interrupts enabled, then it is up to the interrupt service routine to figure out which section needs service.

Once the ACIA operating mode is established, it remains the same as long as the ACIA is not reset by sending CONTROL a pattern of $03. Thus, the operating mode needs to be set up only at the beginning of a sequence of I/O operations; there is no need to reestablish the mode before each operation.

The CONTROL port is write-only; attempts to read from it do not return the last value written into it. Instead, they return the current value of the STATUS port, described later.

15.6.2 Transmitter Data Port

XMT DATA

Once the ACIA operating mode has been established, the processor may transmit characters to the serial data link through the ACIA's *XMT DATA* output port.

Unlike the generalized output interface described in Section 10.3.3 the ACIA has no "XMT GO" bit; a new output operation is begun each time the processor writes a character into XMT DATA.

XMT SR

As shown in Figure 15–31, the transmitted data is double buffered. Initially, after the ACIA is reset, both XMT DATA and *XMT SR* are empty. When the processor writes the first transmitted character into XMT DATA, the ACIA immediately transfers the contents of XMT DATA into XMT SR, a shift register from which the character is shifted into the serial output line with the prescribed format and speed. Since XMT DATA is now empty, the processor may immediately place a second character into XMT DATA. However, the ACIA will not transfer this second character into XMT SR until the first character has been fully transmitted, a format- and speed-dependent wait. In general, the processor can

Transmitter Ready

determine when XMT DATA is empty only by checking the *Transmitter Ready* bit in the STATUS port.

15.6.3 Receiver Data Port

Unlike the generalized input interface described in Section 10.3.1, the ACIA has no "RCV GO" bit. Once the ACIA operating mode has been established in CONTROL, the ACIA immediately starts looking for input characters in the prescribed format.

RCV SR
RCV DATA

Like transmitted data, received data is double buffered. Incoming serial data bytes are assembled and their format checked in the *RCV SR* shift register. Once a complete character has been assembled, it is transferred into *RCV DATA*, where the processor may read it at its leisure. In the meantime, RCV SR is

overrun

available to assemble another incoming character. An *overrun* error occurs only if the processor fails to read the character presently in RCV DATA before a second character is completely assembled in RCV SR.

Receiver Ready

In general, the processor can determine that a new character is present in RCV DATA by checking the *Receiver Ready* bit in STATUS. The ACIA sets Receiver Ready each time that a new character appears in RCV DATA, and clears it each time the processor reads RCV DATA.

15.6.4 Status Port

STATUS

Input/output programs can test the bits in the ACIA's *STATUS* port to determine if operations have been completed and if any errors have occurred.

Bit 1 of STATUS is the Transmitter Ready bit. The ACIA sets this bit on reset and whenever XMT DATA is empty, indicating that the processor may write XMT DATA with a character for the ACIA to transmit. The ACIA clears this bit when the processor writes a new character into XMT DATA. (The bit is also forced to 0 if the CTS input is inactive. The CTS and DCD modem control inputs and status bits are discussed in the next subsection.)

Likewise, bit 0 is the Receiver Ready bit; when this bit is set, RCV DATA contains a new character that a program may read. This bit is cleared on reset and whenever the processor reads RCV DATA. (The bit is also forced to 0 if the DCD input is inactive.)

Three possible receiving errors are indicated by bits 4–6 of STATUS. The *Framing Error* bit is set if a received character does not have the proper number of stop bits (i.e., if a space is detected in the serial input during the stop-bit time). *Parity Error* is set if the received serial input does not have the proper parity. Both of these bits are updated each time that the ACIA puts a new received character into RCV DATA. An *Overrun Error* is set if one or more additional characters are fully received before the processor reads the character presently in RCV DATA. This bit is cleared each time that the processor reads RCV DATA.

Framing Error

Parity Error

Overrun Error

Bit 7 of STATUS is 1 if either the transmitter section or the receiver section of the ACIA has placed an interrupt request on the IRQ output. An interrupt request is made if the transmitter or receiver interrupt has been enabled and the corresponding ready bit in STATUS is 1. (An interrupt request is also made if an active-to-inactive transition is detected on DCD.)

15.6.5   Modem Control Lines

modem control line

request to send (RTS)

In addition to the serial data input and output lines, the ACIA has three *modem control lines* that may be used to indicate or detect certain conditions when the ACIA is connected to a modem. The *request to send (RTS)* output from the ACIA to the modem is intended to indicate that the ACIA would like to send characters to the modem. If the modem has established a connection to another modem and it is in a state in which it can transmit characters, it responds to RTS by activating the *clear to send (CTS)* ACIA input signal.

clear to send (CTS)

The ACIA will not set the Transmitter Ready bit in STATUS while the CTS input signal is inactive. Thus, RTS and CTS form a "handshake" by which a modem or other device can prevent the ACIA from sending characters until it is ready for them. For example, the modem can prevent data transmission until a valid telephone connection has been established. The CTS bit in STATUS is 1 whenever the CTS input signal is inactive.

data carrier detect (DCD)

The *data carrier detect (DCD)* ACIA input signal is normally connected to a modem output signal that indicates whether the modem has detected the presence of another modem at the far end of a telephone connection. The DCD bit in STATUS is set to 1 whenever the DCD input signal changes from active to inactive. This event causes an interrupt request to be placed on the ACIA's IRQ output. The DCD status bit is not cleared until the processor reads STATUS and RCV DATA or resets the ACIA. This convention is useful with telephone links, where a program should detect a loss of the received signal, for example, if the far-end party hangs up.

When the ACIA is connected directly to a terminal without going through a modem, the connections of the modem control leads are system dependent. Quite often the CTS and DCD ACIA inputs are wired so they are always active, and the RTS output is unused.

Many inexpensive printers and other devices may accept data at speeds as high as 19.2 Kbps (approximately 2000 characters per second), even though they can only physically process much lower data rates, say 100 characters per second. For example, a printer may accept characters at the higher speed and store them in an internal buffer, until the buffer becomes full. Such a printer typically has an output signal that indicates that its input buffer is full. If this signal is connected to the ACIA's CTS input, the ACIA is automatically prevented from transmitting additional characters until some of the previous characters have been physically printed and there is once again space in the buffer.

15.7   MC68230 PARALLEL INTERFACE AND TIMER

parallel interface

While serial interfaces are used to connect computers to remote devices, *parallel interfaces* are most often used to connect to local devices, such as switches, lamps, relays, motors, sensors, and data acquisition and conversion devices. A parallel interface typically has an 8- or 16-bit connection to the outside world that can be directly read or written by the processor as an I/O port. Most single-chip microcomputers have one or more built-in parallel ports.

timer/counter

Another important peripheral device is the *timer/counter*. When such a device counts the ticks of a free-running clock, it measures elapsed time and is

timer

called a *timer*; when it counts external events that occur at irregular intervals, it is

counter

called a *counter*. Timer/counters are small peripherals—one or more can be built into a single integrated circuit—and so timer/counters are usually provided on a computer's main printed-circuit board. Also, most single-chip microcomputers have one or more built-in timer/counters.

MC68230 parallel interface and timer (PI/T)

The Motorola *MC68230 parallel interface and timer (PI/T)* contains three 8-bit parallel ports and a 24-bit timer/counter. Its block diagram is shown in Figure 15–33. Its *parallel ports A, B, and C* can be configured in a variety of

parallel ports A, B, and C

input, output, and bidirectional modes; in fact, port bits may be individually configured as inputs or outputs.

handshake lines H1–H4

The *handshake lines H1–H4* are used in most modes to implement handshake protocols with external devices connected to ports A, B, and C, for the purposes discussed in Section 10.3; However, H1–H4 can also be used in certain modes as general input or output lines.

Port C is special; instead of being used for general I/O, certain pins may be individually enabled to perform the special functions listed in Table 15–12. For example, PC5/$\overline{\text{PIRQ}}$ may be configured as an output that generates an interrupt request when an I/O transfer completes on port A or B. In simple 68000 systems, this signal is used as an autovectored interrupt request. In more complex systems, PC6/$\overline{\text{PIACK}}$ is also configured, as an input; when it sees an interrupt acknowledge signal from the processor, the PI/T supplies the interrupt vector. For timer interrupts, PC3/$\overline{\text{TOUT}}$ and PC7/$\overline{\text{TIACK}}$ have similar configuration options.

loopback

The PI/T's programming model has 23 I/O registers and is shown in Figure 15–34. Many of the registers are read/write and have *loopback*; that

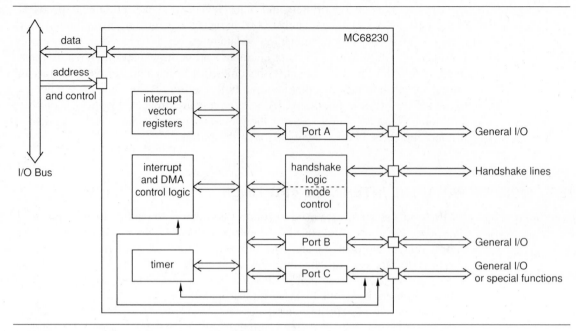

FIGURE 15–33   Simplified block diagram of the Motorola MC68230 PI/T.

is, the last value written to the register can be read back at the same location. However, five of the registers have independent read and write operations, and five are read-only, as indicated in the figure.

The addresses of the I/O registers depend on the system hardware design. In a system with a 16-bit memory and I/O bus, such as a 68000, a register's address is equal to the sum of a base address for the PI/T plus two times the offset shown in Figure 15–34. In the Motorola MC68000 Educational Computer Board, the base address is $010001 (the PI/T is attached to the low-order byte of the 16-bit data bus).

TABLE 15–12   Special functions of port C I/O pins.

Pin	Name	Special Function
7	PC7/$\overline{\text{TIACK}}$	Timer interrupt acknowledge input
6	PC6/$\overline{\text{PIACK}}$	Port interrupt acknowledge input
5	PC5/$\overline{\text{PIRQ}}$	Port interrupt request output
4	PC4/$\overline{\text{DMAREQ}}$	DMA request output
3	PC3/$\overline{\text{TOUT}}$	Timer state or interrupt request output
2	PC2/$\overline{\text{TIN}}$	Timer enable or clock input
1	PC1	None
0	PC0	None

Register	Offset	7	6	5	4	3	2	1	0	
port general control PGCR	$00	port mode control		H34 enable	H12 enable	H4 sense	H3 sense	H2 sense	H1 sense	
port service request PSRR	$01	unused	SVCRQ select		IPF select		port interrupt priority control			
port A data direction PADDR	$02	bit 7	bit 6	bit 5	bit 4	bit 3	bit 2	bit 1	bit 0	
port B data direction PBDDR	$03	bit 7	bit 6	bit 5	bit 4	bit 3	bit 2	bit 1	bit 0	
port C data direction PCDDR	$04	bit 7	bit 6	bit 5	bit 4	bit 3	bit 2	bit 1	bit 0	
port interrupt vector PIVR	$05	interrupt vector number						unused		
port A control PACR	$06	port A submode		H2 control			H2 interrupt enable	H1 SVCRQ enable	H1 status control	
port B control PBCR	$07	port B submode		H4 control			H4 interrupt enable	H3 SVCRQ enable	H3 status control	
port A data PADR	$08	bit 7	bit 6	bit 5	bit 4	bit 3	bit 2	bit 1	bit 0	†
port B data PBDR	$09	bit 7	bit 6	bit 5	bit 4	bit 3	bit 2	bit 1	bit 0	†
port A alternate PAAR	$0A	bit 7	bit 6	bit 5	bit 4	bit 3	bit 2	bit 1	bit 0	*
port B alternate PBAR	$0B	bit 7	bit 6	bit 5	bit 4	bit 3	bit 2	bit 1	bit 0	*
port C data PCDR	$0C	bit 7	bit 6	bit 5	bit 4	bit 3	bit 2	bit 1	bit 0	†
port status PSR	$0D	H4 level	H3 level	H2 level	H1 level	H4S	H3S	H2S	H1S	†
timer control TCR	$10	TOUT/TIACK control			Z D control	unused	clock control		timer enable	
timer interrupt vector TIVR	$11	bit 7	bit 6	bit 5	bit 4	bit 3	bit 2	bit 1	bit 0	
counter preload high CPRH	$13	bit 23	bit 22	bit 21	bit 20	bit 19	bit 18	bit 17	bit 16	
counter preload middle CPRM	$14	bit 15	bit 14	bit 13	bit 12	bit 11	bit 10	bit 9	bit 8	
counter preload low CPRL	$15	bit 7	bit 6	bit 5	bit 4	bit 3	bit 2	bit 1	bit 0	
counter high CNTRH	$17	bit 23	bit 22	bit 21	bit 20	bit 19	bit 18	bit 17	bit 16	*
counter middle CNTRM	$18	bit 15	bit 14	bit 13	bit 12	bit 11	bit 10	bit 9	bit 8	*
counter low CNTRL	$19	bit 7	bit 6	bit 5	bit 4	bit 3	bit 2	bit 1	bit 0	*
timer status TSR	$1A	unused							ZDS	†

† read operations do not necessarily return the last value written
* read-only port

FIGURE 15–34   Programming model of the MC68230 PI/T.

PGCR
PSRR
PACR
PBCR

PSR

        Two registers, *PGCR* and *PSRR*, control the general configuration of the PI/T's three parallel ports, including port modes, handshake operation, and interrupt and DMA support. Two more registers, *PACR* and *PBCR*, control the specific configuration of ports A and B. When ports are configured to generate vectored interrupts, the vector number programmed in PIVR is given to the processor during interrupt acknowledge bus cycles. A status register, *PSR*, can be read to monitor activity on the handshake lines.

PADDR
PBDDR
PCDDR
PADR
PBDR
PCDR

Each port has an associated data direction register, *PADDR*, *PBDDR*, or *PCDDR*, that configures each of its bits to be either an input or an output. Each port also has a data register, *PADR*, *PBDR*, or *PCDR*, that is used to read or write values on the port pins. If a pin is configured as an input, reading the corresponding data register bit returns the value of the pin (possibly latched by a handshake signal), while writing the data register bit has no effect on the pin. If a pin is configured as an output, writing the data register bit affects the output value on the pin (possibly after a handshake), and reading the data register returns the last value written to it. Ports A and B also have alternate read-only registers, *PAAR* and *PBAR*, that always contain the instantaneous value of the port's pins, independent of their data direction and handshake status.

PAAR
PBAR
CNTRH
CNTRM
CNTRL
TCR

The remaining registers in Figure 15–34 are associated with the 24-bit timer/counter, which may be read as three 8-bit ports *CNTRH*, *CNTRM*, and *CNTRL*. Four timer/counter operating modes are configured by bits 2–1 of *TCR*:

00 *System timer.* The counter is decremented on every 32nd tick of the system clock. The system clock frequency is, of course, system dependent. For example, the Motorola MC68000 Educational Computer Board has a system clock frequency of 4 MHz, and so its PI/T counter would be decremented once every 8 microseconds in this mode.

01 *System timer with enable.* This is similar to the previous mode, except that the PC2/TIN pin is used as an enable input. The counter is decremented only if the PC2/TIN pin is 1. This mode is useful for timing the duration of an external signal applied to the PC2/TIN pin.

10 *Counter with 5-bit prescaler.* The PI/T looks for input pulses on the PC2/TIN pin. On every 32nd pulse, it decrements the counter. This mode is useful for counting external events that occur at a very high rate, where the low-order five bits of the total count are insignificant.

11 *Counter.* The PI/T looks for input pulses on the PC2/TIN pin. It decrements the counter once for every pulse received. This mode is useful for counting external events.

In each mode, bit 0 of TCR must be 1 for the counter to be decremented; otherwise, the counter maintains its current value. Bit 4 of TCR determines what happens when the counter is decremented to 0. If this bit is 0, the next tick loads the counter with the contents of the 24-bit preload register (*CPRH*, *CPRM*, *CPRL*); otherwise, the counter "rolls over" to $FFFFFF. Bits 7–5 configure the PC3/TOUT output and PC7/$\overline{\text{TIACK}}$ input:

CPRH
CPRM
CPRL

00x PC3/TOUT and PC7/$\overline{\text{TIACK}}$ are not used by the timer/counter.

01x PC3/TOUT is used as a square-wave timer output—its value is complemented each time that the counter is decremented to 0. PC7/$\overline{\text{TIACK}}$ is not used by the timer/counter.

101 PC3/TOUT is used as a timer interrupt request output—it requests an interrupt each time that the counter is decremented to 0. PC7/$\overline{\text{TIACK}}$ is used as an input for interrupt acknowledge bus cycles—when the processor signals such a cycle, the PI/T gives it an interrupt vector that the programmer *TIVR*   has written into *TIVR*.

100 Similar to the preceding mode, but the interrupt request output is disabled.

111,110 Similar to modes 101 and 100, but supporting autovectored interrupts only. PC7/$\overline{\text{TIACK}}$ is not used by the timer/counter.

When programmed with appropriate values in the control and preload registers, the timer/counter can interrupt the processor at regular intervals. This is very useful in software environments, such as timesharing systems, that must switch among multiple processes at regular intervals to guarantee that each process receives its "fair share" of processing time.

ZDS   The timer/counter can also be used in a polled I/O environment. The *ZDS*
TSR   bit in *TSR* is set to 1 whenever the counter is decremented to 0. Thus, a busy-wait I/O routine may poll ZDS to determine that a certain time has elapsed. The ZDS bit is "sticky;" it is cleared to 0 only when the timer/counter is disabled or when a 1 is written into it (that's right, a 1).

A program may read the counter registers (CNTRH, CNTRM, and CNTRL) at any time. However, the values that are read may be inconsistent if the counter is enabled. This situation is somewhat analogous to what we described for a program-controlled timer/counter in Section 12.4.1. In the present situation, we have a *hardware* process—the PI/T chip itself—that, if enabled, may update the counter between programmed reads of the individual counter bytes.

Actually, the present situation is made worse by a small but nonzero probability that the hardware may update a byte precisely when we are reading it. That is, a byte could change from $00 to $FF as we are reading it, and the processor could interpret this as any value in between, say, $95. Thus, the counter must be disabled for the current count to be read reliably. If the counting rate is slow enough, an acceptable and practical alternative is to read the counter bytes several times, until identical values are obtained.

REFERENCES

The structure, use, and performance of caches is generally covered in books on advanced computer architecture. One of the best references on this topic is Harold Stone's *High-Performance Computer Architecture* (Addison-Wesley, 1987). Caches are also covered in some but not all introductory books, including *Computer Organization* by V. C. Hamacher, Z. G. Vranesic, and S. G. Zaky (McGraw-Hill, 1984, 2nd ed.). The performance gains that are obtained with the MC68020 and MC68030 caches can be estimated using information in the corresponding processor user manuals from Motorola.

The idea of having a small, fast memory to store the most frequently used instructions and data, embodied in the MC68020 and MC68030 caches, is not a new one. The first implementation of this idea is generally credited to the Atlas computer at Manchester University, as described in a 1962 paper by T. Kilburn, D. B. G. Edwards, M. J. Lanigan, and F. H. Sumner, "One-Level Storage System," reprinted in *Computer Structures: Principles and Examples* by D. P. Siewiorek, C. G. Bell, and A. Newell (McGraw-Hill, 1982).

translation lookaside buffer (TLB)

Likewise, the idea of translating logical to physical addresses using translation tables stored in main memory, as embodied in the PMMU, is nothing new. Early mainframe computers, such as the IBM 360/67, implemented this idea, including an address translation cache, which they called a *translation lookaside buffer (TLB)*. For example, see *Computer Structures* or Richard W. Watson's *Timesharing System Design Concepts* (McGraw-Hill, 1970).

Motorola manuals are available for all of the ICs discussed in this chapter, of course. References for the MC68020 and MC68030 processor chips were listed in the previous chapter. The FPU is described in *MC68881 Floating-Point Coprocessor User's Manual* (Motorola publ. MC68881UM/AD, 1985), and the PMMU in *MC68851 Paged Memory Management Unit User's Manual* (Prentice-Hall, 1986). The MC68030's on-chip MMU is described in a chapter of the MC68030 user's manual. Motorola also publishes data sheets for the MC6850 ACIA and the MC68230 PI/T (publ. ADI-860-R2).

EXERCISES

15.1 Draw a block diagram that shows the structure of a 2-way set associative cache.

15.2 Suppose that part of an application program is stored in the MC68020 instruction cache, and the operating system overwrites the program in main memory with a new one. Describe the problems that can occur and how they can be avoided.

15.3 Write a realistic program fragment (one that does something useful) that has much poorer performance with a write-around policy than with a pure write-back policy. The program should repeatedly write to a particular variable, but seldom or never read it. Comment on the likelihood of encountering program fragments with similar behavior in "typical" applications.

15.4 In the MC68030 data cache, the write policy for misses on byte, word, and unaligned longwords when WA = 1 clears the corresponding V bit(s), but does not update the tag(s). Yet it would be more efficient not to affect the cache at all on such misses—the information already in the cache remains valid. Why was this peculiar policy adopted? (You'll have to study the Motorola MC68030 reference manual to figure out the answer.)

15.5 When the MC68881 FPU is used with an MC68020 processor, how does the instruction FMOVE.W FP1,D1 affect the high-order word of D1?

15.6 As defined by the MC68881 FPU, a number in packed decimal real format has somewhat less precision than a number in extended real format. Does this imply that any real number that can be represented exactly in packed decimal real format can also be represented exactly in extended real format? Prove your answer if yes; give counterexamples if no.

15.7 In what ways is the FMOVECR instruction more efficient than an FMOVE with immediate addressing for the src operand? How is your answer affected by the actual value of the immediate data (e.g., 1 vs π)?

15.8 Write an assembly language program for an MC68020-based computer, such as the Macintosh II, that contains an MC68881 FPU. Your program should emulate a simple hand-held calculator, using the numeric keypad of a keyboard for input, and a display for output.

15.9 In the MC68851 PMMU, why is the SG bit normally set in the SRP and DRP?

15.10 Why are type-2 descriptors in the PMMU translation tree most appropriate for memory-resident programs and data that are loaded into memory at system initialization and never swapped out?

15.11 Adapt the keyboard and display drivers in Table 10–5 on page 374 for use with the MC6850.

15.12 After a hardware reset, what are the initial values of each of the registers in the MC68230 PI/T? Explain the rationale for each value.

15.13 Devise an algorithm for reliably reading the 24-bit counter value in the MC68230 PI/T "on the fly," that is, while the counter is enabled. In designing your algorithm, try to make it run as fast as possible, and try to make it work with a timer/counter that is being updated by the hardware by a very fast rate. Describe the circumstances, if any, under which your algorithm fails to return a correct result. (Taking too long or not returning at all would be considered such a failure.)

15.14 Write a "reaction timer" program for the Motorola MC68000 Educational Computer Board that makes use of the MC6850 ACIA and the MC68230 PI/T. After a random wait, the program displays a character on the system console and measures the time that it takes for the user to react by typing a character. The reaction time should be measured to the nearest millisecond and adjusted for transmission time on the serial link and other delays in the display and keyboard that aren't part of the user's reaction time (what are they?). The adjusted reaction time should then be displayed.

CHAPTER 16

An Accumulator Architecture: The Motorola 6809

MC6800

Motorola's *MC6800* was one of the most popular processors of the "microprocessor revolution" of the 1970s. The MC6800 has two 8-bit accumulators, condition bits, and 16-bit index register, stack pointer, and program counter. The MC6809 is Motorola's successor to the MC6800; it extends the original MC6800 architecture by including more registers, instructions, and addressing modes.

The MC6809 integrated circuit contains a CPU only; a system designer must add external memory and I/O to get a complete computer. A number of "turnkey" systems that use the MC6809 CPU are available from different manufacturers. These include Motorola's EXORciser II development system and the Tandy TRS-80 Color Computers.

There are a few intermediate members of the Motorola 6800 family besides the the original MC6800 and the advanced MC6809. The *MC6801* has the same registers and instructions as the MC6800 plus several additional instructions. The *MC6805* is intended for microcontroller applications; it has MC6800-type instructions but only one accumulator, plus it has extensive bit-manipulation instructions. A more recent addition to the family is the *MC68HC11* single-chip microcomputer; it has a superset of the MC6800 registers and instruction set, plus 8 Kbytes of on-chip ROM, 256 bytes of on-chip RAM, and several on-chip peripheral interface circuits. In this chapter, we focus only on the MC6809; other family members are easily understood by anyone familiar with the MC6809, which we'll now refer to simply as the *6809*.

MC6801

MC6805

MC68HC11

6809

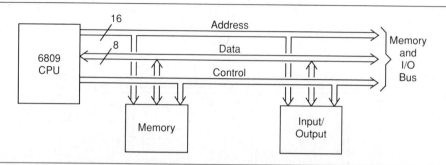

FIGURE 16–1   Structure of a computer that uses the 6809 processor chip.

16.1   BASIC ORGANIZATION

16.1.1   Computer Structure

The basic structure of a 6809-based computer is shown in Figure 16–1. Like the 68000, the 6809 communicates with memory and peripherals using a single memory and I/O bus. This bus contains an 8-bit data bus, a 16-bit address bus, and various control signals, so that the maximum memory size is 2^{16} (64K) bytes. A system designer can use a memory mapping unit such as the Motorola MC6829 to increase the size of the physical memory connected to the CPU, but a program cannot access more than 64 Kbytes at one time.

The 6809 has no I/O instructions, and so it must use memory-mapped I/O. The system designer must allocate a portion of the total memory address space for I/O interface registers. Usually addresses in the upper regions of the address space are used. The 6809 processor supports a three-level vectored priority interrupt system. Additional sublevels and vectors may be provided within each level by external hardware, a system-dependent characteristic.

16.1.2   Processor Programming Model

A, B
X, Y
S, U
PC
DP
CC
D

address register

The internal organization of a 6809 processor is shown in Figure 16–2 and the corresponding programming model is shown in Figure 16–3. There are two 8-bit accumulators (*A* and *B*), two 16-bit index registers (*X* and *Y*), two 16-bit stack pointers (*S* and *U*), a 16-bit program counter (*PC*), an 8-bit direct-page register (*DP*), and a set of 8 condition bits (*CC*). Most instructions manipulate 8-bit data, and the 6809 is considered to be an 8-bit machine. However, some instructions manipulate the two accumulators A and B as a single 16-bit unit called *D* (using A as the most significant byte). Also, several operations are provided for manipulating 16-bit quantities (usually addresses) in the index registers and stack pointers (which we'll call *address registers*).

Of the two stack pointers, S is the system stack pointer—it is automatically used by the processor for pushing and popping registers during subroutine and interrupt calls and returns. The other, U, is a user stack pointer—the programmer

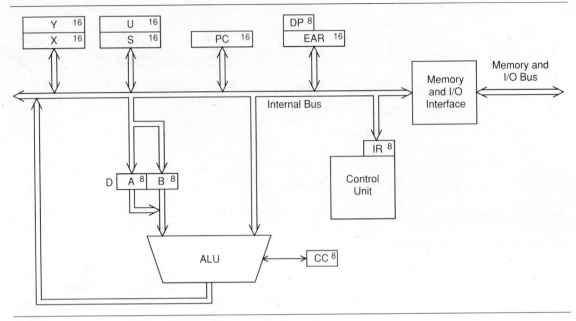

FIGURE 16–2   Internal organization of a 6809 processor.

can use it to create another stack. The processor has special instructions for pushing and popping registers in either stack.

Although the 6809 has two stack pointers, it does *not* have user and supervisor modes like the 68000. In fact, typical programs use U more often as a third index register than as a stack pointer—all addressing modes that use the index registers (X and Y) can use either stack pointer (S or U) as well.

The 6809's N, Z, V, and C condition bits are similar in function to the 68000's. The half-carry bit H is used in BCD operations, as described in Section 8.11. The remaining bits in CC are used in conjunction with interrupt processing, as discussed in Section 16.6.2.

16.1.3 Instruction Formats

A typical 6809 instruction specifies an operation (add, subtract, etc.) and one of several basic addressing modes (inherent, immediate, absolute, or indexed). This combination of operation and addressing mode is encoded in the instruction's opcode.

Most 6809 instructions have an 8-bit opcode. However, the 6809 has more than 256 distinct operation/addressing mode combinations. Therefore, some instructions using 16-bit (2-byte) opcodes, where the first byte is $10 or $11, and the second byte specifies the exact instruction. This encoding scheme easily accommodates the 6809's 268 distinct opcodes.

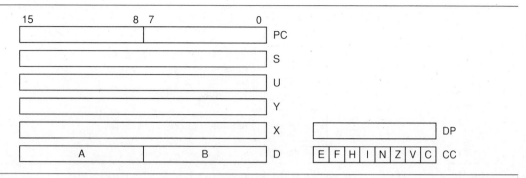

FIGURE 16–3   Programming model for the 6809.

Up to three additional bytes are used with some addressing modes to hold addressing information. With a 2-byte opcode, this yields instructions that are up to five bytes long.

16.2 ASSEMBLY LANGUAGE

Motorola's standard assembly language for the 6809 is similar to the 68000's. However, most of the assembler directives have different names, and of course all of the instruction mnemonics are different. Important Motorola 6809 assembler directives are summarized in Table 16–1.

Most double-operand instructions in 6809 assembly language have their operands in the order "dst,src" since the destination operand is part of the instruction mnemonic and therefore appears first, for example:

```
LDA        SOURCE          A := SOURCE;
```

However, store and transfer instructions have the opposite operand order:

```
STA     DEST          DEST := A;
TFR     A,B           B := A;
```

TABLE 16–1   Motorola 6809 assembly language directives.

		Examples		
Name	Label	Opcode	Operand	Effect
ORG		ORG	$4000	Set starting address of program.
EQU	CR	EQU	$0D	Equate symbol with 16-bit value.
FCB	CBYT	FCB	17,$F9,-1	Fill memory with constant bytes.
FDB	CWRD	FDB	-789,$E800,CAT	Fill memory with constant words.
FCC	STRG	FCC	/ABCDEFG/	Fill memory bytes with ASCII characters.
RMB	TBYT	RMB	10	Reserve memory bytes.
END		END	START	End of assembly; specify starting address.

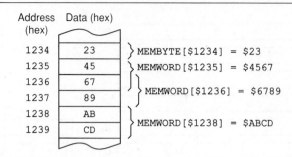

FIGURE 16–4   Memory addressing in the 6809.

16.3   ADDRESSING

inherent
 addressing

Many 6809 instructions use *inherent addressing*, in which the operand, generally a processor register, is specified in the instruction opcode itself. For example, the INCA instruction (opcode $4C) increments accumulator A, while INCB (opcode $5C) increments accumulator B.

word

Other 6809 instructions specify operands in memory. The 6809 memory is byte-addressable, and most instructions specify 1-byte operands. Some instructions access two bytes as a unit—the *word*. In the 6809, a word may start at an even or odd address and occupies two consecutive bytes. The most significant byte of a word is stored in the lower-numbered address, as in the 68000. These concepts are illustrated in Figure 16–4.

The 6809 has a very "regular" instruction set because any instruction that specifies an operand in memory may do so using *any* addressing mode that makes sense. Thus, the addressing modes in this section may be used with just about any operation that specifies an operand in memory. Table 16–2 summarizes the 6809's addressing modes and assembly language notation for each mode.

16.3.1   Immediate

immediate
 addressing

In *immediate addressing*, the instruction contains the operand. This is the only 6809 addressing mode that cannot be used with all memory operations, since it makes no sense with instructions that test a value (the test outcome would always be the same) or store a result (the result would have to be stored in the instruction). Thus, immediate mode can be used with load and add, but not with store, test, increment, rotate, or any single-operand instruction.

#

An immediate operand may be one or two bytes, as needed by the operation. For example, LDA #$15 loads A with an 8-bit operand $15; as shown in Figure 16–5(a), the instruction has two bytes. In Figure 16–5(b), the three-byte instruction LDX #$1234 loads X with a 16-bit operand $1234. In both cases, an assembly language program denotes an immediate operand with the prefix "#"; the assembler knows from the opcode (LDA or LDX) whether an 8-bit or

TABLE 16–2   Memory addressing modes and assembly language notation for the 6809.

Mode	Notation	Next Byte(s)	Operand
Immediate	`#n`	`n[lo]` or `n[hi],n[lo]`	`n`
Absolute	`n` or `>n`	`n[hi],n[lo]`	`MEM[n]`
Direct page	`n` or `<n`	`n[lo]`	`MEM[n[lo]+256*DP]`
Register indirect	`,RR`	`PB`	`MEM[RR]`
Based or indexed (16-bit disp.)	`n,RR` or `>n,RR`	`PB,n[hi],n[lo]`	`MEM[n+RR]`
Based (8-bit displacement)	`n,RR` or `<n,RR`	`PB,n[lo]`	`MEM[xtnd(n[lo])+RR]`
Based (5-bit displacement)	`n,RR`	`PB`	`MEM[xtnd(n[so])+RR]`
Based indexed (16-bit disp.)	`D,RR`	`PB`	`MEM[D+RR]`
Based indexed (8-bit disp.)	`A,RR` or `B,RR`	`PB`	`MEM[xtnd(A or B)+RR]`
Relative (16-bit displacement)	`n,PCR` or `>n,PCR`	`PB,(n-PLC)[hi],` `(n-PLC)[lo]`	`MEM[n]`
Relative (8-bit displacement)	`n,PCR` or `<n,PCR`	`PB,(n-PLC)[lo]`	`MEM[n]`
Auto-increment (by 1 or 2)	`,RR+` or `,RR++`	`PB`	`MEM[RR]`, then `RR := RR + 1 or 2`
Auto-decrement (by 1 or 2)	`,-RR` or `,--RR`	`PB`	`RR := RR - 1 or 2,` then `MEM[RR]`

Notes: n denotes the 16-bit two's-complement value of an expression.
   `MEM[x]` denotes the memory byte or word, as appropriate, starting at address `x`.
   `RR` denotes an address register, X, Y, S, or U.
   `PB` denotes the indexed addressing postbyte.
   `PLC` denotes the address of the byte following the instruction.
   `n[lo]` denotes the low-order byte of n; `n[hi]` denotes the high-order byte; `n[so]` denotes
      bits 4 to 0.
   `xtnd(x)` sign extends x to a 16-bit two's-complement value.
   In based and relative modes, the assembler attempts to use the smallest possible displacement
      size, unless the prefix > or < is used, which forces a 16-bit or 8-bit value, respectively.

16-bit immediate operand is required. Thus, the assembly language instruction
`LDX #1` generates the 3-byte machine instruction shown in Figure 16–5(c).

16.3.2 Absolute

absolute
 addressing
extended
 addressing

In *absolute addressing* (which Motorola calls *extended addressing*), the instruction contains the 16-bit absolute memory address of the operand. As shown in Figure 16–6, a typical instruction using absolute addressing is three bytes long—one byte for the opcode and two bytes for the address.

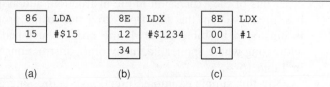

(a)   (b)   (c)

FIGURE 16–5   Immediate addressing: (a) 8-bit operand; (b,c) 16-bit operands.

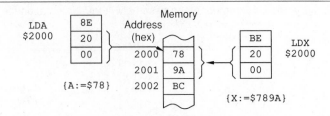

FIGURE 16–6   Typical 6809 instructions using absolute addressing.

The instruction LDA $2000 loads accumulator A with the 8-bit contents of memory location $2000. On the other hand, the instruction LDX $2000 must load register X with a 16-bit quantity. In this case, $2000 is considered to be the address of the first byte of a word. Thus, the high-order byte of X is loaded with MEM[$2000] and the low-order byte of X is loaded with MEM[$2001]. Both instructions LDA $2000 and LDX $2000 contain a 16-bit address, but the processor deduces from the opcode whether it must load a byte or a word starting at that memory address.

16.3.3   Direct Page

direct-page addressing

page number

page address

direct-page number

<

Direct-page addressing partitions the 6809's 64-Kbyte address space into 256 pages of 256 bytes each, as shown in Figure 16–7(a). Thus, a 16-bit address may be partitioned into an 8-bit *page number* and an 8-bit *page address* within the page, as in Figure 16–7(b).

The 6809 has a direct-page register, DP, that a program may load with an 8-bit *direct-page number*. When an opcode specifies direct-page addressing, a full 16-bit address is obtained by concatenating the contents of DP with an 8-bit page address in the instruction, as shown in Figure 16–7(c).

Operands in the direct page may be accessed by short instructions that contain only an 8-bit page address instead of a full 16-bit absolute address. By storing frequently used variables in the direct page, a programmer can significantly reduce the size of a program (and improve its speed, too). Since the programmer specifies the direct-page number in a register, different programs or subroutines can use different regions of memory for the direct page; however, some overhead is required to manage DP.

An assembly language program may indicate direct-page addressing using the prefix "<" before an address expression. The assembler places the 8 low-order bits of the expression in the instruction, and assumes that the programmer has already set up the direct-page register to the proper value. This technique is illustrated in Table 16–3. If the programmer had not indicated direct-page addressing where applicable, many of the instructions would be longer, as shown in Table 16–4.

In this simple example, direct-page addressing actually made the program fragment longer than the corresponding program with absolute addressing. In a

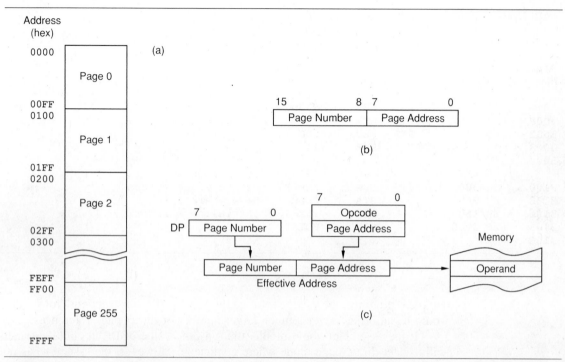

FIGURE 16–7 Paged addressing in the 6809: (a) address space partitioning; (b) address values; (c) address formation using DP.

TABLE 16–3 Excerpt from a program that uses direct-page addressing.

Machine Language		Assembly Language			
Address (hex)	Contents (hex)	Label (sym)	Opcode (mnem)	Operand (sym)	Comments
			ORG	$3000	Begin direct-page
3000	?? ??	POINT	RMB	2	variables and
3002	0D	CARRET	FCB	$0D	constants.
3003	??	CHAR	RMB	1	
3004			...		
			ORG	$3100	Begin program.
3100	86 30	START	LDA	#$30	Direct-page number.
3102	1F 8B		TFR	A,DP	Load DP with page number.
3104	96 02		LDA	<CARRET	Get terminator.
3106	97 03		STA	<CHAR	Save character.
3108	8E 1800		LDX	#$1800	Initialize pointer.
310B	9F 00		STX	<POINT	
310D			...		

TABLE 16–4   The same program without direct-page addressing.

Machine Language		Assembly Language			
Address (hex)	Contents (hex)	Label (sym)	Opcode (mnem)	Operand (sym)	Comments
			ORG	$3000	Begin variables
3000	?? ??	POINT	RMB	2	and constants.
3002	0D	CARRET	FCB	$0D	
3003	??	CHAR	RMB	1	
3004			. . .		
			ORG	$3100	Begin program.
3100	B6 3002	START	LDA	CARRET	Get carriage return.
3103	B7 3003		STA	CHAR	Save character.
3106	8E 1800		LDX	#$1800	Initialize pointer.
3109	BF 3000		STX	POINT	
310C			. . .		

complete program, the overhead of setting up DP (two instructions, four bytes) would be amortized over a much larger number of direct-page references.

If the assembler could predict the run-time value of DP, it could automatically select direct-page mode where applicable. However, the assembler is not smart enough to do this. Instead, the programmer may tell the assembler what value DP will have at run time, using an internal assembler variable called the *direct-page pseudo-register* (DPPR).

direct-page pseudo-register (DPPR)
SETDP

In assembly language, the SETDP pseudo-operation is used to change the value of DPPR. Corresponding to each run-time change of DP, the programmer must insert a SETDP pseudo-operation to tell the assembler the proper value for DPPR. Then the assembler can automatically select direct-page addressing for all instructions that access operands in the direct page, according to DPPR. This is shown in Table 16–5. Even though the "<" prefix is not used, the assembler automatically selects direct-page addressing whenever the high-order byte of an address matches the current value of DPPR. For example, "STA CHAR" generates a 2-byte instruction the first time that it appears. However, the second appearance of "STA CHAR" generates a 3-byte instruction, since CHAR's page ($30) is no longer the direct page.

The assembler initializes DPPR to zero when assembly begins, because the 6809 processor initializes DP to zero whenever it is reset. Thereafter it is the programmer's responsibility to maintain the proper values of DPPR in the assembly language program and DP in the run-time program.

The programmer can always force the assembler to use 16-bit absolute addressing, even when direct-page addressing is applicable, by placing the prefix ">" before an address expression. Likewise the programmer can force direct-page addressing, even when it seems inapplicable, with the "<" prefix.

>
<

When no prefix is used, the assembler chooses either absolute or direct-

TABLE 16–5   Direct-page addressing with direct-page pseudo-register.

Machine Language		Assembly Language			
Address (hex)	Contents (hex)	Label (sym)	Opcode (mnem)	Operand (sym)	Comments
			ORG	$2E00	Begin one direct page.
2E00	??	VAR1	RMB	1	
2E01	??	VAR2	RMB	1	
2E02			...		
			ORG	$3000	Begin another direct page.
3000	?? ??	POINT	RMB	2	
3002	0D	CARRET	FCB	$0D	
3003	??	CHAR	RMB	1	
3004			...		
			ORG	$3100	Begin program.
3100	86 30	START	LDA	#$30	Direct-page number.
3102	1F 8B		TFR	A,DP	Load DP with page number.
3104			SETDP	$30	Tell the assembler about it.
3104	96 02		LDA	CARRET	Get carriage return.
3106	97 03		STA	CHAR	Save character.
3108	8E 1800		LDX	#$1800	Initialize pointer.
310B	9F 00		STX	POINT	
310D	86 2E		LDA	#$2E	New direct-page number.
310F	1F 8B		TFR	A,DP	Load DP with page number.
3111			SETDP	$2E	Tell the assembler about it.
3111	86 11		LDA	#17	Get initial value.
3113	97 00		STA	VAR1	Initialize variables.
3115	97 01		STA	VAR2	
3117	B7 3003		STA	CHAR	
311A			...		

page addressing. For direct-page addressing to be chosen, the high-order byte of the address expression must match the value of DPPR during *pass 1* of the assembly. If the expression contains a forward reference, the assembler assumes that it must use 16-bit absolute addressing.

16.3.4   Indexed Addressing Modes

indexed
addressing

indexed
addressing
postbyte

Motorola's *indexed addressing* for the 6809 is actually a family of addressing modes. When an instruction opcode specifies indexed addressing, the opcode is followed by another byte, called an *indexed addressing postbyte*, that specifies exactly which indexed mode is to be used. In some modes, the postbyte itself is followed by one or two additional bytes of addressing information.

In addition to their typical use with most instructions to specify a source or destination operand in memory, indexed addressing modes can also be used with the LEA (load effective address) instruction. As in the 68000, LEA in the 6809 is sort of a half-hearted load. The instruction LEAx xmode computes the

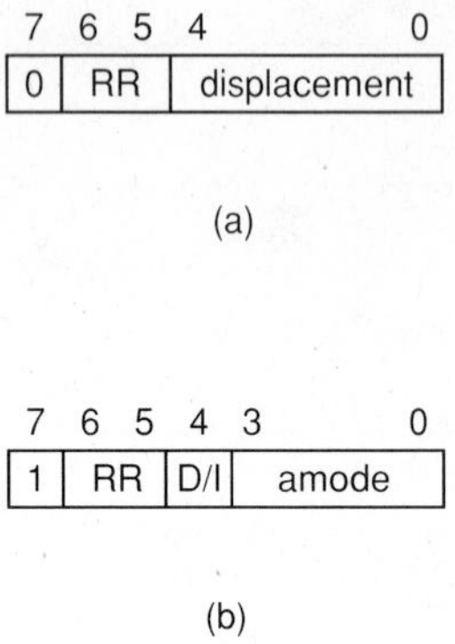

```
7 6 5 4          0
0 | RR | displacement |
```

(a)

```
7 6 5 4 3        0
1 | RR |D/I| amode |
```

(b)

(c)

amode	Addressing mode
0000	Auto-increment by 1 (no indirect)
0001	Auto-increment by 2
0010	Auto-decrement by 1 (no indirect)
0011	Auto-decrement by 2
0100	Register indirect
0101	Based indexed (offset B)
0110	Based indexed (offset A)
0111	Not allowed
1000	Based (8-bit offset)
1001	Based (16-bit offset)
1010	Not allowed
1011	Based indexed (offset D)
1100	Relative (8-bit offset)
1101	Relative (16-bit offset)
1110	Not allowed
1111	Absolute (indirect only)

FIGURE 16–8   Indexed addressing postbyte: (a) based addressing with 5-bit displacement; (b) other modes; (c) encoding of amode field.

address of an operand using an indexed mode **xmode**, and deposits the address in an address register **x** (X, Y, U, or S).

Figure 16–8 shows the layout of the indexed addressing postbyte. A 2-bit RR field in the postbyte usually specifies one of four address registers that may be used in an addressing computation—X, Y, S, or U. If the MSB of the postbyte is 0, then the mode is based addressing with a 5-bit displacement in the low-order bits. If the MSB is 1, then the mode is specified by the four low-order bits of the postbyte. The individual indexed addressing modes are described in detail in the remaining subsections. In most of these modes, the D/I bit is 0. When D/I is 1, an extra level of indirection occurs, as described in the last subsection.

16.3.5   Register Indirect

register indirect addressing

,X

In *register indirect addressing*, the specified address register (RR) contains the address of the operand. For historical reasons, Motorola's standard assembly language notation for indexed and indirect modes is a little strange, as shown in Table 16–2. In general, Motorola's 6809 assembly language uses a comma ",X" where other assembly languages use an at-sign "@X" or parentheses "(X)". Thus, the Motorola instruction LDA ,X is roughly equivalent to the 68000 instruction MOVE.B (A0),D0 (substituting D0 for A and A0 for X).

16.3.6   Based or Indexed

based or indexed addressing

In 6809 *based or indexed addressing*, a constant displacement in the instruction is added to the specified address register to form the effective address of the operand; the contents of the register are not disturbed. The postbyte can call for a

5-, 8-, or 16-bit displacement. As shown in Figure 16–8(a), a 5-bit displacement is encoded as part of the postbyte itself. An 8-bit displacement is placed in a byte following the postbyte, while a 16-bit displacement is placed in two bytes following the postbyte.

The short displacements are treated as signed numbers; their signs are extended to make a 16-bit two's-complement number before adding to the address register. Thus a 5-bit displacement ranges from −16 to +15, and an 8-bit displacement ranges from −128 to +127. The 16-bit displacements may be viewed as either signed or unsigned numbers, since a 16-bit addition gives the same 16-bit result in either case (think about it). According to the definitions of based and indexed addressing in Section 7.3, the 5- and 8-bit displacements yield based addressing, while the 16-bit displacement yields based or indexed addressing according to the application.

The 5-bit displacement mode is very useful, since it allows efficient access of operands in small tables and in stack frames using short, 2-byte instructions (1-byte opcode plus postbyte). In most programs, these short instructions are used much more often than the longest 6809 instructions, which are five bytes long (2-byte opcode plus postbyte plus 2-byte displacement).

The assembly language notation for 6809 based and indexed modes was shown in Table 16–2. The prefixes "<" and ">" may be used to force 8-bit and 16-bit displacements, respectively. If no prefix is given, the assembler automatically selects the shortest displacement mode that works with the given expression. Thus, if the value of the displacement expression is 0, register indirect mode is used; otherwise, if it is between −16 and +15, 5-bit displacement mode is used; otherwise, if it is between −128 and +127, 8-bit displacement mode is used; otherwise, 16-bit displacement mode is used. As with direct-page addressing, the value of the expression should be known during pass 1 of the assembly; otherwise, the assembler selects a worst-case default of 16-bit displacement mode.

<
>

16.3.7 Based Indexed

based indexed addressing

Based indexed addressing forms an effective address by combining a base address and an index value, both of which are contained in registers. In the 6809, any of the address registers X, Y, U, or S may contain the base address, while the index value may be contained in A or B (8 bits, sign extended to 16) or D (16 bits).

As shown in Table 16–2, assembly language programs specify based indexed addressing by using one of the reserved identifiers A, B, or D as the offset for based addressing.

16.3.8 Auto-Increment and Auto-Decrement

auto-increment addressing
auto-decrement addressing

Auto-increment and *auto-decrement addressing* may be used to step through arrays, lists, and other data structures and to manipulate stacks. The 6809 supports these addressing modes for both byte and word operands. Unlike the 68000, which deduces the operand size from the opcode, the 6809 encodes the operand size in the indexed addressing postbyte, and the programmer must explicitly indicate the operand size as shown in Table 16–2. Thus, the following instruction sequence initializes a table of bytes to contain $12:

```
         LDA     #$12
         LDX     #TABBEG        Starting address of table.
ILOOP    STA     ,X+            Initialize table entry.
         CMPX    #TABEND        Past end?
         BNE     ILOOP          Repeat until all entries done.
```

On the other hand, the following sequence initializes a table of words (recall that D is the concatenation of A and B):

```
         LDD     #$1234
         LDX     #TABBEG        Starting address of table.
ILOOP    STD     ,X++           Initialize table entry.
         CMPX    #TABEND        Past end?
         BNE     ILOOP          Repeat until all entries done.
```

What initial values would the table contain if the instruction STD ,X+ were mistakenly used above?

16.3.9   Relative

relative addressing

The 6809 provides *relative addressing* modes with both 8-bit and 16-bit displacements, in which the (sign-extended) displacement is added to the current PC to obtain the effective address of the operand. The 8-bit displacement mode allows efficient access to data nearby the current instruction, while both modes allow data references to be coded in a position-independent manner.

,PCR

In Motorola's 6809 assembly language, the suffix ",PCR" denotes relative addressing, as shown in Table 16–2. The assembler computes the required displacement as the difference between the given address expression (n) and the address following the instruction. As with the direct-page and based and indexed modes, the assembler automatically selects the shortest possible relative mode according to the information that it has during pass 1 of the assembly. The prefixes ">" and "<" force use of the mode with the "greater" and "lesser"

\>

\<

number of displacement bits, respectively.

Relative addressing is often used in jump-type instructions. For the 6809, a programmer could write "JMP <target,PCR" to jump to a target address within 127 bytes of the JMP instruction. However, this is a 3-byte instruction (JMP opcode plus postbyte plus 8-bit displacement). The programmer would be better off using the BRA (branch) instruction, which has an 8-bit opcode and 8-bit displacement, and uses relative addressing inherently. Likewise, for a long jump (more than 127 bytes away), the programmer could write "JMP >target,PCR" (four bytes long) or "LBRA target" (long branch, three bytes long)

Relative addressing is also useful for looking up information in tables in a position-independent manner. For example, suppose the programmer created a 256-byte table N1S[0..255], where N1S[i] contains the number of ones in the binary representation of i:

```
N1S        FCB       0,1,1,2,1,...   256-byte table.
I          RMB       1               Variable i.
```

The following code loads A with the number of ones in I:

```
           LDB       I               Load X with value of i.
           LDA       #0
           TFR       D,X
           LDA       N1S,X           Get value of N1S[X].
```

An alternate version of the code is shown below:

```
           LDB       I               Get value of i.
           LDX       #N1S            Get base address of table.
           LDA       B,X             Get value of N1S[i].
```

However, neither version is position independent, since both contain instructions that fix the absolute addresses of I and N1S at assembly time. A position-independent version may be coded as shown below.

```
           LDB       I,PCR           Get value of i.
           LEAX      N1S,PCR         Get base address of table.
           LDA       B,X             Get value of N1S[i].
```

In the new code, the first two instructions contain *offsets* to I and N1S; absolute addresses are computed at run time by adding the PC and the offsets.

16.3.10 Indirect

Most of the indexed addressing modes can specify an additional level of indirection by setting the direct/indirect bit in the postbyte to 1 (see Figure 16–8). In

*indirect
 addressing*
[]

assembly language, *indirect addressing* is indicated by a pair of square brackets [] surrounding the usual address and mode expression (except that the prefixes ">" and "<" should appear before the brackets, if used).

When indirect addressing is used, an indirect address is calculated in the same way as the effective address in the corresponding nonindirect mode. The memory word starting at the indirect address is then fetched and used as the effective address of the operand. In the case of based and indexed addressing, the mode would therefore be classified as "preindexed indirect".

The 6809 does not support indirection with auto-increment-by-1 and auto-decrement-by-1 modes, since a sane program should use an increment of 2 when stepping through a table of indirect addresses. Also, indirect addressing with the 5-bit displacement mode is not provided, since the direct/indirect bit has been used as the sign of the displacement; the 8-bit displacement mode must be used instead.

TABLE 16–6   Operations coded with and without indirect addressing.

Instructions	With Indirect	Comments
LDX HEAD LDA ,X	LDA [HEAD]	Get first item in queue.
LDX 10,S	LEAX [10,S]	Get address of VAR-type parameter from stack.
LDX 10,S LDA ,X	LDA [10,S]	Get value of VAR-type parameter from stack.
LDX ,X JMP ,X	JMP [,X]	Jump to address in jump table, pointed to by X.
RTS	JMP [,S++]	Return from subroutine.

absolute indirect addressing

Recall that the 6809 provides absolute addressing as a nonindexed mode with a 2-byte absolute address and no postbyte. *Absolute indirect addressing* is provided as one of the indirect indexed modes. For examples of indirect addressing, see Table 16–6, which shows various instruction sequences coded without and with indirect addressing.

16.4 OPERATIONS

We shall classify 6809 instructions into three types: memory reference, register reference, and program control.

16.4.1 Memory Reference

LD
ST
CMP

Instructions that have an operand in memory are listed in Table 16–7. The first part of the table contains three important operations, LD, ST, and CMP, that may be performed on almost any 6809 register, A, B, D, X, Y, U, or S. Even though any of the three operations may be performed on any of the seven registers, it takes 14 lines in the table to specify all of the instruction combinations, because they are so irregularly encoded (compare with MOVE instructions in the 68000).

ADD
SUB

ADC
SBC
AND
OR
EOR
BIT

The second part of the table shows the remaining double-operand instructions, which cannot be performed on address registers. The ADD and SUB instructions may be used with accumulator A or B or on the double-length pseudo-accumulator D, which is the concatenation of A and B. The other arithmetic and logical operations may only be performed on accumulators A and B. ADC uses the C bit for the carry in and the carry out, while SBC uses C as the borrow, as in the 68000. The logical instructions, AND, OR, and EOR, perform bit-by-bit operations in the usual way, while BIT is a "logical comparison" instruction that ANDs its operands and sets the condition bits, but does not store the result.

The third part of the table shows single-operand instructions that may be performed on operands in memory. As shown in the next subsection, these

TABLE 16–7   Memory reference instructions in the 6809.

Mnemonic	Operand	Opcode Byte(s)	HNZVC	Description
LDab	mem	1BMM0110	-**0-	Load accumulator from memory
LDD	mem	11MM1100	-**0-	Load double accumulator from memory
LDxu	mem	1UMM1110	-**0-	Load address register from memory
LDys	mem	$10 1SMM1110	-**0-	Load address register from memory
STab	mem-imm	1BMM0111	-**0-	Store accumulator into memory
STD	mem-imm	11MM1101	-**0-	Store double accumulator into memory
STxu	mem-imm	1UMM1111	-**0-	Store address register into memory
STys	mem-imm	$10 1SMM1111	-**0-	Store address register into memory
CMPab	mem	1BMM0001	u****	Compare accumulator with memory
CMPD	mem	$10 10MM0011	-****	Compare double accumulator with memory
CMPX	mem	10MM1100	-****	Compare address register with memory
CMPY	mem	$10 10MM1100	-****	Compare address register with memory
CMPU	mem	$11 10MM0011	-****	Compare address register with memory
CMPS	mem	$11 10MM1100	-****	Compare address register with memory
ADDab	mem	1BMM1011	*****	Add memory to accumulator
ADDD	mem	11MM0011	-****	Add memory to double accumulator
SUBab	mem	1BMM0000	*****	Subtract memory from accumulator
SUBD	mem	10MM0011	-****	Subtract memory from double accumulator
ADCab	mem	1BMM1001	*****	Add with carry to accumulator
SBCab	mem	1BMM0010	u****	Subtract with carry from accumulator
ANDab	mem	1BMM0100	-**0-	AND memory to accumulator
ORab	mem	1BMM1010	-**0-	OR memory to accumulator
EORab	mem	1BMM1000	-**0-	Exclusive OR memory to accumulator
BITab	mem	1BMM0101	-**0-	Bit test memory with accumulator
CLR	mem-imm	0DDD1111	-0100	Clear memory byte
TST	mem-imm	0DDD1101	-**0-	Test memory byte, set condition bits
NEG	mem-imm	0DDD0000	u****	Negate memory byte
COM	mem-imm	0DDD0011	-**01	Bit-by-bit complement memory byte
INC	mem-imm	0DDD1100	-***-	Increment memory byte
DEC	mem-imm	0DDD1010	-***-	Decrement memory byte
ROR	mem-imm	0DDD0110	-**-*	Rotate memory byte right with C
ROL	mem-imm	0DDD1001	-****	Rotate memory byte left with C
LSR	mem-imm	0DDD0100	-**-*	Logical shift memory byte right
LSL/ASL	mem-imm	0DDD1000	-****	Logical/arithmetic shift memory byte left
ASR	mem-imm	0DDD0111	u**-*	Arithmetic shift memory byte right
LEAxy	indexed	0011000Y	--*--	Load register with effective address
LEAus	indexed	0011001U	-----	Load register with effective address

Notes: In mnemonics, ab denotes A or B; xu denotes X or U; ys denotes Y or S; and so on.
In operands, mem denotes any memory addressing mode; mem-imm denotes any mode except immediate; indexed denotes indexed modes only.
In opcode bytes, B is 1 if ab in the mnemonic is B; U is 1 if xu is U; and so on.
MM selects an addressing mode: 00 = immediate, 01 = direct-page, 10 = indexed, 11 = absolute.
DDD selects a destination addressing mode: 000 = direct-page, 110 = indexed, 111 = absolute.
Effects of instructions on condition bits:
    -: not affected.
    1: always set to 1.
    0: always cleared to 0.
    *: set according to operation result.
    u: undefined.

instructions may also be performed on accumulator A or B. The shift and rotate instructions operate in the usual way and store the lost bit into C.

LEA The last instruction in the table, LEA, loads an address register with the effective address of an operand specified by an indexed addressing mode. Like LEA in the 68000, this instruction is useful for passing the addresses of VAR-type parameters to subroutines. In the 6809, LEA also provides the only convenient way to add constants or accumulator values to address registers, for example:

```
      LEAX    NUM,X        Add the constant value NUM to X,
                             that is, ADDX #NUM.
      LEAY    A,Y          Add contents of accumulator A to Y.
```

In general, a 6809 instruction may use any memory addressing mode for which the instruction makes sense. All instructions set, clear, or hold condition bits HNZVC according to the result of the operation, as shown in the table.

16.4.2 Register Reference

Several useful operations are provided by the 6809's register reference instructions, shown in Table 16–8. The first part of the table contains single-operand instructions on A and B. These are accumulator versions of the single-memory-operand instructions from the third part of Table 16–7.

NOP The second part of the table begins with NOP, which does nothing in its
TFR usual, inimitable fashion. The TFR and EXG instructions allow the contents of
EXG any register to be transferred to or exchanged with a like-sized register. Both of these instructions have a 1-byte opcode followed by another byte with reg1 and reg2 specified in the two 4-bit halves.

ABX The ABX instruction, one byte long, adds B to X as an 8-bit unsigned integer. Almost the same thing can be accomplished by a 2-byte instruction LEAX B,X (which sign extends B). Since ABX is "irregular" (e.g., there is no AAX or ABY), you probably won't remember it, so you might as well forget it! The 6809's designers included ABX for compatibility with the MC6801.

DAA Special arithmetic instructions appear in the third part of Table 16–8. DAA
SEX adjusts accumulator A after a BCD operation as described in Section 8.11. SEX
MUL sign extends an 8-bit value in B to a 16-bit value in A,B (D). The MUL instruction multiplies two 8-bit unsigned numbers in A and B and leaves the 16-bit unsigned result in A,B. This instruction is useful for computing offsets to array items that are more than one byte long, and as a primitive in subroutines for multiplication of larger quantities.

PSH Listed in the last part of the table, PSH and PUL allow registers to be
PUL pushed onto or popped from a stack using either U or S as the stack pointer.
register mask list The instruction opcode byte is followed by a *register mask list* byte that contains one bit position for each register, as shown in Figure 16–9. If the bit is 1, then the register is pushed or popped; otherwise it is not. Thus, zero to eight registers may be pushed or popped by a single 2-byte instruction. The pushing order is governed by the order of the register list, regardless of the order in which the

TABLE 16–8   Register reference instructions in the 6809.

Mnemonic	Operand	Opcode Byte	HNZVC	Description
CLRab		010B1111	−0100	Clear accumulator
TSTab		010B1101	−**0−	Test accumulator, set condition bits
NEGab		010B0000	u****	Negate accumulator
COMab		010B0011	−**01	Bit-by-bit complement accumulator
INCab		010B1100	−***−	Increment accumulator
DECab		010B1010	−***−	Decrement accumulator
RORab		010B0110	−**−*	Rotate accumulator right with C
ROLab		010B1001	−****	Rotate accumulator left with C
LSRab		010B0100	−**−*	Logical shift accumulator right
LSL/ASLab		010B1000	−****	Logical/arithmetic shift accumulator left
ASRab		010B0111	u**−*	Arithmetic shift accumulator right
NOP		00010010	−−−−−	No operation
TFR	reg1,reg2	00011111	−−−−−	Transfer reg1 to reg2
EXG	reg1,reg2	00011110	−−−−−	Exchange reg1 and reg2
ABX		00111010	−−−−−	Add B to X
DAA		00011001	−**u*	Decimal adjust accumulator A
SEX		00011101	−**−−	Sign extend B into A
MUL		00111101	−−*−*	Unsigned multiply A·B, result in A,B
PSHus	reglist	001101U0	−−−−−	Push registers onto stack
PULus	reglist	001101U1	−−−−−	Pull (pop) registers from stack

Notes: `reg1` and `reg2` may be freely chosen from A, B, DPR, and CC, or from D, X, Y, U, S, and
         PC (`reg1` and `reg2` must be the same size).
       `reglist` is a list of zero or more of the registers PC, U (in PSHS) or S (in PSHU), Y, X, DP,
         B, A, and CC.
       Also see notes for Table 16–7.

registers appear in an assembly language statement. Therefore, the instruction
`PSHS A,U,B` pushes U, then B, and then A onto the S stack. Registers are
popped in the opposite order from pushing.

Like the 68000's stack, a 6809 stack grows toward decreasing memory
locations, and the stack pointer points directly to the top item in the stack.
When a 16-bit quantity is pushed, the low-order byte is pushed first, so that
the resulting two bytes in the stack "read" in the correct order, according to
Figure 16–4.

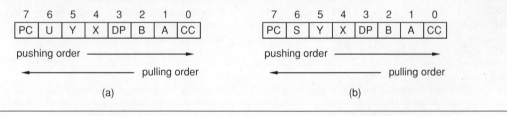

FIGURE 16–9   Register mask list byte: (a) `PSHS` and `PULS`; (b) `PSHU` and `PULU`.

It is up to the programmer to initialize U and S before using PSH or PUL. Also recall that the S stack is also used by subroutine and interrupt calls and returns.

16.4.3   Program Control

JMP

JSR

The 6809's program control instructions are shown in Table 16–9. The JMP and JSR instructions perform unconditional jumps as in the 68000. JMP and JSR may use any memory addressing mode except immediate; the PC is loaded with the effective address specified by the addressing mode.

The JSR instruction saves the return address on a stack pointed to by the S register; RTS pops the return address from the same stack. The BSR instruction is a short form of JSR that uses relative addressing with an 8-bit two's-complement displacement. This 2-byte instruction allows a program to call a nearby subroutine, and it is a byte shorter than JSR using absolute addressing.

RTS

BSR

BRA

Bcc

The BRA and 15 different conditional branch (Bcc) instructions also use relative addressing with an 8-bit displacement and are two bytes long. The conditional branches are the same as the 68000's, described in Section 8.7. When a branch is taken, the displacement is added to the PC to obtain the address of the next instruction. When this addition takes place, the processor

TABLE 16–9   Program control instructions in the 6809.

Mnemonic	Operand	Opcode Byte(s)	HNZVC	Description
JMP	mem−imm	0DDD1110	—————	Unconditional jump
JSR	mem−imm	10MM1101	—————	Jump to subroutine
RTS		00111001	—————	Return from subroutine
BSR	rel8	10001101	—————	Branch to subroutine
BRA	rel8	00100000	—————	Unconditional branch
Bcc	rel8	0010CCCC	—————	Conditional branch
LBSR	rel16	00010111	—————	Long branch to subroutine
LBRA	rel16	00010110	—————	Long unconditional branch
LBcc	rel16	$10 0010CCCC	—————	Long conditional branch
ANDCC	imm	00011100	*****	AND immediate with CC
ORCC	imm	00011010	*****	OR immediate with CC
RTI		00111011	*****	Return from interrupt
SYNC		00010011	—————	Synchronize with interrupt
CWAI	imm	00111100	*****	AND immediate with CC and wait for interrupt
SWI		00111111	—————	Software interrupt
SWI2		$10 00111111	—————	Software interrupt
SWI3		$11 00111111	—————	Software interrupt

Notes: mem denotes any memory addressing mode; imm denotes immediate mode; rel8 denotes relative mode with an 8-bit displacement; rel16 denotes relative mode with a 16-bit displacement.

cc and CCCC denote any of the conditions and their encodings listed in Table 8–9 on page 281.

has already incremented PC to point to the next instruction. Thus, a displacement
of −2, not 0, causes the instruction to branch to itself.

LBSR
LBRA
LBcc

The long branch instructions (LBSR, LBRA, LBcc) are like their shorter
counterparts, except that they give a 16-bit displacement for relative addressing.
Thus, they may specify target addresses anywhere in the 64-Kbyte address space
of the 6809. The main use of LBRA and LBSR is to create position-independent
programs; position independence is maintained because the target address is
specified relative to PC. The same effect could be achieved by JMP and JSR
using one of the indexed modes—PC relative with 16-bit displacement—but the
LBRA and LBSR instructions are one byte shorter and somewhat faster.

ANDCC
ORCC

The ANDCC and ORCC instructions allow a program to clear or set the
condition bits. Referring to the layout of the condition bits in Figure 16–3, we
can see that ANDCC #$F3 clears N and Z, while ORCC #$11 sets I and C.

The instructions in the last part of Table 16–9 will be discussed later, in
connection with input/output and interrupts.

16.5 SAMPLE PROGRAMS

All of the example programs for the 68000 in Chapter 5 have straightforward
counterparts for the 6809. For example, Table 16–10 is a 6809 program that
performs multiplication by repeated addition. We simplified the 6809 version
by reducing the scope of the problem to multiply only bytes, not words, which
are well supported by the 6809 instruction set and registers. Rewriting the
program to multiply words or longwords is more difficult. For example, word
multiplication is performed by the program in Table 16–11. Because there is
only a single 16-bit accumulator (D), many overhead instructions must be used
to shuttle the 16-bit product and loop counter to and from memory.

If the address registers are not being used, they can also be used as 16-
bit accumulators (albeit with somewhat limited functionality), and the word
multiplication program can be simplified as shown in Table 16–12. This is a

TABLE 16–10   Multiplication by repeated addition in the 6809.

```
        ORG    $2000      Multiply MCND by MPY (8-bit inputs and results).
MULT    CLRA              Accumulator A will accumulate product.
        LDB    MPY        Accumulator B holds loop count (multiplier).
        BEQ    DONE       Done if count is down to zero.
LOOP    ADDA   MCND       Else add MCND to product.
        ADDB   #-1        And loop MPY (B) times.
        BNE    LOOP
DONE    STA    PROD       Save product.
        JMP    $F837      Return to operating system.
PROD    RMB    1          Storage for PROD.
MPY     FCB    5          Multiplier value.
MCND    FCB    23         Multiplicand value.
        END    MULT
```

TABLE 16–11   Word multiplication by repeated addition in the 6809.

```
        ORG    $2000    Multiply WMCND by WMPY (16-bit inputs and results).
WMULT   LDD    #0       Location WPROD will accumulate product.
        STD    WPROD    Initialize product to 0.
        LDD    WMPY     Location WCNT will hold the loop count.
        STD    WCNT     Initialize (do loop WMPY times).
        BEQ    WDONE    Done if count is down to zero.
WLOOP   LDD    WPROD    Else add WMCND to product.
        ADDD   WMCND
        STD    WPROD
        LDD    WCNT     And loop WMPY (WCNT) times.
        ADDD   #-1
        STD    WCNT
        BNE    WLOOP
WDONE   JMP    $F837    Return to operating system.
WPROD   RMB    2        Storage for product.
WCNT    RMB    2        Storage for loop count.
WMPY    FDB    123      Multiplier value.
WMCND   FDB    456      Multiplicand value.
        END    WMULT
```

little tricky, in that the LEAX -1, X instruction is used to decrement X. Note that the LEAX and LEAY instructions set the Z bit, as required for this code to work properly, whereas LEAU and LEAS do not.

Depending on the program application, address registers are not always available to hold loop counters as in Table 16–12, and so this "efficient" coding approach is not always possible. In particular, a high-level language compiler normally emits code that uses the address registers for other things, and so it must use more inefficient code, similar to that in Table 16–11, when dealing with 16-bit and larger quantities.

Adapted from the 68000 program in Table 5–10 on page 161, a 6809 program that initializes the components of an array using indirect addressing is

TABLE 16–12   Optimized word multiplication by repeated addition in the 6809.

```
        ORG    $2000    Multiply XMCND by XMPY (16-bit inputs and results).
XMULT   LDD    #0       Accumulator D will accumulate product.
        LDX    XMPY     Register X will hold the loop count.
        BEQ    XDONE    Done if count is down to zero.
XLOOP   ADDD   XMCND    Else add XMCND to product.
        LEAX   -1,X     Subtract 1 from X (XMPY)
        BNE    XLOOP    And loop X (XMPY) times.
XDONE   STD    XPROD    Store product.
        JMP    $F837    Return to operating system.
XPROD   RMB    2        Storage for product.
XMPY    FDB    123      Multiplier value.
XMCND   FDB    456      Multiplicand value.
        END    XMULT
```

TABLE 16–13   Initializing an array using indirect addressing in the 6809.

```
         ORG    $2000
INIT     CLRA              Set components of Q to zero.
         LDX    #Q         Address of first component.
ILOOP    STA    ,X         Set MEM[X] to zero.
         LEAX   1,X        Point to next component.
         CMPX   #QEND      Past last component?
         BNE    ILOOP      If not, go do some more.
         JMP    $F837      Return to operating system.
Q        RMB    5          Reserve 5 bytes for array.
QEND     EQU    Q+5        Address of byte just past array.
         END    INIT
```

shown in Table 16–13. Like the the 68000, the 6809 has auto-increment addressing, and so the STA and LEAX instructions in this example may be replaced with a "STA ,X+" instruction, which stores A and then increments X.

Unlike the original 68000 program, the 6809 program in Table 16–13 does not place the array ending address QEND in an address register such as Y. This would require a "CMPX Y" instruction inside the loop, and the 6809 has no such instruction! In general, 6809 programs do not make as extensive use of address registers as 68000 programs do, because the 6809 has neither a large set of address registers nor a complete set of instructions for operating on them.

A 6809 program that counts the number of "1" bits in a word is shown in Table 16–14. In addition to using subroutines, this program illustrates the use of the stack for storing temporary variables. Such techniques are especially important for accumulator-based machines like the 6809, since there are few registers available for efficiently storing and accessing temporaries.

A 6809 subroutine that uses indexed addressing and an array to discover prime numbers is shown in Table 16–15. Even though we told you to forget it earlier, the ABX instruction is very handy in this program, where it is used to add an unsigned number to X. All of the array indices in this program are treated as unsigned numbers; for example, comparisons use BLS rather than BLE. This is essential for proper program operation because the array is so large. Signed comparisons on array indices 2^{15} or larger would give incorrect results, because these are negative numbers in the 16-bit two's-complement system.

It is interesting that this 6809 program contains only two more instructions than the corresponding 68000 program in Table 7–9 on page 239. Since 6809 instructions are generally shorter than the 68000's, the 6809 program occupies only 71 bytes, compared with the 68000's 84 bytes (assuming absolute short addressing and optimized "quick" instruction formats for the 68000 code). Apparently, the advantages of general registers and double-operand addressing do not come into play in a program that can be efficiently coded with all variables in a small number of registers. In the present example, the 6809's simplicity wins out over the 68000's flexibility, creating shorter instructions and hence a shorter program.

TABLE 16–14   Program that uses subroutines to count the number of "1" bits in a word.

```
        ORG     $2000
MAIN    LDS     #STKE       Initialize SP.
        LDD     TWORD       Get test word.
        JSR     WCNT1S      Count number of 1s in it.
        JMP     SYSRET      Return to operating system.
SYSRET  EQU     $F837       Operating system address.
STK     RMB     16          Space for return addresses and temporaries.
STKE    EQU     *           Initialization address for SP.
TWORD   FDB     $5B29       Test-word to count 1s.
*
*                           Count the number of '1' bits in a word.
*                           Enter with word in D, exit with count in A.
WCNT1S  PSHS    B           Save high-order byte of input word.
        JSR     BCNT1S      Count 1s in low-order byte (A).
        PULS    A           Get high-order byte.
        PSHS    B           Save '1' count.
        JSR     BCNT1S      Count 1s in high-order byte.
        ADDB    ,S+         Pop and add low-order count.
        TFR     B,A         Put result in A.
        RTS                 Done, return.
*
*                           Count number of '1' bits in a byte.
*                           Enter with byte in A, exit with count in B.
BCNT1S  PSHS    A           Save input byte on stack.
        CLRB                Initialize '1' count.
        LDX     #MASKS      Point to 1-bit masks.
BLOOP   LDA     ,X+         Get next bit mask.
        ANDA    ,S          AND with input byte on stack.
        BEQ     BNO1        Is there a '1' there?  Skip if not.
        INCB                Otherwise increment '1' count.
BNO1    CMPX    #MASKE      Past last mask?
        BNE     BLOOP       Continue if not.
        PULS    A           Remove input byte from stack.
        RTS                 Return.
*
*                           Define 1-bit masks to test bits of byte.
MASKS   FCB     $80,$40,$20,$10,8,4,2,1
MASKE   EQU     *           Address just after table.
        END     MAIN
```

A stack-oriented subroutine-calling convention is used by the DIVIDE subroutine in Table 16–16. Register X is used as the frame pointer. A program that calls DIVIDE is shown in Table 16–17. The state of the stack before the DIVIDE subroutine is called is shown in Figure 16–10(a). The calling program reserves two bytes on the stack for REM and QUOT, pushes DVND and DVSR [Figure 16–10(b)], and calls DIVIDE. Then DIVIDE pushes the old value of the frame pointer and CNT onto the stack as shown in Figure 16–10(c). Upon return, the stack is cleaned up, leaving only the output parameters REM and QUOT as shown in Figure 16–10(d).

TABLE 16–15   Subroutine to find primes using an array and indexed addressing.

```
*              This subroutine finds and prints all prime numbers between
*         2 and NPRIME using the 'Sieve of Eratosthenes.' It declares
*         a boolean array PRIME[2..NPRIME], whose components indicate
*         whether or not each number between 2 and NPRIME is prime.
*         For simplicity, one byte is used for each component, with
*         0 = false, 1 = true.
*              The program begins by setting all components true; every
*         integer is potentially a prime. Then it marks the multiples
*         of the first prime (2) as being nonprimes. Then it looks for
*         the next prime and marks off its multiples. This continues
*         until we've marked the multiples of all primes less than
*         PLIMIT, approximately the square root of NPRIME. Now only
*         primes are left marked true, and they are printed.
*
*                            PROCEDURE FindPrimes;
NPRIME  EQU   50000         CONST nPrime = 50000;
PLIMIT  EQU   224             pLimit = 224;
PRIME   RMB   NPRIME-1      VAR prime : ARRAY [2..nPrime] OF boolean;
*                             {register} X : word;
*                             {register} B : byte;
FNDPRM  LDA   #1            BEGIN
        LDX   #2              FOR X := 2 TO nPrime DO
SETEM   STA   PRIME-2,X         prime[X] := true;
        LEAX  1,X               {Set the entire array true.}
        CMPX  #NPRIME
        BLS   SETEM
        LDB   #2            B := 2; {First known prime.}
MARKEM  LDX   #0            REPEAT {Check integers...}
        ABX                   X := B; {...from 2 to pLimit.}
        LDA   PRIME-2,X        IF prime[X] THEN
        BEQ   NOTPRM            BEGIN
        ABX                       X := X + B; {Mark multiples of B...}
CLRLUP  CLR   PRIME-2,X         REPEAT     {...as not prime.}
        ABX                         prime[X] := false; X := X + B;
        CMPX  #NPRIME           UNTIL X > nPrime;
        BLS   CLRLUP            END;
NOTPRM  INCB                  B := B + 1;
        CMPB  #PLIMIT       UNTIL B > pLimit;
        BLS   MARKEM
        JSR   WRMSG1        write('Here are primes from 2 to ');
        LDX   #NPRIME       X := nPrime;
        JSR   PRINTX        writeln(X); {Print the number in X.}
        LDX   #2            FOR X := 2 TO nPrime DO
PRTLUP  LDB   PRIME-2,X       {Print all the primes.}
        BEQ   NEXTP            IF prime[X] THEN
        JSR   PRINTX             writeln(X);
NEXTP   LEAX  1,X
        CMPX  #NPRIME
        BLS   PRTLUP
        RTS                 {All done, return to caller}
        END   FNDPRM        END;
```

TABLE 16–16   DIVIDE subroutine that passes parameters on a stack.

```
*          The offsets below define positions of parameters and local
*          variables in the stack relative to a frame pointer (register X).
CNT        EQU    -1
OLDFP      EQU    0          Old value of frame pointer.
RETADR     EQU    2          Return address.
DVSR       EQU    4          1-byte divisor (input).
DVND       EQU    5          2-byte dividend (input).
REM        EQU    7          1-byte remainder (output).
QUOT       EQU    8          1-byte quotient (output).
*
DIVIDE     PSHS   X          Push old frame pointer onto stack.
           TFR    S,X        Copy SP into X for new frame pointer.
           LDA    #8         Push initial count.
           PSHS   A
           LDA    DVND,X     Put dividend in A,B.
           LDB    DVND+1,X
           CMPA   DVSR,X     Will quotient fit in 1 byte?
           BLO    DIVLUP     Branch if it will.
           JMP    SYSOVF     Else report overflow to operating system.
DIVLUP     ASLB              Left shift A,B with LSB := 0.
           ROLA              A carry here from MSB means
           BCS    QUOT1         high DVND definitely > DVSR.
           CMPA   DVSR,X     Compare high DVND with DVSR.
           BLO    QUOTOK     Quotient bit = 0 if lower.
QUOT1      INCB              Else set quotient bit to 1.
           SUBA   DVSR,X     And update high DVND.
QUOTOK     DEC    CNT,X      Decrement iteration count.
           BGT    DIVLUP     Continue until done.
           STA    REM,X      Store remainder.
           STB    QUOT,X     Store quotient.
           TFR    X,S        Remove local variables.
           PULS   X          Restore frame pointer.
           PULS   Y          Get return address, save in Y.
           LEAS   3,S        Remove input parms (add 3 to SP).
           JMP    ,Y         Return to address contained in Y.
SYSOVF     EQU    $F837      Restart system on overflow.
```

The next example illustrates the 6809's LEA instructions. First, consider the Pascal program shown in Table 16–18. The Swap procedure, which has two VAR-type parameters, could be coded in 6809 assembly language as shown in Table 16–19 using a stack-oriented parameter-passing convention. The main program passes the SWAP subroutine the addresses of two parameters, CAT and AY1[INDEX]. For the first parameter, X is loaded with the address of variable CAT using immediate addressing. For the second parameter, the LEAX AY1-1,X instruction loads X with the address of array element AY1[X]. Without LEAX, the instructions could be coded as follows:

```
           LDD    #AY-1      Get effective base address of AY1.
           ADDD   INDEX      Add index.
           PSHS   D          Pass address of AY1[index] to subr.
```

TABLE 16–17   Program that calls stack-oriented `DIVIDE`.

```
*          Compute PDIVQ := P DIV Q; PMODQ := P MOD Q;
*              where all are 1-byte variables in memory.
DIVPQ     LEAS   -2,S           Make room for output parms (SP := SP-2).
          LDA    P              Push low-order dividend.
          PSHS   A
          CLRA                  Push high-order dividend = 0.
          PSHS   A
          LDA    Q              Push divisor.
          PSHS   A
          JSR    DIVIDE         Do the division.
          PULS   A              Pop remainder and store.
          STA    PMODQ
          PULS   A              Pop quotient and store.
          STA    PDIVQ
          ...
P         RMB    1              Storage for P, Q, PDIVQ, PMODQ
Q         RMB    1                 (all 1-byte variables).
PDIVQ     RMB    1
PMODQ     RMB    1
```

Suppose that we wanted to make this program position independent, so that it may be executed in different memory locations without reassembly. No changes are needed in the `SWAP` subroutine because it uses only registers and variables whose addresses are passed to it at run time. However, the main pro-

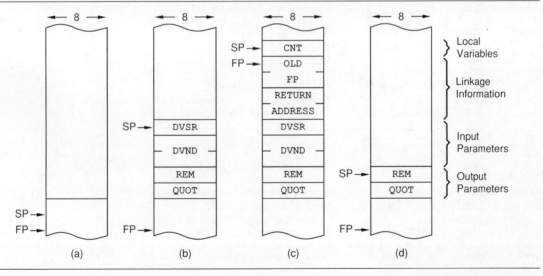

FIGURE 16–10   Stack contents during `DIVPQ` program: (a) at start; (b) just before calling `DIVIDE`; (c) after first four instructions of `DIVIDE`; (d) on return.

TABLE 16–18   Pascal program that uses VAR-type parameters.

```
PROGRAM VarParms (input,output);
VAR cat : byte; index : 1..300; AY1 : ARRAY [1..300] OF byte;
PROCEDURE Swap(VAR v1,v2 : byte);
  VAR temp : byte;
    BEGIN temp := v1; v1 := v2; v2 := temp END;
BEGIN {Main Program}
  ... Swap(cat,AY1[index]); ...
END.
```

gram must be recoded to compute addresses in a position-independent manner. The new main program code is shown below.

```
        LEAX    CAT,PCR         Get address of CAT
        PSHS    X                   and pass to subroutine.
        LEAX    AY-1,PCR        Get effective base address of AY1.
        LDD     INDEX,PCR
        LEAX    D,X             Add INDEX and pass address
        PSHS    X                   of AY1[INDEX] to subroutine.
        LBSR    SWAP            Swap CAT and AY1[INDEX].
```

All of the variable references and even the subroutine jump now use PC-relative addressing. Computing the address of AY1[INDEX] is tricky, because three

TABLE 16–19   Assembly language program using VAR-type parameters.

```
*                               Define offsets to parameters from SP.
RETADR  EQU     0               Offset to return address (top of stack).
AV1     EQU     2               Offset to address of V1.
AV2     EQU     4               Offset to address of V2.
*
SWAP    LDA     [AV1,S]         A-reg gets V1.
        LDB     [AV2,S]         B-reg gets V2.
        STB     [AV1,S]         Store in opposite order.
        STA     [AV2,S]
        LDX     RETADR,S        Get return address.
        LEAS    6,S             Remove return address and parameters
        JMP     0,X                 from stack and return.
*
MAIN    ...                     Main program.
        ...
        LDX     INDEX           Get address of AY1[INDEX]
        LEAX    AY1-1,X
        PSHS    X                   and pass to subroutine.
        LDX     #CAT            Get address of CAT
        PSHS    X                   and pass to subroutine.
        JSR     SWAP            Swap CAT and AY1[INDEX].
        ...
CAT     RMB     1               Variable storage.
INDEX   RMB     2
AY1     RMB     300
```

quantities must be added—the PC, a fixed offset from PC to the effective base address of the array, and an index into the array.

As you can see, writing position-independent code for the 6809 takes more than just writing ", PCR" after each memory reference instruction. Even the code above (and most 6809 position-independent code) is only statically position independent. The program fails if it is dynamically moved after the parameter addresses are computed but before SWAP is executed.

16.6   INPUT/OUTPUT, INTERRUPTS, AND TRAPS

16.6.1   Input/Output

Like the 68000, the 6809 uses memory-mapped I/O. Similar to the 68000 examples in Chapters 10 and 11, I/O devices connected to a 6809 are controlled by interface registers (I/O ports) that are read and written as locations in the memory address space.

Most computers communicate with terminals using the asynchronous serial I/O protocol described in Appendix B. The Motorola MC6850 Asynchronous Communications Interface Adapter (ACIA), introduced in Section 15.6, is used in many 6809 systems to send and receive data in this serial format. The processor controls the ACIA through two input ports and two output ports whose characteristics are described in Section 15.6. A typical system has one ACIA for each serial I/O link, usually at least one for the "system console."

Table 16–20 shows a subroutine CINIT that initializes an ACIA and a subroutine CRTIN that reads and echoes one character each time it is called. By referring to the ACIA description in Section 15.6, you can see how the subroutines initialize the ACIA and then perform busy-wait I/O. The equated symbols in the first four lines of the program may be modified for different ACIA port addresses or mode requirements.

16.6.2   Interrupts

interrupt request (IRQ)

interrupt mask (I)

The 6809 processor has three interrupt request inputs. The first of these is called *interrupt request (IRQ)*. A device interface can interrupt the processor by placing an appropriate logic signal on the IRQ line (or by "tugging" the line, as some hardware designers say). The processor will accept an interrupt request on this line only if the *interrupt mask (I)* bit in the CC register is 0 (see Figure 16–3). Thus, a program can mask interrupts by setting I to 1.

If more than one device interface is capable of tugging IRQ, then the processor must somehow determine which one is doing it. In 6809 systems, this is normally done by software polling. Unlike the 68000, the 6809 processor does not directly support a hardware means for different devices to supply the processor with different interrupt vectors. However, it's possible to "fake it," as discussed later.

TABLE 16–20   ACIA initialization and input/echo subroutines for the 6809.

```
CRTCS    EQU    $E008        Console ACIA control and status.
CRTDTA   EQU    $E009        Console ACIA xmt and rcv data.
CRESET   EQU    $03          ACIA mode control reset.
CMODE    EQU    $11          ACIA mode control:  8 data bits,
*                               no parity, 2 stop bits, RTS active,
*                               divide-by-16 clock, no interrupts.
*
CINIT    LDA    #CRESET      Initialize console ACIA
         STA    CRTCS            by sending master reset...
         LDA    #CMODE           ...and setting proper mode.
         STA    CRTCS
         RTS
*
CRTIN    LDA    CRTCS        Check for character.
         RORA                Receiver data register full?
         BCC    CRTIN        No, busy wait.
         LDA    CRTDTA       Yes, read the character.
CRTWT    LDB    CRTCS        Can we echo the character now?
         RORB                Must wait for transmitter buffer empty.
         RORB
         BCC    CRTWT        No, wait for previous character.
         STA    CRTDTA       OK, echo the received character
         RTS                     and return to calling program.
```

If the processor accepts an interrupt request on IRQ, it performs a whole sequence of actions automatically. First, it saves the entire processor state by pushing PC and all registers except S onto the stack, using S as the stack pointer. Then it sets the I bit in the CC register to 1, which prevents IRQ from causing further interrupts. It also sets the *entire state on stack (E)* bit in CC to 1. Finally, the processor loads the PC with the 16-bit value contained in an interrupt vector stored at memory locations $FFF8 and $FFF9. This value should be the starting address of an interrupt service routine that has been written by a programmer.

entire state on stack (E)

After accepting an interrupt as described above, the processor returns to its normal instruction fetching and execution process. Since the PC has been loaded with the starting address of the interrupt service routine, the next instruction executed will be the first instruction of the interrupt service routine. The interrupt routine services whatever condition caused the interrupt, and causes the interface to remove its request from the IRQ line. Note that before IRQ is cleared, the request is still ignored because I = 1.

RTI

The service routine returns to the interrupted program by executing an RTI instruction. RTI restores the original values of all of the registers, including the PC and CC, by popping them off the stack. Since the value of the I bit is restored to 0 when the saved CC register is popped from the stack, further interrupts may now be accepted when requested on the IRQ line.

A 6809 program that uses interrupts to transmit text strings serially using the MC6850 ACIA is presented in Table 16–21. The ACIA places an interrupt

TABLE 16–21   ACIA output program using interrupts.

```
*            Subroutines STROUT and STRINT are used to transmit text strings
*         using an MC6850 ACIA.  A text string is defined to be a sequence of
*         non-NUL ASCII characters terminated by NUL (0).
*            To transmit a string, a program should call STROUT with the
*         address of the first character of the string.  STROUT turns on the
*         ACIA interrupts, transmits the first character, and returns to the
*         calling program.  Successive characters are transmitted by the
*         interrupt service routine STRINT.
*            The global variable SBUSY, when nonzero, indicates that a string
*         is currently being transmitted.  Thus, when STROUT is entered, it
*         will not start transmitting a new string until it finds that the
*         previous string has been completely transmitted.  STRINT clears SBUSY
*         after transmitting the last character.  Also, the main program must
*         initialize SBUSY to 0 before the first call of STROUT.
*
*         Define ACIA interface registers.
CRTCS   EQU     $E008           ACIA control and status port.
CRTDTA  EQU     $E009           ACIA data port.
CRESET  EQU     $03             ACIA mode control reset.
CMINT   EQU     $31             ACIA mode control:  8 data bits, no parity,
*                                 2 stop bits, RTS active, n/16 clock, ints on.
CMNOINT EQU     $11             ACIA mode control with interrupts disabled.
*
        ORG     $1000
*         Local and global variables.
BUFPNT  RMW     1               Pointer to character being displayed.
SBUSY   RMB     1               Nonzero when string is being displayed.
*
STROUT  TST     SBUSY           Is a previous string being
        BNE     STROUT            displayed?  Wait for it.
        STX     BUFPNT          Save buffer pointer.
        COM     SBUSY           Set SBUSY flag (was $00, now $FF).
        LDA     ,X              Get first character.
        STA     CRTDTA          Transmit it.
        LDA     #CMINT          Enable interrupts.
        STA     CRTCS
        RTS                     Done, return.
*
STRINT  LDX     BUFPNT          Get buffer pointer.
        LEAX    1,X             Bump pointer to next character.
        STX     BUFPNT          Save updated pointer.
        LDA     ,X              Get next character.
        BEQ     STRDUN          Quit if it's a zero.
        STA     CRTDTA          Otherwise transmit it.
        LDA     #CMINT          Enable interrupts.
        STA     CRTCS
        RTI                     Return to interrupted program.
STRDUN  LDA     #CMNOINT        Disable interrupts.
        STA     CRTCS
        CLR     SBUSY           Clear SBUSY flag.
        RTI                     Return to interrupted program.
```

TABLE 16–21   (continued)

```
*         Main program.
MAIN      LDA    #CRESET        Initialize ACIA
          STA    CRTCS             by sending master reset...
          LDA    #CMODE            ...and setting proper mode.
          STA    CRTCS
          CLR    SBUSY          Clear SBUSY flag.
LOOP      ...                   Do some processing.
          LDX    #MSG1          Print the first message.
          JSR    STROUT
          ...                   Do some more processing.
          LDX    #MSG2          Print the second message.
          JSR    STROUT
          ...                   Do some more processing.
          JMP    LOOP
*
MSG1      FCC    'The quick brown fox jumps over the lazy dog.'
          FCB    0
MSG2      FCC    'That was the same old unimaginative message!'
          FCB    0
*
          ORG    $FFF8          IRQ interrupt vector address.
          FDB    STRINT         Address of interrupt service routine.
*
          END    MAIN
```

request on IRQ whenever its transmitter interrupts are enabled and the transmit buffer is empty. Thus, a request is made on IRQ after each character is transmitted. The request on IRQ is removed each time that STRINT begins transmitting another character (by putting it into CRTDTA, which makes the transmitter "not ready"), or when STRINT finds that it has no more characters to transmit (and disables transmitter interrupts).

The main program can transmit a string by calling STROUT with the string's address in X. STROUT transmits the first character, enables the ACIA transmit interrupt, and then returns control to the main program, which may continue to perform useful computation. The remainder of the string is transmitted by the interrupt service routine STRINT, which uses the variable BUFPNT to keep track of which character is being transmitted.

Our example program is somewhat simplified by the fact that only transmit interrupts are enabled. If both input and output interrupts were enabled, then the service routine would have to check both the transmitter and receiver "ready" bits to determine which side of the ACIA caused the interrupt. If there are other devices that can request interrupts on IRQ, then a more general interrupt polling routine is needed.

nonmaskable interrupt (NMI)
fast interrupt request (FIRQ)

In addition to IRQ, the 6809 has two other interrupt request lines, called *nonmaskable interrupt (NMI)* and *fast interrupt request (FIRQ)*. As summarized in Table 16–22, these lines differ from IRQ in their interrupt vector addresses,

TABLE 16–22 Interrupt request lines and vectors in the 6809.

Input or Instruction	Vector Address	Masked by Bit	Sets CC Bits	Clears CC Bits	Pushes Registers
IRQ	$FFF8	I	I, E	none	PC, U, Y, X, DPR, B, A, CC
FIRQ	$FFF6	F	F, I	E	PC, CC
NMI	$FFFC	none	F, I, E	none	PC, U, Y, X, DPR, B, A, CC
RESET	$FFFE	none	F, I	none	
SWI	$FFFA	none	F, I, E	none	PC, U, Y, X, DPR, B, A, CC
SWI2	$FFF4	none	E	none	PC, U, Y, X, DPR, B, A, CC
SWI3	$FFF2	none	E	none	PC, U, Y, X, DPR, B, A, CC

how they are masked, and which registers are pushed onto the stack when the interrupt is accepted. The processor also responds to hardware resets and software interrupt instructions in a manner similar to hardware interrupts, as explained in the next subsection.

The NMI input is similar to IRQ, but it cannot be masked. Interrupts on FIRQ cause only the PC and condition bits (CC) to be stacked, saving execution time in interrupt service routines that don't use many or any registers. The E bit in the saved CC keeps track of whether all the registers were pushed; the RTI instruction looks at this to determine which registers to pop.

faking it

We mentioned previously that the 6809 processor does not directly support a vectoring mechanism whereby different devices that use the same interrupt request line can have different interrupt service routines. However, additional, specialized hardware can provide this capability. For example, suppose that several devices use IRQ. The additional hardware would have to provide priority selection among the devices, and also the capability of responding to read operations on the memory and I/O bus at addresses $FFF8 and $FFF9. Reads of these "pseudo-memory" locations would return a 16-bit value corresponding to the highest priority device currently requesting an interrupt, the address of its interrupt service routine.

SYNC

Two special 6809 instructions are used with interrupts. SYNC suspends instruction fetching and execution until an interrupt request is received on the IRQ, FIRQ, or NMI input. When an interrupt request is finally received, what happens next depends on whether that interrupt is masked in CC. If the interrupt is not masked, then the processor executes an interrupt service routine in the usual way and then returns control to the instruction following SYNC. If the interrupt is masked, then the service routine is not executed, but execution proceeds immediately with the instruction following SYNC. This allows the processor to wait for or synchronize with external events without incurring the overhead of interrupt processing.

CWAI

The CWAI instruction ANDs an immediate byte with CC; this may clear one or both interrupt mask bits. Then it pushes the entire CPU state onto the stack and waits for an interrupt to occur. When an unmasked interrupt finally does occur, the processor state will already have been stacked, and so the interrupt service routine will be entered and executed more quickly. Note that, if the interrupt request occurs on FIRQ, the proper value of E will be set in CC on the stack so that the entire CPU state will be popped by `RTI` on the return.

The 6809 does not have an explicit `test` and `set` instruction for mutual exclusion and synchronization among multiple processes, but the `ASR` instruction may be adapted to perform a locking function in a single-processor environment (see Exercise 16.13).

16.6.3 Traps and Reset

SWI
SWI2
SWI3

The 6809 processor does not trap on abnormal conditions such as illegal instructions, but it does have three explicit trap-type instructions, `SWI`, `SWI2`, and `SWI3`. When one of these instructions is executed, the processor registers are pushed onto the stack in the same way as during an IRQ or NMI hardware interrupt. Then control is transferred to a corresponding interrupt service routine whose 16-bit starting address is found at the interrupt vector address shown in Table 16–22. For example, the starting address for the `SWI` service routine is contained in memory bytes $FFFA and $FFFB. The service routine does some processing and then returns control to the calling program by executing an `RTI` instruction.

reset

The 6809 also uses an interrupt vector when an external *reset* signal is applied to the 6809, typically when power is first applied to the system. In this case, however, it simply loads the PC with the word found at memory address $FFFE. It does not save any registers onto the stack since S may have an arbitrary value.

R E F E R E N C E S

The 6809 was first described in "A Microprocessor for the Revolution: The 6809," a three-part series by Terry Ritter and Joel Boney that appeared in *Byte* [January, February, March, 1979 (Vol. 4, No. 1,2,3)]. Motorola publishes a programming reference manual for the 6809, *MC6809–MC6809E 8-Bit Microprocessor Programming Manual*, [Motorola publication M6809PM(AD), May 1983]. The original version of the book you're now reading was based on the 6809 [*Microcomputer Architecture and Programming* by John F. Wakerly (Wiley, 1981)]. A very comprehensive book on programming the 6809 is Lance Leventhal's *6809 Assembly Language Programming* (Osborne/McGraw-Hill, 1981).

E X E R C I S E S

16.1   What is a "phasing error"?

16.2   Explain any differences in instruction effect, size, or speed between the 6809's register indirect addressing mode and the based mode with a 5-bit offset of 0.

16.3   There are a number of instruction pairs in the 6809 that have exactly the same effect (e.g., `LBRA expr` and `JMP expr,PCR`) or almost the same effect (e.g., `LDX expr` and `LEAX [expr]`, the second instruction does not affect all the condition bits). Find five other such pairs; pairs obtained by simply changing a register name (e.g. `LDY` and `LEAY`) are not allowed. For each pair, either indicate that the instructions have exactly the same effect or explain their differences.

16.4   Suppose that we tried to write a 6809 assembler that could automatically select between `BRA` and `LBRA` instructions according to the distance of the target address from the instruction. What problems occur when the target address expression contains a forward reference? How many passes does the assembler need to resolve such forward references?

16.5   Write a 6809 program similar to Table 16–12 that multiplies two 32-bit quantities and produces a 32-bit result.

16.6   In Table 16–19, why didn't we use `LEAX CAT` instead of `LDX #CAT`?

16.7   Rewrite the sorting program in Table 7–3 for the 6809. Use stacks of bytes instead of stacks of words.

16.8   Rewrite the program in Table 16–15 to use position-independent code.

16.9   Rewrite the word queueing program in Table 8–11 in page 286 for the 6809.

16.10   Rewrite the queue manipulation routines of Table 9–20 on page 338 for the 6809. Be sure to update the prologues as well as the code.

16.11   Rewrite the recursive NIM subroutines of Table 9–22 on page 338 for the 6809.

16.12   Show how a resumption address stored at the top of the S stack can be used to link two coroutines on the 6809, such that a single 6809 instruction can be used to save the resumption address of the current coroutine and resume the other one. Explain why this technique breaks down when there are three or more coroutines.

16.13   Show how to use the 6809's `ASR` instruction on a memory location to perform a locking function equivalent to the one using 68000's `BSET` instruction described in Section 12.3.3.

16.14   Write a complete Pascal simulation of the 6809.

CHAPTER 17

A Classic Mini/Micro Architecture: The DEC PDP-11 and LSI-11

PDP-11/20

PDP-11/34
PDP-11/40
PDP-11/70
PDP-11/03
PDP-11/04
LSI-11/23
PDP-11/23

The PDP-11 was the first minicomputer architecture specifically designed to support an evolving family of computers spanning a range of price and performance. Thus the *PDP-11/20*, introduced in 1970, was just the first in a long series of compatible minicomputers and microcomputers manufactured by Digital Equipment Corporation (DEC). Family members include: *PDP-11/34*, *PDP-11/40* and *PDP-11/70*, high-performance minicomputers supporting large timesharing systems such as UNIX; *PDP-11/03* and *PDP-11/04*, low-end minicomputers for dedicated applications; *LSI-11/23*, a single-board computer module for custom systems; and the *PDP-11/23*, a packaged microcomputer that uses the LSI-11/23.

One measure of the success of a product or idea is how much it is copied. The PDP-11 family introduced (or in a few cases popularized) many features of contemporary minicomputers and microcomputers: memory-mapped I/O; NZVC condition codes; dedicated stack pointer SP for subroutine and interrupt calls; short relative conditional branches; auto-increment, auto-decrement, and immediate addressing modes; multilevel interrupt systems; software interrupts; and byte-addressable memories. Because the PDP-11 architecture embodies so many important minicomputer and microcomputer features, it is an important machine to study even if you don't expect to be using one soon.

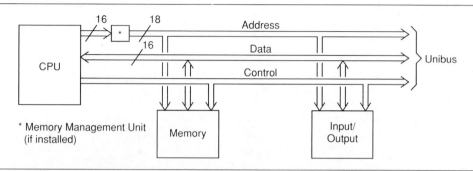

FIGURE 17–1   PDP-11 computer block diagram.

17.1   BASIC ORGANIZATION

17.1.1   Computer Structure

Unibus

Q-bus

The basic structure of a PDP-11 computer is shown in Figure 17–1. The memory and I/O bus, called the *Unibus*, contains a 16-bit data bus, an 18-bit address bus, and various control signals. (LSI-11 systems use the *Q-bus*, which is somewhat different from the Unibus mechanically and electrically, but identical as far as a programmer is concerned.) Only 16 bits of the address bus are used in a basic processor without a memory management unit, since instructions contain only 16-bit addresses. Each address specifies one of 2^{16} (64K) 8-bit bytes, arranged with the lower address assigned to the low-order byte of a word as shown in Figure 5.1.1(b) on page 127.

I/O address space

The PDP-11 has no I/O instructions, and there are no Unibus control signals to distinguish between memory and I/O operations. Instead, the upper 8 Kbytes of the memory address space (the *I/O address space*) are reserved for memory-mapped I/O interfaces. The PDP-11 processor and Unibus support a multilevel, vectored, priority interrupt system.

17.1.2   Processor Programming Model

processor status word (PSW)

general registers (R0–R7)

condition code bits (NZVC)

trace flag (T)

interrupt priority mask (PRI)

program counter (PC)

stack pointer (SP)

The PDP-11 processor is a fine example of a general register machine. As shown in Figure 17–2, the processor state consists of a 16-bit *processor status word (PSW)* and eight 16-bit *general registers (R0–R7)*. Included in the PSW are the four standard *condition code bits (NZVC)*, a 1-bit *trace flag (T)* used by on-line debuggers, a 3-bit *interrupt priority mask (PRI)*, and eight other bits whose meanings depend on the PDP-11 model.

The *program counter (PC)* is one of the general registers, R7. This means that the PC may be used as a source, destination, or address register for any operation, providing a novel means of obtaining some standard addressing modes, as we'll see later. Another one of the general registers also has a special use: R6 is used as a *stack pointer (SP)* to push and pop return addresses during subroutine and interrupt calls and returns.

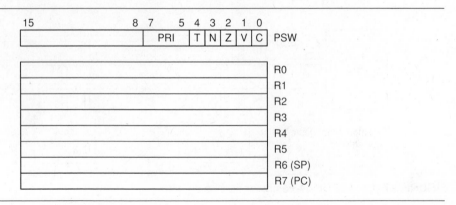

FIGURE 17–2   Programming model for the PDP-11.

17.1.3   Instruction Formats

The major instruction formats of the PDP-11 are shown in Figure 17–3. The fields labeled src and dst specify operands using addressing modes described in Section 17.3. The PDP-11 has a very regular instruction set in the sense that instructions with src and dst fields may specify addressing modes without restrictions. The instruction set is also very regular in the sense that almost every instruction that operates on words can also operate on bytes, as specified by a bit in the opcode field.

As suggested by Figure 17–3, all basic PDP-11 instructions are one word long. For some addressing modes, one word of additional addressing information is appended to the instruction. Thus, an instruction with both src and dst fields may contain up to two words of addressing information, and PDP-11 instruction lengths may vary from one to three words.

17.2   ASSEMBLY LANGUAGE

Standard PDP-11 assembly language uses a free format as defined in Chapter 6. It does not rely on spaces to delimit label and comment fields. Instead, a label is followed by a colon, and a comment is preceded by a semicolon. Thus, all of the following are valid lines of assembly code:

```
START:MOV X,Y;These two lines are really tight.
SUB IND,COUNT
;       The rest of these lines are more typical.
NEXT:   ADD     Z , Y           ;It's nice line up comments
        MOV     Y,X             ;   and other fields, too.
; *** Sometimes we use a whole line for an important message ***
```

Other important features of the assembly language include the following:

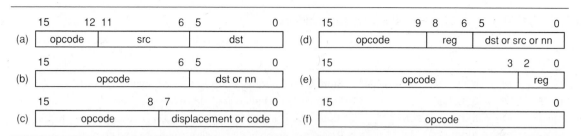

FIGURE 17–3   Major PDP-11 instruction formats: (a) double operand; (b) single operand and JMP; (c) branch and trap; (d) JSR, XOR, and fixed-point arithmetic; (e) RTS; (f) no operand.

- Integer constants are assumed to be in octal, unless followed by a period for decimal.

- An equal sign is used instead of EQU or SET in symbol equations; the value of a symbol may be assigned more than once (as with SET).

- Register numbers are distinguished from memory addresses by preceding them with a percent sign, usually in symbol assignments at the beginning of the program (e.g., SP=%6).

- The program location counter (PLC) is denoted by a period; it may appear on the left-hand side as well as the right-hand side of an "=" symbol assignment.

- There is no ORG directive; instead, a statement like ".=1000" sets the starting value of the PLC.

- One-byte ASCII constants are denoted by preceding an ASCII character with a single quote; for example, 'A yields the value 101_8. Two-byte ASCII constants are denoted by double quotes; for example, "AC yields the value $101_8 + 256 \cdot 103_8 = 041501_8$. Notice that the first character (A) is stored in the least-significant byte.

- Directive names begin with a period. Important PDP-11 assembler directives are listed in Table 17–1.

The next section will give assembly language notation for PDP-11 operand addressing modes; relative addressing is the default. Table 17–2 illustrates some of the features of PDP-11 assembly language.

17.3   ADDRESSING

word

The PDP-11 memory is byte addressable, and many instructions specify 1-byte operands. Most instructions access two bytes as a unit—the *word*. A word has an even address, as does its low-order byte, as shown in Figure 5.1.1(b)

TABLE 17–1   PDP-11 assembly language directives.

Name	Example	Effect
.WORD	WT: .WORD 17,-789.,CAT	Store constant values into successive memory words.
.BYTE	BT: .BYTE 17,99.,'A	Store constant values into successive memory bytes.
.ASCII	AT: .ASCII /ABCDEFG/	Store ASCII character values into successive memory bytes.
.BLKW	BF: .BLKW 10.	Reserve a number of words of memory. BLKW N has the same effect as .=.+(2*N).
=	BE = BF+10.	Equate symbol with 16-bit expression.
.EVEN	.EVEN	Forces the PLC to an even value (i.e., increments it if it is odd). Useful after .BYTE and .ASCII.
.END	.END START	Indicates end of assembly, gives an optional starting address.

on page 127. If an instruction that requires a 1-word operand tries to access an odd address, an error trap occurs. This restriction is made for reasons of efficiency—the PDP-11 memory is physically organized as an array of 16-bit words, so that it is impossible to access in one memory cycle a 2-byte quantity that is split across a word boundary.

TABLE 17–2   PDP-11 assembly language program.

```
                                ;Sample program.
        .=2000                  ;Starts at address 2000 octal.
R0      =       %0              ;Register definitions.
R1      =       %1
SP      =       %6
PC      =       %7
COUNT   =       10.             ;Iteration count.
;
START:  MOV     INIT,SUM;       sum := initialValue;
        CLR     R0
        MOV     TBADDR,R1;      FOR i:=1 TO count DO
LOOP:   ADD     (R1),SUM;          sum := sum + table[i];
        ADD     #2,R1
        INC     R0
        CMP     R0,#COUNT
        BLT     LOOP
        HALT

SUM:    .=.+2                   ;1-word variable.
INIT:   .WORD   17.             ;Initial value.
TBADDR: .WORD   TABLE           ;Starting address of table.
TABLE:  .BLKW   COUNT           ;Reserve COUNT words for table.
        .END    START
```

$$\begin{array}{c} 5 \quad\quad 3 \; 2 \quad\quad 0 \\ \boxed{\text{mode} \;|\; \text{reg}} \end{array}$$

FIGURE 17–4   PDP-11 operand specification.

17.3.1 Basic Addressing Modes

reg
mode

Both single and double operand instructions may have operands in memory; the PDP-11 is a two-address machine. An operand is specified by a 6-bit field in the instruction, consisting of a 3-bit register number and a 3-bit addressing mode designator, as shown in Figure 17–4. The *reg* field specifies one of the eight general registers and *mode* specifies how that register is used to obtain the operand. Mode 0 uses the register itself as the operand; modes 1–7 compute the effective address of an operand in memory, as summarized below.

register direct
addressing

(1) *Register direct.* The operand is reg itself; there is no effective address in memory.

register indirect
addressing

(2) *Register indirect.* The effective address of the operand is taken from reg.

auto-increment
addressing

(3) *Auto-increment.* The effective address of the operand is taken from reg and then reg is incremented by the length of the operand (1 or 2).

auto-increment
indirect
addressing

(4) *Auto-increment indirect.* An indirect address is taken from reg and then reg is incremented by 2. The effective address is taken from the contents of memory at the indirect address.

auto-decrement
addressing

(5) *Auto-decrement.* The reg is decremented by the length of the operand (1 or 2) and then the effective address of the operand is taken from reg.

auto-decrement
indirect
addressing

(6) *Auto-decrement indirect.* The reg is decremented by 2 and then an indirect address is taken from reg. The effective address is taken from the contents of memory at the indirect address.

indexed
addressing

(7) *Indexed.* Register reg and the next word in the instruction stream are added to form the effective address, and the PC is bumped to the next word in the instruction stream. Unless reg = PC, the contents of reg are not disturbed.

indexed indirect
addressing

(8) *Indexed indirect.* Register reg and the next word in the instruction stream are added to form an indirect address. The effective address is taken from the contents of memory at the indirect address.

deferred
addressing

The manufacturer's literature uses the word "deferred" instead of "indirect" when describing modes 1, 3, 5, and 7.

Modes 2 through 5 above increment or decrement register reg by 1 or 2. Thus, they may be used to step forward or backward through tables of bytes or words without extra instructions to update address pointers. Auto-increment and auto-decrement modes also allow any register to be used as a pointer into a stack with standard characteristics:

- The stack pointer always points directly at the top stack item.

- The stack grows by decrementing the stack pointer.

With these conventions, a store instruction using auto-decrement mode pushes an item onto the stack, while load auto-increment pops an item. Thus, any register except PC can be conveniently used as a stack pointer in a program.

The PDP-11 hardware reserves register R6 as a system stack pointer SP, and uses it for interrupt and subroutine calls and returns. The PDP-11's restriction that words have even addresses makes it impractical to store words and bytes in the same stack. Therefore, the hardware forces an entire word to be pushed or popped in byte operations that auto-increment or auto-decrement SP.

17.3.2 PC Addressing Modes

At first glance, it may appear that some important addressing modes are missing in the PDP-11, such as immediate, absolute, and PC relative. However, when reg is PC, these modes are obtained as special cases of the basic modes:

immediate addressing

(1) *Auto-increment PC (immediate).* The effective address is the value of PC; that is, the operand is the next word in the instruction stream. The PC is incremented by 2, bumping it past the operand to the next word. (To keep PC even, it is incremented by 2 even if the operand is a byte.)

absolute addressing

(2) *Auto-increment PC indirect (absolute).* The effective address is taken from the next word in the instruction stream and the PC is incremented by 2.

relative addressing

(3) *PC indexed (relative).* The next word in the instruction stream is read and temporarily saved; PC is incremented by 2. Then the saved value and the new PC are added to form the effective address.

relative indirect addressing

(4) *PC indexed indirect (relative indirect).* The next word in the instruction stream and the new PC are added to form an indirect address. The effective address is taken from the contents of memory at the indirect address.

17.3.3 Addressing Mode Summary

PDP-11 addressing modes and assembly language notation are summarized in Table 17–3. The fourth column shows the value that is stored in the second or third word of the instruction for modes that require additional information.

17.3.4 Pascal Simulation of Addressing Modes

The PDP-11's addressing modes may also be defined by the Pascal simulation in Table 17–4. This code is written in the same style as the 68000 simulation in Table 5–2 on page 138, and it requires the Bits function to be defined similarly—Bits(f,t,w) returns the unsigned integer value of a bit field extending from bit f to bit t in a word w.

TABLE 17–3   PDP-11 addressing modes.

mode	reg	Notation	Next Word	Name
0	0–7	R	not used	Register
1	0–7	(R) or @R	not used	Register indirect
2	0–7	(R)+	not used	Auto-increment
3	0–7	@(R)+	not used	Auto-increment indirect
4	0–7	–(R)	not used	Auto-decrement
5	0–7	@–(R)	not used	Auto-decrement indirect
6	0–7	EXPR(R)	EXPR	Indexed
7	0–7	@EXPR(R)	EXPR	Indexed indirect
2	7	#EXPR	EXPR	Immediate
3	7	@#EXPR	EXPR	Absolute
6	7	EXPR	EXPR-PLC-2	Relative
7	7	@EXPR	EXPR-PLC-2	Relative Indirect

Notes: R = register number; EXPR = expression.
        PLC is the address of the offset word, not the first word of the instruction.

The function RMW in the simulation reads two bytes into a word and detects any attempt to read a word at an odd address. Although it shows the correct effect on the processor state, RMW does not emulate an exact sequence of hardware operations. A typical PDP-11 computer has a 16-bit-wide data path between the processor and memory, and a full word may be read in one step instead of two.

17.3.5 Memory Mapping and Management

page

A memory management unit is available on some PDP-11s to map a 16-bit logical address into an 18-bit or 22-bit physical address, depending on the model. The PDP-11/34, PDP-11/40, and LSI-11/23 use the 18-bit mapping technique shown in Figure 17–5. The map has eight rows, selected by the three high-order bits of the logical address. Therefore, the logical address space is divided into eight 8-Kbyte *pages*. Mapping is accomplished by adding the logical address supplied by the processor to an 18-bit base address in the selected map entry. The 6 low-order bits of the base address are always assumed to be zero, so that each map entry actually specifies only the 12 high-order bits of the base address. Each map entry also contains control and status bits giving information such as the length of the page (in case less than 8 Kbytes are being used) and read/write protection status. The mapping registers appear in the I/O address space, and may be manipulated like other I/O registers.

PDP-11 models with memory management also have user and supervisor operating modes to support operating systems, as in the 68000. In addition, there are separate stack pointers and memory maps for user programs and the operating system (or kernel). Fields in the PSW indicate the current operating mode and which memory map is being used. Interrupts and traps always activate the kernel map, and push information onto the kernel stack. Special instructions allow data to be transferred between the user and kernel address spaces.

TABLE 17–4   Simulation of PDP-11 addressing modes.

```
PROGRAM PDP11 (input,output);
CONST
  PC = 7; SP = 6;
TYPE
  bit = 0..1; byte = 0..255; word = 0..65535; address = 0..65535;
VAR
  R: ARRAY [0..7] OF word; {General registers}
  MEM: ARRAY [address] OF byte; {Main memory}
  EAR, PSW: word;  byteInstr, addrError : boolean;

FUNCTION RMW(addr: address): word; {Read a memory word}
  BEGIN                        {Word must be at even address.}
    IF addr MOD 2 = 1 THEN BEGIN addrError := true; RMW := 0 END
    ELSE BEGIN
        addrError := false;
        ReadMemWord := MEM[addr] + MEM[addr+1]*256;
      END;
  END;

PROCEDURE CalcEAR (opSpec: 0..63);
  VAR mode, reg : 0..7;
  BEGIN
    mode := Bits(5,3,opSpec); reg := Bits(2,0,opSpec);
    CASE mode OF
      0: {register} ; {EAR not used}
      1: {register indirect} EAR := R[reg];
      2: {auto-increment}
        BEGIN EAR := R[reg];
          IF byteInstr AND (reg <> PC) AND (reg <> SP) THEN
            R[reg] := R[reg] + 1 ELSE R[reg] := R[reg] + 2;
        END;
      3: {auto-increment indirect}
        BEGIN EAR := RMW(R[reg]); R[reg] := R[reg] + 2 END;
      4: {auto-decrement}
        BEGIN IF byteInstr AND (reg <> PC) AND (reg <> SP) THEN
            R[reg] := R[reg] - 1 ELSE R[reg] := R[reg] - 2;
          EAR := R[reg];
        END;
      5: {auto-decrement indirect}
        BEGIN R[reg] := R[reg] - 2; EAR := RMW(R[reg]) END;
      6: {indexed}
        BEGIN EAR := RMW(R[PC]); R[PC] := R[PC] + 2;
          EAR := EAR + R[reg];
        END;
      7: {indexed indirect}
        BEGIN EAR := RMW(R[PC]); R[PC] := R[PC] + 2;
          EAR := RMW(EAR+R[reg]);
        END;
    END;
  END;
...
```

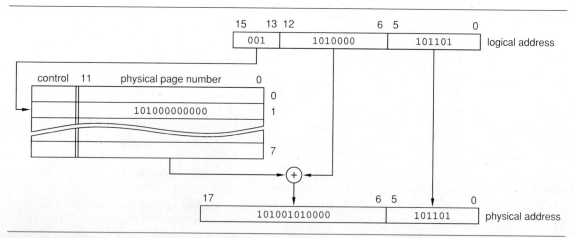

FIGURE 17–5   Mapping of 16-bit logical addresses into 18-bit physical addresses in the PDP-11.

17.4   OPERATION TYPES

We shall classify PDP-11 instructions into five types: double operand, single operand, program control, miscellaneous, and extended.

17.4.1   Double Operand

PDP-11 double-operand instructions, listed in Table 17–5, specify both a source (`src`) and a destination (`dst`) for the operation. The operation order in standard PDP-11 assembly language is left to right, for example, `MOV src TO dst`. Most operations may be performed on either words or bytes. Byte operations on registers access only the low-order byte, except for `MOVB src,reg`, which copies the byte `src` into the low-order byte of `reg` and extends its sign into

TABLE 17–5   PDP-11 double-operand instructions.

Mnemonic	Operands	Format	Description
MOV(B)	src,dst	a	Copy src to dst
ADD	src,dst	a	Add src word to dst
SUB	src,dst	a	Subtract src word from dst
CMP(B)	src,dst	a	Set NZVC according to src minus dst
BIS(B)	src,dst	a	Set corresponding 1 bits of src in dst
BIC(B)	src,dst	a	Clear corresponding 1 bits of src in dst
BIT(B)	src,dst	a	Set NZVC according to src AND dst
XOR	reg,dst	d	Exclusive OR reg into dst

Notes: The notation (B) indicates an instruction that exists for both bytes and words. For example,
MOV moves a word, MOVB a byte.
src and dst are each given by a 6-bit operand specification.
reg is a 3-bit register number.

the high-order byte. All operations set, clear, or hold condition code bits NZVC according to the result of the operation, usually as described in Chapter 8; refer to a PDP-11 processor handbook for the exact rules.

MOV, MOVB

The MOV(B) instruction is the workhorse of the PDP-11 instruction set, accounting for 32% of all the opcodes counted in one study of typical PDP-11 programs. With appropriate addressing modes, one or both operands of MOV may be in memory. Thus MOV performs the functions of both LD and ST found in other architectures, and it performs PUSH and POP when used with auto-decrement and auto-increment addressing. As an added bonus, it allows memory-to-memory data moves without intermediate storage in a register.

ADD
SUB
BIS, BISB
BIC, BICB
XOR
CMP, CMPB
BIT, BITB

The ADD, SUB, BIS(B), BIC(B), and XOR instructions combine src and dst operands and store the result in dst. BIS(B) (bit set) is just another name for logical OR, while BIC(B) (bit clear) performs the logical AND of dst and the *complement* of src. XOR was an addition to the original PDP-11/20 instruction set, which accounts for its restricted format: it allows only a register as source operand. The CMP(B) and BIT(B) instructions compare two operands without modifying them, and set the condition codes according to the result.

17.4.2   Single Operand

PDP-11 single-operand instructions are listed in Table 17–6. Like the double-operand instructions, they all set the condition codes according to their results. Most of the operations are self-explanatory. The shift and rotate instructions operate in the usual way, and all store the lost bit into C. Although SWAB may look like a byte instruction, it swaps the bytes of a word. SXT loads a destination word with all zeroes or all ones depending on whether N is 0 or 1.

SWAB
SXT

TABLE 17–6   PDP-11 single-operand instructions.

Mnemonic	Operands	Format	Description
CLR(B)	dst	b	Clear dst
COM(B)	dst	b	Complement dst (one's complement)
INC(B)	dst	b	Increment dst by 1
DEC(B)	dst	b	Decrement dst by 1
NEG(B)	dst	b	Negate dst (two's complement)
TST(B)	dst	b	Set NZVC according to value of dst
ASR(B)	dst	b	Arithmetic shift right dst
ASL(B)	dst	b	Arithmetic shift left dst
ROR(B)	dst	b	Rotate dst right with C
ROL(B)	dst	b	Rotate dst left with C
ADC(B)	dst	b	Add C to dst
SBC(B)	dst	b	Subtract C from dst
SWAB	dst	b	Swap bytes of dst word
SXT	dst	b	Extend sign (N) into dst word

Notes: The notation (B) indicates an instruction that exists for both bytes and words. For example,
CLR clears a word, CLRB a byte. dst is given by 6-bit operand specification.

TABLE 17-7   PDP-11 program control instructions.

Mnemonic	Operands	Format	Description
BR	rel8	c	Unconditional branch
Bcc	rel8	c	Conditional branch
JMP	dst	b	Jump to effective address of dst
JSR	reg,dst	d	Jump to subroutine
RTS	reg	e	Return from subroutine
MARK	nn	b	Strange stack clean-up
SOB	reg,nn	d	Subtract one and branch if not zero
EMT	code	c	Emulator trap
TRAP	code	c	User trap
BPT		f	Breakpoint trap
IOT		f	Input/output trap
RTI		f	Return from interrupt, allow trace
RTT		f	Return from interrupt, inhibit trace

Notes: rel8 = a target address with 128 words of the instruction.
       cc = one of the conditions listed in Table 8–9.
       nn = 6-bit unsigned integer; dst = 6-bit operand specification.
       reg = 3-bit register number; code = arbitrary 8-bit value.

17.4.3   Program Control

Program control instructions of the PDP-11 are listed in Table 17–7. Among these instructions, the most frequently used are the conditional and unconditional branches, 20% of all the instructions counted in the study mentioned earlier. As indicated in Figure 17–3(c), a branch instruction has an 8-bit opcode and an 8-bit signed displacement. If the branch is taken, the displacement is multiplied by 2 and added to the PC to obtain the address of the next instruction. When this addition takes place, the processor has already incremented PC to point to the next instruction. Thus, a displacement of − 1, not 0, causes an instruction to branch to itself.

BR
BHIS
BLOS

JMP
JSR

    The PDP-11 has 14 different conditional branches and one unconditional branch, precisely the branches that were defined and explained in Section 8.7. There is a slight difference in mnemonics: the 68000's BRA, BHS, and BLS are called BR, BHIS, and BLOS in the PDP-11.

    Other PDP-11 program control instructions are shown in the second part of Table 17–7. JMP and JSR both jump to the effective address specified by dst (register mode is not allowed). Before jumping, JSR reg,dst sets up a subroutine linkage as follows:

(1) Calculate and save the effective address of dst in an internal processor register TMP.

(2) Push the contents of reg onto the stack using SP.

(3) Save the current PC in reg.

(4) Load PC with the saved address from TMP.

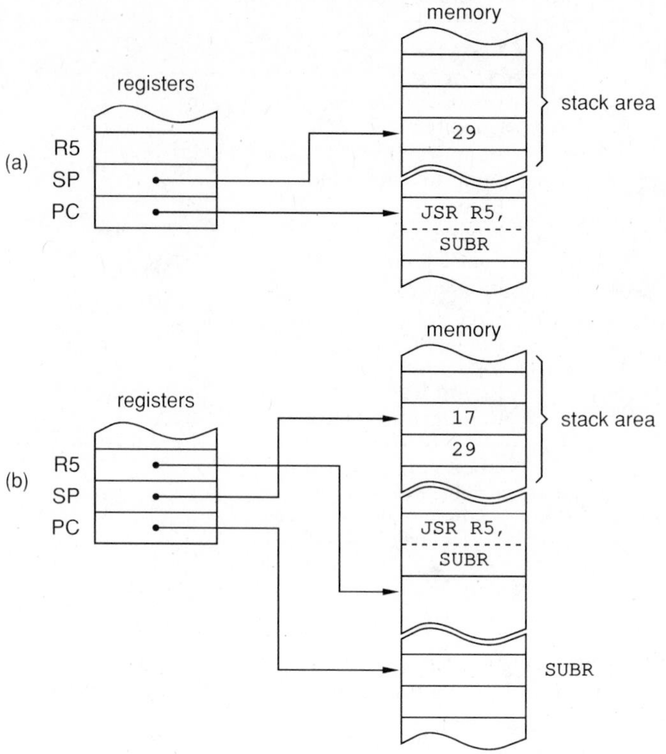

FIGURE 17–6   Effect of JSR R5, SUBR: (a) before; (b) after.

RTS

A subroutine return is made by the RTS reg instruction; the same register reg must be used in the call and the return. The effect of RTS is:

(1) Load PC with the contents of reg.

(2) Pop the value at the top of the stack into reg.

Figure 17–6 shows the effect of executing JSR R5, SUBR. The old value of R5 is pushed onto the stack and the return address is saved in R5. The subroutine must preserve the value of R5 so that a return can be effected by an RTS R5 instruction; this loads PC with the return address and restores the old value of R5. Nested subroutine calls should also use JSR R5, dst to preserve the value of R5 automatically on the stack.

The primary use of JSR and RTS with reg equal to R0 through R5 is in subroutines with in-line parameter areas. In this case, reg will point to the parameter area after the call, and the parameters may be accessed by auto-increment or indexed addressing using reg. However, a more conventional subroutine calling convention is obtained when reg = PC. In this case, the effect of JSR is simply to push the return address (current PC) onto the stack, and the effect of RTS is to pop the return address back into PC, without affecting R0 through R5. Parameters may then be passed in the registers, in main memory locations, on the stack, or using any other convention that the programmer can think of.

MARK nn

The MARK nn instruction pops nn words off the stack and then does the equivalent of an RTS R5, part of a PDP-11 subroutine calling and returning convention that uses R5 as the frame pointer. SOB is a useful loop control

SOB

primitive. After subtracting 1 from the designated register, it branches backward 0 to 63 words (nn) if the register value is nonzero. The remaining instructions in Table 17–7 are explained later, in connection with PDP-11 interrupts and traps.

17.4.4 Miscellaneous

CLx
SEx
HALT
RESET

A few miscellaneous instructions are given in Table 17–8. Individual condition code bits in the PSW are cleared and set by CLx and SEx. HALT stops the processor, leaving the PC pointing at the next instruction that would have been executed. Manual intervention is required to restart the processor. RESET causes a reset pulse to be generated on the Unibus; the effect of this pulse on peripheral devices is device dependent.

WAIT

The WAIT instruction temporarily suspends instruction fetching, resuming processing when any interrupt is received. After the interrupt service routine, instruction execution is resumed at the instruction following the WAIT. Executing a WAIT is more desirable than using a busy-wait loop in some situations; WAIT frees up the Unibus for DMA operations that would otherwise have to compete with the CPU for the bus as the CPU fetches the busy-wait instructions.

We still haven't encountered instructions that read and write the entire PSW as a 16-bit register. Such instructions are not provided in many PDP-11 models; instead, the PSW is accessed as a "pseudo-memory" location 177776_8.

MFPS dst
MTPS src

In LSI-11 models, the PSW is accessed by MFPS dst (Move from PSW) and MTPS src (Move to PSW).

TABLE 17–8   PDP-11 miscellaneous instructions.

Mnemonic	Format	Description
NOP	f	No operation
CL(C,V,N,Z)	f	Clear condition code bit(s)
SE(C,V,N,Z)	f	Set condition code bit(s)
RESET	f	Reset Unibus
HALT	f	Halt the processor
WAIT	f	Wait for interrupt

Notes: Instructions on condition bits may be combined to either set or clear multiple bits in one instruction. For example, CLC|CLZ is a single instruction that clears both C and Z.

TABLE 17–9   Fixed-point arithmetic instructions.

Mnemonic	Operands	Format	Description
MUL	src,reg	d	Multiply reg by src
DIV	src,reg	d	Divide reg by src
ASH	src,reg	d	Arithmetic shift reg according to src
ASHC	src,reg	d	Shift double reg according to src

17.4.5 Extended

extended arithmetic instructions

There are two main types of extended instructions in various PDP-11 models—addressing and arithmetic. The *extended addressing instructions* are used to move data between different address spaces in models with memory management units such as PDP-11/70s and LSI-11/23s. *Extended arithmetic instructions* provide fixed-point and floating-point arithmetic. They are standard on newer PDP-11 models, but optional or unavailable on older models.

MUL

The fixed-point arithmetic instructions are listed in Table 17–9. The MUL instruction computes a double-word product of two signed words and stores the result in reg,reg+1 if reg is even numbered (high-order word in reg). If reg is odd, only the low-order word of the product is stored. In either case, C is set if the product takes more than one word to represent, but held at its previous value otherwise. The V bit is cleared (overflow is impossible), and N and Z are set according to the double-word product value.

DIV

The DIV instruction requires that reg be even, and divides a signed src into the signed double word in reg,reg+1. The quotient appears in reg and the remainder in reg+1. The V bit is set on overflow (zero divisor or quotient too large); C is set on divide-by-0. N and Z are set according to the quotient. The remainder has the same sign as the dividend.

ASH

The ASH instruction arithmetically shifts reg a number of times specified by the src operand, whose low-order six bits are interpreted as a two's-complement number in the range -32 to $+31$. Negative denotes a left shift, positive a right shift. ASHC does the same with a double register, reg,reg+1, if reg is even; otherwise it rotates reg right by |src| bits.

ASHC

Descriptions of floating-point instructions can be found in the appropriate processor handbook—they are not the same in all PDP-11 models.

17.5 SAMPLE PROGRAMS

The simple multiplication program that we showed for the 68000 in Table 5–6 on page 152 is translated into PDP-11 assembly language in Table 17–10. The main difference from the 68000 version of the program is in the use of the ADD instruction. Since the PDP-11 allows memory-to-memory operations, the ADD instruction can work directly on MCND and PROD in memory, without using a

TABLE 17–10   Multiplication by repeated addition.

```
;           Enter with multiplier and multiplicand in locations MPY and MCND.
;           Exit with product in memory location PROD.
            .=25100             ;Program origin.
START:  CLR     PROD            ;Set PROD to 0.
        MOV     MPY,CNT         ;Do loop MPY times.
        BEQ     DONE            ;Done if MPY = 0.
LOOP:   ADD     MCND,PROD       ;Add MCND to PROD
        DEC     CNT             ;   and do loop MPY (CNT) times.
        BNE     LOOP            ;Repeat the loop again.
DONE:   JMP     10000           ;Go to operating system restart address.
*
CNT:    .BLKW   1               ;Loop counter.
MPY:    .BLKW   1               ;Multiplier.
MCND:   .BLKW   1               ;Multiplicand.
PROD:   .BLKW   1               ;Product.
        .END    START
```

temporary register for PROD as in the 68000. Also notice that the loop counter CNT is kept in a memory location.

Although the PDP-11's memory-to-memory operations are convenient, its register-to-register operations are faster. Table 17–11 shows how variables may be kept in registers during loops to obtain the fastest possible execution time.

For example, consider the instruction ADD MCND,PROD. If the variables are kept in registers, the ADD instruction is one word long and only one memory

TABLE 17–11   Multiplication by repeated addition with variables in registers.

```
;           Enter with multiplier and multiplicand in locations MPY and MCND.
;           Exit with product in memory location PROD.
RCNT    =       %0              ;Loop counter.
RMPY    =       %1              ;Multiplier register.
RMCND   =       %2              ;Multiplicand register.
RPROD   =       %3              ;Product register.
            .=25100             ;Program origin.
START:  CLR     RPROD           ;Set RPROD to 0.
        MOVE    MCND,RMCND      ;Put MCND into register for fast loop.
        MOV     MPY,RCNT        ;Do loop MPY times.
        BEQ     DONE            ;Done if MPY = 0.
LOOP:   ADD     RMCND,RPROD     ;Add RMCND to RPROD
        DEC     RCNT            ;   and do loop MPY (RCNT) times.
        BNE     LOOP            ;Repeat the loop again.
DONE:   MOV     RPROD,PROD      ;Save product in memory.
        JMP     10000           ;Go to operating system restart address.
*
MPY:    .BLKW   1               ;Multiplier.
MCND:   .BLKW   1               ;Multiplicand.
PROD:   .BLKW   1               ;Product.
        .END    START
```

TABLE 17-12 Initializing an array of bytes.

```
R0      =       %0
        .=30000            ;Program origin.
INIT:   MOV     #Q,R0      ;Address of first component.
ILOOP:  CLRB    (R0)+      ;Clear component and bump to next.
        CMP     R0,#Q+5    ;Past last component?
        BNE     ILOOP      ;If not, go do some more.
        JMP     10000      ;Go to operating system.
        .=30400            ;New origin for array.
Q:      .=.+5              ;Reserve 5 bytes for array.
        .END    INIT
```

reference is needed to fetch and execute it. If the variables are kept in memory, the instruction is three words long. Three memory references are needed just to fetch the instruction, and three more are needed to read the two operands and write the result. Since the execution times of most instructions are limited by memory access times, the register-oriented instructions are much faster. However, the choice of whether to keep variables in registers or in memory depends not only on program size and speed, but also on program complexity (see Section 13.4).

The program may be further optimized using the PDP-11's SOB instruction as long as the loop count is kept in a register. In this case, the three-instruction loop in Table 17-11 may be replaced with the following code:

```
LOOP:   ADD     RMCND,RPROD    ;Add RMCND to RPROD
        SOB     RCNT,LOOP      ;Repeat loop until CNT = 0.
```

Table 17-12 illustrates auto-increment and byte addressing in the PDP-11. The program declares an array of five bytes, and uses the CLRB instruction to initialize each component. The address of the next component, kept in R0, is a 16-bit quantity even though the components themselves are bytes. Since auto-increment addressing is used with a byte instruction, the processor increments R0 by 1 at each step, not 2.

PDP-11 subroutines are introduced in Table 17-13. The main program initializes SP to point just past the end of a seven-word stack buffer. Successive pushes, such as subroutine calls, decrement SP, so a maximum of seven words may be stored in the stack.

The program also shows the use of the stack for temporary storage. In WCNT1S, it is necessary to save the 1 count of the low-order byte before calling BCNT1S the second time. Instead of using a register or an explicit variable in memory, the program pushes the 1 count onto the stack. Later the program pops the saved 1 count, adding it to the high-order 1 count. A subroutine may mix return addresses and data in the stack as long as it performs an equal number of pushes and pops between the entry and return. It is especially important to balance the number of pushes and pops inside loops, lest the stack systematically grow (or shrink) with each iteration.

TABLE 17-13   Program that uses subroutines to count the number of "1" bits in a word.

```
R0        =      %0
R1        =      %1
R2        =      %2
SP        =      %6
PC        =      %7
SYSRET    =      10000          ;Operating system restart address.
          .=20000              ;Program origin.
STK:      .BLKW  7              ;Space for 7 return addresses.
STKE      =      .              ;Initialization address for SP.
TWORD:    .WORD  55451          ;Test-word to count 1s.
;
MAIN:     MOV    #STKE,SP       ;Initialize stack pointer.
          MOV    TWORD,R0       ;Get test word.
          JSR    PC,WCNT1S      ;Count number of 1s in it.
          JMP    SYSRET         ;Go to operating system.
;
;         Count the number of '1' bits in a word.
;         Enter with word in R0, exit with count in R1.
WCNT1S:   JSR    PC,BCNT1S      ;Count 1s in low-order byte.
          MOV    R1,-(SP)       ;Save '1' count on stack.
          SWAB   R0             ;Count 1s in high-order byte.
          JSR    PC,BCNT1S
          ADD    (SP)+,R1       ;Add low-order count to high-order byte.
          RTS    PC             ;Done, return.
;
;         Count number of '1' bits in a byte. Enter with byte in
;         low-order R0, exit with R0 undisturbed and count in R1.
BCNT1S:   CLR    R1             ;Initialize '1' count.
          MOV    #MASKS,R2      ;Point to 1-bit masks.
BLOOP:    BITB   R0,(R2)+       ;Got a '1'?
          BEQ    BNO1           ;Skip if none.
          INC    R1             ;Otherwise increment '1' count.
BNO1:     CMP    R2,#MASKE      ;Past last mask?
          BNE    BLOOP          ;Continue if not.
          RTS    PC             ;Else return.
;         Define 1-bit masks to test bits of byte.
MASKS:    .BYTE  200,100,40,20,10,4,2,1
MASKE     =      .
          .END   MAIN
```

The BCNT1S subroutine once again illustrates auto-increment and byte addressing. Addresses are 16-bit quantities (R2, #MASKE), but the BITB instruction manipulates 8-bit quantities (MEM[R2] and low-order byte of R0). Notice also how BITB is used to compare two operands logically without disturbing either.

A program that uses two stacks to sort a sequence of input numbers is shown in Table 17–14. Similar to the 68000 program in Table 7–3, this program shows the correspondence between Pascal statements and corresponding PDP-11 assembly language code. The operation of the Pascal program was explained and illustrated in Section 3.4. The power of PDP-11 double-operand addressing is

TABLE 17–14   Sorting subroutine for the PDP-11.

```
;                                   PROCEDURE StackSort; {Based on Table 3-6}
MAXLEN   =      200.;               CONST maxLen = 200;
SIZE     =      201.;                 stackSize = 201;
MINNUM   =      -9999.;               minNum = -9999;
MAXNUM   =      9999.;                maxNum = 9999;
SPL      =      %0;                 VAR spL,spH: address; {Stack pointers
SPH      =      %1;                                for stackL and stackH}
INNUM    =      %2;                   inNum, {Input number}
NNUMS    =      %3;                   nNums  {Number of inputs}
PC       =      %7;                         : integer; {16-bit 2's comp}
STACKL:  .BLKW  SIZE;               stackL, stackH :
STKEL    =      .-2;                  ARRAY [1..stackSize] OF integer;
STACKH:  .BLKW  SIZE;
STKEH    =      .-2;
;                                   BEGIN
SORT:    MOV    #STKEL,SPL;           spL := MemAddress(stackL[stackSize]);
         MOV    #STKEH,SPH;           spH := MemAddress(stackH[stackSize]);
         MOV    #MINNUM-1,@SPL;        MEM[spL] := minNum - 1;
         MOV    #MAXNUM+1,@SPH;        MEM[spH] := maxNum + 1;
         MOV    #1,NNUMS;             nNums := 1;
         JSR    PC,WRMSG1;            writeln('Input sequence: ');
         JSR    PC,READ;             read(inNum);
WHILE1:  CMP    INNUM,#MINNUM;       WHILE inNum >= minNum
         BLT    WHILE4;
         CMP    INNUM,#MAXNUM;            AND inNum <= maxNum DO
         BGT    WHILE4;                 BEGIN
WHILE2:  CMP    INNUM,@SPL;              WHILE inNum < MEM[spL] DO
         BGE    WHILE3;                     {Top of stackL --> stackH.}
         MOV    (SPL)+,-(SPH);              PushH(PopL);
         BR     WHILE2;
WHILE3:  CMP    INNUM,@SPH;              WHILE inNum > MEM[spH] DO
         BLE    OUT3;                       {Top of stackH --> stackL.}
         MOV    (SPH)+,-(SPL);              PushL(PopH);
         BR     WHILE3;
OUT3:    MOV    INNUM,-(SPL);           PushL(inNum);
         JSR    PC,WRNUM;               write(inNum);
         INC    NNUMS;                  nNums := nNums + 1;
IF1:     CMP    NNUMS,#MAXLEN;          IF nNums <= maxLen THEN
         BGT    ELSE1;
THEN1:   JSR    PC,READ;                    read(inNum)
         BR     IFEND1;                 ELSE BEGIN
ELSE1:   JSR    PC,WRMSG2;                  writeln('***Too many inputs');
         MOV    #MINNUM-1,INNUM;            inNum := minNum - 1;
IFEND1:  BR     WHILE1;                 END;
;                                   END; {Inputs are now sorted.}
WHILE4:  CMP    SPL,#STKEL;          WHILE spL <>
         BEQ    OUT4;                   MemAddress(stackL[stackSize]) DO
         MOV    (SPL)+,-(SPH);          {Move everything into stackH.}
         BR     WHILE4;                 PushH(PopL);
OUT4:    JSR    PC,WRMSG3;           writeln; write('Sorted sequence: ');
```

TABLE 17–14   (continued)

```
WHILE5: CMP    SPH,#STKEH;        WHILE spH <>
        BEQ    OUT5;                  MemAddress[stackH[stackSize]) DO
        MOV    (SPH)+,INNUM;      {Print contents of stackH.}
        JSR    PC,WRNUM;          write(PopH);
        BR     WHILE5;
OUT5:   RTS    PC;                {Return to caller.}
        .END   SORT;             END;
```

TABLE 17–15   Program to find primes using an array and indexed addressing.

```
;                                 PROCEDURE FindPrimes;
NPRIME  =      1000.;             CONST nPrime = 1000;
PLIMIT  =      32.;                 pLimit = 32;
PRIME:  .=.+NPRIME-1;             VAR prime:ARRAY [2..nPrime] OF boolean;
        .EVEN;
I       =      %0;                {reg} I, J : word;
J       =      %1;
PC      =      %7;                BEGIN
FNDPRM: MOV    #2,I;              FOR I := 2 TO nPrime DO
SETEM:  MOVB   #1,PRIME-2(I);       {Set the entire array true.}
        INC    I;                   prime[I] := true;
        CMP    I,#NPRIME;
        BLE    SETEM;
        MOV    #2,J;              J := 2; {First known prime.}
MARKEM:;                          REPEAT {Check integers 2 to pLimit.}
        TSTB   PRIME-2(J);          IF prime[J] THEN
        BEQ    NOTPRM;                 BEGIN
        MOV    J,I;                       I := 2 * J;
        ASL    I;
CLRLUP: CLRB   PRIME-2(I);             REPEAT {Mark multiples of J.}
        ADD    J,I;                      prime[I] := false; I := I + J;
        CMP    I,#NPRIME;             UNTIL I > nPrime;
        BLE    CLRLUP;                END;
NOTPRM: INC    J;                   J := J + 1;
        CMP    J,#PLIMIT;         UNTIL J > pLimit;
        BLE    MARKEM;
        JSR    PC,WRMSG1;         write('Primes between 2 and ');
        MOV    #NPRIME,I;         I := nPrime;
        JSR    PC,PRINTI;         writeln(I); {Print the number in I.}
        MOV    #2,I;              FOR I := 2 TO nPrime DO
PRTLUP: TSTB   PRIME-2(I);          {Print all the primes.}
        BEQ    NEXTP;               IF prime[I] THEN
        JSR    PC,PRINTI;              writeln(I);
NEXTP:  INC    I;
        CMP    I,#NPRIME;
        BLE    PRTLUP;
        RTS    PC;                {All done, return to caller.}
        .END   FNDPRM;           END;
```

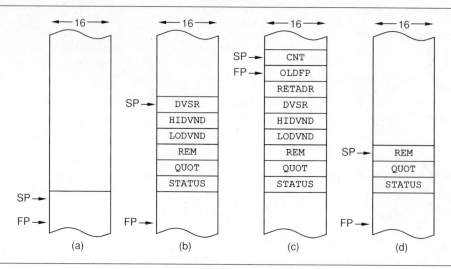

FIGURE 17–7   Stack contents during `DIVPQ` program: (a) at start; (b) just before calling `DIVIDE`; (c) after first three instructions of `DIVIDE`; (d) on return.

best illustrated by popping a word from one stack and pushing it into another with a single one-word instruction like `MOV (SPL)+,-(SPH)`. Without procedures, three or four Pascal statements are needed to do the same thing.

Besides declaring its own two stacks using R0 (`SPL`) and R1 (`SPH`) as stack pointers, the program in Table 17–14 assumes that the operating system has already initialized R6 to point into a return address stack. It further assumes that the operating system has called it by executing a `JSR PC,SORT` instruction, so that it may return by executing `RTS PC`. If a program reinitializes SP to point to its own stack area (as did the program in Table 17–13), it loses any return address on the operating system's stack and therefore must return to the operating system by an absolute jump or a software interrupt.

PDP-11 indexed addressing is illustrated in Table 17–15, a program that finds prime numbers using the sieve of Eratosthenes. Like the 68000 version in Table 7–5 on page 231, the PDP-11 program declares an array of bytes with each component corresponding to a number between 2 and 1000. By marking off multiples of known primes, it eliminates nonprimes until only primes remain.

Section 9.3.6 described a stack-oriented parameter-passing convention; a PDP-11 subroutine that uses this convention is shown in Table 17–16. A main program that calls `DIVIDE` is shown in Table 17–17. Initially the stack has the state shown in Figure 17–7(a). The main program pushes the input parameters onto the stack in the order shown in Figure 17–7(b), and then calls `DIVIDE`. The first three instructions of `DIVIDE` set up the stack frame pointer `FP` and push one local variable, `CNT`, leaving the stack as shown in Figure 17–7(c). The last four instructions clean up the stack and return to the calling program with only the output parameters on the stack, as shown in Figure 17–7(d).

TABLE 17–16   Unsigned division subroutine that passes parameters on a stack.

```
FP        =      %5                    ;Stack frame pointer.
SP        =      %6
PC        =      %7
;                The offsets below define positions of parameters and local
;                variables in the stack relative to the frame pointer (FP).
CNT       =      -2                    ;Loop counter.
OLDFP     =      0                     ;Old value of frame pointer.
RETADR    =      2                     ;Return address.
DVSR      =      4                     ;1-word divisor (input).
HIDVND    =      6                     ;High-order word of dividend (input).
LODVND    =      8.                    ;Low-order word of dividend (input).
REM       =      10.                   ;1-word remainder (output).
QUOT      =      12.                   ;1-word quotient (output).
STATUS    =      14.                   ;0 ==> OK, <>0 ==> overflow (output).
;
DIVIDE:   MOV    FP,-(SP)              ;Push old frame pointer onto stack.
          MOV    SP,FP                 ;Copy SP into FP for new frame pointer.
          MOV    #16.,-(SP)            ;Push initial count.
          CLR    STATUS(FP)            ;Initial status OK.
          CMP    HIDVND(FP),DVSR(FP)   ;Will quotient fit in 1 word?
          BLO    DIVLUP                ;Branch if it will.
          INC    STATUS(FP)            ;Else report overflow.
          BR     CLNSTK
DIVLUP:   ASL    LODVND(FP)            ;Left shift dividend with LSB := 0.
          ROL    HIDVND(FP)            ;A carry here from MSB means
          BCS    QUOT1                 ;  high DVND definitely > DVSR.
          CMP    HIDVND(FP),DVSR(FP)   ;Compare high DVND with DVSR.
          BLO    QUOTOK                ;Quotient bit = 0 if lower.
QUOT1:    INC    LODVND(FP)            ;Else set quotient bit to 1.
          SUB    DVSR(FP),HIDVND(FP)   ;And update high DVND.
QUOTOK:   DEC    CNT(FP)               ;Decrement iteration count.
          BGT    DIVLUP                ;Continue until done.
          MOV    HIDVND(FP),REM(FP)    ;Store remainder.
          MOV    LODVND(FP),QUOT(FP)   ;Store quotient.
CLNSTK:   MOV    RETADR(FP),LODVND(FP) ;Save return addr lower in stack.
          MOV    OLDFP(FP),FP          ;Restore old frame pointer.
          ADD    #LODVND-CNT,SP        ;Remove garbage except LODVND,
          RTS    PC                    ;  which contains return address.
```

Parameters and local variables are accessed within the DIVIDE subroutine by based addressing using fixed offsets from FP. PDP-11 single- and double-operand instructions and addressing modes allow all operations to be performed directly on variables in the stack frame; no processor registers are used as accumulators. However, the speed of the program could be improved by keeping LODVND, HIDVND, DVSR, and CNT in registers during the division loop.

Table 17–18 is a set of queue manipulation subroutines for the PDP-11. Like the 68000 version in Table 9–20, this code is self-documenting, and so we leave you to read it.

TABLE 17–17   Program that calls stack-oriented DIVIDE.

```
;         Compute PDIVQ := P DIV Q; PMODQ := P MOD Q;
;         where all are 1-word variables in memory.
DIVPQ:    ADD    #-6,SP           ;Reserve space for output parameters.
          MOV    P,-(SP)          ;Push low-order dividend.
          CLR    -(SP)            ;Push high-order dividend = 0.
          MOV    Q,-(SP)          ;Push divisor.
          JSR    PC,DIVIDE        ;Do the division.
          MOV    (SP)+,PMODQ      ;Pop remainder and store.
          MOV    (SP)+,PDIVQ      ;Pop quotient and store.
          TST    (SP)+            ;Test status.
          BNE    DIVOVF           ;Branch on overflow.
          ...
P:        .BLKW  1                ;Storage for P, Q, PDIVQ, PMODQ
Q:        .BLKW  1                ;   (all 1-word variables).
PDIVQ:    .BLKW  1
PMODQ:    .BLKW  1
```

17.6   INPUT/OUTPUT, INTERRUPTS, AND TRAPS

17.6.1   Input/Output

The PDP-11 introduced the concept of memory-mapped I/O. It has no I/O in-structions; all devices are controlled by interface registers that are read and writ-ten as locations in the address space. Depending on device complexity, different interfaces have different numbers of registers and assign different functions and meanings to their bits.

As an example, Figure 17–8 shows the interface registers for a typical read/write, character-oriented I/O device, such as a CRT terminal or teleprinter. The physical device consists of two independent logical devices, a "receiver"

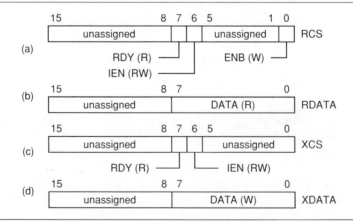

FIGURE 17–8   PDP-11 interface registers: (a) receiver control/status; (b) receiver data; (c) transmitter control/status; (d) transmitter data.

TABLE 17–18 Queue manipulation subroutines for the PDP-11.

```
;
; QUEUE MODULE
;
; This module contains three subroutines for manipulating queues
; of 16-bit words. A queue is defined by a queue descriptor table
; and a block of storage, as shown below.
;
;                                          QUEUE STORAGE BLOCK
;         --------------------             --------------------
; QDTBL |    QHEAD (word)    |   -------->|      (word)        |
;       |--------------------|   |        |--------------------|
;       |    QTAIL (word)    |   |        |                    |
;       |--------------------|   |        |   o  o  o  o       |
;       |    QSTRT (word)    |----         |                    |
;       |--------------------|            |--------------------|
;       |    QEND  (word)    |----------->|      (word)        |
;         --------------------             --------------------
;
; Offsets in descriptor table:
;
QHEAD    =        0
QTAIL    =        2
QSTRT    =        4
QEND     =        6
;
; In this table, the last two words are constants, initialized at
; load time, that give the starting and ending addresses of the block
; of storage (buffer) reserved for the queue itself.  The first and
; second words are reserved to store the queue head and tail (absolute
; memory addresses), and are manipulated by the subroutines.
;
; If a program defines several queues, it allocates a separate queue
; descriptor table and storage block for each one.  For example, the
; statements below define a 5-word queue Q1 and a 100-word queue Q2:
;
;Q1BLK: .BLKW   5              ;Storage block for Q1.
;Q1END  =       .-2            ;Last location in Q1 storage block.
;Q1DT:  .BLKW   2              ;Q1 descriptor table -- QHEAD and QTAIL.
;       .WORD   Q1BLK,Q1END    ;                      QSTRT and QEND.
;
;Q2BLK: .BLKW   100.           ;Storage block for Q2.
;Q2END  =       .-2            ;Last location in Q2 storage block.
;Q2DT:  .BLKW   2              ;Q2 descriptor table -- QHEAD and QTAIL.
;       .WORD   Q2BLK,Q2END    ;                      QSTRT and QEND.
;
; Subroutines are provided to initialize a queue (QINIT), enqueue
; a word (QENQ), and dequeue a word (QDEQ).  Each subroutine must
; be passed the address of the descriptor table for the queue
; to be manipulated.
;
```

TABLE 17-18 (continued)

```
; SUBROUTINE QINIT -- Initialize a queue to be empty.
;
; INPUTS
;    #QDTBL -- The address of the queue descriptor table for the
;              queue to be initialized, passed in register R0.
; OUTPUTS, GLOBAL DATA, LOCAL DATA -- None
; FUNCTIONS
;    (1) Initialize the queue to empty by setting QHEAD and QTAIL
;        in QDTBL equal to the first address in the queue buffer.
; REGISTERS AFFECTED -- CC
;
; TYPICAL CALLING SEQUENCE
;        MOV    #Q1DT,R0
;        JSR    PC,QINIT
;
QINIT:   MOV    QSTRT(R0),QHEAD(R0)   ;Put buffer starting address
         MOV    QSTRT(R0),QTAIL(R0)   ;  into QHEAD and QTAIL.
         RTS    PC                    ;Done, return.
;
; SUBROUTINE QENQ -- Enqueue one word into a queue.
;
; INPUTS
;    #QDTBL -- The address of the queue descriptor table for the
;              queue to be manipulated, passed in register R0.
;    QDATA  -- The word to be enqueued, passed in register R1.
; OUTPUTS
;    QFULL  -- 1 if the queue is already full, else 0;
;              passed in condition bit Z.
; GLOBAL DATA, LOCAL DATA -- None.
; FUNCTIONS
;    (1) If the queue described by QDTBL is full, set QFULL to 1.
;    (2) If the queue is not full, enqueue QDATA and set QFULL to 0.
; REGISTERS AFFECTED -- R2,CC
;
; TYPICAL CALLING SEQUENCE
;        MOV    #Q1DT,R0           ;Enqueue AWORD.
;        MOV    AWORD,R1
;        JSR    PC,QENQ
;        BEQ    OVFL               ;Branch if queue is full.
;
QENQ:    MOV    QTAIL(R0),R2       ;Get queue tail.
         ADD    #2,R2              ;Bump to next free location.
         CMP    R2,QEND(R0)        ;Wrap-around?
         BLOS   QENQ1
         MOV    QSTRT(R0),R2       ;Reinitialize on wrap-around.
QENQ1:   CMP    R2,QHEAD(R0)       ;Queue already full?
         BEQ    QENQ2              ;Return with Z = 1 if full.
         MOV    R1,@QTAIL(R0)      ;Else store QDATA.
         MOV    R2,QTAIL(R0)       ;Update tail.
         CLZ                       ;Set Z := 0 since not full.
QENQ2:   RTS    PC                 ;Return.
```

TABLE 17–18   (continued)

```
; SUBROUTINE QDEQ -- Dequeue one word from a queue.
;
; INPUTS
;   #QDTBL -- The address of the queue descriptor table for the
;             queue to be manipulated, passed in register R0.
; OUTPUTS
;   QEMPTY -- 1 if the queue is empty, else 0; passed in
;             condition bit Z.
;   QDATA  -- The word dequeued, passed in register R1.
; GLOBAL DATA, LOCAL DATA -- None.
; FUNCTIONS
;   (1) If the queue described by QDTBL is empty, set QEMPTY to 1.
;   (2) If the queue isn't empty, dequeue QDATA and set QEMPTY to 0.
; REGISTERS AFFECTED -- R1, CC
;
; TYPICAL CALLING SEQUENCE
;         MOV     #Q1DT,R0        ;Dequeue a word into AWORD.
;         JSR     PC,QDEQ
;         BEQ     UNDFL           ;Branch if queue is empty.
;         MOV     R1,AWORD
;
QDEQ:     CMP     QHEAD(R0),QTAIL(R0)  ;Queue empty?
          BEQ     QDEQ2                ;Return with Z = 1 if empty.
          MOV     @QHEAD(R0),R1        ;Read QDATA word from queue.
          ADD     #2,QHEAD(R0)         ;Bump head to next item in queue.
          CMP     QHEAD(R0),QEND(R0)   ;Wrap-around?
          BLOS    QDEQ1
          MOV     QSTRT(R0),QHEAD(R0)  ;Reinitialize head on wrap-around.
QDEQ1:    CLZ                          ;Set Z := 0 since not empty.
QDEQ2:    RTS     PC                   ;Return.
```

and a "transmitter," each of which uses two interface registers. In a typical PDP-11 installation, the system terminal keyboard is assigned addresses 177560_8 and 177562_8, and its screen or printer is assigned 177564_8 and 177566_8. Each bit of each register is classified as read only, write only, read/write, or unassigned, as explained in Section 10.3.

Three bits control the receiver section of the interface. Writing a 1 in the ENB bit clears RDY in preparation for receiving a character. This also starts motion in the case of a papertape reader or other mechanical device. When a character is received, the interface sets RDY to 1. The character may then be read from the receiver data register RDATA; reading RDATA clears RDY as a side effect. The IEN bit enables the interface to interrupt the processor whenever a character is received. Precisely stated, the interface requests interrupt service from the processor whenever both RDY and IEN are 1.

Only two bits control the transmitter section of the interface. Writing a value in the transmitter data register XDATA automatically starts sending the data to the device and clears the RDY bit. The interface sets RDY to 1 as soon as

TABLE 17–19   PDP-11 input and echo subroutine.

```
RCS    =    177560        ;Receiver control and status.
RDATA  =    177562        ;Received data.
XCS    =    177564        ;Transmitter control and status.
XDATA  =    177566        ;Transmit data.
;
RCVIN: MOVB  #1,@#RCS      ;Initiate read, interrupts off.
RCVWT: TSTB  @#RCS         ;Reader RDY = 1?
       BPL   RCVWT         ;No, busy wait.
       MOVB  @#RDATA,R0    ;Yes, read character.
       BICB  #200,R0       ;Mask off possible garbage.
XMTWT: TSTB  @#XCS         ;Transmitter RDY = 1?
       BPL   XMTWT         ;No, wait for previous character.
       CLR   @#XCS         ;Make sure transmitter interrupts off.
       MOVB  R0,@#XDATA    ;Echo new character
       RTS   PC            ;  and return to calling program.
```

XDATA can accept another character (even though in some cases the character may not yet have been fully transmitted or physically printed). Like the receiver, the transmitter section interrupts whenever both RDY and IEN are 1.

Table 17–19 shows a subroutine that reads and echoes a character using busy-wait I/O with the interface described above. It is called by JSR PC, RCVIN and it returns with the character in R0. The subroutine begins by initializing the receiver and then it waits for a character. After receiving the character, it busy-waits for the transmitter until XDATA is emptied of any previous character; then it echoes the received character and returns immediately.[1]

One advantage of memory-mapped I/O is that all of the addressing modes as well as opcodes may be used to specify I/O interface registers. This makes it very easy to write I/O handlers that can be shared by many devices. For example, in a system with several terminals, the subroutine in Table 17–19 can be modified to work with an interface at any address by having the calling program pass the address of the receiver control/status register in R1, as shown in Table 17–20.

17.6.2 Interrupts

bus request (BR)

The PDP-11 has a multilevel, vectored, priority interrupt system. Each device may be physically connected to one of four priority levels, called BR4, BR5, BR6, and BR7; *BR* stands for *bus request*. The highest priority level is BR7; the LSI-11 has only one level, BR4. Within each level, devices are "daisy-chained" so the one closest to the processor on the bus has the highest priority. For an interrupt to be serviced, the device priority level (BR number) must be higher

---

[1]Normally, relative addressing is used to obtain position-independent programs. However, in Table 17–19, absolute addressing yields position independence because the interface registers are at fixed locations in memory.

TABLE 17–20   PDP-11 shared input and echo subroutine.

```
RCS     =    0              ;Receiver control and status.
RDATA   =    2              ;Received data.
XCS     =    4              ;Transmitter control and status.
XDATA   =    6              ;Transmit data.
;
RCVIN:  MOV    #1,RCS(R1)       ;Initiate read, interrupts off.
RCVWT:  TSTB   RCS(R1)          ;Reader RDY = 1?
        BPL    RCVWT            ;No, busy wait.
        MOV    RDATA(R1),R0     ;Yes, read character.
        BIC    #177400,R0       ;Mask off possible garbage.
XMTWT:  TSTB   XCS(R1)          ;Transmitter RDY = 1?
        BPL    XMTWT            ;No, wait for previous character.
        CLR    XCS(R1)          ;Make sure transmitter interrupts off.
        MOV    R0,XDATA(R1)     ;Echo new character
        RTS    PC               ;  and return to calling program.
```

than the processor priority (PRI) in PSW bits 7–5. Thus, setting the processor priority to 7 effectively disables the interrupt system.

In general, all of the following conditions must be met for an interface to successfully interrupt the processor:

IEN

(1) The *IEN* bit in the interface must be set to 1.

(2) The interface must have experienced an interrupt-generating condition (e.g., RDY = 1 on the terminal interface, block transfer complete or read error on a disk interface).

(3) No interface with a higher BR number may be trying to interrupt.

(4) No interface closer to the processor with the same BR number may be trying to interrupt.

(5) The processor priority (PRI) must be strictly less than the BR number.

When the processor accepts an interrupt request, the interrupting interface identifies itself by placing a unique address on the Unibus (or Q-bus). This address points to an *interrupt vector*, two words of memory containing the starting address of the interrupt service routine and a new PSW. The bottom 400_8 bytes of memory in the PDP-11 address space are reserved in two-word blocks for interrupt vectors (i.e., octal addresses 0, 4, 10, 14, 20, ..., 370, 374). In a typical installation, the interrupt vector for the system terminal keyboard is at address 60_8, and the vector for the screen or printer is at 64_8.

interrupt vector

After an interrupt is accepted, the processor pushes the current PSW into the stack, followed by the current PC. Then it fetches a new value for PC from the first word of the interrupt vector, and a new PSW from the second. Besides new values of the condition codes, the new PSW contains a new value for the processor priority. This value should be greater than or equal to the hardware priority of the interrupting device, to prevent the device from reinterrupting its own service routine if it is very fast.

RTI

RTT

The RTI instruction is used to return from an interrupt service routine. It pops the top word in the stack into the PC, and the next word into the PSW. The RTT instruction operates the same as RTI, except for its handling of the trace trap as explained in Section 17.6.3. User programs should always use RTI.

A program that uses interrupts to print strings of characters is shown in Table 17–21. A string is a sequence of ASCII characters stored one per byte and terminated by a 0 byte. The CRT output initialization routine CRTOUT accepts a pointer to a string to be printed. The variable CRTBSY indicates whether a previous string is still being printed, so that a new operation is not started until the previous one is completed. The initialization routine CRTOUT prints the first character and the remaining characters are printed by the interrupt service routine CRTINT. Notice that CRTINT does not save any processor registers, because its operations are all performed directly in memory with appropriate double-operand instructions and addressing modes. In longer interrupt service routines, it is usually more efficient to save registers on the stack, use them as needed, and then restore them before executing RTI.

17.6.3 Traps

trap instructions

The PDP-11 has several *trap instructions* which appeared in Table 17–7. Executing a trap instruction has the same effect as an interrupt—the current PSW and PC are pushed onto the stack and a new PSW and PC are taken from a vector in memory. As shown in Table 17–22, each of the different trap instructions has a different preassigned *trap vector address*. Except for the vector addresses, all of the trap instructions have the same effect, but their names indicate software applications intended by the original machine designers.

trap vector address

TRAP

EMT

The TRAP and EMT instructions have an 8-bit opcode in the high-order byte, while the low-order byte is not used by the hardware. Therefore, the programmer may place an arbitrary 8-bit code into the low-order byte, to be decoded by the trap handler. The EMT (emulator trap) instruction is used by DEC operating systems for system calls, while TRAP is generally reserved for the user. Table 17–23 shows a handler for the TRAP instruction that performs one of 256 possible actions depending on the code specified in the instruction. This effectively gives the user 256 different one-word subroutine calls. The other two trap instructions, BPT and IOT, are fully encoded 16-bit instructions.

BPT

IOT

The PDP-11 processor also traps on various unusual conditions shown in Table 17–22. For example, a trap is taken through location 4 on any attempt to access nonexistent memory or a word at an odd address.

BPT

trace trap

The BPT instruction traps through location 14, allowing the on-line debugger to insert breakpoints by substituting BPT for user instructions. The *trace trap* is also used by on-line debuggers. If an instruction sets the T bit in the PSW, a trap through location 14 will take place after the execution of the *next* instruction. This allows the debugger to single-step a user program. For ex-

TABLE 17-21 Interrupt-driven CRT output.

```
                .=64                    ;CRT interrupt vector address.
CVECT:  .WORD   CRTINT,200              ;CPU priority = 4.
                .=4000
;               Define addresses of CRT interface registers.
CRTCSR  =       177564                  ;CRT control and status register.
CRTDTR  =       177566                  ;CRT data register.
;
;               Global and local variables.
CRTBSY: .BLKW   1                       ;Nonzero when string is being displayed.
BPNT:   .BLKW   1                       ;Pointer to character being displayed.
;
;               CRT output initialization, pointer to string passed in R0.
;
CRTOUT: TST     CRTBSY                  ;Still printing previous string?
        BNE     CRTOUT                  ;Yes, wait for it.
        INC     CRTBSY                  ;Else mark CRT busy for new string.
        MOV     R0,BPNT                 ;Save pointer to string.
        MOVB    @R0,@#CRTDTR            ;Print first character.
        MOV     #100,@#CRTCSR           ;Turn on CRT interrupts
        RTS     PC                      ;  and return.
;
;               CRT output interrupt handler
;
CRTINT: INC     BPNT                    ;Get pointer to next character.
        TSTB    @BPNT                   ;Is it NUL (0)?
        BEQ     CDONE                   ;We're done if it is.
        MOVB    @BPNT,@#CRTDTR          ;Otherwise print the character
        RTI                             ;  and return.
CDONE:  CLR     CRTBSY                  ;CRT is no longer busy.
        CLR     @#CRTCSR                ;Turn off CRT interrupts
        RTI                             ;  and return.
;
;               Typical main program
MAIN:   MOV     #770,SP                 ;Initialize stack pointer.
        CLR     CRTBSY                  ;Mark CRT not busy.
        CLR     @#177776                ;Set processor priority to 0.
LOOP:   ...                             ;Do some computation.
        ...
        MOV     #MSG1,R0                ;Get address of first message
        JSR PC,CRTOUT                   ;  and print it.
        ...                             ;Do some more computation.
        MOV     #MSG2,R0                ;Get address of second message
        JSR PC,CRTOUT                   ;  and print it.
        JMP     LOOP                    ;Do it all again.
;
MSG1:   .ASCII  'This is a rather unimaginative message.'
        .BYTE   15,12,0                 ;Carriage return, line feed, NUL.
MSG2:   .ASCII  'But this one is even worse.'
        .BYTE   15,12,0                 ;Carriage return, line feed, NUL.
        .END    MAIN
```

TABLE 17–22   PDP-11 trap vector addresses.

Address (octal)	Purpose
000	Reserved
004	Bus errors
010	Illegal and reserved instructions
014	BPT and trace trap
020	IOT
024	Power fail
030	EMT
034	TRAP

TABLE 17–23   Handler for TRAP instruction.

```
        .=34
TVECT:  .WORD   THNDL,340       ;TRAP vector.
        .=5000
;       TRAP handler
THNDL:  MOV     R5,-(SP)        ;Save caller's registers on stack.
        MOV     R4,-(SP)
        MOV     R3,-(SP)
        MOV     R2,-(SP)
        MOV     R1,-(SP)
        MOV     R0,-(SP)
        MOV     12.(SP),R0      ;Get address of instruction after TRAP.
        MOV     -(R0),R0        ;Fetch the TRAP instruction.
        BIC     #177400,R0      ;Get its low-order byte.
        ASL     R0              ;Make it a word offset
        JMP     @TRAPTB(R0)     ;  and jump through table.
;
;       Table of trap routine starting addresses.
TRAPTB: .WORD   T0,T1,T2,...,T255
;
;       Format of typical trap routine.
T0:     ...                     ;Do some computation.
        ...                     ;Parameters in caller's registers may
        ...                     ;  be accessed by offsets from SP
        ...                     ;  (e.g., 10.(SP) = user R5).
        JMP     TRAPEX          ;Go to common trap exit code.
        ...
TRAPEX: MOV     (SP)+,R0        ;Restore caller's registers.
        MOV     (SP)+,R1
        MOV     (SP)+,R2
        MOV     (SP)+,R3
        MOV     (SP)+,R4
        MOV     (SP)+,R5
        RTI                     ;Return to calling program.
```

ample, assume that the CPU is executing the debugger and the current PC and PSW for a user program are stored at the top of stack. Then we can execute one instruction of the user program as follows:

(1) Set the T bit in the copy of the user PSW in the stack to 1.

(2) Execute an RTT. This returns control to the user program and pops the user PSW, setting the real T bit to 1.

(3) One instruction of the user program is executed, and then the trace trap is sprung, returning control to the debugger.

Notice that we specified an RTT instruction above instead of RTI. The RTI instruction is an exception to the general trace rule: if an RTI instruction sets the T bit, then the trace trap occurs immediately. This allows RTIs in user programs to be traced. RTT, on the other hand, allows one instruction of the user program to be executed before the trace trap is sprung.

In rare situations, several traps and interrupts may become pending simultaneously. For example, suppose an instruction sets the T bit, the next creates an addressing error, and at the same time an interrupt request appears. Each PDP-11 model has a fixed set of priorities for handling such cases, as detailed in the model's processor handbook.

R E F E R E N C E S

The PDP-11 was first described in "A New Architecture for Minicomputers — The DEC PDP-11" by C. G. Bell et al. (*AFIPS SJCC Conf. Proc.*, Vol. 36, 1970, pp. 657–675). This article and several original chapters on the PDP-11 architecture appear in *Computer Engineering* by C. G. Bell, J. C. Mudge, and J. E. McNamara (Digital Press, 1978). The study of PDP-11 instruction frequencies that we mentioned in Section 17.4 appears in a Ph.D. thesis, "Analysis and Performance of Computer Instruction Sets," by Leonard J. Shustek (Stanford University, 1978, available from University Microfilms, Ann Arbor, MI).

DEC publishes processor handbooks for all of the different PDP-11 and LSI-11 models; these are generally available from local DEC sales offices. A number of programming textbooks are oriented towards the PDP-11, including *Introduction to Computer Organization and Data Structures: PDP-11 edition* by H. S. Stone and D. P. Siewiorek (McGraw-Hill, 1975) and *Minicomputer Systems* by R. H. Eckhouse and L. R. Morris (Prentice-Hall, 1979, 2nd ed.).

VAX-11   DEC's successor to the PDP-11 architecture, called the *VAX-11*, extends the PDP-11 architecture in many ways. For example, the maximum address size supported by a VAX-11 CPU is 32 bits instead of 16, and the CPU has sixteen 32-bit registers instead of eight 16-bit registers. DEC introduced the first VAX-11 model in 1978; it is described in Chapter 17 of *Computer Engineering*, "VAX-11/780: A Virtual Address Extension to the DEC PDP-11 Family" by William D. Strecker.

EXERCISES

17.1 Assuming that each memory access (read or write) takes 1 microsecond, compare the size and execution time of the multiplication programs in Tables 17–10 and 17–11.

17.2 Assuming that each memory access takes 1 microsecond, compare the size and execution time of the multiplication program in Table 17–11 with that of the same program using the SOB instruction.

17.3 Write a PDP-11 subroutine that adds two 48-bit unsigned integers P and Q, stored in memory words P2,P1,P0 and Q2,Q1,Q0, respectively. The sum should be stored in memory locations S2,S1,S0. When the subroutine returns, C should be set to 1 if the true sum is greater than $2^{48} - 1$, else to 0.

17.4 Translate one of the multiplication or division algorithms in Section 4.8 or 4.9 into an assembly language program for the PDP-11.

17.5 Show how to use auto-increment instead of indexed addressing in the "clear loop" and the "print loop" in Table 17–15.

17.6 Modify the DIVIDE program in Table 17–16 so that the frame pointer is not needed (i.e., SP is used for all stack references).

17.7 Rewrite the DIVIDE program in Table 17–16 using registers to improve the speed of the division loop. What is the effect on the program's length?

17.8 Modify the queue module in Table Table 17–18 to manipulate queues of bytes.

17.9 Rewrite the QENQ subroutine in Table 17–18 so that R2 is no longer needed for temporary storage (use the stack).

17.10 Rewrite the PDP-11 DIVIDE subroutine in Table 17–16 and the main program in Table 17–17 using a stack-oriented subroutine-calling convention that uses the MARK instruction for stack clean up. The convention is explained along with the MARK instruction in PDP-11 processor handbooks. Comment on advantages and disadvantages of this approach.

17.11 Explain how two PDP-11 coroutines can use the instruction JSR PC, @ (SP) + to call each other.

17.12 Rewrite the recursive NIM subroutines in Table 9–22 on page 344 for the PDP-11. Write a main program that analyzes the game for all combinations of values of NHEAP from 2 to 25 and NTAKE from 2 to 6.

17.13 Write a PDP-11 keyboard input and display output module similar to the 6809 module in Table 10–5 on page 374.

17.14 Write a complete Pascal simulation of the PDP-11.

CHAPTER 18

An Evolved Architecture: The Intel 80x86 Family

80x86 family
4004
8008
8086

The roots of the Intel *80x86 family* of microprocessors go back to the first single-chip microprocessors, the Intel *4004* and *8008*. The events leading to introduction of the 80x86 family's first member, the *8086*, were rather blasphemously summarized by one of the 8086's architects:[1]

> In the beginning Intel created the 4004 and the 8008. And these processors were without enough memory and throughput. And Intel said, "Let there be an 8080," and there was an 8080 and Intel saw that it was good....
>
> And Intel said, "Let a new-generation processor serve the midrange market. And let there be true 16-bit facilities in the midrange. And let there be one megabyte of memory and efficient interruptible byte-string instructions and full decimal arithmetic." And Intel saw the collection of all of these things, that it was good, and Intel called it the 8086....
>
> And Intel saw everything that he [*sic*] had made and, behold, it was good.

8080

The original 8086 architecture was derived from the popular *8080* for a good reason—to ensure a measure of software compatibility and thereby preserve the industry's large (at that time) investment in 8080 software. Although 8080 machine language programs cannot be run directly on an 80x86, it is fairly

---

[1] S. P. Morse, in "Intel Microprocessors—8008 to 8086" by S. P. Morse, B. W. Ravenel, S. Mazor, and W. B. Pohlman, in *Computer*, Vol. 13, No. 10, October 1980, p. 46.

CONV-86

straightforward to translate an 8080 assembly language program into an equivalent program for an 80x86. In fact, Intel provides a program, *CONV-86*, that does this automatically.

8088

In the years since the introduction of the original 8086 chip in the late 1970s, Intel has repackaged and extended the 8086 processor architecture in several ways. Shortly after introducing the 8086, Intel announced the *8088*, an "8-bit" microprocessor with exactly the same instruction set and internal architecture as the "16-bit" 8086. The only difference between the two circuits is in their external memory data buses—the 8086 accesses memory 16 bits at a time, while the 8088 accesses only 8 bits at a time.

Because its memory is only 8 bits wide, the smallest 8088-based computer has fewer components and costs less to build than the smallest 8086-based computer. That's the only advantage of an 8088. With its narrow data path to memory, an 8088-based computer is slower than an 8086-based counterpart, and in a large configuration it's not much more inexpensive. For example, a megabyte of memory requires 32 $256K \times 1$ memory chips, whether the chips are arranged 4×8 or 2×16. The 8088 processor chip was used in the original IBM PC family of personal computers, while the 8086 is used in some "turbo" PC clones as well as in the low-end members of IBM's PS/2 family of personal computers.

80186

In the early 1980s, Intel looked for ways to use VLSI technology to develop microprocessors with expanded capabilities (and markets), while still maintaining compatibility with the large installed base of 8086-based computers, application software, and development tools. One result was the *80186*, a single chip that contains an 8086 processor and several useful peripheral circuits: a multilevel interrupt controller, two DMA controllers, three timer/counters, and a master oscillator, and several miscellaneous bus control circuits.

The idea behind the 80186 was to make it possible to build a computer in a smaller number of chips than an equivalent 8086-based computer. This made the 80186 an attractive circuit for "imbedded control" applications, such as test instruments, industrial robots, and telephone switching systems, where the end-user sees not a general-purpose computer, but a specific functional interface provided by a program in the computer. Unfortunately, operational differences between the internal peripherals of the 80186 and the discrete peripheral chips used in standard IBM PCs prevented the 80186 from being used to any large extent in PCs and clones.

80188

Intel introduced the *80188* at the same time as the 80186. The 80188 is to the 80186 as the 8088 is to the 8086—it is identical to the 80186 in all respects except that it has an 8-bit-wide instead of a 16-bit-wide memory data bus. The 80188 finds application in low-cost "imbedded control" applications, where the computer hardware may consist of only a handful of chips including an 80188, perhaps a single 128-Kbyte ROM, and a single 32-Kbyte RAM.

In the future, we can expect to see 80x86-family circuits with even higher levels of integration, for example, with ROM and RAM as well as peripheral controllers packaged in the same chip with an 8086 processor. However, there

TABLE 18–1   Differences among 80x86 family members.

Feature	8086/88	80186/188	80286	80386
Memory data bus width (bits)	8/16	8/16	16	16 or 32
Memory address bus width (bits)	20	20	24	32
Clock cycles per memory access	4	4	3	2
Internal data bus size (bits)	16	16	16	32
Clock cycles for fastest instruction	4	4	3	2
Physical address space (bytes)	2^{20}	2^{20}	2^{24}	2^{32}
Logical address space (bytes)	2^{20}	2^{20}	2^{30}	2^{46}
Memory segmentation	Yes	Yes	Yes	Yes
Maximum segment size (bytes)	2^{16}	2^{16}	2^{16}	2^{32}
Maximum number of segments	n/a	n/a	2^{14}	2^{14}
Memory-mapping algorithm	Shift–add	Shift–add	Table lookup	Table lookup
Memory protection	No	No	Yes	Yes
Memory paging	No	No	No	Yes
Virtual 8086 mode	n/a	n/a	No	Yes
On-chip I/O controllers	No	Yes	No	No

is another dimension to the evolution of the 80x86 family, the *architectural* evolution of the 8086 processor.

80286

8086 emulation mode

Intel began the architectural evolution of the 8086 processor in the early 1980s with the *80286* processor. The 80286 retains the basic programming model and instruction set of the 8086, but it modifies and extends the 8086's memory-mapping scheme to provide memory management (protection) capabilities and to access a somewhat larger memory. It also provides an *8086 emulation mode* in which the extended features are disabled, and the processor behaves exactly like an 8086. Since the 80286 is built with faster technology and has an improved execution unit and memory interface, it runs programs faster than an 8086, whether in native mode or in 8086 emulation mode. IBM PC-ATs and compatibles use 80286s running in 8086 emulation mode, with brief forays into native mode to access so-called "extended memory."

80386

The major limitation of the 80x86 family, from the 8086 through the 80286, is the segmentation of programs and data into 64-Kbyte chunks accessed by 16-bit addresses in a larger physical address space. With the introduction of the *80386* in the mid 1980s, Intel finally caught up with the Motorola 68000's clean 32-bit addressing architecture. In native mode, the 80386 still segments its programs and data, but each chunk may be up to 4 gigabytes long, accessed by a 32-bit address.

virtual 8086 mode

Other important improvements in the 80386 architecture include an expanded programming model with 32-bit-wide registers and instructions to operate on them, a 32-bit-wide data path to memory, and an even faster memory bus architecture. For compatibility with its predecessors, the 80386 can emulate both the 80286 and the 8086 processors. Its *virtual 8086 mode* is especially useful, since it allows the multiple 8086 programs to run on an 80386 system as if each one had its own private 8086 processor and memory; this mode is used in Microsoft's Windows/386 and other operating systems that run PC applications on 80386-based personal computers.

80486

We can expect Intel's next step in the 80x86 family's evolution to appear in the late 1980s, and to be similar to Motorola's evolution from the MC68020 to the MC68030. That is, we can expect the *80486* to have exactly the same programming model and instruction set as the 80386, with its "improvements" consisting of performance enhancements like on-chip cache memory or floating-point processing. At the same time, Intel is addressing the low-end PC market

80386SX

with an 80386 processor, called the *80386SX*, that uses a lower-cost 16-bit-wide memory data bus (*à la* 8086/8088). In the future, we can expect Intel to provide a high-integration chip containing an 80386 processor (*à la* 80186/80188) for the imbedded control market.[2]

Several important differences among 80x86 family members are listed in Table 18–1. In this chapter, we'll describe the complete architecture of the original 8086 processor and, in the last two sections, we'll highlight the major

80x86

extensions provided by the 80286 and 80386 processor architectures. Throughout this chapter, we use the term *80x86* when referring to the instructions and features of the 8086, 8088, 80186, and 80188, and of the 80286 and 80386 in 8086 emulation mode.

18.1 BASIC ORGANIZATION

18.1.1 Computer Structure

The basic structure of an 80x86-based computer is shown in Figure 18–1. The 80x86 processor architecture supports isolated I/O, so that there could be separate buses for I/O and for memory. However, in all of the 80x86-family components introduced so far, the I/O bus and the memory bus both share the same pins. The processor generates bus control signals to indicate whether a particular transaction using the shared pins is for an I/O interface or for memory.

As indicated in Figure 18–1 and Table 18–1, the data part of an 80x86 memory bus may be 8, 16, or 32 bits wide, depending on the family member. The 80386's memory data bus is physically 32 bits wide, but may be dynamically reconfigured to 16 bits—"narrow" memory and I/O subsystems request the processor to perform a 16-bit transfer by asserting a special control signal when they are addressed.

80376

---

[2]Intel initially introduced the *80376* for the imbedded control market. However, the 80376 is simply a half-price 80386SX in which virtual 8086 mode has been disabled. Intel cut the 80376's price to get designers to use it in imbedded control applications, and disabled virtual 8086 mode, which is used in PC-compatible applications, so that it would not compete with the 80386SX in the lucrative PC-compatible market.

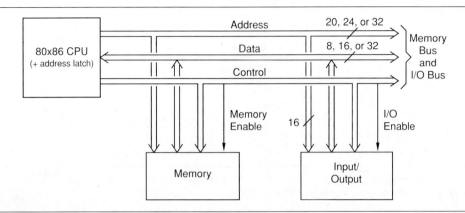

FIGURE 18–1 80x86-based computer block diagram.

The address part of an 80x86 memory bus may be 20, 24, or 32 bits wide, depending on the family member. In the 8086/88 and 80186/188, the address and data buses share the same pins of the IC package. The address comes out on these pins at the beginning of a memory or I/O cycle, and is captured by an *address latch* external *address latch* circuit that drives the Address bus in Figure 18–1. The data transfer takes place on the shared pins at the end of the cycle.

logical address An 80x86 *logical address* consists of a *segment base address* and a 16-bit *segment base* *segment offset*. Even though 80x86 processors have a minimum of 20 address *address* bits to access physical memory, most instructions use only a 16-bit segment *segment offset* offset to address memory. In the 8086/88 and 80186/188, an on-chip memory-mapping unit combines the 16-bit segment offset with a segment base address to obtain a 20-bit physical address, as explained in Section 18.3.10. In the 80286 and 80386, 16-bit segment offsets are translated into 24-bit and 32-bit physical addresses, as explained in Sections 18.7 and 18.8, respectively.

Input/output operations in the 80x86 use a 16-bit address, so that the CPU may access up to 64 Kbytes of I/O interface registers (ports) in addition to the main memory. Of course, memory-mapped I/O may also be used at the discretion of the system hardware designer.

Most 80x86 processors contain a two-level, vectored, priority interrupt system. The 80186 and 80188 processors provide additional interrupt inputs and levels for external and internal I/O devices. Interrupt vectors are contained in the bottom 1 Kbyte of memory.

18.1.2 Processor Programming Model

The processor state of the 80x86 contains a total of fourteen 16-bit registers, as *general registers* shown in Figure 18–2. Intel calls eight registers, AX through DI, *general registers* *(AX–DI)* because they contain data and addresses during computations. However, these registers are fairly specialized, and the 80x86 is hardly a general-register machine

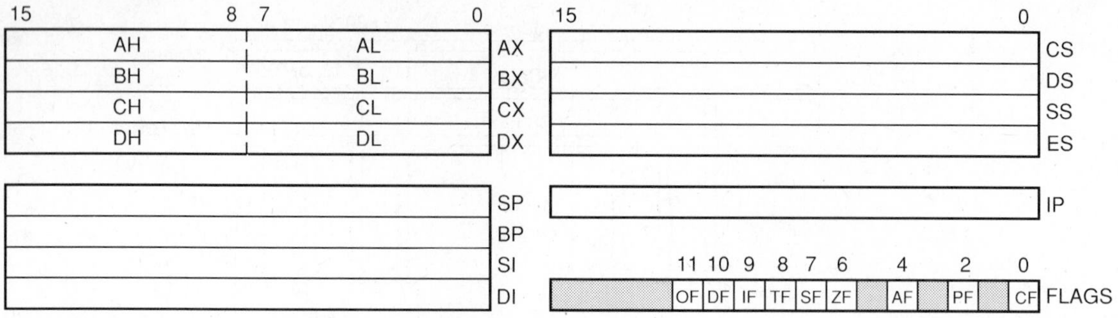

FIGURE 18–2   Programming model of the 80x86.

in the traditional sense of the word. The specialization (i.e., irregularity) of the 80x86 registers is explained by the fact that they were designed to be a compatible superset of the registers of the Intel 8080, an older accumulator-based machine. In a strict taxonomy, the 80x86 processor architecture is more closely related to extended accumulator-based architectures such as the 8080 and the Motorola 6809, than to the 68000. In the 80x86 family, only the 80386 in native mode is a true general-register machine.

data registers (AX–DX)

Four of the 80x86's general registers, AX through DX, are *data registers* primarily intended to hold data. Most 80x86 data-manipulation instructions can operate on either bytes or words; byte-manipulation instructions can access either half of a data register, for example, AH or AL.

address registers (SP–DI)

The other four general registers, SP through DI, are *address registers* intended to hold 16-bit addresses. Register SP is used as a stack pointer to push and pop return addresses during subroutine and interrupt calls and returns. Like the stacks in the 68000 and 6809, the 80x86 stack grows toward decreasing memory locations and SP points directly at the top stack item.

base or index registers (BP, SI, DI, BX)

Address registers BP, SI, and DI may be used as *base or index registers* in various addressing modes as explained in Section 18.3. Just to confuse things, data register BX can also be used as a base or index register (actually, this feature was included for 8080 compatibility).

Besides distinguishing between data registers and address registers, the 80x86 CPU performs certain operations using only one or two specific registers, reinforcing our claim that the registers are not really "general." Special-purpose uses of the registers are outlined in Table 18–2.

At this point, it should be apparent that the 80x86 has a much more irregular register structure than other processors, requiring a programmer or compiler to allocate and keep track of specific registers for specific coding tasks. On the other hand, the implicit use of registers with certain operations and addressing modes allows instructions to be encoded with a smaller number of bits than would be needed for completely general register-selection. Faced with a trade-off between

TABLE 18–2   Special-purpose functions of 80x86 "general" registers.

Register	Description	Special Function
AX	Accumulator	Word multiply, divide, and I/O; optimized
AL	Accumulator (low byte)	Byte multiply, divide, and I/O; translate; decimal arithmetic; optimized
AH	Accumulator (high byte)	Byte multiply and divide
BX	Base	Base register; translate
CX	Count	String operations; loops
CL	Count (low byte)	Dynamic shifts and rotates
DX	Data	Word multiply and divide; indirect I/O
SP	Stack Pointer	Stack operations
BP	Base Pointer	Base register
SI	Source Index	String source; index register
DI	Destination Index	String destination; index register

assembly language programming effort and program size and execution time, the 80x86's designers chose to optimize the latter.

Most 80x86 instructions deal only with the 16-bit segment offset part of a logical address; the segment base address is implied by the contents of one of four *segment registers*, CS through ES in Figure 18–2. After a 16-bit segment offset has been derived from the instruction and general registers using traditional addressing modes, the offset is added to the segment base address to form a 20-bit or wider physical address using rules given in Section 18.3.10. In systems that use 64K or fewer bytes of memory, all of the segment registers may be initialized to provide a segment base address of zero and then ignored.

segment registers (CS–ES)

In one sense, the 80x86's support of memory mapping goes beyond that of the original 68000—the 80x86's memory-mapping scheme is defined as part of the processor architecture and the mapping circuits are contained in the same integrated circuit as the CPU. On the other hand, the 8086/88 and 80186/188 lack two essential ingredients for employing memory management in a multi-programming system: access control bits and a privileged mode of operation. These features were added in the 80286 and 80386 processors.

instruction pointer (IP)

Strangely, the 80x86 does not have a program counter (PC). However, it does have a 16-bit *instruction pointer (IP)* that, except for its name, is just like the PC found in other processors. Intel gives no reason for the name change.

FLAGS
carry flag (CF)
zero flag (ZF)
sign flag (SF)
overflow flag (OF)
auxiliary carry flag (AF)
parity flag (PF)

The 80x86's condition bits and processor control bits are grouped together in a 16-bit register called *FLAGS* that may be pushed onto or popped from the stack as a single unit. FLAGS contains four "standard" condition bits called *carry flag (CF)*, *zero flag (ZF)*, *sign flag (SF)*, and *overflow flag (OF)*. There is also an *auxiliary carry flag (AF)* that is set to the carry or borrow between nibbles during decimal addition and subtraction operations. The *parity flag (PF)* is set to 1 if a result has an even number of 1s.

direction flag (DF)

Three bits in FLAGS are classified as "processor control" bits. Setting the *direction flag (DF)* to 1 causes string-manipulation instructions to use auto-decrement addressing; otherwise they use auto-increment addressing. Setting

interrupt flag (IF)   the *interrupt flag (IF)* allows the processor to accept interrupt requests on its
trace flag (TF)   INTR input. Setting the *trace flag (TF)* causes a trace trap to occur after each
                           instruction is executed, allowing on-line debuggers to single-step programs.

                                   The arrangement of bits in FLAGS is unusual since not all of the condition
                           bits are grouped together; compare with the "system byte" and "user byte"
                           arrangement of the 68000. However, in the present arrangement the low-order
PSW   byte of FLAGS is compatible with the 8-bit *PSW* of the older 8080; bits in the
                           high-order byte of FLAGS did not exist in the 8080.

18.1.3   Instruction Formats

Basic instruction lengths in the 80x86 vary from one to six bytes. The opcode
is always contained in the first byte of the instruction, and successive bytes, if
instruction prefix   any, contain addressing information. In addition, one or more *instruction prefix*
byte   *bytes* may be placed before the opcode byte of any basic instruction to override
                          certain default operation modes; the prefixes allowed in various situations will
                          be discussed later as appropriate.

                                  The 80x86 has many different instruction formats; a few are shown in
                          Figure 18–3. In formats (b), (c), and (e), one or two additional bytes may
                          be appended to the postbyte field for certain addressing modes, yielding the
                          maximum instruction length of six bytes in format (b). Most 80x86 instructions
w   can operate on either words or bytes, as designated by a *w* bit in the opcode
                          byte (w = 1 for words).

                                  Instruction encodings will be discussed as appropriate in the sections on
                          80x86 addressing modes and operations. However, we concentrate mainly on the
                          effects and assembly language format of various 80x86 operations and addressing
                          modes. Readers interested in all of the details of instruction encodings can find
                          them in the manufacturer's literature.

18.2   ASSEMBLY LANGUAGE

ASM-86   Intel's standard assembly language for the 80x86, called *ASM-86*, is very un-
                          usual, complex, and sophisticated.[3] In a small space, we can only touch on
                          the philosophy and basic features of the language, and so you must read Intel's
                          literature to find all of the features of ASM-86 that are used in large programs.

                                  In a typical assembler, the symbol table contains a list of symbols and a
                          value for each symbol. In ASM-86, a symbol can have a 16-bit value. However,
                          ASM-86 implements an unusual concept for assembly languages, namely, that
                          symbols may have other attributes besides value, including "type" and "segment
                          name." We'll discuss the uses of these attributes shortly.

---

[3]Just like the personalities of the 8086's architects, according to a reader who knew them well!

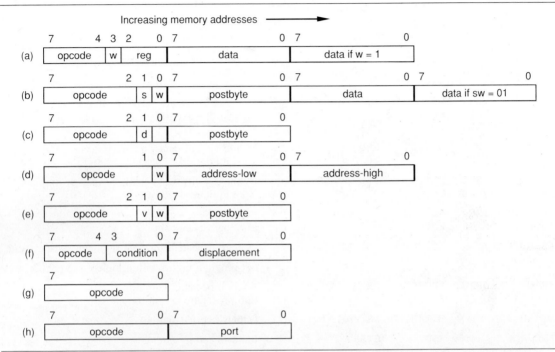

FIGURE 18–3   A few 80x86 instruction formats: (a) immediate to register; (b) immediate to register or memory; (c) memory to or from register; (d) absolute short; (e) shifts and rotates; (f) conditional branches; (g) inherent addressing; (h) input/output with fixed port.

       The basic line format of ASM-86 is simple enough, containing label, opcode, operand, and comments, similar to the free-format assembly language discussed at the end of Section 6.1.1. Comments start with semicolons, and labels of executable instructions are followed by colons. However, labels in directive statements are not followed by a colon. Hexadecimal numbers are denoted a suffix of H; however, for the assembler to distinguish them from symbols they must begin with a decimal digit (e.g., 0BEACH, not BEACH).

EQU

DB
DW
DD
?

DUP

       Important ASM-86 assembler directives are listed in Table 18–3. The EQU directive defines a new symbol as in other assembly languages, except that it gives to the new symbol *all* of the attributes of its operand expression. The DB, DW, and DD directives define byte, word, and double-word data. ASM-86 is unique in that these same statements are used to declare constant data (initialized at load time) and variable storage (uninitialized): an operand of "?" denotes a variable, that is, an uninitialized byte, word, or double word. Multiple operands are separated by commas. Any operand, including "?", may be repeated *n* times by enclosing it in parentheses and then preceding the parenthesized expression with "*n* DUP". The remaining directives in Table 18–3 will be introduced in sample programs later in this chapter.

TABLE 18–3   ASM-86 assembly language directives.

Name	Label	Opcode	Operands	Effect
		Examples		
EQU	CR	EQU	0DH	Equate symbol with operand
DB	CBYT	DB	17,0EFH,-1,CR	Define 1-byte data—memory may or may not
	VBYT	DB	?	be initialized
	MSG1	DB	'IKSTYDK',0	
DW	CWRD	DW	8800H,OFFSET CB	Define 1-word data—memory may or may not
	TWRD	DW	10 DUP (?)	be initialized
DD	CDBL	DD	456789ABH	Define 2-word data—memory may or may not
	VDBL	DD	?	be initialized
SEGMENT	SEG0	SEGMENT		Begin logical segment
ENDS	SEG0	ENDS		End logical segment
ASSUME		ASSUME	CS:SEG0	Declare expected run-time segment register value
ORG		ORG	4000H	Set program origin within logical segment
PROC	DRAW	PROC	NEAR	Begin procedure definition
ENDP	DRAW	ENDP		End procedure definition
EXTRN		EXTRN	OS:FAR	Define external symbol
END		END	START	Indicate end of assembly

symbol type   Each symbol in an ASM-86 program has an associated *symbol type*. Most symbols have one of the following types and associated values:

BYTE PTR
- **BYTE PTR.** The value of the symbol is the 16-bit segment offset (i.e., address in segment) of a 1-byte variable in memory.

WORD PTR
- **WORD PTR.** The value of the symbol is the 16-bit segment offset of a 1-word variable in memory.

DWORD PTR
- **DWORD PTR.** The value of the symbol is the 16-bit segment offset of a 2-word variable in memory.

NEAR PTR
- **NEAR PTR.** The value of the symbol is the 16-bit segment offset of a "nearby" instruction, one that may be referenced by an intrasegment jump or call instruction.

FAR PTR
- **FAR PTR.** The value of the symbol is the 16-bit segment offset of an instruction that can be referenced only by an intersegment jump or call instruction.

NUMBER
- **NUMBER.** The value of the symbol is an arbitrary 16-bit number. The programmer has assigned a symbolic label to the number for documentation purposes.

TABLE 18–4   ASM-86 special operators.

Operator	Converts from	To	Comment
OFFSET	Any PTR	NUMBER	Returns 16-bit segment offset
SEG	Any PTR	NUMBER	Returns 16-bit segment base address
SIZE	Any data PTR	NUMBER	Returns number of bytes allocated for data
LENGTH	Any data PTR	NUMBER	Returns number of bytes, words, or double words
BYTE PTR	Any PTR or NUMBER	BYTE PTR	Segment name (if any) is preserved
WORD PTR	Any PTR or NUMBER	WORD PTR	Segment name (if any) is preserved
DWORD PTR	Any PTR or NUMBER	DWORD PTR	Segment name (if any) is preserved
NEAR PTR	Any PTR or NUMBER	NEAR PTR	Segment name (if any) is preserved
FAR PTR	Any PTR or NUMBER	FAR PTR	Segment name (if any) is preserved

segment name   Any symbol of one of the first five types also has an associated *segment name*. ASM-86 provides a few more types, not discussed here, to facilitate program relocation and linking.

symbol typing   In many cases, *symbol typing* allows the assembler to figure out the programmer's intentions without specific directions. For example, the 80x86 has an INC instruction that increments a byte or word in memory. The assembler determines whether the assembly language instruction

```
        INC     SPOT                ;Add one to variable SPOT.
```

should increment a byte or a word at memory location SPOT according to the type of symbol SPOT, either BYTE PTR or WORD PTR. Other assembly languages would use different opcode mnemonics for byte and word operations (e.g., ADD.B and ADD.W in the 68000).

Typing also allows the assembler to check the consistency of a programmer's statements. For example, the statement INC WELL is an error if the type of WELL is anything but BYTE PTR or WORD PTR. Likewise, the statement

```
        MOV     AL,QUICK
```

is an error if QUICK has type WORD PTR, since this is an attempt to load a byte register with a memory word.

Despite the benefits of typing, some programmers dislike the structure that it imposes. For example, suppose that you declared a 1-word variable,

```
CATS    DW      ?                   ;Counts cats in Kate's kitchen.
```

and for some reason you wanted to read the first byte of the word. If you wrote

```
        MOV     AL,CATS
```

then you would get an error message for trying to load a byte register with a word value. Therefore, ASM-86 provides special operators, listed in Table 18–4, that convert symbols and expressions from one type to another. The correct code for the above example is

```
MOV     AL, BYTE PTR CATS
```

Typing and the absence of opcode size suffixes sometimes create ambiguity. For example, the statement

```
INC     [BX]                    ;Add one to byte pointed to by BX.
```

may be intended to increment a byte, but ASM-86 has no way of determining whether BX points to a byte or word (it doesn't read comments!). In such cases, the programmer must explicitly inform the assembler of the operand's intended type using one of the special operators:

```
INC     BYTE PTR [BX]  ;Add one to byte pointed to by BX.
```

program location counter (PLC)

The *program location counter* (PLC) in ASM-86 has a 16-bit offset value and an associated segment name (as defined by the SEGMENT directive). When PLC is used in an expression, a type must be associated with it as well. Therefore, the PLC may be specified by the reserved symbol THIS followed by a type designator: BYTE, WORD, DWORD, NEAR, or FAR. Thus, you might define the address just past the end of a table of 20 data words as follows:

THIS
BYTE
WORD
DWORD
NEAR
FAR

```
TABLE    DW      20 DUP (?)
TBLEND   EQU THIS WORD
```

LENGTH

relocation and linking

In this definition, ASM-86 gives TABLE a length attribute—the number of bytes allocated by DW. Thus, MOV AX, LENGTH TABLE loads AX with 40.

At this point, we can introduce the concepts of relocation and linking that are embodied in the 80x86 memory-mapping scheme and in ASM-86 and related program development tools. We assume that you are familiar with the general concepts of relocation and linking discussed in Section 6.4.

logical segment

The 8086's designers intended for programs to be broken into modules for code, data, and stack. Each module is stored in a separate *logical segment* that is accessed through an appropriate segment register. The exact physical address used by a logical segment is unimportant as long as the segment registers are maintained properly. Therefore, the binding of each logical segment to a physical base address may be deferred until all of the logical segments (relocatable object modules) of the program are brought together at load time.

In an 80x86 program development system, individual assembly language program modules are assembled by ASM-86, which produces relocatable object modules. The *PLM-86* high-level language for the 80x86 also produces relocatable object modules. Both types of modules may be linked together by the *LINK-86* link editor, which produces a single relocatable object module in which external references have been resolved. The logical segments in a single relocatable object module may be bound to physical addresses using the *LOC-86* relocater, which produces an absolute object module.

PLM-86

LINK-86

LOC-86

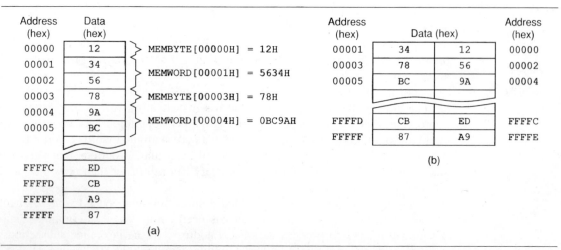

FIGURE 18–4   Memory organizations: (a) 80x86 logical organization, and 8088 and 80188 physical organization; (b) 8086, 80186, and 80286 physical organization.

18.3   ADDRESSING

Most 80x86 instructions specify operands in the general registers or in memory. Typical operands may be a byte or a word, but there are also instructions, described in Section 18.4, that operate on BCD digits, byte strings, and word strings. Most word instructions can access any of the general registers AX–DI in Figure 18–2. Byte instructions treat registers AX–DX as a set of eight 8-bit registers AH–DL shown in Figure 18–2, and cannot access registers SP–DI. In either case, a 3-bit field in the instruction is used to encode the register number.

The 80x86's memory is logically organized as a contiguous list of bytes, as shown in Figure 18–4(a). Bytes in memory are assembled into words with the lower-numbered byte in the least significant position. When we write an instruction from left to right, as in Figure 18–5, word values come out backwards; in fact, 8086 co-architect S. P. Morse has observed that this arrangement could *backwords* be called *backwords storage*!
storage

Unlike other 16-bit processors, the 80x86 architecture does not require memory words to start at even addresses; both instructions and data words may start at even or odd addresses.

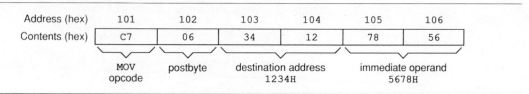

FIGURE 18–5   Layout of bytes in a typical 80x86 instruction, MOV WORD PTR 1234, 5678.

word alignment

The memory connected to an 8088 or 80188 processor is physically as well as logically organized as a list of bytes as shown in Figure 18–4(a). However, the memory connected to an 8086, 80186, or 80286 processor is physically organized as a list of words as shown in Figure 18–4(b). These processors may access a word in one memory cycle if the word starts at an even address (i.e., if the word is *aligned* on a word boundary). If an instruction specifies a word at an odd address, then the CPU must access two memory words and extract the appropriate bytes from each. Although alignment operations are done without explicit program intervention, programs that access aligned words can run faster than ones that access nonaligned words. In particular, programs that keep the stack pointer SP aligned on a word boundary can run faster than ones that push and pop individual bytes.

effective address

Basic 80x86 instructions and addressing modes specify 16-bit segment offsets. After a 16-bit segment offset has been computed, it is combined with a segment register to produce a physical address. In the next nine subsections, we'll describe the traditional addressing modes by which the 80x86 generates 16-bit segment offsets; these modes are summarized in Table 18–5. We'll call the 16-bit segment offset computed by an addressing mode an *effective address* for compatibility with traditional addressing-mode parlance. In the last subsection, we'll describe how 20-bit physical addresses are generated in the 8086/88 and 80186/188.

18.3.1   Postbyte Addressing Modes

addressing-mode postbyte

mod

r/m

Some 80x86 instructions specify their operand addressing modes in the opcode byte, for example, in formats (a) and (d) in Figure 18–3. Other formats, such as (b), (c), and (e), contain an *addressing-mode postbyte*. The postbyte can specify one or two operands and has the layout shown in Figure 18–6.

The postbyte always specifies one operand using the *mod* and *r/m* fields. If the 2-bit mod field contains 11_2, then the operand is a register and the 3-bit r/m field contains the register number. Otherwise, mod and r/m are decoded together to yield one of the memory addressing modes that we discuss later: absolute, register indirect, based, indexed, or based indexed. If the selected mode requires additional addressing information, the information is contained in one or two bytes immediately following the postbyte.

reg

The use of the *reg* field depends on whether the instruction requires the postbyte to specify one or two operands. Instructions such as ADD dst,reg [format (c)] require two operands. In this case, the second operand is always a register whose number is contained in the reg field of the postbyte.

```
 7 6 5   3 2   0
+-----+-----+-----+
| mod | reg | r/m |
+-----+-----+-----+
```

FIGURE 18–6   Layout of the addressing-mode postbyte.

TABLE 18–5   Addressing modes and assembly language notation for the 80x86.

Mode	Notation(s)	Operand
Register	`reg`	`reg`
Immediate	`n`	`n`
Absolute	`addr16`	`MEM[addr16]`
Register indirect	`[rireg]`	`MEM[rireg]`
Based (8-bit displacement)	`[bireg].disp8` `[bireg+disp8]`	`MEM[bireg+disp8]`

Based or Indexed
(16-bit displacement)
	`[bireg].disp16`
	`addr16[bireg]`
	`[bireg+disp16]`
	`[addr16+bireg]`
		`MEM[bireg+disp16]` or `MEM[addr16+bireg]`

Based indexed (no displacement)	`[breg][ireg]` `[breg+ireg]`	`MEM[breg+ireg]`
Based indexed (8-bit displacement)	`[breg].disp8[ireg]` `[breg+disp8+ireg]`	`MEM[breg+disp8+ireg]`
Based indexed (16-bit displacement)	`[breg].disp16[ireg]` `[breg+disp16+ireg]`	`MEM[breg+disp16+ireg]`

Notes: `reg` denotes a general register, AX–DI in word instructions, or AH–DL in byte instructions.
    `rireg` denotes BX, SI, or DI.
    `bireg` denotes BX, BP, SI, or DI.
    `breg` denotes BX or BP.
    `ireg` denotes SI or DI.
    `n` denotes an expression of type `NUMBER` yielding a byte or word value as appropriate for
      the instruction.
    `MEM[x]` denotes the memory byte or word starting at physical address `x+segbase`, where
      `segbase` is the segment's starting physical address implied by one of the segment
      registers as described in Section 18.3.10. If all of the segment registers contain 0,
      then `segbase` is always 0.
    `addr16` denotes an expression of some `PTR` type yielding a logical address in a segment
      that is currently accessible though one of the segment registers, according to the most
      recent `ASSUME` statements. The 16-bit offset part of the logical address is used in the
      instruction, and a segment override prefix is generated if necessary.
    `disp8` denotes an expression of type `NUMBER` yielding an 8-bit displacement value (-128
      through $+127$). `disp16` denotes an expression yielding a 16-bit `NUMBER` (-32768
      through $+32767$). The assembler chooses the shortest possible displacement based on
      the value of the expression.
    The assembler distinguishes between absolute and immediate addressing modes according
      to the type of the operand expression: absolute for `PTR` types, immediate for the
      `NUMBER` type.

On the other hand, instructions such as `ROL dst` [format (e)] require only one operand. In this case, the postbyte's reg field is not needed for operand selection. The reg field is used instead with the opcode byte to specify an operation. For example, the instructions `ROL dst` and `ROR dst` both have the same opcode byte followed by a postbyte; however, `ROL`'s postbyte reg field is 000_2 while `ROR`'s is 001_2.

18.3.2 Register

*register
addressing*

In *register addressing*, the operand is contained in one of the general registers. In the 80x86, register addressing may be specified in the opcode byte as in Figure 18–3(a), or as a postbyte addressing mode as explained earlier. In double-operand instructions, two registers may be specified.

A register number is contained in a 3-bit field. In word instructions (w = 1), this field specifies one of the 16-bit registers, AX–DI in Figure 18–2. In byte instructions (w = 0), it specifies one of the 8-bit registers, AH–DL.

18.3.3 Immediate

*immediate
addressing*

In *immediate addressing*, the instruction contains the operand. In the 80x86, immediate addressing is designated by a particular opcode combination, and is available for most double-operand instructions. Immediate instructions contain an addressing-mode postbyte, so that immediate-to-memory as well as immediate-to-register operations are possible. Instructions for which immediate addressing is *not* available include segment register loads and PUSH.

In a byte instruction (w = 0), an immediate operand is one byte long and appears at the end of the instruction [data in formats (a) and (b) in Figure 18–3]. In a word instruction (w = 1), the immediate operand is usually two bytes long [format (a)]. However, some word instructions can have 1-byte immediate operands specified by an s bit [format (b)]. If s is 1, then a 1-byte immediate value is sign extended to 16 bits before being used in a word operation. This allows small immediate values between −128 and +127 to be added to, subtracted from, or compared with word operands using only one immediate byte instead of two.

18.3.4 Absolute

*absolute
addressing*
direct addressing

*long absolute
addressing*

In *absolute addressing* (which Intel calls *direct*) the instruction contains the 16-bit effective address of the operand. Absolute addressing is a postbyte addressing mode; the 16-bit address follows the postbyte, low-order byte first.

There is also a *long absolute addressing* mode in which the instruction contains a 16-bit segment base address as well as a 16-bit offset (effective address), allowing the program to access any logical memory address directly. However, this mode is available only with jump and call instructions, and not with general data-manipulation instructions. As we'll see later in our sample programs, the lack of long absolute addressing is sometimes very inconvenient.

18.3.5 Register Indirect

*register indirect
addressing*

In *register indirect addressing*, a specified register contains the 16-bit effective address of the operand. This is another mode that may be specified by the addressing-mode postbyte.

The 80x86 contains four base registers: BX, BP, SI, and DI. However, register indirect mode is only available with three of the base registers—BX, SI, and DI. Register indirect addressing with BP must be simulated using based addressing with a displacement of 0.

Register SP, though classified as an address register, is not one of the base registers. The 8086's designers intended for references to data on the stack to use BP as a stack-frame pointer. Notice that the top of stack can be accessed no more efficiently than the middle, because register indirect addressing is not available with BP or SP.

18.3.6 Based

based addressing   *Based addressing* allows access to list items and other data structures when the offset to a particular item is known at assembly time, but the base address of the data structure must be computed at run time. Based addressing is a postbyte addressing mode in the 80x86. Any of the four registers—BX, BP, SI, or DI—may be used as a base register. The effective address of the operand is formed by adding the 16-bit address in the specified base register and an 8- or 16-bit displacement contained in the instruction. The displacement byte(s) immediately follow the addressing-mode postbyte.

In the 8-bit displacement mode, the displacement byte is treated as a signed number in the range −128 through +127. In assembly language programs, the assembler automatically determines whether a long or short displacement should be used when based addressing is specified.

ASM-86 assembly language allows two different notations for based addressing. The first, `[bireg].disp`, is similar to the notation used to access a field in a Pascal record. The second, `[bireg+disp]`, explicitly reminds us of the run-time addition that takes place in based addressing.

18.3.7 Indexed

The 80x86 does not have a separate indexed addressing mode. However, based mode with a 16-bit displacement is logically equivalent to indexed mode. In this case, the instruction contains a 16-bit base address, and the base register contains an index value.

Although any of the 80x86's four base registers may be used in based and indexed modes, the designers of the 8086 intended for BX and BP to be used as base registers and for SI and DI to be used as index registers. Compliance with the designer's wishes is motivated by the implicit use of the base and index registers in certain instructions and by defaults in the memory-mapping hardware described in Section 18.3.10.

While indexed and based addressing modes have the same encoding in 80x86 machine language, ASM-86 assembly language provides separate notations for them. The notation for indexed mode, `addr16[bireg]`, is similar to notations used in high-level languages and other assembly languages.

18.3.8   Based Indexed

based indexed
addressing

Based indexed addressing forms an effective address by adding a base address and a displacement, both of which are contained in registers. This allows both the base address of a data structure and a displacement to one of its components to be computed at run time. Based indexed addressing is a postbyte addressing mode in the 80x86. Either BX or BP may be used as the base register, and either SI or DI may be used as the index register. Thus, there are four different combinations of registers that may be used in based indexed addressing.

The 80x86 embellishes based indexed mode by allowing the instruction to contain an optional 8- or 16-bit displacement that is also added in the effective-address computation. An 8-bit displacement is treated as a signed number in the range −128 through +127. In assembly language programs, the assembler determines from the operand expression whether to use an 8-bit or 16-bit displacement or no displacement. The displacement bytes, if any, follow the postbyte in the assembled instruction.

18.3.9   Relative

relative
addressing

In the 80x86, *relative addressing* is used only in jump, call, conditional branch, and loop control instructions. The effective address is computed as the sum of the IP and an 8- or 16-bit signed displacement contained in the instruction. The IP value used is the address of the byte following the current instruction.

18.3.10   Memory Mapping

In this subsection, we'll discuss the memory-mapping scheme used by the 8086/8088 and 80186/188. The "native-mode" mapping mechanisms of the 80286 and 80386 are described in Sections 18.7 and 18.8. However, the mapping scheme described in this subsection also applies to the 80286 and 80386 in their 8086 emulation modes. We'll continue to use the designation "80x86" as we describe this mapping scheme, which exists in all 80x86-family processors.

segment

At any time, the logical addresses generated by 80x86 instructions may be translated into physical addresses in any of four different 64-Kbyte *segments* of physical memory. The four segments are named according to their intended uses: code, data, stack, and extra. Each of the four 16-bit segment registers (CS, DS, SS, and ES in Figure 18–2) implies the 20-bit physical base address of a 64-Kbyte segment.

paragraph
paragraph
number

In order to derive a 20-bit physical address from the contents of a 16-bit segment register, the memory-mapping unit in the 80x86 conceptually divides the 2^{20}-byte physical memory into 2^{16} 16-byte *paragraphs*; the 16 high-order bits of a 20-bit physical address are its *paragraph number*. Segments always begin on paragraph boundaries, that is, the low-order four bits of segment base addresses are always zero. Thus, segment registers contain not 20-bit addresses, but 16-bit paragraph numbers.

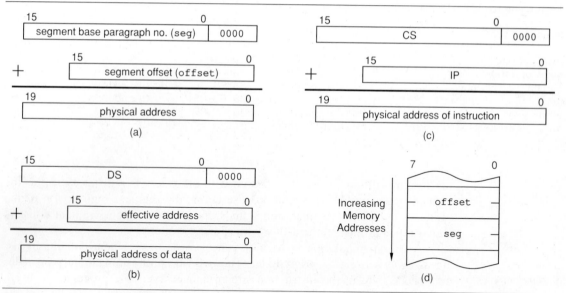

FIGURE 18–7   Logical-to-physical address translation in the 80x86: (a) general computation; (b) instruction fetch; (c) variable references; (d) `seg:offset` format in memory.

As shown in Figure 18–7(a), the 80x86 computes a 20-bit physical address by adding a 16-bit segment offset to a 20-bit segment base address (ignoring any carry beyond the 20th bit). The segment base address is obtained by a simple 4-bit shift of a 16-bit segment base paragraph number. The segment base paragraph number is usually obtained from one of the segment registers, while the segment offset is generally an effective address produced by one of the addressing modes of the previous subsections.

Since there are four different segment registers, a particular one must be selected to provide the segment base paragraph number for each logical-to-physical address translation. Instead of explicitly selecting segment registers by 2-bit fields in instructions, the 80x86 hardware selects a *default segment* according to the purpose of each memory reference.

default segment

Segment defaults are listed in Table 18–6. Instruction bytes are always fetched from the segment indicated by CS, the code segment register. As shown in Figure 18–7(b), IP contains the 16-bit segment offset for the instruction byte, and is added to the shifted CS to obtain the 20-bit physical address of the instruction byte. Likewise, stack operations always read and write bytes in the stack segment indicated by SS.

Most data-manipulation operations access variables in the data segment indicated by DS. As shown in Figure 18–7(c), the effective address obtained from the traditional addressing-mode computation is combined with DS to yield the physical address.

Subroutine parameters and other data on the stack must be accessed in the

TABLE 18–6 Default segment registers for memory reference types.

Reference Type	Segment Register	Alternates	Offset
Instruction fetch	CS (Code Segment)	None	IP
Stack operation	SS (Stack Segment)	None	SP
Variable (except three types below)	DS (Data Segment)	CS, ES, SS	Effective address
BP used as base register	SS (Stack Segment)	CS, ES, DS	Effective address
String source	DS (Data Segment)	CS, ES, SS	SI
String destination	ES (Extra Segment)	None	DI

stack segment; thus, operands accessed with BP as a base register use SS as the segment register. String operations use DS as the segment register for source operands and ES for destination operands; the use of different segment registers allows efficient intersegment block transfers.

segment override prefix

A data-manipulation instruction can override the segment defaults by using a *segment override prefix* byte. The override prefix immediately precedes the opcode byte in the instruction stream and instructs the processor to use a particular segment to access variables, instead of the default. Regardless of the override prefix, all instruction-fetch, stack, and string-destination references use the default segments defined in Table 18–6.

For example, the instruction MOV AL, BYTE PTR 100 loads AL from memory location 100 in the data segment; the corresponding machine instruction is four bytes long (opcode byte, addressing-mode postbyte, and 2-byte absolute address). The instruction MOV AL, ES:BYTE PTR 100 loads AL from memory location 100 in the extra segment; the machine instruction is five bytes long (override prefix followed by the original 4-byte instruction). In both cases, all instruction bytes are fetched from the code segment.

Using the four segment registers, a program may access four disjoint 64-Kbyte regions of physical memory at any time. However, nothing prevents segments from being partially or fully overlapped. Figure 18–8 shows a case in which the code segment is totally disjoint from the others, but the data and extra segments are identical and partially overlap the stack segment.

Although the 80x86 segment size is 64 Kbytes, most programs can use smaller segments. A program may use only part of a 64-Kbyte segment, say the first or last n bytes, according to some software convention. For example, a program might intend to use only the non-overlapping portion of the stack segment shown in Figure 18–8. However, since the 80x86 does not have any "segment length" registers, the unused $64K-n$ bytes of physical memory in a segment are not protected from inadvertent reading or writing by program errors.

A few 80x86 instructions, such as intersegment jumps and calls, specify absolute physical addresses. Such addresses occupy a double word in memory and contain a 16-bit offset and a 16-bit segment base address as shown in Figure 18–7(d). A 20-bit physical address is computed at run time by shifting the segment base address and adding the offset in the usual manner.

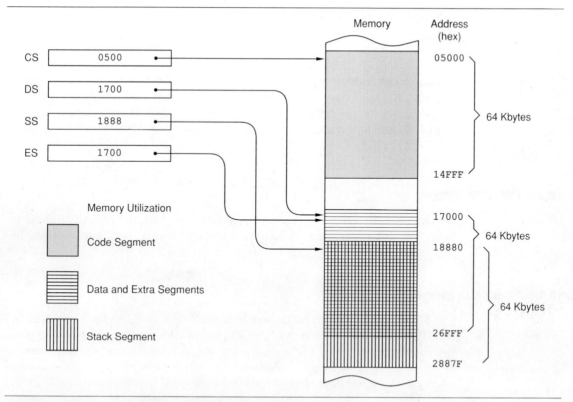

FIGURE 18–8   A possible segment allocation.

A major flaw in the 80x86 architecture is the difficulty in dealing with 20-bit physical addresses at run time, for example, comparing two physical addresses. Many different logical addresses can yield the same physical address. For example, physical address 12345H may be produced by a `seg:offset` of `1000H:2345H` or `1234H:0005H` or any of 4094 other `seg:offset` pairs. Therefore, it is insufficient simply to compare the `seg` and `offset` parts of logical addresses. Instead, the 20-bit physical addresses produced by the logical addresses must be compared.

Unfortunately, the 8086 has no instruction that directly compares the physical addresses produced by a pair of logical addresses. Likewise, it has no "load effective *physical* address" instruction; such an instruction would have to compute a 20-bit physical address from a logical address and deposit it in a pair of registers. Instead, a program that needs to compare physical addresses must use an explicit sequence of instructions to convert logical addresses to physical addresses. For example, in Intel's PLM/86 high-level language, a programmer might declare a logical-address "pointer variable" using the statement

```
DECLARE LIST$HEAD POINTER;
```

and check for the end of a linked list with the statement

```
IF LIST$HEAD = 0 THEN RETURN;
```

Since `LIST$HEAD` is a logical address, the compiled machine code must compute the resulting 20-bit physical address and compare it with 0. Intel's PLM/86 compiler, version 1.1, generates a 44-byte sequence of 21 machine instructions for the `IF` test in the above statement!

18.4 OPERATIONS

We shall classify 80x86 instructions into six types: data movement, arithmetic, logic and shifts, program control, string manipulation, and input/output. Input/output instructions will be discussed in Section 18.6.1.

18.4.1 Data Movement

The 80x86's data movement instructions are listed in Table 18–7. Typical instructions have one operand (`src` or `dst`) specified by an addressing-mode postbyte; such operands may use register, absolute, register indirect, based, indexed, or based indexed addressing. None of the 80x86 data movement instructions affect the condition flags, except for two instructions that explicitly load `FLAGS`.

Although many 80x86 instructions can operate on either bytes or words, 80x86 assembly language mnemonics do not contain size suffixes. Instead, the assembler associates a size attribute with each symbol so that the operand size for an instruction can be deduced from the attributes of symbols in the operand expression.

MOV

As shown in the first part of Table 18–7, the 80x86 has a fairly powerful `MOV` instruction. A `MOV` instruction in the format of Figure 18–3(c) specifies one general-register operand and another general-register or memory operand (*r/m*) using an addressing-mode postbyte. A *word bit (w)* specifies whether a word or byte is to be moved, and a *direction bit (d)* specifies the direction of transfer. Thus, r/m-to-register and register-to-r/m MOVs are possible. Notice that the assembly language operand order (`dst`, `src`) of 80x86 `MOV` and other double-operand instructions is the reverse of the order used in Motorola 68000 assembly language (`src`, `dst`).

r/m
word bit (w)
direction bit (d)

Another `MOV` format, shown in Figure 18–3(b), allows immediate-to-r/m MOVs. There are also `MOV` instructions for transferring data to or from the segment registers. However, notice that there is no "move immediate to segment register" instruction; this omission in the 80x86 instruction set is inconvenient because segment registers often must be loaded with constant values (see sample programs). The `XCHG` instruction swaps the contents of a general register and another general register or memory location.

XCHG

TABLE 18-7　　　Data movement instructions in the 80x86.

Mnemonic	Operands	Size	Description
MOV	dst,src	B,W	Copy src to dst
MOV	dst,data	B,W	Load dst with immediate data
MOV	dst,sreg	W	Load dst with sreg
MOV	sreg,src	W	Load sreg with src
XCHG	dst,reg	B,W	Exchange dst with reg
PUSH	src	W	Push src onto stack
PUSH	sreg	W	Push sreg onto stack
PUSHF		W	Push FLAGS onto stack
POP	dst	W	Pop stack into dst
POP	sreg	W	Pop stack into sreg
POPF		W	Pop stack into FLAGS
LAHF		B	Load AH with low byte of FLAGS
SAHF		B	Store AH into low byte of FLAGS
XLAT		B	Load AL with MEM[BX+AL]
LEA	reg,msrc	W	Load reg with effective address of msrc
LDS	reg,msrc	D	Load DS and reg with double-word msrc
LES	reg,msrc	D	Load ES and reg with double-word msrc

Notes: Instructions operate on bytes (B), words (W), or double words (D). When two operand sizes are allowed, the assembler determines the proper size according to the type of the operand expression.

reg may be any word register AX–DI in word and double-word operations, or any byte register AH–DL in byte operations.

sreg may be any segment register, CS–ES.

A src or dst operand is specified by an addressing-mode postbyte and therefore may use register, absolute, register indirect, based, indexed, or based indexed addressing. The MOV instruction has only one such postbyte; therefore, either src or dst must be a register.

An msrc operand may use any mode except register.

MOV instructions that have AX or AL as one of the operands and an absolute memory address as the other have an optimized encoding with no addressing-mode postbyte [Figure 18–3(d)].

data indicates an immediate operand (an expression of type NUMBER) appropriate to the size of the operation.

PUSH
POP
　　　　　　The PUSH and POP instructions in the 80x86 implicitly use the stack pointed to by SP. Like other stacks in this book, the 80x86 stack grows toward decreasing memory locations and SP points directly at the top stack item. As indicated in the second part of Table 18–7, a general register, segment register, memory operand, or FLAGS may be pushed onto the stack; and the word at the top of the stack may be popped into a register, memory word, or FLAGS. Notice that there is no "push immediate" instruction; a constant value to be pushed must first be loaded into a register.

　　　　　　The last part of the table lists miscellaneous data movement instructions.
LAHF
SAHF
XLAT
LAHF and SAHF move the low-order byte of FLAGS to and from AH; these instructions were included for compatibility with the 8080. The XLAT instruction replaces AL with a byte from a 256-byte translation table pointed to by BX.

LEA

LDS
LES

LEA loads a general register with the effective address of a `src` operand using any postbyte addressing mode except register. The value loaded is the 16-bit offset part of the operand's logical address, not the physical address.

The LDS and LES instructions load a general register and a segment register DS or ES with a 4-byte logical address found in memory in the format of Figure 18–7(d). This allows a segment register and base register to be initialized to a logical address in one step. For example, DS:BX may be initialized to 2000H:7FFFH as shown below:

```
MYSEG   DD      2000H:7FFFH     ;Store logical address value.
        . . .
        LDS     BX, MYSEG       ;Load DS:BX with logical address.
```

There should be a corresponding instruction to load SP and SS in one step, but there isn't. To initialize SP and SS to the logical address above, two instructions must be executed:

```
        MOV     SS, WORD PTR MYSEG+2 ;SS := segment base address.
        MOV     SP, WORD PTR MYSEG   ;SP := segment offset.
```

A problem is that, if an interrupt occurs between the execution of the two MOV instructions, then SS:SP will be in an inconsistent state and the interrupt handler will store data in the wrong place in memory. The 8086's designers discovered this problem and modified the CPU circuit so that interrupts cannot take place immediately after a MOV instruction that stores a value into SS. This is called a *kludge*.

kludge

18.4.2 Arithmetic

CMP

SUB

Arithmetic instructions of the 80x86 are listed in Table 18–8. All of these instructions set the condition flags according to their result, roughly as described in Chapter 8 for the 68000; refer to an 80x86 user's manual for detailed flag settings.

Instructions in the first part of Table 18–8 have a comprehensive and consistent set of formats. For double-operand instructions, there are r/m-to-register, register-to-r/m, and immediate-to-r/m formats available. We observed earlier that the 80x86's general register set is very irregular with respect to addressing modes and special-purpose instructions. However, the present example and others show that the 80x86's basic instructions have a very regular set of formats available.

Most 80x86 arithmetic instructions can operate on bytes or words. There is a complete set of add, add with carry, subtract, and subtract with borrow instructions (CF = 1 indicates a borrow). The CMP instruction performs the same operation as SUB except that it does not store the result. The three single-operand instructions allow a general register or memory operand to be incremented, decremented, or negated.

Instructions in the second group in Table 18–8 allow signed and unsigned multiplication and division of bytes and words. Multiply and divide operations

TABLE 18–8   Arithmetic instructions in the 80x86.

Mnemonic	Operands	Size	Description
ADD	dst,src	B,W	Add src to dst
ADD	dst,data	B,W	Add immediate data to dst
ADC	dst,src	B,W	Add with carry src to dst
ADC	dst,data	B,W	Add with carry immediate data to dst
SUB	dst,src	B,W	Subtract src from dst
SUB	dst,data	B,W	Subtract immediate data from dst
SBB	dst,src	B,W	Subtract with borrow src from dst
SBB	dst,data	B,W	Subtract with borrow immediate data from dst
CMP	dst,src	B,W	Compare dst with src (dst-src)
CMP	dst,data	B,W	Compare dst with immediate data (dst-data)
INC	dst	B,W	Add 1 to dst
DEC	dst	B,W	Subtract 1 from dst
NEG	dst	B,W	Negate dst (two's complement)
MUL	src	B,W	Unsigned multiply AL or AX by src
IMUL	src	B,W	Signed multiply AL or AX by src
DIV	src	B,W	Unsigned divide DX,AX by src
IDIV	src	B,W	Signed divide DX,AX by src
CBW		B	Convert byte in AL to word in AX
CWD		W	Convert word in AX to double word in DX,AX
DAA		B	Decimal adjust AL for add
DAS		B	Decimal adjust AL for subtract
AAA		B	ASCII adjust AL for add
AAS		B	ASCII adjust AL for subtract
AAM		W	ASCII adjust AX for multiply
AAD		*W	ASCII adjust AX for divide

Notes: Instructions operate on bytes (B) or words (W). When two operand sizes are allowed, the assembler determines the proper size according to the type of the operand expression.

In general, a src or dst operand is specified by an addressing-mode postbyte and therefore may use register, absolute, register indirect, based, indexed, or based indexed addressing. However, in instructions with both src and dst operands, there is only one addressing-mode postbyte. Therefore, either src or dst must be a register.

data indicates an immediate operand (an expression of type NUMBER) appropriate to the size of the operation.

MUL
IMUL
DIV
IDIV

SEX

on bytes use AX as a double-length accumulator: MUL and IMUL multiply AL by an 8-bit src, leaving the 16-bit product in AX; DIV and IDIV divide AX by an 8-bit src, leaving 8-bit quotient in AL and 8-bit remainder in AH. Multiply and divide operations on words use DX:AX in an analogous manner: DX holds a 16-bit multiplier, remainder, or high-order word of a 32-bit product or dividend; AX holds a 16-bit multiplier, quotient, or low-order word of a 32-bit product or dividend. Two instructions originally named SEX[4] are consistent with IMUL and IDIV: CBW sign extends the byte in AL into a word in AX, and CWD sign extends the word in AX into a double word in DX:AX.

[4]Stephen P. Morse, *The 8086 Primer*, Hayden, 1980, p. 52.

DAA

DAS

*unpacked BCD
format*

ASCII format

Instructions in the last group of Table 18–8 support arithmetic on decimal numbers in one of two formats. Standard packed-BCD arithmetic (Sections 4.10 and 8.11) is supported by DAA and DAS. The remaining four instructions support *unpacked BCD format*. This format stores one BCD digit per byte; the low-order nibble contains the BCD digit and the high-order nibble is irrelevant. One common unpacked format is *ASCII format*, in which the high-order nibble is always 0011. Thus, each byte contains the ASCII code for a BCD digit. Methods of performing unpacked-BCD arithmetic in the 80x86 are discussed in some of the references at the end of this chapter.

18.4.3 Logicals and Shifts

AND

OR

XOR

NOT

TEST

As shown in the first part of Table 18–9, the 80x86 logical instructions have the same format flexibility as the arithmetic instructions. All of the standard logical instructions—AND, OR, XOR, NOT, and AND-TEST—are provided. However, the 80x86 lacks the static and dynamic bit-manipulation instructions found in the 68000.

TABLE 18–9   Logical and shift instructions in the 80x86.

Mnemonic	Operands	Size	Description
AND	dst,src	B,W	Logical AND src to dst
AND	dst,data	B,W	Logical AND immediate data to dst
OR	dst,src	B,W	Logical OR src to dst
OR	dst,data	B,W	Logical OR immediate data to dst
XOR	dst,src	B,W	Logical Exclusive OR src to dst
XOR	dst,data	B,W	Logical Exclusive OR immediate data to dst
TEST	dst,src	B,W	Set FLAGS according to src AND dst
TEST	dst,data	B,W	Set FLAGS according to immediate data AND dst
NOT	dst	B,W	Invert bits of dst (ones' complement)
SHR	dst,cnt	B,W	Logical shift dst right cnt bits
SHL/SAL	dst,cnt	B,W	Logical/arithmetic shift dst left cnt bits
SAR	dst,cnt	B,W	Arithmetic shift dst right cnt bits
ROL	dst,cnt	B,W	Rotate dst left cnt bits
ROR	dst,cnt	B,W	Rotate dst right cnt bits
RCL	dst,cnt	B,W	Rotate dst left with C cnt bits
RCR	dst,cnt	B,W	Rotate dst right with C cnt bits

Notes: Instructions operate on bytes (B) or words (W). The assembler determines the proper size according to the type of the operand expression.

In general, a src or dst operand is specified by an addressing-mode postbyte and therefore may use register, absolute, register indirect, based, indexed, or based indexed addressing. However, in instructions with both src and dst operands there is only one addressing-mode postbyte. Therefore, either src or dst must be a register.

data indicates an immediate operand (an expression of type NUMBER) appropriate to the size of the operation.

cnt is either "1", specifying a shift count of 1, or "CL", specifying that the shift count is contained in register CL.

The 80x86 contains a complete set of static and dynamic shift and rotate instructions that operate much like the 68000 instructions described in Section 8.9. These instructions have a v bit [Figure 18–3(e)] that indicates whether the shift count is 1 ($v = 0$) or a variable contained in register CL ($v = 1$).

v

18.4.4 Program Control

The 80x86's program control instructions are shown in Table 18–10. The first six instructions handle jumps, subroutine calls, and subroutine returns both within a segment (intrasegment or **NEAR**) and between segments (intersegment or **FAR**). There are several opcodes associated with each mnemonic; the assembler picks the proper opcode according to the type of the operand expression. For example,

NEAR

FAR

TABLE 18–10   Program control instructions in the 80x86.

Mnemonic	Operands	Description
JMP	addr	Jump to address `addr`
JMP	src	Jump to address contained in `src`
CALL	addr	Call subroutine at address `addr`
CALL	src	Call subroutine at address contained in `src`
RET		Return from subroutine
RET	n	Return from subroutine, add n to SP
Jcc	addr8	Conditional branch to address `addr8`
LOOP	addr8	Decrement CX, jump to `addr8` if CX≠0
LOOPE/LOOPZ	addr8	Decrement CX, jump to `addr8` if CX≠0 and ZF = 1
LOOPNE/LOOPNZ	addr8	Decrement CX, jump to `addr8` if CX≠0 and ZF = 0
JCXZ	addr8	Jump to `addr8` if CX = 0
CLC		Clear carry (CF := 0)
CMC		Complement carry (CF := 1−CF)
STC		Set carry (CF := 1)
CLD		Clear direction (DF := 0)
STD		Set direction (DF := 1)
CLI		Clear interrupt-enable (IF := 0)
STI		Set interrupt-enable (IF := 1)
HLT		Halt and wait for reset or interrupt
WAIT		Wait for external event
ESC	opc,srce	Fetch `opc` and `srce` for external processor
NOP		No operation

Notes: addr is a target address in the current segment or a different segment.
   src is a word or double-word operand that contains the target address in the current segment
      or in a different segment, respectively.
   n is a 16-bit number added to SP after the return address is popped.
   cc is a standard 80x86 condition code chosen from the next table.
   addr8 is a target address in the current segment within 128 bytes of the instruction.
   opc is a 6-bit opcode for an external processor. srce is a source operand for the external
      processor, specified by a standard addressing-mode postbyte.

JMP

there are four possible interpretations of the instruction JMP expr in an assembly language program, according to the type of expr:

(1) expr has type NEAR PTR, so that expr denotes an instruction address in the current segment. The assembler generates opcode E8H for an *intrasegment direct jump* with long offset. The opcode is followed by two bytes containing a signed number in the range −32768 through +32767 that is added to IP when the instruction is executed. If the target address is within 128 bytes of the JMP instruction, the assembler may instead generate opcode EBH for a NEAR direct jump with short offset. In this case, the opcode is followed by one byte containing a signed number in the range −128 through +127 that is added to IP when the instruction is executed. In either case, the value of IP used is the address of the byte following the instruction.

intrasegment direct jump

(2) expr has type FAR PTR, so that expr denotes an instruction address in a different segment. The assembler generates an opcode of 9AH for an *intersegment direct jump*. The opcode is followed by two words. The first word is loaded into IP and the second word is loaded into CS when the instruction is executed.

intersegment direct jump

(3) expr has type WORD PTR, so that expr specifies a single-word operand using any of the 80x86's postbyte addressing modes. The assembler generates an opcode of FFH followed by an addressing-mode postbyte with a reg field of 100_2 for an *intrasegment indirect jump*. The operand word specified by the postbyte is loaded into IP when the instruction is executed.

intrasegment indirect jump

(4) expr has type DWORD PTR, so that expr specifies a double-word operand using any of the 80x86's postbyte addressing modes except register mode. The assembler generates an opcode of FFH followed by an addressing-mode postbyte with a reg field of 101_2 for an *intersegment indirect jump*. The first word of the operand specified by the postbyte is loaded into IP and the second word is loaded into CS when the instruction is executed.

intersegment indirect jump

Wheww! It is fortunate that the assembler can sort out all of the cases. Also, notice that the indirect jumps do not jump to their operand address; rather they load IP and possibly CS with values found at the operand address. In a FAR indirect jump, the double-word operand contains seg:offset in the standard format shown in Figure 18–7(d).

CALL

The CALL instruction has the same options and effects as JMP, except that it pushes a return address onto the stack before jumping. In a NEAR CALL, only IP is pushed. In a FAR CALL, first CS and then IP is pushed; this pushing order produces on the stack the standard seg:offset format shown in Figure 18–7(d).

RET

The RET instruction returns from a subroutine by popping a return address from the stack. Since a return address may be one or two words long, two different RET opcodes are needed. A NEAR RET pops a word into IP, while a

TABLE 18–11 Branch conditions in the 80x86.

Type	Mnemonic	Branch If	Condition
Single Bit			
	C	Carry	$CF = 1$
	NC	Not Carry	$CF = 0$
	S	Sign	$SF = 1$
	NS	Not Sign	$SF = 0$
	E / Z	Equal / Zero	$ZF = 1$
	NE / NZ	Not Equal / Not Zero	$ZF = 0$
	O	Overflow	$OF = 1$
	NO	No Overflow	$OF = 0$
	P / PE	Parity / Parity Even	$PF = 1$
	NP / PO	No Parity / Parity Odd	$PF = 0$
Signed			
	L / NGE	Less / Not Greater nor Equal	$(SF \oplus OF) = 1$
	GE / NL	Greater or Equal / Not Less	$(SF \oplus OF) = 0$
	LE / NG	Less or Equal / Not Greater	$((SF \oplus OF) + ZF) = 1$
	G / NLE	Greater / Not Less nor Equal	$((SF \oplus OF) + ZF) = 0$
Unsigned			
	B / NAE	Below / Not Above nor Equal	$CF = 1$
	AE / NB	Above or Equal / Not Below	$CF = 0$
	BE / NA	Below or Equal / Not Above	$(CF + ZF) = 1$
	A / NBE	Above / Not Below nor Equal	$(CF + ZF) = 0$

Notes: + denotes logical OR; $\oplus$ denotes logical Exclusive OR.

FAR RET pops one word into IP, and then a second word into CS. The assembler determines which RET opcode to use according to how the subroutine was declared—PROC NEAR or PROC FAR, with PROC NEAR being the default. As with parameter-passing conventions, it is up to the programmer to ensure that a subroutine and its callers agree on which call and return instructions will be used.

RET n
    The RET n instruction returns from a subroutine and adds n to SP after popping the return address. This instruction is very useful for cleaning up input parameters in stack-oriented parameter-passing conventions. As with RET, there are NEAR and FAR forms of RET n that the assembler chooses as appropriate.

    The 80x86 has sixteen distinct conditional branch instructions of the form
Jcc
Jcc addr8. The branches add a displacement of −128 to +127 to IP if a specified condition is true. The allowable conditions include all of the standard ones described in Section 8.7 plus parity, but Intel's mnemonics for the conditions are different, as shown in Table 18–11.

    The four instructions in the third group of Table 18–10 are useful loop-
LOOP
control primitives. If CX contains a number X, then the LOOP instruction may
LOOPZ
be placed at the end of a loop to execute the loop X times. The LOOPZ and
LOOPNZ
LOOPNZ instructions keep an iteration count in the same way and also allow the
JCXZ
loop to be terminated early by a zero or nonzero result. The JCXZ instruction

may be placed just before a loop controlled by CX in order to skip it completely if CX is already zero.

None of the program control instructions described so far affect FLAGS. The fourth group of Table 18–10 contains instructions whose sole purpose is to manipulate individual bits in FLAGS; their operations are self-explanatory.

A few miscellaneous instructions are listed in the last group in Table 18–10. HLT suspends processing until a reset or interrupt signal is received. WAIT suspends processing until a signal is received on the 80x86's TEST input line, allowing the processor to synchronize with an external event without requiring an interrupt. ESC is used to fetch an opcode and operand for an external coprocessor such as the Intel 8087 Numeric Processor. NOP needs no explanation.

HLT
WAIT

ESC
NOP

18.4.5   String Manipulation

Although the 80x86 does not have auto-increment and auto-decrement addressing modes for its memory reference instructions, it does have a number of special-purpose instructions for processing blocks or strings of data. These instructions are described in Table 18–12. The string instructions are only one byte long, and implicitly use index registers SI and DI to point to the source string and the destination string, respectively. Destination strings are always accessed in the extra segment, via ES. By default, source strings are accessed in the data segment, via DS; however, a segment override prefix may be used to access source strings in a different segment.

At run time, string instructions use either auto-increment or auto-decrement addressing on SI and DI, depending on the value of the DF flag. Each instruction may operate on either byte strings or word strings according to a w bit in the instruction. ASM-86 determines the proper size at assembly time according to the attributes of dummy `ssrc` and `sdst` operands.

repeat prefix

A *repeat prefix* may be used on any string instruction to process a string efficiently in one instruction with the CPU maintaining a loop count in CX. A few examples of program applications for the string-manipulation instructions will be given at the end of the next section.

18.4.6   *80186/188 Extended Instructions*

The 80186 and 80188 processors implement several additional instructions, listed in Table 18–13, that are not present in the 8086 and 8088. These instructions were also carried forward to the 80286 and 80386 processors.

PUSH
IMUL

The PUSH and IMUL instructions have been extended to use immediate operands. Also, IMUL now allows its result to be stored in any register, but in this form only the low-order word of a double-word product is stored. All of the shift and rotate instructions have been extended to accept an immediate shift count in the range 0–255. In the 80286 and 80386, only the five low-order bits of the shift count are used, so that the processor doesn't waste its time doing superfluous shifts.

TABLE 18–12 Block- and string-manipulation instructions in the 80x86.

Mnemonic	Operands	Size	Description
MOVS	sdst,ssrc	B,W	Copy ssrc string element to sdst
CMPS	sdst,ssrc	B,W	Set FLAGS according to sdst − ssrc
SCAS	sdst	B,W	Set FLAGS according to A − dst
LODS	src	B,W	Load A with ssrc
STOS	sdst	B,W	Store A into sdst
REP	minstr		Repeat minstr while CX≠0, that is, WHILE CX <> 0 DO BEGIN CX := CX - 1; minstr END
REPE/REPZ	cinstr		Repeat cinstr while equal/zero and CX≠0, that is, WHILE CX <> 0 DO BEGIN CX := CX - 1; cinstr; IF ZF = 0 THEN EXIT END
REPNE/REPNZ	cinstr		Repeat cinstr while unequal/nonzero and CX≠0, that is, WHILE CX <> 0 DO BEGIN CX := CX - 1; cinstr; IF ZF = 1 THEN EXIT END

Notes: String operations may be performed on byte strings or word strings, depending on a w bit in the instruction's opcode byte.

A denotes AL in byte-string operations, AX in word-string operations.

The CPU implicitly uses ES:DI as a pointer to a destination string and DS:SI as a pointer to a source string (register indirect addressing). It is up to the programmer to ensure that DI, SI, ES, and DS have the proper values at run time.

sdst and ssrc denote the source and destination operands in assembly language string instructions. However, the string instructions are only one byte long, and have no operand fields corresponding to ssrc and sdst. Nevertheless, the ASM-86 examines the attributes of the sdst and ssrc operands to determine the size of the string operation (byte or word), and whether a segment override prefix is needed for the ssrc operand (the sdst operand *must* be in the extra segment). Typically, sdst and ssrc are symbols corresponding to the base addresses of destination and source string buffers, respectively.

Each string instruction has alternate mnemonics, such as MOVSB and MOVSW, in which the operand size is explicitly mentioned and src and dst operands are not written.

Each string instruction automatically updates DI and/or SI after each sdst and/or ssrc string element is processed. The registers are updated by either incrementing or decrementing, depending on the run-time value of DF in FLAGS (DF = 1 for decrementing). Incrementing and decrementing are by 1 or by 2 depending on whether byte strings or word strings are being processed.

minstr denotes a MOVS or STOS instruction. cinstr denotes a CMPS or SCAS instruction. One of the repeat prefixes may be placed before a string instruction to cause it to repeat a number of times under CPU control, as governed by the Pascal algorithms shown. Note that if CX is 0 initially, then instr is skipped. Otherwise, the instruction is repeated until CX has been decremented to 0 or a termination condition on ZF has been reached.

PUSHA
POPA

To reduce the overhead of register saving and restoring in interrupt and general subroutine calls and returns, the PUSHA and POPA instructions push and pop eight general registers. This saves time and program length compared to the alternative of using sequences of PUSH and POP instructions.

ENTER

The ENTER alloc,lev instruction supports a stack-oriented parameter-

TABLE 18–13   Extended instructions in the 80186 and 80188.

Mnemonic	Operands	Size	Description
PUSH	data	B,W	Push immediate `data` onto stack
IMUL	wreg,src,data	B,W	Load `reg` with signed product of `src` and `data`
SHR	dst,icnt	B,W	Logical shift `dst` right `icnt` bits
SHL/SAL	dst,icnt	B,W	Logical/arithmetic shift `dst` left `icnt` bits
SAR	dst,icnt	B,W	Arithmetic shift `dst` right `icnt` bits
ROL	dst,icnt	B,W	Rotate `dst` left `icnt` bits
ROR	dst,icnt	B,W	Rotate `dst` right `icnt` bits
RCL	dst,icnt	B,W	Rotate `dst` left with C `icnt` bits
RCR	dst,icnt	B,W	Rotate `dst` right with C `icnt` bits
PUSHA			Push registers AX, CX, DX, BX, SP, BP, SI, DI onto stack
POPA			Pop registers DI, SI, BP, SP, BX, DX, CX, AX from stack
ENTER	alloc,lev		Create stack frame
LEAVE			Deallocate stack frame
BOUND	wreg,msrc	D	Check register against bounds pair
INS	sdst,DX	B,W	Input string from port specified by DX
OUTS	DX,ssrc	B,W	Output string to port specified by DX

Notes: Instructions operate on bytes (B), words (W), or double words (D). When two operand sizes are allowed, the assembler determines the proper size according to the type of the operand expression.

A `src` or `dst` operand is specified by an addressing-mode postbyte and therefore may use register, absolute, register indirect, based, indexed, or based indexed addressing. An `msrc` operand may not use register addressing.

`wreg` is any word register, AX–DI.

`data` indicates an immediate operand (an expression of type NUMBER) appropriate to the size of the operation.

`icnt` indicates an 8-bit immediate shift count, an expression of type NUMBER in the range 0–255.

`alloc` is a 16-bit unsigned integer that is subtracted from SP to allocate space for local variables.

`lev` is an 8-bit value whose five low-order bits specify the depth of subroutine nesting in a stack-oriented parameter-passing convention.

See Table 18–12 for a discussion of `ssrc` and `sdst` operands.

passing convention for a subroutine at level `lev` of nesting. The first thing **ENTER** does is to push the current frame pointer (BP) onto the stack; this is the beginning of a new stack frame. Then, if `lev` > 0, it pushes the frame pointers of `lev` − 1 outer subroutines and the current subroutine onto the stack. Finally, it loads BP with a pointer to the new stack frame and subtracts `alloc` bytes from SP to allocate space for local variables in the new stack frame.

display

The first `lev` words in the stack frame created by **ENTER** are called a *display* and contain pointers to the stack frames at nesting levels 1 through `lev`. The current subroutine uses the display to access variables of outer-level subroutines, whose addresses are not known until run time. At the end of a

LEAVE

subroutine, the **LEAVE** instruction undoes the effects of **ENTER** by simply setting SP to BP, and popping the old value of BP from stack.

BOUND   Array bounds can be checked with the BOUND `wreg,msrc` instruction. The `msrc` operand is a double word in memory; the first word is a signed lower bound and the second word is a signed upper bound. If array index contained in `wreg` does not lie within the range defined by the bounds pair, then a trap occurs as explained in Section 18.6.3.

                      The last two instructions in Table 18–13 are used for I/O as explained in Section 18.6.1.

18.5 SAMPLE PROGRAMS

                      The simple unsigned multiplication program that we showed for the 68000 in Table 5–6 is recoded for the 80x86 in Table 18–14. In this and the next example, we ignore the 80x86's segment registers and memory-mapping system; this simplification can only be used in 80x86 systems with 64K or fewer bytes of physical memory. The SEGMENT directive tells the assembler that the program

AT   contains one segment (SEG0) starting AT physical address 0000H. It also initializes the program location counter (PLC) to 0, so that assembly begins at offset 0 in the current segment. Within a segment, an ORG statement may be used to set the PLC to another value as shown. Thus, within a segment, we can use ORG statements to locate code and data just as we did with the 68000.

                      The program tells the assembler to ASSUME that all segment registers will contain the base address of SEG0 (0000H) when the program runs. Later we'll show programs that may use multiple segments and more memory.

TABLE 18–14   Multiplication by repeated addition in the 80x86.

```
SEG0      SEGMENT AT 0000H
          ASSUME CS:SEG0, DS:SEG0, SS:SEG0, ES:SEG0
;
          ORG     200H                 ;Program origin within segment.
;
;         Multiplication program works for any two 16-bit unsigned
;         numbers whose product can be expressed in only 16 bits.
;         Enter with multiplier and multiplicand in BX, DX.  Exit
;         with BX and DX undisturbed, CX bombed, and product in AX.
;
START:    MOV     AX,0                 ;Set AX to 0 (initial product).
          MOV     CX,BX                ;CX holds loop count (multiplier).
          JCXZ    OUT                  ;Already done if loop count zero.
MLOOP:    ADD     AX,DX                ;Else add multiplicand to product.
          DEC     CX                   ;Decrement loop count...
          JNZ     MLOOP                ;...and check for termination again.
OUT:      JMP     OPSYS                ;Go to operating system.
;
OPSYS     EQU     NEAR PTR 1000H ;Define OS address in current segment.
;
SEG0      ENDS
          END     START
```

TABLE 18–15   Initializing an array of bytes in the 80x86.

```
SEG0    SEGMENT AT 0000H
        ASSUME CS:SEG0, DS:SEG0, SS:SEG0, ES:SEG0
;
        ORG     200H                ;Program origin within segment.
INIT:   MOV     BX,OFFSET Q         ;Address of first array component.
ILOOP:  MOV     BYTE PTR [BX],0     ;Clear component.
        INC     BX                  ;Bump to next component.
        CMP     BX,OFFSET Q+5       ;Past last component?
        JNE     ILOOP               ;If not, go do some more.
        JMP     NEAR PTR 1000H      ;Go to operating system.
;
Q       DB      5 DUP (?)           ;Reserve 5 bytes for array.
;
SEG0    ENDS
        END     INIT
```

reset
How do the segment registers get set to zero in the first place? When power is applied to the 80x86, and whenever the 80x86 is *reset*, the CPU automatically sets CS to FFFFH and IP to 0000H. Therefore, the first instruction will be fetched from physical memory address FFFF0H. Most 80x86 systems are configured with read-only memory (ROM) at this address, so that the ROM may contain a FAR JMP to the actual starting address of a start-up program. Since the FAR JMP specifies new values for both CS and IP, the system designer can choose any new value for CS, including zero. At reset, the CPU also automatically sets the other segment registers to zero, where they will remain unless explicitly changed.

In Table 18–14, the multiplication program itself is straightforward and uses a loop to generate a product by repeated addition. The program could be optimized by replacing the DEC and JNZ instructions with the LOOP instruction, which performs the equivalent operations. Of course, the biggest optimization could be obtained by replacing the whole loop with the 80x86 MUL instruction, but then it would be an even less interesting example!

Table 18–15 is a program that declares and initializes an array of bytes and illustrates some unusual aspects of ASM-86 assembly language. The first executable instruction uses immediate addressing to load BX with the starting address of the array. Since there are no addressing-mode notations to distinguish between absolute and immediate addressing, ASM-86 must examine the types of its operands to determine the addressing mode. It uses immediate addressing if the source operand is a NUMBER, and absolute addressing if the source operand is a BYTE PTR or WORD PTR. For example, if we were to write

```
INIT:    MOV    BX,Q                ;Address of first component.
```

then ASM-86 would find that the operand Q is of type BYTE PTR; it would therefore assume that we are trying to load BX with the memory byte at address Q (absolute addressing). This is why the OFFSET operator is necessary. Given an expression `expr` of any `PTR` type, `OFFSET expr` returns a 16-bit `NUMBER` equal to the offset part of `expr`. Therefore, the instruction

```
INIT:   MOV     BX,OFFSET Q        ;Address of first component.
```

uses immediate addressing, because its operand has type `NUMBER`. A word rather than a byte move is assembled because `BX` is a word register. If we wrote

```
INIT:   MOV     BL,OFFSET Q        ;Low byte of component address.
```

then the assembler would generate a "move byte immediate" instruction because `BL` is a byte register; the immediate value would be the low-order byte of the offset part of address `Q`. With immediate addressing in general, the assembler determines the operand size from the size of the destination operand.

In the second instruction in Table 18–15, the source operand 0 is clearly a `NUMBER` for immediate addressing, but another special ASM-86 operator is needed just the same. In this case, if we simply wrote

```
ILOOP:  MOV     [BX],0             ;Clear component.
```

then the size of the destination operand would be ambiguous, because `BX` may point to either a byte or a word using register indirect addressing. The `BYTE PTR` operator informs the assembler that the destination operand is a byte, and so a "move byte immediate" instruction is assembled.

ASM-86 can make sense out of arithmetic expressions in operands in most cases. For example, in the `CMP` instruction in Table 18–15, the symbol `Q` has type `BYTE PTR` and therefore `Q+5` is assumed to be a `BYTE PTR` as well. Then `OFFSET Q+5` is a `NUMBER`, and the instruction

```
        CMP     BX,OFFSET Q+5      ;Past last component?
```

uses immediate addressing to compare the value of `BX` with the offset part of the logical address five bytes past the start of array `Q`.

The next two programs in this section use multiple segments and illustrate some of the concepts of relocation and linking that are embodied in the 80x86 memory-mapping scheme and in ASM-86 and related program development tools. In Table 18–16, we have recoded the array initialization program using separate segments for code and data, `CSEG` and `DSEG`.

The sixth line of the program tells the assembler to `ASSUME` that, when the program is run, `CS` will have been loaded with the proper segment base address for the segment named `CSEG`, and `DS` will have been loaded with the base address of `DSEG`. Two new instructions have been added at `INIT` to initialize `DS` to the proper base address for the data segment; note the lack of immediate addressing for segment register loading (...*groan*...). `CS` need not be initialized since it is loaded by the instruction that jumps to `INIT` in the first place.

linking and relocation

external address

This example uses the linking and relocation facilities of ASM-86 in conjunction with LINK-86 and LOC-86. The operating system restart address `OPSYS` is defined as an *external address* in another segment; its value will be

TABLE 18–16   A program with separate segments for code and data.

```
DSEG       SEGMENT                    ;Define data segment.
Q          DB      5 DUP (?)          ;Reserve 5 bytes for array.
DSEG       ENDS
;
CSEG       SEGMENT                    ;Define code segment.
           ASSUME CS:CSEG, DS:DSEG
;
INIT:      MOV     AX,DSEG            ;Initialize segment register.
           MOV     DS,AX
           MOV     BX,OFFSET Q        ;Address of first component.
ILOOP:     MOV     BYTE PTR [BX],0    ;Clear component.
           INC     BX                 ;Bump to next component.
           CMP     BX,OFFSET Q+5      ;Past last component?
           JNE     ILOOP              ;If not, go do some more.
           JMP     OPSYS              ;Go to operating system.
;
           EXTRN   OPSYS:FAR          ;Label OPSYS is defined elsewhere.
;
CSEG       ENDS
           END     INIT
```

supplied when the INIT module is linked with other modules using LINK-86. Also, the starting physical addresses of CSEG and DSEG are not tied down, as SEG0 was tied down by the AT clause in the original program. Instead, LOC-86 performs the final binding of logical segments CSEG and DSEG to physical memory addresses, and it patches all instructions and other locations that are to contain the now-known segment base addresses (e.g., MOV AX,DSEG and JMP OPSYS in Table 18–16).

Subroutines in the 80x86 are introduced in Table 18–17. This program counts the number of "1" bits in a word. The main program initializes the segment registers and SP, loads AX with a test word, and then calls WCNT1S to count 1s in AX. The WCNT1S subroutine performs its task by calling BCNT1S twice to count 1s in the high and low bytes of AX.

Four separate segments are used in Table 18–17: STACK for the return-address stack, MAIND for main program data, MAINC for main program code, and CNTSEG for code for both subroutines. A small data table (MASKS) is included in CNTSEG; this data is put in the code segment because it is "read-only."

Appropriate segment register initializations are made in MAIN. After initialization, the only segment register changes are the ones made to CS by FAR CALL and RET instructions.

Several ASM-86 conventions are used for the first time in Table 18–17. One pseudo-operation, DW, is used to define data words in memory whether the locations are to be initialized or not. Thus, the statement

```
TWORD   DW      1357H                      ;Test word to count 1s.
```

TABLE 18–17   An 80x86 program that uses subroutines to count the number of "1" bits in a word.

```
STACK    SEGMENT                      ;Stack segment for entire program.
         DW      32 DUP (?)           ;Reserve space for stack buffer.
STKE     EQU     THIS WORD            ;Define initialization address for SP.
STACK    ENDS
;
MAIND    SEGMENT                      ;Data segment for main program.
TWORD    DW      1357H                ;Test word to count 1s.
MAIND    ENDS
;
MAINC    SEGMENT                      ;Code segment for main program.
         ASSUME CS:MAINC, DS:MAIND, SS:STACK, ES:MAIND
MAIN:    MOV     AX, STACK            ;Initialize stack segment register.
         MOV     SS, AX
         MOV     SP, OFFSET STKE      ;Initialize stack pointer.
         MOV     AX, MAIND            ;Initialize data segment register.
         MOV     DS, AX
         MOV     ES, AX               ;Initialize extra segment register.
         MOV     AX, TWORD            ;Get test word.
         CALL    WCNT1S               ;Count number of 1s in it.
         JMP     OPSYS                ;Go to operating system.
         EXTRN   OPSYS:FAR            ;Operating system restart address.
MAINC    ENDS                         ;End main program.
;
CNTSEG   SEGMENT                      ;Define new code segment for subroutines.
         ASSUME CS:CNTSEG             ;CS will have new value here.
WCNT1S   PROC    FAR
;
; Count the number of '1' bits in a word. Enter with word in
; AX, exit with count in AX.  WCNT1S splits AX into two bytes,
; and calls BCNT1S to count the number of 1s in each byte.
;
         CALL    BCNT1S               ;Count 1s in AL, leave count in CX.
         PUSH    CX                   ;Save '1' count on stack.
         MOV     AL, AH               ;Count 1s in AH.
         CALL    BCNT1S
         POP     AX                   ;Get low-order count.
         ADD     AX, CX               ;Add high-order count.
         RET                          ;Done, return.
WCNT1S   ENDP                         ;            Continued on the next page.
```

defines a memory word whose contents will be initialized to 1357H at load time, similar to the DC.W statement in the 68000. On the other hand, the statement

```
         DW      32 DUP (?)           ;Reserve space for stack buffer.
```

reserves 32 memory words that will not be initialized at load time, similar to DS.W in the 68000. Finally, STKE is defined as a symbol whose value is the current PLC and whose type is WORD PTR by the statement

```
STKE     EQU     THIS WORD            ;Initialization address for SP.
```

TABLE 18–17   (continued)

```
BCNT1S  PROC    NEAR
;               Count number of '1' bits in a byte. Enter with byte in AL,
;               exit with count in CX.
        MOV     CX, 0               ;Initialize '1' count.
        MOV     SI, 0               ;Index of first mask in table.
BLOOP:  TEST    AL, MASKS[SI]       ;Test a bit of AL.
        JZ      BNEXT               ;Skip if bit is zero.
        INC     CX                  ;Update count if bit set.
BNEXT:  INC     SI                  ;Point to next mask.
        CMP     SI, 8               ;Past last mask?
        JNE     BLOOP               ;No, continue?
        RET                         ;Yes, return.
;
MASKS   DB      1,2,4,8,10H,20H,40H,80H
BCNT1S  ENDP
CNTSEG  ENDS
        END     MAIN
```

Each subroutine in Table 18–17 is preceded by a PROC pseudo-operation to inform the assembler whether the subroutine will be called by a NEAR or FAR CALL. Since WCNT1S is declared by PROC FAR, the assembler uses the FAR format for the CALL WCNT1S instruction in MAIN and for the RET instruction in WCNT1S. The FAR declaration and format are appropriate because MAIN and WCNT1S are in different segments. On the other hand, WCNT1S and BCNT1S are in the same segment, and so BCNT1S may be declared by PROC NEAR. In this case, the assembler uses the NEAR format for the CALL BCNT1S instruction in WCNT1S and for the RET instruction in BCNT1S. When NEAR CALL and RET instructions are executed, CS is neither saved on the stack nor restored, because the subroutine is in the same segment as its caller.

Subroutine BCNT1S checks the bits of AL using indexed addressing to compare AL against each element of a table of eight 1-bit masks. The subroutine could also be recoded to use register indirect addressing instead of indexed, as shown below:

```
        MOV     CX,0                ;Initialize '1' count.
        MOV     SI, OFFSET MASKS    ;Address of first mask in table.
BLOOP:  TEST    AL, [SI]            ;Test a bit of AL.
        JZ      BNEXT               ;Skip if bit is zero.
        INC     CX                  ;Update count if bit set.
BNEXT:  INC     SI                  ;Point to next mask.
        CMP     SI, OFFSET MASKS+8  ;Past last mask?
        JNE     BLOOP               ;No, continue?
        RET                         ;Yes, return.
```

Although the change appears to be straightforward, it contains a subtle bug. Register indirect addressing with SI normally uses DS as the default segment register. However, in the above code, SI contains an offset in the *code* segment, and so segment register CS should be used. The assembler is not smart enough to figure out what segment the programmer expects SI to be pointing into at run time, and therefore it generates a TEST instruction that uses the default segment register DS. To access the desired segment, we must recode the instruction as follows:

```
BLOOP:   TEST    AL, CS:[SI]        ;Test a bit of AL.
```

The "CS:" text tells the assembler to generate a segment override prefix so that segment register CS is used instead of the default DS. So why didn't we have to use a prefix in the original code? In the original statement

```
BLOOP:   TEST    AL, MASKS[SI]      ;Test a bit of AL.
```

the base address MASKS is explicitly mentioned. In this case, the assembler can determine that segment name of MASKS is CNTSEG. Since DS has been ASSUMEd to contain MAIND, address MASKS is not accessible through the default segment register DS. However, CS has been ASSUMEd to contain CNTSEG, and therefore MASKS should be accessible using the CS segment override prefix. The assembler automatically generates the override prefix for the TEST instruction. This example shows why ASSUME statements are needed—they help the assembler make "intelligent" decisions.

Table 18–18 presents another example of indexed addressing in the 80x86, a program that finds prime numbers. Like the 68000 version in Table 7–5, the 80x86 program declares an array of bytes with each component corresponding to a number between 2 and 1000. By marking off multiples of known primes, it eliminates nonprimes until only primes remain.

The FNDPRMS subroutine has its own private code and data segments, PRIMSEG and ARRAYSG. Therefore, it must be called by a FAR CALL, and it must start by initializing DS to point to the private data segment. As a service to its caller, FNDPRM saves and restores the caller's DS using the stack. The caller's CS is saved and restored by the subroutine CALL and RET, of course.

A parameter-passing convention that puts parameters and local variables on a stack was described in Section 9.3.6. An 80x86 subroutine that uses this convention is shown in Table 18–19, and the stack format during the subroutine's execution is shown in Figure 18–9. Much of this code could be rewritten to be more efficient, for example, by using the 80x86 DIV instruction instead of a loop. However, the existing code better illustrates calling conventions and 80x86 instructions.

Note the use of the special WORD PTR and BYTE PTR operators in four of the instructions in the DIVIDE subroutine. This operator is needed to determine the size of the operand—the assembler has no other way of determining whether the programmer intends the pointers to reference words or bytes.

SHORT   In the JMP instruction just before label DIVVY:, the special operator SHORT informs the assembler that the label CLNSTK is within 128 bytes of the JMP instruction. Since CLNSTK is a forward reference, the assembler has no other way of learning its distance during pass 1 of the assembly. The SHORT operator forces

TABLE 18–18 An 80x86 subroutine to find primes using an array and indexed addressing.

```
;                              PROCEDURE FindPrimes;
NPRIME  EQU     1000;          CONST nPrime = 1000;
PLIMIT  EQU     32;              pLimit = 32;
;
ARRAYSG SEGMENT
PRIME   DB      NPRIME-1 DUP (?);VAR prime:ARRAY [2..nPrime] OF boolean;
ARRAYSG ENDS                        {register} SI, DI : integer;
;
PRIMSEG SEGMENT
FNDPRM  PROC    FAR;            BEGIN
        PUSH    DS;             {Save caller's data segment register.}
        MOV     AX,ARRAYSG;     {Initialize data segment register.}
        MOV     DS,AX;
        MOV     DI,2;           FOR DI := 2 TO nPrime DO
SETEM:  MOV     PRIME-2[DI],1;  {Set the entire array true.}
        INC     DI;                prime[DI] := true;
        CMP     DI,NPRIME;
        JLE     SETEM;
        MOV     SI,2;           SI := 2; {First known prime.}
;                               REPEAT {Check integers 2 to pLimit.}
MARKEM: CMP     PRIME-2[SI],0;  IF prime[SI] THEN
        JEQ     NOTPRM;             BEGIN
        MOV     DI,SI;              DI := 2 * SI;
        ADD     DI,SI;              REPEAT {Mark multiples of SI.}
CLRLUP: MOV     PRIME-2[DI],0;         prime[DI] := false;
        ADD     DI,SI;                DI := DI + SI;
        CMP     DI,NPRIME;         UNTIL DI > nPrime;
        JLE     CLRLUP;           END;
NOTPRM: INC     SI;               SI := SI + 1;
        CMP     SI,PLIMIT;      UNTIL SI > pLimit;
        JLE     MARKEM;
        CALL    WRMSG1;         write('Primes between 2 and ');
        MOV     SI,NPRIME;      SI := nPrime;
        CALL    PRINTSI;        writeln(SI); {Print the value in SI.}
        MOV     SI,2;           FOR SI := 2 TO nPrime DO
PRTLUP: CMP     PRIME-2[SI],0;  {Print all the primes.}
        JZ      NEXTP;             IF prime[SI] THEN
        CALL    PRINTSI;             writeln(SI);
NEXTP:  INC     SI;
        CMP     SI,NPRIME;
        JLE     PRTLUP;
        PUSH    DS;             {All done, restore caller's data segment
        RET;                         register and return.}
FNDPRM  ENDP;                   END;
PRIMSEG ENDS;
```

the assembler to generate the short, 8-bit-offset form of the JMP instruction, instead of the 16-bit-offset form that the assembler would have to assume is needed otherwise.

Table 18–20 shows a main program that calls DIVIDE. The parameter-

TABLE 18–19   An 80x86 unsigned division subroutine that passes parameters on a stack.

```
DIVSEG    SEGMENT
          ASSUME CS:DIVSEG
;         The statements below define positions of parameters and local
;         variables in the stack relative to the frame pointer (BP).
CNT       EQU     -1                      ;Loop counter.
OLDBP     EQU     0                       ;Old value of frame pointer.
RETADR    EQU     2                       ;Return address.
DVSR      EQU     6                       ;1-word divisor (input).
HIDVND    EQU     8                       ;High-order word of dividend (input).
LODVND    EQU     10                      ;Low-order word of dividend (input).
REM       EQU     12                      ;1-word remainder (output).
QUOT      EQU     14                      ;1-word quotient (output).
STATUS    EQU     16                      ;0 ==> OK, <>0 ==> overflow (output).
;
DIVIDE    PROC    FAR                     ;Unsigned division subroutine.
          PUSH    BP                      ;Push old frame pointer onto stack.
          MOV     BP, SP                  ;Copy SP into BP for new frame pointer.
          SUB     SP, 1                   ;Allocate local variable space.
          MOV     BYTE PTR [BP].CNT, 16   ;Initialize loop count.
          MOV     WORD PTR [BP].STATUS, 0 ;Initial status OK.
          MOV     AX, [BP].HIDVND         ;Put high DVND in a register.
          CMP     AX, [BP].DVSR           ;Will quotient fit in one word?
          JB      DIVVY                   ;Branch if it will.
          INC     BYTE PTR [BP].STATUS    ;Else report overflow.
          JMP     SHORT CLNSTK
DIVVY:    MOV     BX, [BP].LODVND         ;Put low DVND in a register.
DIVLUP:   SAL     BX, 1                   ;Left shift dividend with LSB := 0.
          RCL     AX, 1                   ;A carry here from MSB means
          JC      QUOT1                   ;  high DVND definitely > DVSR.
          CMP     AX, [BP].DVSR           ;Compare high DVND with DVSR.
          JB      QUOTOK                  ;Quotient bit = 0 if lower.
QUOT1:    INC     BX                      ;Else set quotient bit to 1.
          SUB     AX, [BP].DVSR           ;And update high DVND.
QUOTOK:   DEC     BYTE PTR [BP].CNT       ;Decrement iteration count.
          JG      DIVLUP                  ;Continue until done.
          MOV     [BP].REM, AX            ;Store remainder.
          MOV     [BP].QUOT, BX           ;Store quotient.
CLNSTK:   MOV     SP, BP                  ;Remove local variables.
          POP     BP                      ;Restore old frame pointer.
          RET     6                       ;Discard input parameters and return.
DIVIDE    ENDP
DIVSEG    ENDS
```

passing mechanism used in this program is similar to that of the 68000 DIVIDEL program shown in Section 9.3.6, and the stack has the same states as those shown in Figure 9–5, except that for the 80x86 the stack cells are bytes instead of words.

Table 18–21 is a set of queue manipulation subroutines for the 80x86. Like

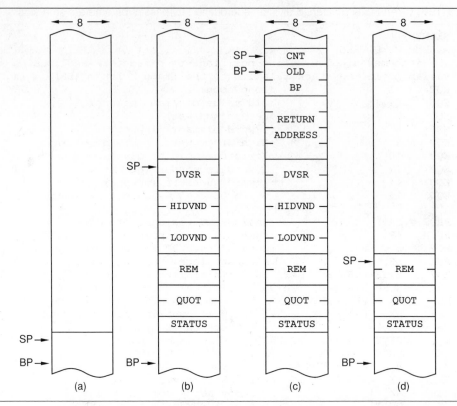

FIGURE 18–9 Stack contents for DIVIDE subroutine: (a) at initialization; (b) just before calling DIVIDE; (c) after the first three instructions; (d) just after returning from DIVIDE.

the 68000 version in Table 9–20 on page 338, this code is self-documenting. However, the fine points of segment utilization need some explanation.

The offsets that define the queue descriptor table (QHEAD, QTAIL, etc.) have type NUMBER and so the assembler does not associate them with a segment. Instructions like MOV SI, [BX].QHEAD use the default segment register DS, and so the queue descriptor table is accessed in whatever segment DS happens to be pointing to. Therefore, the queue-subroutine calling conventions insist that DS contain the segment base address for the queue descriptor table.

Now suppose that we wanted to redefine the queue subroutines so that ES instead of DS contains the segment base address for the queue descriptor table. We could rewrite the "typical calling sequence" as follows:

```
MOV     AX, SEG Q1DT       ;Set up ES with segment #
MOV     ES, AX             ;  of queue descriptor table.
MOV     BX, OFFSET Q1DT    ;Set up BX with offset.
CALL    QINIT              ;Initialize descriptor table.
```

However, in the queue subroutines, the assembler has no way of knowing that ES

TABLE 18–20   An 80x86 program that calls stack-oriented DIVIDE.

```
MAINDAT SEGMENT
P        DW      ?                      ;Storage for P, Q, PDIVQ, PMODQ
Q        DW      ?                      ;   (all 1-word variables).
PDIVQ    DW      ?
PMODQ    DW      ?
MAINDAT ENDS

STACK    SEGMENT                        ;Stack segment for this program
         DW      32 DUP (?)             ;32 words should be plenty.
STKE     EQU     THIS WORD              ;Value of SP when stack is empty.
STACK    ENDS

MAINSEG SEGMENT
         ASSUME CS:MAINSEG, DS:MAINDAT, SS:STACK
                                        ;Compute PDIVQ := P DIV Q; PMODQ := P MOD Q;
                                        ;   where all are 1-word variables in memory.
DIVPQ:   MOV     AX, STACK              ;Initialize SS for stack segment.
         MOV     SS, AX
         MOV     SP, OFFSET STKE        ;Initialize stack pointer.
         MOV     AX, MAINDAT            ;Initialize DS for main data segment.
         MOV     DS, AX
         SUB     SP, 5                  ;Reserve space for output parameters.
         PUSH    P                      ;Push low-order dividend.
         MOV     AX, 0                  ;Push high-order dividend = 0.
         PUSH    AX                     ;(No push immediate instruction.)
         PUSH    Q                      ;Push divisor.
         CALL    DIVIDE                 ;Do the division.
         POP     PMODQ                  ;Pop remainder and store.
         POP     PDIVQ                  ;Pop quotient and store.
         POP     AL                     ;Get status.
         CMP     AL, 0                  ;Test it.
         JNE     DIVOVF                 ;Branch on overflow.
         ...                            ;(rest of program)
MAINSEG ENDS
```

holds the segment base address unless we use explicit segment override prefixes. Thus, we must recode QINIT as follows:

```
QINIT    PROC    FAR
         MOV     AX, ES:[BX].QSTRT      ;Put buffer starting address
         MOV     ES:[BX].QHEAD, AX      ;   into QHEAD and QTAIL.
         MOV     ES:[BX].QTAIL, AX
         RET                            ;Done, return.
QINIT    ENDP
```

Another note on coding is also in order. At the end of QDEQ, ZF must be cleared. Since the 80x86 does not have a single instruction to set or clear ZF, we push the current value of FLAGS when ZF is known to be 0, and pop this desired value later. Without this trick, it would have taken several more instructions to explicitly clear ZF without affecting other registers (see Exercise 18.3).

TABLE 18–21   Queue manipulation subroutines for the 80x86.

```
;
; QUEUE MODULE
;
; This module contains three subroutines for manipulating queues
; of 16-bit words. A queue is defined by a queue descriptor table
; and a block of storage, as shown below.
;
;                                                 QUEUE STORAGE BLOCK
;         --------------------                    --------------------
; QDTBL |    QHEAD (word)     |    -------->|       (word)       |
;       |--------------------|      |      |--------------------|
;       |    QTAIL (word)     |      |      |                    |
;       |--------------------|      |      |                    |
;       |    QSTRT (word)     |----          |    o   o   o   o    |
;       |--------------------|             |--------------------|
;       |    QEND  (word)     |----------->|       (word)       |
;         --------------------              --------------------
;
;
QHEAD    EQU    0                    ;Define offsets in descriptor table.
QTAIL    EQU    2
QSTRT    EQU    4
QEND     EQU    6
;
; In this table, the last two words are constants, initialized at
; load time, that give the starting and ending addresses of the block
; of storage (buffer) reserved for the queue itself.  The first and
; second words are reserved to store the queue head and tail (absolute
; memory addresses), and are manipulated by the subroutines.  The
; queue descriptor table and the queue storage block must be in the
; same segment.
;
; If a program defines several queues, it allocates a separate queue
; descriptor table and storage block for each one.  Different queues
; may be in different segments. The statements below define a 100-word
; queue Q1 and a 5-word queue Q2:
;
;Q1BLK    DW     100 DUP (?)         ;Storage block for Q1.
;Q1END    EQU    (THIS WORD)-2       ;Last word in Q1 storage block.
;Q1DT     DW     ?, ?, OFFSET Q1BLK, OFFSET Q1END   ;Q1 descriptor table.
;
;Q2BLK    DW     5 DUP (?)           ;Storage block for Q2.
;Q2END    EQU    (THIS WORD)-2       ;Last word in Q2 storage block.
;Q2DT     DW     ?, ?, OFFSET Q2BLK, OFFSET Q2END   ;Q2 descriptor table.
;
; Subroutines are provided to initialize a queue (QINIT), enqueue
; a word (QENQ), and dequeue a word (QDEQ).  On entry, each
; subroutine assumes that DS contains the segment base address
; for the queue's segment, and BX contains the segment offset for
; for the descriptor table of the queue.
;
```

TABLE 18–21   (continued)

```
QCODE     SEGMENT
          ASSUME CS:QCODE
;
; SUBROUTINE QINIT -- Initialize a queue to be empty.
;
; INPUTS
;    QDTBL -- The address of the queue descriptor table for the
;             queue to be initialized, passed in registers DS:BX.
; OUTPUTS, GLOBAL DATA, LOCAL DATA -- None
; FUNCTIONS
;    (1) Initialize the queue to empty by setting QHEAD and QTAIL
;        in QDTBL equal to the first address in the queue buffer.
; REGISTERS AFFECTED -- AX
;
; TYPICAL CALLING SEQUENCE
;        MOV     AX, SEG Q1DT      ;Set up DS with segment #
;        MOV     DS, AX            ;  of queue descriptor table.
;        MOV     BX, OFFSET Q1DT   ;Set up BX with offset.
;        CALL    QINIT             ;Initialize descriptor table.
;
QINIT     PROC    FAR
          MOV     AX,[BX].QSTRT     ;Put buffer starting address
          MOV     [BX].QHEAD,AX     ;  into QHEAD and QTAIL.
          MOV     [BX].QTAIL,AX
          RET                       ;Done, return.
QINIT     ENDP
;
; SUBROUTINE QENQ -- Enqueue one word into a queue.
;
; INPUTS
;    QDTBL -- The address of the queue descriptor table for the
;             queue to be manipulated, passed in registers DS:BX.
;    QDATA -- The word to be enqueued, passed in register AX.
; OUTPUTS
;    QFULL -- 1 if the queue is already full, else 0;
;             passed in condition flag ZF.
; GLOBAL DATA, LOCAL DATA -- None.
; FUNCTIONS
;    (1) If the queue described by QDTBL is full, set QFULL to 1.
;    (2) If the queue is not full, enqueue QDATA and set QFULL to 0.
; REGISTERS AFFECTED -- SI, FLAGS
;
; TYPICAL CALLING SEQUENCE
;        MOV     AX, SEG Q1DT      ;Set up DS with segment #
;        MOV     DS, AX            ;  of queue descriptor table.
;        MOV     BX, OFFSET Q1DT   ;Set up BX with offset.
;        MOV     AX, AWORD         ;Enqueue AWORD.
;        CALL    QENQ
;        JZ      OVFL              ;Branch if queue is full.
;
; {Body of QENQ appears on next page}
```

TABLE 18–21   (continued)

```
QENQ      PROC    FAR
          MOV     SI,[BX].QTAIL       ;Get queue tail.
          MOV     [SI],AX             ;Store QDATA at tail (no harm if full).
          ADD     SI,2                ;Bump to next free location.
          CMP     SI,[BX].QEND        ;Wraparound?
          JBE     QENQ1
          MOV     SI,[BX].QSTRT       ;Reinitialize on wraparound.
QENQ1:    CMP     SI,[BX].QHEAD       ;Queue already full?
          JEQ     QENQ2               ;Return with ZF=1 if full.
          MOV     [BX].QTAIL,SI       ;Update tail, ZF=0 still.
QENQ2:    RET                         ;Return.
QENQ      ENDP
;
; SUBROUTINE QDEQ -- Dequeue one word from a queue.
;
; INPUTS
;    QDTBL -- The address of the queue descriptor table for the
;             queue to be manipulated, passed in registers DS:BX.
; OUTPUTS
;    QEMPTY-- 1 if the queue is empty, else 0; passed in
;             condition flag ZF.
;    QDATA -- The word dequeued, passed in register AX.
; GLOBAL DATA, LOCAL DATA -- None.
; FUNCTIONS
;    (1) If the queue described by QDTBL is empty, set QEMPTY to 1.
;    (2) If the queue isn't empty, dequeue QDATA and set QEMPTY to 0.
; REGISTERS AFFECTED -- AX, SI, FLAGS
;
; TYPICAL CALLING SEQUENCE
;         MOV     AX, SEG Q1DT        ;Set up DS with segment #
;         MOV     DS, AX              ;  of queue descriptor table.
;         MOV     BX, OFFSET Q1DT     ;Set up BX with offset.
;         CALL    QDEQ                ;Dequeue a word into AWORD.
;         JZ      UNDFL               ;Branch if queue was empty.
;         MOV     AWORD,AX
;
QDEQ      PROC    FAR
          MOV     SI,[BX].QHEAD       ;Get copy of head.
          CMP     SI,[BX].QTAIL       ;Queue empty?
          JEQ     QDEQ2               ;Return with ZF=1 if empty.
          PUSHF                       ;Else save ZF=0 on stack.
          MOV     AX,[SI]             ;Read QDATA word from queue.
          ADD     SI,2                ;Bump copy head to next item in queue.
          CMP     SI,[BX].QEND        ;Wraparound?
          JBE     QDEQ1
          MOV     SI,[BX].QSTRT       ;Reinitialize copy head on wraparound.
QDEQ1:    MOV     [BX].QHEAD,SI       ;Update real head in memory.
          POPF                        ;Restore ZF=0 from stack since not empty.
QDEQ2:    RET                         ;Return.
QDEQ      ENDP
QCODE     ENDS
```

To illustrate the 80x86's block- and string-manipulation instructions, we reconsider the prime-number program in Table 18–18. The first five executable instructions of the program initialize an array of memory bytes. These instructions could be replaced with a repeated STOS instruction as follows:

```
FNDPRM  PROC   NEAR
        MOV    AX, SEG PRIME      ;Point ES:DI to start of buffer.
        MOV    ES, AX
        MOV    DI, OFFSET PRIME
        MOV    CX, LENGTH PRIME   ;Set up number of array bytes.
        MOV    AL, 1              ;Set up initialization value.
        CLD                       ;Set up DF for auto-increment.
REP     STOS   ES:PRIME           ;Initialize the entire array.
```

Although some overhead is required to set up the registers, the hardware-repeated STOS instruction is much faster than the original software loop. Note that the operand of STOS merely serves to inform the assembler of the element size and segment of the destination string.

Next, in Table 18–22, we consider a subroutine to search for the first occurrence of a character variable in a fixed buffer, coded without the string-

TABLE 18–22   Character search subroutine for the 80x86.

```
;       Find the first occurrence in BUFFER of a character.
;       Enter with:  AL = the character to be found
;       Return with: If character not found: ZF = 0, and ES:DI points just
;                              past the end of BUFFER.
;                    If character found: ZF = 1, and ES:DI points to the
;                              first occurrence of the character in BUFFER
;
ZCODE   SEGMENT
        ASSUME CS:ZCODE, ES:ZDATA
SEARCH  PROC   FAR
        MOV    BX, SEG BUFFER      ;Point ES:DI to start of buffer.
        MOV    ES, BX
        MOV    DI, OFFSET BUFFER
SLOOP:  CMP    AL, ES:[DI]         ;Match?
        JEQ    OUT                 ;Exit with ZF = 1 if match found.
        INC    DI                  ;Bump to next character.
        CMP    DI, OFFSET BUFEND   ;At end?
        JNE    SLOOP               ;No, look some more.
        MOV    AH, 0               ;Not found, set ZF to 0.
        SAHF
OUT:    RET                        ;Return.
SEARCH  ENDP
ZCODE   ENDS
;
ZDATA   SEGMENT
BUFFER  DB     1000 DUP (?)        ;Reserve 1000-byte buffer.
BUFEND  EQU    THIS BYTE           ;Address just past end of buffer.
ZDATA   ENDS
```

manipulation instructions. The subroutine may be optimized by replacing the code beginning at SLOOP with the following:

```
SLOOP:  CLD                         ;Clear DF for auto-increment.
        MOV     CX,LENGTH BUFFER    ;Set up length of BUFFER.
  REPNE SCAS    BUFFER              ;Search for match.
;               If found, DI now points just past matched char, ZF = 1.
        RET                         ;Return.
```

TABLE 18–23   String search subroutine for the 80x86.

```
;       Find the first occurrence in buffer of a specified string.
;       Enter with:  DS:SI = base address of string
;                    DX = length of string
;                    ES:DI = base address of buffer
;                    AX = length of buffer
;       Return with: If string not found: ZF = 0
;                    If string found: ZF = 1, and ES:DI points to the
;                                     first character of the string in buffer
;
ZCODE   SEGMENT
        ASSUME CS:ZCODE, ES:ZDST, DS:ZSRC
STSRCH  PROC    FAR
        MOV     BX, SI              ;Save starting address of string.
        ADD     AX, DI              ;Compute last possible starting
        SUB     AX, DX              ;   address in BUFFER for a match.
        CLD                         ;Clear DF for auto-increment.
        JMP     SHORT CHKLST        ;Make sure string not too long.
CHKSTR: MOV     SI, BX              ;Get starting address of string.
        MOV     CX, DX              ;Get length of string.
        PUSH    DI                  ;Save current starting point in BUFFER.
  REPE  CMPS    BUFF, STRING        ;Check for a match.
        POP     DI                  ;Restore starting point (ZF unaffected).
        JEQ     FNDIT               ;Got a match, return with ZF = 1.
        INC     DI                  ;Try starting with next byte in BUFFER.
CHKLST: CMP     DI, AX              ;Still possible to get a match?
        JBE     CHKSTR              ;Yes, try some more.
NOTFND:                             ;No, return with ZF = 0 (from JBE).
FNDIT:  RET
STSRCH  ENDP
ZCODE   ENDS
;
ZSRC    SEGMENT                     ;Dummy segment for source string.
STRING  DB      ?
ZSRC    ENDS
;
ZDST    SEGMENT                     ;Dummy segment for destination string.
BUFF    DB      ?
ZDST    ENDS
```

TABLE 18–24   A program fragment that eliminates MONEY.

```
ZCALLER SEGMENT
        ASSUME CS:ZCALLER
WANTED  DB      'MONEY'                  ;Desired string.
        ...
START:  MOV     AX, SEG WANTED           ;Set up logical address of
        MOV     DS, AX                   ;  WANTED string in DS:BX.
        MOV     SI, OFFSET WANTED
        MOV     DX, LENGTH WANTED        ;Load DX with length (5).
        MOV     AX, SEG BUFFER           ;Point ES:DI to start of buffer.
        MOV     ES, AX
        MOV     DI, OFFSET BUFFER
        MOV     AX, LENGTH BUFFER        ;Load AX with length (1000).
        CALL    STSRCH                   ;Look for string.
        JNE     TOOBAD                   ;Jump if not found.
FOUND:                                   ;ES:DI points to 'MONEY' in BUFFER.
        MOV     CX, LENGTH WANTED        ;Length of 'MONEY'.
        MOV     AL, ' '                  ;Load AL with ASCII space.
  REP   STOS    ES:BUFFER                ;Replace 'MONEY' with spaces.
TOOBAD: ...
;
ZCALLER ENDS
;
ZDATA   SEGMENT
BUFFER  DB      1000 DUP (?)             ;Reserve 1000-byte buffer.
ZDATA   ENDS
```

The optimized code is obviously shorter, and it is much faster, too. As in the previous example, the operand of SCAS serves merely to inform the assembler of the element size and segment of the destination string.

A subroutine that uses the CMPS instruction is shown in Table 18–23. The STSRCH subroutine finds the first occurrence of a desired string in a buffer. Unlike the previous example, which used a fixed buffer, this subroutine accepts a variable buffer address and size as well as a variable search string. Beginning with the first byte in the buffer, the STSRCH subroutine checks each possible starting address in the buffer to determine whether a copy of the desired string begins there. A method for speeding up the STSRCH subroutine using a combination of SCAS and CMPS instructions is suggested in Exercise 18.10.

A main program that calls the STSRCH subroutine is shown in Table 18–24. The "ES:" prefix on the operand of STOS is redundant since STOS always uses ES for its destination operand. However, "ES:" has another function besides generating a segment override prefix if one is required. It tells ASM-86 to omit its usual comparison of the operand's segment number with the value currently ASSUMEd to be in ES, if any. In this case, the programmer guarantees that ES contains the proper segment number, regardless of what the assembler may think.

18.6 INPUT/OUTPUT, INTERRUPTS, AND TRAPS

18.6.1 Input/Output

The 80x86 uses isolated I/O; it can access 2^{16} bytes of input ports and output ports in an address space separate from the memory address space. Like memory, I/O ports may be accessed one or two bytes at a time. Instructions that access the I/O ports are listed in the first part of Table 18–25.

Unlike most other aspects of the 80x86, the I/O organization and I/O instructions are exceedingly simple. All I/O transfers in the 80x86 use the accumulator AX (word I/O) or its low-order byte AL (byte I/O). The assembler determines the size of the operation according to whether the programmer has written AX or AL in the assembly language instruction.

IN
OUT

The IN instruction moves a byte or word from a specified port to the accumulator; OUT moves from accumulator to port. Ports with small addresses may be accessed more efficiently than other ports, since a port address between 0 and 255 may be specified as an 8-bit immediate value in an I/O instruction. Any port address, between 0 and 65535, may be specified using register indirect addressing with DX. Besides allowing larger port addresses, this mode is useful in shared I/O drivers where the port number must be computed at run time.

Noninterrupt I/O programming practices for the 80x86 faithfully follow the general principles that we presented in Chapter 10.

18.6.2 Interrupts

nonmaskable interrupt (NMI)
vectored interrupt (INTR)

The 80x86 CPU contains a two-level, vectored priority interrupt system with two interrupt request lines, one for each level. The higher priority input is called *nonmaskable interrupt (NMI)* and the lower is called *vectored interrupt (INTR)*. Within each level, a system hardware designer may provide additional interrupt lines and priority by means of external hardware.

TABLE 18–25   I/O, interrupt, and trap instructions in the 80x86.

Mnemonic	Operands	Size	Description
IN	accum,port	B,W	Load accum from input port
IN	accum,DX	B,W	Load accum from input port specified by DX
OUT	port,accum	B,W	Load output port from accum
OUT	DX,accum	B,W	Load output port specified by DX from accum
IRET			Return from interrupt
LOCK			Bus lock prefix
INT	3		Trap using vector 3 (breakpoint trap)
INTO			Trap using vector 4 (overflow trap)
INT	vec		Trap using vector vec

Notes: accum is AL or AX according to the size of the operation, byte or word.
port denotes an 8-bit port number, between 0 and 255.
vec denotes an 8-bit interrupt vector number, between 0 and 255.

TABLE 18–26   Interrupt and trap vectors in the 80x86.

Vector Number	Physical Address (hex)	Interrupt or Trap
0	00000	Divide error trap
1	00004	Single-step (trace) trap
2	00008	NMI interrupt
3	0000C	Breakpoint trap (INT 3 instruction)
4	00010	Overflow trap (INTO instruction)
5–31	00014–0007C	Reserved for Intel products
32–255	00080–003FC	User vectored interrupts

Interrupts in the 80x86 are usually accepted between the executions of individual instructions. An NMI request is generally accepted immediately after the current instruction is executed. An INTR request is accepted only if the IF (interrupt flag) bit in FLAGS is 1. Of course, for any interrupt to be accepted, a device must first generate an interrupt request on the NMI or INTR input line. The conditions for generating an interrupt request are device dependent, but typically the interrupt enable bit in the device interface must be "on" and an I/O event must have occurred at the device. Thus, three conditions are needed for the 80x86 to accept an interrupt:

(1) For INTR, the IF bit in FLAGS must be equal to 1.

(2) The interrupt enable bit in the device interface must be "on."

(3) The interface must have experienced an interrupt-generating event (e.g., character received from keyboard, ready to send character to screen, disk block transfer complete, etc.).

When an interrupt is accepted, the CPU automatically pushes the current values of FLAGS, CS, and IP onto the stack, in the order just given. Then it clears the IF and TF bits in FLAGS to prevent any more vectored interrupts or trace traps from occurring. Finally it loads CS and IP with new values from an *interrupt vector* found in memory, thereby transferring control to an interrupt service routine. The interrupt service routine eventually returns control to the interrupted program by executing an IRET instruction, which restores the old IP, CS, and FLAGS from the stack.

interrupt vector

IRET

The 80x86 allocates the first 1024 bytes of physical memory for a table of interrupt vectors, as shown in Table 18–26. Each vector is four bytes long, containing new values for IP and CS in the format of Figure 18–7(d).

For NMI interrupts and for traps, the CPU fetches the corresponding IP and CS from the vector table and executes the interrupt service routine at the address indicated by the new CS and IP. If the system has multiple devices connected to the NMI request line, then it is up to the service routine to determine which device has interrupted on each occasion.

For INTR interrupts, the CPU allows the interrupting device to place an 8-bit number on the data bus to identify itself. If two or more devices can make a request on INTR simultaneously, external hardware must determine priority, that is, determine which device may place its identifier on the data bus. Then the CPU uses the 8-bit identifier supplied by the device as an index into the vector table. The identifier, which should be between 32 and 255, is multiplied by 4 to obtain the address of the interrupt vector. Thus, each device connected to INTR may have a different interrupt service routine that is automatically selected by the hardware.

The 80x86's INTR input is level sensitive, so that the CPU will accept an interrupt whenever an INTR interrupt request signal is present and the IF bit in FLAGS is 1. The CPU automatically clears IF upon accepting an INTR request to prevent the interrupt service routine from being continuously reinterrupted by the same condition. Once the service routine has removed the condition that caused the interrupt, it may set IF to 1 to allow INTR interrupts from other devices. Alternatively, it may leave IF at 0, so that no further INTR interrupts will be accepted until the service routine exits and restores FLAGS using the IRET instruction.

Since an NMI request cannot be disabled, a different scheme must be used to keep the NMI service routine from being continuously interrupted by the same condition. Therefore, the NMI input is edge sensitive. The 80x86 CPU accepts an NMI request only when it detects an inactive-to-active transition on the NMI input line. Thus, the CPU can accept a second NMI request only after the condition causing the first NMI request has been removed and a second inactive-to-active transition has occurred on the NMI input.

A set of subroutines for displaying strings of characters using interrupt I/O is shown in Table 18–27. The subroutines assume that a Motorola 6850 ACIA is attached to the 80x86 as I/O ports 40H and 42H. They further assume that a string is a sequence of ASCII characters stored one per byte and terminated by a zero byte.

A main program that calls the display subroutines is shown in Table 18–28. The main program sets up the stack pointer and segment registers and then calls INITCRT to reset the ACIA hardware and initialize the ACIA interrupt vector and software busy-flag (CRTBSY). In its main processing loop, the main program passes a pointer to the CRT output routine CRTOUT each time it wants to display a string. CRTBSY is 1 when a previous string is still being displayed, so that a new operation is not started until the previous one is completed. CRTOUT prints the first character of a new string, enables the ACIA to interrupt after the character has been printed, and then returns to the main program.

Remaining characters are printed by the interrupt service routine CRTINT. Before entering CRTINT, the CPU pushes only FLAGS, CS, and IP onto the stack, so CRTINT must preserve any other registers that it uses. Thus AX, BX, DS, and ES are saved on the stack at the beginning of CRTINT and restored at the end.

Some of the code in this example shows the weaknesses of the 80x86 as compared with other advanced microprocessors such as the 68000. Since there

TABLE 18–27 Interrupt-driven CRT output subroutines for the 80x86.

```
;          Define addresses and bit patterns for CRT ACIA.
CRTCS    EQU    40H              ;ACIA control and status port.
CRTDATA  EQU    42H              ;ACIA XMT and RCV data ports.
CRTVECT  EQU    WORD PTR 34      ;ACIA interrupt vector number.
CRESET   EQU    03H              ;ACIA control pattern for reset.
CMODE    EQU    11H              ;Basic ACIA operating mode.
CINTON   EQU    20H              ;ACIA XMT interrupt enable bit.
CINTOFF  EQU    00H              ;ACIA XMT interrupts disabled.
;
IODATA   SEGMENT                 ;Local variables.
CRTBSY   DB     ?                ;Nonzero when string is being displayed.
BPNT     DD     ?                ;seg:offset for char being displayed.
IODATA   ENDS
;
IOCODE   SEGMENT
         ASSUME CS:IOCODE, DS: IODATA
INITCRT  PROC   FAR              ;Initialization procedure for CRT.
         PUSH   DS               ;Save caller's DS.
         PUSH   AX               ;Save caller's AX.
         MOV    AX,IODATA        ;Set up DS to access I/O data.
         MOV    DS,AX
         MOV    AL,CRESET        ;Reset CRT ACIA, no interrupts.
         OUT    CRTCS,AL
         MOV    CRTBSY,0         ;Mark CRT not busy.
         MOV    AX,0             ;Initialize DS to get at
         MOV    DS,AX            ; vector table in low memory.
         MOV    DS:CRTVECT,OFFSET CRTINT ;Initialize CRT
         MOV    DS:CRTVECT+2,SEG CRTINT  ; interrupt vector.
POPRET:  POP    AX               ;Restore caller's AX.
         POP    DS               ;Restore caller's DS.
         RET                     ;Done.
INITCRT  ENDP
;
;          CRT output routine, pointer to string passed in ES:BX.
CRTOUT   PROC   FAR
         PUSH   DS               ;Save caller's DS.
         PUSH   AX               ;Save caller's AX.
         MOV    AX,IODATA        ;Set up DS to access IODATA.
         MOV    DS,AX
WTOUT:   CMP    CRTBSY,1         ;Still busy with previous string?
         JEQ    WTOUT            ;Yes, wait for completion.
         MOV    CRTBSY,1         ;Mark CRT busy for new string.
         MOV    WORD PTR BPNT,BX ;Save pointer to new string.
         MOV    WORD PTR BPNT+2,ES
         MOV    AL,CMODE+CINTOFF ;Set ACIA operating mode,
         OUT    CRTCS,AL         ;  XMT interrupts off.
         MOV    AL,ES:[BX]       ;Get first character.
         OUT    CRTDATA,AL       ;Send it to ACIA.
         MOV    AL,CMODE+CINTON  ;Enable ACIA XMT interrupts.
         OUT    CRTCS,AL
         JMP    POPRET           ;Restore caller's AX and DS and return.
CRTOUT   ENDP
```

TABLE 18–27   (continued)

```
;         CRT output interrupt handler.
CRTINT: PUSH    AX                 ;Save some working registers.
        PUSH    BX
        PUSH    DS
        PUSH    ES
        MOV     AX,IODATA          ;Set up DS to access I/O data.
        MOV     DS,AX
        LES     BX,BPNT            ;ES:BX points to char just displayed.
        INC     BX                 ;Point to next character.
        MOV     WORD PTR BPNT,BX   ;Save updated pointer.
        MOV     AL,ES:[BX]         ;Fetch the character.
        CMP     AL,0               ;Is it NUL (0)?
        JEQ     CDONE              ;We're done if it is.
        OUT     CRTDATA,AL         ;Otherwise display the character,
CRTRET: POP     ES                 ;  restore registers,
        POP     DS
        POP     BX
        POP     AX
        IRET                       ;  and return.
;
CDONE:  MOV     AL,CMODE+CINTOFF   ;Disable ACIA interrupts.
        OUT     CRTCS,AL
        MOV     CRTBSY,0           ;Mark CRT no longer busy.
        JMP     CRTRET             ;Restore registers and return.
IOCODE  ENDS
```

are no "load multiple" and "store multiple" instructions, individual pushes and pops are needed for register saving and restoring.

Especially troublesome is the lack of an absolute addressing mode that allows the segment as well as the offset to be specified in the instruction. For example, in INITCRT we need to set CRTBSY to zero. It would be nice to have an instruction MOV DS:CRTBSY, 0 that contains a two-word logical address (IODATA:CRTBSY) and performs the desired operation in one step. Instead, we must load the segment number into a segment register and then use an instruction such as MOV DS:CRTBSY. If the contents of the registers are not to be disturbed, then the old value of DS must be saved and restored.

The problem above is exacerbated by the lack of immediate addressing with segment register MOVs, so that it takes two instructions to load DS in the first place. In addition, AX must be now saved and restored too. You might wonder, why not PUSH IODATA and then POP DS to avoid destroying AX? Sorry, immediate addressing is not allowed with PUSH either!

We should now say a few words about the interruptibility of 80x86 programs. Although interrupts normally occur between the execution of individual 80x86 instructions, they may also occur in the middle of a repeated string instruction. In this case, the address of the REP prefix of the string instruction is saved on the stack, so that the string instruction starts repeating itself again when

TABLE 18–28   Main program that uses interrupt output routines.

```
ZDATA    SEGMENT                      ;Messages printed by main program.
MSG1     DB      'Correct programs are difficult to write when...'
         DB      0DH,0AH,0            ;Carriage return, line feed, NUL.
MSG1PNT  DD      MSG1                 ;Stores seg:offset of MSG1.
;
MSG2     DB      '...simple operations require many instructions.'
         DB      0DH,0AH,0            ;Carriage return, line feed, NUL.
MSG2PNT  DD      MSG2                 ;Stores seg:offset of MSG2.
ZDATA    ENDS
;
ZSTACK   SEGMENT                      ;Define stack segment.
         DW      32
STACKE   EQU     OFFSET (THIS WORD)
ZSTACK   ENDS
;
ZMAIN    SEGMENT                      ;Main program
         ASSUME CS:ZMAIN, SS:ZSTACK, DS:ZDATA
MAIN:    MOV     AX,ZSTACK            ;Initialize stack pointer.
         MOV     SS,AX
         MOV     SP,STACKE
         MOV     AX,ZDATA             ;Initialize DS.
         MOV     DS,AX
         CALL    INITCRT              ;Initialize CRT software and hardware.
         STI                          ;Enable INTR interrupts.
LOOP:    ...                          ;Do some computation.
         LES     BX,MSG1PNT           ;Get pointer to first message
         CALL    CRTOUT               ; and print it.
         ...                          ;Do some more computation.
         LES     BX,MSG2PNT           ;Get pointer to second message
         CALL    CRTOUT               ; and print it.
         JMP     LOOP                 ;Do it all again.
ZMAIN    ENDS
         END     MAIN
```

the interrupt service routine returns control to it. The instruction resumes properly because its progress is reflected in SI, DI, CX, and FLAGS, which presumably are not altered by the interrupt service routine.

The 80x86 also has a DMA facility that allows other devices to access its memory between the individual bus cycles of an instruction, temporarily suspending the instruction in execution. As discussed in Section 11.5, DMA is used by some I/O devices to transfer blocks of data without processor intervention. DMA may also be used in multiprocessor systems to allow several CPUs to share the same memory.

LOCK   The LOCK prefix may be placed before any 80x86 instruction to forbid DMA access during the execution of that instruction. This allows the programmer to create an "atomic" instruction that executes with the guarantee that no other processor can read or write memory during its execution. LOCK

may be used to create a test-and-set primitive for the purposes discussed in
Section 12.3.4 as follows:

```
CHECK:  MOV    AL,0FFH      ;Get old value of SEMAPH
   LOCK XCHG   AL,SEMAPH    ; and set new value to FF.
        CMP    AL,0         ;Is resource available?
        JNE    CHECK        ;No, wait for SEMAPH to be cleared.
        ...                 ;Yes, use resource.
DONE:   MOV    SEMAPH,0     ;Release resource for others.
```

18.6.3 Traps

The 80x86 has four interrupt vectors for exceptional conditions and trap instructions:

- *Divide error.* A trap occurs if the quotient produced by a DIV or IDIV
  instruction is larger than the specified destination.

- *Trace trap.* A trap occurs after the execution of each instruction for which
  the TF bit was 1 at the beginning of the instruction.

INT 3
- *Breakpoint trap.* A trap occurs if the processor executes an INT 3 instruction.

INTO
- *Overflow trap.* A trap occurs if the processor executes an INTO instruction
  when the OF bit in FLAGS is 1.

A trap has the same effect as an interrupt: the CPU pushes the current FLAGS,
CS, and IP onto the stack, and a new CS and IP are loaded from the an interrupt
vector as specified in Table 18–26.

In on-line debuggers, the trace trap is used to single-step programs, and the
INT 3 instruction (one byte long) is used in the place of executable instructions
to create breakpoints. The divide error trap and the INTO instruction are used
to detect arithmetic errors. The 80x86 also has a general trap instruction, INT

INT vec
vec, which causes a trap using interrupt vector vec. The 8-bit value of vec is
contained in the second byte of the instruction.

18.7 80286 PROCESSOR ORGANIZATION

From a user's point of view, the 80286 processor has three major improvements
over an 8086:

- Faster execution speed is obtained because the 80286's clock runs faster
  and most instructions take fewer clock cycles to execute.

- The maximum size of physical memory is extended from 2^{20} to 2^{24} bytes
  (16 Mbytes).

- A memory management system that enforces access rights and levels of protection is included on-chip.

The 80286 includes the extended instructions of the 80186/88 and has its own extended instructions to support the new addressing and protection features. Its most ubiquitous application is as the main processor in the IBM PC-AT and some PS/2 computers amd compatibles.

18.7.1 Programming Model

reset
real address mode

After a hardware reset, the 80286 enters a so-called *real address mode* and behaves just like an 8086 processor. The same basic register set as the 8086's, shown in Figure 18–10(a), is available, as are all 8086 instructions and 80186 extended instructions. Memory accesses use 20-bit addresses generated by the standard shift-and-add scheme of the 8086. This mode is used by the IBM PC-AT to execute programs written for the original 8088-based IBM PC.

machine status
word (MSW)
protected-mode
enable (PE)
protected mode

An additional register, called the *machine status word (MSW)*, is provided in the 80286 as shown in Figure 18–10(b). Its low-order bit, called *protected-mode enable (PE)*, may be set to 1 to put the processor into a so-called *protected mode* of operation in which the 80286's extended memory mapping and protection

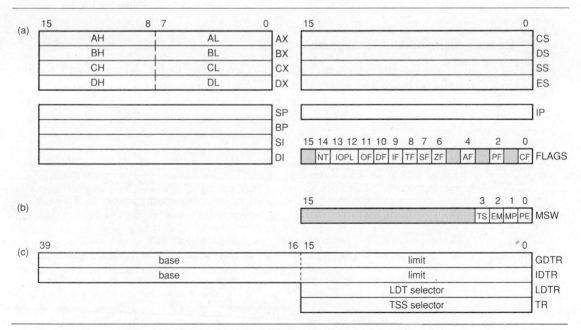

FIGURE 18–10   Programming model of the 80286: (a) basic register set; (b) machine status word; (c) memory mapping registers.

features are activated.[5] The remaining bits MSW bits are used with coprocessors such as the 80287 FPU.

Four more registers, shown in Figure 18–10(c), were added to the 80286 to support its extended memory mapping and protection features. Also, two fields were added to FLAGS. These registers and fields will be described shortly.

18.7.2   Privilege Levels and Protection

*privilege levels
(0–3)*
*current privilege
level (CPL)*
task

In protected mode, the 80286 provides a multilevel protection scheme similar to that of the MC68020 processor with the MC68851 PMMU. While the MC68020 and MC68851 may be programmed to provide supervisor mode plus 1, 2, 4, or 8 privilege levels in user mode, the 80286 scheme is fixed and provides exactly four privilege levels (0–3); level 0 is the most privileged and is equivalent to supervisor mode. A *current privilege level (CPL)*, stored in the low-order two bits of CS, is always associated with the current process (which Intel calls a *task*). A privilege level is also associated with each memory segment. The processor provides well-controlled mechanisms for changing CPL and for protecting more-privileged segments from access by processes with less-privileged CPLs.

*I/O privilege level
(IOPL)*

Certain 80286 extended instructions, including the ones that load MSW and the mapping registers [Figure 18–10(b,c)] can be executed only if CPL = 0. I/O instructions (IN, INS, OUT, OUTS, STI, CLI, LOCK) can be executed only if CPL is at least as privileged as the level given in the *I/O privilege level (IOPL)* field of FLAGS. Most privilege violations cause a trap using vector 13.

18.7.3   Memory Mapping and Management

When the 80286 is running in protected mode, logical addresses still have 32 bits, of which 16 bits are contained in a segment register CS–ES and 16 bits are an offset generated by a traditional addressing mode. Thus, just like a standard 8086 program, an 80286 program can access four 64-Kbyte segments whose

---

[5]The LMSW instruction is used to set PE to 1, but only a hardware reset can clear PE to 0. This is a major flaw in the 80286 architecture, since it makes it difficult to switch back and forth between real and protected modes. The architects probably thought, "Why would anyone ever want to give up our nice mapping and protection features to go back to the 8086's crummy mapping scheme?" However, they failed to anticipate the proliferation of application programs for the 8088-based IBM PC, most of which are incompatible with 80286 protected mode. As a result, to access extended memory on an 80286-based IBM PC-AT, a real-mode program must perform a ridiculous sequence of actions: (1) set up mapping tables to access protected memory as required; (2) enter protected mode by setting PE to 1; (3) perform a block move (MOVSW) between the low 1 Mbyte of memory and extended memory as required; (4) write a shutdown status code in nonvolatile RAM (part of the PC-AT's clock/calendar chip); (5) reset the processor by sending a special command to the keyboard controller chip, which has a spare output connected to the 80286 reset input; (6) after reset, examine the shutdown status code to determine the reason for reset; (7) finding a code of "block move shutdown," return to the user's program. This silly sequence has been observed to occur up to 1000 times per second in certain applications running on the PC-AT.

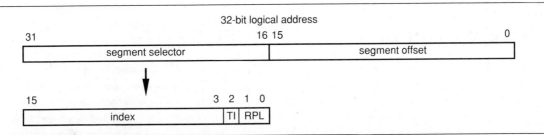

FIGURE 18–11 Format of an 80286 protected-mode logical address and segment selector.

physical base addresses are implied by the segment registers. However, the 80286 does not use the segment register value as a paragraph number.

Instead, as shown in Figure 18–11, an 80286 running in protected mode uses the segment-register part of a logical address as a *segment selector* that chooses a *segment descriptor* from one of two translation tables in main memory:

segment selector

segment descriptor

global descriptor table (GDT)

global descriptor table register (GDTR)

- The *global descriptor table (GDT)* contains descriptors for operating system resources (code, data, and other things) and for utility routines that are shared among user processes. The *global descriptor table register (GDTR)* in Figure 18–11(c) contains the base address in physical memory and the length of the GDT. The GDTR is generally loaded only once, at system initialization.

local descriptor table (LDT)

local descriptor table register (LDTR)

table indicator (TI)

index

- A *local descriptor table (LDT)* contains descriptors for the resources of a particular user process. Each process has its own LDT, as selected by the *local descriptor table register (LDTR)* in Figure 18–11(c). The LDTR is reloaded during context switches.

Within a segment selector, the *table indicator (TI)* bit indicates whether the descriptor is in the GDT (TI = 0) or the LDT (TI = 1). The location of the descriptor within the selected table is given by the *index* field; each table may have up to 2^{13} (8K) 8-byte descriptors. The formats and types of descriptors will be described shortly. Each segment selector has an associated *requested privilege level (RPL)*; a process cannot use a segment selector whose RPL is more privileged than CPL.

requested privilege level (RPL)

Figure 18–12 shows the descriptor format for a code or data segment. The

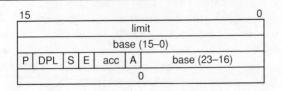

	P = present
	DPL = descriptor privilege level
	S = 1 = segment descriptor
	E = executable
	acc = segment access information
	A = accessed

FIGURE 18–12 Format of an 80286 code- or data-segment descriptor (S = 1).

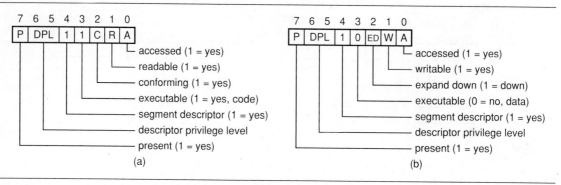

FIGURE 18–13 Format of the access-rights byte: (a) code segment; (b) data segment.

base
limit

base field contains the physical base address of the segment in memory, a 24-bit number. The *limit* field normally specifies the highest valid offset in the segment; for example, if limit = 9ABCH, then valid offsets are in the range 0000H–9ABCH.

access-rights byte

The remaining bits in the descriptor form the *access-rights byte*; they determine the type of the descriptor and the protection for the associated segment or other resource. The *segment (S)* bit is 1 for code and data segments. The *descriptor privilege level (DPL)* field indicates the minimum privilege level required for access to this segment. Both the CPL of the process and the RPL of a selector must be at least as privileged as DPL for access to be granted. Recall that the CPL of a process is contained in the two low-order bits of CS.

segment (S)
descriptor privilege level (DPL)

present (P)
accessed (A)

Virtual memory is supported by the *present (P)* and *accessed (A)* bits. If P indicates that segment is "not present," then an attempt to use the descriptor causes a trap. When a "present" segment descriptor is used, its A bit is set; a virtual-memory operating system uses this information to help decide which segments to swap out of physical memory. However, unlike the MC68881 PMMU, the 80286 does not provide a "modified" bit.

executable (E)
code segment
data segment
acc

The *executable (E)* bit is 1 for a *code segment* and 0 for a *data segment*. Code cannot be fetched from data segments, and nothing can be written in code segments. The format of the *acc* field depends on E.

As shown in Figure 18–13(a), shows the access-rights byte for a code segment. Information in a code segment, such as lookup tables, can be read only if *readable (R)* bit is 1. The *conforming (C)* bit specifies what happens to CPL during an *intersegment call*. Normally, a program can transfer control only to a code segment whose DPL equals CPL. Thus, subroutines in a *nonconforming code segment* (C = 0) can be called only by programs at the same privilege level. However, subroutines in a *conforming code segment* (C = 1) can be called from a less privileged level. The CPL is not changed during the call, so that the subroutine executes at the caller's less privileged level. Conforming code segments are provided for utility routines (e.g., sort) that may be used by different processes at different privilege levels, but that should never have more privilege than their current caller.

readable (R)
conforming (C)
intersegment call
nonconforming code segment
conforming code segment

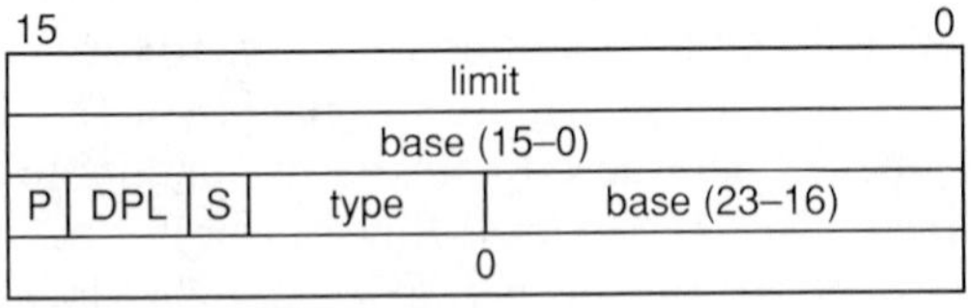

15					0
		limit			
		base (15–0)			
P	DPL	S	type	base (23–16)	
			0		

P = present
DPL = descriptor privilege level
S = 0 = special descriptor
type = type of special descriptor
   0 = invalid descriptor
   1 = available task state segment
   2 = LDT descriptor
   3 = busy task state segment

FIGURE 18–14   Format of a 80286 system segment descriptor (S = 0, type = 0–3).

writable (W)
expand down (ED)

Figure 18–13(b) shows the access-rights byte for a data segment. The *writable (W)* bit determines whether writes are allowed to the segment. The *expand down (ED)* bit governs the interpretation of the limit field. If ED = 0, then the valid range of offsets is 0–limit, as in code segments. However, if ED = 1, then the range is (limit+1)–FFFFH. This is useful for stack segments, which normally start at a high address and grow toward lower addresses. (A *stack segment* is simply a data segment that may contain the system stack, i.e., it may be selected by SS.)

stack segment

type

System segment and control descriptors have their S bit equal to 0, as shown in Figure 18–14. The *type* field distinguishes among several special descriptor types, described in the next three subsections, that are used for task management and transfer of control within and between tasks.

18.7.4   Task Management

In an environment with multiple tasks, each task has its own context—the register values and other information that define the state of the task. The 80286 uses a block of memory called a *task state segment (TSS)* to store the context of a task, consisting of the following information:

*task state segment
(TSS)*

- A selector that indirectly specifies an LDT for the task.

- Saved selector values for the four segment registers (CS–ES).

- Saved values for the eight general registers (AX–DI), FLAGS, and IP.

- Initial values of SS and SP for CPLs 0–2.

back link

- A *back link*—the TSS selector of the task, if any, that called the current task (only if it was invoked by a CALL instruction, interrupt, or trap).

Before starting a particular task for the first time, an operating system must initialize all of the context information in the TSS; but during subsequent context switches, this information is automatically saved and restored by the hardware.

LDT selector
LDT descriptor

The TSS does not specify a task's LDT directly. Instead, it contains an *LDT selector* that selects an *LDT descriptor* (type = 2) in the global descriptor table (GDT). The LDT descriptor contains the actual base address and length of the LDT in physical memory. (The DPL field of an LDT descriptor is not used.)

TSS descriptor
available task
busy task
task register (TR)
TSS selector

The base address and length of TSS itself are specified by a *TSS descriptor* in the GDT. There are two types of TSS descriptors, corresponding to *available tasks* (type = 1) and *busy tasks* (type = 3). At all times in protected mode, the *task register (TR)* in Figure 18–10(c) contains a *TSS selector* that locates a TSS descriptor, which in turn specifies a TSS for the currently executing task.

A system with *n* tasks typically has *n* TSSs and LDTs, each of which has a descriptor in the GDT. During a context switch, the operating system loads TR with a TSS selector that locates the tasks's TSS, and it loads LDTR with an LDT selector that locates the task's LDT. When LDTR is loaded, the processor copies the LDT's base address and length from the selected LDT descriptor into programmer-invisible processor registers, and uses this information whenever a segment selector specifies the LDT (TI = 1).

The simplest way for a program to start or resume a task is to execute an intersegment JMP where the segment selector portion of the destination address is a TSS selector. The CPL of the current task and the RPL of the TSS selector must be at least as privileged as the DPL of the destination TSS descriptor. When executing the JMP, the processor automatically saves the context of the current task (AX–DI, CS–ES, FLAGS, and IP) in the current TSS, and it marks the current TSS descriptor "available" (type = 1). Then it loads TR with the new TSS selector and loads the processor registers (AX–DI, CS–ES, FLAGS, IP, and LDTR) from the destination TSS, and it marks the destination TSS descriptor "busy" (type = 3). (Note that the segment offset portion of the JMP instruction's destination address is not used.) This task JMP facility is normally used by an operating system to transfer control from a task that is going to sleep (perhaps waiting for an I/O event to occur) to one that is ready to be awakened.

Tasks may also be started or resumed by an intersegment CALL instruction with a TSS selector. This differs from a task JMP in two important ways. First, the calling task is considered to remain busy, and so its TSS descriptor is *not* marked available. Second, the *nested task (NT)* bit in FLAGS is set to 1 and the TSS selector of the calling task is saved in the back link field of the new task's TSS. This back link allows the new task to resume the calling task at a later time: if the processor executes an IRET instruction while NT is 1 then, instead of the usual IRET sequence, it restores the context of the task specified by the back link in the current TSS. The task CALL facility is most commonly used by background tasks that wake up at unscheduled times to service I/O events (typically interrupts) and then return control to the current foreground task.

nested task (NT)

18.7.5 Gates

gate descriptor

Another type of special descriptor is the *gate descriptor* (type = 4–7), shown in Figure 18–15. When the segment selector part of a logical address specifies a gate, the segment offset part of that logical address is not used; the gate itself provides a transfer address.

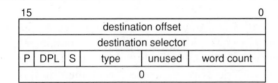

15					0
destination offset					
destination selector					
P	DPL	S	type	unused	word count
0					

P = present
DPL = descriptor privilege level
S = 0 = special descriptor
word count = # of words to copy (call gate only)
type = type of special descriptor
      4 = call gate
      5 = task gate
      6 = interrupt gate
      7 = trap gate

FIGURE 18–15   Format of a 80286 gate descriptor (S = 0, type = 4–7).

call gate
call gate
 descriptor

destination selector

destination offset

In particular, a *call gate* provides a controlled entry point to a subroutine that executes at a level the same as or more privileged than its caller. A *call gate descriptor* (type = 4) may be selected as the destination for an intersegment JMP or CALL instruction. The *destination selector* field of such a descriptor is like a segment selector; it specifies a code-segment descriptor in the GDT or LDT. The *destination offset* field specifies the subroutine entry point within the selected code segment;

Both a minimum and a maximum privilege level check are performed during a JMP or CALL through a call gate. First, the CPL of the caller must be at least as privileged as the DPL field in the call gate descriptor, or the gate cannot be used. Second, the CPL of the caller must be the same as (for a JMP) or no more privileged than (for a CALL) the CPL of the called subroutine, which is contained in the subroutine's code-segment descriptor, as specified by the call gate's destination selector field.

If a subroutine that is CALLed through a call gate executes at a level more privileged than its caller, then a more trusted stack is used. That is, the CALL instruction automatically loads SS and SP with new values taken from the corresponding field of the current TSS. It saves the return address on the new stack, and copies up to 31 words from the caller's stack to the new stack, as

word count

specified by the *word count* field of the call gate descriptor.

As in the MC68020 with MC68851 PMMU, call gates are used by less-privileged routines to request services that must be executed by more-privileged routines. For example, an application program would use a call gate to invoke a file-system routine to read a file, and the file-system routine might use a call gate to invoke a kernel routine that allocates memory buffers.

task gate

Another type of gate that can be the destination of an intersegment JMP or CALL is the *task gate* (descriptor type = 5). The destination selector field of a task gate is a TSS selector, and the destination offset and word count fields are not used. A task gate can perform a context switch to a task that runs at a level more privileged than the current task. For example, a user task could JMP to a task gate to return control to the operating system while waiting for an I/O event to occur. A intersegment JMP with a TSS selector cannot be used in this situation, because a task is not allowed to invoke a more privileged task in this way; a task gate must be used.

18.7.6   Interrupts and Traps

In protected mode, 80286 interrupts and traps are serviced through an *interrupt descriptor table (IDT)* whose physical address and size are contained in the *interrupt descriptor table register (IDTR)* shown in Figure 18–10. Like the GDT and LDT, the IDT contains 4-word descriptors, up to 256 of them in this case. Only task gate, *interrupt gate* (type = 6), and *trap gate* (type = 5) descriptors are allowed in the IDT.

When an interrupt or trap occurs, the interrupt vector number (0–255) selects a descriptor from the table. If the descriptor is a task gate, then the processor automatically performs a context switch to the specified task, as described in the previous subsection. If the descriptor is an interrupt or trap gate, then the interrupt is serviced within the current task. Among other things, this means that the interrupt service routine must explicitly save and restore any registers that it uses. When an interrupt gate is used, the processor clears the IF bit in FLAGS to prevent further interrupts; with a trap gate, IF is not affected.

Interrupt and trap gates provide reasonably fast entry into interrupt service routines. However, they have the same usage restrictions as call gates. In particular, the service routine must execute at a level at least as privileged as its caller. In general, this implies that interrupt service routines must run at the most privileged level (CPL = 0), since hardware interrupts are unpredictable and may occur when the processor happens to be executing a kernel task (CPL = 0). For an interrupt service routine to be executed at a less privileged level, it must be invoked by a task gate, which is slower than an interrupt or trap gate.

18.7.7   Extended Instructions

Compared with the 80186, the only instruction-set extensions in the 80286 are ones that deal with the new registers and protection features, as listed in Table 18–29. The first instruction loads the MSW, and is used to set the PE bit to put the 80286 into protected mode after the other registers and the translation tables have been initialized. The SMSW instruction reads the MSW, which is used not only to verify the value of PE, but also to read the other MSW bits when a coprocessor's activities must be coordinated with the 80286's after a context switch.

The remaining instructions in the table can be executed only in protected mode. Instructions in the third group load and store the remaining new registers, TR, GDTR, IDTR, and LDTR. The load instructions can be executed only when CPL = 0, the most privileged mode of operation, and are typically used in an operating system's kernel during system initialization and task switching. The store instructions can be executed at any privilege level. As a result, the 80286 does not support virtual machine operation: an application that *thinks* it is running with CPL = 0 and controlling these registers can read them (as well as the CPL in CS) and find out that it isn't. (Compare with MC68010 and MC68020 virtual machine support as discussed in Section 14.1.)

TABLE 18-29   Extended instructions of the 80286.

Mnemonic	Operands	Size	Description
LMSW	src	W	Load MSW with `src`
SMSW	dst	W	Store MSW into `dst`
LTR	src	W	Load TR with `src`, a TSS selector
STR	dst	W	Store MSW into `dst`
LGDT	msrc		Load GDTR with five memory bytes starting at `msrc`
SGDT	mdst		Store GDTR into six memory bytes starting at `mdst`
LIDT	msrc		Load IDTR with five memory bytes starting at `msrc`
SIDT	mdst		Store IDTR into six memory bytes starting at `mdst`
LLDT	src	W	Load LDTR with `src`, an LDT selector
SLDT	dst	W	Store LDTR into `dst`
CLTS			Clear TS flag in MSW
LAR	reg,src	W	Load `reg` with access-rights byte of descriptor selected by `src`
LSL	reg,src	W	Load `reg` with limit field of descriptor selected by `src`
VERR	src	W	Verify that segment selected by `src` is readable
VERW	src	W	Verify that segment selected by `src` is writable
ARPL	dst,reg	W	Adjust RPL of `dst` to be no more privileged than `reg`

Notes: `reg` may be any word register AX–DI.

A `src` or `dst` operand is specified by an addressing-mode postbyte and therefore may use register, absolute, register indirect, based, indexed, or based indexed addressing.

An `msrc` or `mdst` operand may use any mode except register.

The `CLTS` instruction is used in the operating system code that coordinates a coprocessor's activities with the 80286's after a context switch. It can be executed only when CPL = 0.

Instructions in the last group of the table are used to validate segments without causing protection violations. The `src` and `dst` operands of these instructions are segment selectors, in the format of Figure 18-11. If necessary, each instruction reads the descriptor specified by the selector in order to complete its action.

The `LAR` and `LSL` instructions first determine whether the segment selected by their `src` operand is accessible at the current privilege level; if it is, then the access-rights byte or limit field of the segment descriptor is loaded into `reg`. Also, Z is set or cleared to indicate whether or not the segment is accessible.

The `VERR` and `VERW` instructions go one step further. The `src` operand must select a code or data segment (special segments were allowed with the previous instructions), and it must be readable or writable for Z to be set.

The `dst` operand of the `ARPL` instruction must be a segment selector, usually a parameter supplied by a caller. `ARPL` adjusts this selector's RPL field to be no more privileged than the RPL field of `reg`, usually the CPL of the caller. Thus, a privileged routine uses `ARPL` to prevent its less-privileged callers from successfully fabricating pointers to and accessing privileged resources.

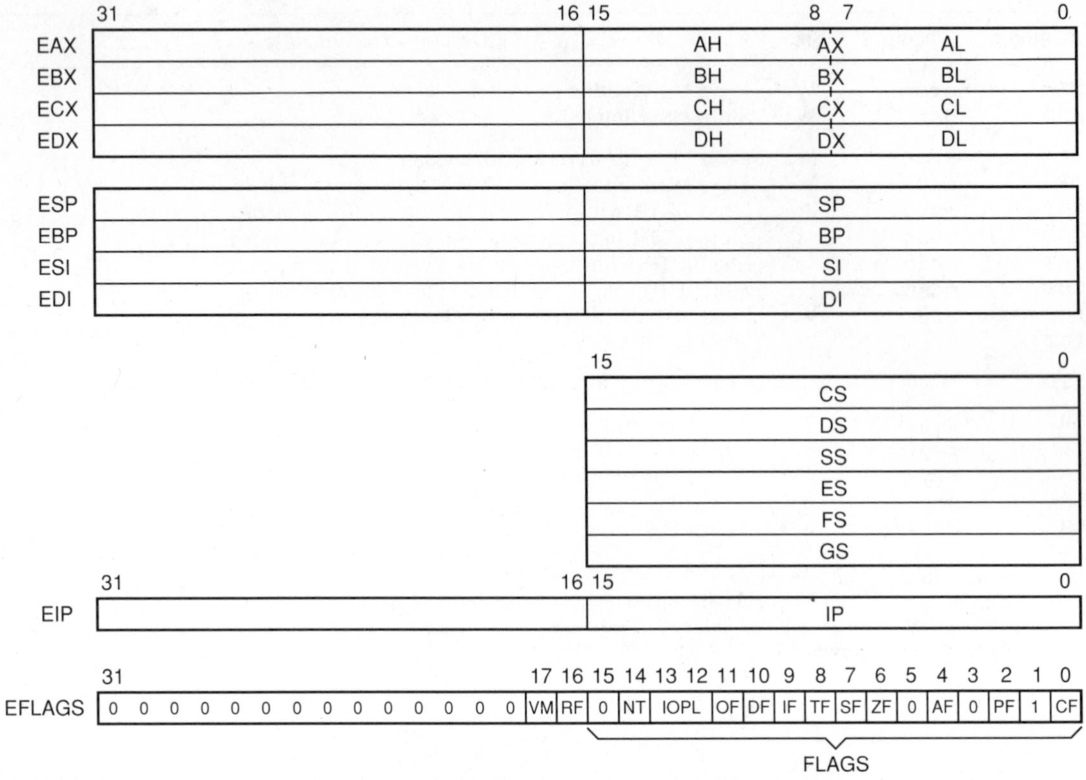

	31	16 15	8 7	0
EAX		AH	AX	AL
EBX		BH	BX	BL
ECX		CH	CX	CL
EDX		DH	DX	DL

	31	16 15	0
ESP			SP
EBP			BP
ESI			SI
EDI			DI

	15	0
	CS	
	DS	
	SS	
	ES	
	FS	
	GS	

	31	16 15	0
EIP			IP

EFLAGS (bit positions 31 ... 17 16 15 14 13 12 11 10 9 8 7 6 5 4 3 2 1 0):

0 0 0 0 0 0 0 0 0 0 0 0 0 0 | VM | RF | 0 | NT | IOPL | OF | DF | IF | TF | SF | ZF | 0 | AF | 0 | PF | 1 | CF

FLAGS

FIGURE 18–16   Basic register set in the 80386 programming model.

18.8   80386 PROCESSOR ORGANIZATION

Like the 80286 before it, the 80386 processor is a compatible extension of previous 80x86 architectures. Major improvements over the 80286 architecture include the following:

- The processor's registers and arithmetic units are 32 bits wide, and the instruction set is extended to support 32-bit addresses and data.

- The main memory and the data path to it can be 32 bits wide, so instructions and data can be read and written up to twice as fast.

- The maximum size of physical memory is extended from 2^{24} to 2^{32} bytes (4 gigabytes).

- Faster execution speed is obtained because the 80386's clock runs faster and most instructions take fewer clock cycles to execute.

- The on-chip memory management system supports paging.

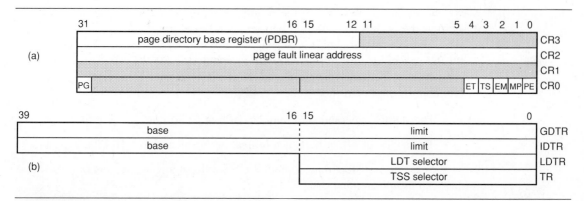

FIGURE 18–17   System registers in the 80386: (a) control registers; (b) memory mapping registers.

18.8.1 Programming Model

FS
GS
extended registers

The 80386 registers that are accessible by a typical user program are shown in Figure 18–16. All of the basic 80x86 register set is present, and two more "extra" segment registers, *FS* and *GS*, are provided. All of the registers except the segment registers are extended to 32 bits; compare with the basic register set of the 80286, shown in Figure 18–10(a). Each 32-bit register is named like its 16-bit low-order part, with a prefix of "E" indicating "extended."

CR0
paging (PG)
extension type
 (ET)
CR3
CR2

The 80286's MSW register is expanded into four 32-bit registers in the 80386, as shown in Figure 18–17(a). Register *CR0* contains all the bits of the 80286's MSW, plus a *paging (PG)* bit that enables paging and an *extension type (ET)* bit that selects whether an 80287 or an 80387 coprocessor is connected to the processor. Register *CR3* contains the base address of the "page directory" when paging is enabled, and *CR2* is loaded with the offending "linear address" if the processor tries to access an inaccessible page. Identical to the 80286, the 80386 has four registers, shown in Figure 18–17(b), that support memory mapping and task switching features.

debug registers
 (DR0–3,6–7)

Not shown in the figures, the 80386 has six *debug registers (DR0–3,6–7)* that support a sophisticated debugging facility whereby the programmer may specify up to four breakpoint addresses and conditions. If the processor reads or writes data at or fetches an instruction from a breakpoint address, a trap occurs.

18.8.2 Operating Modes

reset
real address mode

After a hardware reset, the 80386 enters a *real address mode* similar to the 80286's, and behaves just like an 8086 processor. Only the low-order word of each extended register is accessible, and the processor executes all standard 8086 instructions and 80186 extended instructions. Memory accesses use 20-bit addresses generated by the standard shift-and-add scheme of the 8086. This mode is sometimes used by the Compaq DeskPro 386 and other compatibles to execute programs written for the original 8088-based IBM PC. However, we'll see that the 80386 has another, better way of executing 8088/8086 programs.

protected mode

Like the 80286, the 80386 has a PE bit in CR0 that may be set to 1 to put the processor into *protected mode* to enable the 80386's extended registers, instructions, memory mapping, and protection features.[6] Several options are available in protected mode:

- The default operand size may be 16 bits or 32 bits.

- The segment offset part of a logical address can have 16 bits or 32 bits.

- Segment registers may contain 80286-style segment selectors or 8086-style paragraph numbers.

We'll show how these options are selected shortly. In general, regardless of the option selections, instruction opcodes and addressing modes for 8086 and 80286 instructions are the same as in the original processors, allowing compatibility at the object-code level with existing 80x86 programs.

18.8.3   Memory Mapping, Protection, and Tasks

The memory mapping, protection, and task management features of the 80386 are a superset of the ones available in the 80286, including the same registers, tables, and descriptor types. However, the last word of each descriptor, normally 0 in the 80286, has additional fields that enable the 80386's features. Depending on how these fields are used, an 80386 can run user programs that were originally written for the 16-bit 80286, or new programs that were specifically designed to use the 80386's 32-bit addressing and data manipulation capabilities.

18.8.4   Descriptor Formats and Address and Data Sizes

base

linear address

Figure 18–18(a) shows the format of an 80386 data-segment descriptor. The *base* field now has 32 bits and therefore can specify an address anywhere in a 4-gigabyte physical memory. The sum of base and the segment offset part of a logical address is 32 bits wide and is called a *linear address*. If paging is disabled (PG = 0 in CR0), then the physical memory address equals the linear address; if paging is enabled (PG = 1), then the linear address is translated through two more levels of tables to obtain a 32-bit physical address, as explained later.

limit

granularity (G)

A data-segment descriptor's *limit* field is expanded to 20 bits, so that a segment can contain up to 2^{20} bytes (1 Mbyte). Better yet, the *granularity (G)* bit, when 1, indicates that limit is multiplied by 2^{12}, so that the maximum segment size is 2^{32} bytes, equal to the physical address space of the machine. With this option, the 80386 is the first 80x86 processor that can directly access a 4-gigabyte linear address space, just like the 68020.

---

[6]But unlike the 80286, the 80386 also allows you to clear PE to get back into real address mode.

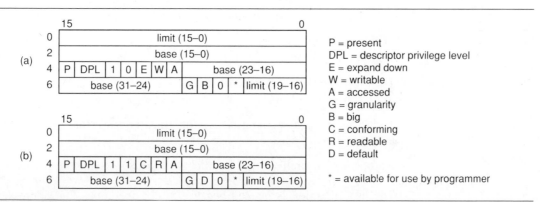

FIGURE 18–18   Segment descriptors in the 80386: (a) data segment; (b) code segment.

big (B)

   The *big (B)* bit is the final addition to the 80386's data-segment descriptor format. This bit tells the processor the size of the stack pointer to use for implicit stack references, for example, when handling interrupts and when executing CALL, RET, PUSH, and POP instructions. If B = 0 then SP (16 bits) is used; if B = 1 then ESP (32 bits) is used.

   Figure 18–18(b) shows the format of an 80386 code-segment descriptor. It has the same new fields as a data-segment descriptor, except that B has been

default (D)

replaced with a *default (D)* bit. When the descriptor for the currently executing code segment has D = 0, the processor uses a default operand size and segment offset size of 16 bits. That is, word instructions (ones with w = 1 in Figure 18–3) use only the low-order 16 bits of the general registers, and the segment offsets resulting from effective-address calculations are 16-bit numbers. When D = 1, the defaults are 32 bits. In this case, word instructions access 32-bit double words in the extended general registers and memory, and segment offsets have 32 bits, providing linear addressing of up to 4 gigabytes in a single segment. Regardless of the value of D, byte instructions (w = 0) have 8-bit operands.

   Since each code segment specifies its own default, 16- and 32-bit code modules can be mixed in a single program. For example, a program's 16-bit modules may have originally been written for the 80286, while its 32-bit modules may be new code that employs 32-bit arithmetic or accesses data structures larger than 64 Kbytes. In addition, the size defaults set by D may be overridden

operand-size
 override prefix

on an instruction-by-instruction basis within a code module. The *operand-size override prefix* causes the instruction that follows it to use the opposite operand

address-size
 override prefix

size from what is specified by D. The *address-size override prefix* does the same for effective addresses. One or both prefix bytes may be used with an instruction. Although most 16-bit modules will not employ any 32-bit overrides, the operand-size override prefix is often used in 32-bit modules to access 16-bit data.

   To run properly in protected mode on the 80386, a user program that was originally written for the 80286 must observe the following rules:

- The program must run properly on the 80286 in protected mode.

- The G bit in all segment descriptors must be 0, and limit(19-16) must be 0, thus limiting segment size to 64 Kbytes as in the 80286.

- The D bit in code-segment descriptors must be 0, thus forcing the processor to use only 16-bit registers and 16-bit segment offsets.

- The B bit in stack-segment descriptors must be 0, so that SP, not ESP, is used for implicit stack references.

- No opcodes or prefixes that are illegal in the 80286 may be used.

The last condition is needed because 32-bit operations and addresses, as well as extended 80386 instructions, are available through instruction prefixes and opcodes that are illegal (and cause traps) in the 80286. This is both good and bad—an existing 80286 program can be optimized to use 80386 features, but an 80286 program that encounters a hidden (or masked) bug when running on the 80386 may do something completely unpredictable.

A user program that takes full advantage of the 80386's large linear address space and 32-bit operations generally has the following characteristics:

- The G bit in all segment descriptors is 1, so that segment size may be as large as 4 gigabytes, with a granularity of 4 Kbytes.

- The D bit in code-segment descriptors is 1, so that 32-bit operations and addresses are the default. The address-size prefix is not used (16-bit addresses are almost useless in a large segment), but the opcode-size prefix may be used to perform 16-bit data operations.

- The B bit in stack-segment descriptors is 1, so that ESP is used for implicit stack references.

- New instructions and the two new extra-segment registers are used freely.

18.8.5 Paging

In protected mode, the 80386 can use a two-level translation scheme to map 32-bit linear addresses into 32-bit physical addresses, as shown in Figure 18–19. The page size is fixed at 4 Kbytes, and the translation tables also have a fixed size of 4 Kbytes.

page directory

Paging is enabled when the PG bit in CR0 is 1. In this case, processor register CR3 contains the base address in physical memory of a *page directory*. Depending on the operating system design, one page directory may be shared by all tasks, or each task may have its own page directory, so that CR3 is changed during context switches.

In any case, a page directory has 1024 (2^{10}) 4-byte entries, and is indexed by the 10 high-order bits of a linear address. Each entry either is marked "not

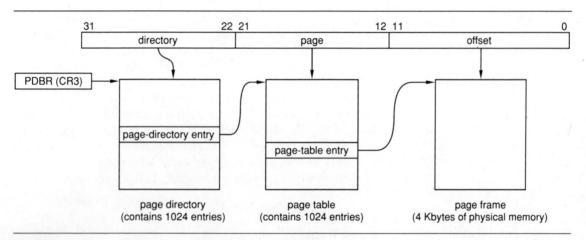

FIGURE 18-19   Page address translation in the 80386.

page table

present" or contains the base address in physical memory address of a second-level *page table*, which also has 1024 4-byte entries. If the second-level page table is present, then the middle 10 bits of the linear address are used to index it. The selected page table entry either is marked "not present" or contains the base address in physical memory of a page. The low-order 12 bits of the linear address are added to the page's base address to form the physical address corresponding to the original linear address.

If a task uses the maximum of 4 gigabytes of physical memory, then it must have one page directory and 1024 page tables; a total of 1025 pages of memory must be used for translation tables. On the other hand, a smaller task may use far fewer tables. For example, even if 1023 of the page directory's entries are marked "not present," the single remaining entry can select a page table that locates 1024 "present" pages, a total of 4 Mbytes of physical memory.

Figure 18-20 shows the detailed format of a page directory or page table entry. Since pages, page directories, and page tables are all 4 Kbytes long and must start on a page boundary, the table entries (as well as CR3) contain only the 20 high-order bits of the physical base address. In addition to the present bit (P), the low-order bits of a table entry include protection bits (U and W) and usage information (D and A).

The protection bits augment the protections provided by segment descrip-

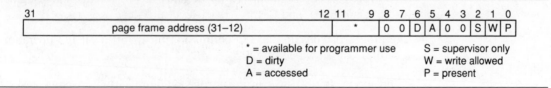

FIGURE 18-20   Format of an 80386 page-directory or page-table entry.

tors. If the protections specified by the segment descriptor, page directory, and
page table entries are different, the most restrictive protection applies. The pro-

user level

cessor is running at *user level* when CPL = 3 and, in this case, only pages with
U = 1 can be accessed. Furthermore, such pages can be written at user level only

supervisor level

if W = 1. The processor is running at a *supervisor level* when CPL = 0, 1, or 2;
in this case, any page may be read or written independent of U and W.

The processor does not have to look up paging information in main mem-

*translation
  lookaside buffer
  (TLB)*

ory on every access. Like the MC68851 PMMU, it has a small, programmer-
invisible memory, called a *translation lookaside buffer (TLB)*, that stores recent
translations. The TLB is a 4-way set-associative cache with eight entries per set;
it is automatically flushed whenever CR3 is changed. Two *test registers (TR6–7)*

*test registers
  (TR6–7)*

are used to test the TLB.

18.8.6   Input/Output, Interrupts, and Traps

The 80386's I/O mechanisms in protected mode are similar to the 80286's,
including the use of IOPL to determine the privilege level required for I/O instructions to be executed. The 80386's interrupt and trap mechanisms are also
similar.

*I/O permission bit
  map*

A major enhancement in the 80386 is the provision of an optional *I/O
permission bit map* in the TSS. This bit map has one bit for every I/O address
in a certain range, starting at 0 and possibly going all the way to 64K. If the
processor tries to execute an I/O port operation that is prohibited by IOPL, it
then consults the bit map. If the address has a corresponding bit in the map, and
if the bit is 0, then the I/O operation is allowed; otherwise, an exception occurs
as usual. This facility allows user programs to operate directly on "private" I/O
ports, such as individual user device interfaces, while still protecting general I/O
resources, such as disks, from malicious mischief.

18.8.7   Virtual 8086 Mode

*virtual 8086
  (V86) mode*

While operating in protected mode, the 80386 processor may be put into *virtual
8086 (V86) mode* by setting the VM bit in CR0 to 1. This has several effects:

- The high-order word of a 32-bit logical address is used as an 8086-style
  paragraph number instead of an 80286/386-style segment selector.

- Even though no segment descriptors are used, the processor behaves as if
  D = 0 for the code segment (16-bit default), B = 0 for the stack segment
  (use SP, not ESP), and CPL = 3 (user-level privilege).

- The processor consults the I/O permission bit map for all I/O operations,
  regardless of the value of IOPL.

Using V86 mode, the 80386 can create one or more virtual-machine tasks to
run programs originally written for the 8086. With paging enabled and multiple

page directories, each V86 task can have a private area of the 80386's physical memory to emulate an 8086's 1 Mbyte of physical memory. This technique is used by virtual-machine operating systems such as Windows/386 to run multiple 8086 programs concurrently on an 80386.

In V86 mode, just as in non-V86 protected mode, the extended registers, instructions, and addressing of the 80386 are available through previously illegal instruction prefixes and opcodes. As we explained before, this implies that 8086 programs can be optimized to use 32-bit features, or they can be run unmodified, with the possibility of crashing in new and exciting ways. However, since V86 tasks run with CPL = 3, errors in a particular V86 task running under a robust operating system should not affect other V86 tasks or the system as a whole.

18.8.8   Extended Addressing Modes

The 80386 features that we've described so far are used primarily by operating system software. But the 80386 also has features that benefit user programs.

In protected mode, either 16- or 32-bit addressing is selected, depending on the D bit in the code-segment descriptor and an optional address-size instruction prefix. When 16-bit addressing is selected, the 80386's addressing modes, as encoded in an instruction's addressing-mode postbyte (Figure 18–6), are precisely the same as the 8086's.

When 32-bit addressing is selected, the encoding of the postbyte and the resulting addressing modes are completely different. The available addressing modes are as follows:

register addressing
- *Register.* Any of the 32-bit general registers EAX–EDI may be specified. A corresponding 16- or 8-bit register is used for word or byte operations.

absolute addressing
- *Absolute.* The 32-bit segment offset part of a memory operand's effective address follows the postbyte.

register indirect addressing
- *Register indirect.* Any 32-bit general register except ESP or EBP may contain the segment offset part of the effective address.

based short addressing
- *Based short.* An 8-bit signed displacement following the postbyte(s) is added to any 32-bit general register except ESP to get the segment offset.

based long addressing
- *Based long.* A 32-bit displacement following the postbyte(s) is added to any 32-bit general register except ESP to get the segment offset.

Thus, unlike the 8086, the 80386 allows almost general selection of registers in addressing modes. EBP is omitted from register indirect mode to provide an encoding for absolute, and ESP is omitted from register indirect and based modes to provide an encoding for *based indexed addressing* modes. In these
based indexed addressing
modes, a *second* postbyte specifies the base register (any general register), an index register (any but ESP), and a scale factor for the index register (1, 2, 4,

or 8). The segment offset is obtained by adding the scaled index register, the base register, and the displacement, if any, specified by the first postbyte.

When ESP or EBP is used as a base register, SS is the default segment register in the address calculation, similar to the 8086. For all other addressing modes, DS is the default. However, the defaults may be overridden as in the 8086 using instruction prefixes, including new ones that select FS and GS.

18.8.9 Extended Instructions

The 80386 has all of the extended instructions of the 80286. In addition, all of its instructions use 32-bit operands as appropriate when 32-bit operation is selected. The 80386 also has several new instructions, listed in Table 18–30.

LSS
LFS
LGS
MOV

MOVSX
MOVZX

The LSS instruction corrects an oversight in the original 8086 design, providing a way to load SS and SP in a single step. LFS and LGS are the corresponding instructions for the new extra-segment registers.

The two MOV instructions provide the means for loading and storing the 80386's new control, debug, and test registers. The MOVs can be executed only when CPL = 0, and they operate on 32 bits regardless of the size option in effect. In support of the 80386's "variable" general register widths, the MOVSX and MOVZX allow a byte or word operand to be moved into a wider register with either its sign bit or 0s filling the high-order bits of the register.

TABLE 18–30   New instructions of the 80386.

Mnemonic	Operands	Size	Description
LSS	reg,src	D	Load SS and reg with double-word src
LFS	reg,src	D	Load FS and reg with double-word src
LGS	reg,src	D	Load GS and reg with double-word src
MOV	reg,spcl	D	Load reg with special register
MOV	spcl,reg	D	Load special register with reg
MOVSX	reg,src	B,W	Load reg with sign-extended src
MOVZX	reg,src	B,W	Load reg with zero-extended src
BTS	src,ireg	W/D	Copy, then set to 1, bit ireg of src operand
BTR	src,ireg	W/D	Copy, then reset to 0, bit ireg of src operand
BTC	src,ireg	W/D	Copy, then complement, bit ireg of src operand
BT	src,ireg	W/D	Copy bit ireg of src operand into CF
BSF	reg,src	W/D	Load reg with index of rightmost 1 in src
BSR	reg,src	W/D	Load reg with index of leftmost 1 in src
SHLD	dst,reg,icnt	W/D	Left shift dst by icnt bits, filling from reg
SHRD	dst,reg,icnt	W/D	Right shift dst by icnt bits, filling from reg

Notes: src and dst operands are specified by an addressing-mode postbyte and may use any 80386 addressing mode.
reg may be any general register, as appropriate for the size of the operation.
ireg may be any general register or an 8-bit immediate value.
icnt specifies the source of the shift count, either CL or an 8-bit immediate value.
spcl may be CR0, CR2, CR3, DR0, DR1, DR2, DR3, DR6, DR7, TR6, or TR7.

BTS	The next instructions in the table are comparable to the 68000's bit ma-
BTR	nipulation instructions. A word or double-word `src` operand may be located,
BTC	and one of its bits may be set, reset, complemented, or tested. The operand size
BT	depends on the size option currently in effect. The `BSF` and `BSR` instructions
BSF	find the `src` operand's leftmost or rightmost 1 bit. Note that the 80386 does
BSR	not have bit *field* instructions.
SHLD	The last two instructions in the table simplify multiprecision shifts. `SHLD`
	replaces `dst` with the result of shifting the double-size operand `dst:reg` left
SHRD	by `icnt` bits. `SHRD` does a similar right shift, using the operand `reg:dst`.

R E F E R E N C E S

The 8086 processor architecture evolved from the 8080, which evolved from the 8008, which Intel originally developed as a custom chip according to the specifications of one of its customers in about 1970. The history of this evolution has been traced in "Intel Microprocessors—8008 to 8086," by S. P. Morse, B. W. Ravenel, S. Mazor, and W. B. Pohlman (*Computer*, Vol. 13, No. 10, October 1980). A discussion of the 8086 in particular appeared in "The Intel 8086 Microprocessor: A 16-bit Evolution of the 8080," by Morse, Pohlman, and Ravenel (*Computer*, Vol. 11, No. 6, June 1978).

A discussion of 8086-family hardware and software, from the 8086 through the 80286, can be found in *Microcomputer Systems: The 8086/8088 Family* (Prentice-Hall, 1986, 2nd ed.), by Y.-C. Liu and G. A. Gibson. Another very readable introduction to 8086 hardware and software is *The 8086 Primer* by 8086 co-architect Stephen P. Morse (Hayden, 1980). More recently, Morse has co-authored a book with E. J. Isaacson and D. J. Albert on *The 80386/387*

80387

Architecture (Wiley, 1987). (The *80387* is a floating-point coprocessor for the 80386.) Another comprehensive 80386 book is *80386 Technical Reference* by Edmund Strauss (Brady, 1987). Naturally, Intel publishes plenty of technical information on the 80x86 family, including hardware and software reference manuals for all of the processors in the family.

E X E R C I S E S

18.1 Write an 8086 subroutine that sets the contents of a memory byte at logical address `seg:offset` to zero, assuming that the values of `seg` and `offset` are known at assembly time. This sounds like absolute addressing—it should be easy, right? Your subroutine must make no assumptions about the contents of the segment registers and it may not disturb the contents of any processor register.

18.2 Write an 8086 subroutine that sets or clears ZF according to whether or not DS:BX and ES:DX point to the same physical memory address. Your subroutine may not disturb the contents of any processor register.

18.3 Write an 8086 subroutine that clears ZF to 0 without affecting any other condition bits or processor registers.

18.4 An alternative to the DF bit in the 8086 is having separate string-manipulation instructions for auto-increment and auto-decrement. How many more opcodes would be needed without DF?

18.5 Write an 8086 subroutine that adds two 24-bit unsigned integers P and Q, stored in memory bytes P2,P1,P0 and Q2,Q1,Q0, respectively. The sum should be stored in memory locations S2,S1,S0. When the subroutine returns, CF should be set to 1 if the true sum is greater than $2^{48} - 1$, else to 0.

18.6 Rewrite the sorting program of Table 7–3 for the 8086.

18.7 Rewrite the sorting program of Table 7–3 for the 8086, using string-manipulation instructions to improve the speed of the program where possible. (*Hint:* Reverse the order of one of the stacks.)

18.8 Show the statements needed in Table 18–18 for the FNDPRM procedure and the PRIME array to occupy different segments.

18.9 Rewrite the queue module of Table 18–21 to manipulate queues of bytes. As much as possible, make the new code independent of queue element size (byte or word).

18.10 Show how to speed up the string search subroutine in Table 18–23 by using the SCAS instruction to look for occurrences of the first character of the specified string in BUFFER, and then using CMPS to check for a complete match.

18.11 Rewrite the string search subroutine and calling program in Tables 18–23 and 18–24 so that a string or buffer is defined to be arbitray-length sequence of nonzero bytes, terminated by a zero byte. The new subroutine must compute the length of the search string and search buffer at run time.

18.12 Rewrite the recursive NIM subroutines in Table 9–22 for the 8086. Write a main program that analyzes the game for all combinations of values of NHEAP from 2 to 25 and NTAKE from 2 to 6.

18.13 Write an 8086 keyboard input and display output module similar to the 68000 module in Table 10–5.

18.14 Write a complete Pascal simulation of the 8086.

18.15 Draw a figure that shows the relationships among the GDT, LDTs, LDT descriptors, GDTR, and LDTR in the 80286.

18.16 Compare the memory mapping approaches of the MC68851 and the 80286.

18.17 Compare the subroutine calling restrictions that are imposed by the MC68020 and MC68851 with those of the 80286 in protected mode.

18.18 List all of the conditions that must be true for the 80286 LAR or LSL instruction to set Z.

18.19 Compare the memory mapping approaches of the MC68851 and the 80386.

CHAPTER 19

A Hypothetical Stack Machine: The H11

stack machine

A *stack machine* has neither general registers nor accumulators, only a stack pointer SP that points to a pushdown stack in memory; all operations are performed on the stack. Many of Hewlett-Packard's desktop and hand-held calculators (and many imitators) are stack machines. The HP 300 and HP 3000 mini-computers are also stack machines. (Perhaps HP is trying to make up for the lack of stack in its first minicomputer, the HP 2116.) Also, most accumulator-based and general-register processors have at least a few stack-oriented instructions.

None of the real processors discussed in in this book are pure stack machines. However, the PDP-11, a general-register processor, has instructions that easily simulate those of a pure stack machine. It is instructive to study the architecture of a simple, hypothetical stack machine based on these PDP-11 instructions.

19.1 PROCESSOR AND MEMORY ORGANIZATION

Figure 19–1 shows the internal organization of a hypothetical stack machine. At the end of this chapter, we'll show how the PDP-11 can easily simulate this machine; for now, we'll call the hypothetical machine the *H11*.

H11

The H11's organization is similar to that of a simple accumulator-based machine, except that it uses a 16-bit *temporary register (TEMP)* in the place of an accumulator A. As shown in the H11's programming model, Figure 19–2, TEMP is not accessible to the programmer; it is only used during the execution of each instruction to temporarily hold an operand.

temporary register (TEMP)

The H11 has a byte-addressable memory of 64 Kbytes, organized as shown in Figure 5.1.1(b). Thus, addresses are two bytes long. Data manipulated by an

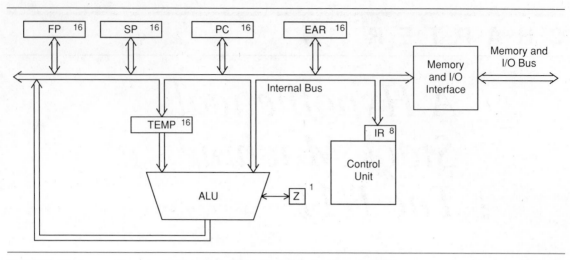

FIGURE 19–1   Organization of a hypothetical stack machine, the H11.

stack pointer (SP)

frame pointer (FP)

program counter (PC)

zero bit (Z)

effective address register (EAR)

H11 program is stored in a pushdown stack in memory. The instructions that we describe here manipulate only 16-bit (2-byte) data. As shown in Figure 19–3, high memory is used for the stack, which grows downward, and low memory is used for instructions and "global" data. The *stack pointer (SP)* points to the top of the stack, using the same conventions as the stack pointers of all the other processors in this book. A *frame pointer (FP)* normally contains the address of a location somewhere inside the stack.

Other programmer-visible registers in the H11 are the *program counter (PC)* and the *zero bit (Z)*. The *effective address register (EAR)* is programmer invisible; it temporarily holds operand address for instructions that use absolute addressing.

19.2 INSTRUCTION SET

The instruction set of the H11 is listed in Table 19–1. Instructions in the first group are used to push and pop arbitrary data on the stack. Any word in memory

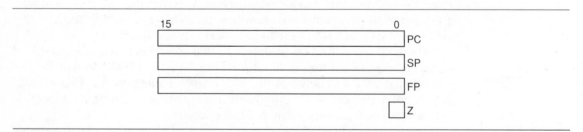

FIGURE 19–2   Programming model of the H11.

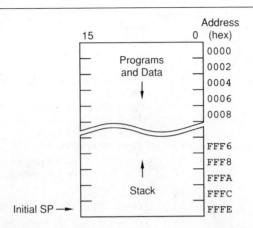

FIGURE 19–3   Memory organization of the H11.

PUSH

TOS

POP

may be pushed onto the stack by a PUSH addr instruction, which specifies a 16-bit absolute address in two bytes following the opcode. Likewise, the word at the top of the stack (*TOS*) may be popped into any memory location by means of a POP addr instruction. When a word is pushed, SP is decremented by two; then the word is stored at the memory address indicated by the new value of SP (which must be even). A word is popped by storing the TOS into the specified memory address and then incrementing SP by two. Figure 19–4 illustrates the contents of memory for a sequence of several pushes and pops.

Several other PUSH and POP instructions are provided: PUSH #data

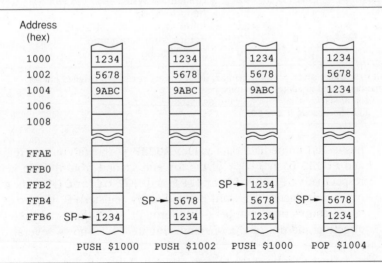

FIGURE 19–4   Memory contents after various stack pushes and pops.

TABLE 19–1   Machine instructions of the H11.

Mnemonic	Operand	Length (bytes)	Opcode (hex)	Description
PUSH	addr	3	01	Push MEMW[addr] onto stack
PUSH	#data	3	02	Push data onto stack
PUSH	offset(FP)	2	03	Push MEMW[FP+offset] onto stack
PUSHT		1	04	Push TOS onto stack
PUSHS		1	05	Push SOS onto stack
PUSHF		1	06	Push FP onto stack
POP	addr	3	07	Pop TOS, store into MEMW[addr]
POP	offset(FP)	2	08	Pop TOS, store into MEMW[FP+offset]
CLR		1	10	Clear TOS
COM		1	11	Ones' complement bits of TOS
NEG		1	12	Negate TOS (two's complement)
SWAB		1	13	Swap bytes of TOS
ADD		1	14	Pop TOS, add to new TOS
AND		1	15	Pop TOS, logical AND to new TOS
CMP		1	16	Pop TOS, compare with new TOS
MUL		1	17	Pop TOS, SOS, and push TOS·SOS
LD	r,#data	3	20+r	Load r with data
LD	r,addr	3	22+r	Load r with MEMW[addr]
LDFS		1	24	Load FP with a copy of SP
ST	r,addr	3	26+r	Store r into MEMW[addr]
ADD	r,#offset	2	28+r	Add offset to r
VAL		1	30	Replace TOS with MEMW[TOS]
STOW		1	31	Store TOS into MEMW[SOS], pop both
BNE	offset	2	40	Branch if Z=0
BEQ	offset	2	41	Branch if Z=1
BRA	offset	2	42	Branch always
JMP	addr	3	50	Jump to addr
JSR	addr	3	51	Jump to subroutine at addr
RTS		1	52	Return from subroutine
NOP		1	00	No operation

Notes: data = 16-bit data value; addr = 16-bit memory address; offset = 8-bit signed integer.
  MEMW[n] = memory word at address n; n must be even.
  TOS = word at top of stack; SOS = second word on stack.
  r = FP or SP; add 1 to opcode if r = SP.

PUSHF
PUSHT
PUSHS

pushes an immediate data value; PUSHF pushes a copy of register FP; PUSHT and PUSHS push a copy of the top and second from the top items in the stack, respectively. PUSH offset(FP) and POP offset(FP) push and pop memory words "near" the word pointed to by register FP. Here offset is an 8-bit two's-complement number (−128 through +127) that is added to FP to obtain the effective address of the operand. Figure 19–5 shows several operations using FP.

Instructions in the second group in Table 19–1 perform arithmetic and logical operations on data at the top of the stack. As shown in Figure 19–6, single-

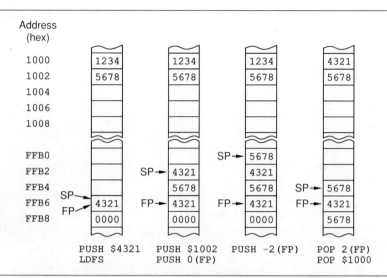

FIGURE 19–5   Stack contents after operations using the frame pointer.

operand instructions modify the value stored at the top of the stack. Double-operand instructions combine two operands at the top of the stack, replacing them with the result of the operation. These are called *zero-address instructions*, because they contain no address specifications; they implicitly manipulate the top one or two stack items.

zero-address instruction

The third group contains "housekeeping" instructions for SP and FP. The fourth group provides a method of indirect addressing for accessing array elements and other data by means of pointers computed at run time. If the address of a variable is stored on the top of the stack, VAL replaces the address with the value of the variable itself. STOW performs the inverse operation, storing the data word from the top of the stack at an address contained in the second word on the stack (one below the top).

VAL
STOW

All of the instructions in the first four groups set Z to 1 if they produce

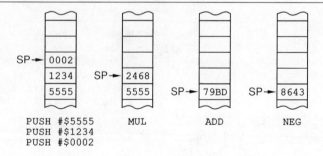

FIGURE 19–6   Effects of single- and double-operand instructions.

BEQ   a zero result, to 0 otherwise. BEQ and BNE test Z and branch as in the 68000.
BNE   The other instructions in the fifth group also operate the same as in the 68000.

19.3 SAMPLE PROGRAMS

Our standard algorithm for multiplying two numbers by repeated addition is coded for the H11 in Table 19–2. The state of the stack at various points in the program is shown in Figure 19–7. There are at most five items on the stack at any time. Although SP changes as the stack expands and shrinks during each iteration of the loop, the frame pointer FP always provides a fixed reference address for accessing CNT and PROD.

An array initialization program for the H11 is shown in Table 19–3. This program also illustrates the use of the STOW, CMP, and PUSHS instructions. As an exercise, you should sketch the contents of the stack during the execution of the program.

TABLE 19–2   Multiplication by repeated addition on the H11.

Machine Language		Assembly Language			
Address	Contents	Label	Opcode	Operand	Comments
			ORG	$2A40	Multiply MCND by MPY.
2A40		SPROD	EQU	-2	Offset to PROD in stack frame.
2A40		SCNT	EQU	-4	Offset to CNT.
2A40		SMCND	EQU	-6	Offset to MCND.
2A40		*	Assume SP has already been loaded on entry.		
2A40	24	START	LDFS		Set up frame pointer.
2A41	04		PUSHT		Push a word onto the stack.
2A42	10		CLR		Clear it (initial PROD).
2A43	01 2C00		PUSH	MPY	Set CNT equal to MPY.
2A46	01 2C02		PUSH	MCND	Make a copy of MCND in stack.
2A49	50 2A58		JMP	IN	Do the loop MPY times.
2A4C	02 FFFF	LOOP	PUSH	#-1	Decrement CNT.
2A4F	14		ADD		
2A50	08 FC		POP	SCNT(FP)	
2A52	04		PUSHT		Make a copy of MCND.
2A53	03 FE		PUSH	SPROD(FP)	
2A55	14		ADD		
2A56	08 FE		POP	SPROD(FP)	
2A58	03 FC	IN	PUSH	SCNT(FP)	Push a copy of CNT.
2A5A	40 F0		BNE	LOOP	Continue if not yet zero.
2A5C	29 06	DONE	ADD	SP,#6	Else clean up stack.
2A5E	50 1000		JMP	$1000	Return to operating system,
2A61		*			PROD is at top of stack.
2A61			ORG	$2C00	
2C00	0005	MPY	DC.W	5	Multiplier value.
2C02	0017	MCND	DC.W	23	Multiplicand value.
2C04			END	START	

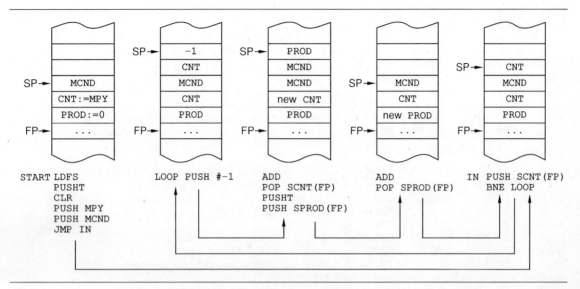

FIGURE 19–7 Stack contents after execution of instructions in multiplication program.

19.4 STRENGTHS AND WEAKNESSES OF STACK MACHINES

Stack machines show their greatest strength in evaluating complicated expressions. To show this, we'll look at some expressions involving multiplication and addition.

The H11 MUL instruction multiplies the top two words on the stack and replaces them with a 1-word product. If the product requires more than one word to express, then the high-order bits are lost. The 68000 MULU.W instruction also multiplies a register by an operand, leaving a longword product in the register; we can ignore the high-order word of the product if we know that results can always be expressed in a single word.

Some Pascal assignment statements using addition and multiplication are coded for the 68000 and the H11 in Table 19–4. Although the H11 requires more instructions than the 68000 to evaluate each expression, its individual instructions are shorter, making the overall H11 program slightly shorter. A stack machine can have shorter instructions than a general-register machine because it does not need any bits to encode register numbers. Compare the 3-byte PUSH and POP instructions in the H11 with the 4-byte MOVEs in the 68000. Both specify a 16-bit memory address, but the 68000 instructions "waste" an extra byte to provide more choices of registers and addressing modes.

Although stack machines may have slightly shorter programs, they are not necessarily faster than general-register machines. Because execution of a typical instruction can be overlapped with fetching the next instruction, the speed of a modern computer processor tends to be limited by the speed of the memory system. Therefore, a good approximation of the relative execution speed of a

TABLE 19–3   Initializing an array on the H11.

Machine Language		Assembly Language			
Address	Contents	Label	Opcode	Operand	Comments
			ORG	$3000	Initialize an array to 0.
3000		*	Assume SP has already been loaded on entry.		
3000	02 3100	INIT	PUSH	#Q	Base address of array.
3003	04	ILOOP	PUSHT		Get a copy of array address.
3004	04		PUSHT		Push 0 (initial value).
3005	10		CLR		
3006	31		STOW		Initialize an array location.
3007	02 0002		PUSH	#2	Update array address.
300A	14		ADD		
300B	02 310A		PUSH	#Q+10	Past end?
300E	16		CMP		
300F	40 F2		BNE	ILOOP	Continue if not.
3011	29 02		ADD	SP,#2	Else clean up stack.
3013	50 1000		JMP	$1000	Go to operating system.
3016			ORG	$3100	
3100	??	Q	RMW	5	Reserve 5 words.
310A			END	INIT	

program can be obtained by simply counting the number of times it accesses memory (i.e., reads or writes it) while fetching and executing its instructions.

In Table 19–4, we have counted the number of bytes of memory that are accessed during the 68000 and H11 expression evaluation programs. The H11 programs, although slightly shorter in bytes, take much more execution time than the 68000 programs. This is directly attributable to the fact that the only "working register," where arithmetic operations take place, is the top of the stack. And the top of stack is stored in memory, which we claim is the bottleneck in the system!

In order to get around the memory bottleneck, many real stack machines are designed to keep the top few items of the stack in "scratchpad" processor registers, in a way transparent to the programmer. When the top of stack is accessed by a program, the hardware accesses memory only if the processor stack registers have become full or empty because of too many more pushes than pops or vice versa. Even after going through all this trouble, computer architects still debate whether a stack machine can be made to run as fast as a general-register machine designed with an equal amount of circuitry and engineering effort.

The main advantage of stacks is not in expression evaluation anyway. Rather, stacks are the most natural data structure for saving return addresses and other information during subroutine calls. And as we learned in Chapter 9, they can also be used to store subroutine parameters and local variables in both assembly and high-level language programs.

TABLE 19–4   Assignment statements in general-register and stack machines.

Statement	68000 Instructions		H11 Instructions		Stack Contents
P:=Q*R+S+T	MOVE.W Q,R0	(4,6)	PUSH Q	(3,7)	Q
	MUL R,R0	(4,6)	PUSH R	(3,7)	Q, R
	ADD S,R0	(4,6)	MUL	(1,7)	Q*R
	ADD T,R0	(4,6)	PUSH S	(3,7)	Q*R, S
	MOVE.W R0,P	(4,6)	ADD	(1,7)	Q*R+S
			PUSH T	(3,7)	Q*R+S, T
			ADD	(1,7)	Q*R+S+T
			POP P	(3,7)	empty
		(20,30)		(18,56)	
P:=(Q+R)*(S+T)	MOVE.W Q,D0	(4,6)	PUSH Q	(3,7)	Q
	ADD R,D0	(4,6)	PUSH R	(3,7)	Q, R
	MOVE.W S,D1	(4,6)	ADD	(1,7)	Q+R
	ADD T,D1	(4,6)	PUSH S	(3,7)	Q+R, S
	MUL D1,D0	(2,2)	PUSH T	(3,7)	Q+R, S, T
	MOVE.W D0,P	(4,6)	ADD	(1,7)	Q+R, S+T
			MUL	(1,7)	(Q+R)*(S+T)
			POP P	(3,7)	empty
		(22,32)		(18,56)	
P:=(Q*R+S*T)*(U+V)	MOVE.W Q,D0	(4,6)	PUSH Q	(3,7)	Q
	MUL R,D0	(4,6)	PUSH R	(3,7)	Q, R
	MOVE.W S,D1	(4,6)	MUL	(1,7)	Q*R
	MUL T,D1	(4,6)	PUSH S	(3,7)	Q*R, S
	ADD D1,D0	(2,2)	PUSH T	(3,7)	Q*R, S, T
	MOVE.W U,D1	(4,6)	MUL	(1,7)	Q*R, S*T
	ADD V,D1	(4,6)	ADD	(1,7)	Q*R+S*T
	MUL D1,D0	(2,2)	PUSH U	(3,7)	Q*R+S*T, U
	MOVE.W D0,P	(4,6)	PUSH V	(3,7)	Q*R+S*T, U, V
			ADD	(1,7)	Q*R+S*T, U+V
			MUL	(1,7)	(Q*R+S*T)*(U+V)
			POP P	(3,7)	empty
		(32,46)		(26,84)	

Notes: Parentheses indicate instruction length in bytes and number of memory bytes accessed (read
        or written) during instruction fetching and execution.
        Commas separate entries in Stack Contents column; rightmost entry is top of stack.

Luckily, we don't need a pure stack machine to get the benefits of stacks
for calling subroutines. Because stacks are so useful in this situation, almost all
modern processors have registers and instructions that can be used to manipulate
data and addresses in stacks.

TABLE 19–5 PDP-11 equivalents of H11 instructions.

H11 Instruction	PDP-11 Instruction(s)	Description
PUSH addr	MOV @#addr,-(R6)	Push MEMW[addr] onto stack
PUSH #data	MOV #data,-(R6)	Push data onto stack
PUSH offset(FP)	MOV offset(R5),-(R6)	Push MEMW[FP+offset] onto stack
PUSHT	MOV (R6),-(R6)	Push TOS onto stack
PUSHS	MOV 2(R6),-(R6)	Push SOS onto stack
PUSHF	MOV R5,-(R6)	Push FP onto stack
POP addr	MOV (R6)+,@#addr	Pop TOS, store into MEMW[addr]
POP offset(FP)	MOV (R6)+,offset(R5)	Pop TOS, store into MEMW[FP+offset]
CLR	CLR (R6)	Clear TOS
COM	COM (R6)	Ones' complement bits of TOS
NEG	NEG (R6)	Negate TOS (two's complement)
SWAB	SWAB (R6)	Swap bytes of TOS
ADD	ADD (R6)+,(R6)	Pop TOS, add to new TOS
AND	COM (R6)	Pop TOS, logical AND to new TOS
	BIC (R6)+,(R6)	
CMP	CMP (R6)+,(R6)	Pop TOS, compare with new TOS
MUL	MOV (R6)+,R1	Pop TOS,SOS, push TOS·SOS
	MUL (R6)+,R1	(1-word result, ignore overflow)
	MOV R1,-(R6)	
LD r,#data	MOV #data,r	Load r with data
LD r,addr	MOV @#addr,r	Load r with MEMW[addr]
LDFS	MOV R6,R5	Load FP with a copy of SP
ST r,addr	MOV r,@#addr	Store r into MEMw[addr]
ADD r,#offset	ADD #offset,r	Add offset to r
VAL	MOV @(R6)+,-(R6)	Replace TOS with MEMW[TOS]
STOW	MOV (R6)+,@(R6)+	Store TOS into MEMW[SOS], pop both
BNE offset	BNE offset	Branch if Z=0
BEQ offset	BEQ offset	Branch if Z=1
BRA offset	BR offset	Branch always
JMP addr	JMP addr	Jump to addr
JSR addr	JSR PC,addr	Jump to subroutine at addr
RTS	RTS PC	Return from subroutine
NOP	NOP	No operation

Notes: r = SP or X
   H11 SP = PDP-11 R6; H11 FP = PDP-11 R5.
   PDP-11 R1 is used as scratchpad for MUL.

19.5 THE PDP-11 AS A STACK MACHINE

The PDP-11 can simulate most of the H11's operations with single instructions, as shown in Table 19–5. The table uses the PDP-11's R6 to simulate the H11 stack pointer, and R5 for the H11 index register X. The data-manipulating instructions could be adapted to work on bytes as well as words, leaving it to the programmer to always keep track of whether the top of stack contains a byte or a word. However, for byte operations, one of the registers R0 through R5 must be used as the stack pointer, because the PDP-11 hardware forbids auto-incrementing or auto-decrementing R6 by only 1.

E X E R C I S E S

19.1   Using the same structure as the program in Table 5–12 on page 166, write a bit-counting subroutine for the H11. Values passed to and from the subroutine should be contained in the stack, not fixed memory locations. Use the SWAB instruction to allow you to process the high and low bytes of a word separately. You need not assemble the program.

19.2   Assemble the following H11 subroutine by hand, producing a listing in the format of Table 19–2. Also, add comments that explain what the subroutine does.

```
            ORG     $3000
VSUM        LDFS
            PUSH    #V
            PUSHT
            CLR
            PUSH    VADDR(FP)
LOOP        VAL
            ADD
            PUSH    VADDR(FP)
            PUSH    #2
            ADD
            PUSHT
            POP     VADDR(FP)
            PUSH    #V+LEN
            CMP
            BNE     LOOP
            PUSH    RADDR(FP)
            POP     VADDR(FP)
            PUSH    SUM(FP)
            POP     RADDR(FP)
            ADD     SP,#4
            RTS
RADDR       EQU     0
VADDR       EQU     -2
SUM         EQU     -4
LEN         EQU     20
V           DS.B    LEN
            END     VSUM
```

19.3   Sketch the contents of the stack, registers, and memory during the execution of the array initialization program in Table 19–3.

19.4   Suppose that the H11 were designed so that the top four words of the stack may be shadowed in processor registers. Write a Pascal algorithm that describes how the processor should manage these registers as the stack grows and shrinks. Your algorithm should strive for the best possible performance, that is, the fewest possible number of main-memory accesses by the processor.

19.5   Recompute the timing numbers for the H11 in Table 19–4 assuming that the top four words of the stack may be shadowed in processor registers. Also state your assumptions on how the processor manages these registers as the stack grows and shrinks.

19.6   Write a Pascal simulation of the H11.

APPENDIX A

The ASCII Character Code

A.1   ASCII ENCODING

ASCII

The most commonly used character encoding in computers is *ASCII* (pronounced ass'-key), shown in Table A–1. The code contains the uppercase and lowercase alphabet, numerals, punctuation, and various nonprinting control characters that are sometimes used in serial communications links.

ASCII is a 7-bit code, so its characters are stored one per byte in most computers. The MSB of an ASCII byte is usually unused and set to zero. However, ASCII bytes received from a serial communication link may use the MSB as a parity bit or may have the MSB set to some arbitrary value. Therefore it is wise for a program to clear the MSB of a received ASCII byte before comparing it with other ASCII bytes.

Notice that the numeric and alphabetic codes are ordered, so that character sequences may be sorted lexicographically using numeric comparisons of the corresponding character codes. Also, there is a simple relationship between uppercase and lowercase letters, so that lowercase letters may be converted to uppercase by subtracting 0100000.

A.2   ASCII AND TERMINALS

A few words should be said about the relationship between the ASCII characters and the keyboards and screens of typical terminals. Typically each key transmits one of three or four possible ASCII codes, depending on whether or not the SHIFT and CTRL keys on the keyboard are depressed at the same time as the key. Thus, typing L by itself transmits a lowercase "l", binary code 1101100. Holding down SHIFT and typing L transmits an uppercase "L", binary code 1001100. Holding down CTRL and typing L transmits binary code 0001100, regardless of the position of the SHIFT key on most keyboards.

TABLE A–1 American Standard Code for Information Interchange (ASCII), Standard No. X3.4–1968 of the American National Standards Institute.

$b_3b_2b_1b_0$	row (hex)	$b_6b_5b_4$ (column)							
		000 0	001 1	010 2	011 3	100 4	101 5	110 6	111 7
0000	0	NUL	DLE	SP	0	@	P	`	p
0001	1	SOH	DC1	!	1	A	Q	a	q
0010	2	STX	DC2	"	2	B	R	b	r
0011	3	ETX	DC3	#	3	C	S	c	s
0100	4	EOT	DC4	$	4	D	T	d	t
0101	5	ENQ	NAK	%	5	E	U	e	u
0110	6	ACK	SYN	&	6	F	V	f	v
0111	7	BEL	ETB	'	7	G	W	g	w
1000	8	BS	CAN	(	8	H	X	h	x
1001	9	HT	EM	)	9	I	Y	i	y
1010	A	LF	SUB	*	:	J	Z	j	z
1011	B	VT	ESC	+	;	K	[	k	{
1100	C	FF	FS	,	<	L	\	l	|
1101	D	CR	GS	–	=	M	]	m	}
1110	E	SO	RS	.	>	N	^	n	~
1111	F	SI	US	/	?	O	_	o	DEL

Control Codes

NUL	Null		DLE	Data link escape
SOH	Start of heading		DC1	Device control 1
STX	Start of text		DC2	Device control 2
ETX	End of text		DC3	Device control 3
EOT	End of transmission		DC4	Device control 4
ENQ	Enquiry		NAK	Negative acknowledge
ACK	Acknowledge		SYN	Synchronize
BEL	Bell		ETB	End transmitted block
BS	Backspace		CAN	Cancel
HT	Horizontal tab		EM	End of medium
LF	Line feed		SUB	Substitute
VT	Vertical tab		ESC	Escape
FF	Form feed		FS	File separator
CR	Carriage return		GS	Group separator
SO	Shift out		RS	Record separator
SI	Shift in		US	Unit separator
SP	Space		DEL	Delete or rubout

In general, a control code in column 0 or 1 of Table A–1 is obtained by holding down the CTRL key and typing the character from the same relative position in column 4 or 5. Thus, holding down CTRL and typing C (i.e., typing CTRL–C) transmits the binary code 0000011, the ASCII control code named ETX. Many computer systems use these control codes as special system commands, for example, CTRL–C to return control to an executive, CTRL–O to suspend the current output, CTRL–U to cancel the current input line, and so on.

Note that the ESC key found on most terminals sends a particular ASCII code (0011011), while the CTRL key performs a mapping on other key codes as described above. The BREAK key places an abnormal condition on the serial data link, as described in Appendix B. In some systems this abnormal condition is detected and used as another system command, but it is not an ASCII character.

A typical CRT display ignores most control codes that it receives, but there are five control codes that all CRT displays respond to:

SP Prints a blank space.

BS Moves the cursor (current printing position) one space left.

CR Moves the cursor to the beginning of the current line. Some terminals are configured to also move the cursor to the next line when CR is received.

LF Moves the cursor down one line. Some terminals are configured to also move the cursor to the beginning of the line when LF is received.

BEL Produces an audible sound (usually a beep) at the terminal.

escape sequences

Some "smart" CRT screens respond to special *escape sequences*, typically consisting of an ESC character followed by one or more additional characters. For example, a terminal might respond to ESC H by "homing" the cursor (moving it to the upper left-hand corner of the screen), and to ESC J by clearing all of the text from the current cursor position to the end of the screen. Different escape sequences are defined for different smart terminals.

APPENDIX B

Serial Communication

Serial data links are commonly used by computers to communicate with both local and remote terminals. *Serial* communication means that information transmitted from source to destination is carried over a single pathway. Within the immediate physical confines of a computer system, the use of serial links is most often motivated by cost considerations—serial links can reduce packaging and cabling cost and reduce the number and complexity of components for sending and receiving data. Outside the computer system, use of a serial communication link is often forced by the very nature of the available data transmission media—telephone lines and radio waves can only send one analog signal at a time.

In this appendix we describe the simple serial data links that are most often used by computers to communicate with local and remote terminals.

B.1 SERIAL DATA LINKS

simplex

A *simplex* serial data link transmits data in only one direction. A connection from a computer to a remote printer could be a simplex serial data link.

full duplex

There are usually two serial data links between a computer and a terminal, one for transmission in each direction. This is called *full-duplex* operation and is illustrated in Figure B–1. Transmission in the two directions is independent and simultaneous. A typical terminal consists of a keyboard and a screen or hardcopy printing mechanism. Even though they may be packaged together, the keyboard and screen are logically independent devices. When a character is typed at the keyboard, it is not automatically printed. In most full-duplex systems, the computer must receive each character and send a copy of it back to the terminal; this is called *echo*. A few full-duplex systems have terminals hard-wired to locally print all typed characters, saving the computer the overhead of echoing them. This mode of operation is sometimes called *echo-plex*. (The "half-duplex" option provided on many terminals is really echo-plex.)

echo

echo-plex

737

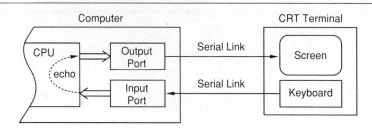

FIGURE B–1 Full-duplex serial communication link.

half duplex

Bidirectional communication can also be achieved with a single link as shown in Figure B–2, but only in one direction at a time. A special control sequence is needed to "turn the line around" whenever the direction of transmission is changed. This is called *half-duplex* operation. Local printing of typed characters is essential with ha f-duplex links, because of the high overhead that would be incurred if the computer had to turn the line around to echo each character. Most serial links in use today are full duplex.

bit rate

The rate of transmission of a data stream in bits per second (bps) is called the *bit rate*. This rate is sometimes mistakenly called the "baud rate." The bit rate and the baud rate are usually equal, but not always; the exact definition of baud rate must wait until we discuss modems. Serial transmission rates for typical computer terminals range from 75 to 19200 bps (19.2 Kbps). The

bit time

reciprocal of the bit rate is called the *bit time*—the time that it takes to transmit one bit.

By far the most common character encoding in minicomputer and microcomputer systems is ASCII, which represents each character by 7 bits (see Appendix A). A character is transmitted over the link one bit at a time, with two to four control bits added to each character. Thus, 9 to 11 bits are required to transmit one character, and the typical bit transmission rates mentioned above yield about 8 to 2000 characters per second. A typical 24×80 CRT screen contains 1920 characters, so it can be completely filled in one second by a 19.2 Kbps data link.

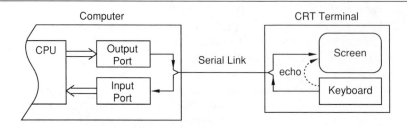

FIGURE B–2 Half-duplex serial communication link.

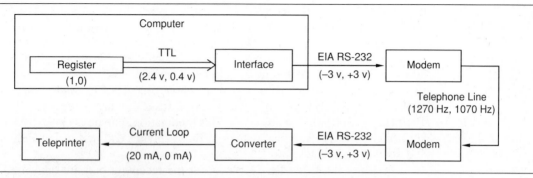

FIGURE B–3   Encodings of (mark,space) in a serial communication link.

Standard bit rates are 75, 110, 134.5, 150, 300, 600, 1200, 2400, 4800, 9600, 19200, and 38400 bps. The standard bit rates form a geometric progression, except for 110 bps, used by old-fashioned ASR-33 teleprinters and similar equipment, and 134.5 bps, used by some old-fashioned IBM printing terminals. Modern CRT terminals have switch-selectable bit rates up to a maximum of 9600 to 38400 bps.

Most often the same bit rate is used for both directions in a full-duplex serial communication link. This is especially true in communications between a computer and a local terminal, since data is carried over relatively inexpensive, short, high-bandwidth copper wires.

split bit rate   On the other hand, there is nothing to prevent different bit rates from being used in a so-called *split bit rate* arrangement. This is advantageous for connections to remote equipment connected by telephone lines or other expensive links with limited bandwidth. A human can type only so fast, even with a repeat key, and so a bit rate supporting more than 15 characters per second from a keyboard to the computer is wasteful. On the other hand, a computer can easily send data to a CRT continuously at rates of 100 characters per second or higher. Therefore, one popular split bit rate arrangement used a 150 bps link from terminal to computer, but 1200 bps from computer to terminal.

mark   A simple serial communication link uses the signals *mark* and *space* to
space   encode the binary digits 1 and 0, respectively. The names mark and space go back over 100 years to the days of printing telegraphy, in which a the presence or absence of a signal caused a pen to make a mark or leave a space on a moving piece of paper. These unusual names also remind us that the physical values used to represent 1 and 0 depend on the type of physical link. In fact, each bit takes on several different physical representations during its journey from source to destination, as shown by the example in Figure B–3.

transistor-   Within a computer, 1s and 0s of a character are represented by a sequence
transistor logic   of standard voltage levels for a particular logic family, say *transistor-transistor*
(TTL)   *logic (TTL)*. An interface in the computer converts TTL levels to another standard

RS-232

*modem
(modulator/-
demodulator)*

telephone link

set of voltage levels prescribed by EIA (Electronic Industries Association) standard *RS-232*, and connects to a device called a *modem (modulator/demodulator)*.

A standard *telephone link* cannot transmit and receive absolute voltage levels, only sounds whose frequency components are between approximately 300 and 3000 Hz. Therefore the modem converts RS-232 voltage levels into tones that can be transmitted over a telephone line. For example, the modem could transmit a 1270 Hz tone whenever an RS-232 mark level is present, and 1070 Hz for an RS-232 space level. This modulation scheme is called *frequency-shift keying (FSK)*. Another modem at the receiving end can detect FSK tones and convert them back into RS-232 levels.

*frequency-shift
keying (FSK)*

current loop

In Figure B–3, the RS-232 levels at the receiving end are converted to a *current-loop* interface—a pair of wires in which a 20 milliampere (mA) current represents a mark and 0 mA represents a space. The resulting sequence of on/off currents controls the motion of a teleprinter's mechanical wheels and cams that finally print a character. Alternatively, the RS-232 levels could be connected to a typical CRT terminal which is designed to accept RS-232 levels directly.

Most serial communication links are full duplex, so that Figure B–3 should really show another serial link in the reverse direction. However, another telephone line and pair of modems usually is not required for the reverse link. Most modems can provide a full-duplex connection using a single telephone line. They do this by using a different pair of frequencies for communicating in the reverse direction, for example, 2225 Hz for a mark and 2025 Hz for a space. The choice of transmitting and receiving frequencies for the computer and terminal is predetermined by convention in any given system. The modem handles the links in both directions simultaneously.

The bit rate that can be received reliably by a particular modem is limited. For example, suppose we tried to send data at 9600 bps using the FSK modulation scheme described above. Then one bit time would correspond to only about one-eighth of a sine wave period at a transmitting frequency of 1270 Hz. Such a tiny slice of a sine wave cannot be reliably detected at the receiving end after passing through the distortions of the telephone network.

Modulation and demodulation schemes more sophisticated than FSK are used in high bit-rate modems. It may seem paradoxical that it is indeed possible to send 9600 bits per second over a telephone link that has a bandwidth of only about 3000 Hz. Such high bit rates are achieved by modulation techniques in which each transmitted signal element has more than two values. For example, most 1200 bps modems use a modulation scheme that transmits only 600 signal elements per second, where each signal element can have one of four values, representing the four possible combinations of two bits. The number of signal elements per second is called the *baud rate*. In low speed modems the bit rate and baud rate are usually equal; in high speed modems they usually are not.

baud rate

Inexpensive, low-speed modems transmit and receive data at 300 to 2400 bits per second. When a terminal is connected directly to a computer without using a telephone link and modems, it is usually practical to use a much higher bit rate such as 9600 or 19200 Kbps.

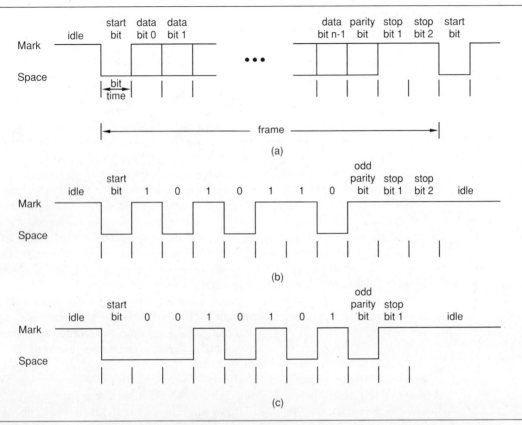

FIGURE B–4   Asynchronous serial data: (a) general bit format; (b) typical teleprinter format; (c) typical high-speed terminal format.

B.2   ASYNCHRONOUS SERIAL COMMUNICATION FORMAT

asynchronous link   The majority of serial communication links now in use are *asynchronous links*. "Asynchronous" means that the transmitter and receiver do not share a common clock, and no clock signal is sent with the data. So how does the receiver know when the data bits begin and end? We shall describe a simple algorithm that can be used if the transmitter and receiver agree on a standard bit rate and format.

asynchronous   The standard *asynchronous serial bit format* used by computers and ter-
serial bit format   minals is shown in Figure B–4(a). When the transmitter is idle (no data being sent), the line is maintained in a continuous mark state. The transmitter may
start bit   initiate a character at any time by sending a *start bit*, that is, by putting the line in the space state for exactly one bit time. It then transmits the data bits, least significant first, optionally followed by an even or odd *parity bit*. An even (odd)
parity bit   parity bit is chosen in such a way that the total number of 1s among the data

stop bit

bits and parity bit is even (odd). Finally, the transmitter maintains the mark state for 1, 1.5, or 2 bit times—so-called *stop bits*.

frame

The period of time from the beginning of the start bit to the end of the stop bits is called a *frame*. After the stop bits, the transmitter may immediately send a new start bit if it has another character to send. Otherwise, it may maintain the mark state as long as it is idle. A new start bit may be sent at any time, not necessarily an integral number of bit times since the last stop bit.

An old-fashioned teleprinter operating at 110 bps transmits a start bit, 7 ASCII data bits, an odd parity bit, and two stop bits, as shown in Figure B–4(b) for the character 0110101 (ASCII '5'). Since 11 bits are required to send each character, at 110 bps there are 10 characters per second.

Terminals operating at 300 bps and higher usually transmit a start bit, 7 ASCII data bits, a parity bit, and one stop bit, as shown in Figure B–4(c) for the character 1010100 (ASCII 'T'). Since only 10 bits are needed for each character, at 300 bps there are 30 characters per second. The usage of the parity bit varies widely among different systems. There are three possibilities: even, odd, or no parity. These possibilities are compounded by the fact that most terminals and computers can send and receive an optional eighth data bit before the optional parity bit. There are four possibilities for the eighth bit: not transmitted, constant 1, constant 0, or useful data. The last case creates an additional 128 non-ASCII characters that may be transmitted between the terminal and computer for extended character sets or special functions.

In a serial communication link, the transmitter and receiver must agree upon all of the parameters of the bit format in Figure B–4(a), including a nominal bit time (or equivalently, bit rate). Since transmitter and receiver have different clocks, they will have slightly different bit times. The decoding procedure described below allows a difference of up to a few percent in the bit times.

For optimum immunity to signal distortion, noise, and clock inaccuracies, the receiver should sample each incoming bit in the middle of its bit time. This can be accomplished by the following algorithm, which samples the input signal at a frequency that is m times the bit rate; typical values of m are 8, 16, 32, and 64.

(1) *Start-bit detection.* Sample the input for a space. After the first detection of a space, be sure that the input remains in the space state for $(m/2) - 1$ more sample times. If successful, we are now approximately at the middle of the start bit. Otherwise, we have detected a noise pulse and we should start again.

(2) *Data-bit sampling.* After m more sample times after start bit detection, read the first data bit from the input. Repeat a total of n times for n data bits, and repeat if necessary for the parity bit. Each bit will be sampled approximately in the middle of its bit time. Place the assembled character in a buffer for the processor or terminal to read.

(3) *Stop-bit detection.* After m more sample times, sample the input for the mark state (stop bit). Repeat if there are two stop bits. If the input is in the space state, set a "framing error" status flag along with the received character. Set a "character received" flag for the processor and return to step 1.

The leading edge of the start bit signals the beginning of a character, and the time of its occurrence provides a timing reference for sampling the data bits. The stop bits provide time for "clean-up" required between characters on older terminals, and also provide a degree of error detection. If the line is not *framing error* in the mark state when a stop bit is expected, a *framing error* is said to occur. Framing errors occur most often when the receiver erroneously synchronizes on a space bit that is not the real start bit. Proper resynchronization can always be accomplished if the transmitter is idle (sending mark) for one frame or longer. Unfortunately, if synchronization is lost when the transmitter is sending at full speed, in general it will not be regained until an idle frame occurs.

When the line is continuously held in the space state for one frame or *break* longer, a *break* is said to occur. The "BREAK" key on many keyboards actually holds the line in the space state for as long as the key is depressed. The serial interfaces on most computers have the capability of detecting break as a special condition. Many software systems then treat break as an extra, special-function character. However, break must be used cautiously in remote communication links, because most modems automatically disconnect from the telephone line if a break is held too long.

Index

Boldface type is used to indicate page numbers on which the corresponding index terms are defined or used in an important way. The index terms usually appear in the left-hand margin on such pages.

Index terms that one might associate with a processor (e.g., "addressing") are, in fact, associated with the 68000. Index terms associated with other processors are indicated as such (e.g., "addressing, 80x86").

Processor and coprocessor instructions and pseudo-operations are indexed beginning on page 760.